# From Mesolithic to Mot

## The archaeology of the M1 (Junction 6a-10) Widening Scheme, Hertfordshire

by Dan Stansbie, Paul Booth, Andrew Simmonds,
Valerie Diez and Seren Griffiths

with contributions by
*Rebecca Bridgman, Lisa Brown, John Cotter, Rebecca Devaney, Denise Druce,
Luke Howarth, Nicholas Márquez-Grant, David Mullin, Rebecca Nicholson, Cynthia Poole,
Ian Scott, Ruth Shaffrey, Wendy Smith, Ben Stern, Lena Strid and Leo Webley*

Illustrations by
*Daniel Bashford, Hannah Kennedy, Sophie Lamb, Sarah Lucas and Magdalena Wachnik*

Oxford Archaeology Monograph No. 14
2012

Published by Oxford Archaeology as part of the Oxford Archaeology Monograph Series

Designed by Oxford Archaeology Graphics Office

Edited by Richard Gregory

This book is part of a series of monographs which can be bought from all good
bookshops and internet bookshops. For more information visit www.oxfordarch.co.uk

ISBN 978 0 904220 65 0


Typeset by Production Line, Oxford
Printed in Great Britain by Berforts Information Press, Eynsham, Oxford

# Contents

## Chapter 1: Introduction *by Paul Booth*

## Chapter 2: Junction 8 Southbound *by Dan Stansbie*

# Chapter 5: Junction 9 *by Andrew Simmonds*

# Chapter 6: Areas M, P and Junction 10 *by Dan Stansbie*

## Chapter 7: The Finds

## Chapter 8: Environmental evidence

## Chapter 9: Radiocarbon dating *by Seren Griffiths, Dan Stansbie and Rebecca Nicholson*

## Chapter 10: Overview *by Dan Stansbie, Paul Booth and Seren Griffiths*

# List of Figures

# List of Tables

# Summary

A programme of archaeological work was undertaken by Oxford Archaeology in advance of engineering works to relieve congestion along the M1 between Junctions 6a to 10, a length of about 15km, stretching roughly south to north from a point east of Hemel Hempstead to just south of Luton, on the Bedfordshire border. The work was commissioned by Atkins Heritage, acting on behalf of Balfour Beatty/Skanska Joint Venture who undertook the M1 widening scheme for the Highways Agency.

Significant remains of prehistoric, Roman and medieval date were encountered. Important evidence for late Mesolithic and early Neolithic activity, including pit features, was recovered from Junction 9. Later prehistoric evidence was less concentrated; ephemeral features adjacent to The Aubreys hillfort were poorly dated, but cremation burials and scattered features of late Bronze Age date came from Junction 8 Southbound, which also produced probable Iron Age features, with other evidence of this period coming from Junction 8 Northbound and the adjacent Buncefield Depot site. The most widespread evidence was from the late Iron Age and Roman periods. Significant settlement-related features of this date occurred at Junction 8 Northbound and Junction 9, and to a lesser extent at the intervening Site M. Ditched trackways and enclosures were characteristic of all these sites, and further probable trackway ditches were present at Site P. Structural evidence was minimal, except for hearths and ovens, and the sites seem to have been of fairly low status and concerned with mixed agriculture. The evidence for earlier Roman occupation was generally stronger than that for the late Roman period. At Junction 8 Northbound, however, an east-west trackway seems to have survived as a landscape feature and in the 12th and 13th centuries was adjoined by a ditched enclosure containing a post-built structure. A few medieval features were also encountered in areas just to the north of Junction 8 Northbound, but were otherwise absent, nor were any significant post-medieval features found.

# Acknowledgements

Oxford Archaeology would like to thank Balfour Beatty/Skanska Joint Venture who funded the archaeological programme, and particularly Liam McGirl, Steve Gray and Steve Todd for their help. The work was expedited by Andrew Holmes of Atkins Heritage and was also monitored by Simon West for St Albans District Council.

At Oxford Archaeology the project was initiated by Richard Brown. The evaluation and excavation fieldwork stages were managed by Valérie Diez, with supervision in the field by Ross O'Maolduin and Austin Ainsworth. The main members of the fieldwork team were Michael Baddiel, Veronica Bisio, Rosie Blackwell, Abigail Brown, Ralph Brown, Jessica Bryan, Peter Burge, Gaylin Carter, Lawrence Coalter, Robert Cole, Sharon Cook, Mike Donnelly, Patrick Dresch, Mark Gibson, Rebecca Griffin, Kat Grindley, Mike Kershaw, Laura King, Neil Lambert, Sarah Lane, Steve Laurie-Lynch, Laura Maccalman, Roberta Marziani, Bryan Mathews, Rowan Mcalley, Janice Mcleish, Hefin Meara, Chris Naisbit, Sam Oates, Lucy Offord, John Onraet, Hugo Pinto, Emily Plunkett, Russel Prost, Sophie Prost, C Ross, Mark Stedman, Alexandra Stevenson, Peter Stock, Dan Watkeys, Dan Wheeler, Victoria Wilkinson, Kate Woodley and Alistair Zochowski. The work of the post-excavation assessment and analysis and reporting stages was managed by Paul Booth, and the majority of the post-excavation analysis was undertaken by Andrew Simmonds and Dan Stansbie. Support was provided by Leigh Allen (finds management), Rebecca Nicholson (environmental management), Louise Loe (osteology management) and Nicola Scott (archive management). Thanks are owed to all the specialists and illustrators for their contributions, and to Anna Hodgkinson for work on the CAD drawings

Ros Niblett kindly read and commented on a draft of the publication report, offering many helpful insights for which the authors are extremely grateful. Duncan Garrow read and commented on the Mesolithic and Neolithic part of the discussion.

# Chapter 1: Introduction

*by Paul Booth and Dan Stansbie*

This volume presents the results of archaeological excavations undertaken, mostly in 2006-7, in advance of engineering works to relieve congestion along the M1 between Junctions 6a and 10, within Hertfordshire and Bedfordshire. The work was undertaken by Oxford Archaeology (OA) and was commissioned by Atkins Heritage, acting on behalf of Balfour Beatty/Skanska Joint Venture who undertook the M1 widening scheme for the Highways Agency.

## SITE LOCATION, GEOLOGY AND TOPOGRAPHY

The sites (Figs 1.1-2) lie on both sides of the M1 between Junction 6a and Junction 10, a length of about 15km, stretching roughly south to north from a point east of Hemel Hempstead to just south of Luton, on the Bedfordshire border (from *c* TL 115 038 to TL 087 184).

The underlying geology is Upper Chalk (Fig. 1.3), which for much of the length of the route is overlain by clay-with-flints and associated deposits of pebbly clay and sand, the latter seen, for example, in the vicinity of The Aubreys (Sherlock 1922; Sherlock and Pocock 1924). Soils are mainly clayey soils of the Carstens series, frequently flinty with a silty plateau drift and modern landscape use consists principally of arable agriculture. The topography of the route, which in broad terms lies on the dip slope of the Chilterns, is mostly undulating plateau. More specifically, the southern part of the route lies close to the watershed located between the valleys of the Gade to the west and the Ver to the east. Further north it then draws closer to the west side of the Ver, after which it crosses this valley in the vicinity of Junction 9, just north of Redbourn, before resuming the plateau location in its northernmost stretch.

Current water levels in this area may be lower than at any time since the end of the Ice Age. This is largely due to the large-scale extraction of water related to the growth of the modern towns of the region, which has resulted in significant reductions in the volume of water in the River Ver. Many of the small dry tributary valleys of the Ver, for example those at Friar's Wash, The Aubreys and St Michaels, St Albans, had at least seasonal streams in them in the past (R Niblett pers. comm.).

## ARCHAEOLOGICAL AND HISTORICAL BACKGROUND

An archaeological statement was produced as part of the Environmental Impact Assessment (EIA) for the scheme in September 1994 by St Albans Museum in association with Hertfordshire County Transportation Design services for the Highways Agency (Highway Agency 1994). This work was confined to a 500m-wide corridor centred on the line of the motorway, within which approximately 16 sites were identified in the SMR (now HER) and the records of the St Albans Museum. In addition, a surface collection survey, undertaken as part of the EIA, identified a further 31 potential sites, indicated by the presence of archaeological finds (mostly medieval and later building materials, prehistoric flint and pottery). A programme of geophysical survey was also undertaken.

The following brief summary of the archaeological background to the project is based, in part, on this information and where appropriate, site reference numbers within this chapter (prefixed with an 'A') correspond to the scheme-specific numbering system set out in the Archaeological Design produced by Atkins Heritage (2005). However, to provide a wider background, particularly for successive periods of prehistory, it also draws on a variety of other sources, both site specific and more synthetic in character, which are vital for interpretation of the developments in the wider region from the late Iron Age onwards. The synthetic works consulted include, a review of the archaeology of the Chilterns (Holgate 1995a) and a more recent survey of the archaeology of St Albans (Niblett and Thompson 2005).

### Lower Palaeolithic

Lower Palaeolithic settlement in the Chiltern region is indicated by the discovery of four intact flint-working areas in brick pits at Caddington, Gaddesden Row, Whipsnade and Round Green, Luton, by Smith in the early 20th century (Holgate 1995b, 6). Over 2000 flints were recovered from Caddington and reinvestigation of the site by Sampson in the 1970s recovered faunal remains and pollen dating to the Ipswichian interglacial (*c* 125,000 bp) (ibid., 6). Lower Palaeolithic worked flint has also been recovered from gravel deposits at Rickmansworth and Hitchin, in Hertfordshire and from Limbury in Bedfordshire, although this

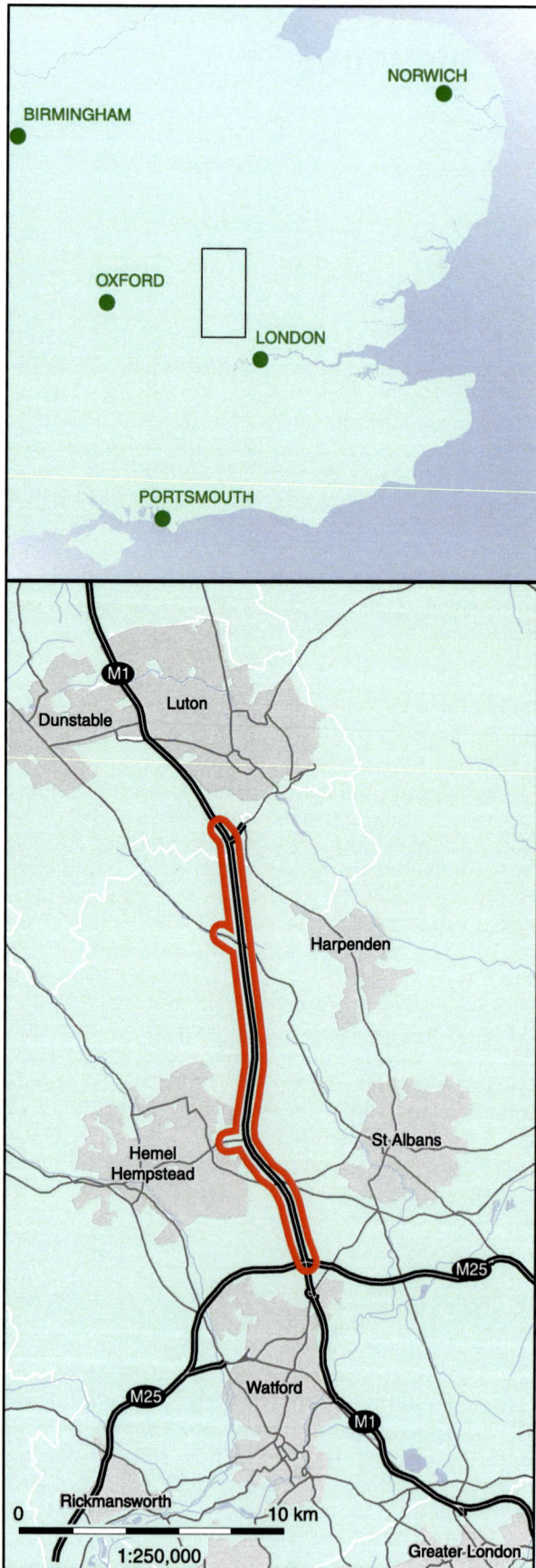

*Fig. 1.1  Site location*

material was not *in situ* (ibid.). In addition, Palaeolithic handaxes have been discovered at Slip End and in the vicinity of Redbourn, whilst field-walking in the environs of St Albans has produced flint assemblages including lower Palaeolithic material (ibid.).

## Upper Palaeolithic and Mesolithic

In contrast to the earlier period, evidence for upper Palaeolithic activity in the Chiltern environs is limited. The only material of early upper Palaeolithic date comprises leaf points or leaf-shaped spearheads from Broxbourne, Hertfordshire (ibid., 6-7). Sites dating to after the Devensian maximum (in the 10th millennium BC) include Three Ways Wharf, Uxbridge and Broxbourne Site 106 (ibid., 7) and, further afield, Gatehampton Farm, Goring, Oxfordshire (Barton 1995). Early Mesolithic activity, however, is relatively widespread, with assemblages of worked flint, including broad blades, occurring in the lower stretches of the Colne and Lea, in similar locations to late upper Palaeolithic sites (ibid., 8). Late Mesolithic occupation was more widespread, being mainly situated along the river valleys of the Chiltern region (ibid.). Sites with later Mesolithic flint assemblages include: Stratford's Yard, Chesham; Redbourn; The Grove, Watford; Low Farm, Fulmer; Gerrard's Cross; and Tolpit's Lane Site B, Moor Park. The excavations at Stratford's Yard revealed a buried land surface with an *in situ* flint scatter (Stainton 1989, 50). Excavations at The Grove found evidence for repeated intermittent occupation on the edge of the Gade and similar evidence comes from Aldwickbury, Harpenden, on the margin of the Lea (AOC Archaeology Group 2002; R Niblett pers. comm.) Other late Mesolithic sites in the Ver valley include settlement at Redbourn and Friar's Wash (Holgate 1995b, 9).

## Neolithic and early Bronze Age

Monuments belonging to the early Neolithic period are all located on the periphery of the Chiltern region, either on the scarp, or in the middle Thames and Stort valleys (Holgate 1995b, 10). Early Neolithic settlement sites are also scarce and apparently mostly situated on the upper slopes of the Chiltern scarp or dip slope (ibid., 10), with early Neolithic pottery and flint having been recovered from beneath Bronze Age barrows at Whiteleaf Hill, Buckinghamshire (Hey *et al.* 2007) and Five Knolls barrow, Bedfordshire. A Neolithic polished axe has been discovered near Redbourn. In addition, early Neolithic pits have been excavated near Maiden Bower, Old Parkbury, Hertfordshire and at Foxholes Farm, Hertfordshire (Holgate 1995b, 11). An early Neolithic building measuring 7m wide by at least 9m long, and radiocarbon dated (HAR-3484) to 3513-3389 cal BC, has been excavated at Gorhambury (Neal *et al.* 1990, 9). At Radlett airfield a watching brief in 1992 by Verulamium Museum recorded a penannular ditch associated with early Neolithic pottery (R Niblett pers. comm.). The density of settlement in the region increased during the late Neolithic, with settlement spreading to the valley bottoms. Several sites, including Old Parkbury, Foxholes Farm, Codicote, Baldock and Blackhorse Road, Letchworth, all in Hertfordshire, comprised scatters of pits containing pottery, animal bone and worked flint (Holgate 1995b, 12). Late Neolithic to early Bronze Age occupation has been recorded at Feldon Lane (Hemel Hempstead) and on the Berkhamsted bypass at Rucklers Lane (R Niblett pers. comm.; McDonald 1996).

Evidence for early Bronze Age activity is dominated by round barrows and ring-ditches, which cluster along the Chiltern scarp (Holgate 1995b, 14). Flint scatters containing early Bronze Age material are closely associated with these monuments, suggesting that the scarp may also have been the main focus of settlement (ibid., 15). About 14 ring ditches (generally described as Bronze Age in date) have been recorded on air photographs within 15km of the M1 corridor. In addition, fragments of early and middle Bronze Age pottery are recorded on later occupation sites in the area, such as Folly Lane, St Albans, Colney Street and The Grove, near Watford, and King Harry Lane, St Albans (R Niblett pers. comm.; Longworth 1989, 53-8). A number of the late Neolithic flint scatters also contain early Bronze Age material, so there may have been some settlement continuity on these sites (Holgate 1995b, 14). Furthermore, at Cheapside Farm, between St Albans and Harpenden, a large collection of late Neolithic and early Bronze Age flint suggested the presence of a truncated occupation site situated on the plateau (R Niblett pers. comm.). A Bronze Age metal hoard found near Westwick Farm is also recorded in the HER (A51) and in the wider region there is a large late Bronze Age hoard from Watford (Coombs 1979).

**Later prehistoric: middle-late Bronze Age and Iron Age**

The majority of evidence for later prehistoric settlement in the Chilterns comes from fieldwalking (Bryant 1995, 17), but settlement sites, including early and middle Iron Age hillforts and smaller farmsteads belonging to the late Bronze and Iron Ages, are also known from other evidence.

Late Bronze Age-early Iron Age settlement is known from Puddle Hill, Foxholes Farm, Cole Green, Pea Lane and Bottom House Lane, all on the Berkhamsted bypass (ibid., 19) and also occurs at the hillfort at Ivinghoe Beacon (Cotton and Frere 1968). In addition, excavations at Rucklers Lane on the Berkhampstead Bypass have also produced evidence for late Bronze Age/early Iron Age occupation (R Niblett pers. comm.). Two late Bronze Age roundhouses and eight four-post structures were excavated at Oakwood, Berkhamsted (McDonald 1996, 23), and

a probable Bronze Age roundhouse was excavated in Westwood Quarry, about 500m west of The Grove site, near Watford; environmental evidence also suggests that during the Bronze Age woodland was cleared and arable farming was practised close to this site (R Niblett pers. comm.). Late Bronze Age occupation is also known from much nearer to the M1 project area at Buncefield Lane, Hemel Hempstead, where pits, postholes, a ditch and a buried soil horizon were discovered dating to the late Bronze Age/early Iron Age (McDonald 2003, 51). At Gorhambury linear ditches may be part of a late Bronze Age field system (Neal *et al.* 1990, 10), whilst evidence of bronze working has been found at Half Hide Lane, Turnford and Prior's Wood, Hertford (Bryant 1995, 19). Concentrations of Ewart Park metalwork hoards correspond to clusters of settlements, particularly around the Hitchin gap and in the Lea Valley, and a Bronze Age metal hoard has been found near Westwick Farm (ibid.). Few settlements can be definitively assigned to the early Iron Age, but the earliest defences of the hillforts at Ravensburgh Castle and Maiden Bower were constructed in this period, and there was early Iron Age occupation at Puddle Hill (ibid., 21).

Middle Iron Age settlement is known from Puddle Hill, Foxholes Farm, Barley and Leavesden Airfield (Brossler *et al.* 2009); at Puddle Hill there were four successive rectilinear enclosures (Bryant 1995, 22). Middle Iron Age pottery has been recorded on later Iron Age sites at Mackerye End, Harpenden (R Niblett pers. comm.), and King Harry Lane, St Albans (Longworth 1989, 53). In addition, many enclosures attributed to the late Iron Age in the St Albans area have only been recorded on aerial photographs and may be of early or middle Iron Age date (R Niblett pers. comm.). At least four hillforts in the Chiltern Region, including Cholesbury, Ravensburgh Castle, Wilbury Hill and Maiden Bower, were either constructed in the middle Iron Age, or had their defences reconstructed at that time. Evidence for Iron Age activity in the vicinity of the scheme is mostly localised in two areas. The area between Blunts Lane and Bedmond Lane (Area T) was identified in the St Albans District Plan as being of high archaeological potential on the basis of scattered flint finds and suggested Iron Age enclosures visible on aerial photographs. It has also been suggested that the Devil's Dyke, Wheathampstead, may date to the late 2nd century BC (Thompson 1979, 178). A copper-alloy knife dating to the late 3rd or early 2nd century BC has also been discovered in the St Albans area, west of the town (Megaw *et al.* 1999).

A major earthwork, The Aubreys, a Scheduled Ancient Monument (SAM), lies adjacent to, and has been clipped by, the M1 on its eastern boundary. This earthwork is defined for most of its oval circuit by two substantial banks and ditches enclosing an area of *c* 8ha. Its dating is not completely certain, and while it is commonly referred to as an Iron Age hillfort, topographically the site is positioned on

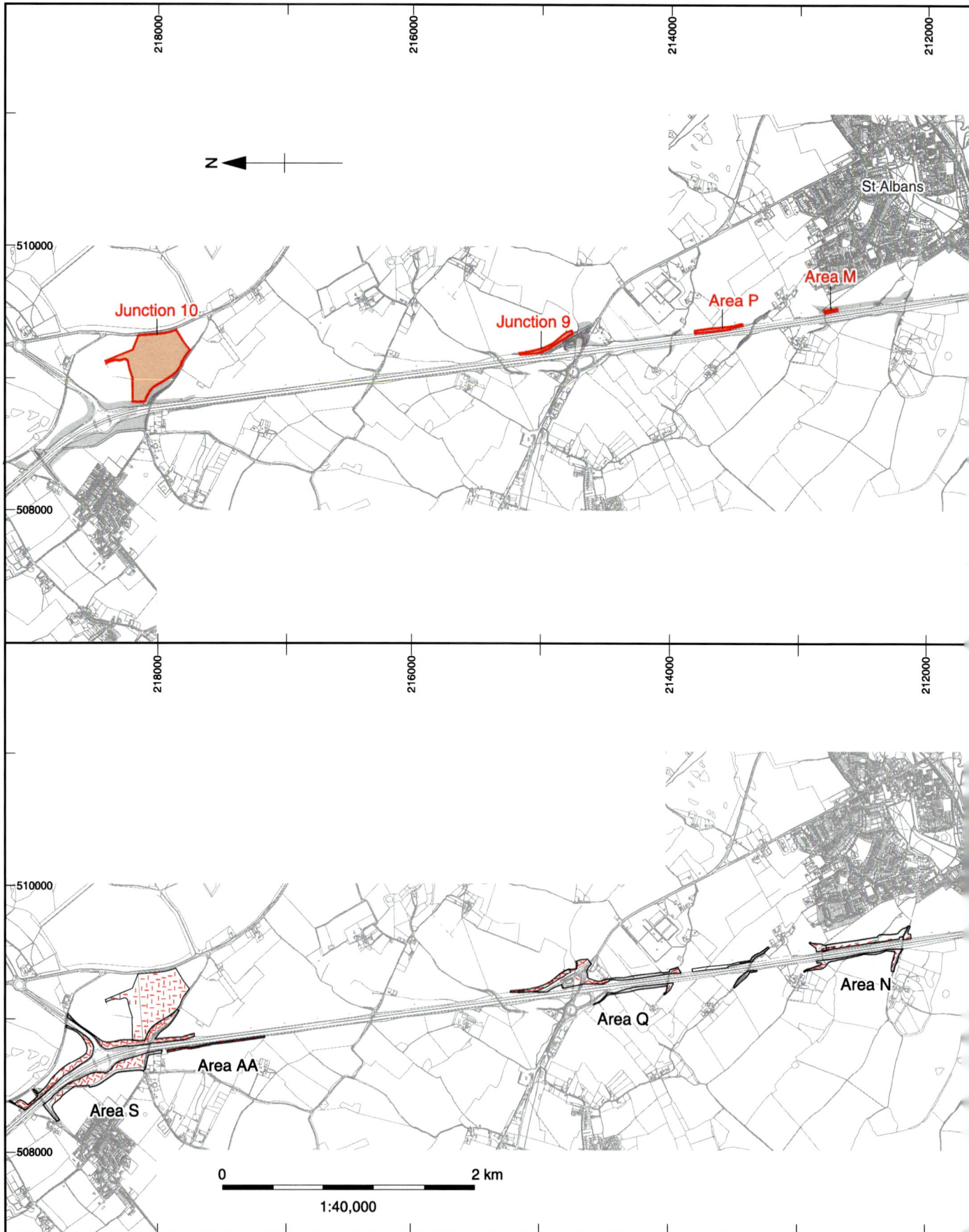

*Fig. 1.2  Location of sites and evaluation trenches*

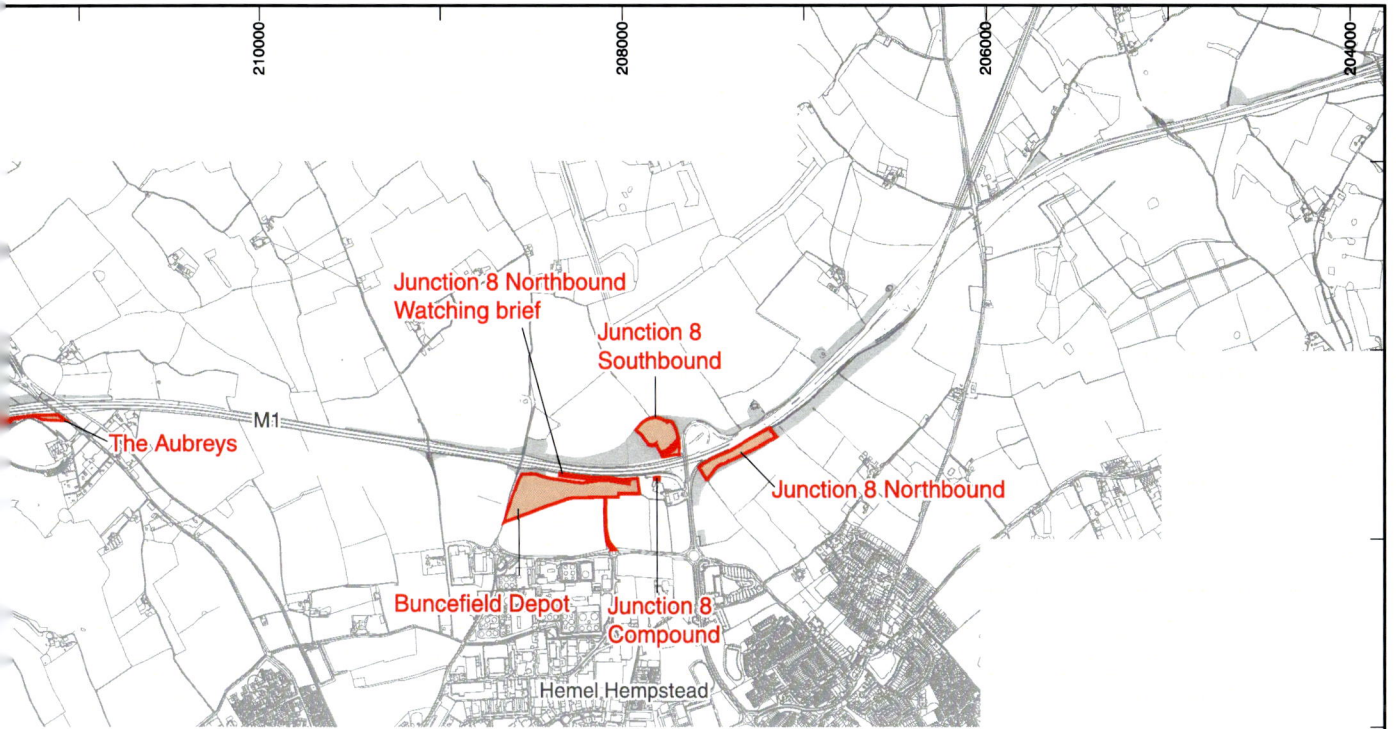

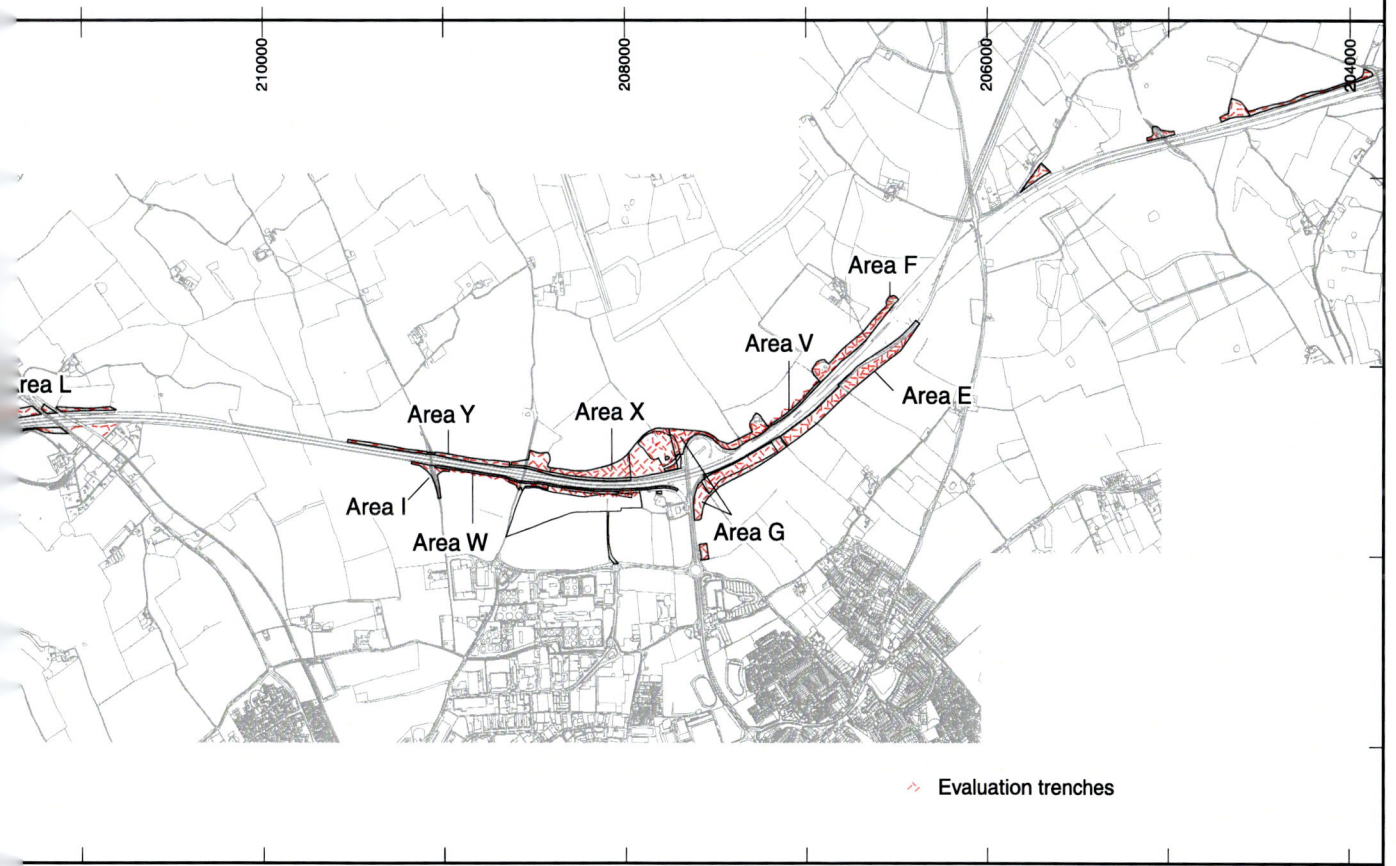

Evaluation trenches

sloping ground above the River Ver valley. Residual flint finds from the ditches have been dated to the early Neolithic, but there is no evidence for the nature and chronology of activity within the earthwork. A minor and inconclusive excavation occurred in the 1930s (Atkins 2005, A39). Geophysical survey and trial trenching undertaken in advance of the M1 widening scheme established the continuation of the outer defences on the east side and suggested a possible middle Iron Age date for their construction, but the amount of dating evidence was extremely small. The Iron Age is also represented in the immediate vicinity of the scheme by a number of cropmark features comprising enclosures and other ditches (ibid., A52, A63 and A67), but these are only dated on morphological criteria.

## Late Iron Age

The density of late Iron Age settlement in the area was high, and over 150 late Iron Age settlements are known from the Chiltern region (Bryant and Niblett 1997, 271). Late Iron Age settlement appears to have been concentrated in the river valleys of the Bulbourne and the Lea, and of the Ver, Mimram and Rib, tributaries of the Colne and Lea, which cut the Chiltern dip slope (ibid., fig. 27.2). Late Iron Age enclosures in the Bulbourne valley at Cow Roast and Ashridge covered an area of over 300ha and excavation has revealed evidence of a major iron-working centre, exploiting local bog ore on a massive scale (Morris and Wainwright 1995; Bryant and Niblett 1997, 272). All of these settlement foci, with the exception of the Cow Roast/Ashridge complex and Wheathampstead, have produced evidence of high-status burial. A high-status late Iron Age burial was also found at Harpenden during the construction of the Luton and Dunstable branch of the Great Northern Railway in 1867 (Bagshawe 1928; Freeman and Watson 1949). Imported pottery, metalworking debris and coinage were present at Verulamium in the Ver valley and imported pottery has been recovered from Braughing in the Rib valley (Bryant and Niblett 1997, 271-8). The Braughing complex was particularly important as a major centre of exchange and distribution in the 1st century BC, as considerable quantities of imported Continental pottery have been found at this site (ibid., 276). However, it appears to have gone into decline as Verulamium started to grow in size. All of these settlement complexes have been compared to Continental oppida, although some of their characteristics, particularly the density of settlement within them, are notably different (ibid., 279) and subsequent work at some of these sites has cast doubt on this interpretation (Bryant 2007, 73). Given the extent of these sites, and their largely rural nature, it seems that they could account for the majority of settlement in the region. The Verulamium complex lay close by, to the south-east of the M1 widening excavations, and must have provided a focus for late Iron Age activity along the line of the M1. Furthermore, at least some of the cropmarks of rectangular enclosures in the hinterland of Verulamium may represent sites where occupation started in the late Iron Age (R Niblett pers. comm.).

## Roman

At its southern end the scheme lies only 3km west of St Albans (Roman Verulamium) and the whole of the scheme area therefore lies within the hinterland of the Roman city, and Roman sites are frequent in the area. Environmental evidence suggests a relatively densely occupied hinterland for Verulamium in the mid 1st century AD. Pollen evidence from the River Ver, at St Albans, for example, shows that the landscape upstream of Verulamium was largely in agricultural use during the Roman period and only contained small areas of remnant woodland (Dimbleby 1978). In addition, pollen evidence from the mid-1st-century funerary shaft at Folly Lane supports this, whilst the discovery of animal dung and trampled soil from the same feature suggested the presence of nearby stockyards (Niblett 1999, 62). The NMR lists four Roman roads that are known, or thought to exist, along the route of the scheme, or to cross it (Atkins 2005, A58-61). The main one of these (ibid., A60) is Watling Street, the course of which is followed approximately by the modern A5183 and A5, and which intersects the M1, as well as the River Ver, at Junction 9. Although the route of Roman Watling Street runs through the Junction 9 area, the location of the present works did not provide scope for examination of the line of this road or its relationship with the River Ver. Indeed, much, if not all, of this evidence will have been destroyed by the original construction of Junction 9. The three other roads are all ones identified by The Viatores (1964, 34) and comprise their roads 163, 165 and 169b, although no evidence for them was uncovered during the M1 widening scheme excavations. Of these, a road running west from St Albans to join the well-known alignment of Akeman Street in the Bulbourne valley was the most important and would have crossed the line of the M1 in the vicinity of Junction 7 (cf Margary 1973, 155-6).

Knowledge of the Roman rural settlement pattern in this area is dominated by the evidence for villas and shrine complexes. The villa complexes at Gorhambury, which had high-status pre-conquest origins (Neal *et al.* 1990), and Gadebridge Park (Neal 1974), respectively 2km east and 4.5km west of Junction 8, have both been the subject of major excavations. Several other villa sites in the area have also been examined in part (eg Neal 1976). There are a further four known villas in the area between the rivers Gade and Ver, including those at Kings Langley, Park Street and Childwickbury. In addition, probable villas exist at Netherwild and Munden (Hunn 1995a, 81), but a potential villa site near the southern end of the present project area,

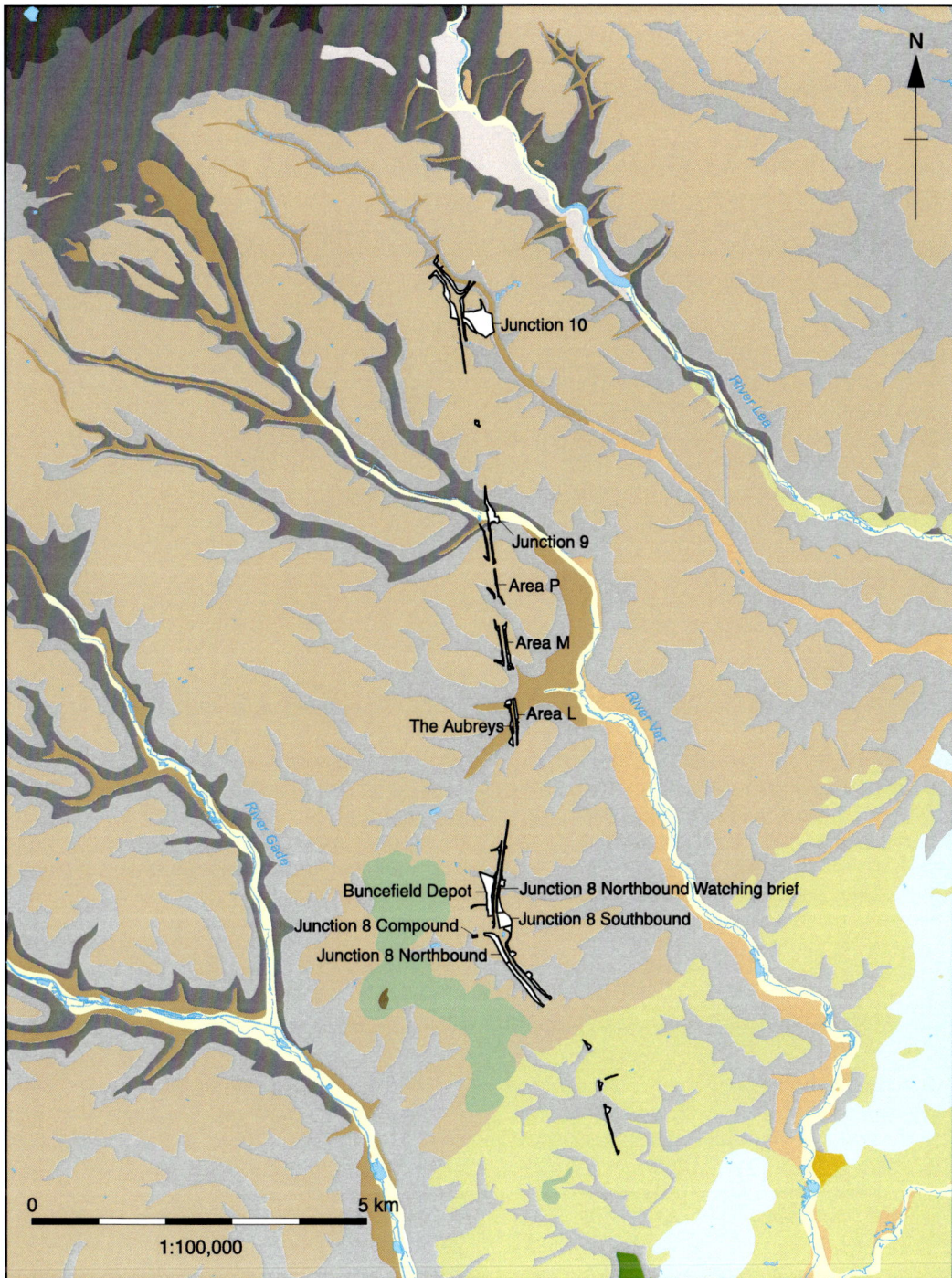

*Fig. 1.3  Geology*

just east of Potters Crouch (Atkins 2005, A37), has been discounted (R Niblett pers. comm.).

Villas appear to be absent on the Chiltern dip slope to the east of Verulamium (Hunn 1995a, 91), where the local superficial geology produces soils that are generally infertile. The villa at Mackerye End, Harpenden, developed on the site of an established late Iron Age farmstead, as did the Romanised building/villa at Fairfolds Farm, Sandridge. Further villas are known from aerial photographic evidence, or are suspected, at Harpenden, Gaddesden and Frithsden, Berkhamsted. Roman pottery from the site of the farmstead at Prae Wood may be evidence for its continued use, while an aisled building occupied the centre of the post-conquest enclosure, south of the King Harry Lane cemetery (Niblett 2005a, 123-4).

Shrine complexes are known from Annables Cottages, near Friars Wash, close to Watling Street and the River Ver, where there were two adjacent temple structures (Wessex Archaeology 2009), and Wood Lane End, just to the west of Junction 8, where a large temple and associated buildings, including a bath house, were discovered (Neal 1983; 1984). In addition, an early 2nd-century temple/mausoleum complex has been excavated at Rothamstead, Harpenden, and this was possibly associated with a suspected villa near Harpenden church, or at Hatching Green (Lowther 1937).

Roman tiles and masonry remains were seen in the vicinity of Junction 8 of the M1 during its original construction, but the real nature of this evidence is very unclear. It may indicate that there was a small villa or farmstead at this location, with a building of rectangular plan (Anthony 1960, 8; Hunn 1995a, 83). However, the present work suggests continuity of settlement from the late Iron Age and the presence of reused building materials rather than a more substantial structure. Lower status Roman rural sites are rare on the Chiltern dip slope (Hunn 1995a, 91), but sites of varying degrees of status and complexity are known to the north of Gorhambury, at Old Jeromes West, at Prae Wood, at Breakspears and at Boxfield Farm, 22km to the north of St Albans (ibid., 83-4). In addition, rural settlements are known from Harpenden, Redbourn, Kettlewells and Bladder Wood (ibid., 84). A low-status rural site is also known from Bishops Stortford where an extensive settlement, comprising ditches, pits, gullies and spreads of domestic debris, grew up at Thorley (R Niblett pers. comm.). Other rural settlements include Harpenden, Fairfolds Farm, Sandridge and Gaddesden Row (R Niblett pers. comm.). To the south, excavation at Leavesden Airfield recorded a complex of ditched enclosures, pits and postholes, dating from the middle Iron Age to the late Roman period, along with a kiln producing grog-tempered pottery, which was dated to the late 1st century AD (Brossler *et al.* 2009). A further, and perhaps earlier, kiln has been excavated recently during work associated with widening of the M25 at Bricket Wood (OA forth-

coming). Excavations at Westwood Quarry, near The Grove site in Watford, recorded three rectilinear enclosures (R Niblett pers. comm.) and field walking on the enclosures at Old Jeromes East and Beech Hyde Farm have produced late Iron Age pottery and Roman pottery and tile (R Niblett pers. comm.). A sub-rectangular ditched enclosure on the line of the Redbourn bypass, excavated in 1983, dated to between the late Iron Age and the early 2nd century and produced metalworking slag (R Niblett pers. comm.). Kiln sites belonging to the Verulamium region pottery industry are also known from the area, but these are concentrated along the route of Watling Street, south of Verulamium, between it and Sulloniacis (eg Hunn 1995a, 85; Bird 2005; Smith *et al.* 2008).

## Saxon and medieval

The medieval period is well represented along the route. Many of the farmsteads and manorial complexes in the area have early medieval origins, with materials dating from this period still evident in their fabric. Although evidence for Saxon activity on the Chiltern dip slope is scarce, settlement dating to the 7th century is known from Foxholes Farm, Hertford, Old Parkbury, Colney Street, Bricket Wood and Aldenham. In addition, a 7th-century burial is known from Wheathampstead (Wingfield 1995, 39), whilst an Anglo-Saxon cemetery of 39 inhumation graves from King Harry Lane was probably established during, or following, the middle of the 7th century (Ager 1989, 226). Other possible evidence for early Saxon burial comes from the 'mound of the banners' at Redbourn, close to the line of Watling Street (Williamson 2010, 155). This site was dug into by the monks of St Albans Abbey in the 12th century, who reported the remains of skeletons and iron weapons, which may have been early Saxon in date (ibid., 155).

It is possible that there was significant increase in woodland in the region at some point in the early medieval period, although the extent of this is unclear (ibid., 77). That there was survival of a post-Roman British enclave in the Chilterns, incorporating St Albans, is a long-standing hypothesis, most recently examined at length by Baker (2006) and potentially supported by Niblett's review (2005b) of the post-Roman (as opposed to early Anglo-Saxon) evidence for St Albans itself. In the 8th century St Albans was part of the kingdom of Mercia, under Offa who founded the Abbey of St Alban on, or near, a late Roman church. Hemel Hempstead, Redbourn and Wheathampstead are all also mentioned in late Saxon charters (Williamson 2010, 151, 155, 172).

The evidence for settlement in the St Albans region between the late Roman period and the 10th century is limited, with no archaeological or historical evidence to suggest that the known medieval settlements existed before the 10th century (Hunn 1995b, 46). Although the sites of the five parish churches of Redbourn, St Michaels, St Peters, St Stephens and Sandridge are not mentioned in Domesday book, they were nevertheless probably established by the late 10th century (ibid., 47). Two of these, Redbourn and Sandridge, were probably sited adjacent to settlements (ibid.), whilst the church of St Mary in Redbourn (Atkins 2005, A11) retains fabric which dates to around 1100. Overall the medieval settlement pattern can be characterised as dispersed (ibid., 50), with St Albans forming a large central focus, which was surrounded by hamlets and individual farmsteads. Only two settlements (Redbourn and Sandridge) had village-like characteristics (ibid.). The place-name Potterscrouch was recorded as early as 1346-7, but there is no evidence for pottery production there (McCarthy and Brooks 1988, 435-6).

### Post-medieval and 20th century

The dominance of the agricultural economy continued into the post-medieval period, although in recent years the construction of the motorways and the expansion of London's satellite towns have changed the character of the area, and have led to the growth of urban settlements in Hertfordshire, such as Hemel Hempstead. Villages such as Redbourn have also expanded; their growth characterised by recent housing estates. These changes are important in that they represent a time of significant development in Britain's 20th-century cultural heritage.

More specifically, the direct impact of the original M1 construction on the landscape was very striking and was, in terms of its disregard for the landscape and the historic boundaries within it, comparable in its effect to the major phase of railway construction in the 19th century. This was also the first substantial stretch of motorway to be constructed in England, as the earlier Preston bypass was just eight miles long. The 61-mile length of the M1 from Watford to Daventry was opened in November 1959 and incorporated, amongst other things, new developments in bridge construction technology. The effect of the motorway on the evolution of settlement patterns in this part of Hertfordshire was less direct, although its presence did encourage secondary eastward expansion of the 'new town' of Hemel Hempstead.

### THE PROJECT

The scheme involved the asymmetric widening of the motorway by an extra lane to relieve congestion along the corridor. Existing junctions were adapted to reduce the level of accidents and some modifications to slip and approach roads were also made. Accompanying mitigation took the form of activities such as planting and most existing structures were demolished or altered. Many of these late 1950s concrete structures (bridges and underpasses) were of interest in their own right and were the

subject of a separate recording project (OA 2006a).

An Environmental Statement (ES) for the scheme was produced in 1994 (Highways Agency 1994) based on a full EIA. The Archaeological input to the ES was prepared in September 1994 by St Albans Museum in association with Hertfordshire County Transportation Design Services. It identified several sites of potential archaeological significance on the basis of site walkover, limited geophysical survey and existing knowledge. In total, nine sites were identified in the ES, and the commitments established at the Public Inquiry (PI) included further evaluation and mitigation at these sites. Moreover, further assessment concluded that the scope of the preliminary survey work needed to be expanded in respect of the rest of the scheme area. This led to extensive evaluation trenching being undertaken in locations which were not identified as archaeologically sensitive at the PI, in order to reduce the risk of discovering remains during the watching brief, which was required during construction. In addition, a record was made of changes to the historic landscape through an innovative photographic project, but this was separate from the work reported in this volume.

A complex system of area nomenclature was developed (Table 1.1). Evaluation trenching (Fig. 1.2) in Area S (Junction 10) was undertaken in December 2005 and January 2006 and was reported on in March 2006 (OA 2006b). Evaluation of a proposed borrow pit area immediately south-east of Junction 10, in Bedfordshire, took place in February 2006 and was also reported upon in March of that year (OA 2006c). Areas Q, L, M and N were subjected to a programme of trial trenching from January to April 2006 in line with a Written Scheme of Investigation (WSI) prepared by Oxford Archaeology (OA 2005). The results were presented in a report (OA 2006d) which also included an account of a watching brief undertaken near Junction 9. Evaluation trenching in Areas T, A, B, D, F, V, G, X, H, J, Y, I, W and E was undertaken from November 2005-May 2006 and the results of this work were presented in a further report (OA 2006e).

The results of the various phases of evaluation were used as the basis for establishing a programme of further mitigation works (Atkins 2006). The principal mitigation strategies are listed in Table 1.1 and the excavations and watching briefs were undertaken from autumn 2006-summer 2007. Substantive results were derived from excavation at three sites (Junction 8 Southbound; Junction 8 Northbound; and Junction 9) with smaller bodies of information recovered from The Aubreys and Areas M and P, and minor observations at locations in the vicinity of Junction 8 Northbound and at Junction 10. All of these are presented in summary in this volume, whilst records of observations from other areas are retained in the project archive.

A programme of post-excavation assessment work was undertaken in 2007 and a revised report was submitted in March 2008 (OA 2008). This report outlined the nature of the records and the character of the archaeological features and finds with an assessment of their significance, and set out proposals for further analysis and reporting. The results of this programme of work form the basis of the work presented in this volume.

## MITIGATION: AIMS, METHODOLOGY AND ARCHIVE

The main aims of the mitigation fieldwork programme were very broadly defined, with an emphasis on basic characterisation of sites in terms of their function and date. Particularly in terms of prehistoric archaeology, this broad-based approach reflects the relative lack of detailed evidence dating to this period in the vicinity of the scheme. The primary objectives were, therefore, to define the nature of landuse and its evolution and development through time, relating such developments, where possible, to the wider landscape. Given the lack of comparative excavation data from the area, similarly broad objectives were defined in relation to the examination of medieval features at Junction 8 Northbound.

It was possible, however, to pose more specific questions for sites of Roman date, although the need for accurate basic characterisation remained paramount. Attention was focussed on defining the balance between the evidence for domestic occupation and types of activity, and the origins and sequence of such occupation, particularly with regard to continuity of settlement from the late Iron Age. The principal wider question for examination concerned the role of these sites within the hinterland of Verulamium, the dominant focus in the local and regional settlement pattern, and the extent to which it was possible to identify evidence that would illustrate the connections, if any, between the rural settlements and this Roman city.

*Table 1.1: M1 sites listed in geographical order from north to south (based on Atkins 2006, section 4.2.3)*

| ES number/ evaluation area | Additional evaluation area | Description of site and reason for evaluation | Evaluation result |
|---|---|---|---|
| | S (includes OA site AA) | Junction 10 area. Prehistoric, Roman and medieval. Predominantly Roman potential | Positive. Possible field system of ditches with five/six possible pits. Focus of site a possible ring ditch with one worked flint. No other dating material |
| | Borrow Pit Area | Borrow Pit Area east of Junction 10 Prehistoric, Roman and medieval. Predominantly Roman potential | Positive but limited. Series of field boundaries and five possible gullies in concentrated area. Possible prehistoric settlement. Dating material primarily post-medieval in date. Possibly connected with Area S |
| | R | Coles Lane crossing. Prehistoric potential | Not evaluated due to limitations of access – reverted to a scheme-wide watching brief as proposed at PI |
| | Q | Area around Junction 9 and the A5 Watling Street. High Roman potential (also prehistoric and medieval) | Positive. Series of ditches containing Iron Age/Roman material and some containing Mesolithic, Neolithic and Bronze Age material. Large amount of 2nd-century AD pottery and building material. Stakeholes, postholes, other occupation debris. Roman roadside activity and occupation? Stratified deposits and concentrated features |
| | Junction 9 compound | Junction 9 compound. Potential prehistoric, medieval and Roman remains | Negative |
| 6/P (including OA site Z) | | Struck flint scatter and geophysical anomalies. Prehistoric and medieval potential | Not evaluated due to limitations of access – evaluation watching brief employed |
| | O | Lybury Lane crossing. Prehistoric and medieval potential | Not evaluated due to limitations of access – reverted to a scheme-wide watching brief as proposed at PI |
| 7/M | | Flint scatters and geophysical anomalies north of The Aubreys. Iron Age/prehistoric potential | Positive. Trackway and boundary ditches (Iron Age and Roman). Possible yard surface and postholes. Some Iron Age and Roman finds. Dispersed archaeology and not deeply stratified |

**Fieldwork methodology**

Fieldwork methodologies followed standard agreed procedures set out in a series of site specific WSIs (OA 2006f; 2006g; 2006h; 2006i; 2006j). Excavation areas were stripped with a 360° tracked machine, fitted with a toothless ditching bucket, under direct archaeological supervision. Machine excavation proceeded to the first archaeological horizon or to the underlying natural geology, whichever was encountered first.

In the principal excavation areas base plans were produced digitally. Sections and detailed plans of complex areas and archaeological interventions were drawn by hand and integrated with the main site plans. A representative sample of the features and deposits revealed was excavated by hand to determine their depth, extent and nature. Finds, where present, and environmental samples, where appropriate, were recovered and all artefacts were retained. All features and deposits encountered were issued a unique context number and recording followed procedures laid down in the *OA Fieldwork Manual* (Wilkinson 1992). Photographs, including a record of each intervention, were taken using colour-slide and black-and-white print film.

The procedures for targeted watching briefs and other watching brief areas followed those set out above, with the exception that, in some cases, base plans were prepared by hand using local grids. Fixed points on these grids were subsequently surveyed and related to National Grid Reference (NGR) co-ordinates.

**Post-excavation methodologies**

The excavation and watching brief site records were subject to assessment in 2007 (OA 2008). A context database was compiled for all the principal sites

| Report | Further mitigation | Mitigation result | In present volume |
|---|---|---|---|
| 5038930/TE/DO/EHE/007 | Excavation, targeted watching brief, Junction 10 | Minor features, mostly undated | Y |
| 11.4.2006 | Excavation, Borrow Pit Area | see above | Y |
| - | Scheme-wide watching brief | - | N |
| 5038930/TE/DO/EHE/011 | Excavation, Junction 9 | Prehistoric and late Iron Age-Roman features | Y |
| - | - | - | N |
| - | Evaluation watching brief | Roman linear features | Y |
| - | Scheme-wide watching brief | - | N |
| 5038930/TE/DO/EHE/011 | Targeted watching brief, Nicholls Farm | Late Iron Age and Roman linear features | Y |

and hand-drawn plans were digitised and incorporated into the digital base plans for each site. Features were assigned to broad period-based phases (late Neolithic-early Bronze Age, late Bronze Age-early Iron Age, Roman and medieval), using key stratigraphic sequences and spot dates provided by the pottery assessments and, in the case of the earlier prehistoric features, the flint assessment. Phase plans were produced for all of the sites and, in some cases, major features were assigned to feature groups.

All of the artefacts were assessed. In the case of the principal artefact groups (pottery, ceramic building material and lithics) the material was fully recorded. In most cases, recording was restricted to the establishment of chronology, in order to assist the development of schemes of phasing for each site, while an assessment of each assemblages' character and potential for further analysis was also undertaken.

Animal bone, like the principal artefact categories, was fully recorded at this stage, but additional work was confined to assessing the potential of the material for further analysis. Environmental samples were assessed by category and, although full recording was not undertaken, provisional assessments of the character of the material were made and its potential for further work determined.

The post-excavation assessment report has formed the basis for the results outlined in this volume. However, in addition, site sequences have been examined in more detail and site narratives expanded and amended accordingly. Artefact assemblages have also been analysed in the light of revised phasing and selected environmental samples have been fully examined. The site narratives and specialist reports presented in this volume are nevertheless quite condensed, and further analytical data can be found in the project archive.

Within this volume, reports are presented on the results of work at the principal sites examined during the project, although in some cases the results were disappointing and the scale of reporting is therefore limited. The sites are described separately, proceeding in geographical sequence from south to north (Chapters 2-6). Reports on artefactual and ecofactual material consider the finds from all the sites together, but with a clear distinction between each assemblage (Chapters 7-8), which are then followed by a report on the programme of radiocarbon dating (Chapter 9). A final discussion (Chapter 10) attempts to place the results from each individual site together, within a developing chronological framework.

## Archive

Quantification of aspects of the project archive was set out in the post-excavation assessment report (OA 2008). The finds, paper record and digital archive will be deposited with the Verulamium Museum. Owing to increasing inaccessibility to microfilm services the basic digital archive will take the form of a pdfA scan of the hard-copy records. These pdfA scans will be preserved on the OA South archive server and a copy on disk will accompany the hard copy deposited within the project archive. Born digital data, such as jpeg digital images and databases or geomatics data, which are not suitable for hard copy, will also be stored in this way. In time it is hoped that these digital archives will be made publicly available through the internet, but in the interim anyone unable to access the hard copy or museum disk copy may approach OA South for acces

# Chapter 2: Junction 8 Southbound

*by Dan Stansbie*

## SITE LOCATION

The Junction 8 Southbound (Junction 8S) site was centred at NGR TL 094 079, east of both Hemel Hempstead and the M1 (see Fig. 1.2). The excavation area lay to the north of what was then the Junction 8 slip road and occupied an area of approximately 4.1ha. The local geology comprises clay-with-flints, overlying Upper Chalk (see Fig. 1.3), and the area has a relatively flat topography, with a maximum height of 136m above Ordnance Datum (aOD).

## SUMMARY (Fig. 2.1)

Activity at Junction 8S can be divided into five broad phases. Flint tools and flint-working debris, mostly dating from the late Neolithic and early Bronze Age periods, were recovered from the fills of pits and tree-throw holes across the site, suggesting that people were moving through the area and possibly using it for short-term occupation in these periods. Most of this material came from pits dating to the late Bronze Age or early Iron Age, but some came from features which were otherwise without finds and could therefore be related to Neolithic/early Bronze Age occupation. Late Bronze Age-early Iron Age pits and postholes, some of which formed two distinct clusters in the northern half of the site, indicate settlement during this period. Following the cessation of this activity, the site appears to have been unoccupied until the early Roman period, when two ditches, probably defining a sub-rectangular enclosure extending beyond the limit of excavation, were established in the north-eastern corner of the site. Two large quarry pits, cutting the enclosure ditch and dated to the late 1st-2nd centuries AD, were probably contemporary with a third quarry pit in the south-western corner of the site. A single pit containing middle-late Roman pottery lay in the south-eastern corner of the site, suggesting some level of activity on, or near, the site in this period. Following the end of the Roman period, there is no evidence of activity until the establishment of field boundary ditches in the 19th or early 20th centuries.

## NEOLITHIC AND EARLY BRONZE AGE ACTIVITY (Fig. 2.2)

### Summary

The evidence for Neolithic and Bronze Age activity suggests flint working and possibly temporary occupation. Flint tools and working debris from this period were scattered widely over the site, but were mostly residual in later pits and ditches. However, a pit (5081), lying in the south-western part of the site contained cremated animal bone, possibly a token deposit, which produced a late Neolithic radiocarbon date. A second pit (5064), lying in the far south-western corner of the site produced six flint flakes and may also have been of Neolithic or early Bronze Age date. In addition, four pits (5088, 5096, 5172 and 5226) contained burnt unworked flint, but no other finds, and could therefore date to this period.

### Late Neolithic pit 5081 (Figs 2.2-3)

Pit 5081 was an isolated feature lying in the southern central part of the site. The pit was sub-circular in plan, with a flattish base and steeply sloping sides. It measured 0.79m in diameter by 0.1m in depth and was filled with a single deposit of clay silt, with frequent inclusions of charcoal flecks, burnt clay and flint. The pit contained a small quantity of burnt animal bone, which could not be identified to species. This material produced a radiocarbon determination (NZA-32714) of 3800-3640 cal BC (95.4% confidence; or 3760-3650 cal BC, 68.2% confidence). In addition, the pit produced pottery and worked flint.

### Possible Neolithic and early Bronze Age pits

#### *Pit 5064* (Figs 2.2 and 2.4)

Pit 5064 was sub-circular in plan, measured 0.74m in diameter by 0.54m in depth, and had a U-shaped profile. The pit contained two fills of silty clay, with occasional inclusions of natural flint, and produced six worked flint flakes.

#### *Pits 5088, 5096, 5172 and 5226* (Figs 2.2-4)

The pits were sub-circular, or oval, in plan and averaged 0.95m in diameter by 0.12m in depth. In profile they were bowl- or saucer-shaped and their fills comprised single deposits of clay silt, containing moderate to frequent sub-angular flint. Pits 5088, 5096 and 5172 each produced a single fragment of burnt flint, which in the case of pit 5088 was possibly worked. Pit 5226 produced 12 fragments of burnt unworked flint.

## LATE BRONZE AGE-EARLY IRON AGE ACTIVITY (Fig. 2.5)

### Summary

Late Bronze Age-early Iron Age activity was largely restricted to two concentrations of pits; pit group 7785 located in the north-western corner of the site, close to the north-western limit of excavation, and pit group 7786 located in the central-eastern part of the site, close to the north-eastern limit of excavation. In addition, isolated pits of this date were scattered across the site. These included pits 5094 and 5173 in the southern part of the site and pits 5006 and 5009 in the north-eastern part of the site, close to the limit of excavation. A tree-throw hole (5203) in the central southern part of the site also produced late Bronze Age-early Iron Age pottery. Two four-post structures (5034 and 5189) lay close to the south-eastern limit of excavation. The site also produced two late Bronze Age/early Iron Age unurned and unaccompanied cremation burials (5066 and 5244), one in the south-western corner of the site close to the limit of excavation and the other in the northern-central part of the site.

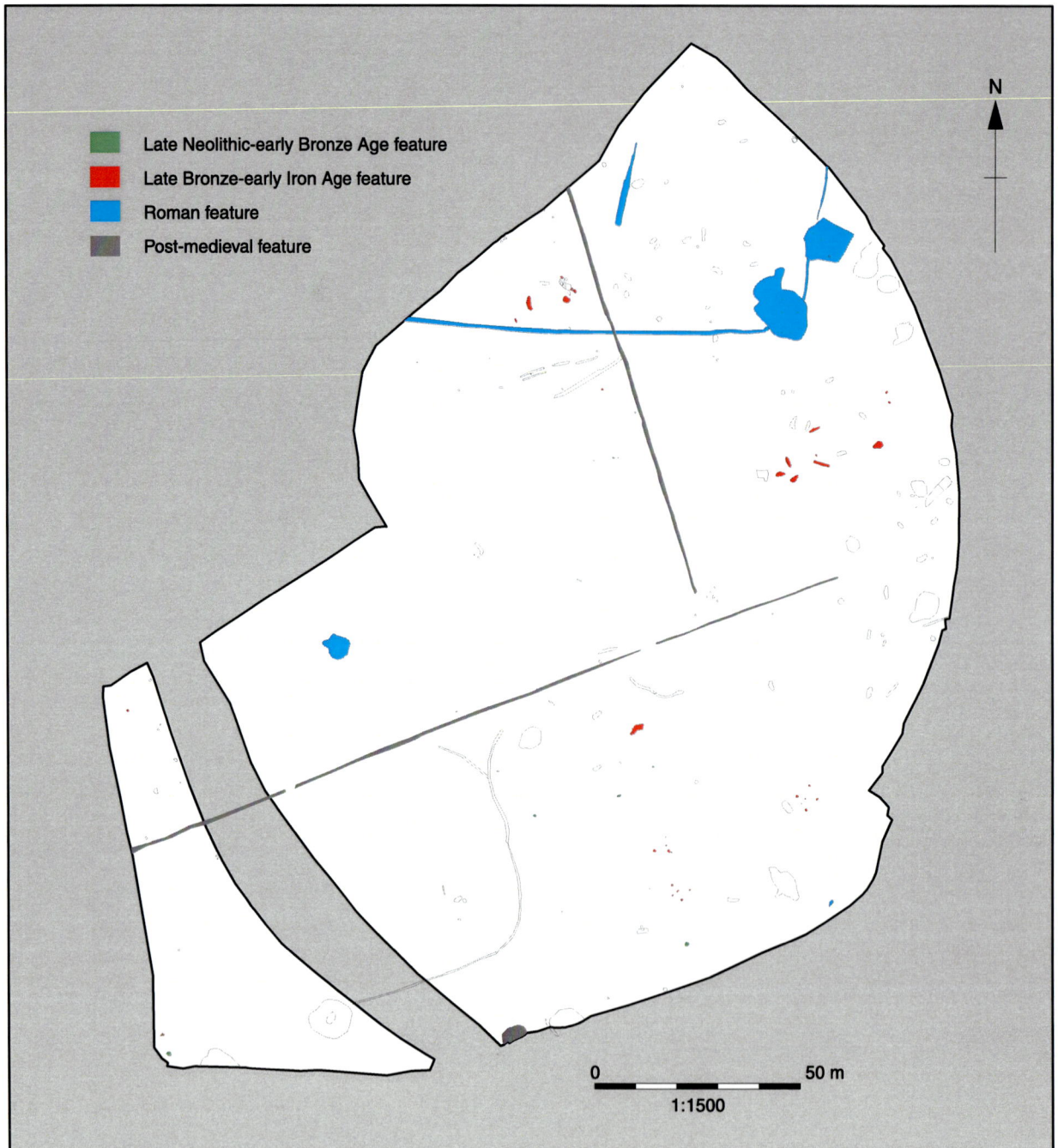

*Fig. 2.1 Junction 8S, plan of all features*

**Pit group 7785** (Fig. 2.6)

Pit group 7785 comprised a concentration of ten pits (5234, 5236, 5246, 5441, 5446, 5448, 5459, 5461, 5465 and 5474) including a number of inter-cutting features, although some (5234, 5236, 5246 and 5474) were part of a dispersed linear scatter orientated NE-SW. The pits were largely sub-circular or oval in plan, with bowl- or saucer-shaped profiles, and averaged 0.71m in diameter by 0.25m in depth. They were filled with sequences of silty clays, or clay silts, which contained moderate inclusions of sub-angular flint and charcoal flecks. The pit fills produced 78 sherds of late Bronze Age-early Iron Age pottery, weighing 445g, in flint- and sand-tempered fabrics, along with 30 worked flints and 32 burnt unworked flints.

**Pit group 7786** (Fig. 2.7)

A second concentration of eight pits (5021, 5023, 5055, 5106, 5422, 5424, 5426 and 5428) and two tree-throw holes (5345 and 5433) lay in the central part of the site, close to the eastern limit of excavation. This was a more dispersed group, with no inter-cutting features, which formed a linear scatter, aligned NE-

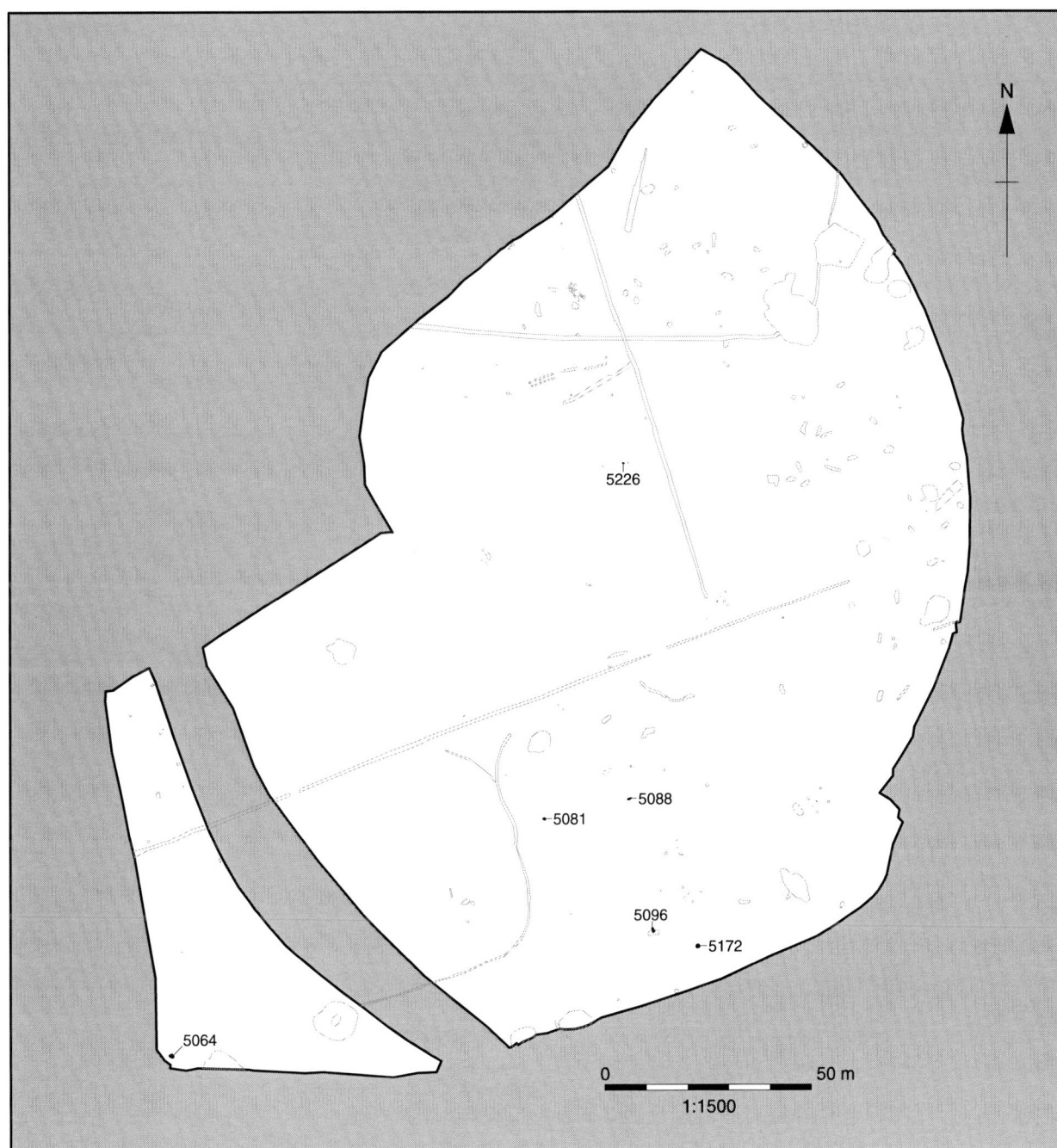

*Fig. 2.2   Junction 8S, plan of Neolithic and early Bronze Age activity*

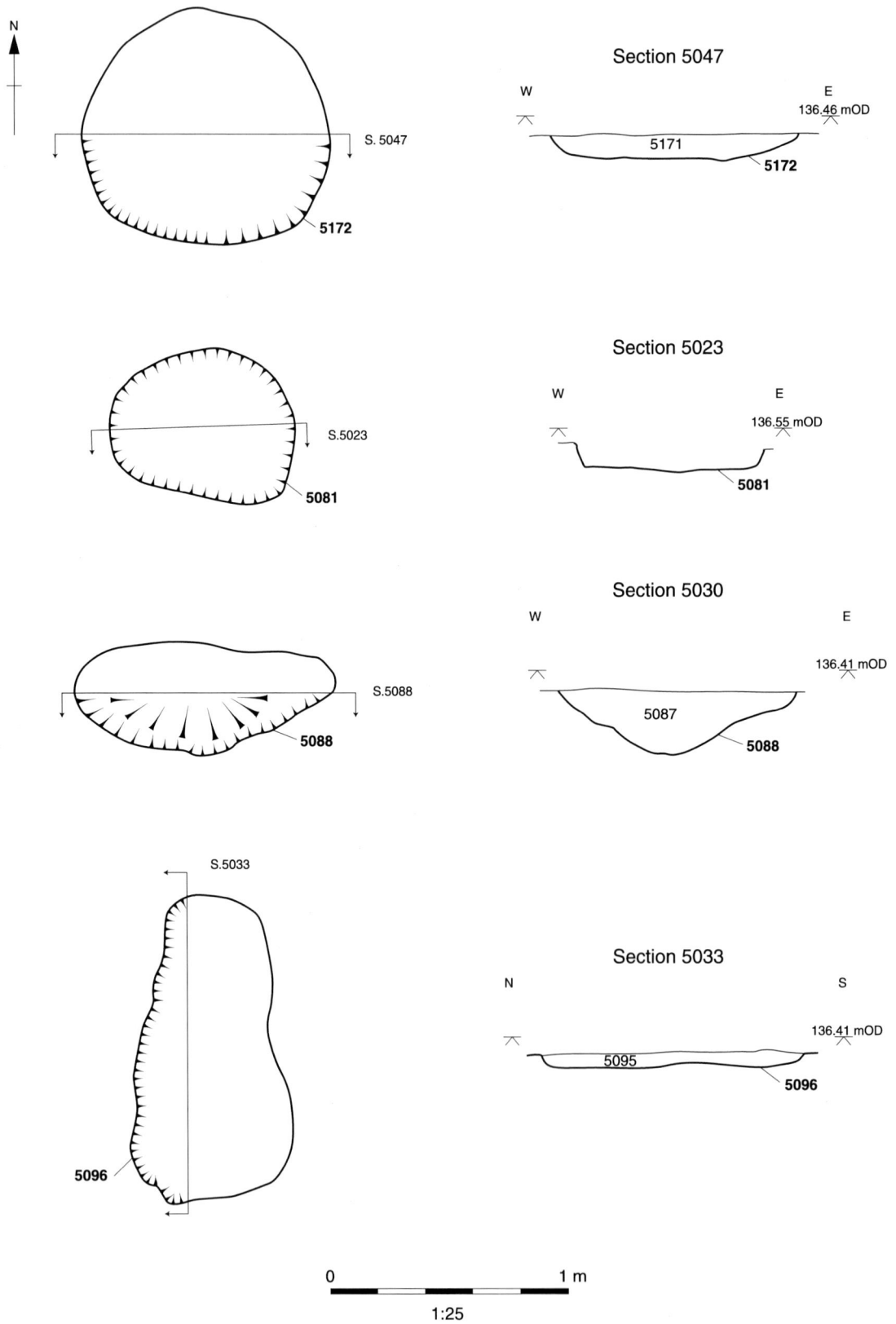

*Fig. 2.3   Junction 8S, detail plans and sections of late Neolithic and early Bronze Age pits*

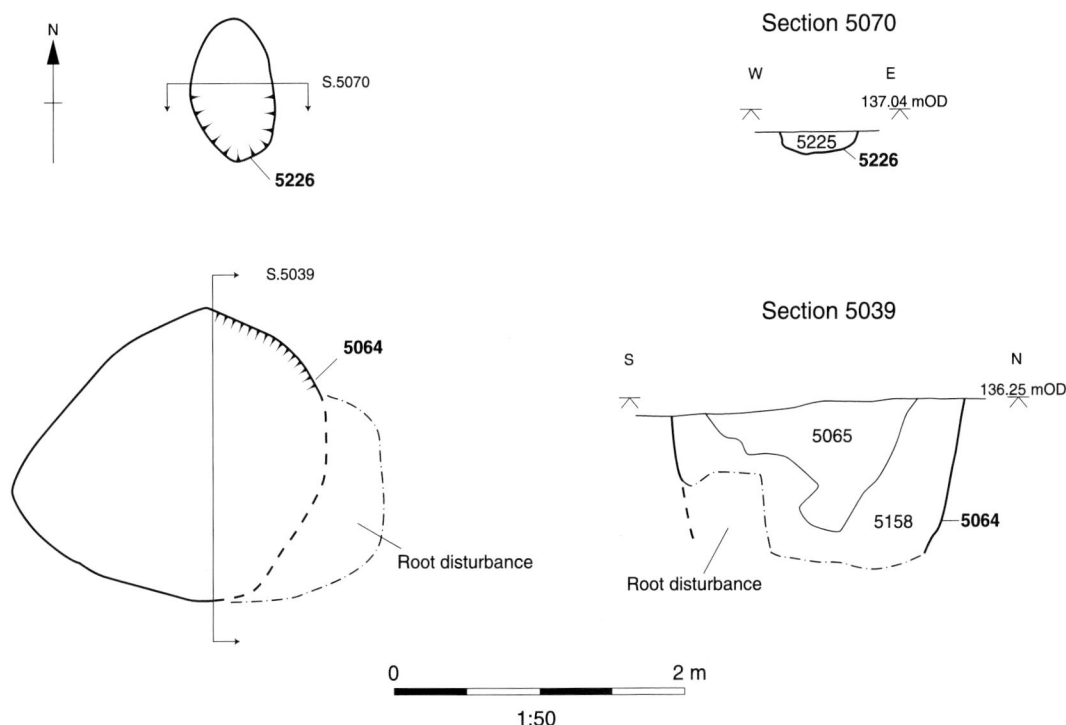

*Fig. 2.4 Junction 8S, detail plans and sections of late Neolithic and early Bronze Age pits*

SW. These pits were largely oval or sub-circular in plan, with bowl-shaped profiles, and averaged 1.32m in diameter by 0.23m in depth. The pits all contained single fills, mostly comprising silty clays and clay silts, with occasional inclusions of sub-angular flint gravel and charcoal flecks. The pit fills produced 338 sherds of late Bronze Age-early Iron Age pottery, weighing 924g, and three fragments of burnt unworked flint.

A short (3.9m) length of gully (5450) aligned almost east-west was associated with this pit cluster. It was 0.74m wide and 0.24m deep, and was bowl-shaped in profile, having a concave base and steeply sloping sides. The single fill comprised a clay silt with frequent flint fragments, but it contained no finds.

### Pits 5094 and 5173, and tree-throw hole 5203 (Fig. 2.5)

Pits 5094 and 5173 were located 2.77m apart in the central-southern part of the site. Pit 5094, the more westerly of the two, was sub-circular in plan, with a concave profile and was 0.68m in diameter and 0.11m deep. The pit contained a single fill of clay silt. Pit 5173 was also sub-circular in plan and had a flat base, with vertical sides. It measured 0.7m in diameter by 0.29m in depth and contained two fills of clay silt, with occasional inclusions of flint fragments and charcoal flecks. The pits produced three sherds of late Bronze Age-early Iron Age

pottery, along with a single fragment of burnt unworked flint from pit 5173.

Tree-throw hole 5203, which lay *c* 28m north of pits 5094 and 5173, was irregular in plan and profile, measuring 3.9m in length by 1.25m in width and 0.56m in depth. The feature contained three fills of silty clay with occasional fragments of flint and charcoal. The fills produced two sherds of late Bronze Age-early Iron Age pottery, weighing 4g, along with two flint flakes and one burnt unworked flint.

### Pits 5006 and 5009 (Fig. 2.5)

Pits 5006 and 5009 were situated at the north-eastern limit of the excavation. Pit 5006 was sub-circular in plan and had a flat base, with steeply sloping sides. The pit measured 1.4m in diameter by 0.45m in depth and contained two fills of clay silt, with occasional inclusions of flint fragments. Pit 5009 cut pit 5006 and was sub-circular in plan, and irregular in profile. It was 0.95m in diameter and 0.53m deep and contained three fills of silty clay, with occasional inclusions of flint fragments and occasional charcoal flecks. Pit 5006 produced a single flint blade and a single sherd of late Bronze Age pottery, while pit 5009 contained no finds.

### Post-built structures 5034 and 5189 (Figs 2.8-9)

Structure 5034, which lay in the south-eastern corner of the excavation, comprised five postholes

17

(5035, 5037, 5041, 5042 and 5044) forming a square measuring 4 x 4m, with a single posthole in the centre. The postholes were all sub-circular, measured 0.53m in diameter by 0.12m in depth on average, and had shallow bowl-shaped profiles, suggesting that they had been truncated. Structure 5189 lay in the southern-central part of the excavation, measured 5.5 x 4.5m and was less regular in plan than structure 5504, although it also consisted of five postholes (5190, 5192, 5194, 5196 and 5198), suggesting a sub-rectangular plan with one post in

the centre. The postholes were again sub-circular in plan, with irregular rather than bowl-shaped profiles. They measured 0.43m in diameter by 0.19m in depth on average and contained fills of sandy clay, with frequent inclusions of flint fragments and charcoal flecks. Structure 5034 produced a single unidentified fragment of fired clay, while structure 5189 produced five sherds of late Bronze Age-early Iron Age pottery, weighing 20g, a flint flake and a fragment of burnt unworked flint.

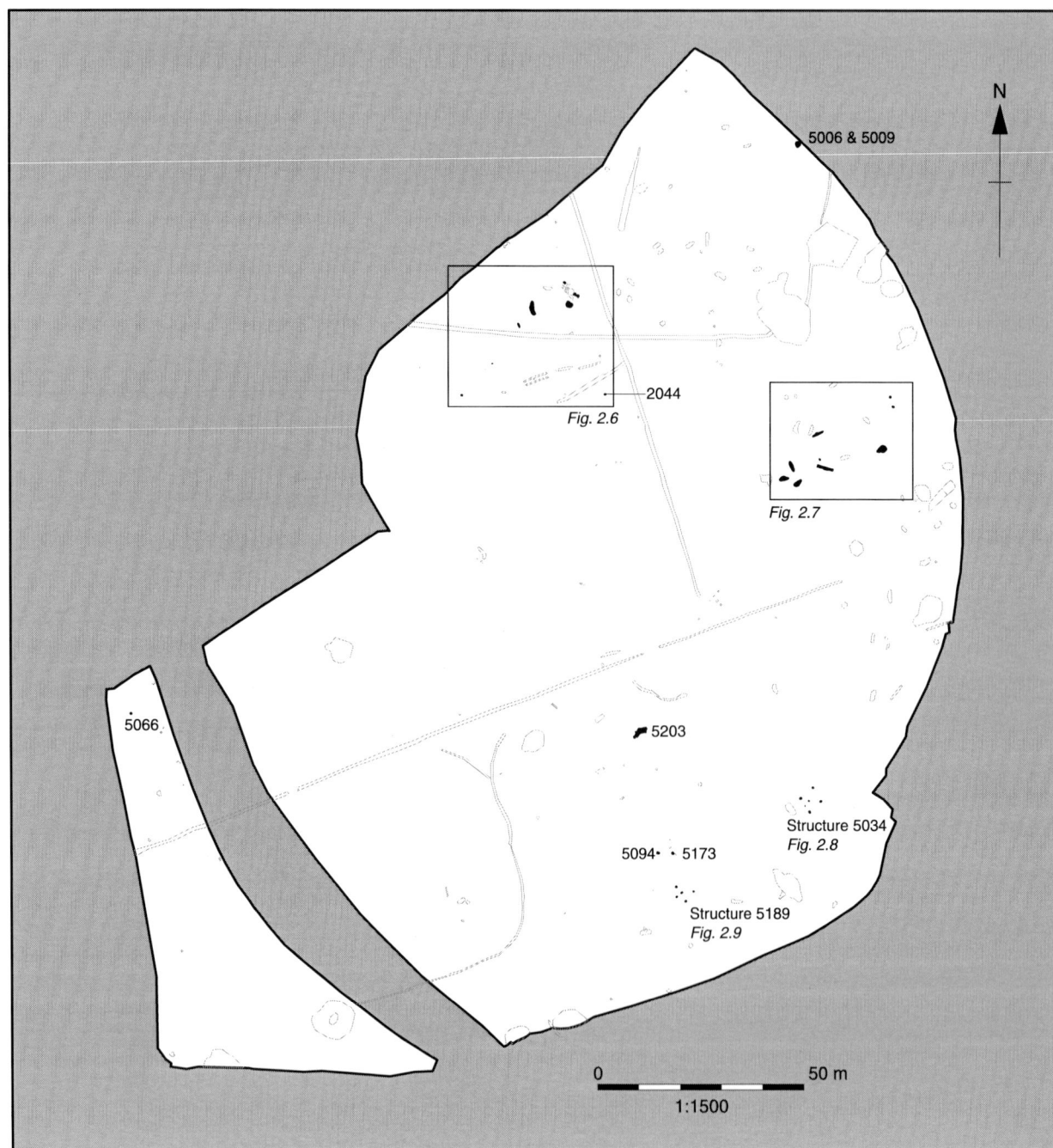

*Fig. 2.5   Junction 8S, late Bronze Age-early Iron Age activity*

*Fig. 2.6 (facing page)   Junction 8S, detail plan and sections of pit group 7785*

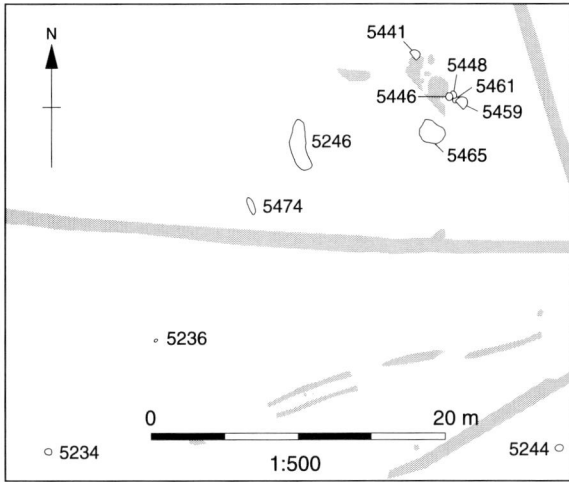

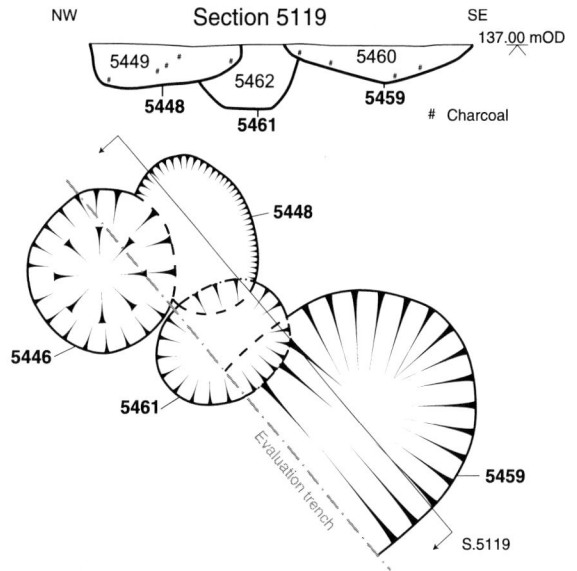

### Section 5119

NW · SE · 137.00 mOD

5449 · 5462 · 5460 · **5459**

**5448** · **5461**

\# Charcoal

**5448**

**5446**

**5461**

**5459**

Evaluation trench

S.5119

### Section 5091

SW · NE · NW · SE · 136.58 mOD

5283 · 5247 · **5246**

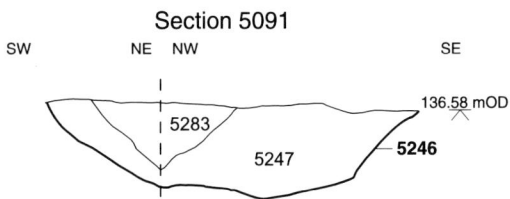

### Section 5118

NE · SW · 137.00 mOD

5463

5464 · **5465**

### Section 5111

NW · SE · 136.36 mOD

5442 · **5441**

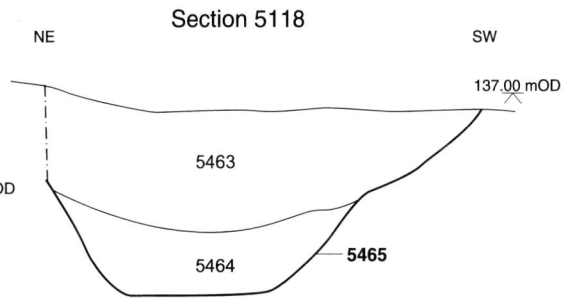

**5441**

Evaluation trench

S.5111

**5465**

S.5118

Evaluation trench

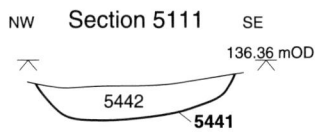

### Section 5124

ENE · WSW · 136.95 mOD

5475 · 5476 · **5474**

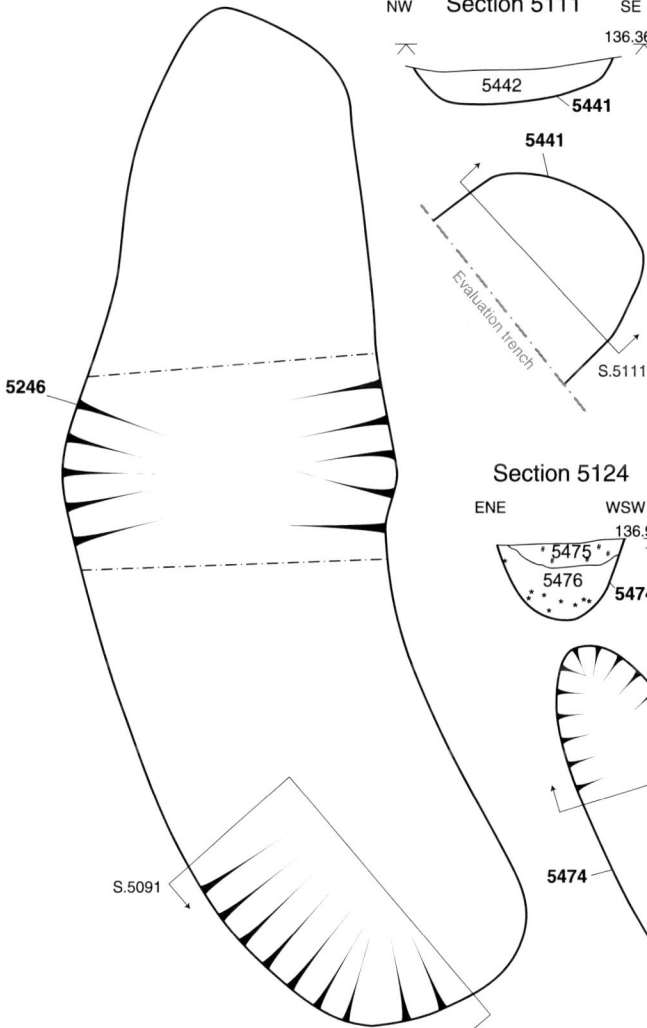

**5246**

S.5091

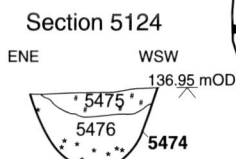

S.5124

**5474**

### Section 5073

NW · SE · 137.32 mOD

5235 · **5234**

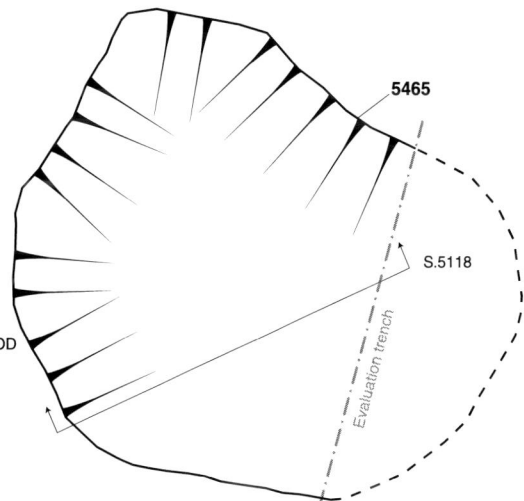

### Section 5074

SE · NW · 137.24 mOD

5237 · **5236**

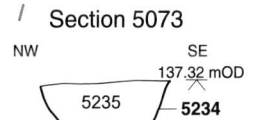

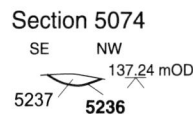

**5236**

S.5074

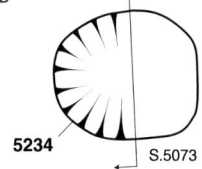

**5234**

S.5073

0 · 1 m

1:25

19

**Cremation burials 5066 and 5244** (Figs. 2.5 and 2.10)

Two unurned, unaccompanied cremation burials (5066 and 5244) of late Bronze Age date were contained in sub-circular pits averaging 0.57m in diameter. The cremated bone from these deposits produced radiocarbon determinations (NZA-32713 and NZA-32715) of 1370-1090 cal BC (95.4% confidence; or 1260-1130 cal BC, 68.2% confidence) and 1130-900 cal BC (95.4% confidence; or 1050-920 cal BC, 68.2% confidence) respectively. No finds were recovered from the fills of either pit.

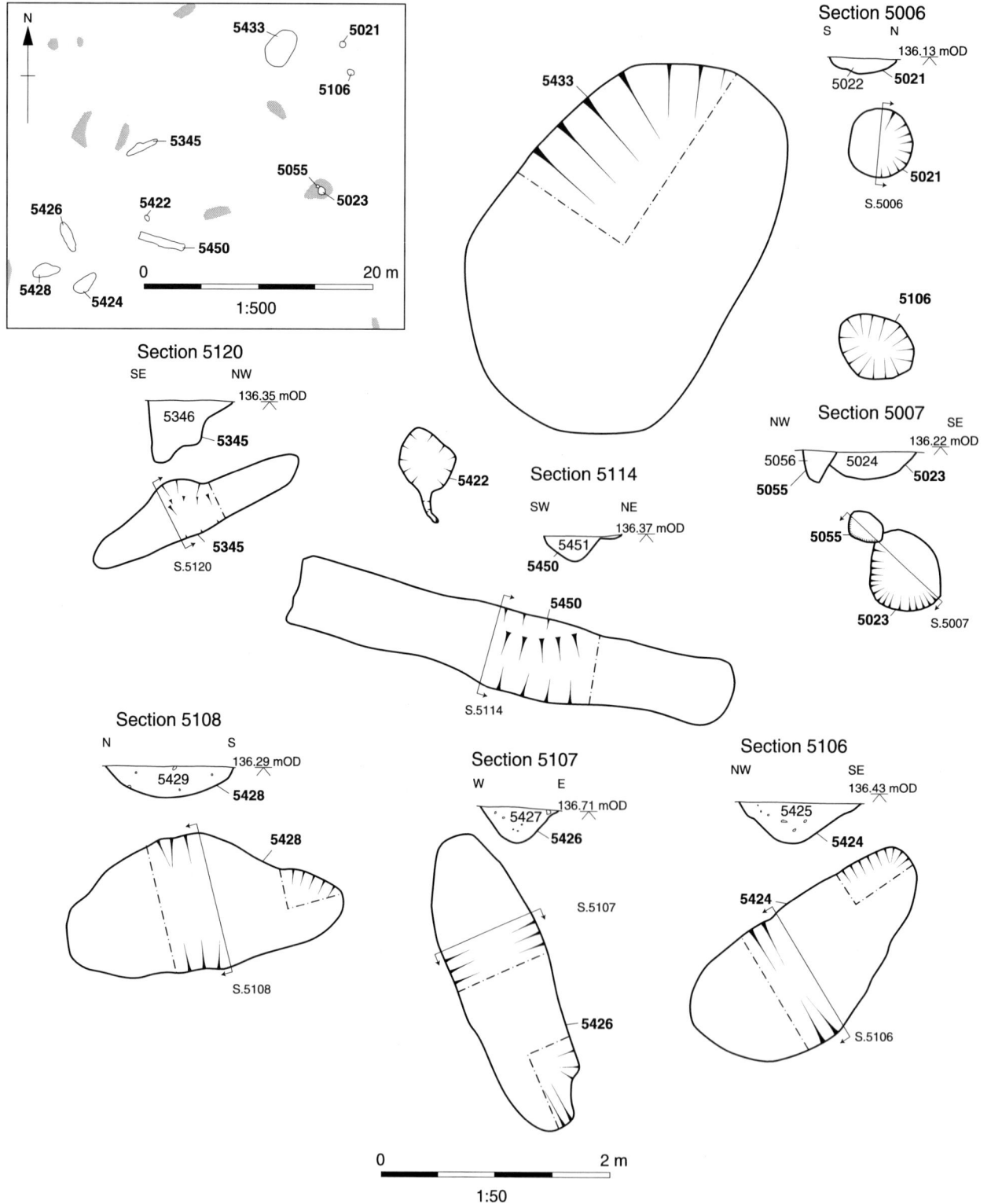

*Fig. 2.7 Junction 8S, detail plan and sections of pit group 7786 and gully 5450*

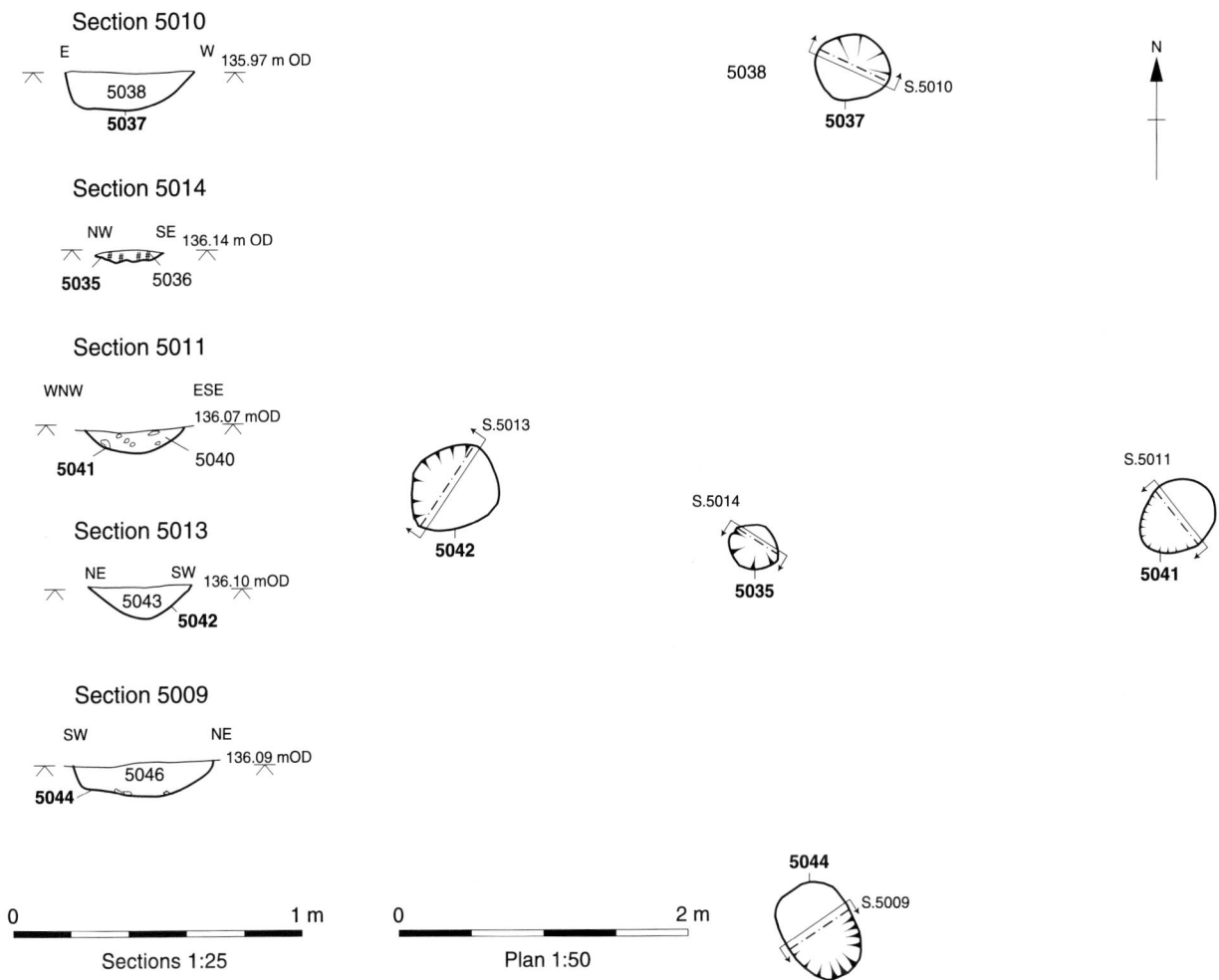

*Fig. 2.8  Junction 8S, detail plan and sections of structure 5034*

## EARLY-MIDDLE ROMAN ACTIVITY (Fig. 2.11)

### Summary

During the mid-late 1st century AD part of a substantial rectilinear enclosure (5500) was established in the north-eastern corner of the site. Within the space defined by the enclosure was a NE-SW-orientated linear ditch (5501). However, there was no evidence for occupation or any other kind of Roman activity within the enclosure, a fact that may be due to heavy post-Roman truncation of the soils in this area. Pottery from the fills of enclosure ditches 5500 and 5501 dates from the late Iron Age-early Roman period, suggesting that these features may have gone out of use by the late 1st century AD; however, the assemblages are small and abraded and could therefore be residual. Other probable early-middle Roman features included quarry pit 5155, situated in the south-western corner of the site, and quarry pit 5025, which cut enclosure ditch 5500 in the north-eastern corner of the site. Both quarry pits

produced early-middle Roman pottery. Also probably dating to the early Roman period, on the basis of its similarity in size and shape, was quarry pit 5265, situated 20m south-west of quarry pit 5025, which also cut enclosure ditch 5500.

### Enclosure 5500 (Fig. 2.11)

Enclosure 5500 was defined by a rectilinear boundary ditch, which was orientated east-west and returned to the NNE at its eastern end, running beyond the limit of excavation at both ends. The distance from the east/west-aligned boundary to the northern limit of excavation was approximately 40m and from the north-western limit of excavation to the NNE return approximately 95m. It is clear that this boundary ditch formed part of a much larger enclosure running beyond the limits of excavation to the north and west. The ditch was *c* 0.5m wide on average but in places was up to 1m across, and it varied in depth from approximately 0.1m at its western end to

Section 5058

Section 5055

Section 5059

Section 5057

Section 5056

0            1 m

Sections 1:25

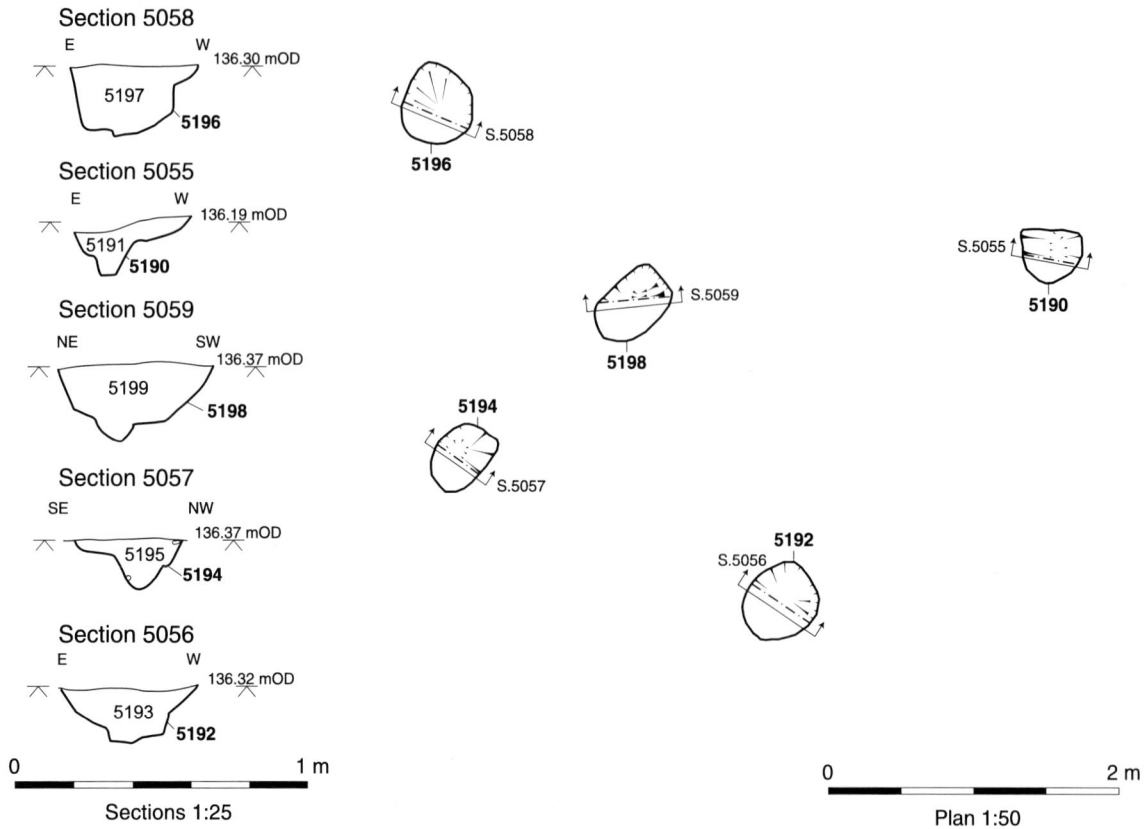

*Fig. 2.9 Junction 8S, detail plan and sections of structure 5189*

0.28m at its north-eastern end. Similarly, the ditch profile varied from bowl-shaped at the western end to V-shaped at the north-eastern end. No recuts were visible. The single ditch fill comprised clay silt, with frequent inclusions of flint fragments and occasional charcoal flecks. Finds from this fill were scarce, comprising six sherds (14g) of late Bronze Age-early Iron Age pottery and two sherds (7g) of late Iron Age-early Roman pottery, along with four flint flakes and four fragments of burnt unworked flint.

**Ditch 5501** (Fig. 2.11)

Within the enclosure, ditch 5501 was aligned NNE-SSW, almost exactly parallel to the eastern side of the enclosure but 46m west of it. At its south-western end the ditch had a rounded terminus some 19m north of the southern side of the enclosure. North of this point it survived for a length of 20m, at which point it apparently petered out, probably as a result of truncation. The maximum width of ditch 5501 was 1.6m and its maximum depth was only 0.13m, giving a very shallow profile with gently sloping sides. The ditch fills comprised silty clay with occasional inclusions of flint fragments and occasional charcoal flecks. The upper fill produced five sherds of late Iron Age-early Roman pottery, weighing just 9g.

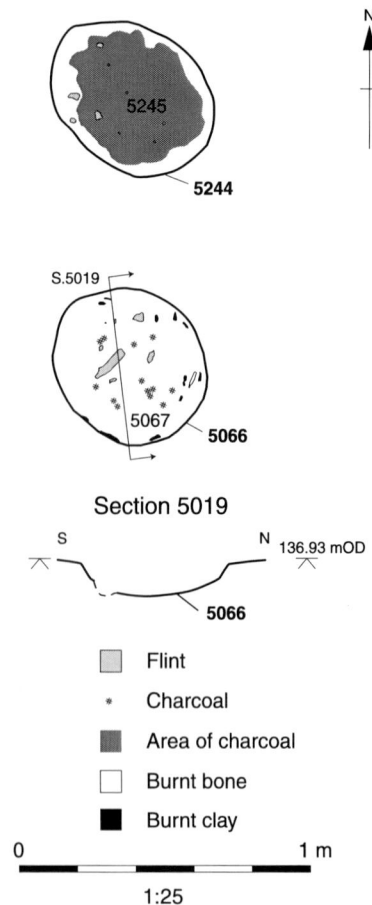

0            2 m

Plan 1:50

Section 5019

| | |
|---|---|
| ▨ | Flint |
| * | Charcoal |
| ▨ | Area of charcoal |
| ☐ | Burnt bone |
| ■ | Burnt clay |

0            1 m

1:25

*Fig. 2.10 Junction 8S, detail plans of cremation burials 5066 and 5244, and profile of cremation burial 5066*

**Quarry pits 5025, 5265 and 5155** (Figs 2.11-12)

Quarry pit 5025 was irregular in plan, with a concave base and steeply sloping convex sides. The pit measured *c* 10m across by 2.1m in depth and contained three fills of silty clay, with occasional inclusions of flint fragments. The upper fill produced 50 sherds of early Roman pottery, weighing 151g, along with 90 fragments of brick and tile, weighing 567g, 16 worked flints and 43 fragments of burnt unworked flint.

Quarry pit 5265 was irregular in plan and measured 17m NW-SE by 10.8m NE-SW. The pit had a concave base and steeply sloping concave sides and was up to 1.8m deep. It contained three fills, all consisting of silty clay, with occasional flint inclusions and charcoal flecks. No finds were recovered from these fills.

Quarry pit 5155 was 6m long, 5.5m wide and 1.3m deep. In profile the pit was irregular and it contained a single fill of clay silt, with occasional inclusions of flint gravel. The fill produced a single tiny fragment of a south Spanish amphora, weighing 1g, and five fragments of animal bone, weighing 5g.

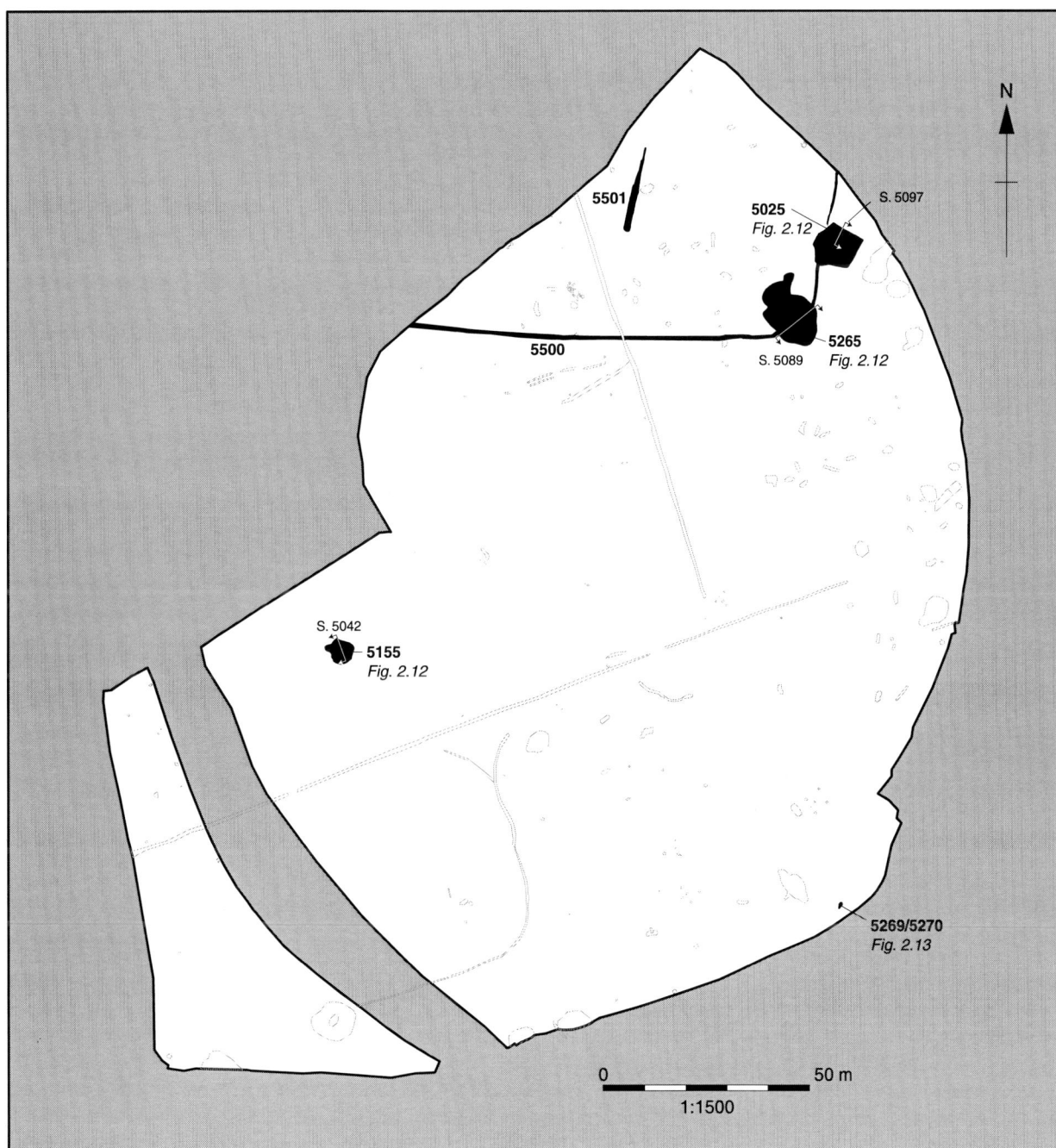

*Fig. 2.11   Junction 8S, Roman activity*

23

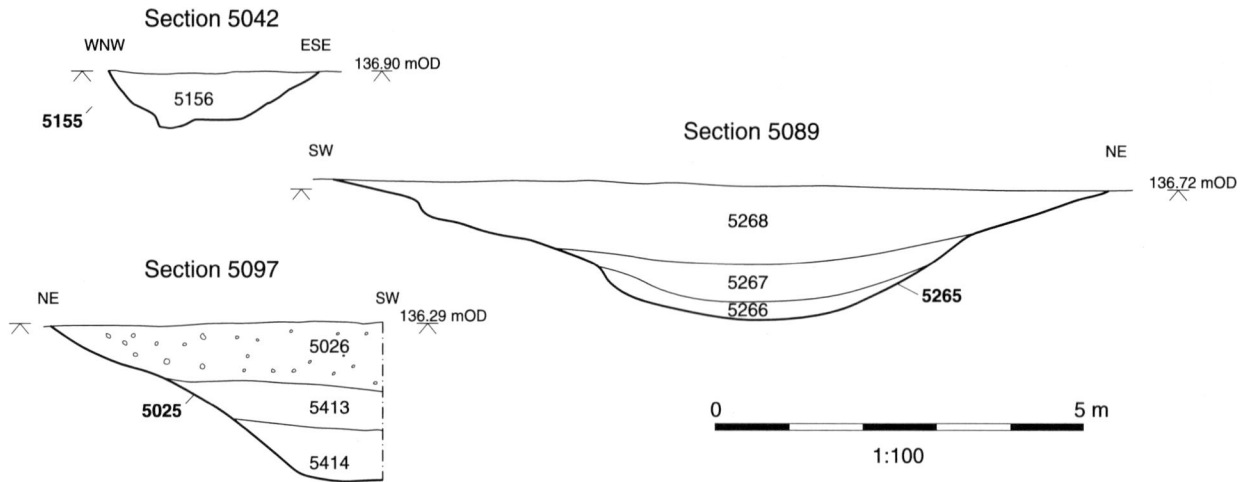

*Fig. 2.12   Junction 8S, sections of quarry pits 5025, 5265 and 5155*

## MIDDLE-LATE ROMAN ACTIVITY (Fig. 2.11)

### Pits 5269 and 5270 (Fig. 2.13)

Only two pits (5269 and 5270) situated in the south-eastern corner of the site, close to the edge of excavation, were potentially of middle-late Roman date. Pit 5269 was irregular to oval in plan and measured 1.5m in length by 0.96m in width and was 0.66m deep. The fills comprised silty clay with frequent flint inclusions and produced two sherds (15g) of late Roman pottery, along with seven sherds (12g) of late Bronze Age-early Iron Age pottery and a single flint flake. Pit 5269 was cut by pit 5270, which also had a single fill of silty clay and produced a single fragment of Roman tile.

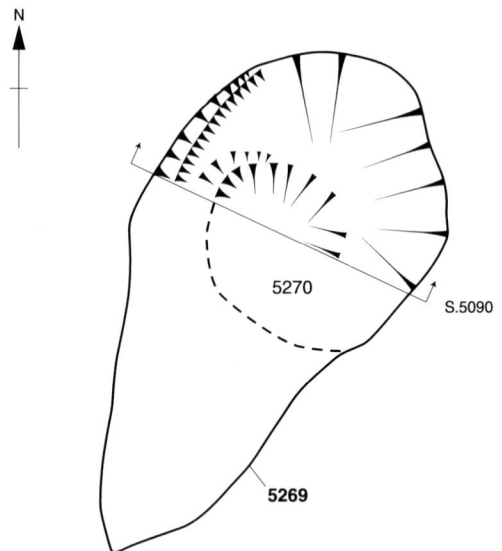

## POST-MEDIEVAL ACTIVITY (Fig. 2.14)

Post-medieval activity comprised two linear field boundary ditches (5502 and 5503) dating to the 19th and early 20th centuries. Ditch 5502 was aligned SW-NE and ran across the centre of the site at a right angle to ditch 5503, which was orientated NW-SE and ran across the northern part of the site.

A quarry pit (5057), measuring 5.1 x 3.2 x 0.75m, was dated to this period by ceramic building material recovered from its single fill. It is also possible that some of the other large quarry pits, assigned to the Roman period on the basis of limited artefactual evidence, were of this much later period, with the associated finds being redeposited.

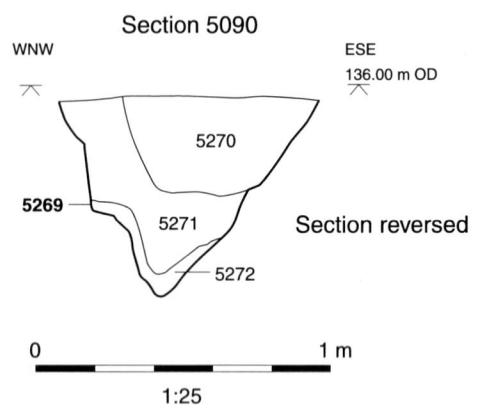

*Fig. 2.13  Junction 8S, detail plan and section of pit 5269*

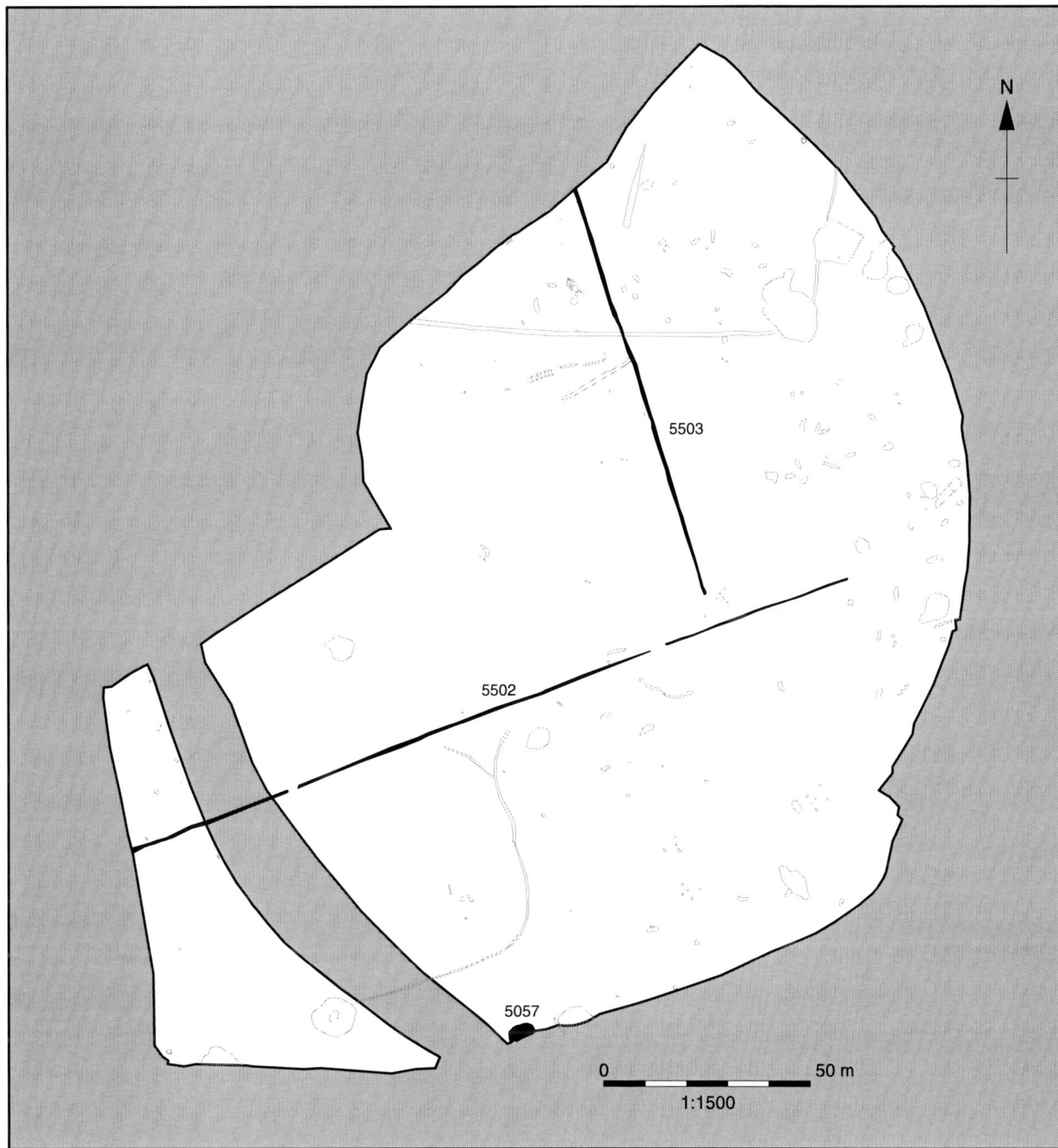

Fig. 2.14   Junction 8S, post-medieval activity

# Chapter 3: Junction 8 Northbound and minor sites to the north

*by Dan Stansbie*

## JUNCTION 8 NORTHBOUND

### Site location

The excavation area at Junction 8 Northbound (Junction 8N) was centred on NGR TL 094 072, immediately to the south of Junction 8 of the M1 and to the east of Hemel Hempstead (see Fig. 1.2). It lay west of the motorway and to the south of the Junction 8 slip road and occupied an area of approximately 3ha. The local geology comprises clay-with-flints, overlying Upper Chalk (see Fig. 1.3). The topography of the northern part of the Junction 8N site, and other adjacent areas examined to the north, was relatively flat, with a maximum height of 137m aOD to the north, and *c* 132m aOD within the Junction 8N area. The southern part of the Junction 8N excavation area sloped down gradually to the south, to a height of 125m aOD.

### Site layout (Fig. 3.1)

Evidence for settlement at Junction 8N may be divided into two broad periods, which also correspond to two geographically distinct parts of the road cutting. The earlier activity, belonging to the late Iron Age-early Roman and middle Roman periods, with scattered later Roman features, consisted of a series of enclosures occupying the south-eastern half of the excavated area. Immediately north-west of the Roman activity, occupying the north-western part of the site, was an area of medieval settlement, dating to the late 12th-13th centuries, and comprising a post-built structure, groups of pits and several enclosure gullies.

### Late Iron Age-early Roman activity (50 BC-AD 70) (Fig. 3.2)

#### Summary

The earliest phase of activity was represented by a substantial WSW-ENE-aligned ditch (7676), with a row of evenly spaced, square postholes, suggesting a fenceline or possible bank revetment on the southern side of the ditch. To the north-west of ditch 7676 was an irregular boundary (7187), aligned roughly north-south and defined by a series of ditch segments, one of which was cut by early Roman trackway ditch 6365 (see below). The position of these two feature groups suggests a relationship between them, but the significance of 7676, without obviously related enclosure features, is unclear. South of the fenceline was beam-slot 7229 with two postholes (112211 and 112213) to its south-west, suggesting the presence of a building, while approximately 15m north of ditch 7676 was a large pit (6780), which produced late Iron Age-early Roman pottery.

#### Ditches

*Ditch 7187* (Figs 3.2 and 3.4)

Ditch 7187 was a segmented boundary ditch, aligned roughly north-south, that was traced over a length of approximately 80m northwards from a point some 15m north-west of the terminal of ditch 7676. The ditch segments were up to 1m wide and ranged between 0.02m and 0.35m in depth. They were generally flat based with gently sloping sides and filled with silty clay, with frequent inclusions of flint and occasional charcoal flecks.

*Ditch and post-line 7676* (Fig. 3.3)

Ditch 7676 projected approximately 40m from the eastern edge of the excavated area on an ENE-WSW alignment. The ditch was 1.6m wide and 0.74m deep, had a V-shaped profile, and was filled with a single deposit of silty clay, containing occasional flint inclusions. The ditch ended in a rounded terminal that appeared to be well defined in plan but was not excavated. It had been recut along its south-eastern-facing edge by a U-shaped feature, measuring 1.3m wide and 0.15m deep. A large group of grog-tempered pottery, including two medium-mouthed jars was recovered from the fill of 7676, but the recut was not well dated. Immediately south of and parallel to ditch 7676 was an alignment of 16 square or sub-circular postholes, with side lengths of between 0.33m and 0.58m, and depths of 0.05-0.26m. These were filled with deposits of silty clay with frequent inclusions of flint and occasional charcoal flecks.

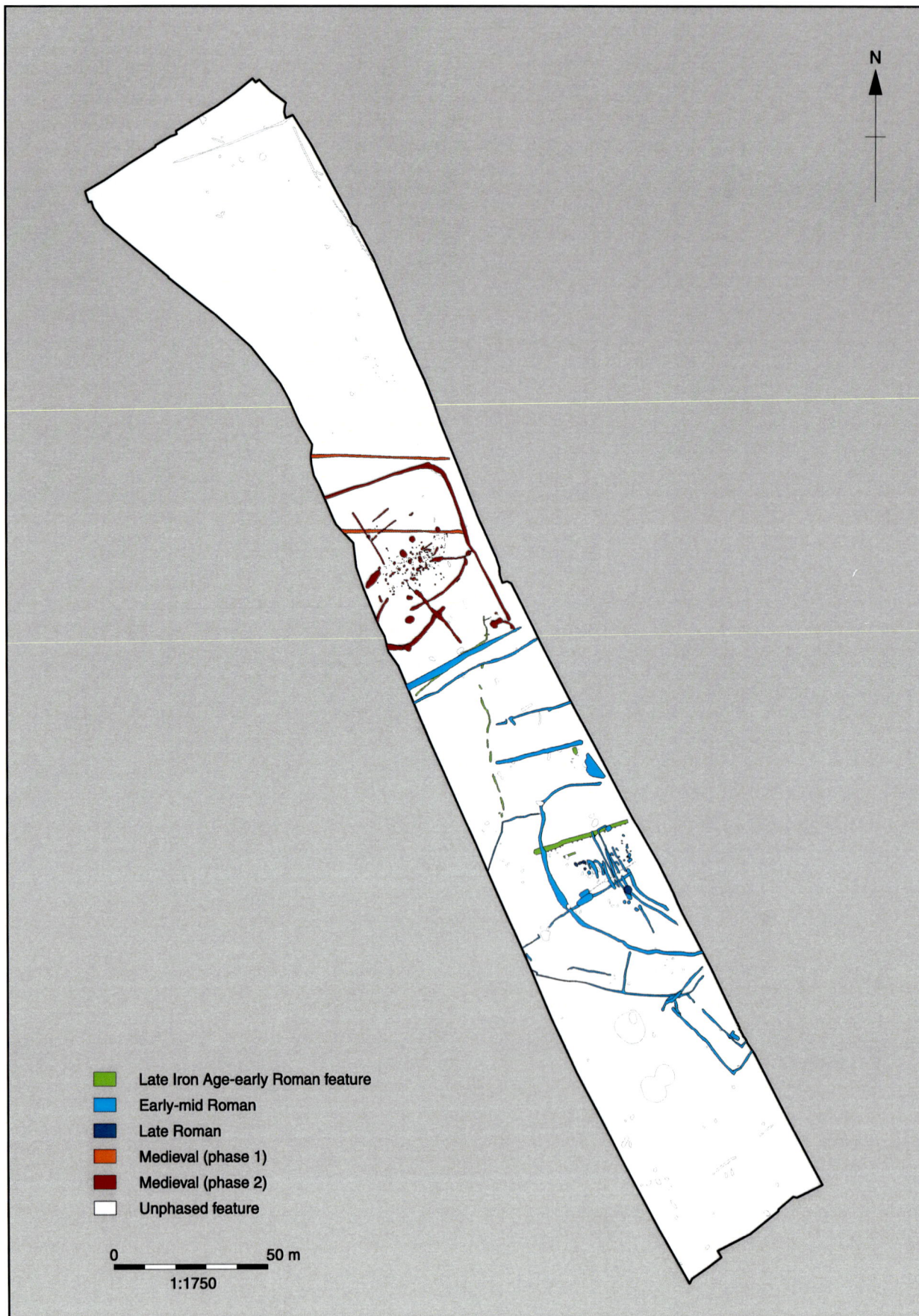

Fig. 3.1   *Junction 8N, plan of all features*

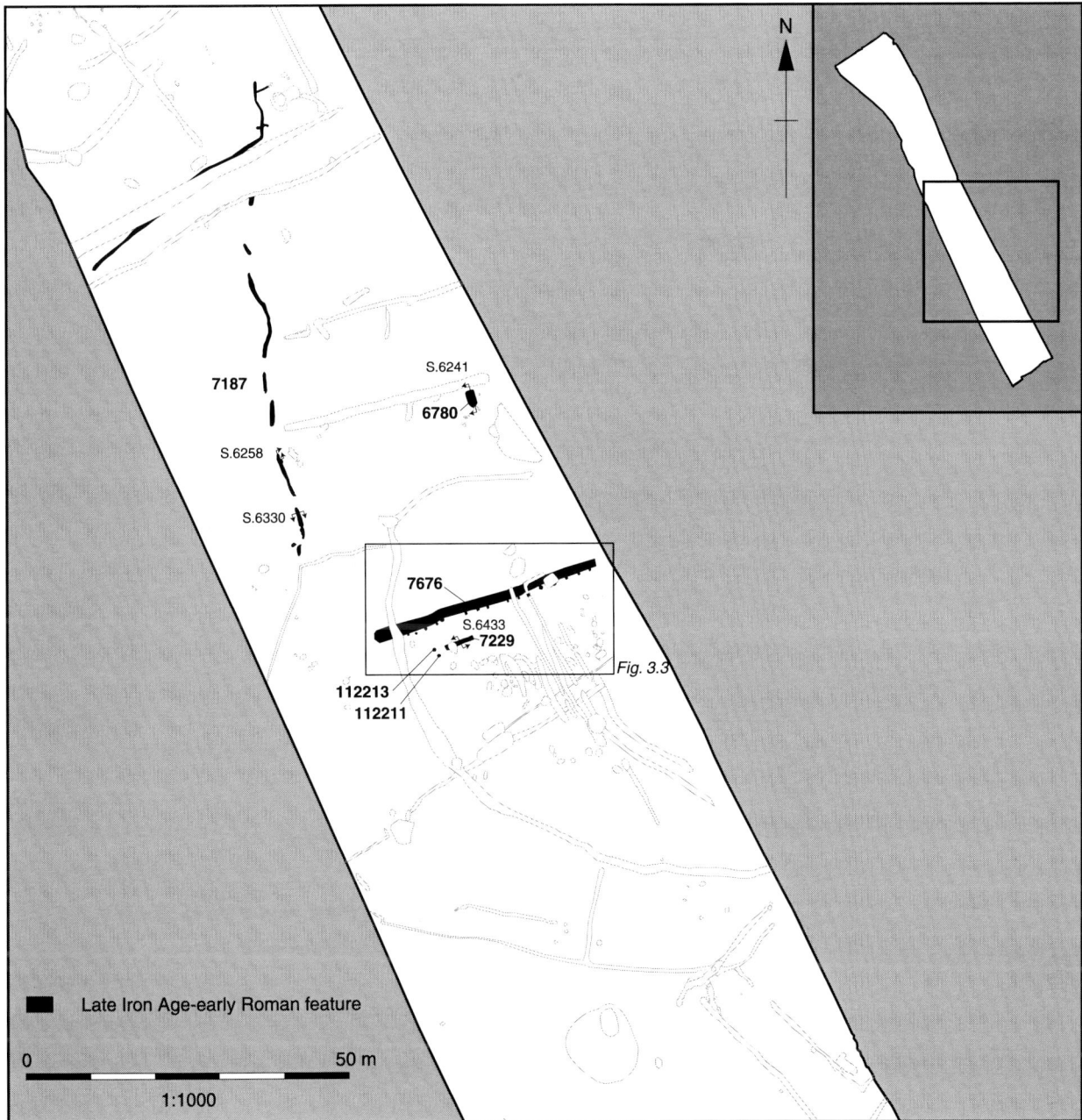

*Fig. 3.2 Junction 8N, late Iron Age-early Roman activity*

### Structures and pits

*Structural features* (Figs 3.3-4)

Some 4m south of ditch 7676 and parallel to it was a possible beam-slot (7229), which measured 4.5 x 0.68 x 0.28m, and had a flat base with steeply sloping/near-vertical sides. Its primary fill (7231) comprised abundant inclusions of burnt flint and charcoal in a black silty-clay matrix, while the upper fill (7230), an orange-brown clay, also contained much burnt, as well as unburnt, flint. Three sherds of late Iron Age-early Roman pottery were recovered from this feature during the evaluation.

Postholes 112211 and 112213, excavated during the evaluation, had respective diameters of 0.25m and 0.37m, and depths of 0.14m and 0.24m, and lay approximately 1m south-west of beam-slot 7229. Both these features had single fills of silty clay, which did not produce any finds. Despite the lack of dating evidence from these postholes, their position relative to possible beam-slot 7229 suggests that they may have been part of a structure.

*Pit 6780* (Figs 3.2 and 3.4)

Pit 6780 north of ditch 7676 was sub-rectangular, measuring 2.4 x 1.3 x 0.42m. The pit had a flat base and steeply sloping sides and its fills consisted of silty clay, with occasional inclusions of flint and

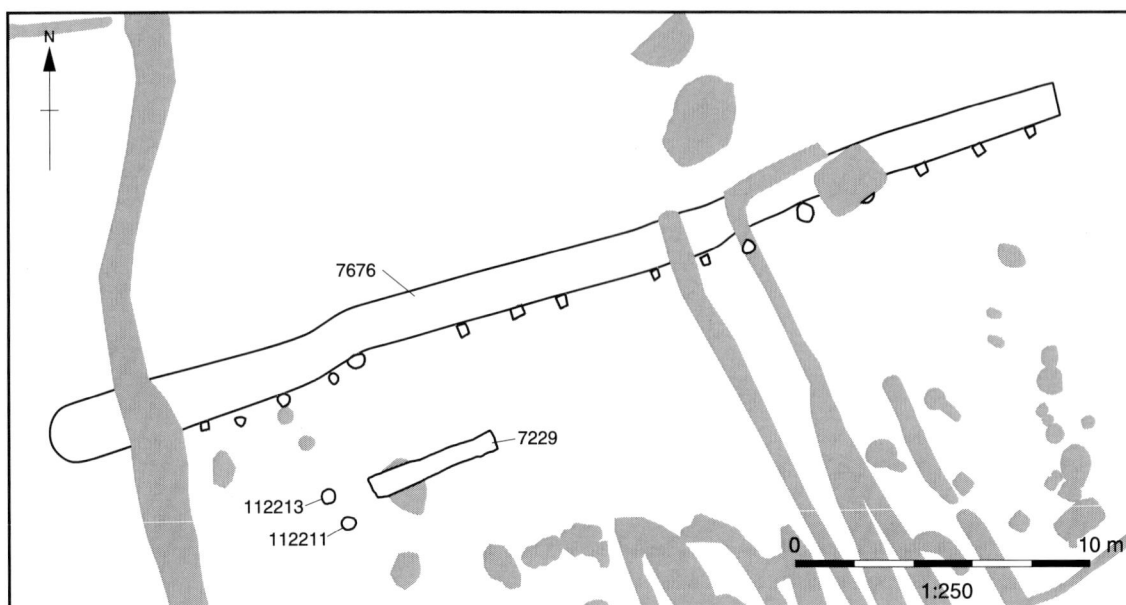

*Fig. 3.3   Junction 8N, detail plan of ditch and post-line 7676, postholes 112213 and 112211, and beam-slot 7229*

charcoal flecks. The fills produced 66 sherds of late Iron Age-early Roman pottery, representing several grog-tempered vessels, including a high-shouldered jar.

### Early-middle Roman activity (AD 43-200)
(Fig. 3.5)

*Summary*

Early-middle Roman activity at Junction 8N was characterised by a series of irregular-shaped enclosures, along with field boundaries and a trackway. The largest enclosure lay in the central-southern part of the site. Its north, west and south sides were defined by ditch 7700 cutting late Iron Age ditch 7676. The enclosure was subdivided internally by a series of linear and curvilinear ditches (7701) and contained scatters of pits (groups 7107 and 7065), along with two ovens (7259 and (7335) and a large quarry pit (7124), in the north-eastern corner of the enclosure. Abutting enclosure 7700 to the south and west were four smaller, but still substantial, sub-rectangular enclosures (7277, 6624, 6622 and 6150/6104). Cremation burials 6289 and 6293 were found within enclosures 6624 and 6622 respectively though, as these were associated with grog-tempered pottery dated to the late Iron Age-early Roman period, it is possible that they predated the enclosures. To the north-west of enclosure 7700, ditches 6713 and 6768 may have represented field boundaries, or possibly a further rectilinear enclosure. Beyond these ditches to the north-west was an ENE-WSW-aligned trackway (6365).

*Enclosures*

*Enclosure 7700, ditch group 7701 and ditch 7702 (Figs 3.6-7)*

Enclosure 7700 was probably oval in plan, though it extended beyond the limit of excavation to the east. It was defined by a curvilinear ditch on its northern, western and southern sides. Within the excavated area the enclosure measured approximately 77m NW-SE by 33m SW-NE and the enclosure ditch ranged from 1-2m in width and 0.35-0.75m in depth. The ditch was V-shaped in profile and its fills comprised silty clay, with frequent inclusions of flint and charcoal flecks. The lower fills of this ditch contained late Iron Age-early Roman pottery, while the middle and upper fills produced early-middle Roman pottery, suggesting that although first established in the late Iron Age-early Roman period the ditch remained in use throughout the early and middle 2nd century, finally going out of use towards the end of that century.

Within the space defined by the enclosure ditch, and separating its south-western half from its north-western half, was a series of at least three curvilinear and linear ditches suggesting an internal subdivision of the enclosure (ditch group 7701). These ditches represented at least three phases of boundary recutting and contained late 2nd-century pottery, indicating that they went out of use at about the same time as ditch 7700, although the absence of grog-tempered material from their fills may suggest that they were established somewhat later. Ditch group 7701 was aligned roughly NW-SE and measured approxi-

Section 6433

NW    SE SE    NW

7230    128.19 mOD

7231

**7229**

— Carbonised Wood

**7348**    **7229**

**7229**

S.6433

N

S.6241

**6780**

Section 6241

NNW    SSE

129.56 mOD

6779

6781    **6828**

**6780**

**6830**

**6828**

Ditch group 7187

Section 6330    Section 6258

ENE    WSW    E    W S    N

129.38 mOD    6835    129.79 mOD

7072    7073    6836    **6837**

0    2 m

1:50

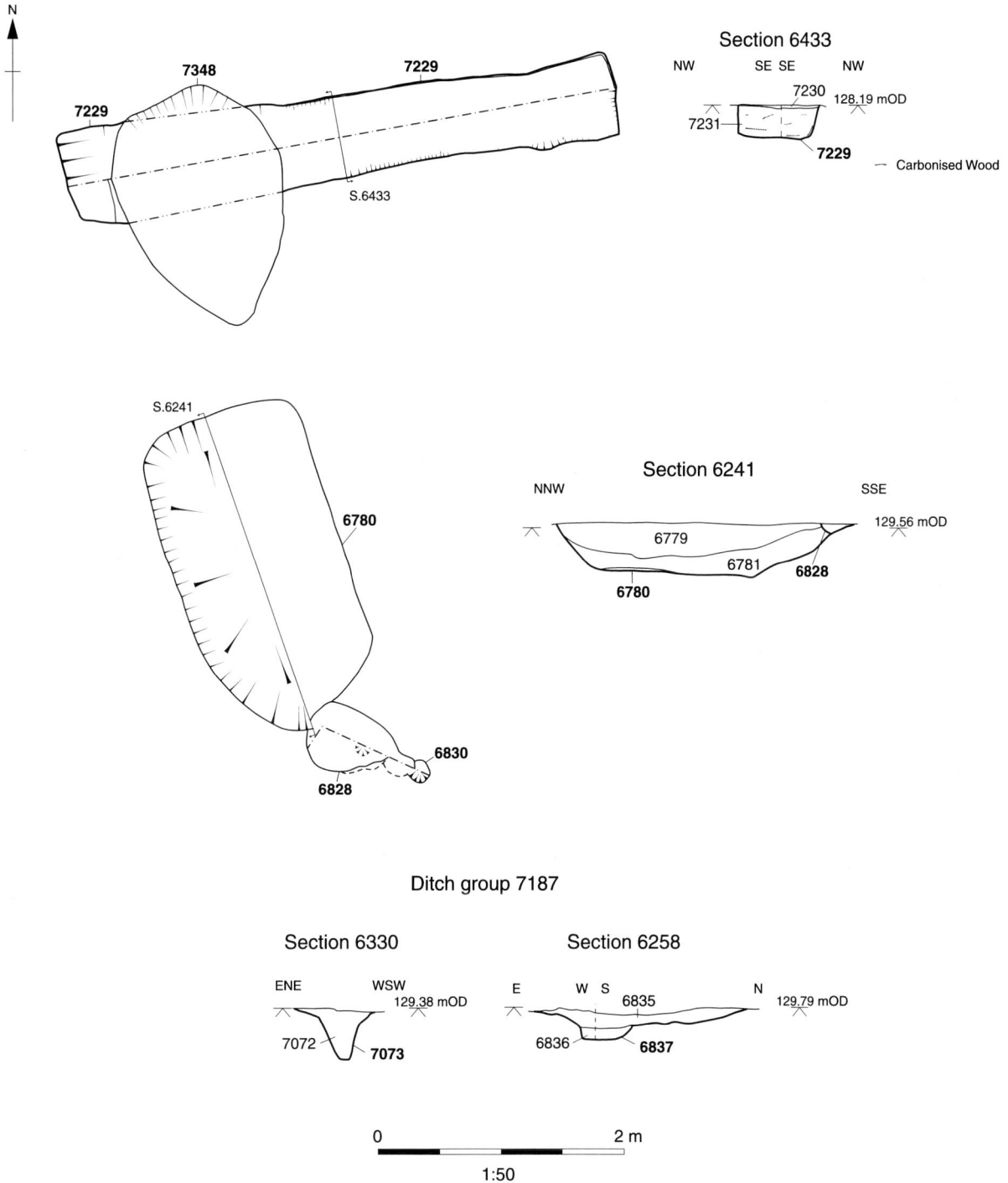

*Fig. 3.4   Junction 8N, detail plan and sections of beam-slot 7229 and pit 6780, and sections of ditch 7187*

mately 32m in length by 0.8m wide and was between 0.13m and 0.4m deep. The ditches generally had flat bases, with steeply sloping sides and were filled with single deposits of silty clay containing frequent flint inclusions.

Ditch group 7702 cut elements of ditch group 7701, was aligned NE-SW and further subdivided the enclosure formed by ditches 7700 and 7701 into two parts; one to the north-west and one to the

south-east. Ditch 7702 was linear, orientated NE-SW and measured approximately 25.5m in length. It varied very considerably in width, from 0.32-1.1m, and was generally extremely shallow, typically not more than 0.12m deep. The ditch had a flat base with steeply sloping sides and was filled with a single deposit of clay silt with frequent to moderate flint inclusions. Cutting ditch group 7702, ditch group 7703 re-established the NW-SE axis of ditch

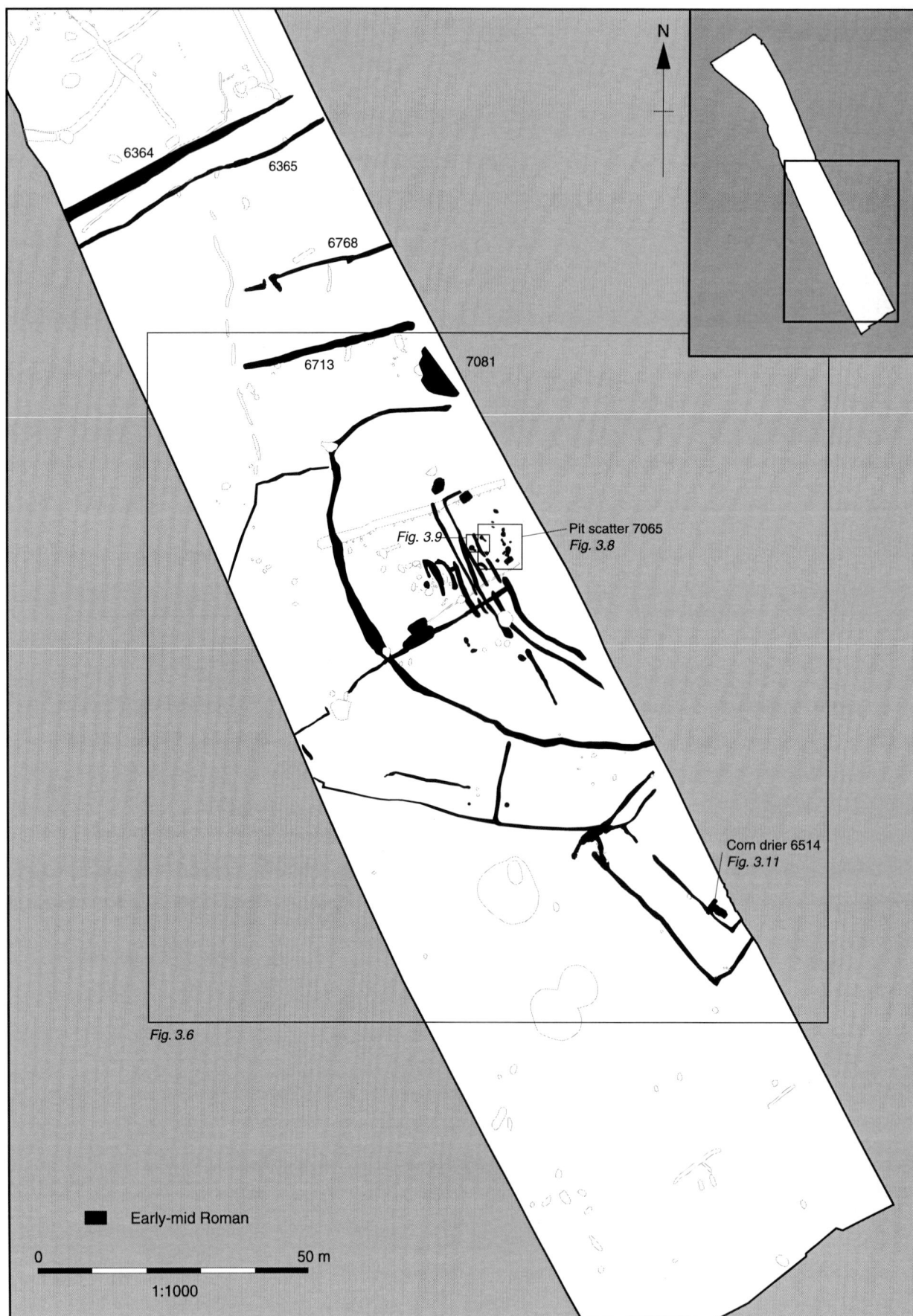

*Fig. 3.5 Junction 8N, early-middle Roman activity*

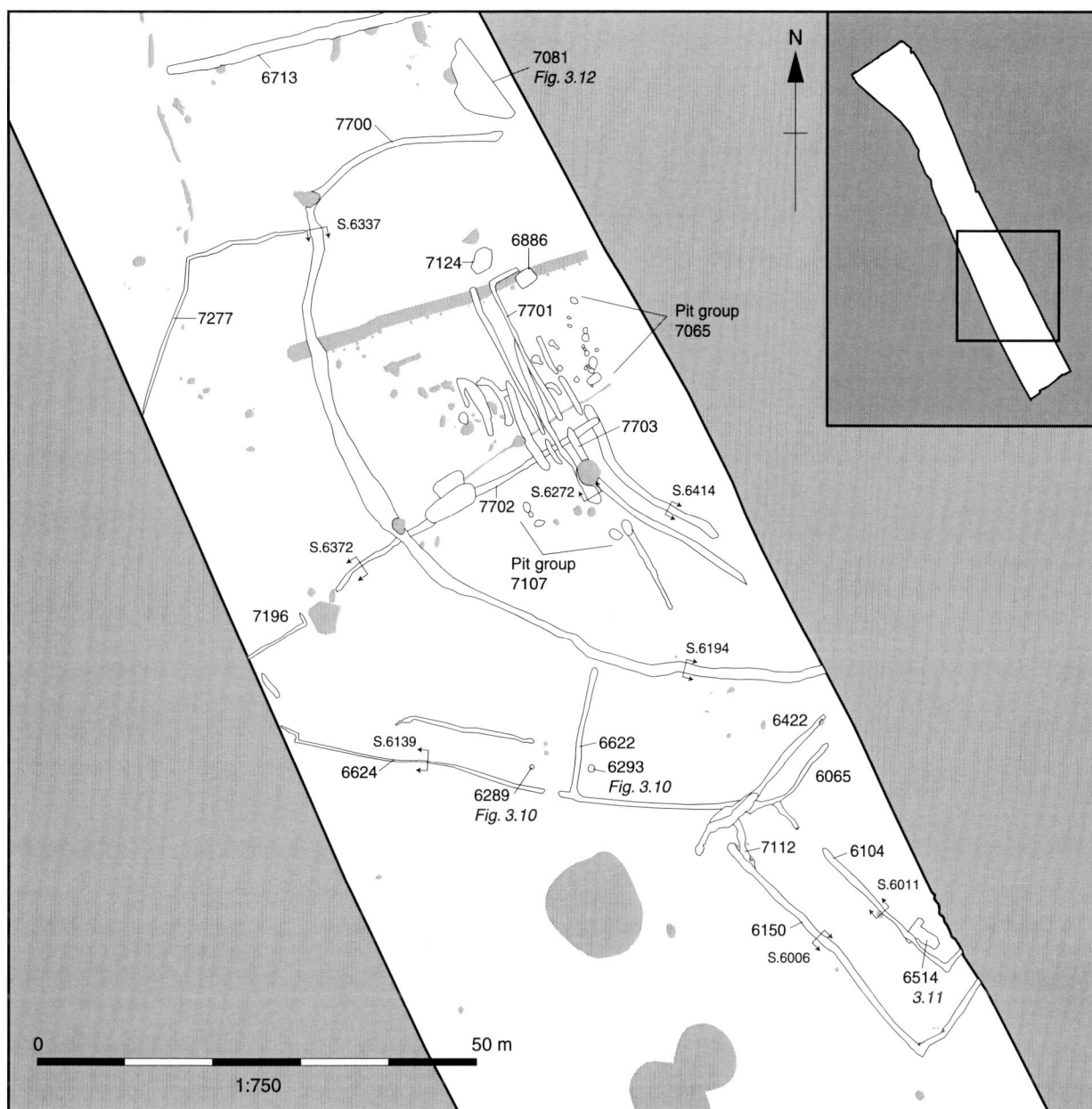

*Fig. 3.6   Enclosure complex at the south-eastern end of Junction 8N*

group 7701. Ditch group 7703 was linear, measured approximately 37m in length and ranged between 1.23m and 0.62m in width.

*Enclosures 7277, 6624 and 6622* (Figs 3.6-7)

Abutting ditch 7700 to the south-west were three contiguous enclosures (7277, 6624 and 6622) of irregular plan, defined by less substantial boundary ditches. The pottery from the fills of these ditches dates to the late 1st-2nd century, suggesting that they may have been established slightly later than ditch 7700, although they probably silted up at about the same time.

Enclosure 7277, the most northerly, had an irregular polygonal plan and measured 38.5m NW-SE by at least 20m NE-SW. The angle of the north-west

corner of this enclosure was exactly in line with the southern end of the earlier segmented ditch (7187). This might suggest either that the north-west arm of the enclosure ditch superseded and obliterated a southward continuation of ditch 7187, or that ditch 7187 was perhaps, despite the dating evidence contained within it, not earlier than, but rather broadly contemporary with the other features of the early Roman phase, being aligned on the corner of enclosure 7277 rather than preceding it. Either way, the ditch defining enclosure 7277 measured 0.7-1.12m in width by 0.42-0.6m in depth, narrowing to 0.29m in width and 0.17m in depth at its north-eastern end. It was V-shaped in profile, with a single fill of clay silt, with occasional to moderate inclusions of flint.

Ditch 7196 formed the common boundary between the south-east side of this enclosure and the north-western side of enclosure 6624. A 4.9m gap in this ditch-line (filled by later features) presumably allowed access between the two enclosures. Ditch 7196 measured approximately 21m in length and varied in width between 0.3m and 0.82m, with a depth of between 0.04m and 0.12m. The ditch had a flat base with steeply sloping sides and was filled with a silty clay containing frequent inclusions of flint. There may have been an 'external' entrance to enclosure 7277 on its south-western side, which lay beyond the limit of the excavation.

Enclosure 6624 was also irregularly polygonal in form, with dimensions of *c* 16-23.5m, NNE-SSW, by 25-38+m, WNW-ESE. An offset in the boundary line on its southern side, close to the site baulk, may suggest that there was an entrance at the western end of this enclosure just beyond the limit of excavation. However, there was also reasonably clear evidence for an entrance in the south-eastern corner of this enclosure, where the outer enclosure ditch appeared to terminate *c* 4.5m from the south-west corner of the adjacent enclosure (6622) to the east. The enclosure ditch/gully was U-shaped in profile and varied from 0.29-0.73m in width and 0.13-0.38m in depth. It contained a single fill of clay

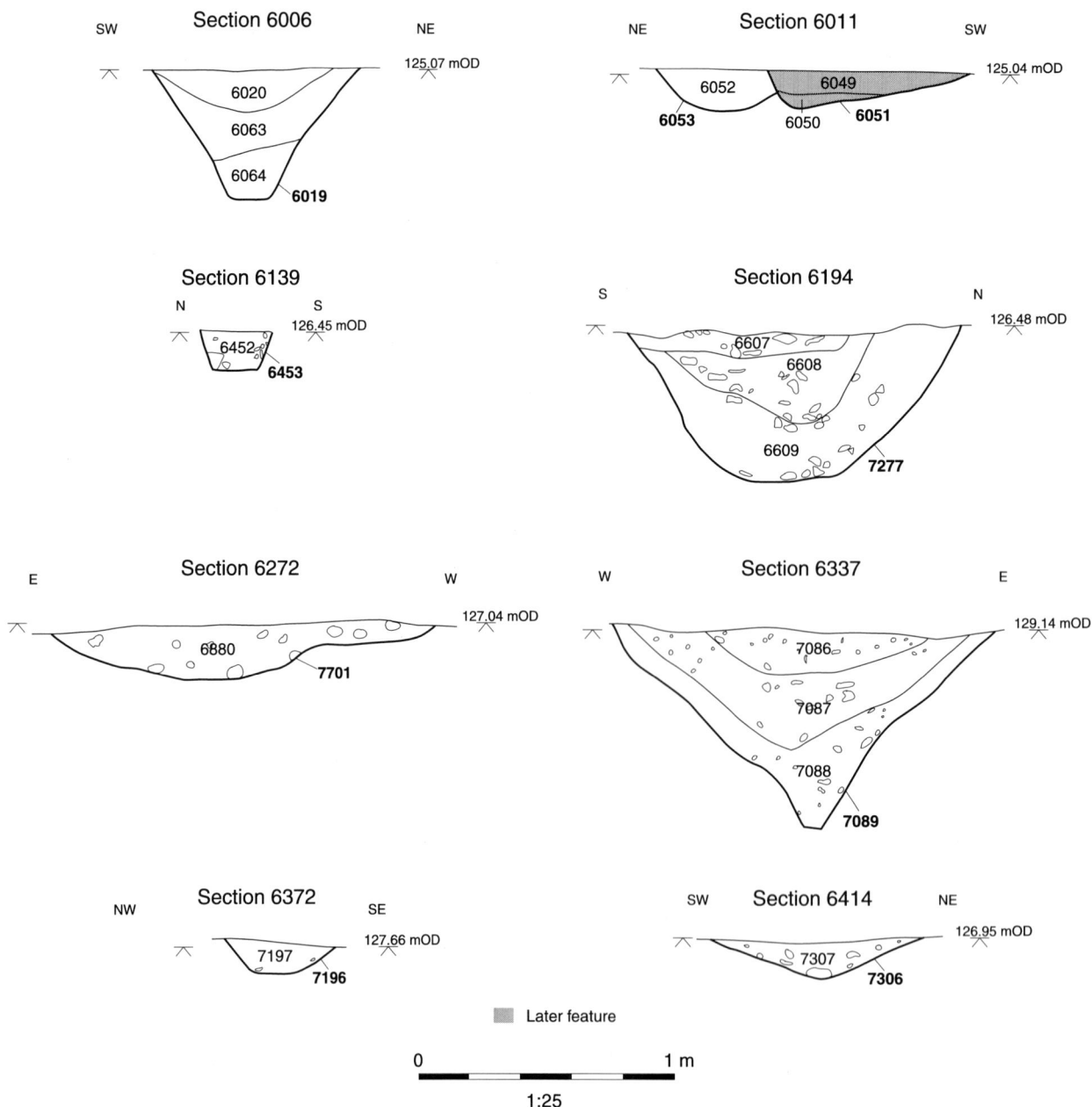

*Fig. 3.7 Sections of features associated with the enclosure complex at the south-eastern end of Junction 8N*

silt, with inclusions of flint and frequent charcoal flecks.

Enclosure 6622 was sub-rectangular in shape with approximate maximum dimensions of 28.5m, east-west, by 16m, north-south, although the enclosure may have extended just beyond the limit of excavation to the east, where an entrance may have been present. A gap of *c* 1m between the enclosure ditch and enclosure 7700 in the north-western corner of the enclosure may have served as a means of access between enclosure 6622 and enclosure 6624 to the west. The enclosure ditch was U-shaped in profile and measured 0.8m in width by 0.23-0.47m in depth. It contained two fills, a primary fill of clay with frequent inclusions of flint, overlain by a secondary fill of silty clay

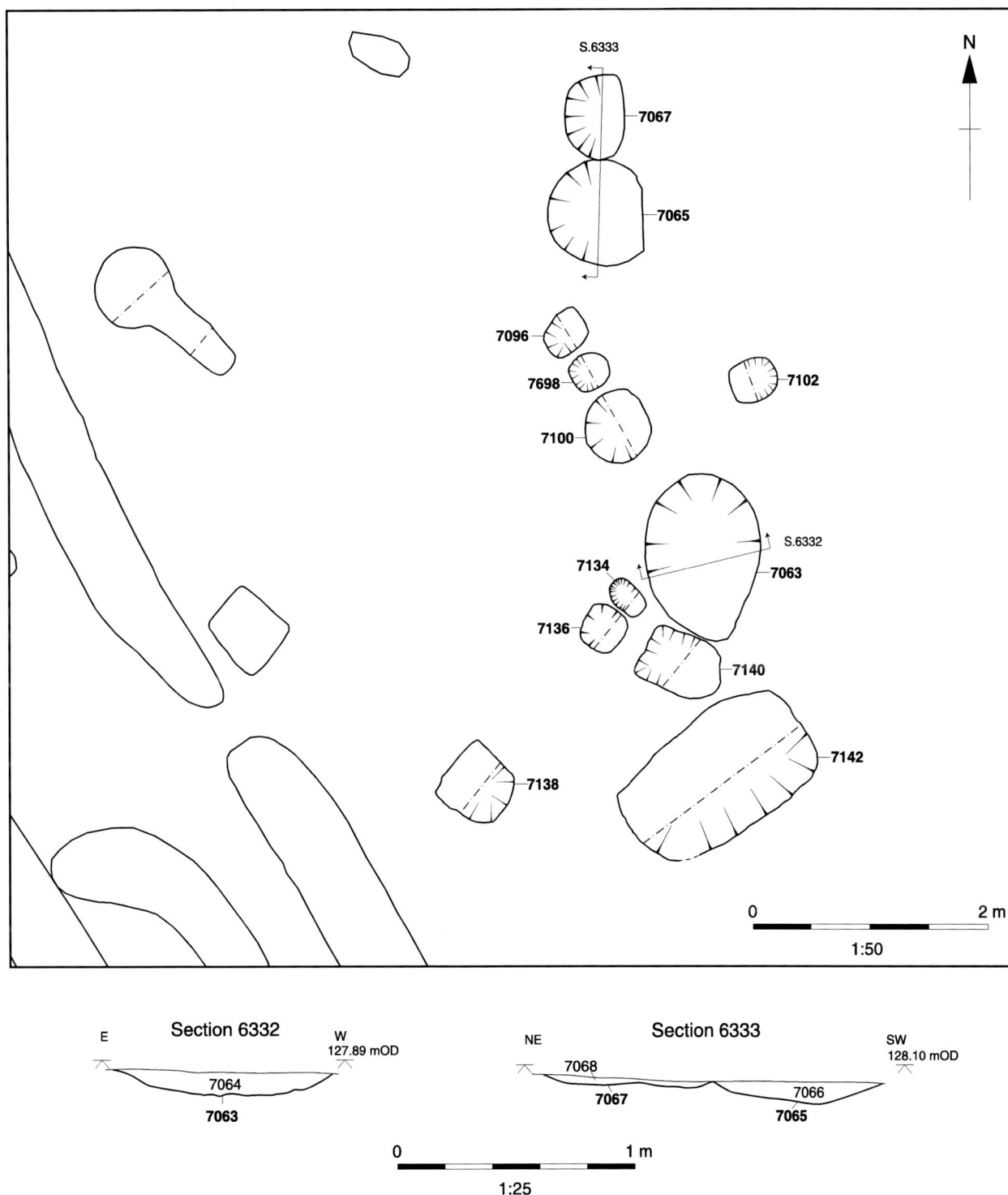

*Fig. 3.8   Junction 8N, detailed plan and sections of pit group 7065*

with frequent flint inclusions and occasional charcoal flecks. Understanding of the south-eastern side of this enclosure was made difficult due to the apparent superimposition of enclosure 6150 (see below). However, two parallel ditches (6422 and 6065) were present in this area and it is likely that the outer (6065), ending in terminal 6068, which lay 8m south of enclosure 7700, was the main ditch defining the south-eastern side of enclosure 6222.

### Internal features (pits, ovens and cremations) (Figs 3.6 and 3.8-10)

Lying within the area defined by ditches 7700 and 7701 were a number of discrete features, some of which occurred in groups. These included a group of pits (7065), along with two ovens (7259 and 7335) containing 1st-2nd-century pottery, lying north-east of ditch 7701 in the north-eastern part of the enclosure. A further scatter of four pits (7107), containing pottery of the same date, lay in the south-western part of the enclosure. A large quarry pit (7124) containing 1st-2nd-century pottery and a fragment of human skull lay in the north-eastern part of the enclosure.

Pit 6886 lay to the north of pit scatter 7065 and was sub-rectangular in plan, with a flat base and steeply sloping sides (Fig. 3.6). It was 2.18m long by 1.7m wide and 0.4m deep, and had two fills. These comprised a lower fill of clay, with frequent inclusions of flint and charcoal, and an upper fill of silty clay, with similar inclusions.

Pit Scatter 7065 comprised 11 sub-circular pits and one sub-rectangular pit lying to the north-east of ditch 7701 (Fig. 3.8). In profile, the majority of these pits were flat based with steep sides, and all were fairly shallow. They ranged in diameter from 0.22-1.1m and were between 0.05m and 0.4m in depth. The pit fills comprised silty clay with moderate inclusions of flint and charcoal flecks.

Pit scatter 7107 consisted of four pits, all of which produced pottery of late 1st- or 2nd-century date (Fig. 3.6). The pits were all oval in plan, with either shallow saucer-shaped or irregular profiles, and measured 0.78-1.25m in diameter and between 0.13m and 0.8m in depth. The pits all had single fills of sandy clay with inclusions of flint, chalk fragments and charcoal flecks.

Pit 7124 was irregular in plan, with an undulating base and irregular sides (Fig. 3.6). The pit measured

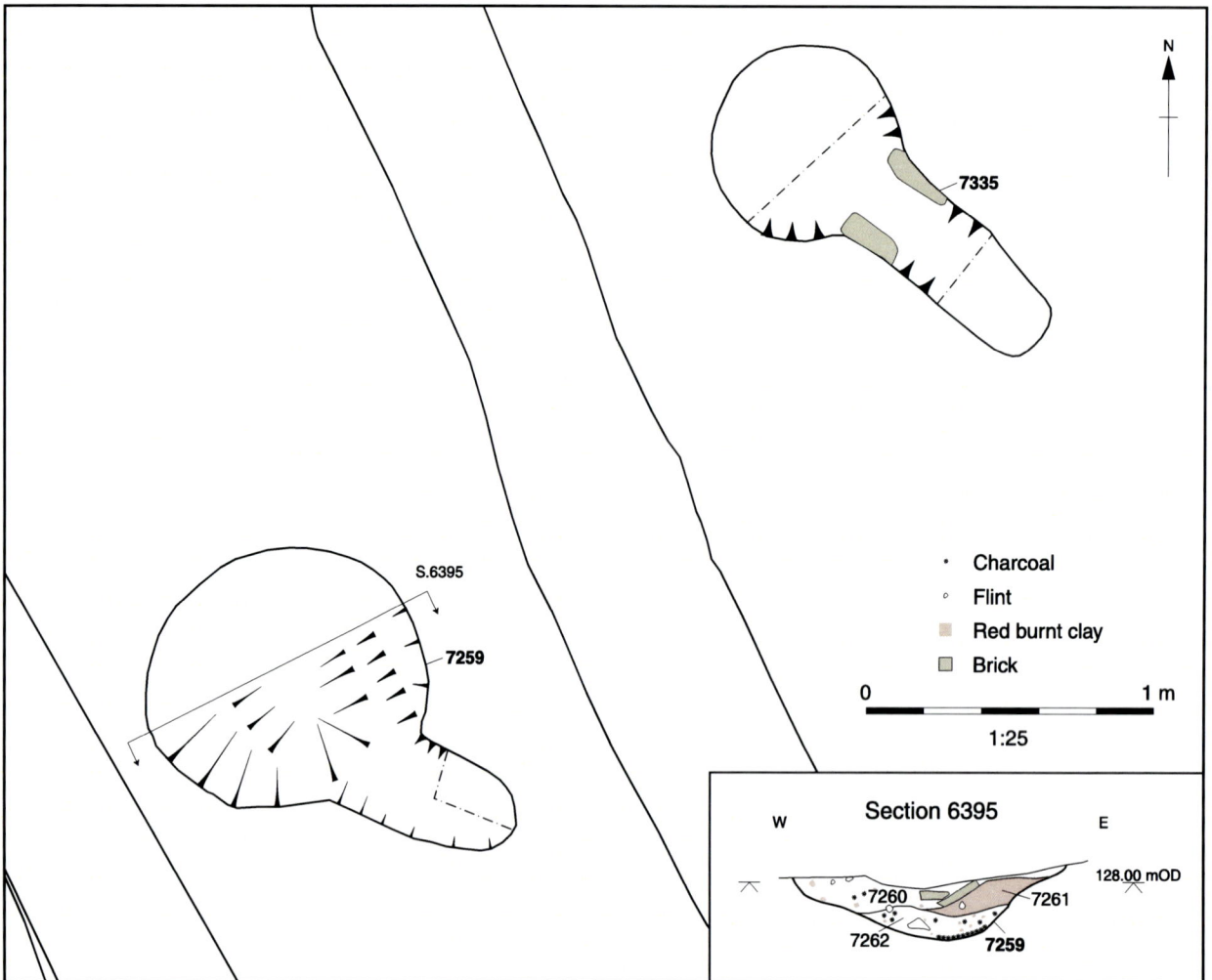

*Fig. 3.9 Junction 8N, detail plans of ovens 7259 and 7335, and section of oven 7259*

3.1 x 2.4 x 0.75m and had three fills of silty clay, with frequent inclusions of flint. The basal fill of the pit produced 13 sherds of 1st-2nd-century pottery, along with a fragment of quern stone and fragments of human skull. A dump of charcoal at the top of this fill produced a further six sherds of 2nd-century pottery, along with a cattle humerus and mandible, and 75 fragments of other animal bone. Seven sherds of 1st-century pottery came from the secondary fill.

Oven 7259 comprised a sub-circular pit, measuring 1m in diameter by 0.21m in depth, with concave sides and a flat base (Fig. 3.9). The oven was stoked by means of a NW-SE-orientated flue measuring 0.5 x 0.3m, which varied in depth between 0.05m and 0.18m. The base of the flue sloped towards the oven pit and the substrate into which the pit was cut was discoloured through burning. The basal fill of the oven comprised a sterile burnt clay silt with frequent fragments of charcoal. Overlying this, on the eastern side of the oven pit, was a burnt clay silt, with occasional flint inclusions, which did not extend into the flue. The upper fill of the feature extended throughout the oven pit and the flue and comprised a deposit of clay silt, with occasional inclusions of flint, frequent large fragments of brick, which probably derive from the oven structure, and two sherds of Roman greyware.

Oven 7335 consisted of a sub-circular pit 1.4m in diameter by 0.35m in depth, with a 1.25m-long flue aligned NW-SE. This flue had a single brick lining either side of its entrance and measured 0.75m in width by 0.27m in depth (Fig. 3.9). The basal fill of the oven, which extended over the base of the pit and the flue, comprised a 0.15m-thick layer of charcoal-rich silt with no finds. Overlying the basal fill within the oven pit was a clay silt, with frequent inclusions of mortar fragments and moderate charcoal fragments. In the flue the basal fill was overlain by a silty clay with occasional flint inclusions. Neither of these upper fills produced any finds.

Cremation burial 6289 was contained within a shallow sub-circular pit measuring 0.59m in diameter by 0.09m in depth (Figs 3.6 and 3.10). The cremated bones had been placed within a grog-tempered vessel, which unfortunately could not be identified to type as later truncation had removed its rim. Two other similarly damaged grog-tempered ancillary vessels were placed alongside the cremation urn on the base of the pit, but no other finds were recorded from the feature. The pottery vessels were overlain with a deposit of silty clay containing occasional charcoal flecks and fragments of flint, which filled the pit.

Cremation burial 6293 was contained in a shallow, sub-circular pit which measured 0.85m in diameter by 0.07m in depth (Figs 3.6 and 3.10). The cremated bones had been placed on the base of the pit cut, in the northern-central part of the pit. Although these bones were not contained in a cremation urn, it is possible that they may originally have been placed in an organic container such

as a bag or a box. Accompanying the burial, and placed on the base of the pit cut around the cremated bone, were three ancillary vessels comprising a platter and a carinated cup in grog-tempered ware and a beaker in 'Belgic' sandy ware. Overlying the pottery vessels and filling the grave pit was a single deposit of silty clay containing occasional flint inclusions.

### *Enclosure 6150/6104* (Fig. 3.6)

Abutting enclosure 6622, to its south-east, was a partly double-ditched (6150 and 6104) sub-rectangular enclosure, which extended beyond the limit of excavation to the north-east. Pottery from the fills of these ditches was of mid-late 2nd-century date. These sherds suggest that the enclosure went out of use at approximately the same time as those to its north, although the apparent use of part of the

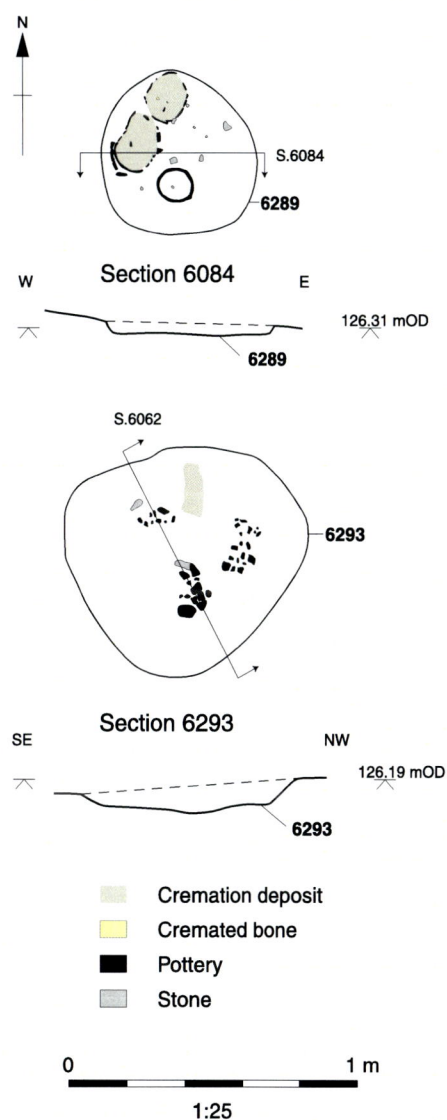

*Fig. 3.10  Junction 8N, detail plans and profiles of cremation burials 6289 and 6293*

boundary ditch of enclosure 6622 on its north-western side suggests that it may have been established slightly later. Moreover, the fact that a corn drying oven (6514), situated to the south-east of enclosure 6622, was cut by ditch 6104 would seem to support this argument.

The enclosure measured *c* 32m NW-SE by at least 15m SW-NE. Part of the south-eastern boundary of enclosure 6622 seems to have been utilised as the putative inner ditch of enclosure 6150/6104 on its north-western side. The south-eastern and south-western boundaries of the enclosure were defined by two L-shaped ditches, set *c* 6-7m apart on the south-west side but only 3m apart on the south-east side. The inner ditch (6104) had an extant length of *c* 30m, including a 3.5m-wide gap for an entrance towards its north-western end. In profile, the ditch was bowl-shaped and measured 0.5-0.78m in width by 0.07-0.31m in depth. The single ditch fill comprised silty clay with occasional flint inclusions. The outer ditch (6150) measured 43.5m in length

with no breaks, but it terminated some 1.8m south of the southern boundary ditch of enclosure 6622, suggesting the presence of a narrow entrance in the north-west corner of 6150/6104. Ditch 6422, which cut across the boundary of enclosure 6622, slightly reducing that enclosure in size on its south-east side, seems to have formed the outer boundary on the north-west side of enclosure 6150/6104. The complex sequence of features located at the north-west corner of the enclosure is not entirely clear. The north-western 'entrance' of enclosure 6150/6104 (see above) seems to have been blocked by a short length of slightly curving ditch (7112). However, this ditch was itself cut by ditch 6150 and may have belonged to an early version of the enclosure, superseded by the more rectilinear form suggested by ditches 6150 and 6422, and incorporating the north-west corner entrance. Ditch 6150 differed from ditch 6104, being V-shaped in profile and measuring 0.58-1m in width by 0.4-0.58m in depth. The ditch had three fills, the lowest of which comprised a clay silt,

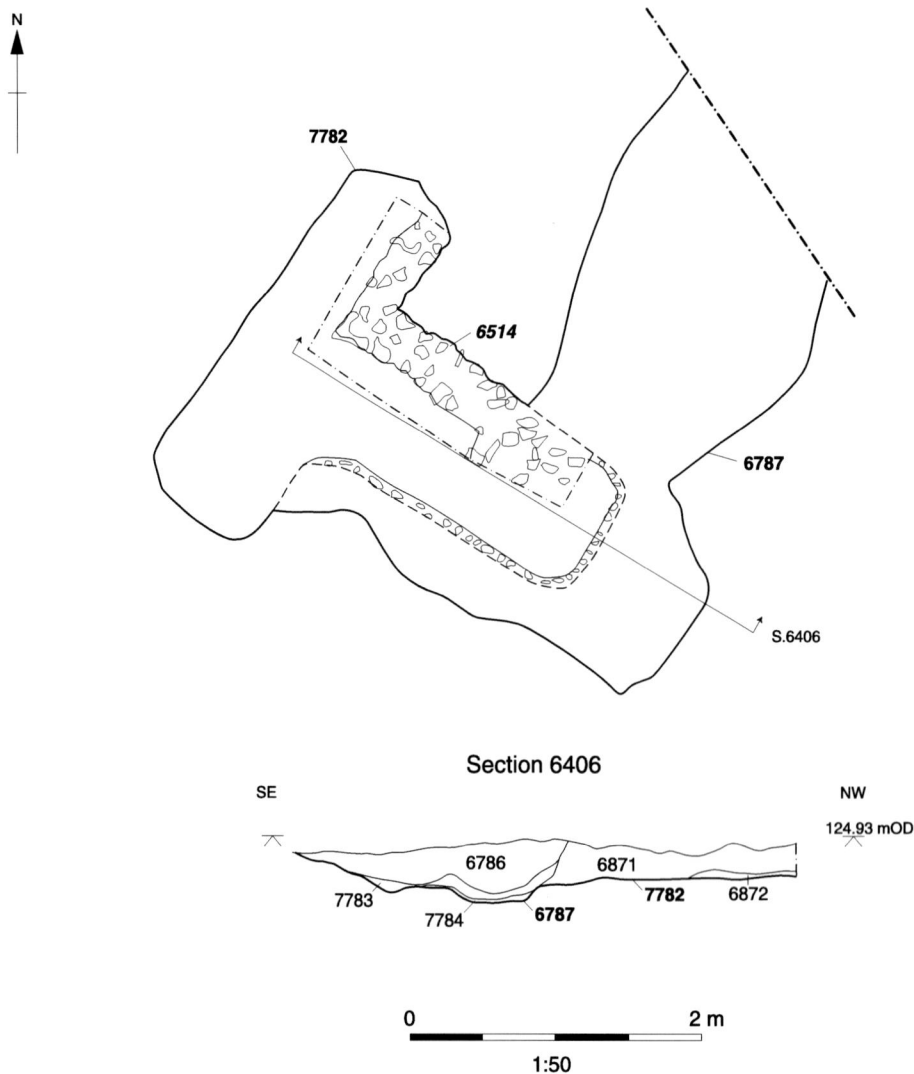

*Fig. 3.11   Junction 8N, detail plan and section of corn dryer 6514*

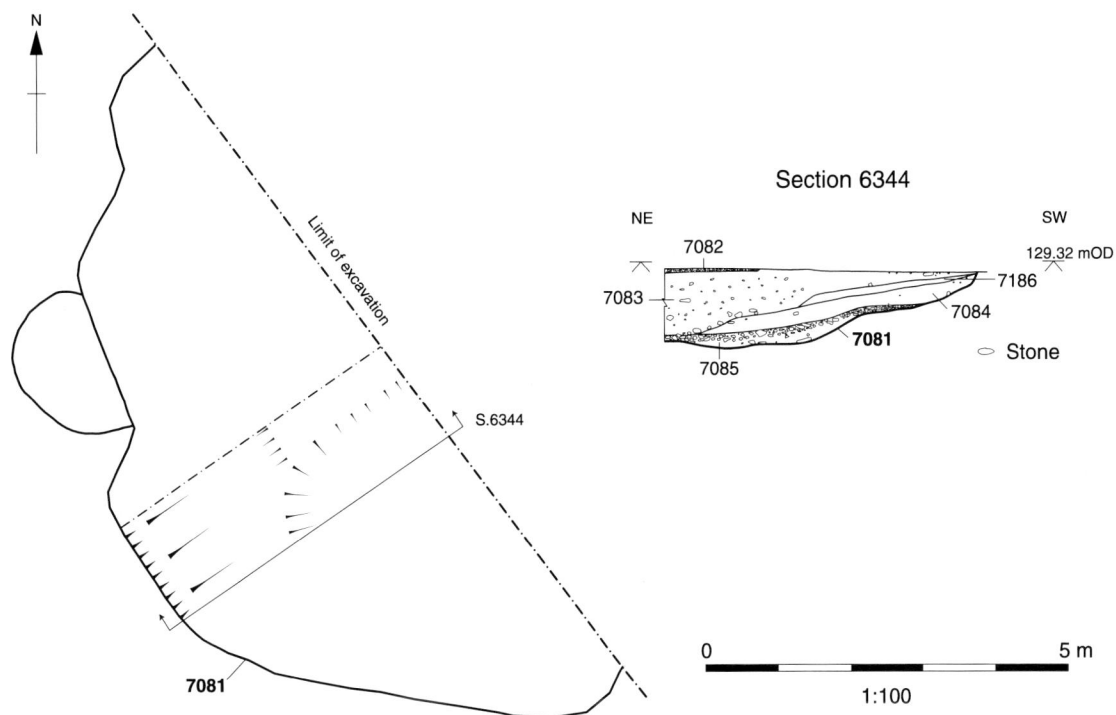

*Fig. 3.12   Junction 8N, detail plan and section of quarry pit 7081*

with occasional flint inclusions, while the upper two consisted of silty clay, with more frequent flint and occasional charcoal.

### *Internal features: corn dryer 6514* (Fig. 3.11)

The only other significant feature in the area occupied by enclosure 6150/6104 was a corn drying oven (6514). This was situated towards the south-west corner of the inner enclosure and was cut by its ditch (6104). The corn dryer may therefore have predated the enclosure altogether, although this assumes that the inner and outer ditches (6150 and 6104) were contemporary which, while likely, is not certain.

The oven was T-shaped in plan and aligned NW-SE but, in addition to the damage caused by the cutting of ditch 6104, it was poorly preserved at its south-eastern end. The structure, of flint nodules (averaging 0.14m in length) bound with a mixture of chalk and clay, with occasional tile elements, was set in a NW-SE-aligned pit measuring *c* 3.7m long and 0.4m deep. The main flue was *c* 2.25m long, 0.6-0.65m wide and 0.25m deep, while the cross bar of the 'T' was 0.2-0.25m wide and, if reconstructed symmetrically about the central axis of the main flue, would have been *c* 2.6m long. A layer of charcoal mixed with clay silt lay over the base of the structure at its north-eastern end, within the cross bar of the T-shaped structure. Overlying this was a mixture of silty clay, chalk and ash which filled the cross bar and the flue. Curiously, the stokehole seems to have been an irregular pit (6787), measuring 2.1 x 1.6 x 0.37m,

set on the north-east side of the flue at its south-eastern end. The stokehole was filled with three layers of silty clay and charcoal containing inclusions of flint gravel and chalk.

### *Features north of enclosure 7700*

#### *Quarry pit 7081* (Figs 3.5 and 3.12)

Situated immediately to the north of enclosure 7700, quarry pit 7081 extended beyond the limit of excavation to the north-east and contained late 1st-2nd-century pottery. Within the excavated area it was sub-circular in plan, measuring at least 4.4 x 2.75m, and was up to 1.16m deep with an irregular profile. The pit had a primary fill of silty clay and angular flint pebbles, overlain by three deposits of silty clay with flint inclusions.

#### *Ditches 6713 and 6768* (Fig. 3.5)

Ditches 6713 and 6768 were situated to the north-west of enclosure 7700 and were approximately 14m apart with 6713, the more southerly of the two, a further 13m distant from enclosure 7700. Pottery dating indicates that they went out of use in the early 2nd century, although they were probably established at the same time as the enclosures to their south. The ditches respected the line of late Iron Age-early Roman ditch 7187 to their west, suggesting that this feature survived as a boundary marker, if not an open ditch into the early Roman period. Ditch 6713 was orientated ENE-WSW and

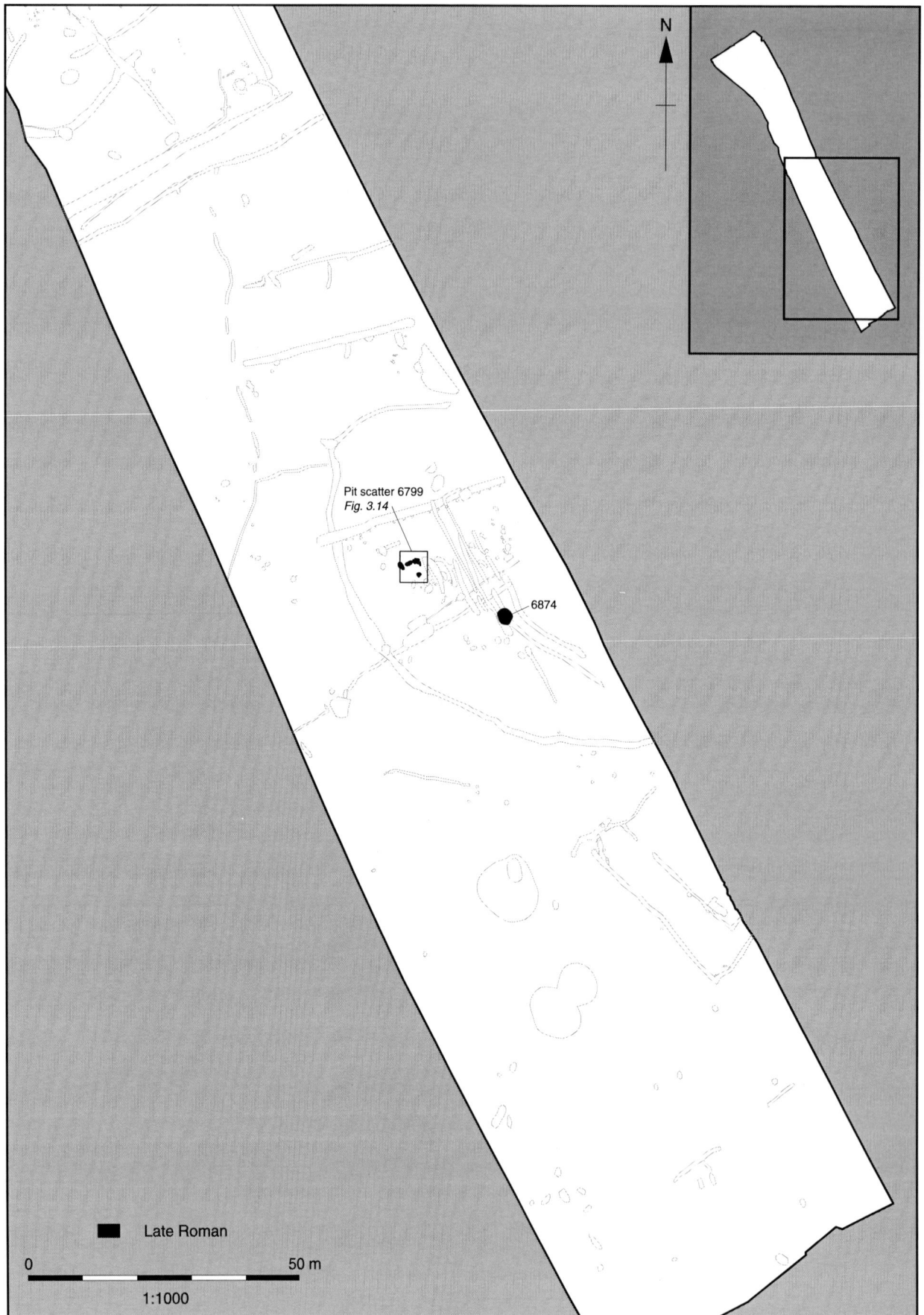

Fig. 3.13   *Junction 8N, late Roman activity*

projected 32m from the eastern site baulk. It was 1.2m wide and 0.35–0.44m deep with a U-shaped profile. Its fills comprised silty clay, with frequent to occasional flint inclusions. Ditch 6768 was also orientated ENE-WSW and projected in total some 28m from the eastern site baulk. It was less regular in plan than ditch 6713, having a short south-eastward return towards its western end, at a point where there was a small break in the principal alignment which was then resumed for a further 4.5m. The ditch therefore incorporated several compo-nents which were probably not all exactly contem-porary. It was up to 1.1m wide and ranged from 0.37-0.55m in depth. In profile, the ditch was flat based with steeply sloping sides and its fills comprised silty clay with frequent inclusions of flint and moderate charcoal flecks.

### Trackway 6364/6365 (Fig. 3.5)

To the north of ditch 6768 two ditches (6364 and 6365) defining a 3-4m-wide trackway ran some 46m across the full width of the site from ENE to WSW,

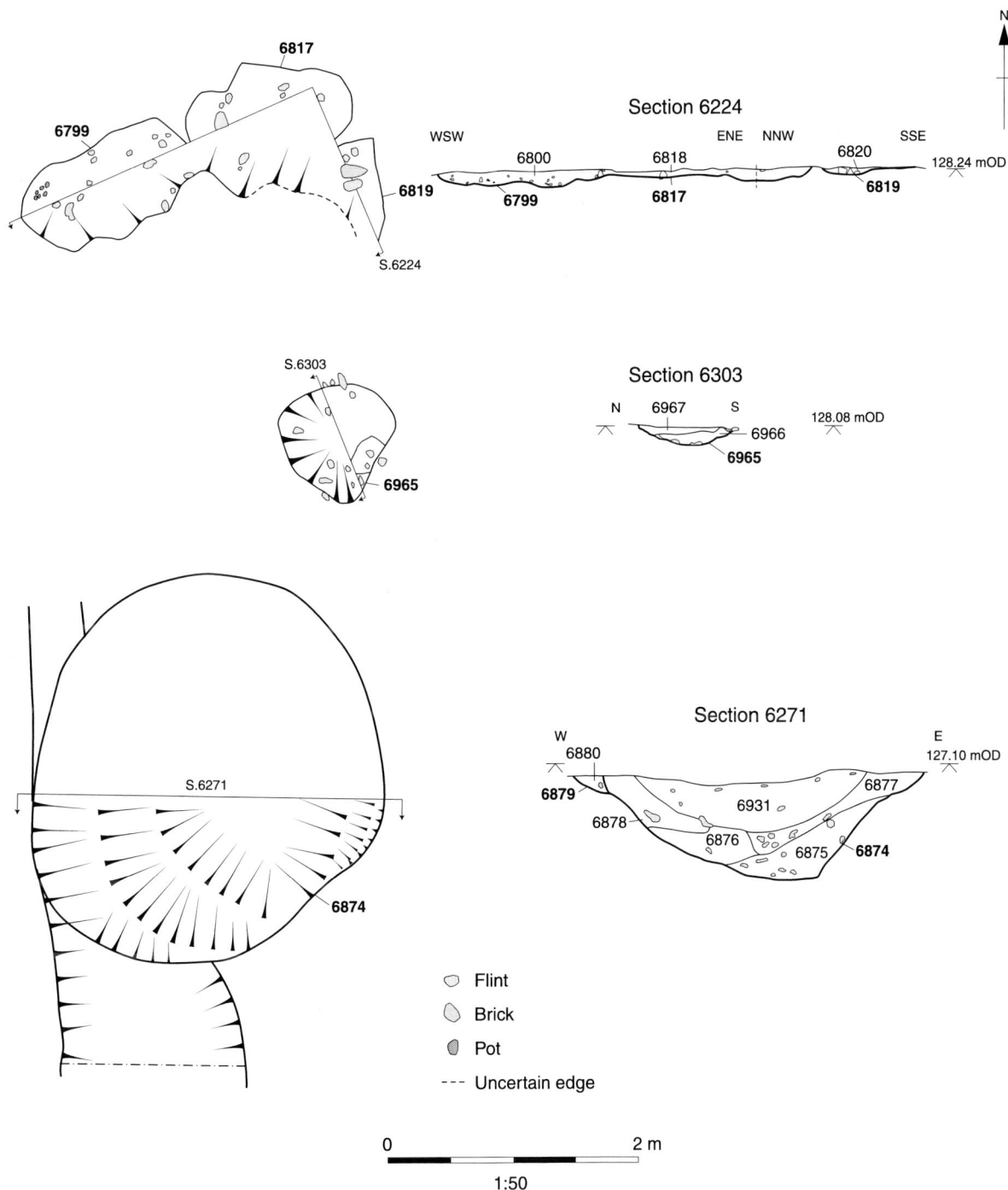

Fig. 3.14   *Junction 8N, detail plans and sections of pit scatter 6799 and pit 6864*

roughly parallel to the line of ditches 6713 and 6768, and some 20m distant from the latter. Pottery from the fills of ditch 6364 suggests that the feature went out of use at the end of the 2nd century, at the same time as the enclosures to its south-east. The northern boundary ditch (6364) varied in width between 0.76m and 1.8m and was 0.54-0.58m in depth, whilst the southern boundary (ditch 6365) was 0.65-0.86m wide and 0.26-0.36m deep. The ditches had bowl-shaped profiles and their fills comprised silty clays, with inclusions of flint and charcoal flecks.

## Late Roman activity (AD 250-410) (Figs 3.13-14)

Very few features were assigned to the late Roman period on the basis of associated finds. The activity comprised a pit scatter (6799) along with a large quarry hollow or pit (6874), all situated in the south-eastern part of the site, within the area of early-middle Roman enclosure 7700.

Pit scatter 6799 (Fig. 3.14) consisted of four shallow sub-circular pits (6799, 6817, 6819 and 6965) and/or postholes, with bowl-shaped profiles. These features ranged from 0.25-1.19m in diameter and were between 0.06m and 0.13m deep. They were filled with deposits of silty clay, with frequent inclusions of flint.

Pit 6874 (Fig. 3.13) measured 3m in diameter and was 0.8m deep. It was filled with a mixture of silty clay and flint nodules and produced substantial amounts of late Roman pottery, brick and tile.

## Medieval activity (late 12th-13th centuries) (Fig. 3.15)

### Summary

The medieval activity, most if not all of which dated to the late 12th-13th centuries, occupied the part of the site to the north of the early Roman trackway. It is divisible into two broad stratigraphic phases. Features assigned to the first phase comprised two east-west-aligned boundary ditches (6095 and 6449), set approximately 26m apart, and a small oven or kiln (6585). These features produced no secure dating evidence, but are believed to be medieval in date on the basis of their spatial relationship with the medieval settlement.

The first phase boundary ditches were super-seded by an L-shaped ditch (6119), running NNW from Roman trackway ditch 6364, which it respected, before cutting ditch 6095 and kiln 6585, and returning to the WSW where it ran beyond the limit of excavation. Ditch 6109 defined an enclosure

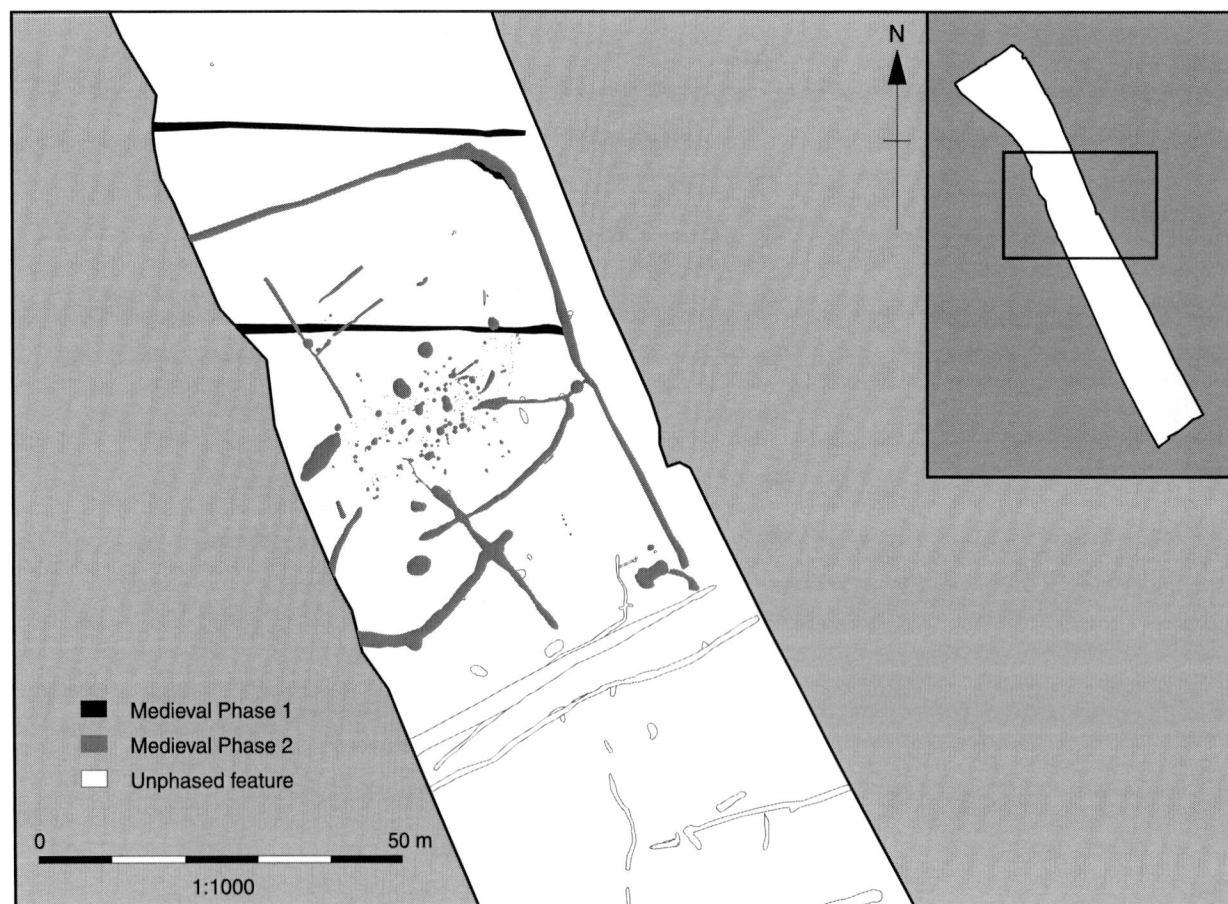

Medieval Phase 1
Medieval Phase 2
Unphased feature

0　　　　　　　　　　50 m
1:1000

*Fig. 3.15　Junction 8N, medieval activity*

measuring 67-72m NNW-SSE, aligned on the route of the Roman trackway, which may therefore have marked the line of a track or boundary that was still in use in the medieval period. Lying within the enclosure, defined by ditch 6119, was a substantial rectangular post-built structure (6961). The building was surrounded by several pits (6030, 6054, 6188, 6363, 6406 and 6497) and was flanked by a number of probable drainage gullies (6300, 6402, 6403, 7006 and 7704) to the south-east. Evaluation trench 1126 which lay to the south-west of the medieval settlement, produced evidence of several SW-NE-orientated gullies and a layer, which produced 13th-century pottery, suggesting that occupation continued beyond the limit of excavation to the south-west. To the north-west of structure 6961 a group of three narrow linear gullies (6515, 6524 and 6538) may have represented palisade slots dividing up yards or working areas.

### Phase 1 (?late 12th-13th centuries) (Fig. 3.16)

#### Ditches 6095 and 6449

These east-west-aligned ditches were parallel to each other some 25-26m apart and extended the entire width of the excavated area (c 50m). Ditch

6095 varied from c 0.5-1m in width and 0.2-0.3m in depth. It had a flat base and steeply sloping sides and was filled with a single deposit of silty clay, with occasional flint inclusions. Ditch 6449 was also variable in width. Where it was best preserved, adjacent to the west baulk of the site, it was 1.3m wide and 0.42m deep with a shallow V-shaped profile. The ditch fill contained a single deposit of sandy silt with occasional inclusions of flint.

#### Oven/kiln 6585 (Fig. 3.17)

Oven/kiln 6585 lay 2m south of ditch 6449 towards the eastern edge of the site and directly beneath the north-east corner of the later enclosure defined by ditch 6119. It was sub-circular in plan, with a south-east-aligned flue (6174), which had been partially cut away by ditch 6169. There was no evidence for a stokehole, which may have been completely cut away by the same ditch. The kiln measured 1.88m in length by 1.5m wide and was 0.6m deep, and was lined with irregularly laid flint nodules in a crushed chalk 'mortar'. The flints ranged from 0.1-0.5m in size and the junction of the chamber with the flue was marked by a very large piece of flint on each side. The flue measured between 1.05m and 0.85m in depth and was lined with identical materials to the oven. The backfill of the kiln comprised flint nodules, chalk

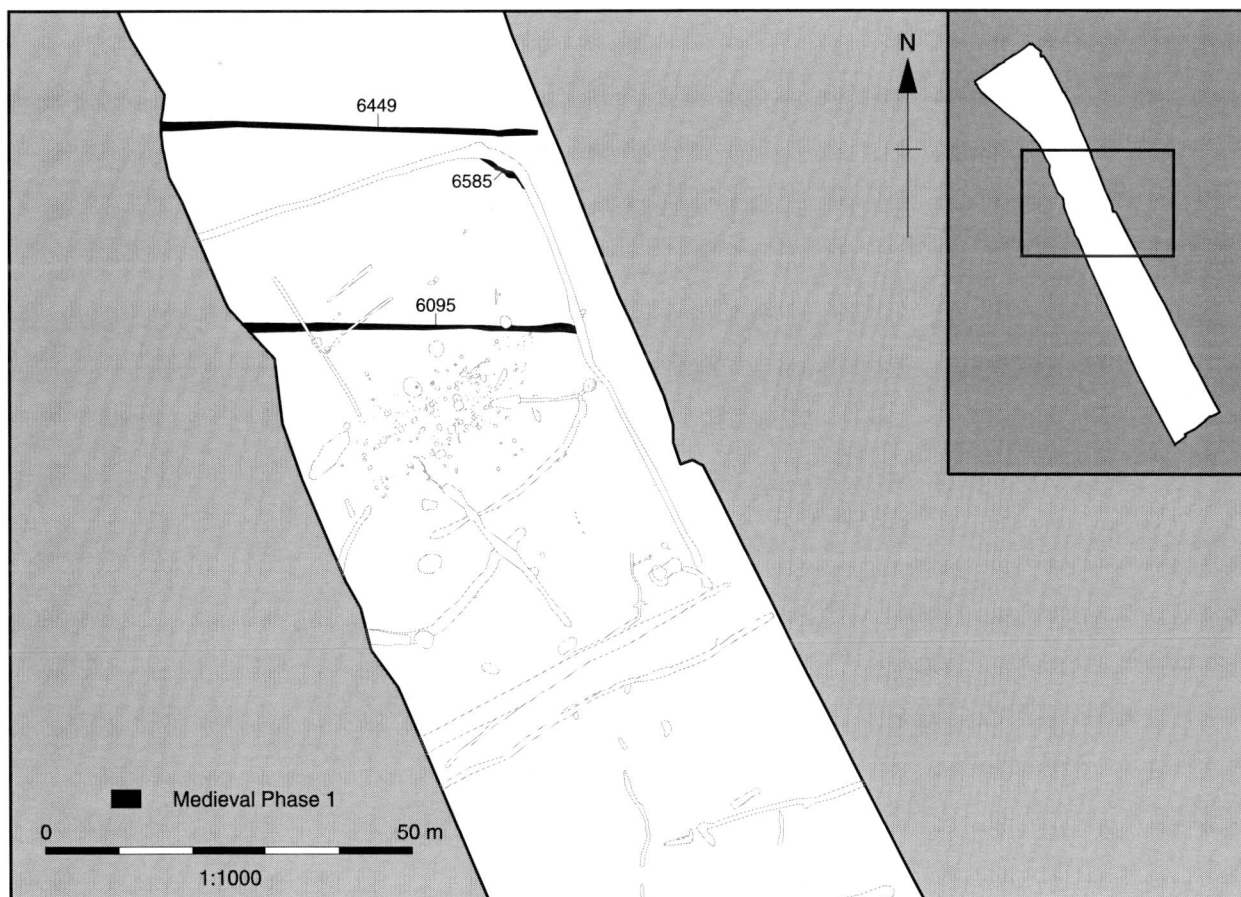

*Fig. 3.16  Junction 8N, medieval phase 1 plan of all features*

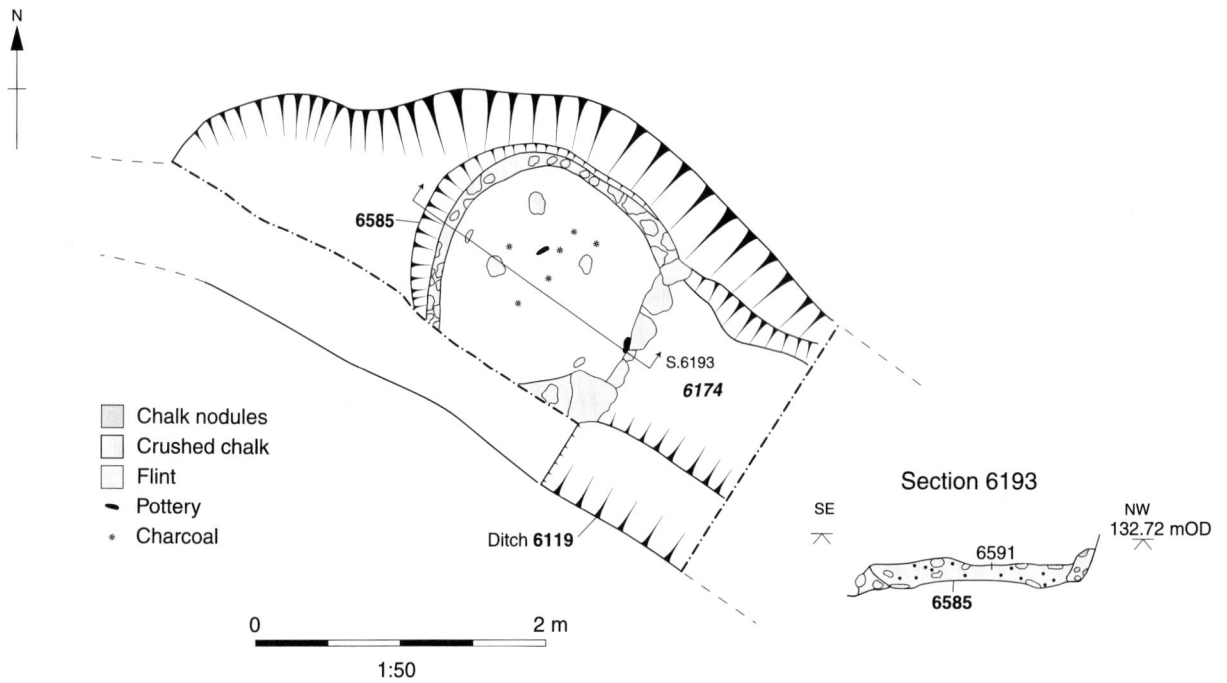

*Fig. 3.17  Junction 8N, detail plan and section of oven/kiln 6585*

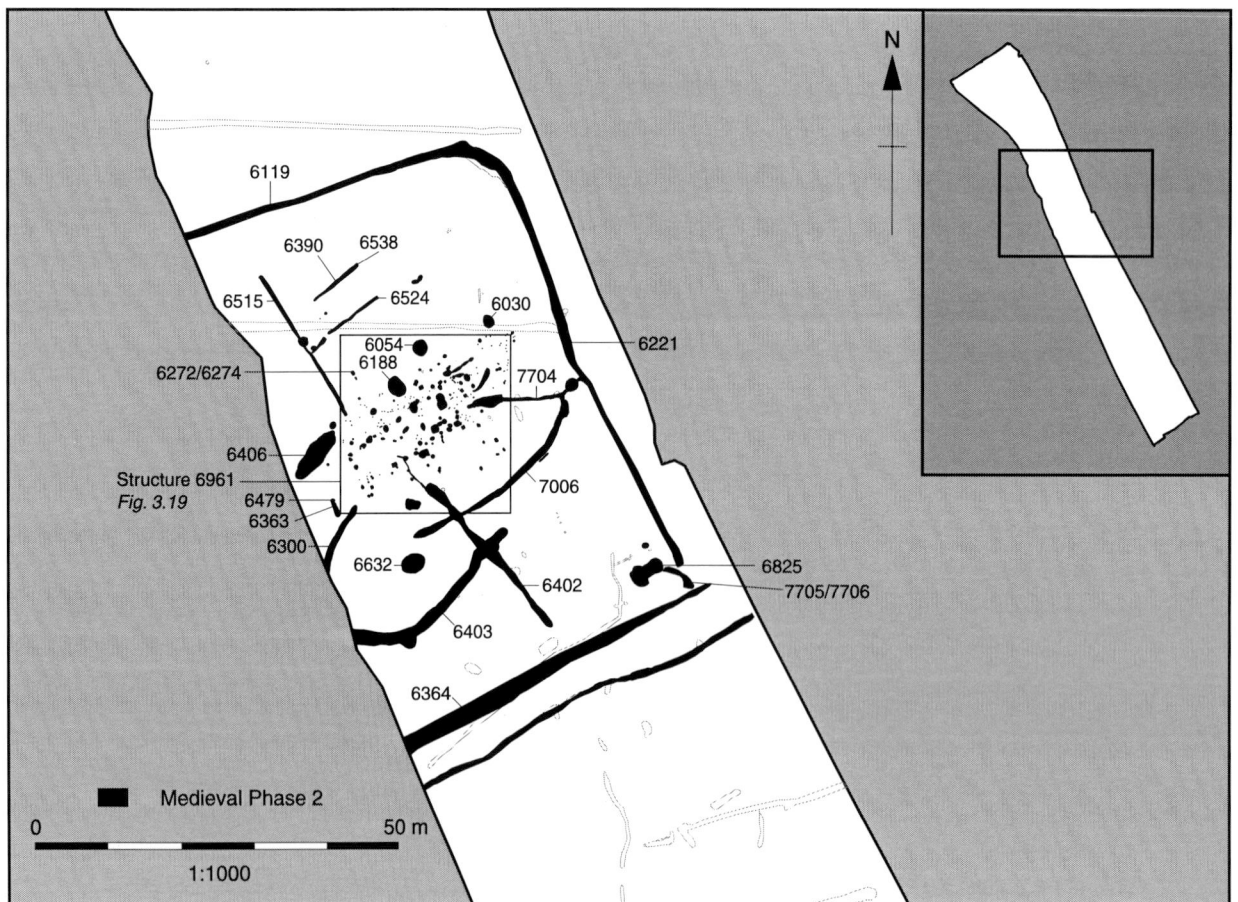

*Fig. 3.18  Junction 8N, medieval phase 2 plan of all features*

and silty clay and contained a moderate quantity of Roman ceramic building material, possibly originally incorporated into the structure. It also produced a little medieval pottery as well as charred cereal remains and charcoal (see Chapter 8). The backfill of the flue was identical to that of the kiln, although it appeared to have accumulated in several layers and did not contain charred plant remains.

### Phase 2 (late 12th-13th centuries) (Fig. 3.18)

#### Enclosures and ditches

Ditch 6119 was L-shaped in plan, aligned SSE-NNW and then returning to the WSW from its northern end, and was traced for a total length of *c* 102m. The eastern arm of the ditch appeared to terminate *c* 3.5m north of the earlier trackway ditch (6364), which formed the south boundary of the medieval settlement complex, but at this point the ditch was only 0.07m deep and it is possible that this was not its real terminus. The ditch varied from 0.95-1.65m in width and was up to 0.6m deep. Generally, it had steeply sloping sides, giving a V-shaped or slightly wider, flat-bottomed profile. Its typical single fill comprised silty clay, with moderate to frequent inclusions of flint and occasional charcoal flecks.

At the point of intersection with east-west ditch 6095, assigned to the previous phase (see above), there was evidence of an earlier cut (6221) on the same alignment as 6119. This earlier cut did not extend south of ditch 6095 and seems therefore to have terminated at the intersection, though it is clear that 6221 was the later of the two features. Ditch 6221 was at least 1.4m wide with sides sloping gently in the upper part of the profile and then steepening above the flat base of the feature, which was 0.56m deep and filled with a single deposit of yellow-brown clay silt. The ditch could not be traced more than *c* 4m north of the point of intersection with 6095, so its significance is uncertain. If it marked an earlier phase of enclosure 6119 this must have been smaller than in the form represented by ditch 6119 itself.

#### Post-built structure 6961 (Figs 3.19-21)

Some 63 postholes were interpreted as components of a NE-SW-aligned post-built structure (6961). This structure lay at the centre of the exposed portion of the enclosure, perpendicular to the eastern arm of the enclosure ditch. The postholes were generally sub-circular in plan, with flat bases and vertical sides, ranging between 0.25m and 0.85m in diameter and 0.05-0.48m deep (Table 3.1). The shallow nature of some of these postholes suggests considerable truncation. The posthole fills comprised silty clay with occasional to moderate inclusions of flint, chalk and charcoal flecks. Only four postholes contained more than a single fill and one post-pipe was observed (in 6999), although it is possible that some were missed because of the homogeneous nature of the posthole fills.

Due to the number of features within the footprint of the building, its layout was ambiguous and there was clearly some rebuilding or repair, including possible rearrangement of the internal features, or an earlier/later phase of activity. There are two main possibilities: first that the postholes represent one large building; and second that two smaller structures are represented. If the postholes do represent a single structure then the building measured 24.3m long by 5.5-6m wide, with a possible 3m-wide entrance, approximately half way along the building's length, on its north-western side. This possible entrance was defined by postholes 7542 and 7022, both of which measured approximately 0.5m in diameter and were 0.2m deep. The north-western wall of the putative structure comprised a single continuous, but irregularly spaced line of postholes, with a beam-slot (6942/6944) at the north-eastern end and little evidence of any rebuilding, although posthole 6433 may have replaced posthole 6435. The north-eastern end of the structure was defined by two groups of two postholes (7167/7170 and 6342/6540), with postholes 6342 and 6540 representing the south-eastern corner of the building. Outlying posthole 7534 may have been the north-eastern corner post. The south-eastern wall of the structure was similar in construction to the north-western one, but had fewer and less substantial postholes (possibly due to greater levels of truncation at this point) and more evidence of rebuilding. On the south-eastern side posthole 7045 may have been replaced by posthole 7175, or posthole 7043, and the line of the wall altered at some point to incorporate postholes 6327 and 7562. The south-western end of the putative structure was more clearly defined, with six postholes, including two closely spaced postholes (6361/6527 and 7558/7051) at each corner. A gap of 4m in the south-western wall at the south-western end of the building may have provided an alternative entrance.

The second option, incorporating two putative structures rather than one, is in many ways the more convincing scenario. In this case a larger structure, measuring 15.75 x 5.5m was accompanied by a smaller structure measuring 6 x 6m immediately to its north-east. The larger structure would have been similar in construction to the putative large structure discussed above, although in this case postholes 7542 and 7175 would have marked the corners of the north-eastern wall-line of the building. The smaller building would have incorporated many of the postholes from the north-eastern end of the larger structure discussed above and included beam-slot 6942/6944. In this case, however, postholes 6948, 6439, 7180 and 6623 would have marked the line of the south-western wall of the smaller structure, with postholes 6494 and 6496 possibly serving as extra support for its roof.

There were a number of features, including pits and postholes, within the footprint of the structure, but few of them could be related to the structure/

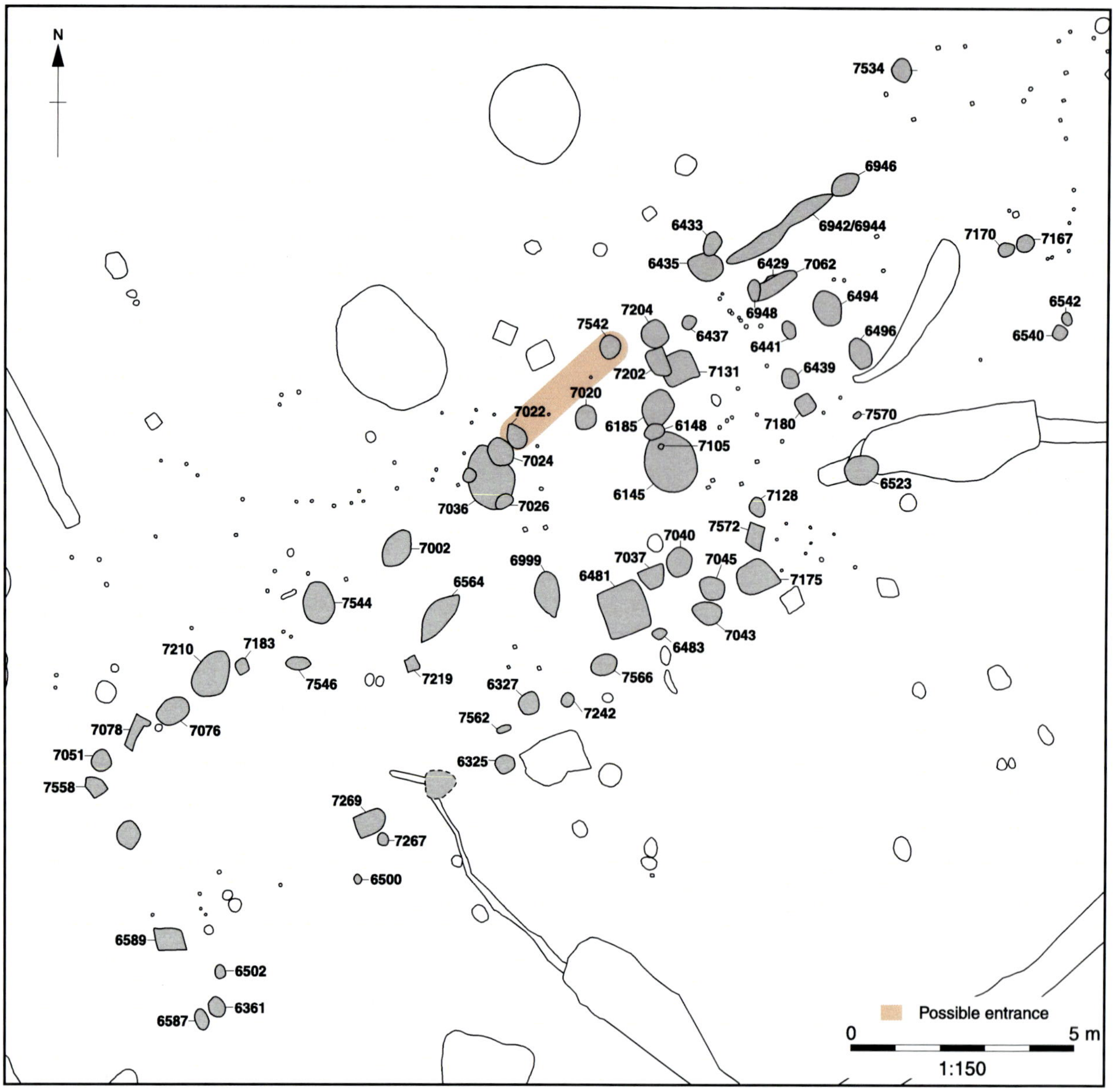

*Fig. 3.19   Junction 8N, detail plan of structure 6961*

structures or its/their use and not all of them were necessarily contemporary. Oval feature 6999, which measured 0.85m long and 0.19m deep, showed clear evidence of a post-pipe and may have been a posthole supporting the roof of the structure. Square posthole 7219 may have fulfilled a similar function. Large pit 6145, which was sub-circular in plan and measured up to 1.45m across by 0.5m in depth, had been backfilled with at least three deposits of silty clay and gravel, containing high concentrations of charcoal and ceramic building material, which may relate to the demolition of the building(s). The remaining internal features comprised randomly placed pits/postholes varying from sub-rectangular to sub-circular in plan. These features were up to 1.2m long, ranged between 1.04m and 0.45m in diameter, and were all between 0.06m and 0.37m deep.

Finds from the structure/structures were restricted in scope, comprising small groups of fairly abraded late 12th-13th-century pottery. The largest individual assemblage was a group of 25 sherds, weighing 55g, from posthole 7175. However, this material provides relatively little information about the detailed chronology and function(s) of the building(s).

*Pits 6030, 6054, 6188, 6363, 6406 and 6632 (Fig. 3.18)*

This group of pits was scattered around post-built structure 6961, with pits 6030, 6054, 6188 and 6406 located close to its north-west side, pit 6363 positioned outside and parallel to the south-west end of the structure, and pit 6632 located some distance to the south. Pits 6030, 6054, 6188 and 6632 were sub-circular to oval in plan, pit 6406 was much larger and more elongated, whilst pit 6363, also

46

*Table 3.1: Details of structure 6961*

| Feature | Diameter or length/ width (m) | Depth (m) | Dating |
|---|---|---|---|
| 6145 | 1.45 | 0.5 | None |
| 6148 | 0.2 | 0.16 | Late 12th-13th-century pottery |
| 6185 | 0.9 | 0.19 | None |
| 6327 | 0.59 | 0.09 | None |
| 6429 | 0.4 | 0.37 | Late 12th-13th-century pottery |
| 6433 | 0.43 | 0.11 | None |
| 6435 | 0.98 | 0.05 | None |
| 6437 | 0.4 | 0.06 | None |
| 6439 | 0.52 | 0.03 | None |
| 6441 | 0.47 | 0.06 | Late 12th-13th-century pottery |
| 6481 | 0.98 | 0.16 | Late 12th-13th-century pottery |
| 6494 | 0.96 | 0.12 | none |
| 6496 | 0.53 | 0.06 | Late 12th-13th-century pottery |
| 6498 | 0.28 | 0.04 | Late 12th-13th-century pottery |
| 6523 | 0.75 | 0.8 | Late 12th-13th-century pottery and metalwork |
| 6564 | 1.22 | 0.3 | Late 12th-13th-century pottery |
| 6589 | 0.67 | 0.06 | None |
| 6942 | 1.71 x 0.3 | 0.14 | Late 12th-13th-century pottery and metalwork |
| 6944 | 1.63 x 0.31 | 0.07 | Late 12th-13th-century pottery |
| 6946 | 0.78 | 0.48 | Late 12th-13th-century pottery |
| 6948 | 0.5 | 0.5 | Late 12th-13th-century pottery |
| 6999 | 0.85 | 0.19 | None |
| 7002 | 0.85 | 0.19 | Late 12th-13th-century pottery |
| 7020 | 0.55 | 0.5 | None |
| 7022 | 0.21 | 0.2 | None |
| 7024 | 0.55 | 0.21 | None |
| 7026 | 0.28 | 0.21 | None |
| 7035 | 1.6 | 0.26 | None |
| 7037 | 0.45 | 0.24 | None |
| 7040 | 0.62 | 0.28 | Late 12th-13th-century pottery |
| 7045 | 0.48 | 0.22 | None |

*Table 3.1: Details of structure 6961 - continued*

| Feature | Diameter or length/ width (m) | Depth (m) | Dating |
|---|---|---|---|
| 7046 | 0.8 | 0.22 | None |
| 7051 | 0.56 | 0.1 | Late 12th-13th-century pottery |
| 7062 | 1.2 x 0.69 | 0.27 | Late 12th-13th-century pottery |
| 7076 | 0.84 | 0.17 | None |
| 7128 | 0.5 | 0.29 | None |
| 7175 | 0.8 | 0.14 | None |
| 7177 | 0.48 | 0.06 | None |
| 7180 | 0.48 | 0.1 | None |
| 7183 | 0.42 | 0.3 | None |
| 7210 | 1.06 | 0.52 | None |
| 7215 | 0.25 | N/A | None |
| 7217 | 0.18 | N/A | None |
| 7219 | 0.3 | 0.09 | None |
| 7221 | 0.29 | 0.25 | None |
| 7223 | 0.24 | 0.07 | None |
| 7242 | 0.36 | 0.1 | Late 12th-13th-century pottery |
| 7246 | 0.6 | 0.03 | None |
| 7248 | 0.38 | 0.12 | None |
| 7267 | 0.25 | 0.05 | None |
| 7269 | 0.53 | 0.1 | None |
| 7277 | 0.57 | 0.11 | Late 12th-13th-century pottery and metalwork |
| 7512 | | | None |
| 7516 | | | None |
| 7542 | 0.5 | N/A | None |
| 7544 | 0.9 | N/A | None |
| 7546 | 0.5 | N/A | None |
| 7558 | 0.5 | N/A | None |
| 7560 | 0.2 | N/A | None |
| 7562 | 0.35 | N/A | None |
| 7566 | 0.6 | N/A | None |
| 7572 | 0.55 | N/A | None |
| 7590 | N/A | N/A | None |

elongated, might perhaps have been an irregular slot, rather than a pit, and incorporated a posthole (6479) at its north-west end. The four ovoid pits ranged from 1.7-3.5m in length and were between 0.07m and 0.85m deep. With the exception of pit 6054, which had an irregular profile, they all had flat bases and steep sides. Pit 6406, measured 8.2 x 2.96m in plan and was up to 0.68m deep, while the linear 'pit' 6363 was 2.4m long and 0.7m wide and had a maximum depth of 0.29m. This pit also had an irregular profile, steep sided on the south-west side and sloping on the north-east, with a slight longitudinal step in its base.

The pit fills varied, though most comprised clay silt, with variable inclusions of flint, chalk and charcoal flecks. Pit 6406 had a sequence of five fills, including a layer of burnt material, which appeared to represent discrete episodes of deliberate back-filling/dumping. The generally regular profiles of these pits suggest that they were dug as rubbish

pits, rather than being infilled quarry pits. The pit fills contained assemblages of late 12th-13th-century pottery.

*Drainage ditches 6300, 7704, 7006, 6403 and 6402 (Fig. 3.18)*

Curvilinear ditches 7704, 7006, 6300 and 6403, were all contemporaneous and aligned broadly NE-SW. Judging from their scale they probably served to drain surface water, with ditches 7704 and 6300 perhaps draining water away from the corners of structure 6961. However, along with enclosure boundary ditch 6119 they divided the south-east corner of the enclosure into two sub-rectangular enclosures, measuring 21m NW-SE by 20m WSW-ENE, and 24m WSW-ENE by 13m NW-SE respectively. These may have been used for corralling animals and/or other agricultural activities and, with the addition of a gate between ditches 7006 and 6403, would have served to keep animals away from structure 6961. At some point, after the silting up of ditches 7006 and 6403, they were replaced by NW-SE-aligned linear ditch 6402, which was dug at a right angle to structure 6961 and may have served a more straightforward function draining water away from the building.

Gully 6300 was curvilinear, measuring approximately 7m long by 0.7m wide and 0.17-0.3m deep. The gully was orientated SW-NE running beyond the limit of the excavation to the south-west and terminating close to the south-western corner of building 6961. It was flat based, with steeply

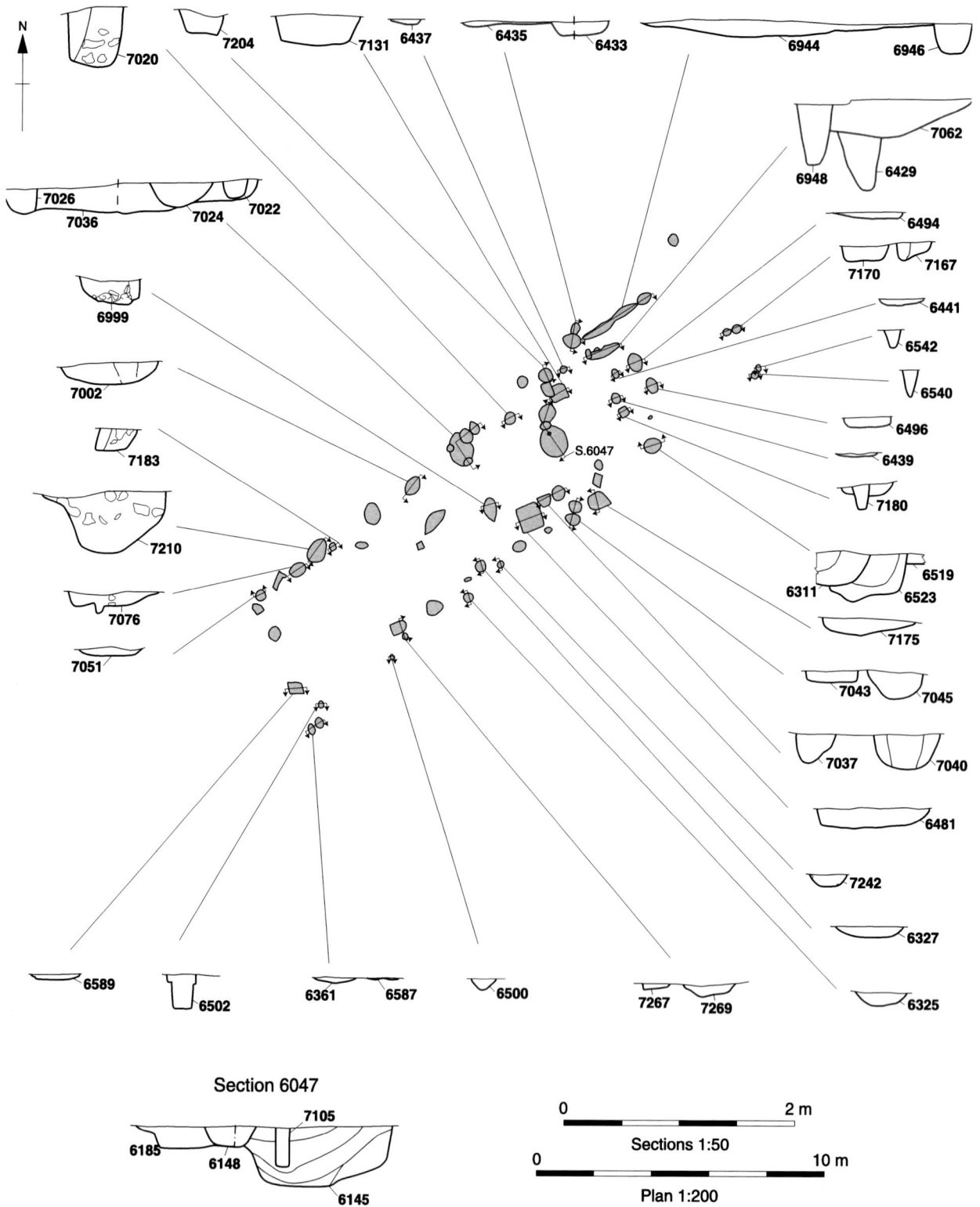

Fig. 3.20  *Junction 8N, sections of features forming structure 6961*

*Fig. 3.21   Junction 8N, post-built structure 6961, looking north-east*

sloping sides and had two fills comprising silty clay, with frequent flint inclusions. Gully 7704 was linear, orientated SE-NW, with a terminus at the south-eastern corner of building 6961, and measured approximately 13m long, 0.5m wide and 0.14m deep. In profile, the gully had a flat base and steep sides and its fill comprised silty clay with frequent flint inclusions. Gullies 7006 and 6403 were slightly curved, but aligned broadly NE-SW. Gully 7006 had a flat base, with steeply sloping sides and measured approximately 23.5m long, 0.6m wide and 0.12-0.44m deep. The gully fills comprised silty clay, with moderate to frequent inclusions of flint, charcoal and chalk. Gully 6403, measuring 12m long, 0.7m wide and 0.58–0.68m deep, had a flat base with steep sides and its fills comprised silty clay, with frequent inclusions of flint and occasional charcoal flecks. Gully 112609, in evaluation trench 1126, may have been a south-western continuation of gully 6403. Gullies 7006 and 6403 were later filled in and replaced by a NW-SE-aligned gully (6402), which also cut them. This gully was 25.3m long, 0.8m wide and 0.32-0.54m deep, and had an irregular profile. Its fills comprised silty clay, with frequent inclusions of flint and occasional charcoal.

*Gullies/beam-slots north-west of the building* (Fig. 3.18)

A group of three linear gullies lay immediately to the north-east of building 6961. Gully 6515 was aligned NW-SE at a right angle to the building, while gullies 6524 and 6538 were aligned NE-SW, parallel to the building. Gully 6538 was cut by sub-circular posthole 6398, about halfway down its length. These gullies, although open to the north-east, may have been palisade slots, dividing up working areas, or animal pens. Together gullies 6515, 6524 and the north-western wall of structure 6961 may have defined a rectangular yard measuring 13.5m NW-SE by 12.5m NE-SW. A further NW-SE-aligned gully (6272/6274), approximately 1m in length, lay in the middle of this area and may have been associated with it. To the north-west of this yard, gullies 6515, 6538 and 6524 may have defined a second but smaller sub-rectangular yard measuring 12m NE-SW by 4.4m NW-SE. Gully 6515 was 17.5m long, 0.4m wide and 0.08-0.15m deep, and had a flat base, with steeply sloping sides. It contained a single deposit of silty clay, with occasional flint inclusions and frequent charcoal flecks. Gully 6524 was 11m long, 0.8m wide and 0.08m deep. It had a flat base and vertical sides and was filled with a single deposit of sandy silt, with inclusions of flint and charcoal flecks. Gully 6538 was 8m long by 0.5m wide and 0.1-0.27m deep. It too had a flat base and near vertical sides, and was filled with a single deposit of sandy silt, with occasional inclusions of flint and occasional charcoal flecks. The gully was cut by a sub-circular posthole, measuring 0.18m wide and 0.28m deep, about halfway down its length. Short linear gully 6272/6274 was 0.36-0.22m wide and 0.1-0.05m deep, and had a single fill of silty clay with occasional flint inclusions.

**6577**

N

S.6249

**6825**

### Section 6249

WSW                   7048     7048      ENE

131.46 mOD

**6825**

6823

6824

**6577**

**6825**

6578

**6825**

☐ Lime mortar
☐ Flint
* Charcoal

0                    2 m

1:50

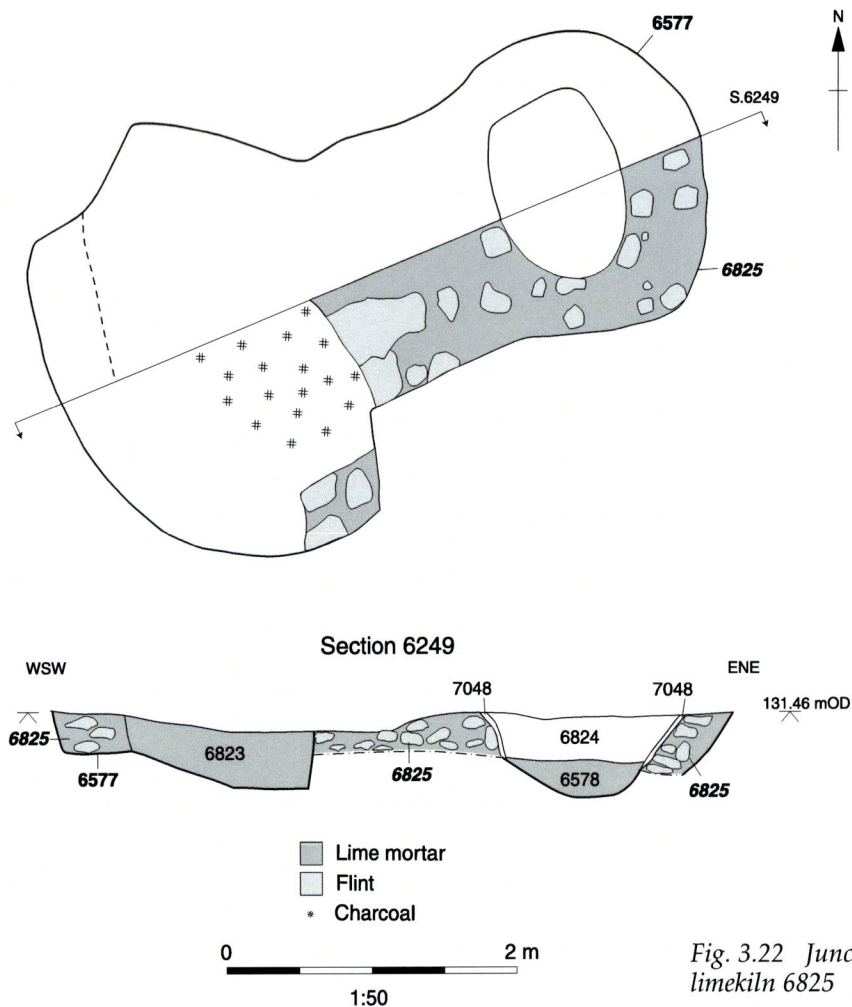

Fig. 3.22  *Junction 8N, detail plan and section of limekiln 6825*

Fig. 3.23   *Junction 8N, limekiln 6825, looking south-west*

50

*Other structures* (Figs 3.22-3)

In the south-east corner of the enclosure, close to ditch 6109 and to Roman trackway ditch 6364 was a limekiln (6825). The kiln was keyhole shaped and measured 4.46 x 3.02m. The firing chamber was set in a sub-circular pit (6577), 2m in diameter and 0.52m deep, and was lined with flint nodules bonded with lime mortar. The maximum size of the flint nodules used was 0.4 x 0.45m and the smallest measured 0.04 x 0.02m. The east-west-oriented flue, which extended from the western side of the firing chamber, was 1.5m long, 1.6m wide and 0.52m deep. The flue appears to have been lined with identical materials to the firing chamber, although this had been extensively robbed, more so on the southern side of the structure. The stokehole, at the western end of the structure, comprised a sub-circular pit 2.9m in diameter and 0.38m in depth, which was partially lined with the same materials as the rest of the structure, though these had been even more comprehensively robbed. The firing chamber had a 0.24m-thick basal fill consisting entirely of lime mortar and the entire inside wall of the chamber was lined with a layer of lime mortar up to 0.05m thick. Overlying the basal fill was a demolition layer comprising silty clay with large flint nodules. The stokehole was filled entirely by a deposit of lime mortar. The limekiln was associated with two shallow gullies (7705 and 7706) to its south-east, measuring respectively 3m long by 0.5m wide, and 5.5m long by 0.5m wide.

## BUNCEFIELD DEPOT WATCHING BRIEF

(Fig. 3.24)

### Site location

This site, centred on NGR TL091 081, covered an area of approximately 12.1ha immediately east of Buncefield Depot, north of the Junction 8 compound and to the west of the M1. The local geology comprises clay-with-flints, overlying Upper Chalk. The area was relatively level in the southern part of the site, but sloped down to the north, with an overall drop from *c* 137m aOD to *c* 125m aOD.

### Summary

Evidence of activity at Buncefield depot was restricted to a thin scatter of pits and linear features over a very substantial area. Four pits (510, 516, 521 and 532) and a short stretch of ditch (506) were dispersed across the site, and contained late Bronze Age-early Iron Age pottery. A number of other small pits and ditches were observed during the watching brief, but none of them had clear spatial relationships with dated features, or contained any dating evidence, and therefore they are not described further.

### Pits 510, 516, 521 and 532

Pit 510 was an isolated feature roughly in the centre of the site. Pits 516 and 521 were adjacent to each other, some 200m further to the NNW, and pit 532 lay another 40m distant. These features were generally sub-circular in plan, with shallow bowl-shaped profiles and varied from 1.56-2.8m in diameter and were 0.2-0.53m deep. The pit fills comprised clay silt, with moderate to frequent inclusions of flint and charcoal flecks. The fills of pit 510 only produced a single sherd of prehistoric pottery, but the other features contained late Bronze Age-early Iron Age assemblages.

### Ditch 506

Towards the southern end of the site, ditch 506 was aligned NNE-SSW and was traced for a distance of approximately 70m. Neither end of the feature was clearly defined (probably owing to truncation) and it is likely to have extended further in both directions, perhaps turning slightly more to the south-west at its southern end. To the north, a further length of ditch (505) is almost certain to have been a continuation of the line of 506 giving a minimum length of at least 105m. The ditch was up to 1.5m wide, but only 0.3m deep, and had a rounded base with steeply sloping sides. The fill comprised silty clay with occasional inclusions of flint and chalk, and produced a single sherd of later prehistoric pottery.

## JUNCTION 8 COMPOUND (Fig. 3.25)

### Site Location

The Junction 8 compound was located at NGR TL 092 079, immediately to the north of Junction 8 of the M1. The small excavation area lay to the west of the motorway and the Junction 8S excavation area, and encompassed an area of approximately 320m². The local geology comprises clay-with-flints, overlying Upper Chalk, and the area has a relatively flat topography, with a maximum height of 136m aOD.

### Summary

The features at the Junction 8 Compound comprised a ditch (5513) and a group of pits and postholes (5550). Ditch (5513) bisected the site, running approximately north-south. The pits and postholes (5509, 5514, 5516, 5518, 5520, 5522, 5524, 5526, 5528 and 5532) were largely concentrated to the west of the ditch, although pit 5509 cut the ditch and pit 5514 lay to its east. In addition to the pits, there was a single tree-throw hole (5530). None of the features produced much dating evidence, although 11th-13th-century pottery from the fills of pits 5514 and 5520 suggests that the whole complex may have been medieval in date.

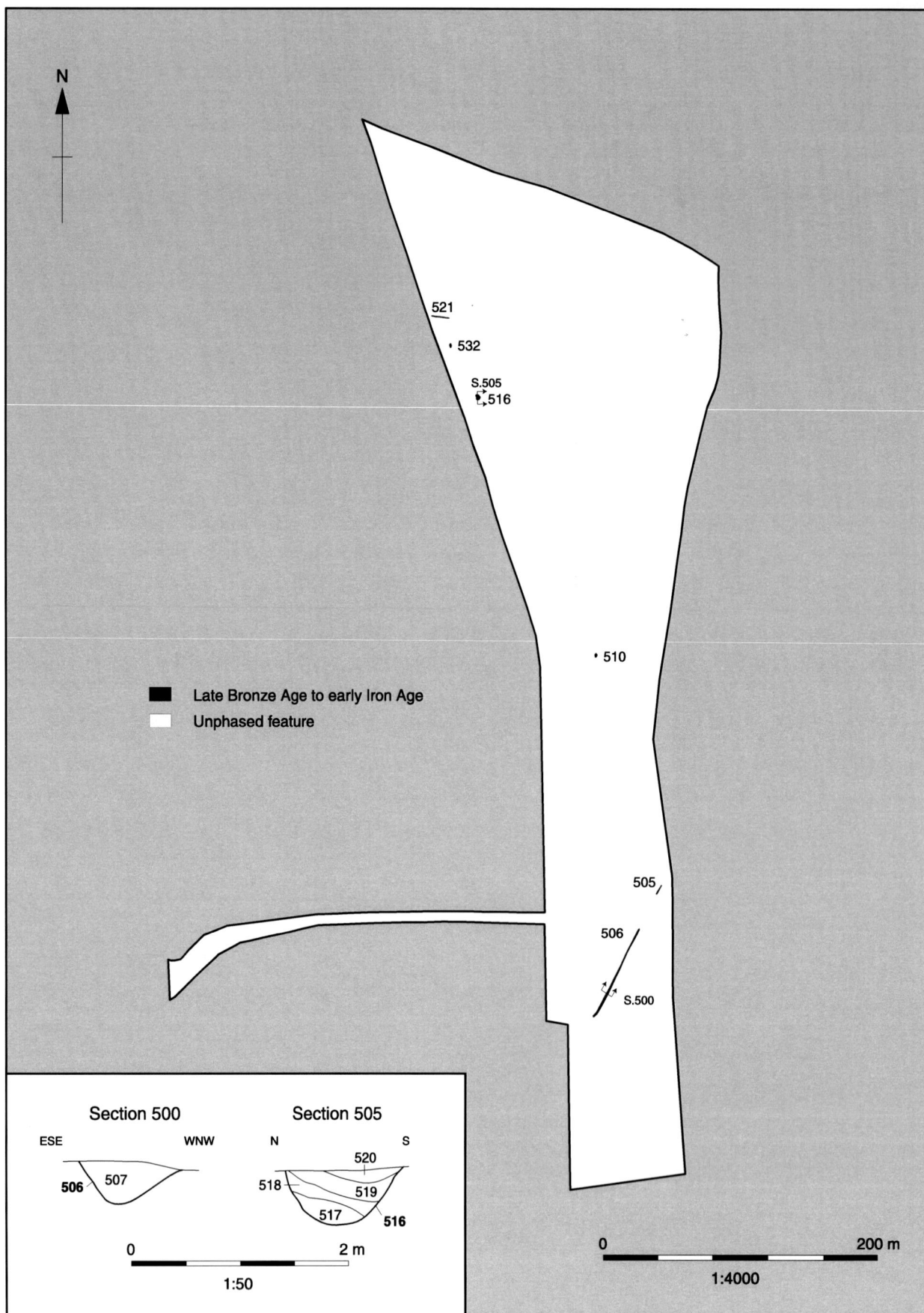

*Fig. 3.24   Buncefield Depot Watching Brief, late Bronze Age-early Iron Age features, with sections*

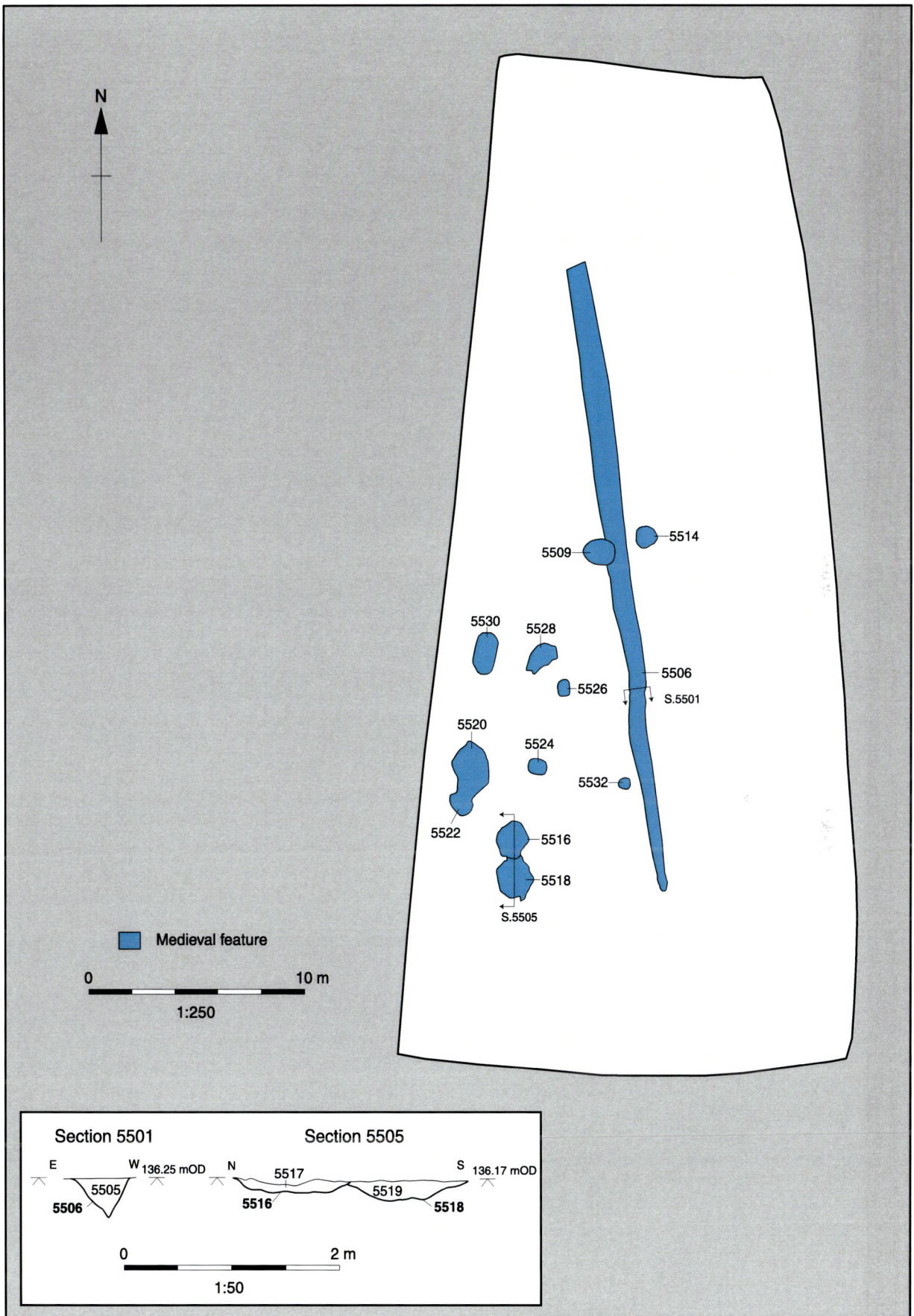

N

5514

5509

5530    5528

5526

5506

S.5501

5520

5524

5532

5522

5516

5518

S.5505

■ Medieval feature

0                    10 m

1:250

Section 5501          Section 5505

E        W 136.25 mOD        N        5517        S 136.17 mOD

5505                                                      5519

**5506**        **5516**                **5518**

0                    2 m

1:50

*Fig. 3.25   Junction 8 Compound, medieval features, with sections*

Section 5404

Section 5618

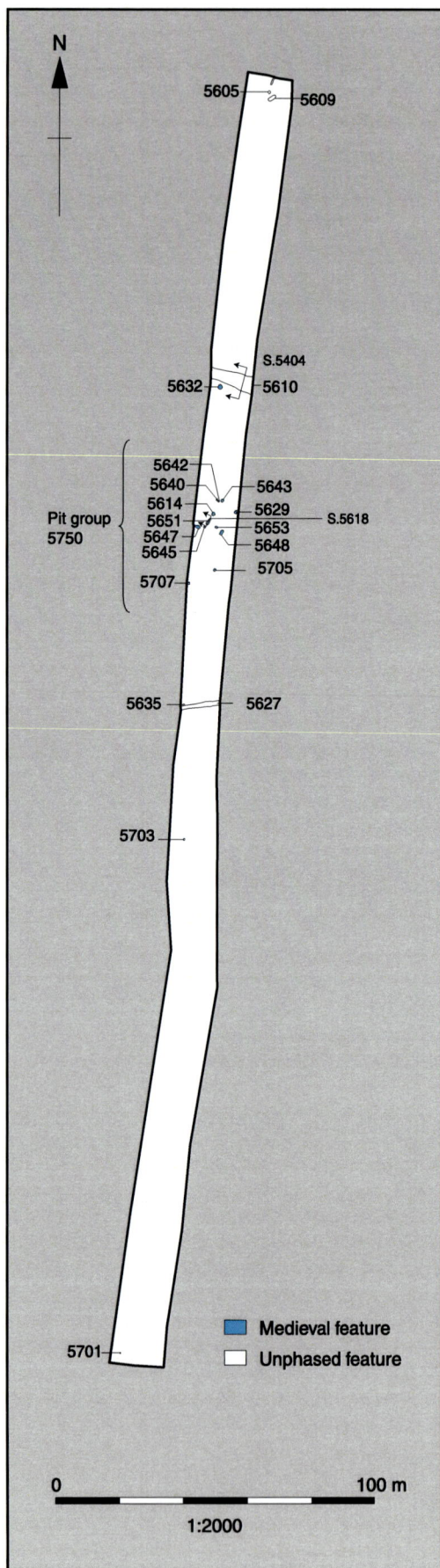

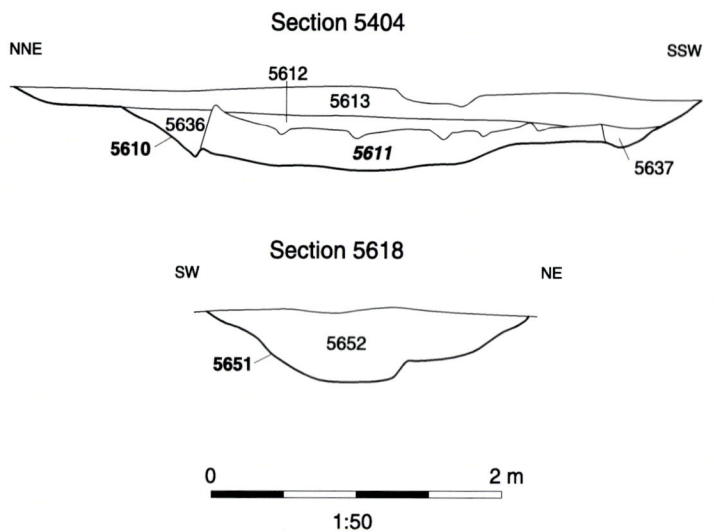

*Fig. 3.26 (left and above) Junction 8 targeted watching brief, Roman and medieval activity, with sections*

### Ditch 5513

Ditch 5513 was a linear feature aligned approximately north-south. It was traced for a length of almost 18m south from the point where it was obscured by a modern feature and it appeared to fade out at its southern end. The ditch was V-shaped in profile and varied from 0.25-0.82m wide and 0.25-0.36m deep. The single ditch fill comprised silty clay, with moderate flint inclusions and occasional charcoal flecks.

### Pit group 5550

Pit group 5550 comprised a scatter of ten very shallow pits and postholes, sub-circular or irregular in plan, with bowl-shaped or irregular profiles. All the features were 0.08-0.18m deep and all contained single fills of clay silt, with occasional to moderate inclusions of flint and charcoal flecks. Their other dimensions suggest at least two slightly different types of feature. Pits 5509, 5516, 5518, 5520 and 5528 were all similar in size, measuring 0.94-1.05m across, while 5514, 5522, 5524 and 5526 had 0.56-0.69m diameters. It is not possible to determine if these features were pits or postholes. Feature 5532, noticeably smaller than the others with a 0.32m diameter, may well have been a posthole rather than a pit, but neither this nor any of the other features had evidence for a post-pipe or any indication of materials used as post-packing. The disposition of the features, however, perhaps suggests an L-shaped 'structure', possibly a fenceline, formed by features 5514, 5526, 5524 and 5532, with all the other features lying to the west and south.

### Tree-throw hole 5530

Tree-throw hole 5530 was irregular in plan with a bowl-shaped profile, measuring 0.9 x 0.5 x 0.13m. It was filled with a single deposit of clay silt, containing very occasional flint inclusions.

## JUNCTION 8 TARGETED WATCHING BRIEF
(Fig. 3.26)

### Site Location

A watching brief was carried out on a long narrow area (approximately 0.6ha) to the north-west of Junction 8, centred on NGR TL 092 081. The area lay immediately to the west of the M1 and to the east of the Buncefield Depot watching brief area. The underlying geology comprises clay-with-flints, overlying Upper Chalk, and the area has a generally flat topography with a maximum height of 134m aOD.

### Summary

A watching brief carried out to the north-east of the compound area revealed scatters of pits or postholes, a linear ditch and a possible sunken trackway or hollow-way. The remaining features were isolated and produced no dating evidence and are therefore not described further.

### Pit Group 5750

Pit group 5750 comprised a scatter of ten pits/postholes (5614, 5629, 5640, 5645, 5647, 5648, 5651, 5654, 5705 and 5707) concentrated within a small area in the northern half of the site, measuring *c* 25m north-south. These features were generally sub-circular or sub-rectangular in plan with flat bases and steeply sloping or concave sides. One pit (5651) measured 2 x 0.8 x 0.48m, while the remaining features were between 0.37m and 0.78m in diameter and 0.1-0.64m deep. The pits were filled with silty clay containing moderate to frequent flint inclusions and moderate to frequent charcoal flecks. Very little dating evidence was recovered from any of these features, with only four sherds of Roman pottery recovered from the entire area. Three of the sherds (dating to the mid-late 1st century) came from the upper fill of pit or posthole 5629. During excavation six of these features (5629, 5648, 5663, 5661, 5614 and 5643) were thought to represent postholes and a beam-slot, belonging to a rectangular building, perhaps *c* 5.5m wide, 8-9m long and aligned approximately NE-SW. However, the individual features seem quite large for such a building and their profiles are more like those of pits than postholes. If they do indeed represent a building then it seems likely to have been medieval in date, given the similarity in construction and close proximity to the 12th-century building from the main Junction 8N excavation area.

### Hollow-way 5610

Approximately 33m to the north of the pit scatter/building, hollow-way 5610 was aligned WNW-ESE and ran across the width of the site (here only 13m), continuing beyond the limits of excavation at both ends. The excavated section of the hollow-way was 4.76m wide and 0.56m deep, with an uneven base which contained a cobbled surface (5611), measuring 2.7m wide and consisting of flint nodules ranging in size from 0.1-0.36m. Flanking the cobbled surface were two shallow ditches. The more northerly of these (5636) measured 0.2m in depth, whilst that to the south (5637) measured 0.14m deep. Both the cobbled surface and the ditches were overlain by deposits of clay silt containing moderate inclusions of small flint fragments. Like the pit scatter/building to its south-west, this feature may have been medieval rather than Roman in date.

# Chapter 4: The Aubreys

*by Paul Booth and Dan Stansbie*

## SITE LOCATION

This was a limited excavation confined largely to a very narrow strip of land immediately west of the current M1, centred on NGR TL 084 118 (see Fig. 1.2). It lay at the eastern edge of the Iron Age hillfort at its lowest point (c 99m aOD) in the shallow dip sloping down north-eastwards towards the upper Ver valley at Redbourn. The underlying geology comprised Upper Chalk (see Fig. 1.3).

## SITE LAYOUT AND SUMMARY (Fig. 4.1)

The excavation area comprised a narrow, irregular strip immediately to the east of the hillfort falling into two parts. The area had a combined length of 429m (roughly north-south) and a maximum width of 71m at its northern end, and a maximum width of 31m at its southern end. Within this excavation area the hillfort ditch was revealed in two places; ditch 261 ran across the southern part of the excavation area on a NE-SW alignment, while ditch 27 ran across the central part of the excavation area from SE-NW. To the south-east of ditch 261 was a scattered group of sub-circular and irregular pits (group 217). Beyond these, to the south-east, was a NE-SW-aligned gully (236/238) and two more pits (230 and 252). Two pits and a ditch terminal (13, 211 and 216), all undated, were located in the central part of the site. To the north of ditch 27 was a substantial pit or ditch (42/85) running beyond the western limit of excavation. This feature may have been a ditch terminal, representing part of an outer ditch running outside the known hillfort ditch. To the north of ditch 42/85 was a dense cluster of shallow gullies, hollows and possible postholes, and to the north of these a NW-SE-aligned gully (6/20), measuring 30m in length and running beyond the eastern baulk.

## STRATIGRAPHIC NARRATIVE

### The Hillfort Ditch 27/261

#### Ditch 27 (Figs 4.2-3)

The principal hillfort ditch (27/261), the easternmost part of which lay beneath the existing M1 embankment, was examined at two points. In the northern part of the excavation area a 40m length of the ditch was revealed (27), although for much of this distance only the inner, western edge was seen, while in the southern part of the excavation area the ditch (261) was traced for a distance of 70m. One main section was cut through each of these two parts. The section examined in the northern part of the excavation area was some 8m wide and 2.7m deep. The profile was variable, being broad with gently sloping sides in the upper part, and with a step on the inner (west) side, while the lowest part was a more steeply sided cut 1.6m across and 0.8m deep, with a flat-bottomed V-shaped profile. There was no suggestion, however, that the lower part of the ditch represented a separate phase of hillfort construction. The basal fill (35) was of dark brownish-grey silty clay with very frequent flint lumps. This was overlain, in the upper part of the steep-sided ditch bottom and in the lower part of the wider profile, by a more gradually accumulated layer (34), up to 0.66m thick, of clayey silt with few flint inclusions. A shallow deposit (32) above this contained much flint and gravel and may represent a short-term infill episode, but it was of even thickness across the ditch and therefore did not derive solely from the rampart to the west. Subsequent fills reflect further gradual infill of the ditch. At the top of the sequence, fill 28, up to 3.8m across and 1.1m deep, is likely to have been the fill of a shallow sloping-sided and round-bottomed recut of the ditch, adjacent to the rampart. This appears to have been dug after the ditch had completely infilled and its date is unknown.

#### Ditch 261 (Figs 4.3-4)

The section of the ditch examined in the southern part of the excavation area was more truncated, and survived as a feature c 5.6m wide and 2.1m deep. The profile was more regular than that seen to the north and was essentially a shallow V shape with the basal section slightly more steep sided. The character of the fills in this section was broadly similar to that seen further north, although there were numerous variations of detail. The secondary fill (263) contained much more flint than fill 34 (see above), and the counterpart of the latter may have been fill 264, which overlay fill 263. Again, there was no suggestion of distinctly differential fill or collapse from the rampart side of the ditch. Equally, however, there was no evidence for the probable late recut seen in the section cut across ditch 27 (see

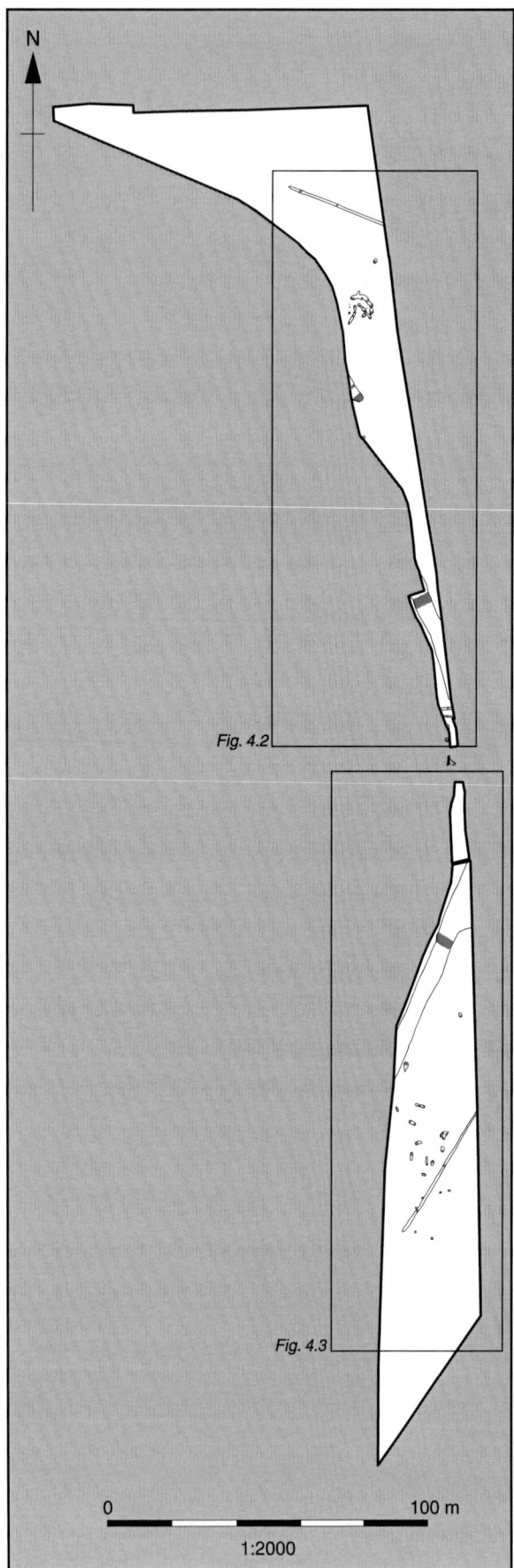

*Fig. 4.1  The Aubreys, plan of all features*

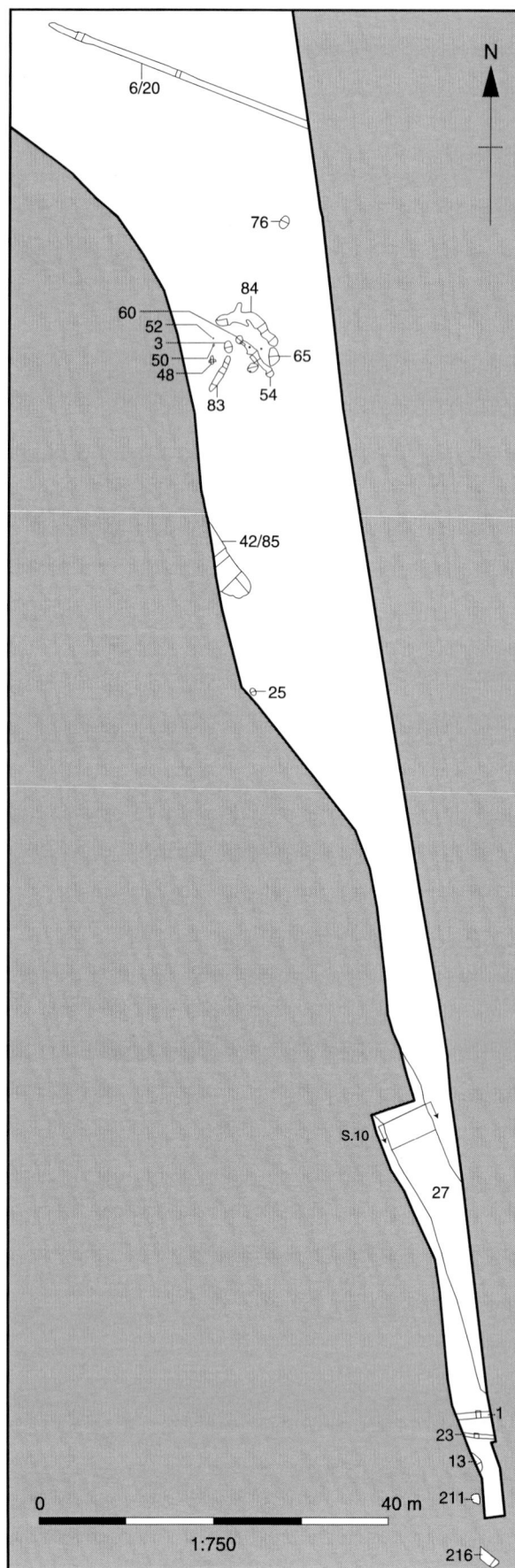

*Fig. 4.2  The Aubreys, detail plan of the hillfort ditch and northern feature group*

above). The only artefacts recovered from either section were a few struck flint fragments; no pottery or other Iron Age material of any kind was found.

**Ditch 42/85** (Fig. 4.2)

Some 55m north of the point where ditch 27 disappeared into the western site baulk a substantial feature (42/85) projected from the same baulk at an oblique angle. The minimum surviving length of this feature was *c* 9.5m. Towards the tip of the terminal the feature was 3m wide and only 0.65m deep, and cut a possible tree-throw hole which lay on its north-eastern side. Some 2.3m further north the ditch was up to 0.9m deep but only a 2.1m width survived within the excavated area; the full original width and depth of the ditch are therefore unknown. Two small pottery sherds came from the main fill (86) of the more northerly intervention in this feature; one was possibly late Iron Age in date and the second, an abraded fine oxidised fragment, may have been Roman.

It is possible that feature 42/85 was simply a large pit, but the similarity of its orientation to that of the outer hillfort ditch is striking. The feature has

the character of a ditch terminal and may therefore represent a further ditch, presumably of limited extent, running parallel to and outside the line of the main 'outer' ditch (27). It is just possible that feature 42/85 related to the augmentation of the defences in the vicinity of an entrance, an idea that could be supported by the geophysical survey of the site which appears to show a break in the line of the outer rampart, and possibly even in the associated ditch, at about this point (Stratascan 1995, fig. 33). The significance of such a break would be uncertain as there is no indication of a corresponding break in the inner rampart at this point. Apparent differences in character (of depth and main fills) between ditches 27 and 42/85, might suggest that the latter was not contemporary with the main phase of the 'hillfort', but variations in ditch character might be expected in the vicinity of an opening. Given this, the presence of an opening in the outer rampart and ditch remains speculative.

**Gully, hollow and posthole group** (Fig. 4.2)

North of ditch 42/85 a complex cluster of features, consisting of shallow gullies, hollows and possible

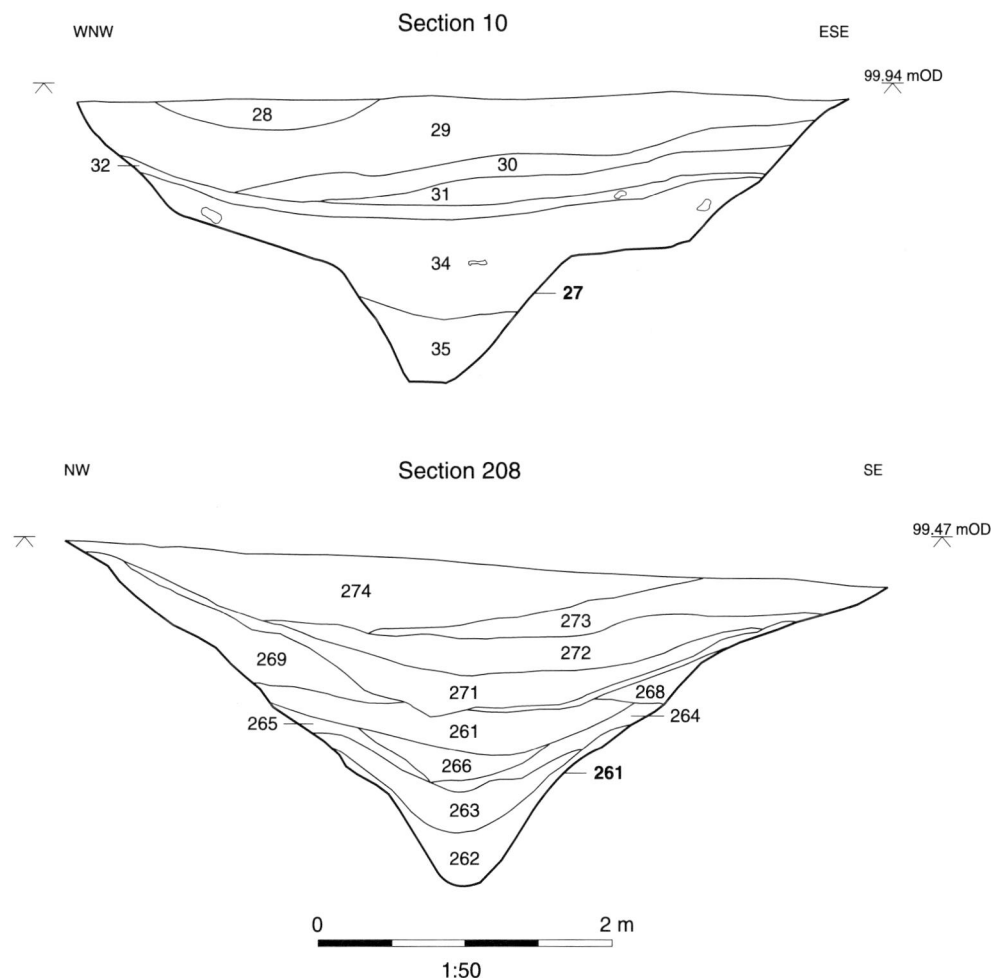

*Fig. 4.3  The Aubreys, sections through the hillfort ditch and pit groups*

postholes, occupied an area a little less than 10 x 10m. An irregular gully (group 54) up to *c* 5.9m long, 0.8m wide and 0.28m deep (but typically more shallow) was considered to be the primary feature, but a further gully (group 83), 4.5m long and up to 0.8m wide, lay roughly at right-angles to it and may have been related. North-east of 54 was a similar, larger gully (group 84) up to 1.2m wide and 0.35m deep, defining the north-eastern limit of this group of features. Other features in the area were three irregular pits, at least one of which was interpreted as a tree-throw hole, and six possible postholes, of which three (48, 50 and 52) formed a south-north line at the western edge of the feature complex. Just east of these, and between the north-west and north-east terminals of gullies 83 and 54 respectively was an oval-shaped hearth (3), measuring 1.2 x 1 x 0.06m, with a fire-reddened base and charcoal staining in the fill, which also contained two flint flakes. Flints were also recovered from gully 54 and pit 65 in this complex (two and four pieces respectively), but these were not closely datable.

## Ditch/gully 6/20 (Fig. 4.2)

The only significant feature north of this complex was a NW-SE-aligned ditch/gully (6/20) up to *c* 0.75m wide and 0.38m deep, which was traced for some 30m from the east edge of the site. Beyond this point the feature faded out and no clearly defined terminus was seen.

## Pits 13 and 211, and ditch terminus 216 (Fig. 4.2)

In the central area of the site three features, pits 13 and 211, and a possible ditch terminus (216) on a NW-SE alignment, were located west of the line of the outer ditch of the hillfort. None of these features were dated. Two east-west-aligned gullies (1 and 23) were also located in the same area, just north of pit 13. Of these, the former certainly and the latter probably cut the post-medieval subsoil, so a fairly recent date is likely, although they contained no finds.

## Pit group 217 (Fig. 4.4)

A group of pits was located in the southern part of the site. Pits 246 and 244 were relatively isolated, but to the south pits 205, 258, 256, 217, 219, 226, 254, 209, 241, 222, 243 and 248 formed a reasonably coherent group. These pits varied in depth from 0.12-0.64m (although ten features had depths in a range of 0.18-0.52m) and all had gently rounded profiles. While some were irregular in plan, with 258 and 219, and perhaps 209 and 241, possibly representing tree-throw holes, a notable characteristic of a number of these pits was their oval shape. The functional significance of this, if any, is uncertain, and most had only a single silty clay fill. Only one feature (218) produced pottery; eight sherds of coarsely flint-tempered material, perhaps of middle Bronze Age date.

## Pits 250 and 252, and ditch 236/238 (Fig. 4.4)

Two further pits (250 and 252) lay immediately south of the main cluster. They were separated from it by a NE-SW-aligned ditch (236/238), traced for a minimum distance of some 40m. This ditch was up

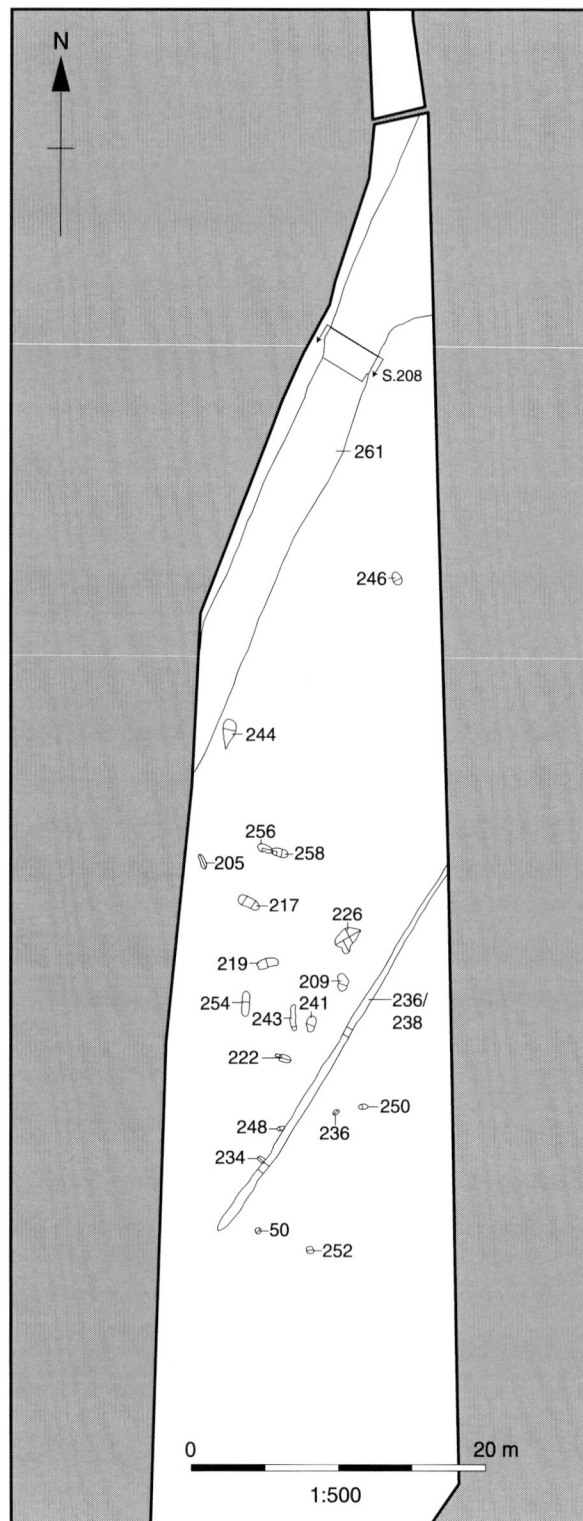

*Fig. 4.4 The Aubreys, detail plan of the hillfort ditch and southern pit group*

to 0.86m wide and 0.3m deep, with moderately sloping sides and a rounded base and had a single sterile clayey silt fill.

## PHASING

The almost total lack of finds and stratigraphic relationships makes interpretation of many of the features problematic. The outer ditch of the hillfort can be assigned to the Iron Age by association, but not on any other criteria, while the possible additional ditch terminal in the northern part of the site may have been filling in the Roman period, but the evidence is exiguous. The three features (pits 13 and 211, and ditch terminus 216) in the central part of the site were located west of the line of the outer hillfort ditch. Although it is possible that they lay on the inner lip of this ditch, it is more likely that the area in which they were located was occupied by the associated rampart. While it is possible that these features post-dated the removal of the rampart at this point, as is almost certainly the case with adjacent east-west-aligned gullies 1 and 23, their character does not support this suggestion. On balance, therefore, they are more likely to predate the hillfort.

This may have implications for the other groups of essentially undated features. Interpretation of the northern cluster of gullies, pits and postholes is very uncertain. The function of the probable hearth (3) within this group is reasonably certain, and the close spacing of the other features suggests that they were perhaps contemporaneous, but beyond this there is no certainty. Whether the features can be seen as forming irregular structures of two phases is very unclear. As recorded they do not readily permit any obvious reconstruction. A later prehistoric (but pre-hillfort) date might be suggested by a very small number of flint fragments from the hearth and two of the associated features, but this material could be residual and was not chronologically diagnostic.

The group of pits at the southern end of the site is similarly problematic. However, if feature 217 is dated by the associated pottery to the middle Bronze Age this may suggest a date for the other pits in its vicinity, and perhaps support the suggestion that occasional flints of generic late Neolithic-Bronze Age character from other features outside the rampart were not residual in the contexts in which they occurred.

Apart from the hillfort ditch, the only significant linear features were the ones found at the north and south margins of the excavated area. Their alignments are very roughly at right-angles to each other and also seem to reflect broadly the alignment of the outer ditch of the hillfort. On this basis it is likely, though not demonstrable, that they post-date the hillfort. For example, although speculative, such ditches could have formed part of a field system of late Iron Age or Roman date.

# Chapter 5: Junction 9

*by Andrew Simmonds*

## SITE LOCATION

The excavation at Junction 9, the interchange of the M1 with the A5/A5183, was located on the north-western side of the junction at NGR TL 090 146 (see Fig. 1.2). It comprised a long, relatively narrow area that extended alongside the exit slip road of the southbound carriageway and measured *c* 440 x 25m, encompassing a total area of 1.03ha (Fig. 5.1). The site was situated on the northern slope of the shallow valley of the River Ver, and sloped down from 125m aOD at its northern end to 105m aOD at the south, where it levelled off somewhat (Fig. 5.2). The area of the excavation was bisected by a haul road that crossed it *c* 160m from the northern end.

The excavation was carried out in a series of stages. This presented particular problems in terms of recording, as it was not possible to see the site in its entirety during excavation or, in some instances, to establish the full extent of individual features. The long and narrow shape of the area investigated also had consequences for the interpretation of the features revealed. The most serious obstacle was presented by the temporary haul road that extended obliquely across much of the southern part of the excavation. This was eventually re-routed and the area beneath it examined at a later stage in the project. However, it is clear that some truncation of the archaeological features beneath this road had occurred, particularly as the density of features uncovered was substantially less than in the adjacent areas. This was confirmed by a small number of features that were partly uncovered adjacent to the haul road, but whose continuations within its footprint were not found when this area was stripped.

## ARCHAEOLOGICAL DESCRIPTION

### Complex of prehistoric features in the central part of the excavation (Figs 5.3-5)

A dense scatter of pits and postholes, as well as four gullies, was exposed in the southern part of the excavation (Figs 5.3-4). Many of these features contained assemblages of worked prehistoric flint, including seven particularly large assemblages with 192-654 pieces. However, the majority of the flint consisted of knapping debris, with few chronologically diagnostic pieces, and consequently only 13 features could be assigned a more precise date. Ten of these datable assemblages were late Mesolithic in

character and three were late Neolithic. The dating of five of the pits with typologically Mesolithic flint assemblages and one with a Neolithic assemblage was confirmed by the results of radiocarbon determinations (see Chapter 9). Five pits contained fragments of pottery, but these were very small and are likely to be intrusive, as may be the cereal grain from pit 2070 that yielded a radiocarbon determination (NZA 32695) of cal AD 120-380 (95.4% confidence; or cal AD 130-330, 68.2% confidence).

The main concentration of features was located south-west of the temporary haul road and comprised a total of 69 pits, and also two gullies, of which all but eight of the pits were investigated by hand excavation. A rather sparser scatter of 42 pits and a single gully was exposed within the footprint of the haul road, but only 11 of these features were excavated. A further 22 pits were located east of the haul road, and six of these were sampled by hand excavation. A separate cluster of 12 pits was situated further north and may represent a separate area of activity.

The pits were typically circular or oval in plan, with moderate or steep sides. They were rarely of any great depth, and although the deepest pit had a depth of 0.6m, the average depth was 0.25m and few examples measured more than 0.35m deep. The larger examples were generally oval in shape and were 1.5-2m long, although they were no deeper than the smaller examples and typically had rather flat bases. The smaller pits were more frequently circular or sub-circular in shape and varied from steep-sided features to more shallow scoops, although the latter could be the truncated bases of pits that were formerly more substantial. It is possible that some of these features may in fact have been tree-throw holes rather than deliberately dug pits. Although the regular shapes and fairly straight-sided profiles of many of the features suggest an anthropogenic origin, some had more irregular forms, such as the banana shape of pit 2297 and, to a lesser extent, the D shape of pit 2094, which could be considered to be characteristic of tree-throw holes. Most of the pits were filled with a single deposit of orange-brown clay and flint gravel that was not dissimilar to the surrounding natural geology. This suggests that each pit was backfilled in a single event, and the absence of any primary fills or other accumulation of sediment in the bases of the majority of the pits indicates that, in most instances, this was done

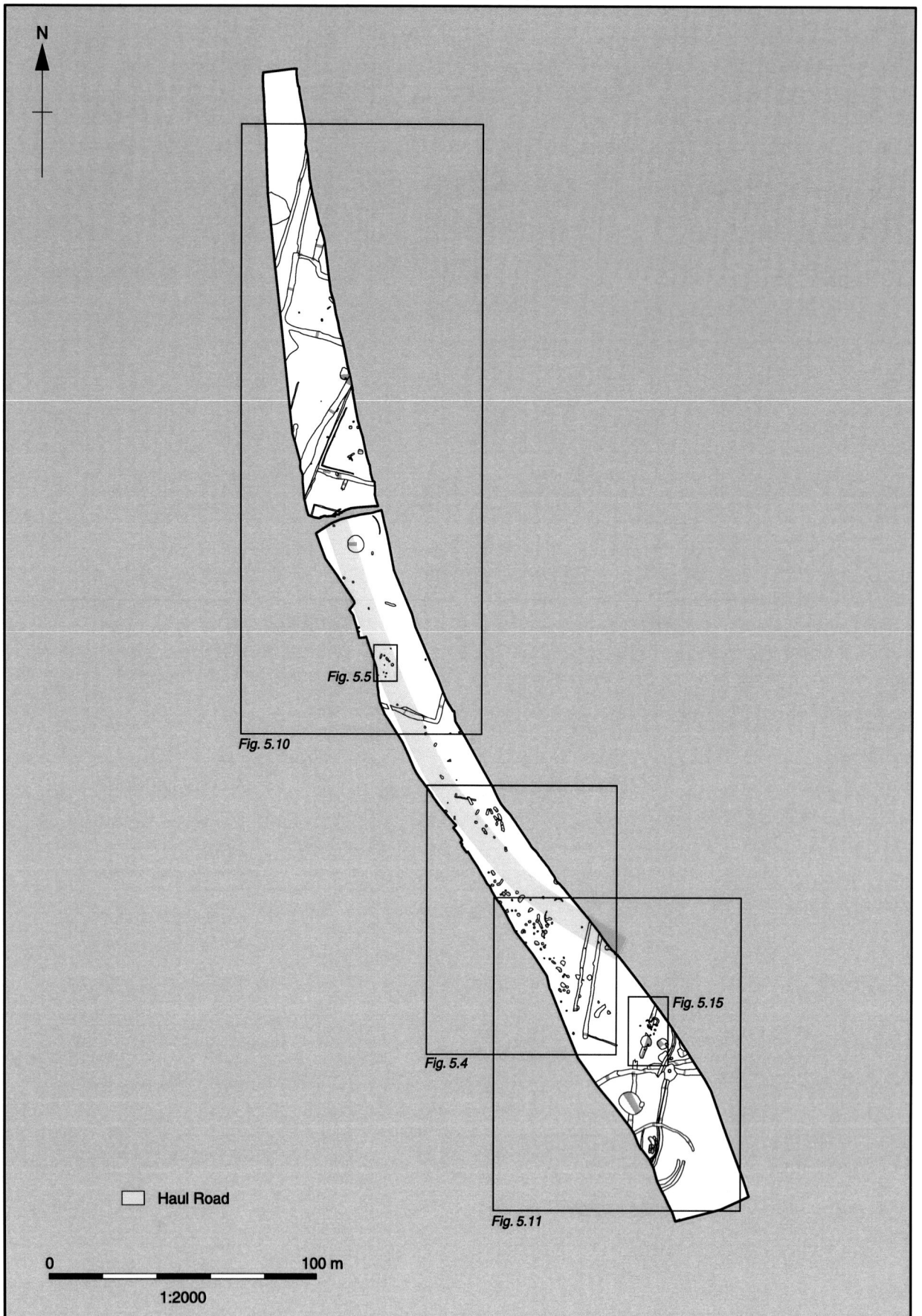

N

Fig. 5.5

Fig. 5.10

Fig. 5.15

Fig. 5.4

Fig. 5.11

Haul Road

0                    100 m

1:2000

*Fig. 5.1   Junction 9, all archaeological features*

*Fig. 5.2   Junction 9, view to the south along the northern part of the excavation*

*Fig. 5.3   Junction 9, prehistoric pits being excavated in the southern part of the excavation*

when little time had elapsed following the digging of the feature.

Many of the pits may also have been dug as post settings. Indisputable evidence for this was limited to only a small number of features, but definite post-pipes were observed in the sections of three pits (2070, 2080 and 2182), and in two other examples (2078 and 2337) deposits of flint gravel were concentrated on one side of the feature and could conceivably have served as packing. A more tenuous post-pipe was identified in pit 2110. In addition, the middle part of the base of pit 2148 appeared to form a distinct socket, while a possible ramp on the northern side of the pit may have been intended to facilitate the insertion of a post. Indeed, the shape and dimensions of many of the pits would be consistent with such a function, although the plan of a coherent structure could not be discerned from their distribution.

The northern group comprised a cluster of 12 pits situated *c* 80m from the main concentration (Fig. 5.5). Two of the pits in this group were oval (2454 and 2510), but the majority were more circular and relatively small in diameter, and were generally of a size that would be consistent with them functioning as postholes. Only four pits were sampled by excavation, including one of the oval examples, and these were all found to be very shallow, the deepest measuring only 0.2m. Few artefacts were recovered from this group. Only two of the excavated pits yielded worked flint, comprising seven pieces from pit 2454 and three from pit 2450, and lithics were also collected from the surfaces of unexcavated pits 2506 and 2510. An assemblage of late Iron Age and early Roman pottery, amounting to six sherds (9g), was recovered from pit 2450, but the small quantity and sherd size are consistent with this material being intrusive.

## Mesolithic features (Figs 5.4 and 5.6-8)

The seven pits (2064, 2090, 2094, 2096, 2100, 2110 and 2316) for which Mesolithic dates were estab-

lished were all located within the main concentration of pits (Fig. 5.4). With the exception of the sub-circular pit 2090 (Fig. 5.6), they were all oval in shape and toward the upper end of the range of sizes, with dimensions ranging between 1.6 x 1.15m and 2.9 x 1.7m (Fig. 5.7). Pit 2094 was the deepest, at 0.55m, but the others were all rather shallower, with depths of between 0.2m and 0.4m. This group of features included six of the seven pits that yielded particularly large flint assemblages.

Pit 2094 produced the largest assemblage, comprising 654 worked flints weighing 662g. This was a large pit, measuring 2.9 x 1.7 x 0.55m, and was recorded as having two main fills (2093 and 2162), although they differed only in the proportion of flint gravel inclusions and may in reality have been a single deposit. A total of 308 pieces of worked flint were recovered from the lower fill (2162) and a further 338 from the upper fill (2093). Six flakes were also recovered from a pocket of flint gravel near the surface of the feature (2154). The assemblage included two microliths, a number of narrow blades and bladelets and nine cores. The Mesolithic date of this assemblage was supported by a radiocarbon determination (NZA-32690) of 5230-4980 cal BC (95.4% confidence; or 5210-4990 cal BC, 68.2% confidence). A few charred fragments of hazel nutshell were also recovered from soil samples, as were some cereal remains, although the latter are likely to have been intrusive.

The next largest flint assemblage was the group of 409 flints from pit 2064. This pit was somewhat unusual in having a very gravelly deposit (2176) filling much of its southern half, overlain by a more conventional fill (2063) that occupied the remainder of the feature. A total of 53 pieces of worked flint was recovered from the earlier fill, but the majority of the assemblage came from context 2063, including a microlith, eight cores and more than 20 narrow blades and bladelets. Hazel nutshell fragments were again present, and a small quantity of oak charcoal was identified. Intrusive cereal fragments, in this case identified as spelt, were also observed. A radiocarbon determination (NZA-32800) of 5290-4940 cal BC (95.4% confidence; or 5220-5000 cal BC, 68.2% confidence) was obtained for one of the fragments of hazel nutshell.

Pit 2100 was another flat-based, oval-shaped pit which measured 1.8 x 1.1 x 0.3m. It contained a single fill (2099) from which 356 pieces of worked flint were recovered during hand excavation. This assemblage included some 15 blades and blade-like flakes, a single microlith and two core rejuvenation pieces. No soil samples were collected from this feature.

Pit 2316 was similar to pit 2100, but slightly smaller, and also possessed a single fill (2317). A

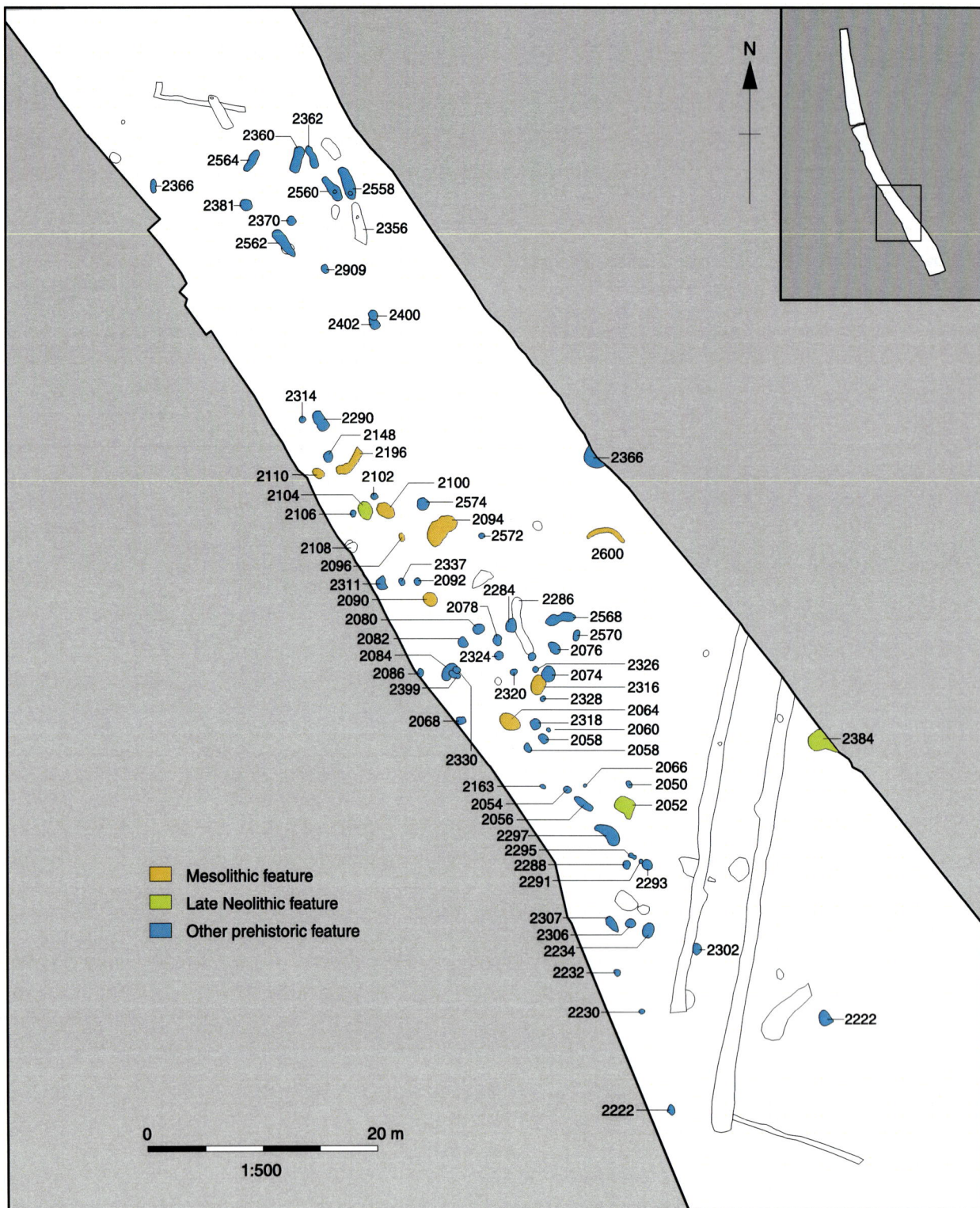

*Fig. 5.4   Junction 9, plan of the main concentration of prehistoric pits in the central area of the excavation*

total of 216 worked flints, including blades, blade-lets, cores and a microlith were recovered, and sieving of soil samples resulted in the collection of fragments of hazel nutshell and oak charcoal. A radiocarbon determination (NZA-32692) of 5210-4930 cal BC (95.4% confidence; or 5200-4990 cal BC, 68.2% confidence) was obtained for one of the fragments of hazel nutshell.

Pit 2090 measured 1.8 x 1.25m, and at 0.4m deep was one of the deeper pits. Its fill (2089) yielded an assemblage of 226 worked flints, 12 of which were classified as blades and blade-like flakes, and are indicative of a late Mesolithic date.

Pit 2110 may have been dug as a post setting, as a possible post-pipe (2165) was identified, consisting of relatively stone-free soil that contrasted with the

more gravelly packing material (2109) around it. The post-pipe appeared to be associated with a socket in the otherwise flat base of the feature. The assemblage of 32 pieces of worked flint from this feature came from both deposits and included a Mesolithic obliquely blunted point and a blade, whilst a single-platform core came from the post-pipe.

The smallest of the Mesolithic features was pit 2096, which was sub-circular in plan, measuring 0.8 x 0.5 x 0.26m. It contained an assemblage of 56 worked flints, which again included blades and narrow flakes. Hazel nutshells were recovered from a bulk soil sample and one of these yielded a radio-carbon date (NZA-32691) of 5310-5000 cal BC (95.4% confidence; or 5230-5060 cal BC, 68.2% confidence).

A further six pits (2362, 2330, 2068, 2398, 2058 and 2299) each contained a microlith, but the lithic assemblage from these features included no other diagnostic pieces that would enable them to be attributed conclusively to the Mesolithic period. Moreover, in a single pit (2384) a microlith was associated with an otherwise late Neolithic flint assemblage.

Four curvilinear gullies (2196, 2287, 2356 and 2600) were identified within the pit complex, three of which produced lithic assemblages indicative of a Mesolithic date (Fig. 5.8). Gully 2287 was slightly curved and extended for a total length of *c* 5m. It was 0.8m wide and 0.3m deep, with a slightly irregular profile and a concave base. It contained a single fill of gravelly clay (2071) from which were recovered 187 worked flints, including four multi-platform cores and a small number of blades and blade-like flakes. The gully was cut half way along its length by pit 2284 and at its southern end by pit 2286.

The northern end of gully 2196 had been destroyed by the truncation associated with the temporary haul road. The surviving part of the feature was *c* 3m long and 0.6m wide, with a depth of 0.35m. It appeared to have silted up gradually, and contained a gravelly lower fill (2142) that was overlain by a main fill of reddish-brown clay (2195). An assemblage of 192 pieces of worked flint was recovered from this gully, including a microlith, ten blades and blade-like flakes, and two core-related flakes. Most of these flints came from the upper fill, from which a fragment of hazel nutshell yielded a radiocarbon determination (NZA-32689) of 5220-4850 cal BC (95.4% confidence; or 5210-4940 cal BC, 68.2% confidence).

Gully 2356 was located to the north of the main concentration of pits, on the eastern side of the haul road. It was *c* 5m long, 0.83m wide and 0.31m deep, with steep sides and a flat base. It was filled with a deposit of gravelly clay that contained a total of 158 worked pieces with cores, bladelets and two microliths present. Two elongated pits or short lengths of gully (2358 and 2558) lay on the same alignment as this feature, and it is possible that they represented three segments of a segmented gully. Feature 2558 was not excavated, but feature 2358

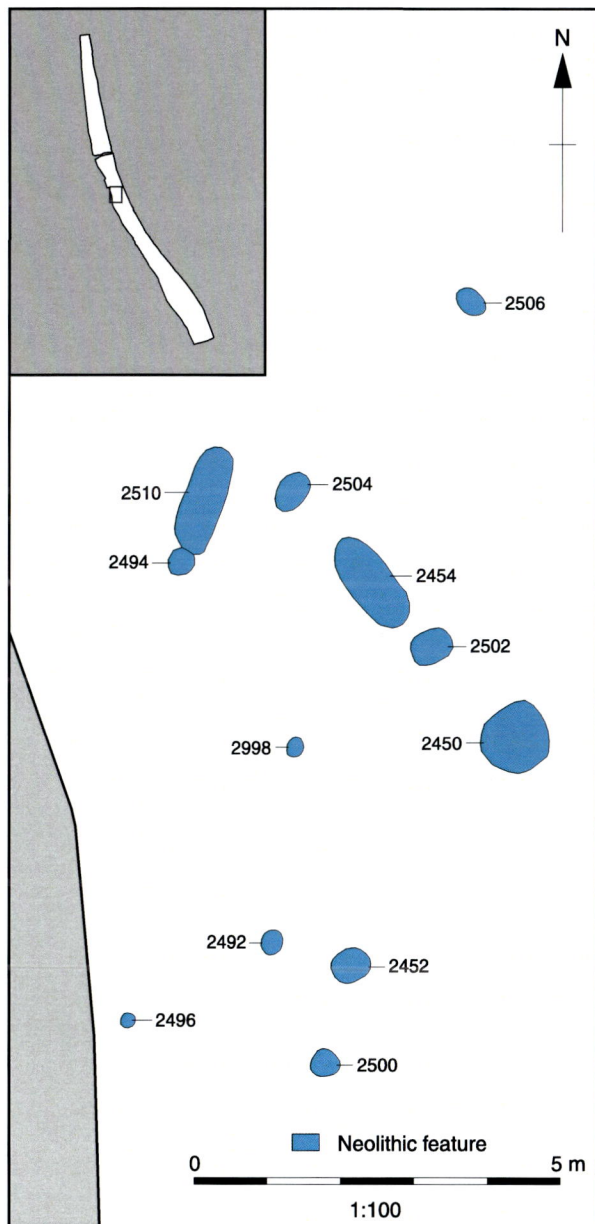

*Fig. 5.5  Junction 9, plan of the northern group of prehistoric pits*

*Fig. 5.6   Junction 9, late Mesolithic pit 2090, viewed from the north-east*

was found to have a similar profile to gully 2356 and was slightly shallower with a 0.25m depth. A total of 25 pieces of worked flint was recovered from feature 2358, as well as 18 collected from the surface of feature 2558, but none of these were chronologically diagnostic. However, several other elongated pits were situated in the immediate vicinity and it is possible that the shared alignment of these features with gully 2356 is merely fortuitous.

Gully 2600 measured 3.5m in length and was quite sharply curved. It had steep sides and a flat base and was 0.15m deep. It was filled with a single, homogenous deposit of silt and gravel from which no finds were recovered.

### Late Neolithic pits (Figs 5.4 and 5.9)

Three pits within the main concentration were attributed to the late Neolithic period (2052 and 2104), as well as a third pit (2384) at the eastern edge of the excavation.

Pit 2052 was located towards the northern end of the main concentration of pits. It was somewhat irregular in plan and measured 1.7 x 1.1m. It was steep sided with a flat base and was the deepest of the three late Neolithic pits, with a depth of 0.5m. A thin layer of flint gravel, derived from the substrate into which the feature had been cut, lay across the base, to a depth of 0.08m, above which the remainder of the pit was filled with a deposit of silty soil (2051). This latter deposit contained a total of 204 worked flints including 11 scrapers, as well as 152 pieces of burnt unworked flint. The broad nature of many of the flakes from the pit and the presence of end and side scrapers suggests a late Neolithic date, and a radiocarbon determination (NZA-32683) of 2620-2340 cal BC (95.4% confidence; or 2570-2460 cal BC, 68.2% confidence) was obtained for a fragment of hazelnut shell from fill 2051.

Pit 2104 was oval in plan, measuring 1.6 x 1.1m, but was extremely shallow with a depth of only 0.15m. It contained a small assemblage (30 pieces) of worked flint including a late Neolithic chisel arrowhead (SF 2027).

Pit 2384 was only partly exposed at the eastern edge of the excavation and, like pit 2052, appeared to be irregular in plan. It measured at least 1.7 x 1.55m, but was only 0.2m deep. The assemblage of 69 pieces of worked flint recovered from its fill included six multi-platform cores indicative of a late Neolithic date.

### Later prehistoric activity

A small quantity of late Bronze Age-early Iron Age and middle Iron Age pottery was recovered, suggesting that there was limited later prehistoric activity preceding the main late Iron Age-early Roman occupation phase. This pottery came from: the tops of two Mesolithic pits (2100 and 2316); a Roman pit (2108); an undated, pit within the complex of earlier prehistoric features; early Roman ditch 2736; and long-lived Roman ditch 2490. While the fresh character of a few of the sherds probably indicates that the activity from which they derive was located nearby, no features could be confidently assigned to this period.

### Late Iron Age and Roman agricultural activity

The excavation revealed part of a complex of enclosures, trackways and associated boundary ditches representing an agricultural landscape that appears to have been in continuous use for several centuries, from the late Iron Age or early Roman period through to at least the later 3rd century. Although stratigraphic and ceramic dating evidence suggests periodic refurbishment of these features and alterations to individual parts of the

Section 2045

NW                                          SE
                                                88.93 mOD
          2063        2176
                                    2064

S.2045

**2064**

N

Section 2051

SE                              NW
                                    89.43 mOD
          2089            **2090**

**2090**

S.2051

Section 2027

NW          SE NE              SW
                                    89.63 mOD
    2154              2093
                2162        **2094**

**2094**          S.2027

Section 2088

       SE      NW
                  89.59 mOD
       2095    **2096**

S.2088

**2096**

Section 2023

S                                N
                                    88.93 mOD
          2099
                    **2100**

**2100**

S.2023

Section 2034

    NW      2165      SE
                        89.84 mOD
    2109      2109    **2110**

S.2034

**2110**

Section 2080

SW                        NE
                            89.05 mOD
          2317      **2316**

2074

**2316**

S.2080

0                          2 m

1:50

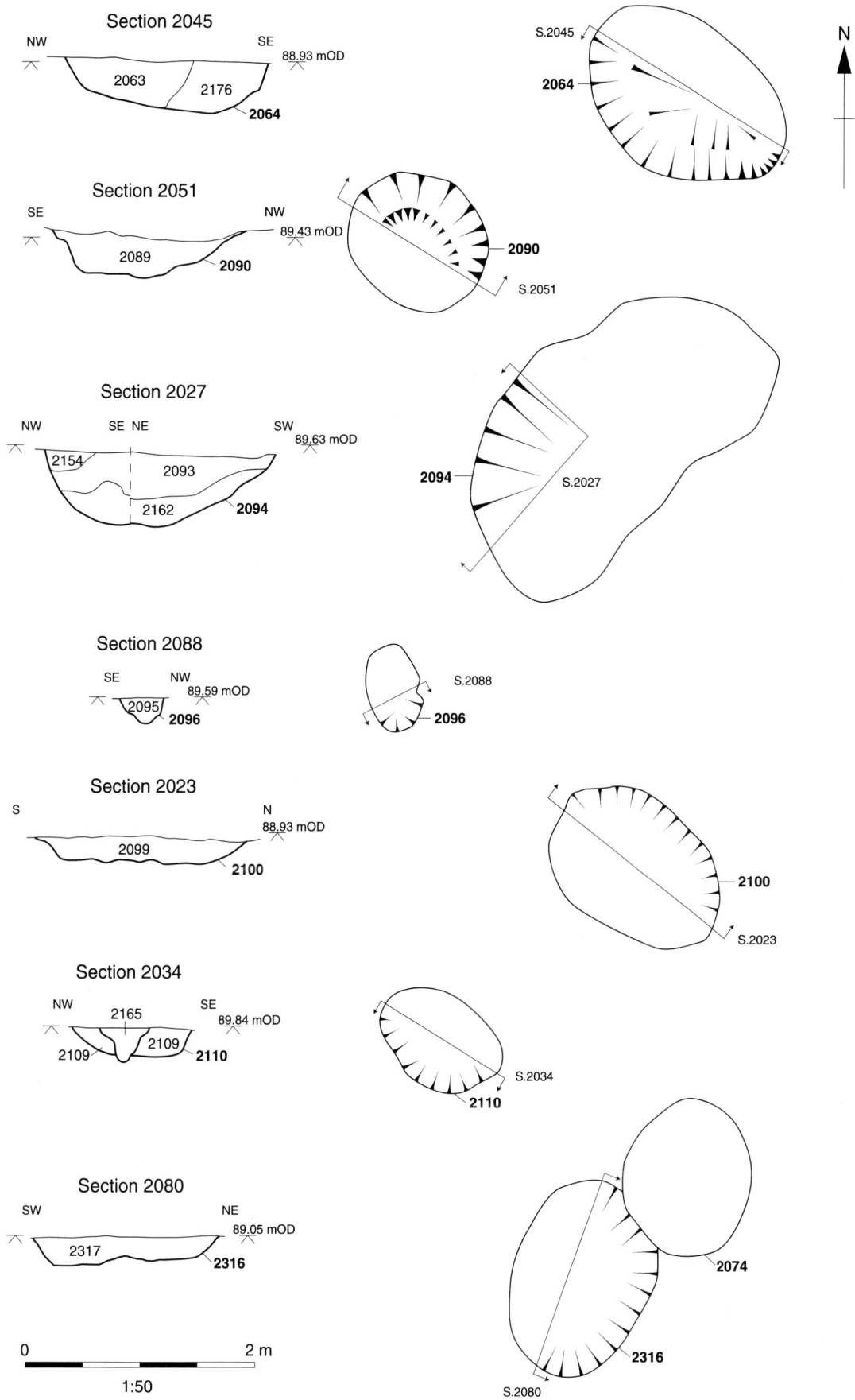

*Fig. 5.7   Junction 9, detailed plans and sections of Mesolithic pits 2064, 2090, 2094, 2096, 2100, 2110 and 2316*

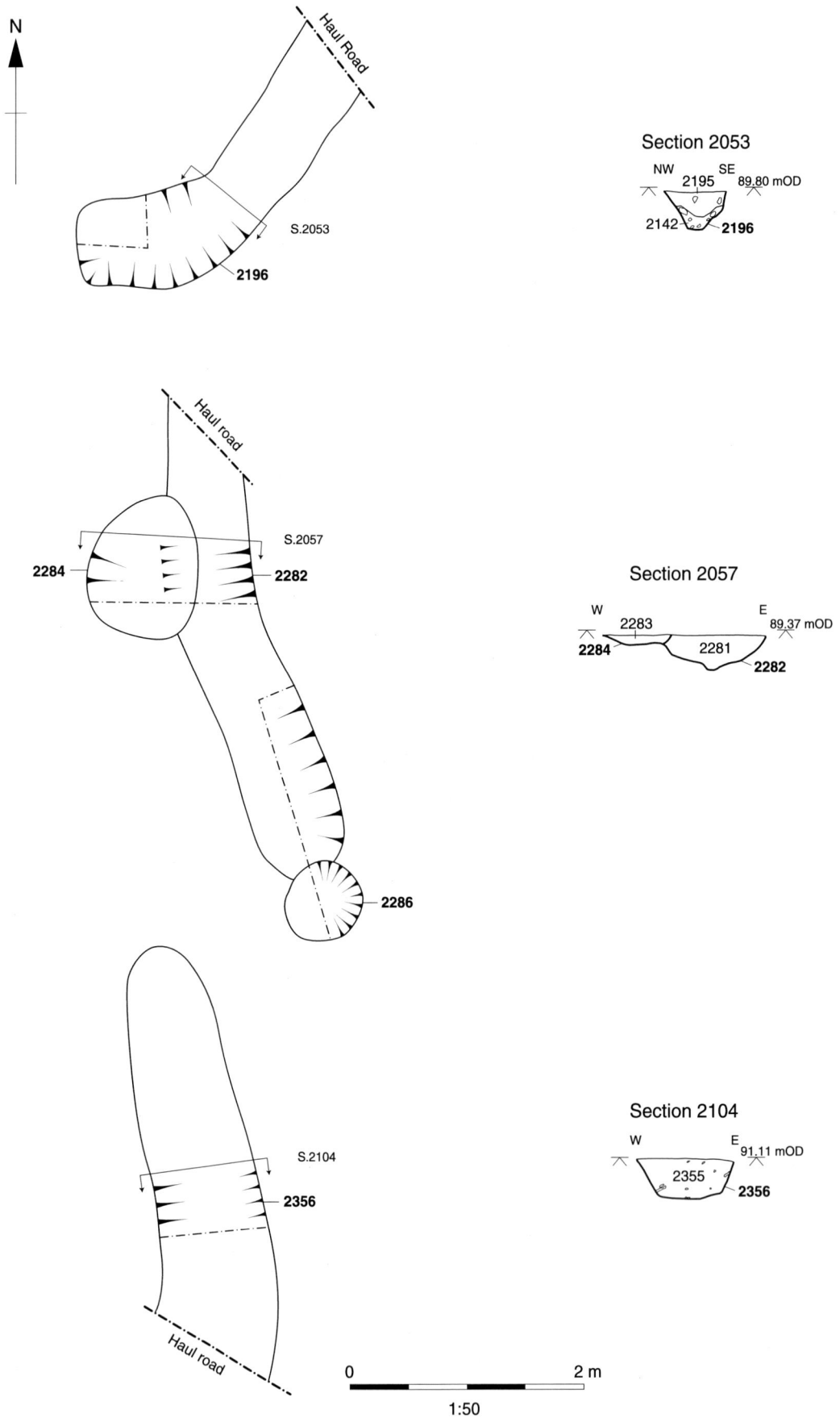

N

Haul Road

S.2053

**2196**

Section 2053

NW    SE   89.80 mOD
2195
2142   **2196**

Haul road

S.2057

**2284**   **2282**

Section 2057

W       E   89.37 mOD
2283
**2284**   2281   **2282**

**2286**

Section 2104

W       E   91.11 mOD
2355   **2356**

S.2104

**2356**

Haul road

0           2 m

1:50

*Fig. 5.8   Junction 9, detailed plans and sections of gullies attributed to the late Mesolithic period*

complex, the basic organisation of the landscape remained essentially the same throughout its use. This system followed the NNE-SSW orientation of the original boundary ditches and this persistence between phases suggests that the boundaries were marked by above-ground features, such as banks and/or hedges, which continued to exist into subsequent phases, after the associated ditches had silted up.

### The earliest phase of the field system (late Iron Age-early Roman) (Figs 5.10-11)

The initial phase of the field system comprised three principal boundary ditches (2188, 2739 and 2745/2747) that were laid out on the slope of the valley of the River Ver. These boundaries lay on roughly parallel NNE-SSW orientations and were

associated with a small number of ditches defining intervening subdivisions. The precise date at which these boundaries and associated features were first established is somewhat uncertain. The ditches which defined them were the earliest features in their respective stratigraphic sequences, but contained little or no artefactual material. Where pottery was present it consisted of fragments from 'Belgic', largely grog-tempered jars with a broad late Iron Age-early Roman date range, probably ending no later than AD 70. It is impossible to be certain whether these assemblages were deposited before or after the Roman conquest, although the absence of demonstrably Romanised types could be interpreted as indicating an earlier date. In two instances (ditches 2594 and 2749) sherds of post-conquest date were present, but these features may represent boundaries that were added after the

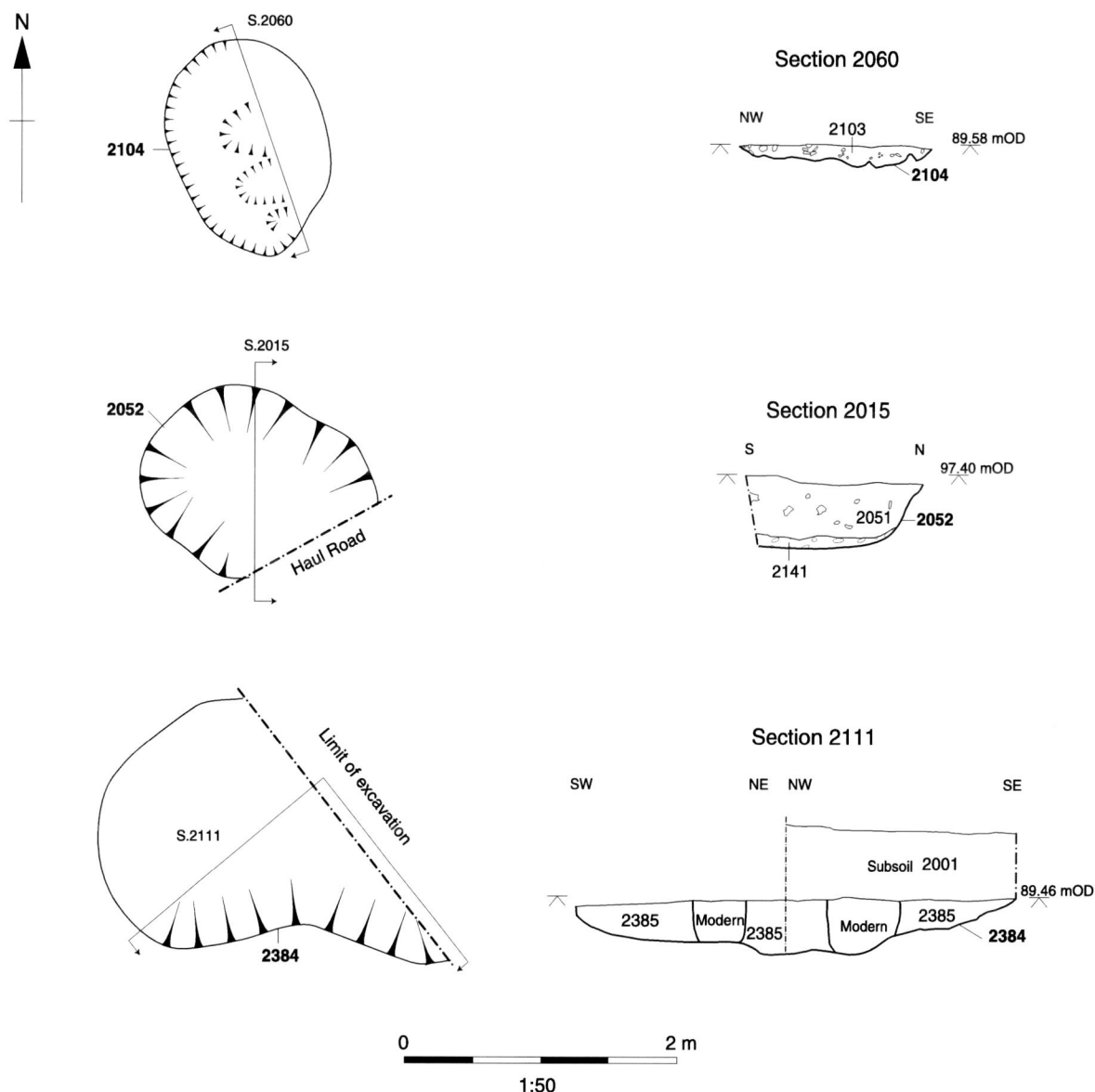

*Fig. 5.9  Junction 9, detailed plans and sections of pits attributed to the late Neolithic period*

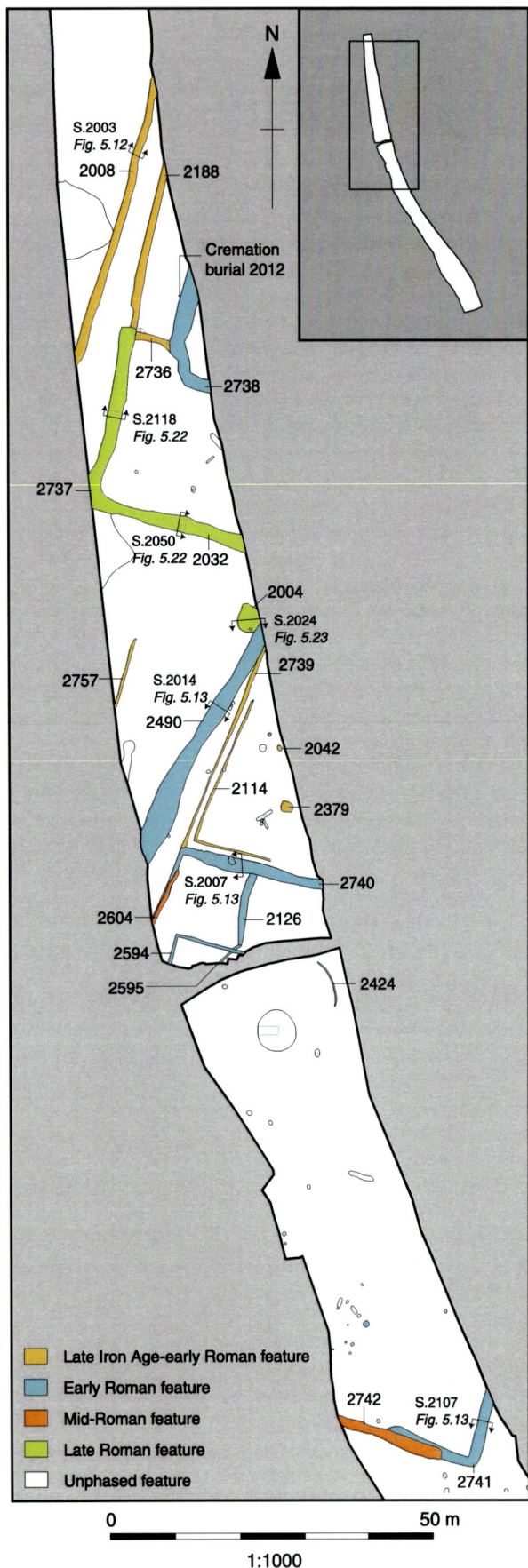

*Fig. 5.10 Junction 9, late Iron Age and Roman activity (northern end of Junction 9)*

main divisions had been established rather than necessarily indicating a post-conquest date for the entire complex.

### Establishment of boundary ditches in the northern part of the excavation (Figs 5.10 and 5.12)

The most westerly of these boundaries was defined by ditch 2188, part of which was uncovered near the northern end of the excavation. The ditch was exposed for a length of *c* 25m, and continued to the north beyond the edge of the excavation. To the south it had been cut away by ditch 2737, which appeared to represent a redefinition of this part of the boundary during the later part of the Roman period. It is possible that ditch 2188 defined the eastern side of a trackway, the western side of which was represented by ditch 2008. Certainly the two ditches were approximately parallel, in addition to which they were of similar proportions, both measuring *c* 1.1m wide and 0.5m deep with V-shaped profiles. The putative trackway widened a little at its western end and very slight changes in the ditch alignments adjacent to the site baulk may indicate that the trackway branched or perhaps turned to the west, just beyond the excavated area. No finds were recovered from either ditch, but two small fragments of pottery dating from the late Iron Age or early Roman period were recovered from ditch 2736. This latter ditch extended ESE at right-angles to the two ditches (2008 and 2188) and may have been a return of ditch 2188, or a contemporary boundary that branched off it. This could not be confirmed, however, as the relationship between ditches 2188 and 2736 did not survive, having been cut away by the digging of ditch 2737. Ditch 2736 had also been truncated to the east by a second later Roman ditch (2738).

An isolated cremation burial (2012) was located *c* 5.5m east of ditch 2188. The burial had been substantially truncated by subsequent ploughing, with the result that only the lowest 0.05m of the base survived and the western half had been mostly destroyed. The fragmentary cremated remains, probably from a single adult individual, had been placed in a late Iron Age pedestal urn, of which only part of the base survived. The soil matrix around the bone fragments comprised clean reddish-brown silty clay (2013), from which only a few small flecks of charcoal were recovered through sieving.

The next major boundary was represented by ditches 2114 and 2739, which were not quite parallel with ditch 2188, but lay on a generally similar orientation *c* 30m to the east. These ditches were only 0.7-1m apart and were clearly too close together to have defined the sides of a trackway. They may instead have flanked a bank formed from their up-cast that was perhaps surmounted by a hedgerow. The dimensions recorded for ditch 2739 were rather varied, ranging from 0.76m wide and 0.56m deep at its northern end to a depth of only 0.27m further south, perhaps indicating some degree of differen-

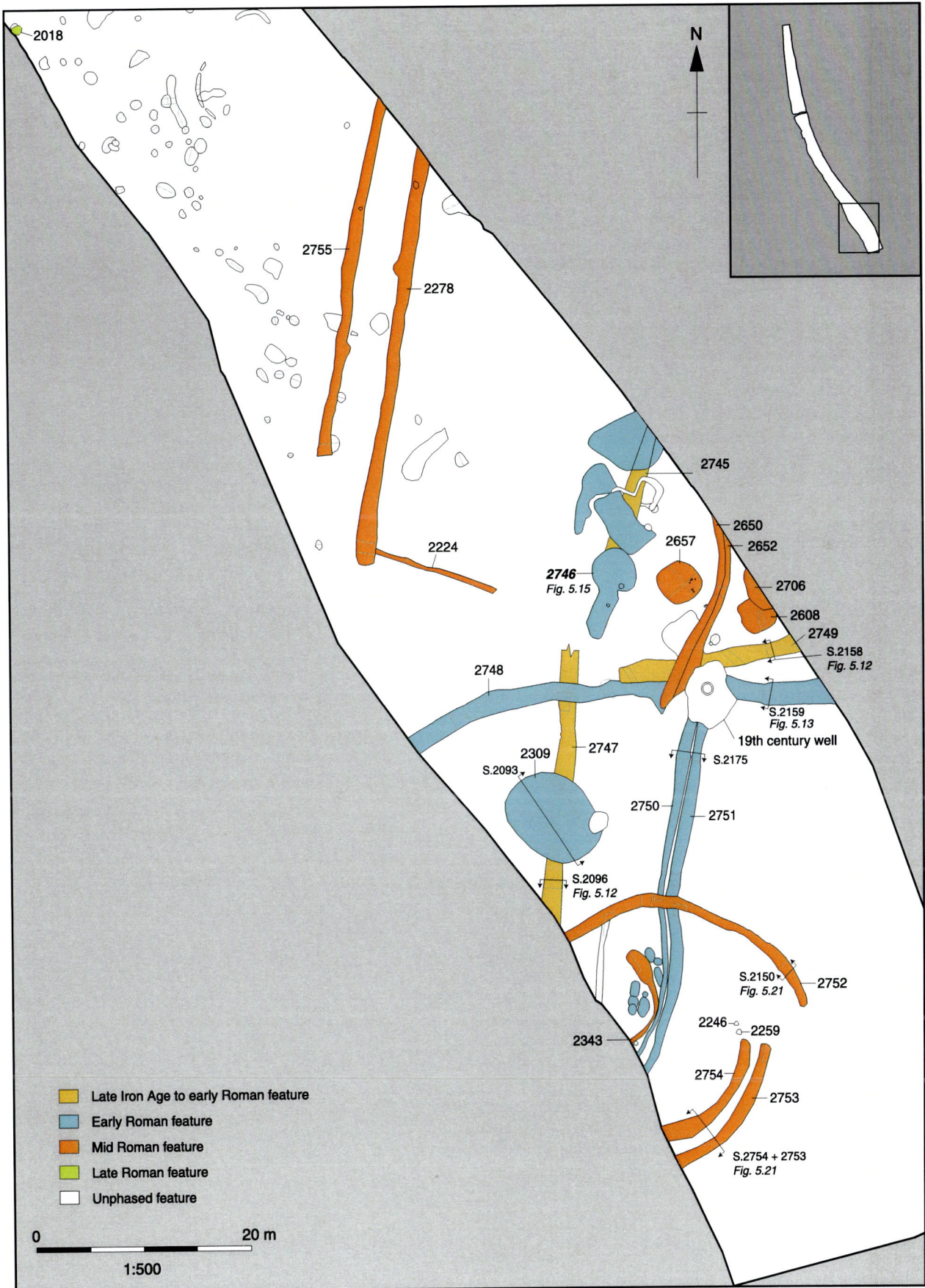

*Fig. 5.11   Junction 9, late Iron Age and Roman activity (southern end of Junction 9)*

tial truncation. The greatest of these depths would be consistent with those of the ditches defining the putatively contemporary trackway to the north-west. The ditch was exposed for a total length of *c* 33m and, like ditch 2188, continued to the north beyond the edge of the excavation, and was cut away to the south by a later ditch (2740) that may represent a redefinition of part of the same boundary. A small assemblage of very fragmentary late Iron Age-early Roman pottery, weighing 83g, was recovered from its fill. Ditch 2114 was considerably less substantial, measuring only 0.3m wide and 0.15m deep. It extended for *c* 22.5m, terminating or petering out within the site at its northern end and turning through a right angle to the east for a distance of 12m at its southern end, presumably to define part of an enclosure or other subdivision abutting the eastern side of the main boundary.

Two features located within the area enclosed by ditch 2114 contained pottery dating from the late Iron Age-early Roman period. Pit 2042 was a shallow scoop only 0.1m deep, which contained six small pottery sherds and a small amount of animal bone and sheep or goat teeth, while pit 2379 was somewhat more substantial, measuring 1.8m in diameter and 0.45m deep. A single pottery sherd was recovered from its fill (2380).

An unexcavated ditch (2757) was situated *c* 18m west of the boundary defined by ditches 2114 and 2739 on a parallel orientation and may therefore have been contemporary. The feature was exposed for a length of 11m, apparently terminating or petering out at its northern end and extending beyond the edge of the excavation to the south. No features in the central part of the excavation were attributed to this phase.

### *Establishment of boundary ditches in the southern part of the excavation* (Figs 5.11-12)

At the southern end of the excavation, ditches 2745 and 2747 are likely to have defined a boundary contemporary with the initial phase of the principal boundaries in the northern part of the site, and on a similar NNE-SSW orientation. Ditch 2747 extended for *c* 24m from the south-west edge of the site. It is unclear if the ditch terminated or was simply obscured beyond this point. A similar alignment was maintained further north by ditch 2745, but this feature was heavily truncated by a series of irregular hollows and soil spreads, and at its southern end was completely removed by the later kiln/oven 2746 (see below). It is possible that ditches 2745 and 2747 were part of the same feature, but if so its line was lost just to the south-west of the kiln. Certainly they lay on approximately the same alignment, and both ditches were substantial features, measuring more than 1.5m wide and 0.7m deep. Ditch 2749 lay on an east-west alignment and is likely to have defined a boundary arranged at a right angle to that represented by ditches 2745 and 2747. It extended for *c* 17m from the eastern edge of the excavation

and terminated at its western end, 3.8m from ditch 2747. It was relatively insubstantial, with a depth of only 0.2m, and yielded a small assemblage of pottery.

### Early Roman activity (*c* AD 43-120)

During the early decades of the Roman period, alterations were made to the existing field system. In the northern part of the excavation new ditches were dug that appear to have defined rectilinear enclosures lying on the same orientations as the earlier boundaries, and more extensive alterations were made to the boundaries at the southern end of the site.

### *Enclosure defined by ditches 2740 and 2741* (Figs 5.10 and 5.13)

Two L-shaped ditches (2740 and 2741) were established that appear to have defined the north-western and south-eastern corners of a large enclosure that measured at least 70 x 70m. The north-western corner was represented by ditch 2740, which extended for 22m from the eastern edge of the excavation before turning through a right angle to the south and extending for a further 12m, continuing beyond the western edge of the site. The latter part of the ditch lay on the same alignment as the earlier boundary, defined by ditches 2114 and 2739, and it is probable that the digging of the new ditch had removed the southern part of those features. The ditch was quite wide and flat based, measuring 1.5m across and up to 0.46m deep. It was

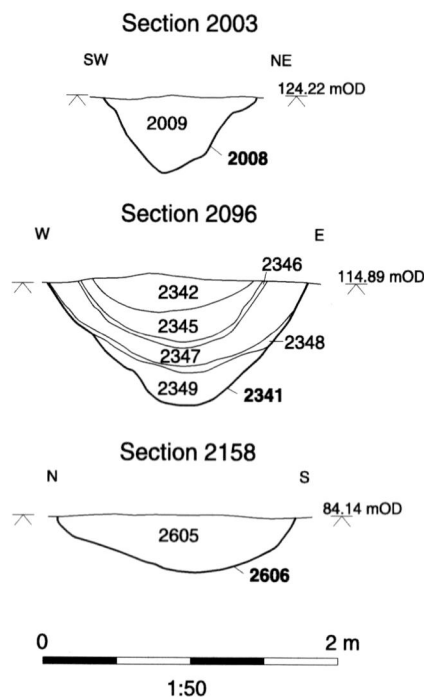

Fig. 5.12  *Sections of late Iron Age-early Roman boundary ditches*

recorded as having two and, in some places three fills, the earliest of which contained a lid in Verulamium region white ware suggesting that the feature was dug after *c* AD 50. The subsequent fills contained larger quantities of pottery indicating that the ditch had silted up gradually over the course of the 2nd century. Ditch 2741, which defined the south-eastern corner of the enclosure, extended for 11m from the eastern edge of the site before turning through a right angle to the west and then apparently terminating some 13m west of the turn. This left an opening measuring at least 8m, between the end of the ditch and the western edge of the excavation. This opening may represent an entrance into the enclosure or may have been blocked by hurdles or a hedgerow with no accompanying ditch. The ditch was of similar width to ditch 2740 and was 0.47-0.78m deep. The pottery assemblage recovered from ditch 2741 was much smaller than that from ditch 2740 and may reflect a shorter period of use, as at least part of the ditch was superseded by ditch 2742 during the 2nd century, whereas ditch 2740 continued in use.

### Curvilinear gullies (2595 and 2424) within the enclosure (Fig. 5.10)

Two lengths of curvilinear gully, that may have defined or formed parts of one or more circular structures, were located in the northern part of the enclosure. Gully 2595 was a curving feature located immediately north of the haul road that bisected the excavation. The gully was exposed for a length of only 4.2m and continued beyond the excavated area into the footprint of the haul road, but did not extend into the area on the south side of this route. Fifty sherds (182g) of pottery were recovered from it and these included sherds that could only be attributed broadly to the late Iron Age-early Roman period that were mixed with pieces that date from the early decades of the Roman period. A similar curving gully (2424) was located *c* 12m to the east, to the south of the haul road. It was not certain whether these gullies were the remains of two separate structures or whether they were parts of a single, larger enclosure. Neither length of gully survived to a depth of more than 0.19m and it is possible that other portions of these features had been destroyed by truncation caused by more recent ploughing. No evidence was recovered from either gully to suggest that they were associated with domestic occupation, and they were not obviously associated with any other features.

### Other features within the enclosure (Fig. 5.10)

The curvilinear gullies were not long lived, as feature 2595 was cut by a field boundary ditch (2594) which contained an assemblage of pottery dated to the early part of the Roman period. This was an L-shaped ditch that lay on the same orientation as the main enclosure and may have defined a subdivision within it. The ditch was particularly steep sided and measured 0.6m wide and 0.6m deep. It may have been associated with a wide, but shallow, ditch (2126) with a 0.08m depth that branched off the south side of ditch 2740, and extended between this boundary and ditch 2594.

The only discrete and possible contemporary feature was a shallow, concave pit or scoop (2450) that was located in the southern part of the enclosure. It measured 0.9m in diameter, by 0.11m deep, and had a distinctly darker-greyer fill than the prehistoric pits in this part of the site. It contained six small sherds of pottery (9g) including two of greyware, as well as a small quantity of ceramic building material.

### Possible enclosure defined by ditch 2738 (Fig. 5.10)

Ditch 2738 may have defined the south-western corner of another enclosure. As exposed, ditch 2738 was L-shaped in plan, albeit with a curving rather than a right-angled corner. It extended north-south for 17.5m from the baulk at the edge of the excavation and turned to the east, extending for a further 7.5m before continuing beyond the same baulk. In doing so, it removed the eastern part of the earlier ditch 2736 and it was uncertain whether it followed an alignment initially established by that earlier ditch, or whether it represented an entirely new boundary. The new ditch was certainly more substantial than any of its predecessors in this part of the site, measuring up to 2.7m wide and 1m deep. The pottery assemblage from its three fills was small and consisted mostly of earlier material, but included a sherd from a greyware jar dated to after AD 120 from its uppermost fill, indicating that it remained open into the 2nd century.

### Linear boundary ditch 2490 (Figs 5.10, 5.13 and 5.24)

A substantial linear boundary ditch (2490) was established adjacent to the western side of the enclosure defined by ditches 2740 and 2741. The ditch measured 2.55m wide and as much as 1.2m deep and extended across the entire width of the excavation. It diverged somewhat from the orientation established by the ditches of the earlier phases, but may have been intended to replace the boundary formerly defined by ditches 2739 and 2740, albeit on a slightly eccentric alignment.

The ditch was open for some considerable period of time, at least into the 3rd century, and appears to have been used as a locale for the dumping of domestic debris, presumably from nearby residential occupation. In contrast with the generally small quantities of pottery recovered from the other ditches, ditch 2490 yielded a very large assemblage of 2262 sherds (33kg), amounting to more than half the pottery from the Junction 9 excavation. Much of this material (more than 13kg) was recovered from a dump of charcoal-rich soil (2139), which also yielded an assemblage of charred plant remains that may have derived from crop processing, cooking and other domestic activities. An iron disc (see Fig. 7.23.9) was a notable individual object from this deposit. Significant quantities of cultural material were also recovered from the subsequent fills, particularly the uppermost fill. The ditch also contained a small quantity of ceramic building material and was one of the few features from which animal bone was recovered, albeit not in large quantities, as well as an assemblage of metal finds that included a carpenter's gouge (SF 2047), an armlet (SF 2008), a copper-alloy bow brooch (SF 2011) and possibly part of a hipposandal.

Section 2007

Section 2107

Section 2159

Section 2175

Section 2014

0                    2 m

1:50

*Fig. 5.13  Sections of early Roman boundary ditches*

## Reorganisation of the boundaries in the southern part of the excavation (Figs 5.10-11 and 5.13)

The boundaries that had previously been established at the southern end of the site did not continue in use into this period, as they were slighted by a series of new features. The principal element of the new arrangement was a slightly circuitous ditch (2748) that extended across the area of the excavation on an east-west alignment, and cut across the boundary that had previously been defined by ditch 2747. Ditch 2748 measured up to 2.2m wide and 0.4m deep, with steep sides and a flat base, and yielded an assemblage of 19 sherds (176g) of pottery, mostly small but including three slightly larger pieces from an oxidised curving-sided bowl that is unlikely to date from before c AD 70.

A pair of closely spaced gullies (2750 and 2751) extended south from ditch 2748. They may have been contemporary features that branched off the main boundary ditch, although the stratigraphic relationship had been destroyed by the construction of a modern well. The gullies, both c 1m wide and 0.2-0.3m deep, contained no artefacts, but they were both earlier than ditch 2752, which dated from no earlier than c AD 120. This, combined with the fact that they apparently respected the boundary defined by ditch 2748 and had a slightly curvilinear character reminiscent of that ditch, suggests that they date to the early Roman period.

Toward their southern end, the two gullies deviated slightly, apparently in order to bypass a group of shallow hollows (2212, 2214, 2248, 2250, 2252, 2333, 2339 and 2363). The dimensions of these hollows varied from a diameter of 0.5m, to 1.8 x 1.05m, but none was more than 0.18m deep, and they had similar dark brown fills. It is uncertain whether they were archaeological in origin or were natural features, such as tree-throw holes, but the deviation of gullies 2750 and 2751 indicates that they were in existence at the time the gullies were dug. A single small sherd of Nene Valley colour-coated ware recovered from pit 2248 may be intrusive.

### Kiln/oven 2746 (Figs 5.11 and 5.14-17)

It is likely that during this phase structure 2746, which has been interpreted as a kiln or oven, and its associated features were constructed and used. The function of the structure provided something of a conundrum. It was rather too large for a domestic structure and was not situated within a domestic context, but neither was there clear evidence for an industrial use in the form of metalworking debris or ceramic wasters, or for a role in crop processing, as very few charred plant remains were recovered.

The structure was located a short distance north of ditch 2748, and had been dug into the fill of ditch 2745, which had clearly silted up by this time. The installation comprised a roughly circular pit, presumably the firing chamber, that measured 4m in diameter and 1.2m deep, with a flue 4.7m long

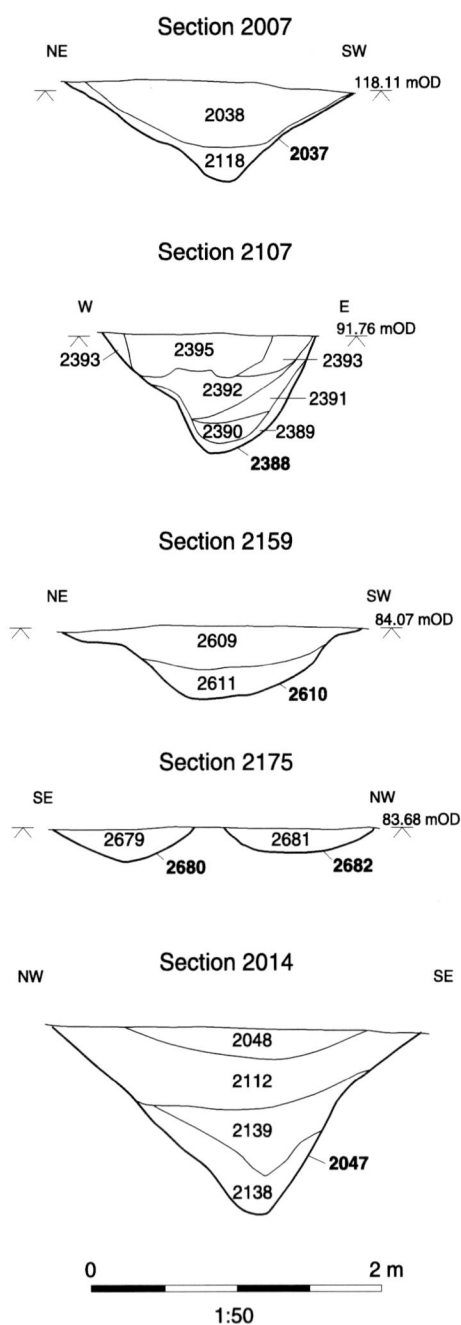

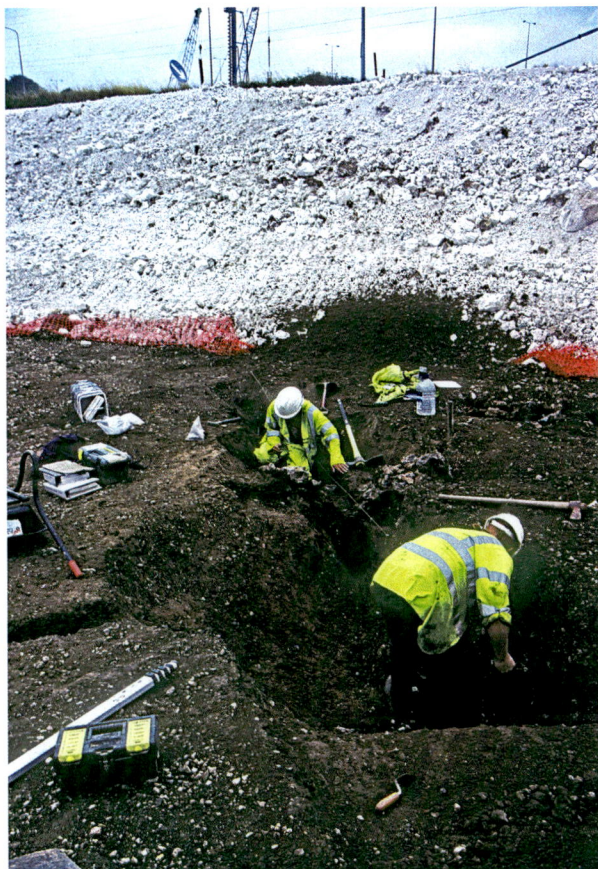

*Fig. 5.14  Junction 9, kiln 2746, viewed from the north-east*

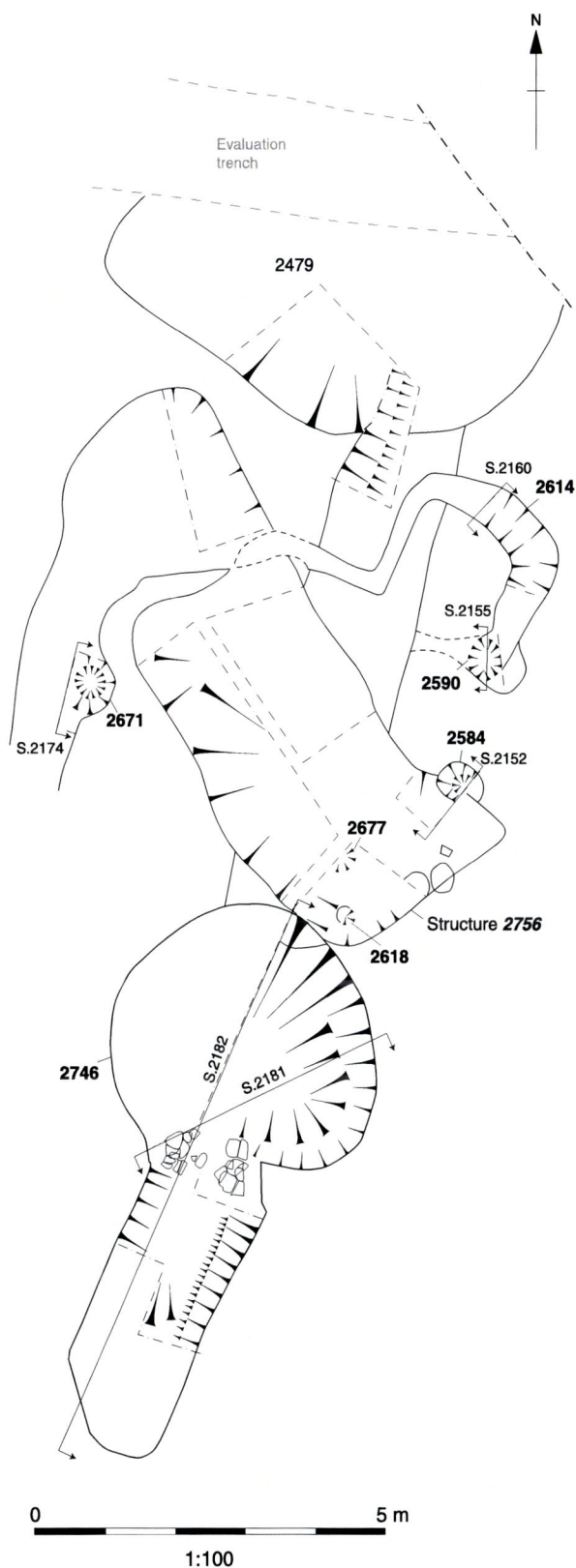

*Fig. 5.15  Junction 9, detail plan of kiln 2746 and associated features*

and 1.7m wide projecting from its southern side. The flue sloped down from ground level at its southern end to a maximum depth of 0.7m where it joined the chamber. A pair of stone piers (2642 and 2709) had been constructed flanking the opening between the pit and the flue. These were formed from large, naturally occurring nodules of unshaped flint, and reddening of the lower nodules attested to the high temperatures reached within the structure. The base and the lower parts of the sides of the firing chamber were similarly discoloured, and the earliest deposit within it comprised a thin, 0.05m-thick, deposit of charcoal, presumably spent fuel from the final firing of the structure (2721). A similar deposit (2725) was located on the base of the flue, where it overlay a thin layer of chalk rubble (2726) and a deposit of purple, heat-discoloured soil (2730), which was situated amongst a sequence of localised deposits of naturally accumulated silt at the mouth of the flue (2727, 2729, 2731 and 2732). Deposit 2721 was immediately overlain by chalk rubble (2720). This may have derived from partial collapse of the rear, northern side of the firing chamber, or possibly indicates the use of the oven for lime production. Either way, evidence for further use of the kiln was provided by the deposition of a layer of red, heat-discoloured soil (2714), which spilled over into the flue, and a thin lens of

**Section 2181**

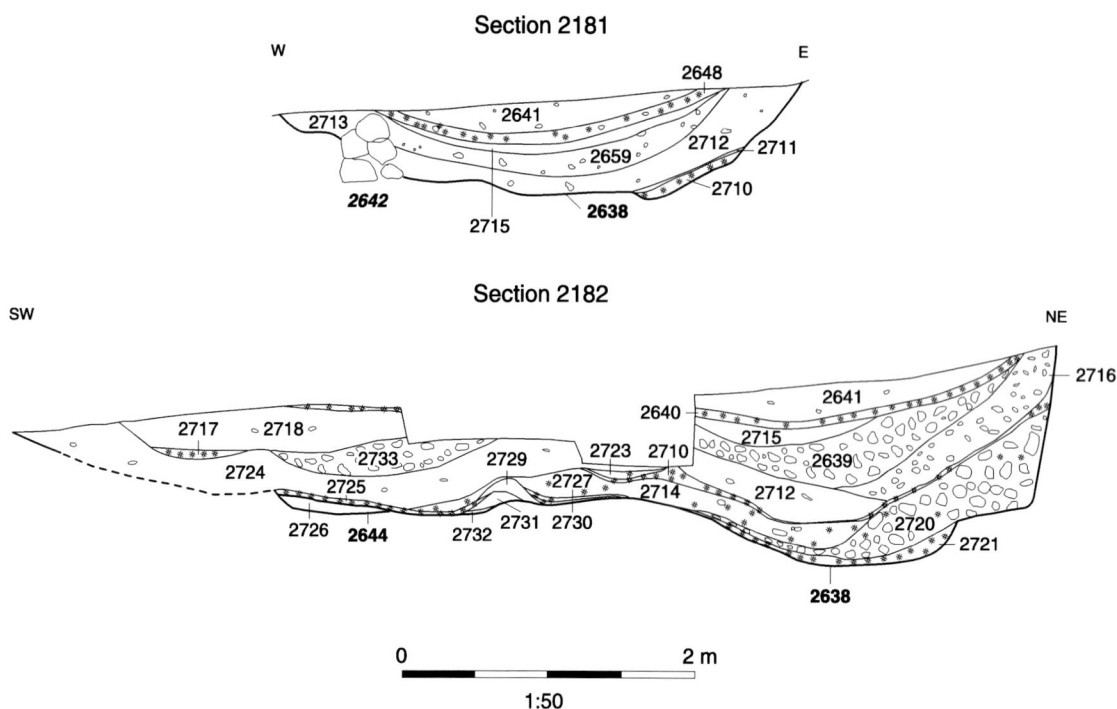

**Section 2182**

0    2 m

1:50

*Fig. 5.16   Junction 9, section of kiln 2746*

charcoal (2710) that was associated with a small patch of burnt silt (2723). The structure was subsequently backfilled with a sequence of layers that alternated layers of silty soil (2712/2724, 2715/2718, 2640 and 2641/2687) and dumps of flint gravel (2716 and 2639/2733). A layer of large flint nodules situated at the mouth of the flue (2722) may derive from part of the superstructure associated with the piers.

The kiln/oven is not well dated. Only two sherds came from deposits earlier than those associated with the backfilling of the feature, but the material is consistently early, including only one sherd certainly later than *c* AD 70 and two undiagnostic sherds of general 'Roman' date from the upper fills of the structure. While most of the pottery might

*Fig. 5.17   Junction 9, section of kiln 2746, viewed from the south-east*

have derived from the ditch into which the oven was cut, the absence of any significantly later pottery suggests that it can be assigned to the early Roman period.

### Post-built structure 2756 and other features associated with kiln/oven 2746 (Figs 5.13 and 5.18-19)

North of the kiln was a series of irregular hollows, a gully or beam-slot (2614) and a number of postholes and possible stakeholes, many cut into the upper fill of ditch 2745. It is likely that these features belonged to structures associated with the operation of the kiln, although it might have been expected that features of this sort would have been concentrated in the area at the mouth of the flue, rather than behind the kiln. Again, artefactual evidence provides no information about the nature of possible activity in this area and little definition with regard to dating. The relationships between the hollows and the structural features were somewhat obscure; the soil spreads filling the hollows appeared to overlie the postholes, but it was uncertain whether this indicated that the hollows themselves were later in date than the structures, or should be associated with their use.

Three postholes stood out on account of their unusual depth (2584, 2590 and 2671). Although none of these features measured more than 0.3m in diameter, all were more than 0.6m deep, and the deepest (2671) exceeded 0.85m. The lower part of each posthole was filled with a deposit of charcoal-rich soil, which was overlain in each case by a main

Section 2152

NE    SW

85.05 mOD

2581

2582

2583 / 2584

Section 2155

N    S    85.10 mOD

2586

2587

2588

2589 — 2590

Section 2160

W    E
85.08 mOD

2612
2614

Section 2174

SW    NE    85.10 mOD

2585

2669

2671

2670

0 ——————— 1 m

1:25

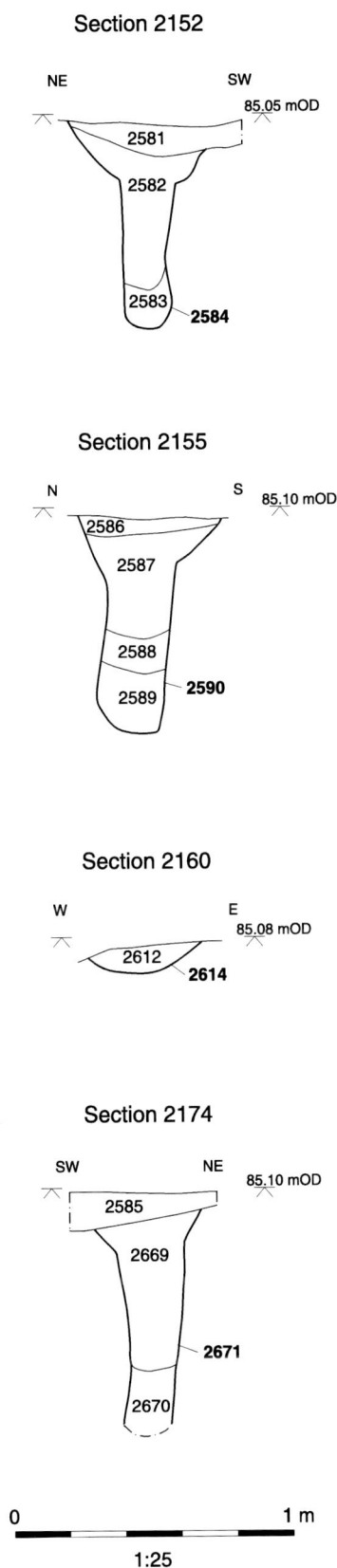

*Fig. 5.18 Junction 9, sections of structure 2756*

fill of clay and flint gravel. The similarities between these postholes leave little doubt that they were part of a single structure (2756). Their spatial arrangement would be consistent with their defining three corners of a rectangular, post-built structure with dimensions of *c* 5.5 x 1.75m, the putative fourth corner of which would have been sealed beneath part of a soil spread that was not removed during the excavation. Although the precise function of the structure is uncertain, its position adjacent to the kiln and its orientation, which was square-on to the kiln, indicate that the two were associated. Posthole 2590 contained a small assemblage of 33 sherds (245g) of pottery with a date range of AD 70-120, and a similar date range was assigned to pottery from a short, sharply angled length of gully (2614) that joined with it. The stratigraphic relationship between these features was not established, but the gully may have served as a beam-slot associated with the structure. The remaining postholes and stakeholes formed no coherent plan.

Contemporary with these features, but located on the other side of ditch 2748, was a large waterhole (2309), which was only partly examined as its base was not reached. The weathered upper cone of this oval cut measured 8.7 x 7.25m, and the feature was at least 2.95m deep. The lowest fill encountered (2332) was a gravel deposit at least 0.75m deep. This produced a small quantity of animal bone and an assemblage of charred plant remains dominated by cereal chaff. Although no dating material was recovered from fill 2332, the overlying layer (2313) contained 14 sherds of pottery, including South Gaulish samian ware, not necessarily later than the early 2nd century. The uppermost fill, a dark clay deposit with few inclusions (2310), appeared to represent tertiary silting and contained no artefactual material.

**Mid-Roman activity (*c* AD 120-200)**

*Modifications to the boundaries in the northern part of the excavation* (Fig. 5.10)

Only minor modifications were made to the boundaries exposed at the northern end of the excavation during the 2nd century, presumably because the existing boundary features were still serviceable. Evidence was identified for the recutting of at least two parts of the ditch defining the rectangular enclosure that had been established during the early Roman period. Part of the western side, adjacent to the north-western corner was, re-dug as a 0.5m-wide gully (2604) which was 0.16m deep, and rather more substantial recutting was undertaken near the south-eastern corner. The latter excavation comprised the digging of a 1.7m-wide ditch (2742), which was up to 0.6m deep, that extended eastwards into the site for 17m, blocking the possible entrance through the original ditch before reaching a rather square-ended terminal short of the corner of the enclosure.

**Section 2093**

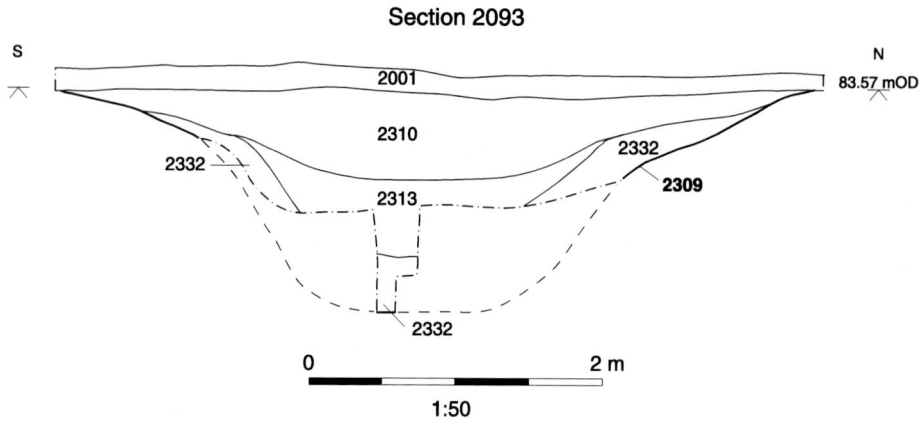

*Fig. 5.19  Junction 9, section of early Roman waterhole 2309*

### Reorganisation of the boundaries in the southern part of the excavation (Figs 5.11 and 5.20-1)

In contrast to the northern part of the excavation, which appears to have been characterised during the mid-Roman period by a continuity of the existing boundaries, the area at the southern end was substantially reorganised during the 2nd century. The principal east-west-aligned boundary represented during the early part of the Roman period by ditch 2748, was cut by a new north-south-aligned boundary, defined by a pair of gullies (2650 and 2652) that extended on a slightly curving alignment for 18m before continuing beyond the eastern edge of the excavation.

Some 30m west of this new boundary, a trackway was established, defined by parallel ditches, some 3.5-4m apart, which ran from the north-east edge of the site but possibly terminated within the excavated area. The western ditch (2755) was traced

*Fig. 5.20  Junction 9, the 2nd-century circular enclosure at the southern end of the excavation, viewed from the south-west*

**Section 2150**

NE · · · · · · · · SW

2257

2258 · · · · · **2256**

**Section 2754** · · · · **Section 2753**

NW

2169

SE

2173 / **2174**

2170

**2172**

2171

0 · · · · · · · · 2 m

1:50

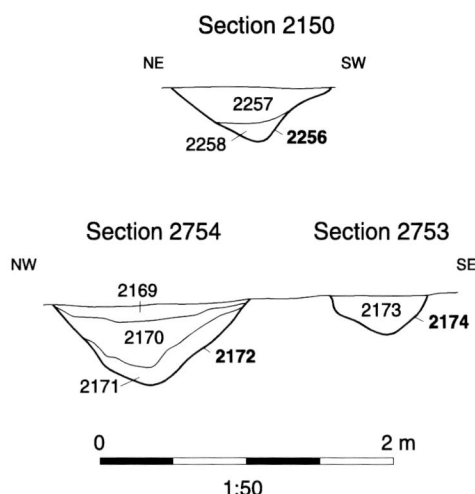

*Fig. 5.21 Sections through the ditches of the 2nd-century circular enclosure at the southern end of the excavation*

southwards for at least 33m, but then became less clear and was not identified in the later machine-cleared strip at the west edge of the site. The eastern ditch (2278) was similarly not seen in this area, but probably terminated at about this point, whereas the apparent absence of 2755 is not considered conclusive. A 12m length of narrow gully (2224) ran at right-angles to the line of 2278 and was apparently cut by it. Its eastern end was not identified. Both features produced pottery assemblages of 2nd-mid-3rd-century date.

Near the southern end of the excavation, three curvilinear ditches (2752, 2753 and 2754) may have defined an enclosure that cut across the boundary defined during the early part of the Roman period by gullies 2750 and 2751. The western part of the putative enclosure lay beyond the edge of the excavation, and consequently it could not be demonstrated conclusively that the ditches joined up to form a single enclosure, although they had similar fills of dark, charcoal-rich soil. However, from the evidence revealed within the excavation, they appeared to enclose a sub-circular area with a diameter of *c* 19m. The northern part of the enclosure was represented by a curvilinear ditch (2752) that was exposed for a length of 24m, while the southern part of the circuit was formed by two closely spaced ditches (2753 and 2754). The terminals of the northern and southern ditches were not aligned directly on each other, but were somewhat off-set, and defined an east-facing entrance, measuring 4m wide. A small pit (2246) adjacent to the terminus of gully 2754 might have been associated with an entrance into the enclosure, perhaps forming part of a gateway. The ditches themselves were of relatively small proportions, typically measuring *c* 1m wide and 0.3m deep. Another curving ditch (2343) may represent a subdivision within the enclosure. The

assemblage of charred plant remains recovered from ditch 2752 was dominated by cereal chaff, perhaps suggesting that crop processing was carried out within or close to the enclosure. Minimal pottery evidence was recovered, but was consistent with the suggestion that the ditches were broadly contemporary with each other and of 2nd-century date.

It was probably during this phase that the soil spreads filling the hollows associated with kiln/oven 2746 developed, since a 2nd-century date has been assigned to the relatively large group of *c* 65 sherds of pottery in soil spread 2488, a layer that sealed several of the postholes in this area. Further shallow pits or hollows were situated to the east of this area, none of which was more than 0.3m deep. Hollow 2657, which lay immediately east of the kiln, produced 232 mostly small pottery sherds dated to the 2nd century, and hollow 2608, adjacent to the eastern edge of the excavation, although not directly dated, was cut by an unexcavated pit/hollow (2706) which had 2nd-century pottery on its surface.

**Mid-late Roman activity (3rd-4th century)** (Figs 5.4, 5.10 and 5.22-4)

Artefactual material dating from the late Roman period was only recovered from features exposed in the northern and central parts of the excavation; indeed, in the southern part of the site no evidence was found for activity dating from after *c* AD 200. The features that could be attributed to the later period comprised a well and two ditches, the latter both apparently respecting the arrangement of the boundaries that had been established during earlier periods and representing modifications to the existing layout, rather than the

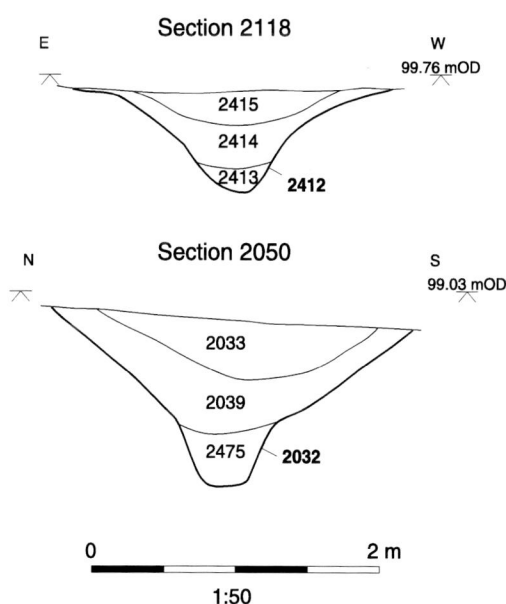

**Section 2118**

E

W

99.76 mOD

2415

2414

2413 / **2412**

**Section 2050**

N

S

99.03 mOD

2033

2039

2475 / **2032**

0 · · · · · · · · 2 m

1:50

*Fig. 5.22 Sections of late Roman boundary ditches*

81

**Section 2024**

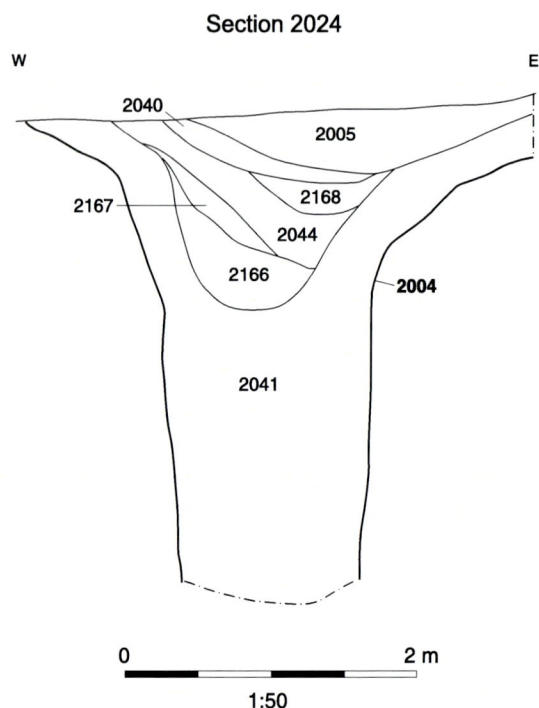

*Fig. 5.23   Section of late Roman well 2004*

imposition of a new scheme. This was exemplified by ditch 2737, which lay on the same alignment as late Iron Age-early Roman ditch 2188 and is likely to have been a deliberate recutting of part of the boundary that had been defined by the earlier ditch. The new ditch was much more substantial than its predecessor, measuring more than 2m wide and up to 0.65m deep, and produced a small group of pottery including four sherds from a Nene Valley colour-coated ware bowl dating from the first half of the 4th century. Ditch 2032 was

equally substantial and extended across the width of the excavated area from the southern end of ditch 2737. The relationship between the two ditches was partly obscured by the western edge of the excavation and was not investigated, but ditch 2032, like ditch 2737, yielded late Roman pottery from its upper fill, in this instance comprising Nene Valley white ware and a sherd from a late Dressel 20 amphora.

Well 2004 was recorded as having cut the western edge of ditch 2490, but in reality it is more likely that the two features were open at the same time. This is suggested by the dating evidence recovered from the well, which was contemporary with that from the upper fill of the ditch, and by the fact that the ditch was cut only by the weathering cone of the well, which may have formed through erosion of the upper part after the well had passed out of use, rather than by the well shaft itself. The weathering cone was quite substantial, giving the well a diameter of *c* 4m at the surface, but beneath this the well consisted of a simple earth-cut shaft measuring only *c* 1.2m across. The upper part of the well was excavated by hand to a depth of 1.2m and the shaft was then machine excavated to a depth of 3.2m, at which point the bottom had still not been reached. Most of the excavated part of the feature was filled with a thick, homogeneous deposit of orange-brown clay (2041), above which had been deposited a dump of flint and chalk (2166) and a final sequence of layers similar in character to the main fill, but containing varying proportions of flint gravel (2005, 2040, 2166, 2167 and 2168). Fill 2041 contained a pottery assemblage, weighing 0.8kg, with a similar composition to that recovered from ditch 2490, as did the uppermost fill (2005), which also produced four 4th-century Roman coins, the latest of which dates from AD 341-8.

*Fig. 5.24   Late Roman boundary ditch 2490, viewed from the south-west*

A single small pit (2108) dating from the late Roman period was located within the concentration of prehistoric features in the central part of the excavation, where it cut an earlier posthole (2182). The pit was oval in plan, with a maximum dimension of 1m, and had a 0.35m-deep concave, bowl-shaped profile. A deposit of silty gravel (2181) lay against the north-western side of the pit, overlain by a main fill of clay soil (2107) which, in addition to a residual assemblage of 84 pieces of worked flint, contained two late Roman coins, the later of which was an issue of Constantine dated AD 313-15.

## JUNCTION 9 WATCHING BRIEF

The watching brief to the south of the existing junction recorded a pit and a ditch terminal, both of Roman date. The pit (2904=2906), which was somewhat irregular in shape, measured 5.5 x 1.7 x 0.25m, contained an unusual bow brooch of 1st-century date (SF 2072; see Fig. 7.23.7) and a small quantity of pottery. The ditch terminal appeared to be the south-western end of a ditch aligned NE-SW, although the rest of the line of the feature could not be defined. A handful of sherds of late Iron Age or early Roman pottery was recovered from its fill.

# Chapter 6: Areas M, P and Junction 10

*by Dan Stansbie*

## AREA M

### Site location and summary

Area M, centred on NGR TL 095 125, occupied a long narrow strip on the east side of the M1 about 1km north of The Aubreys (see Fig. 1.2). The underlying geology in this area is Upper Chalk, overlain by clay-with-flints (see Fig. 1.3). The ground sloped up to north and south from a low point in the centre, varying between 131m aOD at its lowest point and 134m aOD at its highest. The archaeological features consisted principally of ditches, possibly forming trackways and enclosures, and while these were clearly of more than one phase the pottery dated consistently to the late Iron Age-early Roman period, and there was no evidence for significant activity after the 1st century AD.

### Phasing

Activity at Area M can be divided into two main phases. In the first phase, dating to the middle-late Iron Age, two ditches (3022 and 3008), with a posthole (3034) to their east, defined a NE-SW-aligned boundary running across the site. In the second phase, dating to the early Roman period, these were infilled and replaced by a series of ditches (3052, 3012, 3004 and 3006) on the same alignment as the Iron Age boundary. The ditches may have defined two trackways, the first (3052 and 3012) running SW-NE, before turning east across the line of the earlier boundary ditch, and the second (3004 and 3006) continuing to the north-east. Alternatively, these features may have comprised successive boundary ditches for enclosures located to their east. In addition, there were three short stretches of inter-cutting ditch (3057, 3061 and 3059), on an east-west alignment, close to the southern limit of the excavated area. A 3rd-4th-century coin came from the topsoil.

### Middle-late Iron Age activity (Fig. 6.1)

#### Summary

Middle-late Iron Age activity comprised ditches 3008 and 3022, gully 3024 and pit 3034. Although the linear features cannot have been exactly of the same date, as they were inter-cutting, they appear to have been broadly contemporary.

#### Ditches 3008 and 3022, and gully 3024

Ditches 3008 and 3022 defined a single boundary, possibly the edge of an enclosure. The enclosure boundary was approximately 65m in length, aligned roughly north-south and turned a rounded corner to the west at its northern end. Here it ran beyond the limit of excavation, while to the south it petered out a few metres short of the edge of the site. Ditch 3008 formed the northern arm and north-east corner of the boundary, giving a minimum east-west dimension of *c* 15m for the possible enclosure. This ditch had a U-shaped profile and was up to 0.9m wide and 0.18m deep. The fills comprised silty clays, with frequent flint inclusions and occasional charcoal flecks. Ditch 3008 produced 12 sherds of Iron Age and late Iron Age-early Roman pottery, weighing 29g, along with 11 fragments of worked flint. Cutting ditch 3008 at its southern end was a short length of gully (3024), aligned roughly east-west and linking 3008 with the longer north-south-aligned ditch 3022. Gully 3024 was only 1.9m long, 0.34m wide and 0.15m deep, with a gently concave base and steeply sloping sides. Its fill comprised clay silt, with frequent flint inclusions. The gully was cut by ditch/gully 3022, which continued the line of ditch 3008 southwards, with a slight eastward kink in the alignment at the midpoint of the feature, which had a surviving length of 47 m. The ditch/gully was 0.4m wide and 0.12m deep, with a flat base and steeply sloping sides. The single fill consisted of a clay silt, with frequent inclusions of flint, and produced no finds aside from a single flint flake.

#### Pit 3034

A small pit (3034) lay approximately 7m to the east of ditch 3022, about halfway down its length. The pit was sub-circular in plan, U-shaped in profile and measured 0.7m in diameter with a 0.12m depth. Its fill comprised silty clay, with occasional inclusions of flint and charcoal flecks.

### Early Roman activity (Fig. 6.1)

#### Summary

The early Roman activity comprised seven ditches, potentially defining two trackways together with the edge of an enclosure, or possibly representing successive boundaries of two enclosures. Together

## Section 3001

W                           E
99.15 mOD

3005
3014
3016 — 
**3004**

## Section 3024

NE                       SW
99.15 mOD

3009
3017 / **3008**

0                   2 m

1:50

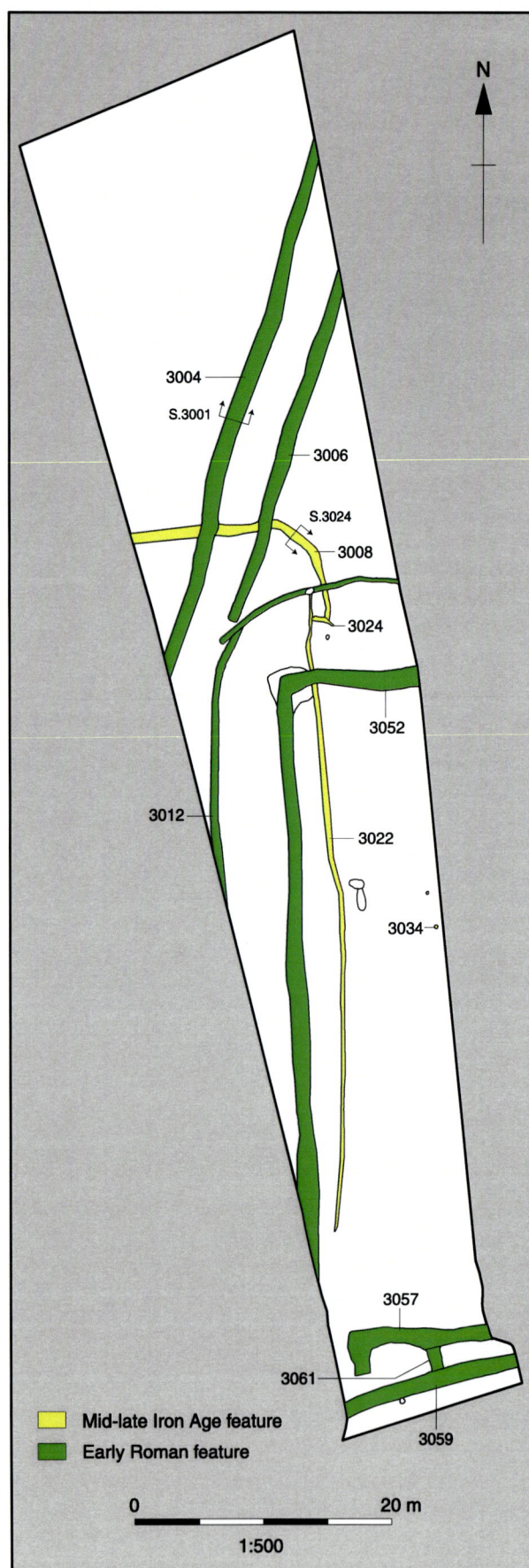

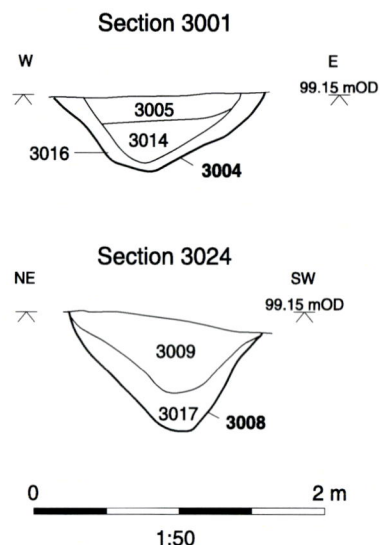

*Fig. 6.1 (left and above)   Site M, mid-late Roman activity, with sections*

ditches 3012 and 3052 may have defined a narrow trackway, at least 49m in length and 5m wide, cutting across the line of middle-late Iron Age ditch 3022. Alternatively, they may have represented successive boundary ditches for an enclosure which lay predominantly to the east. To the north-east of ditches 3052 and 3012, ditches 3004 and 3006 continued on a NNE-SSW alignment. Together these ditches may have defined a second, narrow trackway, 3m in width, or may have formed successive boundary ditches for an enclosure, which again lay predominantly to the east.

At the southern limit of the excavation ditches 3057 and 3059, on an east-west alignment, may have defined the southern limit of the possible enclosure bounded by ditch 3052 to the north-west, but more likely related to a possible enclosure lying to the south, further components of which were not observed.

### Ditch 3052 (Fig. 6.2)

A 45m length of the north-south arm of probable enclosure ditch 3052 lay within the excavated area. At its northern end it turned to the east, ran for 10m and then beyond the limit of excavation. The corner of this probable enclosure was therefore square. The ditch was 1.2m wide, 0.94m deep and was V-shaped in profile. It was filled with silty clay, with frequent flint inclusions, and produced 478 sherds of early Roman pottery, weighing 2746g, two fragments of tile and three flint flakes.

### Ditch/gully 3012 (Fig. 6.2)

Feature 3012 lay north and west of ditch 3052, 4.5-5m distant and roughly parallel to it on the west

## Section 4001

N                                                                    S
                                                              99.85 mOD

4007          4005

4004

4006

## Section 4002

WNW                    ESE
                  100.92 mOD

4009
          4008

0                                    2 m

1:50

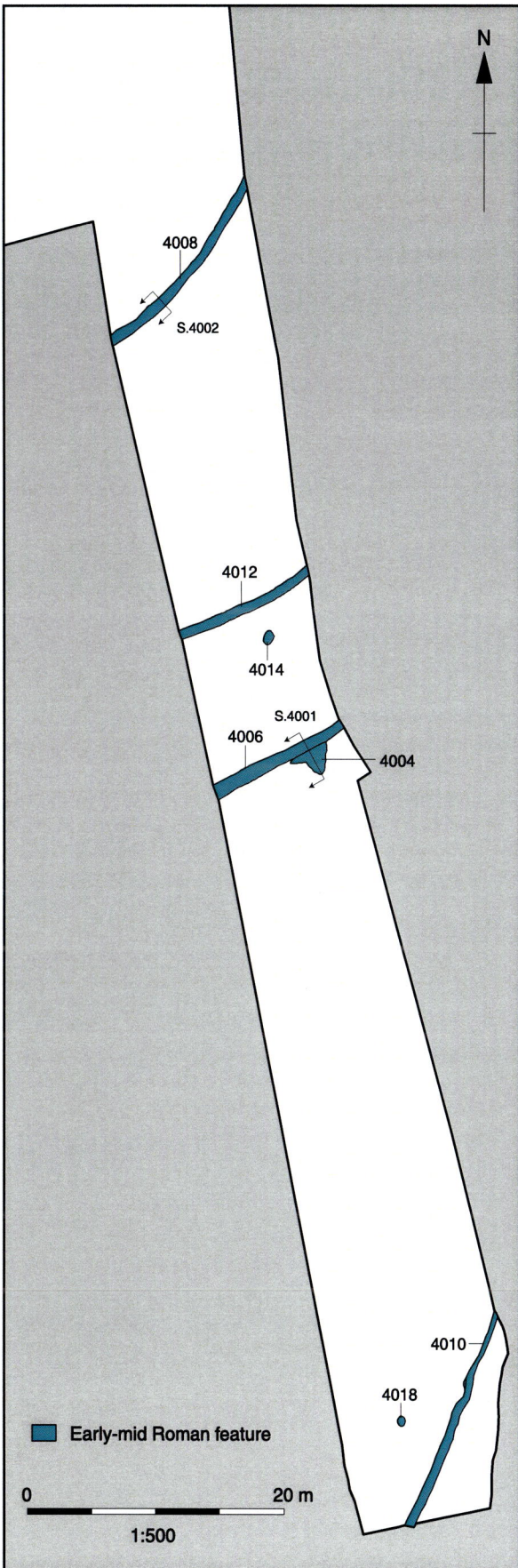

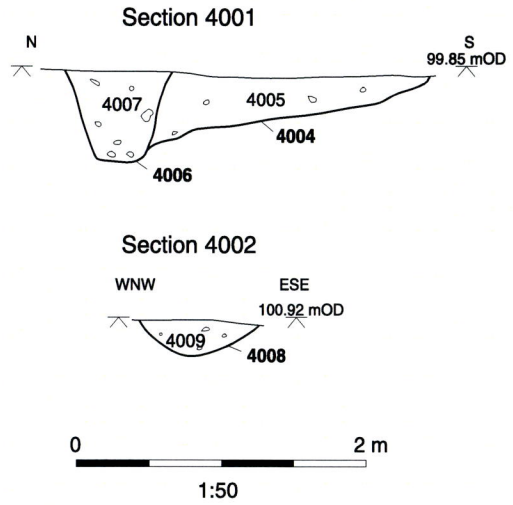

*Fig. 6.2 (left and above)   Site P, early-mid Roman activity, with sections*

and up to 6.5m distant on the north side, where the correspondence of alignment was less precise and the gully was more curvilinear in plan. A length of approximately 37m lay within the excavated area. The gully ranged from *c* 0.35-0.7m wide and was up to 0.35m deep, with a V-shaped profile. It had been recut at least once. The fills comprised silty clay, with the upper fills partially consisting of flint cobbles. Inclusions consisted of frequent charcoal flecks and fragments of flint. In addition, the fills produced a single sherd of Roman pottery, along with four sherds of prehistoric material, weighing 13g, a single flint flake and a fragment of burnt unworked flint.

### Trackway ditches 3004 and 3006 (Fig. 6.2)

Parallel ditches 3004 and 3006, set 3-3.5m apart, defined a probable trackway aligned NNE-SSW and contiguous gully 3012, which may have defined the outer boundary of an adjacent enclosure (see above). The easterly ditch (3006) had a surviving length of *c* 28m and terminated at the outer north-west corner of the possible enclosure, adjacent to gully 3012. The ditch was up to 1.1m wide and 0.3m deep, with a bowl-shaped profile. It was filled with deposits of silty clay, with moderate inclusions of flint and charcoal flecks, which produced four sherds of early Roman pottery, weighing 5g.

Ditch 3004 to the west was up to 1.2m wide and 0.5m deep and a 42m length lay within the excavated area. The ditch had a bowl-shaped profile. Its fills comprised silty clay with occasional stone inclusions and contained a single sherd (8g) of middle Iron Age pottery, five sherds (9g) of early Roman pottery and three flint flakes.

### *Ditches 3057, 3059 and 3061* (Fig. 6.2)

Of these three ditches, the most northerly, east-west-aligned ditch 3057, extended 12m from the east baulk of the site and was 1m wide and 0.34m deep. It appeared to turn sharply to the south at its western end, but the extent of the southward projection is unknown. The ditch had a flat base with steeply sloping sides and it contained a single fill, with occasional inclusions of flint and charcoal flecks. Ditch 3059 to the south extended the full width of the site (at this point 13.5m) on an ENE-WSW alignment. It was up to 1.4m wide, 0.3m deep and like 3057 was flat based with steeply sloping sides. The fill of ditch 3059 comprised silty clay, with occasional flint inclusions and charcoal flecks, and it produced two sherds of late Iron Age-early Roman pottery, weighing 9g.

Lying between, and cut by, ditches 3057 and 3059 was a 1.7m-long, north-south-aligned ditch (3061). This feature had a flat base and was 1m wide and 0.16m deep. The single fill consisted of silty clay, with frequent inclusions of flint and occasional charcoal flecks. Feature 3061 was not traced either north of 3057 or south of 3059. The significance of this is uncertain, but excavation of the intersection of 3061 and 3057 suggested that there was a slightly curving junction in their eastern angle, which might imply that 3061 was originally continuous with an early phase of 3057. On this basis it can be tentatively suggested that 3061 and the eastern part of 3057 initially formed the north-west corner of an enclosure, which was later extended to the west (by a secondary phase of ditch 3057 incorporating the corner observed at the west end of that ditch). It might be further speculated that the north side of the enclosure was then subsequently redefined south of its original position by ditch 3059. However, the principal problem with this hypothesis is the lack of evidence for the southerly continuation (beyond 3059) of either 3061 or the extended version of 3057, but the poor definition of the southward arm of the latter suggests that there were difficulties with the identification of features in this area.

### AREA P

#### Site location and summary

Area P, centred on NGR TL 093 136, was located on the east side of the M1 about 1km north of Area M and 2km north of The Aubreys (see Fig. 1.2). The underlying geology of the site comprises clay-with-flints overlying Upper Chalk (see Fig. 1.3) and it lies on relatively high ground (140m aOD), with slopes down to the north-east, east and south. The excavations revealed four ditches, two of which (4008 and 4010) were isolated features and two defined a possible trackway (4006 and 4012). Other features discovered in this area included a scatter of pits, all probably of early-middle Roman date.

### Ditches 4006, 4008, 4010 and 4012 (Fig. 6.2)

The principal features in this area were four ditches. At the north end of the site ditch 4008 ran roughly NE-SW across the area on a slightly curving alignment. It measured 0.8m wide, 0.28m deep and had a bowl-shaped profile, with a fill comprising clay silt, with occasional flint inclusions. Ditch 4008 was roughly paralleled by a straighter NNE-SSW-aligned ditch (4010), located some 80-90m to the south at the southern extremity of the site. Ditch 4010 had a bowl-shaped profile and measured 0.6m wide by 0.16m deep. Its fill comprised clay silt with occasional inclusions of flint.

Between these two features was a further pair of ditches, 4012 to the north and 4006 to the south. These were 10m apart and aligned approximately ENE-WSW, both turning slightly more northerly at the eastern edge of the site. Ditch 4012 had a regular, shallow V-shaped profile and was 0.8m wide and up to 0.32m deep, with a fill comprising clay silt, with frequent flint inclusions. Ditch 4006 was more steeply V shaped and measured 0.72m wide by *c* 0.6m deep. It was filled with silty clay containing moderate flint inclusions and occasional charcoal flecks.

#### Pits 4014 and 4018 and tree-throw hole 4004 (Fig. 6.2)

A few scattered pits were present. Pit 4014, which was sub-circular and measured 1.2m in diameter by 0.33m deep, lay just south of ditch 4012 and an irregular feature (4004), measuring 2.98m long by 0.45m deep, which was probably a tree-throw hole, was cut by the southern edge of ditch 4006. Pit 4018, which was also sub-circular, up to 0.68m across and 0.3m deep, lay some 5m west of ditch 4010 at the south end of the site. All of these features were filled with single deposits of clay silt with inclusions of flint and charcoal flecks.

#### Chronology and phasing

Pottery was recovered from the fills of all the ditches and from pit 4014. The groups from ditches 4008 and 4012 contained very small sherds (respectively 15 sherds weighing 13g and 22 sherds weighing 82g) of late Iron Age-early Roman character. In contrast, ditches 4006 and 4010 produced larger groups (392 sherds weighing 3324g and 98 sherds weighing 762g) of more substantial sherds, both groups dated around the end of the 2nd-early 3rd century. The pottery from pit 4014 was less diagnostic but a similar date is very likely. Other finds comprised worked flints and fragments of animal bone from ditch 4008 and pit 4014, and brick and tile from ditches 4008 and 4012, and pit 4014.

Superficially the dating evidence indicates an early Roman date for the two northerly ditches and a middle Roman date for the two to the south.

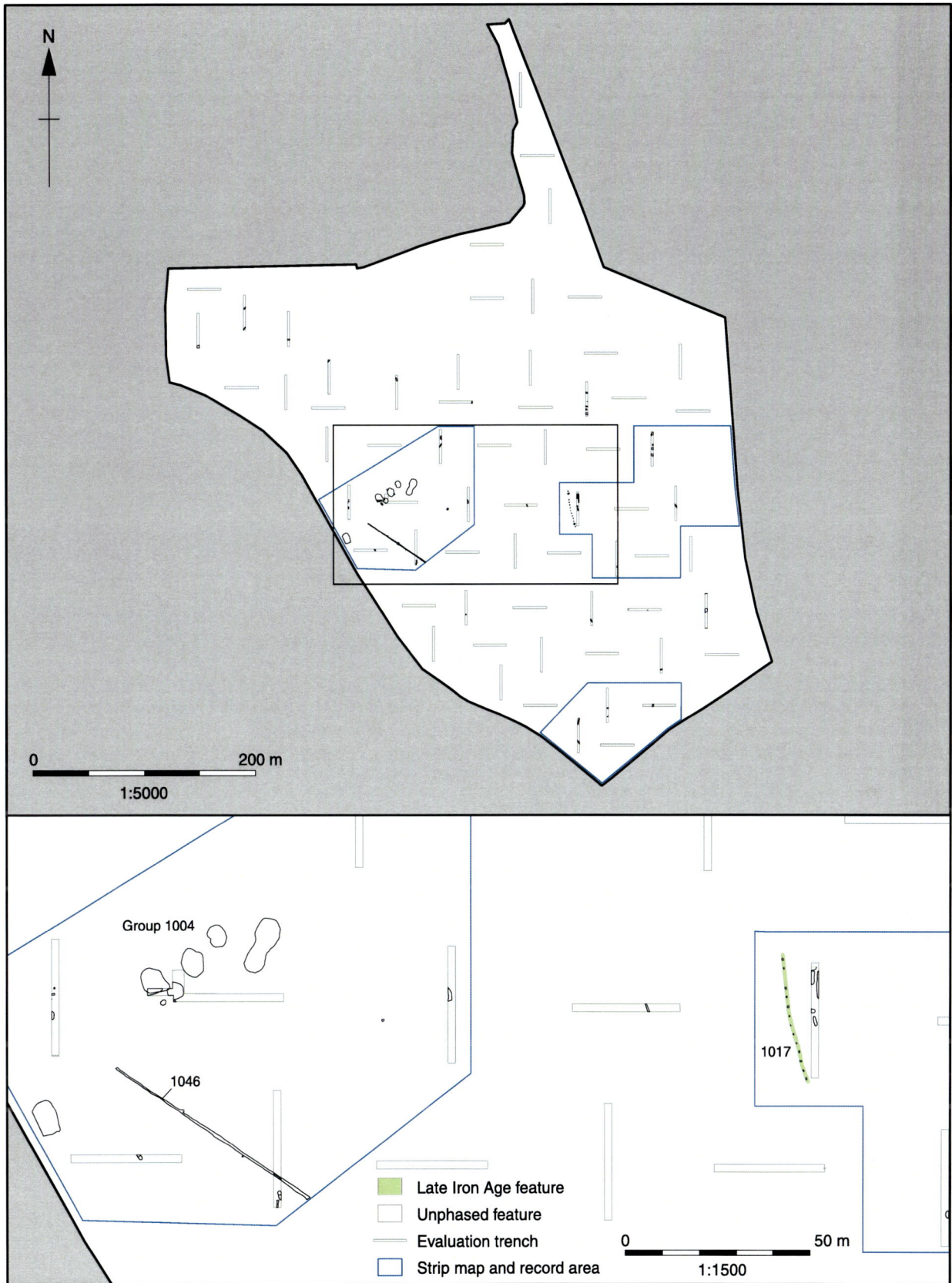

N

0        200 m

1:5000

Group 1004

1046

1017

Late Iron Age feature

Unphased feature

Evaluation trench

Strip map and record area

0        50 m

1:1500

*Fig. 6.3    Junction 10, plan of all features*

However, the parallel layout of ditches 4012 and 4006 suggests, notwithstanding their rather different sizes, that these were contemporary features, perhaps defining an ENE-WSW-aligned trackway. It is possible that all the features on the site were of the same date, but the presence of some late Iron Age-early Roman pottery indicates some activity of that period in the vicinity, and it can be suggested that ditch 4008 at the north end of the site was perhaps the earliest feature. In view of the absence of features, or deposits indicating domestic activity, the quantities of pottery deposited in ditch 4010 and, in particular, in 4006, are notable. The latter assemblage included samian ware and amphora sherds as well as locally and regionally produced coarse wares. If ditch 4006 did define the south edge of a trackway it may be that the pottery contained within it was brought from a nearby settlement located alongside the trackway. Whether this settlement lay to east or west of the present site is, however, unknown.

## JUNCTION 10

### Site Location and summary

The limited Junction 10 excavations took place within an irregularly shaped area of approximately 30ha centred on NGR TL 092179 lying south-east of Junction 10 of the M1 and bounded on the east by the A1081, and on the south by the minor road to Slip End (see Fig. 1.2). The underlying geology comprised clay-with-flints overlying Upper Chalk (see Fig. 1.3) and the site area sloped down from west to east (from *c* 150m aOD to *c* 132m aOD), lying on the west side of a shallow dry valley.

The excavations concentrated on two areas roughly measuring 138 x 110m and 158 x 130m. The westernmost area contained a scatter of quarry pits and a stretch of ditch (1046) orientated NW-SE, none of which contained any dating evidence. The eastern area contained a posthole alignment or possible fenceline (1017), also orientated NW-SE. Limited evidence suggests that the alignment may have dated to the late Iron Age-early Roman period.

### Quarry pit group 1004 (Fig. 6.3)

The quarry pit group comprised five sub-circular pits with flat bases and steeply sloping or stepped sides. The pits generally ranged between 0.7m and 1.4m in diameter and 0.43m and 1.73m in depth, although pit 1004 was much more substantial, being 12m long, 5.35m wide and 1.73m deep. All of the pits contained single fills of clay silt, with flint inclusions, apart from pit 1004, which held six fills.

### Ditch 1046 (Fig. 6.3)

Ditch 1046 ran roughly north-west for a distance of *c* 62m from the south-east edge of the western area ending in a well-defined terminal. It was up to 0.8m wide and 0.45m deep and had a flat base with near-vertical sides. The ditch fills comprised clay silts with inclusions of flint fragments. A V-shaped recut with an identical fill was observed cutting the secondary ditch fill, but it is unclear whether or not this ran along the entire length of the ditch, as the ditch was only subjected to a single 1m-long archaeological intervention.

### Fenceline 1017

Fenceline 1017 comprising 13 sub-circular postholes, was located towards the west edge of the eastern area. The alignment was almost north-south and extended for 32m, with no clear sign at either end that it continued further than this distance. The postholes were generally flat based with steeply sloping sides and typically measured 0.55m in diameter by 0.16m in depth. Their fills comprised silty clay with inclusions of moderate sub-angular flint and they were generally spaced between 2m and 3m apart, with a gap of 5m separating the two most northerly features from the rest. One of the postholes in this alignment produced two sherds of late Iron Age-early Roman grog-tempered pottery and a single sherd of sand and limestone-tempered material.

### Other features

A thin scatter of possible pits and postholes was mapped across part of the Junction 10 area, including examples within the two areas given more detailed attention. None of these features was dated and their interpretation is uncertain.

# Chapter 7: The Finds

FLINT *by David Mullin and Rebecca Devaney*

## Introduction

A total of 4772 pieces of worked flint and 638 fragments (9872g) of burnt unworked flint were recovered from excavations along the route of the M1 (Table 7.1). In addition, 2000 pieces of worked flint and 141 fragments (5183g) of burnt unworked flint were recovered from the earlier programme of evaluations and fieldwalking, though these are not discussed in detail. The flint from the excavations was recovered from 294 contexts. Most contexts (a total of 217) contained less than ten pieces of flint, but a total of 65 contexts contained between ten and 100 pieces and 12 contexts contained over 100 pieces of flint. By far the largest assemblage from the site was that from Junction 9, where substantial amounts of Mesolithic material were recovered from a series of pits. This material was recorded and assessed by Rebecca Devaney. The present report, using the data, was compiled by David Mullin, who also considered the wider context.

## Methodology

The worked flint was catalogued according to a standard typology. Information about burning, breaks, condition, raw material and technology was recorded. In addition, cores were weighed and burnt unworked flint was quantified by count and weight. The data were entered into an MS Access database.

## Raw material

Where identifiable, the most predominant raw material is gravel flint. In general, these pieces have a thin and abraded cortex and are likely to be locally derived, perhaps sourced from river gravel deposits. A smaller amount of chalk-derived flints, which are identified by a thick white cortex, was also present. The sites are situated on chalk bedrock and so this material is also likely to be local in origin.

## Condition

The condition of the assemblage is reasonably good. Of the worked flints, 35% are in a fresh condition and only 56% exhibit slight post-depositional damage. Only a small proportion of the assemblage (8%) is more heavily damaged. Where present, the damage is most frequently seen on vulnerable unretouched edges and implies some post-depositional disturbance. The amount of surface alteration is minimal with the majority of the assemblage (81%) remaining uncorticated.

## Technology and dating

The majority of the assemblage is technologically later prehistoric (later Neolithic and Bronze Age) in date. The presence of rejuvenation flakes, chips and irregular waste, and the relatively low number of larger flakes and tools, suggest that much of the assemblage is knapping waste.

Unretouched debitage dominates the assemblage (4611 pieces; 97%). Of this total, 3684 pieces are flakes and 256 are blades, blade-like flakes and bladelets. Technologically, the assemblage comprises pieces (mainly flakes) with clear points and cones of percussion, pronounced ventral ripples and hinge terminations. These characteristics are most commonly associated with the hard-hammer flint industries of later prehistory. A proportion of the assemblage (mainly blades) exhibits features such as platform-edge abrasion, punctiform butts and dorsal-blade scars, characteristics known to be associated with the more careful, soft-hammer, blade-based industries of the Mesolithic and earlier Neolithic.

In total, 116 cores (2% of the assemblage) were recovered. The majority were utilised for the production of flakes and range in size from a small unclassifiable/fragmentary core of 7g to a large multi-platform flake core of 339g. An opposed-platform blade core, which was neatly worked for the production of bladelets, is probably late Mesolithic or earlier Neolithic in date.

Forty-five retouched tools were recovered, which at 1% of the assemblage is an unusually low proportion. This material is dominated by microliths, half of which are scalene microtriangles (Jacobi 1978, 16) and all are typical later Mesolithic types. Although all of the microliths were recovered from excavations at Junction 9, only one context contained more than one microlith.

The chisel arrowhead is a small example and can be broadly dated to the later Neolithic (Green 1984, 19). The remaining tools are chronologically undiagnostic, but are consistent with the rest of the predominantly later prehistoric assemblage.

## The assemblage

Small amounts of flint were recovered from Area M, Area P and the Borrow Pit Area, with more substantial assemblages from Junction 8N, Junction 8S and Junction 9. The sites are dispersed and will be considered separately, but their assemblages are summarised alongside each other in Table 7.1.

### Area M

A total of 48 flints was recovered from this site, the majority comprising waste flakes, but one single platform core was also recovered from context 3039.

### Area P

A total of eight flints, predominantly waste flakes, was recovered from this site. None was diagnostic of date, but the blade may be late Mesolithic/early Neolithic in date.

### Borrow Pit Area

Two undiagnostic waste flakes were recovered from this site.

### Junction 8N

The majority of the 113 flints recovered from Junction 8N comprised waste flakes, although the remaining material had a relatively high proportion of blades and blade-like flakes. These probably represent a late Mesolithic/early Neolithic presence.

### Junction 8S

A slightly greater number of flints was recovered from the southbound section of Junction 8, but again these were dominated by waste flakes. A small number of blades, blade-like flakes and the presence of a single-platform core from context 5628 probably represent a late Mesolithic/early Neolithic presence. Context 5026 contained a total of 23

*Table 7.1: Summary of flint by excavation area and flint category*

| Flint Category | Excavation area | | | | | | |
| --- | --- | --- | --- | --- | --- | --- | --- |
| | Area M | Area P | Borrow Pit | Junction 8N | Junction 8S | Junction 9 | Total |
| Flake | 45 | 6 | 2 | 88 | 113 | 3430 | 3684 |
| Blade | | 1 | | 3 | 6 | 98 | 108 |
| Blade-like flake | | | | 2 | 3 | 71 | 76 |
| Bladelet | | | | 4 | 1 | 67 | 72 |
| Core-face/edge-rejuvenation flake | | | | 2 | 1 | 5 | 8 |
| Rejuvenation-flake tablet | | | | | | 1 | 1 |
| Irregular waste | 1 | 1 | | 8 | 4 | 104 | 118 |
| Chip | 1 | | | 1 | 6 | 536 | 544 |
| Opposed-platform blade core | | | | | | 1 | 1 |
| Single-platform flake core | 1 | | | | 1 | 9 | 11 |
| Opposed platform flake core | | | | | | 3 | 3 |
| Multi-platform flake core | | | | 2 | 1 | 47 | 50 |
| Keeled/non-discoidal flake core | | | | | | 6 | 6 |
| Core on a flake | | | | | | 4 | 4 |
| Unclassifiable/fragmentary core | | | | 1 | 3 | 19 | 23 |
| Tested nodule | | | | 2 | | 16 | 18 |
| Microlith | | | | | | 18 | 18 |
| Chisel arrowhead | | | | | | 1 | 1 |
| End scraper | | | | | | 7 | 7 |
| End and side scraper | | | | | | 3 | 3 |
| Side scraper | | | | | | 2 | 2 |
| Scraper on a non-flake blank | | | | | | 1 | 1 |
| Retouched blade | | | | | | 1 | 1 |
| Retouched flake | | | | | 1 | 9 | 10 |
| Serrated flake | | | | | | 1 | 1 |
| Miscellaneous retouch | | | | | | 1 | 1 |
| Total | 48 | 8 | 2 | 113 | 140 | 4461 | 4772 |
| Burnt unworked count | 3 | 3 | | 325 | 155 | 152 | 638 |
| Burnt unworked weight (g) | 9 | 14 | | 2972 | 3550 | 3327 | 9872 |

worked flints, mostly undiagnostic flakes, whilst a retouched flake was recovered from context 5460. The flint was recovered from the fills of pits and tree-throw holes across the site, some from features which were otherwise without finds and could therefore be contemporary with the production of the tools themselves.

### Junction 9

By far the largest assemblage of worked flint was recovered from Junction 9. This comprised 4461 items weighing 9594g (Table 7.1). The largest assemblages of flint were recovered from a series of 41 pits within a larger cluster of 69 pits (Table 7.2) and three gullies. All of the pit assemblages were dominated by waste flakes, which comprised as much as 97% of some of these assemblages, with a minimum of 80% from any one pit. Very few formal tools were present in the pits, with only a single scraper and four retouched flakes in the assemblage. Eighteen microliths were recovered from the pits (Table 7.3; see Fig. 5.4). Only one context contained more than a single example and never more than two were

*Table 7.2: Pits containing flint from Junction 9*

| Feature | Type | Dimensions (length x width x depth (m) /sides) | Worked flint pieces | Other finds/comment |
|---|---|---|---|---|
| 2094 | Pit | 1.65+ x 1.60 x 0.55, Sh | 665 | Late Mesolithic date |
| 2064 | Pit | 1.75 x 1.50 x 0.38, Sh | 411 | Late Mesolithic date |
| 2100 | Pit | 1.80 x 0.58 x 0.30, Sh | 365 | Late Mesolithic date |
| 2090 | Pit | 1.80 x 1.24 x 0.40, Sh | 234 | Late Mesolithic date |
| 2316 | Pit | 1.60 x 1.14 x 0.20, S | 222 | Late Mesolithic date |
| 2052 | Pit | 1.50 x 1.11 x 0.57, S | 208 | Late Neolithic date |
| 2189 | Pit | 1.60 x 0.80+ x 0.22, Sh | 93 | |
| 2108 | Pit | 1.00 x 0.95 x 0.35, Sh | 85 | |
| 2290 | ?Pit | 1.20 x 0.70 x 0.35, Sh | 71 | |
| 2384 | Pit | 3.00 x 1.60+ x 0.75, S | 69 | Two fragments of pot |
| 2299 | Pit | 1.00 x 0.67 x 0.43, S | 65 | |
| 2096 | Pit | 0.80 x 0.50 x 0.26, S | 56 | Late Mesolithic date |
| 2058 | Pit | 1.03 x 0.80 x 0.34, S/V | 48 | |
| 2324 | Post hole | 0.80 x 0.60 x 0.35, V | 48 | |
| 2318 | Pit | 0.86 x 0.84 x 0.19, S/Sh | 46 | |
| 2084 | Pit | 1.68 x 0.90 x 0.10, Sh | 40 | |
| 2311 | Pit | 1.06 x c 0.85 x 0.19, I | 37 | |
| 2076 | Pit | 1.35 x ? x 0.25, Sh | 32 | |
| 2104 | Pit | 1.60 x 1.10 x 0.15, I | 31 | Chisel arrowhead |
| 2370 | Pit | 0.80 x 0.72 x 0.40, S | 30 | |
| 2358 | Pit | 1.90 x 1.00 x 0.25, S | 27 | |
| 2297 | Pit | 2.26 x 1.05 x 0.42, S | 26 | |
| 2062 | Pit | 0.85 x 0.64 x 0.47, V | 21 | |
| 2320 | Pit | 0.69 x 0.67 x 0.16, Sh | 20 | |
| 2398 | Pit | 1.14 x 0.97 x 0.19, Sh | 20 | |
| 2068 | Pit | 0.70 x 0.58 x 0.14, Sh | 14 | |
| 2381 | Pit | 1.02 x 0.98 x 0.25, S | 12 | |
| 2360 | Pit | 2.20 x 0.80 x 0.30, Sh | 11 | |
| 2074 | Pit | 1.30 x 1.08 x 0.18, Sh | 10 | |
| 2454 | Pit | 1.40 x 0.57 x 0.16, Sh | 7 | |
| 2234 | Pit | 1.30 x 1.22 x 0.30, I | 6 | |
| 2510 | Pit | 1.45 x 0.50 | 6 | |
| 2102 | Pit/Posthole | 0.60 x 0.54 x 0.17, S | 5 | |
| 2060 | Posthole | 0.59 x 0.47 x 0.28, V | 4 | |
| 2544 | Pit/ Posthole | 1.70 x 0.85 | 4 | |
| 2570 | Pit/ Posthole | 1.00 x 0.60 | 4 | |
| 2366 | Pit | 1.54 x 0.84+ x 0.10, I | 3 | |
| 2704 | Pit | 1.50 x 1.50 x 0.30, S | 3 | |
| 2050 | Pit | 0.60 x 0.92 x 0.40, V | 2 | |
| 2163 | ?Pit | 0.75 x 0.47 x 0.07, Sh | 2 | |
| 2222 | ?Pit | c 0.70 x 0.63 x 0.10, S | 2 | |
| 2386 | Pit | 1.35 x 1.03 x 0.44, I | 2 | 11 fragments of pot |
| 2470 | Pit/ Posthole | 0.65 x 0.45 | 2 | |

present in any pit. A single microlith (SF 2025) does not fit easily into Jacobi's (1978) classification, but the majority (a total of nine) are scalene microtriangles of type 7a2. A further three are type 5c, three examples of type 6 and one of type 5b are also present. An obliquely blunted point completes the assemblage. Cores from the pits are dominated by multi-platform cores, mainly used for the production of blades and blade-like flakes.

Whilst large quantities of worked flint were recovered from 20 pits, with more than 2000 pieces being recovered from a total of six pits, the remaining 21 pits contained very few items (Table 7.2), predominantly non-diagnostic waste flakes (Tables 7.4-5). Assessing the date and function of these pits is extremely difficult and it is not possible to be certain if they form a contemporary group or are part of a long history of pit deposition. The late Neolithic assemblage and radiocarbon date from pit 2052 and the chisel arrowhead from pit 2104 may suggest the latter.

The richest pit was 2094 (contexts 2093, 2154 and 2162) which contained 662 worked flints weighing 665g (Table 7.4). These were dominated by waste flakes and chips, but ten cores were present, as were two microliths of Jacobi's (ibid.) 7a2 form, and narrow blades and bladelets, indicating a Mesolithic date. This is supported by a radiocarbon determination (NZA-32690) of 5230-4980 cal BC (95.4% confidence; or 5210-4990 cal BC, 68.2% confidence) from this feature. Further pits which returned Mesolithic radiocarbon dates included pit 2096, which contained a total of 56 worked flints (Table 7.4), again including blades and narrow flakes. This pit was radiocarbon dated (NZA-32691) to 5310–5000 cal BC (95.4% confidence; or 5230-5060 cal BC, 68.2% confidence). A total of 222

worked flints (Table 7.4) including blades, bladelets, cores and a microlith of Jacobi's (ibid.) 7a2 form were recovered from pit 2316 (context 2317), which returned a radiocarbon determination (NZA-32692) of 5220-4930 cal BC (95.4% confidence; or 5210-4990 cal BC, 68.2% confidence). Pit 2064 (context 2063) contained a total of 411 worked flints (Table 7.4), including a further microlith of Jacobi's (ibid.) type 5c and ten cores. A total of 32 (9%) of the items recovered from the pit were blades, bladelets and blade-like flakes (Table 7.5). This pit produced a radiocarbon determination (NZA-32800) of 5290-4940 cal BC (95.4% confidence; or 5220-5000 cal BC, 68.2% confidence).

The fills of at least seven other pits and a posthole were dominated by waste flakes and chips (Table 7.4), but the presence of microliths, alongside blades and blade-like flakes and the absence of other diagnostic implements, such as scrapers and arrowheads, suggest a probable late Mesolithic date. A total of 234 worked flints were recovered from pit 2090 (context 2089) and, although a small proportion (a total of 12) were classified as blades and blade-like flakes, the assemblage was dominated by waste flakes and chips which form 93% of the material recovered (Table 7.5). A total of 15 blades and blade-like flakes, a single microlith of Jacobi's (ibid.) 7a2 form and two core-rejuvenation pieces were recovered from pit 2100 (context 2099) which contained 365 worked flints, whilst microliths were also recovered from the fills of pits 2384, 2299, 2058 and 2318, where they occurred alongside blades and bladelets except in pit 2384, which had no bladelets (Table 7.4). Blade-based material also formed the majority of the flint recovered from pit 2311, where it formed 11% of the total contents of the pit (Table 7.5).

*Table 7.3: Microliths from pits at Junction 9*

| Context | SF no. | Description |
|---|---|---|
| 2057 | 2023 | Jacobi 1978 7a2. Direct retouch on all edges; scalene microtriangle; tiny |
| 2063 | | Jacobi 1978 type 5c. Lightly burnt |
| 2067 | 2032 | Jacobi 1978 type 5c |
| 2087 | 2022 | Jacobi 1978 7a2. Direct retouch on all edges; scalene microtriangle |
| 2093 | 2010 | Jacobi 1978 7a2. Direct retouch on all edges; scalene microtriangle |
| 2093 | 2013 | Jacobi 1978 7a2. Direct retouch on all edges; scalene microtriangle |
| 2099 | 2033 | Jacobi 1978 7a2. Scalene microtriangle |
| 2539 | 2049 | Obliquely blunted point; direct retouch distal right creates point at distal end |
| 2195 | 2026 | Jacobi 1978 7a2. Direct retouch on all edges; scalene microtriangle |
| 2300 | 2025 | Minimal direct retouch on both lateral edges; forms point at distal end |
| 2317 | 2031 | Jacobi 1978 7a2. Direct retouch on all edges; scalene microtriangle |
| 2319 | 2029 | Jacobi 1978 7a2. Direct retouch on all edges; scalene microtriangle |
| 2331 | 2028 | Jacobi 1978 type 6. Distal trimming |
| 2355 | 2034 | Jacobi 1978 Type 5c. Direct retouch on left side; point at proximal end; direct and inverse retouch at the distal end |
| 2355 | 2036 | Probably Jacobi 1978 Type 6. Direct retouch on both edges; point at proximal end |
| 2361 | 2035 | Jacobi 1978 Type 6. Direct retouch on both edges; point at distal end; light on ventral surface; reused flake? |
| 2385 | 2038 | Jacobi 1978 7a2, scalene microtriangle |
| 2399 | 2037 | Jacobi 1978 5b. Direct retouch on all edges |

Table 7.4: Contents of Mesolithic pits from Junction 9 with more than 30 worked flints

| Pit | Blade | Bladelet | Blade-like flake | Chip | Flake | Unclassifiable waste | Retouched flake | Flake core | Multi-platform core | Single-platform core | Unclassifiable core | Core flake rejuvenation | Microlith | Scraper | Tested nodule | Burnt unworked |
|---|---|---|---|---|---|---|---|---|---|---|---|---|---|---|---|---|
| 2094 | 6 | 7 | 4 | 77 | 529 | 13 | 0 | 1 | 6 | 2 | 1 | 1 | 2 | 0 | 3 | 10 |
| 2064 | 13 | 14 | 7 | 41 | 307 | 11 | 2 | 2 | 11 | 0 | 0 | 0 | 1 | 0 | 1 | 1 |
| 2100 | 11 | 10 | 4 | 53 | 272 | 8 | 0 | 0 | 0 | 0 | 4 | 2 | 1 | 0 | 0 | 0 |
| 2090 | 7 | 4 | 1 | 68 | 150 | 3 | 0 | 0 | 0 | 0 | 0 | 0 | 0 | 0 | 1 | 0 |
| 2316 | 3 | 3 | 3 | 28 | 174 | 5 | 0 | 0 | 2 | 0 | 0 | 1 | 1 | 1 | 1 | 0 |
| 2189 | 2 | 0 | 0 | 14 | 75 | 2 | 0 | 0 | 0 | 0 | 0 | 0 | 0 | 0 | 0 | 0 |
| 2108 | 1 | 2 | 2 | 12 | 65 | 1 | 0 | 2 | 0 | 0 | 0 | 0 | 0 | 0 | 0 | 0 |
| 2290 | 1 | 0 | 0 | 6 | 58 | 2 | 0 | 0 | 0 | 0 | 0 | 0 | 0 | 0 | 0 | 4 |
| 2384 | 2 | 0 | 0 | 1 | 56 | 2 | 0 | 0 | 6 | 0 | 0 | 0 | 1 | 0 | 1 | 0 |
| 2299 | 2 | 1 | 3 | 6 | 50 | 0 | 1 | 0 | 1 | 0 | 0 | 0 | 1 | 0 | 0 | 1 |
| 2096 | 1 | 0 | 0 | 0 | 54 | 0 | 0 | 0 | 0 | 0 | 1 | 0 | 0 | 0 | 0 | 0 |
| 2058 | 1 | 1 | 0 | 7 | 36 | 3 | 0 | 0 | 0 | 0 | 0 | 0 | 1 | 0 | 0 | 0 |
| 2324 | 0 | 4 | 0 | 10 | 28 | 3 | 0 | 0 | 0 | 0 | 0 | 0 | 0 | 0 | 0 | 1 |
| 2318 | 1 | 1 | 1 | 8 | 32 | 2 | 0 | 0 | 0 | 0 | 0 | 0 | 1 | 0 | 0 | 0 |
| 2084 | 0 | 1 | 2 | 7 | 30 | 0 | 0 | 0 | 0 | 0 | 0 | 0 | 0 | 0 | 0 | 0 |
| 2311 | 1 | 3 | 0 | 12 | 20 | 0 | 0 | 0 | 0 | 0 | 0 | 0 | 0 | 0 | 0 | 1 |
| 2076 | 0 | 0 | 0 | 2 | 29 | 0 | 0 | 0 | 0 | 0 | 1 | 0 | 0 | 0 | 0 | 0 |
| 2370 | 0 | 0 | 0 | 6 | 14 | 4 | 1 | 0 | 0 | 0 | 0 | 0 | 0 | 0 | 0 | 3 |
| TOTAL | 52 | 51 | 27 | 358 | 1979 | 59 | 4 | 5 | 26 | 2 | 7 | 5 | 9 | 1 | 7 | 21 |

*Table 7.5: Mesolithic pit assemblage composition (%)*

| Pit | Blade-based pieces | Waste | Cores | Core rejuvenation flake | Microlith | Scraper | Retouched flake | Tested nodule | Burnt unworked |
|---|---|---|---|---|---|---|---|---|---|
| 2094 | 3 | 94 | 1.5 | 0.2 | 0.3 | 0 | 0 | 0.5 | 2 |
| 2064 | 8 | 88 | 4 | 0 | 0.5 | 0 | 0.5 | 0.5 | 0.5 |
| 2100 | 7 | 92 | 1 | 0.5 | 0.3 | 0 | 0 | 0 | 0 |
| 2090 | 5 | 93 | 0 | 0 | 0 | 0 | 0 | 0.5 | 0 |
| 2316 | 4 | 93 | 1 | 0.5 | 0.5 | 0.5 | 0 | 0.5 | 0 |
| 2189 | 2 | 97 | 0 | 0 | 0 | 0 | 0 | 0 | 0 |
| 2108 | 6 | 90 | 2 | 0 | 0 | 0 | 0 | 0 | 0 |
| 2290 | 1 | 93 | 0 | 0 | 0 | 0 | 0 | 0 | 6 |
| 2384 | 3 | 85 | 0 | 0 | 1 | 0 | 0 | 1 | 0 |
| 2299 | 9 | 86 | 0 | 0 | 1 | 0 | 1 | 0 | 1 |
| 2096 | 2 | 96 | 0 | 0 | 0 | 0 | 0 | 0 | 0 |
| 2058 | 4 | 93 | 0 | 0 | 2 | 0 | 0 | 0 | 0 |
| 2324 | 8 | 85 | 0 | 0 | 0 | 0 | 0 | 0 | 2 |
| 2318 | 6 | 92 | 0 | 0 | 2 | 0 | 0 | 0 | 0 |
| 2084 | 7 | 93 | 0 | 0 | 0 | 0 | 0 | 0 | 0 |
| 2311 | 11 | 87 | 0 | 0 | 0 | 0 | 0 | 0 | 3 |
| 2076 | 0 | 97 | 3 | 0 | 0 | 0 | 0 | 0 | 0 |
| 2370 | 0 | 80 | 3 | 0 | 0 | 0 | 3 | 0 | 1 |

Besides the finds from pits, three gullies contained flint-rich fills. Gully 2072 (context 2071) contained 187 worked flints including four multi-platform cores and a small number of blades and blade-like flakes. Gully 2196 (context 2195) contained 186 flints including a microlith of Jacobi's (ibid.) 7a2 form, ten blades and blade-like flakes, and two core-related flakes, whilst gully 2356 (context 2355) contained a total of 158 worked pieces with cores, bladelets and two microliths of Jacobi's (ibid.) Type 5c and 6 present. The narrowness of the flake scars on the cores, along with the predominantly blade and narrow flakes present suggests a late Mesolithic date for this material, which is supported by a radiocarbon date (NZA 32689) of 5220–4850 cal BC (95.4% confidence; or 5210-4940 cal BC, 68.2% confidence) from gully 2196.

Post-Mesolithic worked flint from Junction 9 includes a late Neolithic chisel arrowhead (Fig. 7.1.1) recovered from context 2103 in pit 2104. Pit 2108 (context 2107) contained a total of 84 flints including two multi-platform cores, which are probably later Neolithic in date, and six multi-platform cores were among the 69 worked flints from pit 2384 (context 2385), which also contained pottery. Pit 2052 contained a total of 204 worked flints, as well as 152 burnt unworked pieces. This material was predominantly waste flakes, but 11 scrapers (Fig. 7.1.2-12) were also recovered, as well as four retouched flakes and a core. The broad nature of many of the flakes from this pit and the presence of end and side scrapers suggests a late Neolithic date for the feature, as the material is in fresh condition and does not appear to have been redeposited. This is supported by a radiocarbon date (NZA 32683) of 2620-2340 cal BC (95.4% confi-

dence; or 2570-2460 cal BC, 68.2% confidence) obtained from this pit.

Pit 2189 (context 2190) contained a total of 93 flints, predominantly flakes and chips which were not diagnostic. A further 26 pits contained between one and 85 pieces of flint and of these a total of 11 contained less than ten pieces; five between 11 and 20; four between 21 and 30; and nine between 31 and 85. None of this material is particularly diagnostic and only in one instance (pit 2386) does it occur with pottery (Table 7.2)

**Discussion**

The material from the M1 widening scheme is dominated by undiagnostic waste flakes and chips, with very few formal tools and cores present. The majority of the material is residual within later features, although a small proportion of the material appears to be *in situ*. Most significant is the flint recovered from a series of pits at Junction 9.

The flint from the pits at Junction 9 is dominated by waste flakes and chips and there is a lack of cores and almost complete absence of formal tools. The large amount of waste, and the presence of tested nodules and some heat-treated flint, suggest that this material represents the by-products of flint-knapping episodes and may indicate that the tools produced, and the cores from which they were struck, were removed from the site for use elsewhere. The number of pits, and their distribution, is suggestive of repeated visits to the site during which time the waste from knapping episodes was incorporated into the fills of pits alongside other material such as hazelnut shells and charcoal. The radiocarbon dating programme (see Chapter 9) indicates that this activity may have

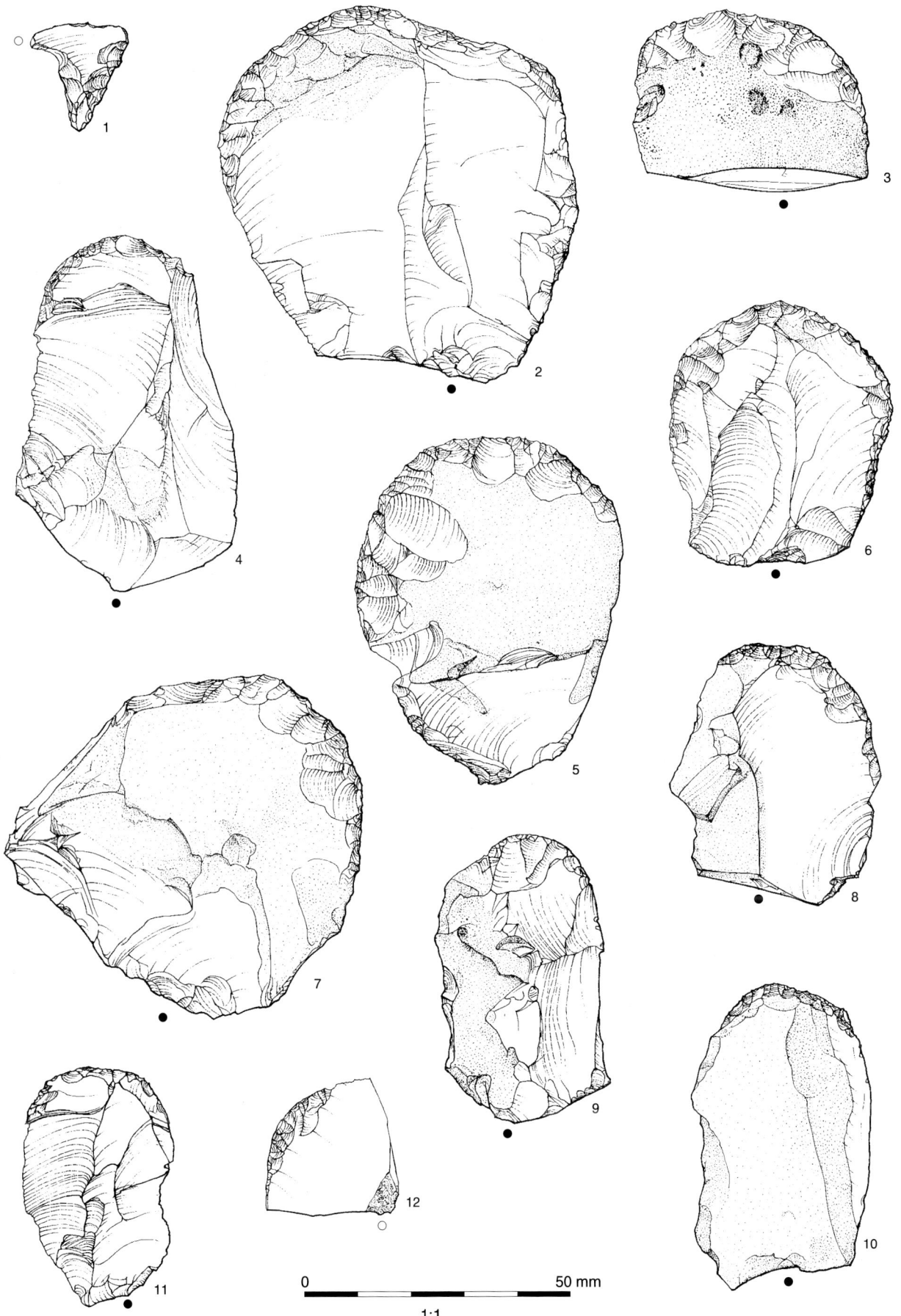

Fig. 7.1   The flint

taken place over a relatively short period of time, potentially less than 100 years, and probably represents several discrete episodes of activity. This is supported by the limited range of materials recovered from within the pits, including a chronologically restricted set of microliths, but it is difficult to find a mechanism which explains why some pits were filled with large numbers of waste flakes, whilst others contained very few (Table 7.2). It is unlikely that this is the result of truncation, as some of the deeper pits on the site contained the least numbers of worked flint (Table 7.2), and it may be that there is an element of selection, although it is not possible to understand the criteria by which pits which received the greatest amount of material were chosen.

The microliths from Junction 9 are predominantly scalene microtriangles of type 7a2 (Jacobi 1978), although types 5 and 6 microliths are also present. This style of microlith was utilised towards the end of the Mesolithic, probably forming part of composite tools (ibid.). Sites containing microliths alongside large assemblages of flakes and blades are known from Stratford's Yard, Chesham (Stainton 1989) and the Colne Valley (Lacaille 1963), but whilst these are late Mesolithic narrow-blade assemblages, they contain very few microtriangles. The assemblages from these sites are markedly different from those on the M1 widening and contain microburins, which are not recorded in the M1 assemblage, scrapers and tranchet axes. It is tempting to see these sites as representing the by-products of longer-term activity, in contrast to the sorter-term repeated visits to what is now Junction 9. The assemblage of flakes and microliths from the M1 can also be paralleled at two sites in Somerset, where similar assemblages were recovered from pits. At Blackmoor, Charterhouse (Lewis 2007), an assemblage of waste flakes, blades and a small number of cores was recovered from a 0.5m-deep pit or posthole. At Langleys Lane, Midsomer Norton, a series of pits containing flakes, blades and microliths, as well as a small assemblage of animal bone and charcoal, was associated with what appears to be a spring, sealed by a layer of tufa (J Lewis and R Davies pers. comm.). Although, at the moment, no radiocarbon dates are available from these sites, the similarity of the lithic assemblages and their circumstances of deposition, have strong parallels with the material from the M1.

Other Mesolithic flint has been recovered from the local area at Chalton and Caddington, to the north of Junction 9, and Meoslithic artefact scatters from the region tend to be focussed on river valleys such as the Colne, Misbourne, Chess, Ver and Lea (Holgate 1995b). The Junction 9 site is close to the headwaters of the Ver, in a valley side location, which fits well with this pattern. Mesolithic material has been recovered from further down the valley at Redbourn and Friar's Wash and from the Park Street Roman Villa, leading Holgate (ibid., 9)

to suggest that the entire valley was exploited for its wild resources during the later Mesolithic. The material from the majority of these sites is, however, unpublished and it is not possible to offer a comparison of the assemblages from these sites with those recovered during the M1 widening scheme.

The small amount of flint from Junction 8S includes blades, blade-like flakes and a single-platform core, which are diagnostically late Mesolithic/early Neolithic in date. The radiocarbon date (NZA-32714) of 3800-3640 cal BC (95.4% confidence; or 3760-3650 cal BC, 68.2% confidence) from pit 5081 places this assemblage in the early Neolithic, but the flint assemblage is relatively small and does not offer enough data to enable any significant typological or technological differences to be identified between the late Mesolithic assemblage from Junction 9 and that from Junction 8S. A further five pits at Junction 8S (5064, 5088, 5096, 5172 and 5226) contain typologically Neolithic to early Bronze Age flint, but these cannot be assigned a narrower range within this time span.

A total of four pits at Junction 9 can be assigned a date in the late Neolithic and the radiocarbon date from pit 2052 confirms the typological dating of the flint. Although the worked flint from the pit is fairly typical of the period, the number of scrapers (predominantly side scrapers) is noteworthy. Similar pits containing later Neolithic material including Grooved Ware and animal bone have been recorded at Puddlehill, Bedfordshire and Letchworth, Hertfordshire (ibid.), and surface scatters of Neolithic to Bronze Age flintwork are known from the Dunstable/Luton area of south Bedfordshire (Hudspith 1995). However, these remain unpublished and it is not possible to make any comparisons between these sites and the material recovered during the M1 widening scheme excavations. The presence of late Neolithic pits so close to those of Mesolithic date at Junction 9 is interesting, but activity at this site appears to be separated by a period of over two thousand years (see Chapter 9). Nevertheless, the occurrence of Neolithic sites close to those of Mesolithic date can be observed at Stonehenge and other sites in southern Britain (Allen and Gardiner 2002), but the reasons for the apparent monumentalisation of areas previously exploited in the Mesolithic is not clear. This process did not happen at the Junction 9 site and there is clearly no causal relationship between the presence of Mesolithic pits and Neolithic monuments. The tradition of deposition of selected assemblages of material culture, including worked flint, within pits has been discussed at length by Thomas (1999) who considers it to be a way of formally drawing attention to specific parts of the landscape. The material recovered from Junction 9 suggests that this tradition may have a longer history than previously anticipated.

**THE PREHISTORIC POTTERY** *by Leo Webley and Lisa Brown*

## Introduction

Prehistoric ceramics predating the late Iron Age were found during the evaluation and mitigation fieldwork at seven of the M1 sites: Buncefield Depot; Junction 8S; Junction 8N; The Aubreys; Area M; Junction 9; and Junction 10. The assemblage comprises 988 sherds, weighing 4373g. Most of the material dates to between the late Bronze Age and the middle Iron Age, but sherds of possible late Neolithic date were found at The Aubreys.

## Methodology

The pottery was recorded following the guidelines of the Prehistoric Ceramics Research Group (PCRG 1997). Data entered onto a MS Access database included quantification by sherd number and weight, fabrics (based on principal inclusion type), form, surface finish and decoration. No carbonised organic residues, soot or limescale were observed, probably due in part to the generally poor condition of the assemblage.

## Condition

With an overall mean sherd weight of only 4.4g, the condition of the assemblage is poor and many sherds are abraded or have missing surfaces. The few large sherds were all recovered from pits in the Buncefield Depot and Junction 8S sites, and a selection of these are illustrated (Fig. 7.2).

## Fabrics

The pottery has been ascribed to 12 broad fabric groups, described in Table 7.6. The majority of the assemblage contains calcined (burnt) flint inclusions. As the underlying geology of the M1 widening footprint is frequently flinty Carstens series clayey soils, this group of fabrics could have been produced from entirely locally derived raw materials. A smaller proportion of sandy wares was also present, and a near negligible number of sherds with shell inclusions (11 sherds) from Area M could have been manufactured from shelly Oxford Clays located some 10-15km to the north of the site. A fabric group with organic inclusions preserved as flat vesicles indicates a practice of deliberate combining of vegetable matter, possibly in the form of manure, with potting clay to improve plasticity and/or firing.

The distribution of fabrics by sherd count and weight within each site is presented in Table 7.7.

## Site assemblages

The pottery is described within site groups. Some identifications are tentative, given the poor condition of much of the material, and the fact that few local or near-regional prehistoric assemblages are currently available for comparison.

### Buncefield Depot

Buncefield Depot produced 301 sherds (2042g), all of which can be placed in the post-Deverel-Rimbury tradition of the late Bronze Age/early Iron Age (Barrett 1980). Most of the material is flint tempered, with some sandy and vegetable-tempered sherds also present. A number of diagnostic vessel fragments were recovered from pit 516 and associated spread 521/522. Fill 519 of the pit contained: part of a round-shouldered bowl or jar with a slightly everted rim; an everted rim from a vessel decorated with fingernail impressions on its neck; sherds of a further coarse vessel decorated with fingertip impressions (Fig. 7.2.1-2); and a body sherd from a fine, carinated bowl. Layer 521 produced part of a fine, bipartite 'furrowed' bowl with an upright rim and a fragment of a fine,

*Table 7.6: Prehistoric pottery fabric descriptions*

| Fabric | | Description |
|---|---|---|
| A1 | Fine sandy | Moderate to abundant quartz sand < 0.5mm; rare iron oxide < 2mm visible in some sherds |
| A2 | Coarse sandy | Moderate to abundant quartz sand < 1mm; rare iron oxide < 2mm visible in some sherds |
| AF1 | Sand and fine flint | Moderate to abundant quartz sand < 1mm; sparse calcined flint < 1mm |
| AF2 | Sand and coarse flint | Moderate to abundant quartz sand < 1mm; sparse, poorly sorted calcined flint < 5mm |
| AL1 | Sand and limestone | Moderate quartz sand < 0.5mm; rare limestone < 5mm, rare flint < 5mm, rare iron oxide < 2mm |
| F1 | Fine flint | Moderate calcined flint < 1mm; sparse quartz sand < 0.5mm |
| F2 | Coarse flint | Moderate calcined flint < 5mm; sparse quartz sand < 0.5mm |
| F3 | Coarse, poorly sorted flint | Moderate, poorly sorted calcined flint < 8mm; sparse quartz sand < 0.5 mm. Hard |
| S1 | Fine shell | Moderate shell < 1mm; sparse quartz sand < 0.5mm; sparse iron oxide < 1mm. Soapy feel |
| V1 | Vegetable inclusions | Moderate to abundant flat voids from vegetable inclusions < 5mm |
| VA1 | Vegetable inclusions and sand | Moderate flat voids from vegetable inclusions < 5mm; moderate quartz sand < 0.5mm; rare, poorly sorted flint < 5mm; rare calcareous inclusions < 1mm. Friable |
| VA2 | Vegetable inclusions and sand | Moderate flat voids from vegetable inclusions < 5mm; moderate sand < 0.5mm. Hard |

*Table 7.7: Quantification of prehistoric pottery fabrics (sherd count and weight) by site*

| | Buncefield Depot | Junction 8S | Junction 8N | The Aubreys | Area M | Junction 9 | Junction 10 |
|---|---|---|---|---|---|---|---|
| A1 | 13 (70g) | 229 (310g) | 42 (107g) | | 3 (8g) | 23 (157g) | |
| A2 | | | 5 (12g) | | 11 (45g) | | |
| AF1 | 144 (943g) | 6 (27g) | | | 1 (2g) | 1 (2g) | |
| AF2 | | | 2 (18g) | | 2 (7g) | 7 (57g) | |
| AL1 | | | | | | | 1 (5g) |
| F1 | 85 (376g) | 52 (166g) | 14 (43g) | | 2 (6g) | 21 (23g) | |
| F2 | 42 (507g) | 212 (1166g) | 10 (58g) | | 2 (7g) | 9 (18g) | |
| F3 | | | | 8 (20g) | | | |
| S1 | | | | | 11 (20g) | | |
| V1 | 1 (7g) | 3 (12g) | 1 (1g) | | 2 (3g) | | |
| VA1 | 16 (139g) | | | | | | |
| VA2 | | | 7 (31g) | | | | |
| Total | 301 (2042g) | 502 (1681g) | 81 (270g) | 8 (20g) | 34 (98g) | 61 (257g) | 1 (5g) |

burnished, carinated bowl with a flaring rim (Fig. 7.2.3-4). Layer 522 contained a fine sandy sherd decorated with two incised lines and two impressed dots inlaid with white paste (not illustrated).

Elsewhere, pit 532 (fill 533) contained a large group of sherds (1037g), most of which belonged to a single coarse vessel; a shouldered jar decorated with fingertip impressions on its shoulder. The vessel forms and types of decoration seen at this site indicate a date in the early Iron Age (*c* 800-400 cal BC) and possibly in the earlier part of this period.

### Junction 8S

Junction 8S produced 502 sherds (1681g) of prehistoric pottery. Most of the material is in flint-tempered fabrics and can be broadly dated to the late Bronze Age/early Iron Age. In most cases, only small undiagnostic sherds were recovered.

Eight small, shallow pits (5234, 5236, 5441, 5446, 5448, 5461, 5465 and 5474) within a group (7785) of ten, together produced a small collection of 78 sherds with a mean sherd weight of under 6g. Although the features were not strictly contemporary, as some were inter-cutting, all except pit 5236 produced flint-tempered fabrics consistent with a late Bronze Age/early Iron Age date. Pit 5465 (fill 5464) produced a single large fragment from a round-bodied jar with a slightly everted rim (Fig. 7.2.5). Pit 5236, which contained only sandy wares (fabric A1) may be a middle Iron Age feature, but cannot be more precisely dated due to the absence of featured sherds.

A second concentration of eight shallow pits (7786) and two features interpreted as tree-throw holes (5345 and 5433) occupied the central part of this site. Of this group, the single fills of pits 5021, 5023, 5106 and 5424 produced a total of 338 sherds (924g) of prehistoric pottery, most of it flint-tempered material of late Bronze Age or early Iron Age type. Pit 5023 (fill 5024) contained the largest group (130 sherds; 650g), most belonging to a single

vessel. Although this vessel is too fragmented and incomplete to be reconstructed, it was probably a jar with a flaring rim. In addition to the flint-tempered sherds, a few contexts (notably fill 5107 of pit 5106) contained sandy sherds. These, like the material from pit 5236, may be of middle Iron Age date.

Posthole 5192 (fill 5193) contained a T-shaped rim, probably from a late Bronze Age/early Iron Age jar (Fig. 7.2.6). Jars with T-shaped rims are often associated with early Iron Age assemblages, an example from pit 1013 at Buncefield Lane (see above) being a case in point. However, the complete absence of decoration in the Junction 8S assemblage suggests that it may have an earlier emphasis than that from Buncefield Depot, perhaps falling within the post-Deverel-Rimbury plain-ware tradition of *c* 1150–800 cal BC.

### Junction 8N

Junction 8N produced 81 sherds (270g) of prehistoric pottery. A number of flint-tempered sherds can be broadly dated to the late Bronze Age/early Iron Age. Most of these are very small and abraded, and much of the material was residual within late Iron Age and early Roman ditch fills. The one notable exception is a large fragment of a shouldered jar with an upright flat-topped rim from fill 6196 of posthole 6195 (Fig. 7.2.7). All of the pottery is undecorated except for a residual body sherd from context 6417 which had fingertip impressions.

Middle Iron Age activity is represented by a small number of undecorated sherds in sandy and vegetable-tempered fabrics. Of three rim fragments, at least one, from fill 6783 of pit 6782, derives from a slack-shouldered jar (Fig. 7.2.8).

### The Aubreys

Pits 207 (fill 206) and 218 (fill 213) produced eight sherds (20g) of pottery in a fabric with poorly sorted flint inclusions. These are early prehistoric, possibly

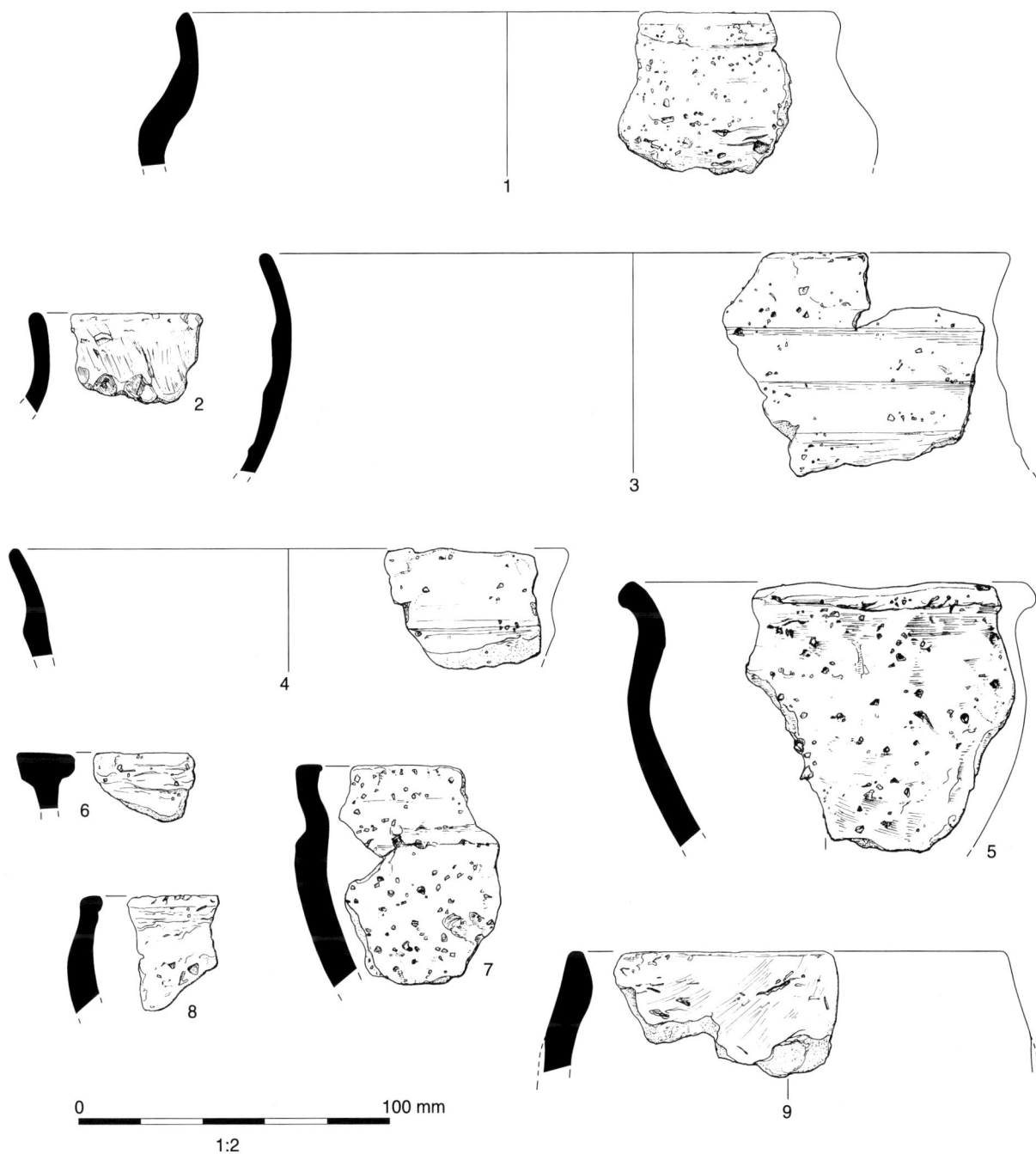

*Fig. 7.2  Prehistoric pottery*

dating to the late Neolithic or early Bronze Age, which would be consistent with the occurrence of numerous flints of that date recovered from locations across the scheme (see above).

### Area M

Area M produced 34 sherds (98g) of prehistoric pottery. The material is highly fragmented, and dating is difficult. A few flint-tempered sherds, likely to be of late Bronze Age/early Iron Age date, include a small fragment of a flat-topped rim; however, an early prehistoric attribution for some of the flint-tempered material cannot be ruled out. Some sandy sherds might date to the middle Iron Age, although again no featured sherds were present. Eleven sherds from ditch 3008 (fills 3009 and 3017) are in a fabric containing fine shell inclusions, which is not paralleled elsewhere in the M1 investigations; an Iron Age date can be tentatively suggested for these.

### Junction 9

Junction 9 produced 61 sherds (257g) of prehistoric pottery. A few very small fragments of flint-

101

tempered pottery are likely to date to the late Bronze Age/early Iron Age, though they could be residual. More clearly represented are middle Iron Age sherds in sandy fabrics, including rim sherds from a slack-shouldered bowl or jar from pit 2108 (fill 2107) (Fig. 7.2.9). Two sherds in fabric S1 from ditch 2047 (fill 2138) belong to an ovoid jar with an upright rounded rim and horizontal combing or scoring on the body. This has been dated to the middle or, more likely, late Iron Age as the sherds were found in association with grog-tempered late Iron Age pottery.

A radiocarbon date (NZA-32692) of 5220-4930 cal BC (95.4% confidence; or 5210-4990 cal BC, 68.2% confidence) was obtained on a charred hazelnut shell from pit 2316 (context 2317); pottery fragments in this deposit, weighing 10g must have been intrusive. The pottery is a coarse flint-tempered ware (F2), which corresponds with late Bronze Age/early Iron Age vessel forms elsewhere on the site.

### Junction 10

Posthole 1009 produced a single residual sherd weighing only 5g, in a fabric containing coarse limestone and iron-oxide inclusions not paralleled elsewhere in the M1 investigations. The date of this is unclear, though it could be Iron Age.

## Discussion

The prehistoric pottery assemblages from the M1 sites are small and poorly preserved. Nevertheless, given the scarcity of late Bronze Age to middle Iron Age assemblages elsewhere in Hertfordshire, and especially south of the Chiltern ridge, the material represents a useful addition to the existing local ceramic record. The pottery from Buncefield Depot is of particular interest as it includes a number of distinctive early Iron Age vessel forms.

### Distribution and provenance

The bulk of the prehistoric pottery from all of the sites came from over 30 pits located at The Aubreys, Buncefield Depot, Junction 8S, Junction 8N and Junction 9. Pits are a common catchment for material on prehistoric sites. Most of the pits, however, contained fewer than 20 sherds (and generally under eight). The exceptions were pit 532 at Buncefield Depot (130 sherds; 1037g) and pits 5023 (130 sherds; 625g) and 5106 (168 sherds; 223g) at Junction 8S. In all three cases, these sherd groups almost certainly represented fragments of single vessels, as they were in identical fabrics with some visible joins. Since the vessels from pit 532 and pit 5023 were early Iron Age, and that from pit 5106 more probably middle Iron Age, however, no particular pattern of chronologically significant deposition practice seems apparent. In fact, since these larger vessel fractions are highly fragmented, they may have entered their respective pits by much the

same means as the rest of the pottery. Accidental inclusion in a deliberate backfill of occupation-rich soils (such as a midden) is one possibility.

Much of the rest of the prehistoric pottery was residual in the fills of ditches in Area M and Junction 8N. Several postholes (most at Junction 8S and Junction 8N) and irregular hollows, recorded as tree-throw holes (eight of the latter located at Junction 8S), accounted for the remainder.

### Regional affinities

Knowledge of later prehistoric ceramic development in south Hertfordshire prior to the late Iron Age ('Belgic') horizon is currently limited. However, the assemblage from pit 532 at Buncefield Depot could be broadly contemporary with the group from pit 1013 at nearby Buncefield Lane, Hemel Hempstead, which included a shouldered jar, a fine carinated bowl and a fine hemispherical bowl decorated with incised lines, associated with a radiocarbon date of 810-515 cal BC (McDonald 2003). Somewhat further afield, Ivinghoe Beacon, some 15km to the west of the M1 on the Chiltern Hills of Buckinghamshire, represents a type-site for pottery dating to the 8th-6th centuries cal BC. The range of ceramics collected here during excavations carried out in the 1960s includes coarsely made hemispherical bowls and shouldered jars with finger-impressed decoration (Cotton and Frere 1968). Small, isolated groups of similar, but unpublished material, are known from Hawthorn Hill, near Letchworth and Bedfordshire sites at Kempton, Sandy and Totternhoe (Cunliffe 2005, 97).

Pottery recovered from Great Wymondley, near Letchworth in the 1930s represents a slightly later ceramic development (5th-3rd centuries cal BC) that includes carinated bowls with flaring rims associated with shouldered jars (Tebbutt 1932). Similar early Iron Age bowls have also been recovered from Puddlehill, Bedfordshire (Matthews 1976). These assemblages, however, include bowls with incised or scratched zigzag decoration of a type not present in the M1 assemblage, which suggests either stylistic or chronological disparity between the assemblages.

## Catalogue of illustrated sherds

1    Buncefield Depot: shouldered jar/bowl, early Iron Age. Ctx 519
2    Buncefield Depot: rim with fingernail impressions on neck, early Iron Age. Ctx 519
3    Buncefield Depot: bipartite furrowed bowl, early Iron Age. Ctx 521
4    Buncefield Depot: carinated flared-rim bowl, early Iron Age. Ctx 521
5    Junction 8S: round-bodied jar, late Bronze Age/early Iron Age. Ctx 5464
6    Junction 8S: T-shaped rim, late Bronze Age/early Iron Age. Ctx 5193
7    Junction 8N: shouldered jar, late Bronze Age/early Iron Age. Ctx 6196

8    Junction 8N: slack-shouldered jar, middle Iron Age. Ctx 6783

9    Junction 9: slack-shouldered bowl/jar, middle Iron Age. Ctx 2107

## THE LATE IRON AGE AND ROMAN POTTERY
*by Dan Stansbie*

### Introduction and Methodology

Late Iron Age and Roman pottery was recovered during the evaluation and mitigation stages of the excavations. The material from the evaluation is discussed as a block, while the assemblages from the mitigation phases of the work, including the watching briefs, are discussed individually (see below).  Six sites within the mitigation phase (Junction 8N, Junction 9, Junction 10, Area M, Area P and The Aubreys) produced assemblages of late Iron Age and Roman date. Overall 12,059 sherds weighing 100kg were recovered. The material was fully recorded on a MS Access database and fabrics were identified using codes based on the national Roman pottery fabric reference collection (Tomber and Dore 1998) and used by Lyne (1999) in his report on the pottery from Folly Lane, Verulamium. However, where a fabric was not covered by either of these systems the OA standard recording system for Iron Age and Roman fabrics was used (Booth 2007). Where necessary, the pottery was examined under a binocular microscope at x20 magnification to aid in identification of the fabric. Reference was also made to: the City of London corpus (Davies *et al.* 1994); Hawkes and Hull's (1947) report on the pottery from Camulodunum and Thompson's (1982) corpus (for 'Belgic' forms); Going's (1987) report on the pottery from Chelmsford; and Young's (1977) corpus of the Oxfordshire industry. Vessel form typology follows the OA standard recording system and where relevant reference is made to regional and international corpora. The OA recording system divides vessels into 13 classes: A-amphorae; B-flagons/jugs; C-jars; D-jar/bowls; E-beakers; F-cups; G-tankards and mugs; H-bowls; I-bowls/dishes; J-dishes and platters; K-mortaria; L-lids; and M-miscellaneous. The pottery was divided into four ceramic phases: late Iron Age-early Roman (50 BC-AD 70); early Roman (AD 43-120); middle Roman (AD 120-250); and late Roman (AD 250-410). In the following report pottery described as being of a particular ceramic phase will have derived from a context or contexts assigned to that phase on both ceramic and other criteria. Such groups frequently contained redeposited material of earlier date which is included in the phase group statistics.

### Condition

An average sherd weight of 8g suggests that the condition of the pottery was poor. However, this figure is influenced by large amounts of very abraded residual material within the assemblage and belies the presence of a substantial number of well-preserved groups.

### Pottery from the evaluation (Table 7.8)

Late Iron Age and Roman pottery from the evaluation comprises 498 sherds, weighing 4606g. With an average sherd weight of 9g the pottery is generally in moderate condition, although there are some large well-preserved groups of sherds and some groups were heavily abraded. The material from the evaluation is dominated by pottery of broad Roman date, which accounts for 46% by weight. This is supplemented by late Iron Age-early Roman pottery, which accounts for 18% by weight and early Roman pottery, which also takes an 18% share. The remainder of the assemblage comprises middle Roman pottery at 11% by weight and late Roman pottery at 7% by weight.

The late Iron Age-early Roman assemblage is composed largely of body sherds of grog-tempered ware (GROG), with several jars, including a high-shouldered jar, and a necked bowl also present. In addition, there is a butt-beaker in 'Belgic' sandy ware. The early Roman assemblage is also dominated by body sherds of grog-tempered ware, with a single grog-tempered jar. This is supplemented by a bead-rimmed jar in unsourced reduced coarse ware (UNSREC), a medium-mouthed jar in shelly ware and body sherds in 'Belgic' sandy ware

*Table 7.8: Evaluation. Late Iron Age and Roman pottery*

| Fabric | Nosh | % Nosh | Weight (g) | % Weight |
|---|---|---|---|---|
| BATAM | 1 | <1 | 122 | 2.6 |
| CGSA | 1 | <1 | 2 | <1 |
| E30 'Belgic' sandy fabrics | 28 | 5.6 | 196 | 4.2 |
| E40  shell-tempered fabrics | 5 | <1 | 19 | <1 |
| GROG | 264 | 52.6 | 1794 | 38.2 |
| HARSH | 25 | 5 | 295 | 6.4 |
| HADOX | 1 | <1 | 2 | <1 |
| HGWREC | 2 | <1 | 12 | <1 |
| LCVRE3 | 5 | 1 | 12 | <1 |
| LNVCC | 1 | <1 | 1 | <1 |
| MISC | 2 | <1 | 2 | <1 |
| OXFRS | 3 | <1 | 48 | 1 |
| OXFRSM | 3 | <1 | 6 | <1 |
| PNKGT | 9 | 1.8 | 610 | 13.2 |
| R90 coarse tempered fabrics | 4 | <1 | 76 | 1.6 |
| SGSA | 2 | <1 | 24 | <1 |
| UNSOX | 14 | 2.8 | 186 | 4 |
| UNSOXC | 36 | 7.2 | 181 | 3.9 |
| UNSBB | 10 | 2 | 118 | 2.5 |
| UNSREC | 46 | 9.2 | 603 | 13 |
| UNSREF | 12 | 2.4 | 55 | 1 |
| VERWH | 24 | 4.8 | 242 | 5.2 |
| Total | 498 | 100 | 4606 | 100 |

(E30). Furthermore, there is a single sherd of Dressel 20 amphora (BATAM) and a form 15/17 dish in South Gaulish samian ware (SGSA).

The bulk of the middle Roman assemblage comprises unsourced reduced coarse ware (UNSREC) and Verulamium-region white ware (VERWH), with a single medium-mouthed jar in the former and a reeded-rim bowl in the later. In addition, there is a reeded-rim bowl in unsourced oxidised ware, a jar in Highgate Wood C ware (HGWREC) and a single body sherd of lower Nene Valley colour-coated ware (LNVCC).

The late Roman assemblage was small and was not dominated by any individual fabric, although Harrold shelly ware (HARSH) is most common with 16 sherds belonging to a medium-mouthed jar. This is supplemented by a bowl in Oxfordshire colour-coated ware (OXFRS) and body sherds of Oxfordshire white-ware mortaria (OXFWHM), pink grogged ware (PNKGT) and Central Gaulish samian ware (CGSA). Like the late Roman material, pottery that can only be assigned a broad Roman date range is not dominated by any individual fabric. Unsourced reduced coarse ware (UNSREC) is prominent, however, with several jars including lid-seated and medium-mouthed types, and this is supplemented by body sherds and medium-mouthed jars in Harrold shelly ware (HARSH) and a flagon and a jar in Verulamium-region white ware (VERWH). Moreover, there are body sherds of Highgate Wood C (HGWREC), pink grogged ware (PNKGT) and Hadham oxidised ware (HADOX).

**Pottery from Junction 9** (Table 7.9)

In total 4936 sherds of late Iron Age and Roman pottery, weighing 54kg were recovered from Junction 9. With an average sherd weight of 11g the pottery is in moderate condition, although some groups are particularly well preserved and a number of sherds are clearly residual, being heavily abraded. The assemblage from Junction 9 is dominated by material from contexts of early Roman date, which accounted for 60% of the assemblage by weight. This is supplemented by smaller amounts of late Iron Age-early Roman pottery at 10% by weight, middle Roman pottery at 17% by weight and late Roman pottery at 11% by weight. The remaining 2% are accounted for by material that can only be assigned a broadly Roman date range.

The late Iron Age-early Roman assemblage is overwhelmingly dominated by grog-tempered wares (GROG), with vessels in this fabric largely being made up of medium-mouthed jars, supplemented by several high-shouldered jars, a lid-seated jar and a storage jar. Also present are a carinated bowl and several lids. The grog-tempered material is supplemented by shelly fabrics (E40), 'Belgic' sandy fabrics (E30), in which there is a butt-beaker and a single sherd of flint-tempered material (E60).

The early Roman assemblage consists of a more diverse range of fabrics, although it is still largely

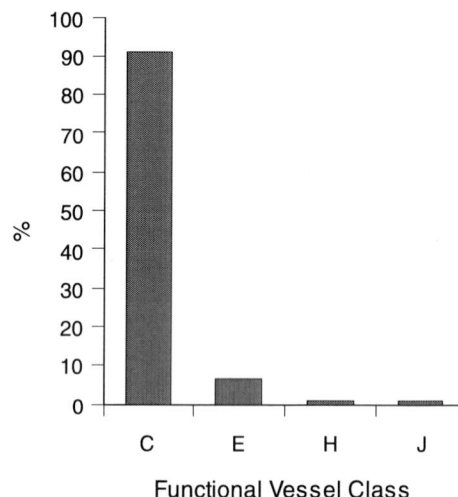

*Fig. 7.3   Late Iron Age-early Roman functional vessel class (%)*

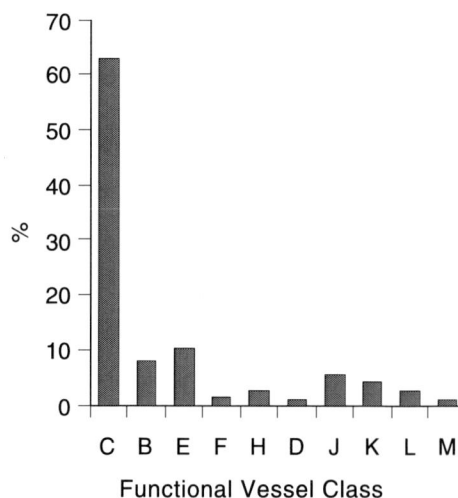

*Fig. 7.4   Early Roman functional vessel class (%)*

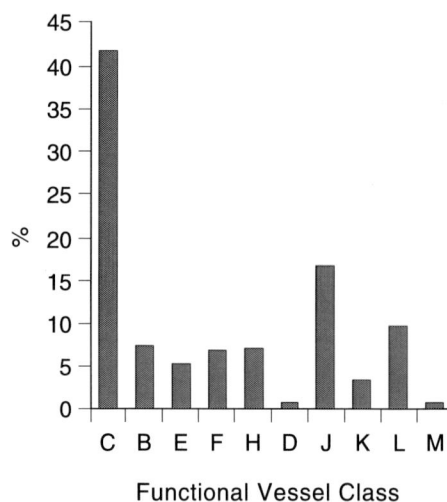

*Fig. 7.5   Middle Roman functional vessel class (%)*

dominated by grog-tempered wares, which account for 63% by weight (much of this material is likely to be residual). Vessels in grog-tempered ware largely comprise high-shouldered and medium-mouthed jars, with some lid-seated and bead-rimmed examples. In addition, there are grog-tempered butt-beakers, carinated bowls, a globular bowl and a platter. No other fabrics are present in such substantial amounts within the early Roman assemblage, although pink grogged wares (PNKGT), unsourced reduced coarse wares (UNSREC) and Verulamium-region white wares are the next most common fabric types at 7%, 6% and 5% by weight, respectively. Reduced-ware vessels also largely comprise medium-mouthed jars, although other types, including lid-seated vessels, are also present and the jars are supplemented by beakers (including poppy-head beakers), bowls and platters. The Verulamium-region white wares include ring-necked flagons, medium-mouthed and neckless jars and reeded-rim bowls. The only vessels present in pink grogged

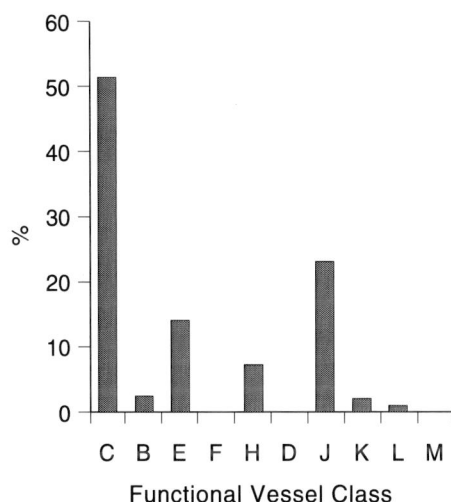

Fig. 7.6  Late Roman functional vessel class (%)

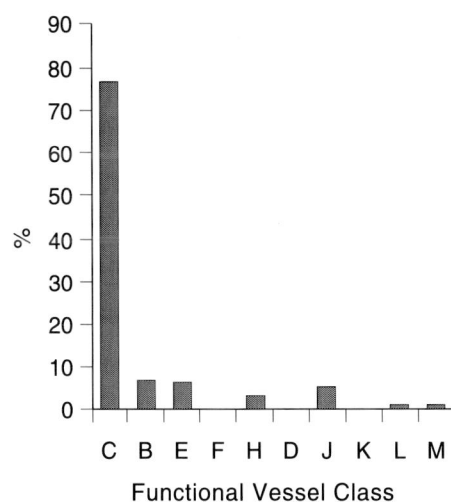

Fig. 7.7  Roman functional vessel class (%)

ware are storage jars. There is a small amount of samian ware, all from South Gaulish (SGSA) production centres, consisting of forms 18 and 18/31dishes, forms 27, 33, 24/25 and 35 cups, and a form 37 bowl. The remaining fabrics in the early Roman assemblage are all present in small amounts of less than 5% by weight (Table 7.9). Notable among these fabrics are body sherds of Dressel 20 (BATAM) and Gallic (GALAM) amphorae, a flanged bowl in local mica-dusted ware, a platter (CAM16) in *terra nigra* (GABTN), body sherds of North Gaulish white ware (NOGWH), body sherds and a storage jar in Harold shelly ware (HARSH) and body sherds of Highgate Wood C ware (HGWREC).

The middle Roman assemblage comprises a diverse range of fabrics, none of which really dominate. The most common of these are again unsourced reduced coarse wares and Verulamium-region white wares, which together account for 40% of the assemblage by weight. Vessels in these fabrics largely consist of jars, including medium-mouthed, wide-mouthed and neckless varieties, with several reeded-rim bowls in Verulamium-region white ware. The small amount of samian ware mostly came from Central (CGSA) and South Gaulish (SGSA) production centres, with a very small amount (less than 1% by weight) of East Gaulish (EGSA) material. Vessels in these fabrics include: form 18/31 dishes; forms 27, 33 and 35 cups; a form 36 dish; and a form 37 bowl. Apart from pink grogged ware (PNKGT), Verulamium-region white-ware mortaria (VERWHM) and unsourced black-burnished wares (UNSBB), the remaining fabrics are all present in small amounts of less than 5%. These fabrics include body sherds of Hadam oxidised wares (HADOX) and Hadham oxidised white-slipped wares (HADWS), along with plain-rimmed dishes, a bead-rimmed dish and a cooking jar in black-burnished ware (BB1), and several jars in Harold shelly wares (HARSH).

Like the middle Roman assemblage, the late Roman pottery is not dominated by a particular fabric, although unsourced reduced wares are most common at 27% by weight, with vessels in this fabric largely consisting of jars, including medium- and wide-mouthed types and cooking jars, supplemented by flanged- and bead-rimmed dishes. Body sherds and jars in unsourced black-burnished wares (UNSBB) are next most common at 8% by weight. These are supplemented by small quantities of regional imports and specialist wares, including: body sherds; a plain-rimmed dish and a flanged dish in black-burnished ware (BB1); body sherds of Dressel 20 and Gallic amphorae (BATAM and GALAM); body sherds and a jar in Harold shelly ware (HARSH); body sherds, a flagon and a bowl/jar in Hadham oxidised ware (HADOX); body sherds and a triangular-rimmed dish in lower Nene Valley colour-coated wares (LNVCC); and a variety of Oxfordshire products including bowls in Oxfordshire colour-coated ware (OXFRS) and a bowl in Oxfordshire parchment ware (OXFPA).

*Table 7.9: Junction 9. Late Iron Age and Roman pottery*

| Fabric | Nosh | % Nosh | Weight (g) | % Weight |
|---|---|---|---|---|
| BATAM | 28 | <1 | 1439 | 2.6 |
| BB1 | 27 | <1 | 408 | <1 |
| CGSA | 13 | <1 | 61 | <1 |
| COLWH | 25 | <1 | 76 | <1 |
| COLCC | 6 | <1 | 17 | <1 |
| E20 'Belgic' fine sandy fabrics | 1 | <1 | 19 | <1 |
| E30 'Belgic' coarse sandy fabrics | 21 | <1 | 55 | <1 |
| E40 shelly fabrics | 205 | 4 | 1676 | 3 |
| E60 | 1 | <1 | 5 | <1 |
| EGSA | 9 | <1 | 87 | <1 |
| GABTN | 3 | <1 | 66 | <1 |
| GALAM | 6 | <1 | 305 | <1 |
| GROG | 2068 | 42 | 27534 | 51 |
| HADOX | 55 | 1 | 433 | <1 |
| HADRE | 7 | <1 | 86 | <1 |
| HADREWS | 14 | <1 | 66 | <1 |
| HADWS | 2 | <1 | 12 | <1 |
| HARSH | 58 | 1 | 459 | <1 |
| HGWREC | 16 | <1 | 40 | <1 |
| LNVWH | 1 | <1 | 15 | <1 |
| LONMD | 4 | <1 | 7 | <1 |
| M23 Mancetter/Hartshill mortaria | 1 | <1 | 42 | <1 |
| MISC | 10 | <1 | 9 | <1 |
| NOGWH | 4 | <1 | 48 | <1 |
| O80 oxidised coarse tempered fabrics | 1 | <1 | 180 | <1 |
| OXFPA | 1 | <1 | 30 | <1 |
| OXFRS | 8 | <1 | 77 | <1 |
| OXFRSM | 1 | <1 | 8 | <1 |
| PNKGT | 212 | 4.2 | 3654 | 6.7 |
| Q20 white-slipped oxidised ware | 2 | <1 | 22 | <1 |
| Q30 white-slipped reduced ware | 24 | <1 | 184 | <1 |
| Q51 Upchurch white-slipped oxidised ware | 2 | <1 | 19 | <1 |
| ROBSH | 5 | <1 | 34 | <1 |
| SGSA | 64 | 1.2 | 170 | <1 |
| UNSBB | 227 | 4.5 | 2280 | 4 |
| UNSOXC | 149 | 3 | 792 | 1 |
| UNSOXF | 21 | <1 | 46 | <1 |
| UNSREC | 814 | 16 | 5602 | 10 |
| UNSREF | 82 | 1.6 | 336 | <1 |
| UNSWS | 5 | <1 | 12 | <1 |
| VERRE | 42 | <1 | 407 | <1 |
| VERWH | 564 | 11.4 | 3911 | 7.1 |
| VERWHM | 37 | <1 | 2237 | 4 |
| VERWS | 1 | <1 | 22 | <1 |
| W10 fine white fabrics | 9 | <1 | 18 | <1 |
| W20 sandy white fabrics | 15 | <1 | 40 | <1 |
| W41 south-east English white/buff fabrics | 3 | <1 | 50 | <1 |
| Total | 4936 | 100 | 54,443 | 100 |

Also present are Oxfordshire white-ware mortaria (OXFWHM) and body sherds of Colchester colour-coated ware (COLCC) and white ware (COLWH). Quantities of grog-tempered material (GROG), which represent 18% of the assemblage by weight, and Verulamium-region white ware at 4% by weight indicate high-levels of residuality within the assemblage. The remaining fabrics were all present in small quantities of less than 5% by weight (Table 7.9).

Pottery which can only be assigned a broadly Roman date range is largely made up of unsourced reduced fabrics, supplemented by unsourced oxidised fabrics, Verulamium-region white wares and grog-tempered wares. The remaining fabrics are all present in small quantities of less than 5% (Table 7.9).

**Pottery from Junction 9 watching brief** (Table 7.10)

A small group of nine sherds weighing 31g was recovered from a single context (ditch 609), during the watching brief on Junction 9. These were all early Roman in date, comprising two ring-necked flagons and some body sherds in Verulamium-region white ware (VERWH) and a jar in Hadham reduced ware (HADRE).

*Table 7.10: Junction 9 watching brief. Late Iron Age and Roman pottery*

| Fabric | Nosh | % Nosh | Weight (g) | % Weight |
|---|---|---|---|---|
| VERWH | 8 | 89 | 19 | 61 |
| HADRE | 1 | 11 | 12 | 39 |
| Total | 9 | 100 | 31 | 100 |

**Pottery from Junction 8N** (Table 7.11)

Late Iron Age and Roman pottery from Junction 8N totalled 5419 sherds, weighing 34kg. The pottery is generally in poor condition, having an average sherd weight of 6g, but some groups were well preserved, comprising large unabraded sherds, and much of the more abraded material is residual. The assemblage from Junction 8N is dominated by middle Roman material, which accounts for 39% of the assemblage by weight. This is supplemented by early Roman material at 24% and late Iron Age-early Roman material at 17%. The remainder of the assemblage is made up of late Roman pottery comprising 7% by weight and pottery of broadly Roman date at 12%. The remaining 1% represents undated material.

The late Iron Age-early Roman pottery is overwhelmingly dominated by grog-tempered wares (GROG), which comprise 96% of the assemblage by weight. Vessels in these fabrics are largely jars, including medium-mouthed, high-shouldered and bead-rimmed varieties, along with a storage jar and a pedestal jar. These are supplemented by a butt-beaker in North Gaulish white ware (NOGWH). The remaining fabrics include a sherd of Dressel 20 amphora (BATAM), sherds of shelly fabric and a sherd of unsourced reduced coarse ware (UNSERC).

The early Roman assemblage is likewise dominated by grog-tempered wares (GROG) at 48% by weight, but these are supplemented by unsourced reduced coarse wares (UNSERC), which account for 21% by weight. Vessels in these fabrics are mostly medium-mouthed jars, with occasional high-shouldered and lid-seated examples in grog-tempered ware. In addition to the grog-tempered wares and unsourced coarse reduced ware fabrics, neckless jars, bowls and ring-necked flagons in Verulamium-region white ware (VERWH) accounted for 13% of the assemblage by weight. The remaining fabrics are all present in small quantities of less than 5% (Table 7.11) and include: jars in local mica-dusted ware (LONMD); a storage jar in Harrold shelly ware (HARSH); body sherds in Upchurch fine reduced ware (UPCFR); body sherds from Dressel 20 amphorae (BATAM); and South Gaulish samian ware (SGSA). Vessels in South Gaulish samian ware largely comprised form 18 dishes, but these were supplemented by a form 36 dish, a form 27 cup and a form 24/25 cup.

The middle Roman assemblage is more diverse in terms of fabrics than either the late Iron Age-early Roman or early Roman assemblages, with a large component of residual grog-tempered material accounting for 24% by weight. Vessels in grog-tempered ware (GROG) consist exclusively of jars, including medium-mouthed and bead-rimmed types. The most common fabric after grog-tempered ware is unsourced reduced coarse ware (NUSREC) at 19% by weight, and this is supplemented by Verulamium-region white ware (VERWH), which accounts for 13% by weight. Vessels in unsourced coarse reduced ware consist largely of jars, including two cooking jars; these are complemented by a jar/bowl, several bowls, a platter, plain rimmed dishes and lids. The majority of vessels in Verulamium-region white ware are also jars or bowls, largely of the neckless variety. There is also a tazza, with finger impressions around the rim. Samian ware (accounting for around 3% of the assemblage by weight) largely consists of form 18 and 18/31 dishes from Central Gaulish (CGSA) production centres, supplemented by several cups including form 27s and a form 33, a form 37 bowl and a form 36 dish. In addition, there is a South Gaulish (SGSA) form 33 cup and an East Gaulish (EGSA) form 38 bowl. The remaining fabrics are all present in small quantities, accounting for less than 5% by weight. Notable among these fabrics are: plain-rimmed dishes and drop-flanged bowls in black-burnished ware (BB1); a wide-mouthed jar and a beaker in Hadham white-slipped reduced ware (HADREWS); mortaria in Oxfordshire and

Verulamium-region white ware (OXFWH and VERWH); an indented beaker in lower Nene Valley colour-coated ware (LNVCC); a beaker in Upchurch fine oxidised ware (UPCFO); a bowl in Oxfordshire colour-coated ware (OXFRS); a jar/bowl in Hadham oxidised ware (HADOX); a body sherd of Verulamium-region amphora (A24); body sherds of

*Table 7.11: Junction 8. Late Iron Age and Roman pottery by sherd count and weight*

| Fabric | Nosh | % Nosh | Weight (g) | % Weight |
|---|---|---|---|---|
| A24 Verulamium region amphorae | 1 | <1 | 118 | <1 |
| BATAM | 59 | 1 | 1824 | 5 |
| GALAM | 9 | <1 | 139 | <1 |
| BB1 | 45 | <1 | 447 | 1.3 |
| HARSH | 70 | 1 | 484 | 1 |
| E30 'Belgic' coarse sandy fabrics | 70 | 1 | 171 | 1 |
| E40 shell-tempered fabrics | 49 | <1 | 432 | 1.2 |
| GROG | 2043 | 38 | 13597 | 39 |
| COLC | 1 | <1 | 1 | <1 |
| HADOX | 18 | <1 | 72 | <1 |
| LNVCC | 34 | <1 | 115 | <1 |
| LONMD | 19 | <1 | 145 | <1 |
| NOGWH | 1 | <1 | 17 | <1 |
| OXFRS | 4 | <1 | 27 | <1 |
| UNSCC | 10 | <1 | 36 | <1 |
| OXFWHM | 15 | <1 | 779 | 2 |
| VERWHM | 16 | <1 | 623 | 1.8 |
| MISC | 4 | <1 | 2 | <1 |
| PNKGT | 41 | <1 | 857 | 2.5 |
| UNSOXC | 193 | 3.5 | 751 | 2.2 |
| UNSOXF | 34 | <1 | 97 | <1 |
| UPCFO | 1 | <1 | 3 | <1 |
| HADREW | 5 | <1 | 35 | <1 |
| Q20 white-slipped oxidised fabrics | 6 | <1 | 52 | <1 |
| Q30 white-slipped reduced fabrics | 28 | <1 | 89 | <1 |
| VERWS | 48 | <1 | 248 | <1 |
| HADRE | 3 | <1 | 24 | <1 |
| LNVRE | 2 | <1 | 9 | <1 |
| R90 coarse tempered fabrics | 8 | <1 | 101 | <1 |
| UNSBB | 135 | 2 | 891 | 3 |
| UNSREC | 1429 | 26 | 6214 | 18 |
| UNSREF | 74 | <1 | 454 | <1 |
| UPCFR | 33 | <1 | 195 | <1 |
| VERRE | 66 | 1 | 367 | 1 |
| CGSA | 55 | <1 | 370 | <1 |
| EGSA | 5 | <1 | 7 | <1 |
| SGSA | 44 | <1 | 254 | <1 |
| OXFWH | 1 | <1 | 35 | <1 |
| VERWH | 729 | 13 | 3918 | 11 |
| W41 south-east English white/buff fabrics | 12 | <1 | 18 | <1 |
| Total | 5419 | 100 | 34,013 | 100 |

Dressel 20 amphorae (BATAM); and body sherds of Gallic amphorae (GALAM).

Unsourced reduced coarse wares (UNSREC) dominate the late Roman assemblage at 48% by weight. Vessels in this fabric are largely drop-flanged bowls, although there is also a beaker and two jars. The next most common fabrics are unsourced black-burnished wares (UNSBB) at 9% by weight and Verulamium-region white wares at 8%. Only one vessel (a jar) is present in Verulamium-region white ware and it can be assumed that this material is residual. Vessels in unsourced black-burnished ware (UNSBB) are restricted to a single drop-flanged bowl. Body sherds of pink grogged ware (PNKGT) and a single storage jar account for 9% by weight and two mortaria in Oxfordshire white ware (OXFWHM) account for 8%. The remaining fabrics are all present in small quantities, each accounting for less than 5% by weight. Notable among these fabrics are: Gallic amphorae (GALAM); body sherds and drop-flanged bowls in black-burnished ware (BB1); body sherds and bag-shaped beakers in lower Nene Valley colour-coated ware (LNVCC); Harold shelly ware (HARSH), including a storage jar; and Hadham oxidised ware (HADOX), including a jar/bowl.

Pottery from Junction 8N that could only be assigned a broad Roman date range include grog-tempered wares (GROG), unsourced reduced coarse wares (UNSREC) and Verulamium-region white wares (VERWH), which together account for 59% of the unphased assemblage by weight. Vessels in these fabrics are largely jars, although there is one unguentarium in Verulamium-region white ware. Body sherds of Dressel 20 amphora (BATAM) also make up a significant proportion of this assemblage at 16% by weight. With the exception of pink grogged ware (PNKGT) at 7% by weight the remaining fabrics are all present in small quantities of less than 5% by weight (Table 7.11).

### Funerary pottery from Junction 8N

The late Iron Age-early Roman assemblage from Junction 8N also included pottery from two cremation burials (6289 and 6293). Cremation burial 6289 contained three grog-tempered vessels, comprising one cremation urn and two ancillary vessels. None of these vessels could be identified to type with any certainty, as they were all very fragmented and had lost their rims. Cremation burial 6293 produced three ancillary vessels, but no urn. These comprised a platter and a carinated cup in grog-tempered ware and a beaker in 'Belgic' sandy ware.

### Catalogue of funerary pottery

*Cremation burial 6289*

Jar/beaker. Fabric GROG. SF 6051
Jar/beaker. Fabric GROG. SF6052
Jar/beaker. Fabric GROG. SF 6053

*Cremation burial 6293*

1    Platter. Fabric GROG. SF 6054
     Carinated cup. Fabric GROG. SF 6055
     Beaker. Fabric GROG. SF 6056

### Pottery from the Junction 10 Borrow Pit Area

Two sherds of grog-tempered ware (GROG), weighing 8g and dating to the late Iron Age-early Roman period, were recovered during the excavations at the Junction 10 Borrow Pit.

### Pottery from The Aubreys (Table 7.12)

Four sherds of late Iron Age-Roman pottery, weighing 23g, were recovered from The Aubreys. These comprise a sherd of unidentifiable material (MISC), a sherd of unsourced oxidised ware (UNSOXC) and two sherds of unsourced reduced coarse ware (UNSREC). The latter three sherds are broadly Roman in date.

*Table 7.12: The Aubreys. Late Iron Age and Roman pottery*

| Fabric | Nosh | %
Nosh | Weight
(g) | %
Weight |
|---|---|---|---|---|
| Misc | 1 | 25 | 1 | 4 |
| UNSOXC | 1 | 25 | 2 | 8.6 |
| UNSREC | 2 | 50 | 20 | 86.9 |
| Total | 4 | 100 | 23 | 100 |

### Pottery from Area M (Table 7.13)

Some 614 sherds of late Iron Age-Roman pottery, weighing 3146g, were recovered during the excavations at Area M. With an average sherd weight of 5g the pottery is generally in poor condition, although some groups contain well-preserved material. The assemblage is dominated by pottery from early Roman contexts, which accounts for 88% of the assemblage by weight. The remainder is accounted for by late Iron Age-early Roman pottery at 11% and pottery of broad Roman date at 1%.

The late Iron Age-early Roman pottery largely consists of grog-tempered ware (GROG), in which there are two jars, plus body sherds of Dressel 20 amphora (BATAM) and 'Belgic' sandy ware (E20). The early Roman pottery is also dominated by grog-tempered ware (GROG), which accounts for 38% of the phase assemblage by weight. Several jars are present in this fabric, along with a butt-beaker and two lids. The grog-tempered ware is supplemented by a medium-mouthed jar in unsourced black-surfaced ware, which accounts for 22% of the assemblage by weight, and body sherds of unsourced reduced coarse ware (UNSREC), along with two jars and a lid, which account for 13%. The remainder of the assemblage comprises five body sherds of

*Table 7.13: Area M. Late Iron Age and Roman pottery*

| Fabric | Nosh | % Nosh | Weight (g) | % Weight |
|---|---|---|---|---|
| BATAM | 6 | <1 | 630 | 11.4 |
| E20 'Belgic' fine sandy fabrics | 2 | <1 | 9 | <1 |
| GROG | 214 | 35 | 1391 | 44 |
| NOGWH | 10 | 1.6 | 13 | <1 |
| SGSA | 18 | 3 | 123 | 3.9 |
| UNSOXC | 7 | 1.14 | 27 | <1 |
| UNSOXF | 11 | 1.7 | 17 | <1 |
| UNSBB | 145 | 23.6 | 599 | 19 |
| UNSREC | 57 | 9.2 | 356 | 11 |
| UNSREF | 47 | 7.6 | 75 | 2.3 |
| VERWH | 3 | <1 | 3 | <1 |
| W41 south-east English white/buff fabrics | 94 | 15.3 | 173 | 5.4 |
| Total | 614 | 100 | 3146 | 100 |

Dressel 20 amphora (BATAM), body sherds of North Gaulish white ware (NOGWH), Verulamium-region white ware (VERWH) and south-east English white ware (W41), along with several form 18/31 dishes, a form 15/17 dish and a form 24/25 cup in South Gaulish samian ware (SGSA). Pottery of broad Roman date comprises body sherds of grog-tempered ware (GROG) and unsourced reduced coarse ware (UNSREC).

## Pottery from Area P (Table 7.14)

A total of 577 sherds, weighing 4405g, was recovered during the excavations at Area P. With an average sherd weight of 8g the pottery was in poor to moderate condition, although some groups of large, well-preserved sherds were recovered. The assemblage is dominated by middle Roman pottery, which accounts for 93% of the assemblage by weight. The remainder is accounted for by late Iron Age-early Roman material at 2% and pottery of broadly Roman date at 5%. The late Iron Age-early Roman material consists of body sherds and a medium-mouthed jar in grog-tempered ware (GROG). Jars and bowls in Verulamium-region white ware (VERWH) dominate the middle Roman assemblage, taking a 37% share of the phase group by weight. These are supplemented by jars and bowls in unsourced reduced coarse ware (UNSREC), which account for 18%, jars including medium-mouthed and lid-seated types in Harrold shelly ware (HARSH) at 15% and body sherds of pink grogged ware (PNKGT), which account for 8%. The remaining fabrics are all present in small amounts of 5% or less. Notable among these fabrics are: body sherds from Campanian and Gallic amphorae (CAMAM1 and GALAM); body sherds of black-burnished ware (BB1); plain-rimmed dishes in unsourced black-burnished ware

*Table 7.14: Area P. Late Iron Age and Roman pottery*

| Fabric | Nosh | % Nosh | Weight (g) | % Weight |
|---|---|---|---|---|
| BATAM | 25 | 4 | 809 | 18 |
| BB1 | 4 | <1 | 18 | <1 |
| CAMAM1 | 1 | <1 | 107 | 2.4 |
| CGSA | 18 | 3 | 84 | 1.9 |
| GALAM | 1 | <1 | 119 | 2.7 |
| GROG | 70 | 12 | 295 | 6.6 |
| HADOX | 1 | <1 | 1 | <1 |
| HARSH | 90 | 15.5 | 455 | 10.3 |
| LNVCC | 12 | 2 | 48 | 1 |
| LNVRE | 1 | <1 | 6 | <1 |
| PNKGT | 10 | 1.7 | 262 | 5.9 |
| Q30 white-slipped reduced fabrics | 7 | 1.2 | 34 | <1 |
| UNSBB | 21 | 3.6 | 78 | 1.77 |
| UNSOXC | 39 | 6.7 | 107 | 2.4 |
| UNSREC | 126 | 21.8 | 579 | 13.1 |
| UNSREF | 20 | 3.4 | 135 | 3 |
| UPCFR | 2 | <1 | 7 | <1 |
| VERRE | 3 | <1 | 57 | 1.2 |
| VERWH | 125 | 21.6 | 1193 | 27 |
| Total | 577 | 100 | 4405 | 100 |

(UNSBB); body sherds in lower Nene Valley colour-coated ware (LNVCC); several form 36 dishes, a form 18/31 dish and a form 37 bowl in Central Gaulish samian ware (CGSA); and some residual jars in grog-tempered ware (GROG). Pottery of broadly Roman date comprises a variety of fabrics, including: a jar in unsourced reduced coarse ware (UNSREC); body sherds of black-burnished ware (BB1); lower Nene Valley colour-coated ware (LNVCC); Hadham oxidised ware (HADOX); and Verulamium-region white ware (VERWH).

## Discussion

### Junction 9

Like the assemblage from Junction 8N the late Iron Age-early Roman pottery from Junction 9 largely consisted of medium-mouthed and high-shouldered jars in grog-tempered fabrics, with a single carinated bowl also present. These were supplemented by small amounts of late Iron Age sandy and shelly fabrics, including a butt-beaker. Small quantities of unsourced reduced coarse ware, Verulamium-region white ware and Hadham oxidised ware from this phase must have been intrusive.

During the early Roman period, grog-tempered fabric still accounted for just over half of all pottery recovered from the settlement, with the bulk of this material being represented by medium-mouthed, high-shouldered and bead-rimmed jars, along with butt-beakers and carinated bowls. These were supplemented by jars and bowls, along with a small number of poppyhead beakers in locally made (but unsourced) reduced coarse wares and jars, bowls and flagons in Verulamium-region white ware. Non-local regionally produced fabrics were in relatively short supply in this period, but accounted for a higher proportion of the assemblage at Junction 9 than at Junction 8N (see above). Such material included south Spanish and Gallic amphora, Highgate Wood reduced ware, pink grogged ware, Much Hadham oxidised ware, North Gaulish white ware and the base of a platter in *terra nigra*. Dishes and cups in South Gaulish samian ware, and a bowl in London mica-dusted ware were also supplied during this phase.

By the beginning of the middle Roman phase the pottery supply was dominated by a combination of local unsourced reduced coarse wares and Verulamium-region white wares. Vessels in these fabrics included medium-mouthed jars and bowls. Supplementing these two main fabric types were small quantities of black-burnished wares, locally produced shell-tempered fabrics, pink grogged wares, locally produced oxidised sandy wares and unsourced black-burnished wares. Vessels in these fabrics consisted of jars. Fine and specialist wares remained in relatively short supply in the middle Roman period, but included south Spanish and Gallic amphorae and cups, dishes and a bowl in South, Central and East Gaulish samian, Much Hadham oxidised ware, and Highgate Wood reduced ware. Also present in very small quantities were Nene Valley colour-coated wares, Mancetter-Hartshill mortaria and Oxfordshire colour-coated wares. A platter in *terra nigra* and some North Gaulish white ware were clearly residual. Deposits of middle Roman pottery were clearly mixed with earlier material during the recutting of enclosure ditches at Junction 9, as at Junction 8N, and this is demonstrated by the presence of relatively substantial quantities of grog-tempered body sherds from this phase.

Pottery supply to Junction 9 in the late Roman period saw the continued dominance of locally made unsourced reduced coarse wares, although, as would be expected, the proportion of Verulamiumn region white ware declined relative to the middle Roman period and the Verulamium material that was present during this phase must have been residual. Once again jars were common in these fabrics, although the proportion of dishes in unsourced reduced coarse ware increased. These fabrics were supplemented by jars in unsourced black-burnished wares, black-burnished wares, pink grogged wares, locally produced sandy oxidised wares, locally produced shelly fabrics and late Roman shell-tempered wares. As might be expected for a later Roman assemblage, the proportion of fine and specialist wares increased in this phase. Fine and specialist wares included: Nene Valley colour-coated ware; Oxfordshire colour-coated ware; Oxfordshire parchment ware; Much

Hadham oxidised ware; Much Hadham reduced white-slipped ware; Verulamium-region white-slipped ware; Colchester colour-coated ware; and Colchester white ware, although some of these may have been residual by this time. Vessels included two bowls, one in Nene Valley colour-coated ware and one in Oxfordshire colour-coated ware, and a flagon in Hadham oxidised ware. Also present were south Spanish and Gallic amphorae and some residual South and Central Gaulish samian, along with some residual grog-tempered body sherds.

### The pottery from Junction 9 in its regional context

The late Iron Age-early Roman pottery from Junction 9 is comparable to that from Junction 8N and to that from most low-status rural sites of this period in the region (see above). In contrast to the assemblage from Junction 8N, the similarity to assemblages from other sites in the region continued into the early Roman period. The dominance of Verulamium-region white wares and locally produced unsourced reduced coarse wares can be paralleled at sites such as Foxholes Farm, Boxfield Farm, Folly Lane, Buncefield Lane, Hemel Hempstead and Gadebridge, although the proportions of fine and specialist wares and regional imports at some of these sites is greater than that seen at Junction 9. This may be explained by the higher status of some of these settlements. Middle Roman pottery supply continued to reflect the pattern seen at many other sites in the region (see above), with high proportions of Verulamium-region white ware and locally made unsourced reduced coarse wares, but relatively low quantities of fine and specialist wares and regional imports reflecting the site's rural character. Late Roman pottery supply, with a slight increase in fine and specialist wares and a fall off in Verulamium-region products, is also typical of the region.

### Junction 8N

The late Iron Age-early Roman pottery from Junction 8N was dominated by locally produced grog-tempered wares, with medium-mouthed, high-shouldered or bead-rimmed jars being the most common vessel forms. Imports, table wares and fine wares were very rare in this phase, being represented by a single butt-beaker in North Gaulish white ware. A single sherd of locally made unsourced reduced coarse ware in this phase may have been intrusive.

By the early Roman period, grog-tempered wares, which were still the dominant fabric type, were being supplemented with locally made unsourced reduced coarse ware fabrics, including some fine white-slipped fabrics and Verulamium-region white wares. Jars were the most common vessels in these fabrics and included medium-mouthed jars and lid-seated examples in grog-tempered ware, with flagons, bowls and a mortarium also present in Verulamium-region white ware. In addition, there were small amounts of unsourced oxidised wares and medium-mouthed jars in unsourced black-burnished wares. Fine and specialist wares had increased as a proportion of the overall assemblage, but were still in relatively short supply. These included south Spanish amphorae, a medium-mouthed jar in London mica-dusted ware and dishes and cups in South Gaulish samian ware.

In many ways the mid-Roman period saw a continuation of the early Roman pattern of supply, with unsourced coarse reduced wares and Verulamium-region white wares playing a dominant role; although vessels in these fabrics now included a higher proportion of bowls and dishes. Grog-tempered wares still represented a significant proportion of the assemblage in this phase, although this material must have been largely residual, its presence probably accounted for by the recutting of enclosure ditches which remained open and largely unmodified through these periods. Also present was a small quantity of black-burnished ware, including plain-rimmed dishes and a bowl. The overall quantities, if not the proportions, of fine and specialist wares had increased by the middle Roman period and new regional fabrics, such as Nene Valley and Oxfordshire colour-coated wares, Hadham oxidised wares and Upchurch fine reduced ware had appeared, although the last of these may have been residual in this period. Vessels in these fabrics included bowls, jars and beakers. Fine and specialist wares included south Spanish, Gallic and Verulamium-region amphorae and bowls, cups and dishes in South, Central and East Gaulish samian. The presence of Upchurch products in Hertfordshire is unusual and outside the normal distribution of the products of this industry, but the identification of the material is secure.

Late Roman pottery supply to Junction 8N continued the trends seen in the middle Roman phase, with jars and dishes in unsourced reduced coarse wares dominating. The unsourced reduced coarse wares were supplemented by relatively small quantities of residual Verulamium-region white wares, pink grogged ware and unsourced black-burnished ware. Grog-tempered wares were no

longer present. Fine and specialist wares comprised a slightly greater proportion of the pottery than that seen in the middle Roman phase, including several beakers in Nene Valley colour-coated ware, along with Oxfordshire white-ware mortaria, some Hadham oxidised wares, including a jar and a jar/bowl, and some Gallic amphorae. Also present was a sherd of Hadham reduced ware with a white slip. Small quantities of shelly fabrics were present throughout the Roman occupation at Junction 8N, but never made a significant contribution in any phase.

*The pottery from Junction 8N in its regional context*

The late Iron Age-early Roman assemblage from Junction 8N is typical of assemblages from this period in Hertfordshire and in southern Britain generally, being dominated by jars in grog-tempered ware. The typical composition of assemblages from this type of site in southern Britain has been clearly demonstrated by Evans (2001, 26). By the early Roman period, and continuing into the middle and late Roman periods, the composition of the Junction 8N assemblage appears to diverge from that of many other contemporary assemblages from Hertfordshire. Whereas the assemblage from Junction 8N continued to be dominated by reduced coarse wares of unknown, but probably, local origin and grog-tempered wares, with small amounts of fine and specialist wares, including Upchurch products, coming into use in the later periods, assemblages from other sites in Hertfordshire included much higher proportions of Verulamium-region white wares and greywares, supplemented by Highgate Wood fabrics in the early period and by high proportions of Hadham wares, Oxfordshire colour-coated wares and Nene Valley colour-coated wares in the later periods. Such assemblages include those from Boxfield Farm (Waugh 1999), the Villas at Gorhambury (Parminter 1990) and Gadebridge (Neal 1974), and the field systems at Buncefield Lane, Hemel Hempstead (Going 2003). One exception to this pattern is the assemblage from Canon's Corner (Biddulph 2001), dating from the second half of the

*Table 7.15: Late Iron Age-early Roman vessel class by feature type (%EVE). All sites*

| Vessel Class | Ditches | Pits | Postholes | Waterholes | Layers | Total Eves |
|---|---|---|---|---|---|---|
| Jars | 63 | 29.5 | 7.2 | - | - | 3.45 |
| Amphorae | - | - | - | - | - | - |
| Flagons | - | - | - | - | - | - |
| Jar/bowls | - | - | - | - | - | - |
| Beakers | 64 | 36 | - | - | - | 0.25 |
| Cups | - | - | - | - | - | - |
| Bowls | - | 100 | - | - | - | 0.06 |
| Platters/dishes | - | - | - | - | - | - |
| Mortaria | - | - | - | - | - | - |
| Lids | 50 | 50 | - | - | - | 0.16 |
| Miscellaneous | - | - | - | - | - | - |

2nd century to the end of the Roman period, which is dominated by miscellaneous sand-tempered wares, both oxidised and reduced, and has relatively small amounts of Verulamium-region white ware and fine and specialist wares. The relative lack of Verulamium ware at Canon's Corner is probably due to chronological factors, but this does not explain the variation in fine and specialist wares, which may be due to its geographical position, further away from regional suppliers of specialist wares than the other examples, as well

its peripheral status (Smith 2001, 38). The differences between the Junction 8N assemblage and those from most of the sites mentioned above may also be accounted for by the status of the Junction 8N settlement. There is a lack of excavated evidence for lower-status Roman rural settlement in Hertfordshire (notwithstanding Hunn's (1996) survey of late Iron Age and Roman enclosures) resulting in a lack of data directly comparable with the Junction 8N assemblage. The nearby site at Buncefield Lane was also considered to be of low

*Table 7.16: Early Roman vessel class by feature type (%EVE). All sites*

| Vessel Class | Ditches | Pits | Postholes | Waterholes | Layers | Total Eves |
|---|---|---|---|---|---|---|
| Jars | 95.5 | 2.6 | - | - | 1.7 | 22.84 |
| Amphorae | 100 | - | - | - | - | 0.04 |
| Flagons | 63.2 | 8.3 | - | - | 28.3 | 4.41 |
| Jar/bowls | 100 | - | - | - | - | 0.3 |
| Beakers | 100 | - | - | - | - | 3.51 |
| Cups | 81.7 | 9.7 | - | 8.5 | - | 0.02 |
| Bowls | 95.8 | 4.1 | - | - | - | 0.96 |
| Platters/dishes | 100 | - | - | - | - | 2.03 |
| Mortaria | 88.5 | 11.4 | - | - | - | 0.35 |
| Lids | 93 | - | - | - | 7 | 0.68 |
| Miscellaneous | 100 | - | - | - | - | 0.12 |

*Table 7.17: Middle Roman vessel class by feature type (%EVE). All sites*

| Vessel Class | Ditches | Pits | Postholes | Waterholes | Layers | Total Eves |
|---|---|---|---|---|---|---|
| Jars | 71.2 | 16 | 1 | - | 11.5 | 16.48 |
| Amphorae | - | - | - | - | - | - |
| Flagons | 100 | - | - | - | - | - |
| Jar/bowls | 50 | 50 | - | - | - | 1.04 |
| Beakers | 57 | 43 | - | - | - | 1.14 |
| Cups | 30.7 | 54.3 | - | - | 14.9 | 1.14 |
| Bowls | 73.2 | 26.7 | - | - | - | 1.46 |
| Platters/dishes | 51.1 | 45 | <1 | - | 3.19 | 3.13 |
| Mortaria | 87.6 | 12.3 | - | - | - | 0.65 |
| Lids | 27 | 68.5 | - | - | 4.5 | 1.97 |
| Miscellaneous | - | 100 | - | - | - | 0.2 |

*Table 7.18: Late Roman vessel class by feature type (%EVE). All sites*

| Vessel Class | Ditches | Pits | Postholes | Waterholes | Layers | Total Eves |
|---|---|---|---|---|---|---|
| Jars | 87 | 3.8 | - | 9.1 | - | 16.48 |
| Amphorae | - | - | - | - | - | - |
| Flagons | 45.7 | 54.2 | - | - | - | 0.35 |
| Jar/bowls | 16.6 | - | 83.3 | - | - | 0.06 |
| Beakers | 75 | - | 16.6 | 8.3 | - | 0.6 |
| Cups | - | - | - | - | - | - |
| Bowls | 37 | 30 | 33 | - | - | 1.32 |
| Platters/dishes | 54 | 15 | - | 30.1 | - | 0.78 |
| Mortaria | 66.6 | 33.3 | - | - | - | 0.18 |
| Lids | 44.4 | - | 55.5 | - | - | 0.09 |
| Miscellaneous | - | - | - | - | - | - |

status, but in that case the assemblage was small (Going 2003) and the significance of conclusions drawn from it is therefore uncertain.

## Area M

Apart from two sherds in an unsourced fine sandy fabric, the late Iron Age-early Roman assemblage from Area M comprised grog-tempered fabrics (GROG), in which there were two jars. By the early Roman period, the assemblage was dominated by grog-tempered wares and locally produced reduced sandy fabrics. Medium-mouthed jars were the dominant vessel type in the grog-tempered fabrics, while jars were also available in the reduced fabrics. These were supplemented by small quantities of unsourced sandy oxidised ware, unsourced black-burnished wares (UNSBB) and Verulamium-region white wares (VERWH). Imports and regional fabrics were in short supply, consisting of south Spanish amphorae (BATAM), dishes and a cup in South Gaulish samian (SGSA) and some sherds of North Gaulish white ware (NOGWH). Also present were some sherds of fine pink/buff south-east English fabric (W41). Pottery supply to Area M during the late Iron Age and early Roman periods was typical of southern British low-status rural settlement (Evans 2001, 26).

## Area P

Pottery supplied to Area P during the late Iron Age-early Roman period consisted entirely of grog-tempered fabrics and included a medium-mouthed jar. During the middle Roman period the assemblage was dominated by jars, including medium-mouthed and lid-seated types in Verulamium-region white wares, unsourced reduced coarse ware and locally produced shell-tempered fabrics. These were supplemented by small quantities of fine and specialist wares, including bowls and dishes in Central Gaulish samian (CGSA), south Spanish amphorae (BATAM), Campanian amphorae (CAM AM1) and Gallic amphorae (GALAM). Also supplied in small amounts were some regional specialist wares including black-burnished ware (BB1), pink grogged ware (PNKGT), a dish in Nene Valley colour-coated ware (LNVCC) and Upchurch fine reduced ware (UPCFR), the presence of which is unusual for the region (see above). Plain-rimmed dishes in unsourced black-burnished ware (UNSBB) were also available. As with Area M, the pottery supply to Area P was typical of a low-status rural settlement (Evans 2001, 26) being dominated by jars in both phases.

## Deposition/distribution

The composition of assemblages from different feature types by vessel class was quantified using estimated vessel equivalents (EVEs). For the purpose of this analysis features were divided into five broad categories: ditches; pits; postholes; water-holes; and layers. Vessels were classified using the standard OA recording system (Booth 2007). The results of the analysis were disappointing, with the majority of all vessel types being confined to ditches in all phases and at all sites (Tables 7.15-18 present data by period for all the sites combined). In the late Iron Age-early Roman phase (Table 7.15) jars and beakers were mostly deposited in ditches, with smaller quantities deposited in pits and bowls being the only vessel type entirely deposited in pits. By the early Roman period (Table 7.16) the vast majority of all vessel classes were deposited in ditches, with some types including jar/bowls, beakers and platters/dishes being entirely confined to ditches. In the middle and late Roman periods (Tables 7.17-18) a wider range of vessel classes were deposited in pits, postholes, waterholes and layers, but most vessel classes were still recovered principally from ditches. The early Roman pattern in particular contrasts strongly with work done by Pitts (2005, 152, table 2) on late Iron Age-early Roman sites in Essex, where drinking and eating vessels such as beakers, bowls and platters were more strongly represented in pits, although it should be noted that the majority of jars at all of the sites were deposited in ditches. The pattern seen in the M1 widening assemblages is probably best explained as a function of the relative lack of pits from the sites, although this begs the question of why there were so few pits, given that some of the enclosures seem to represent domestic occupation. The pattern of deposition therefore possibly represents a particular local mode of disposal, or behavioural pattern.

## Functional analysis: pottery consumption and social stratification

The functional composition of the assemblages (composition by functional vessel class) for each site is described below and the data analysed for information on pottery use, consumption and social stratification. Tables 7.19-22 show the proportions of different functional vessel classes by site and phase, using EVEs as a measure.

The Junction 9 assemblage had a functional vessel class profile displaying the classic characteristics of a rural settlement throughout the Roman period (see Evans 2001), being dominated by cooking and storage jars (Table 7.19). In the late Iron Age-early Roman period, jars accounted for 86.3% of all vessels present (by EVE), with drinking/eating vessels accounting for only 6.5%. By the early Roman and middle Roman periods the proportion of jars had fallen, but they were still dominant at 60.5% and 62.3% of EVEs respectively. Eating/drinking vessels in these periods never exceeded 36% of EVEs. In the late Roman period the proportion of jars increased once more to 70.2% of EVEs with eating/drinking vessels accounting for 29%. The data therefore suggests that the inhabitants of the settlement at Junction 9 occupied the lower end of the social spectrum through the Roman period, with proportions of cooking/storage vessels to eating/drinking vessels comparing well to those on other 'basic' rural sites from throughout the province (Evans 2001), especially in the late Iron Age-early Roman period. Levels of eating/drinking vessels in the early and middle Roman periods, although relatively high, still fall within the upper range of values recorded for lower-status rural assemblages and the level of eating/drinking vessels in the late Roman period is exceptionally low. Where drinking and eating vessels were supplied in the late Iron Age-early Roman and early Roman phases they were mostly in locally produced fabric types, with regional and Continental imports, including decorated samian, being scarce, a pattern which appears to back up the evidence of the vessel forms. However, some pottery from further afield, including Highgate Wood C fabrics, south Spanish and Gallic amphorae, North Gaulish white ware and *terra nigra*, was available, showing that the settlement was not completely isolated. In the middle Roman period, eating/drinking vessels were again overwhelmingly supplied in locally produced fabrics, with regional wares and Continental imports, being restricted to small amounts of Hadham oxidised ware, black-burnished ware and Central Gaulish samian, this last with a very low ratio of decorated to undecorated forms. By the late Roman period, imports were more strongly represented among the eating/drinking vessels, with products of the major regional industries, including the Nene Valley and Oxfordshire, available, although it should be remembered that these formed a minor component of the assemblage.

The assemblage from Junction 8N was also dominated by jars throughout the late Iron Age-early Roman, early Roman and middle Roman phases, although the proportion of jars declined steeply by the middle Roman period (Table 7.20). In the late Iron Age-early Roman period, jars were complemented by beakers and dishes/platters, although these types never accounted for more than 13.2% of EVEs. A wider range of vessel types was available in the early and middle Roman periods, including types related to eating, drinking and food preparation, such as beakers, cups, bowls and mortaria, but these never accounted for more than 22% of EVEs in the early Roman period, or 45% in the middle Roman period. By the late Roman period the percentage of jars had fallen to 14.7% and the assemblage was now dominated by dishes/platters at 50.2% of EVEs, with other eating/drinking vessels constituting 35% of the assemblage. The percentage of jars, in this case, seems particularly low, but the overall late Roman assemblage was very small, comprising some 2.31 EVEs in total, and this fact may have skewed the data set. The data for the late Iron Age-early Roman phases fit the profile of a 'basic' rural site as defined by Evans (2001) and this suggests that the inhabitants occupied the lower end of the social scale, with their pottery mostly consisting of cooking and storage jars, mostly procured from local sources. However, eating and drinking vessels were supplied and where they were present they tended to occur in regionally produced or Continental fabrics such as Verulamium-region white ware, black-burnished ware and South or Central Gaulish samian ware. In

*Table 7.19: Junction 9 functional vessel class by phase (EVEs)*

| Phase | Jars | Flagons | Beakers | Cups | Bowls | Jar-Bowls | Dishes/Platters | Mortaria | Lids | Misc | Total |
|---|---|---|---|---|---|---|---|---|---|---|---|
| RO | 0.83 | - | - | - | 0.13 | - | 0.04 | - | 0.03 | - | 1.03 |
| LIA-ER | 1.96 | - | 0.09 | - | 0.06 | - | - | - | 0.16 | - | 2.27 |
| ER | 14.7 | 2.92 | 3.53 | 0.38 | 0.81 | - | 0.57 | 0.58 | 0.66 | 0.12 | 24.27 |
| MR | 5.11 | 0.65 | 0.26 | 0.62 | | | 1 | 0.25 | 0.3 | | 8.19 |
| LR | 3.83 | - | 0.14 | - | 0.61 | 0.01 | 0.7 | 0.12 | 0.04 | - | 5.45 |
| Total | 26.43 | 3.57 | 4.02 | 1 | 1.61 | 0.01 | 2.31 | 0.95 | 1.19 | 0.12 | 41.21 |

*Table 7.20: Junction 8N functional vessel class by phase (EVEs)*

| Phase | Jars | Flagons | Beakers | Cups | Bowls | Jar-Bowls | Dishes/Platters | Mortaria | Lids | Misc | Total |
|---|---|---|---|---|---|---|---|---|---|---|---|
| RO | 3.04 | 0.32 | 0.43 | - | 0.08 | - | 0.31 | - | - | 0.06 | 4.24 |
| LIA-ER | 2.08 | - | 0.28 | - | - | - | 0.04 | - | - | - | 2.4 |
| ER | 6.14 | - | 0.23 | 0.18 | 0.24 | 0.3 | 0.75 | 0.1 | - | - | 7.94 |
| MR | 9.95 | 1 | 0.88 | 0.89 | 0.8 | 0.14 | 2.11 | 0.48 | 1.7 | 0.2 | 18.15 |
| LR | 0.34 | 0.19 | 0.46 | | 1.04 | 0.05 | 0.12 | 0.06 | 0.05 | | 2.31 |
| Total | 21.55 | 1.51 | 2.28 | 1.07 | 1.12 | 0.49 | 4.37 | 0.64 | 1.75 | 0.26 | 35.04 |

addition, sherds of North Gaulish white ware and Upchurch fine reduced ware suggest some more long distance contacts, while sherds from a locally made mica-dusted vessel indicate at least occasional access to higher-status ceramics. By the middle Roman period, drinking/eating vessels formed a higher proportion of the assemblage, a chronological pattern also recognised by Evans (ibid., 28), but jars were still dominant and this probably reflects relatively low social status. Despite this, the presence of regionally produced and Continental fabrics such as Upchurch fine oxidised ware, Oxfordshire colour-coated ware, samian ware and sherds of south Spanish and Gallic amphorae again indicate some long-distance contacts in this period. The late Roman dominance of drinking/eating vessels over cooking/storage related ones may be partially explained by chronology, but this is a pattern more commonly associated with sites at the higher end of the social spectrum and is therefore anomalous. It may be explained by the small size of the late Roman sample relative to the rest of the assemblage (see above). The continuation of long-distance contacts seen in the earlier phases is demonstrated by a similar range of regional and Continental fabrics, although with the addition of Nene Valley colour-coated wares in this phase.

Cooking/storage jars accounted for 100% of the vessels supplied to Area M during the late Iron Age-early Roman period, falling to 59.1% in the early Roman period, when eating/drinking vessels accounted for 28.2% (Table 7.21). Again the data fits the profile for a rural settlement at the lower end of the social scale, but the presence of Dressel 20 amphorae sherds in the late Iron Age-early Roman phase, and of south-east English white ware, along with presumably residual North Gaulish white ware, in the early Roman phase indicates that even this relatively minor settle-

ment had access to wider pottery supply networks.

Like Area M, the Area P assemblage was completely dominated by jars in the late Iron Age-early Roman phase and continued to be dominated by them into the middle Roman phase, when eating/drinking vessels accounted for 17.8% of EVEs (Table 7.22). Despite the dominance of locally produced material, sherds of Gallic and Campanian amphorae indicate some far-flung contacts. In addition, eating/drinking vessels were supplied in regional and Continental fabrics, including Nene Valley colour-coated ware and Central Gaulish colour-coated ware. Two body sherds of Upchurch fine reduced ware also indicate the capacity to acquire pottery from beyond the immediate region. As with Area M, the Area P data suggest a rural site, with inhabitants at the lower end of the social spectrum.

The pottery from The Aubreys and the Junction 10 Borrow Pit Area did not produce any EVEs data and could not be analysed in functional terms. When compared together (Figs 7.3-7) the functional vessel class data conform with the pattern revealed for the individual sites, with jars (C) dominating throughout the Roman period, but declining steadily in favour of eating/drinking vessels into the middle and late Roman periods. This confirms the overall impression of the users of these sites as representing a rural population at the lower end of the socio-economic scale.

## Catalogue of illustrated vessels

### *Junction 8* (Fig. 7.8)

1 Medium-mouthed jar (cd 740). Fabric UNSREC. Ctx 6118

2 Medium-mouthed jar (cd 730). Fabric UNSREC. Ctx 6118

*Table 7.21: Site M functional vessel class by phase (EVEs)*

| Phase | Jars | Flagons | Beakers | Cups | Bowls | Jar-Bowls | Dishes/Platters | Mortaria | Lids | Misc | Total |
|---|---|---|---|---|---|---|---|---|---|---|---|
| RO | 0.07 | - | - | - | - | - | - | - | - | - | 0.07 |
| LIA-ER | 0.29 | - | - | - | - | - | - | - | - | - | 0.29 |
| ER | 1.75 | - | 0.12 | 0.05 | - | - | 0.67 | - | 0.37 | - | 2.96 |
| Total | 2.11 | | 0.12 | 0.05 | | | 0.67 | | 0.37 | | 3.32 |

*Table 7.22: Site P functional vessel class by phase (EVEs)*

| Phase | Jars | Flagons | Beakers | Cups | Bowls | Jar-Bowls | Dishes/Platters | Mortaria | Lids | Misc | Total |
|---|---|---|---|---|---|---|---|---|---|---|---|
| RO | 0.24 | - | - | - | - | - | - | - | - | - | 0.24 |
| LIA-ER | 0.27 | - | - | - | - | - | - | - | - | - | 0.27 |
| MR | 3.8 | - | - | - | 0.44 | - | 0.41 | - | 0.11 | - | 4.76 |
| Total | 4.31 | - | - | - | 0.44 | - | 0.41 | - | 0.11 | - | 5.27 |

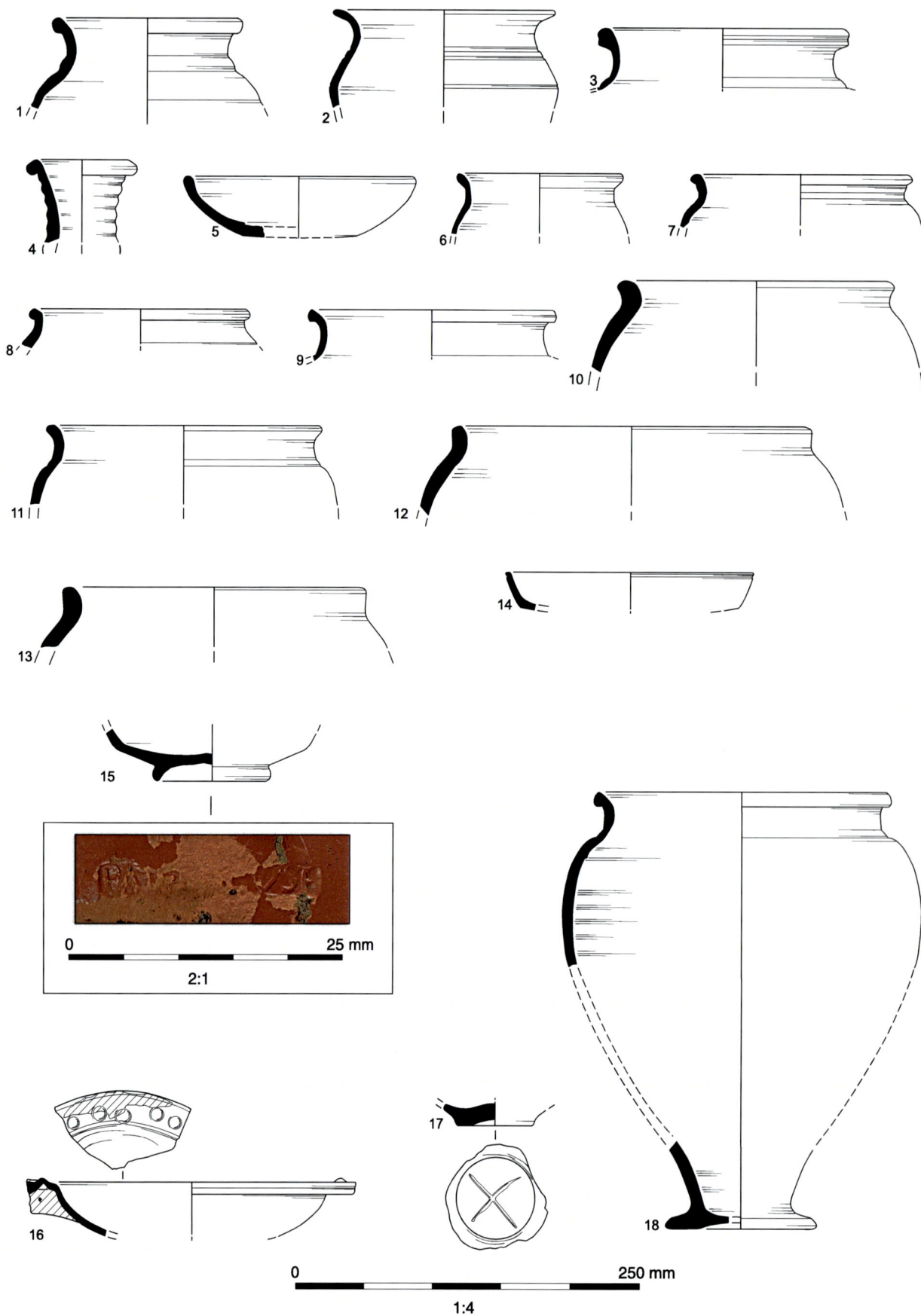

*Fig. 7.8   Late Iron Age and Roman pottery from Junction 8*

3    Medium-mouthed jar (cd 740). Fabric UNSREC. Ctx 6118

4    Ring-necked flagon (bb 235). Fabric VERWH. Ctx 6118

5    Platter (jc 110). Fabric UNSREF. Ctx 6755

6    Medium-mouthed jar (cd 730). Fabric UNSBB. Ctx 6755

7    Medium-mouthed jar (cd 730). Fabric UNSBB. Ctx 6755

8    Medium-mouthed jar (cd 730). Fabric UNSBB. Ctx 6755

9    Medium-mouthed jar (cd 740). Fabric LONMD. Ctx 6755

10   Medium-mouthed jar (cd 730). Fabric GROG. Ctx 6755

11   High-shouldered (necked) jar (ce 730). Fabric GROG. Ctx 6755

12   Medium-mouthed jar (cd 730). Fabric GROG. Ctx 6755

13   Medium-mouthed jar (cd 730). Fabric GROG. Ctx 6755

14   Form 18 dish (j). Fabric SGSA. Ctx 6755

15   Samian stamp (paterclvsf). Ctx 6697

16   Dish (jb 400), possible imitation metal vessel. Fabric UNSOXC. Ctx 7263

17   Jar base with 'x' graffito. Fabric VERWH. Ctx 6420

18   Pedestal jar (cp 740). Fabric GROG. Ctx 6757

### Cremations 6289 and 6293 (Fig. 7.9)

19   Jar/beaker (c/e). Fabric GROG. Ctx 6290 (crem 6289). SF 6051

20   Platter (jc 210). Fabric GROG. Ctx 6294 (crem 6293). SF 6054

21   Butt-beaker (ee 240). Fabric GROG. Ctx 6249 (crem 6293). SF 6055

22   Carinated cup (fd). Fabric GROG. Ctx 6294 (crem 6293). SF 6055

### Site M (Fig. 7.10)

23   Medium-mouthed jar (cd 740). Fabric UNSBB. Ctx 3150

24   Form 24/25 cup. Fabric SGSA. Ctx 3150

25   Form 15/17. Fabric SGSA. Ctx 3150

26   Lid (l). Fabric UNSREC. Ctx 3150

27   Bead-rimmed jar (ch 210). Fabric UNSREC. Ctx3 150

28   Medium-mouthed jar (cd 730). Fabric GROG. Ctx3 150

### Junction 9 (Figs 7.11-12)

29   Lid-seated jar (cj 810). Fabric UNSBB. Ctx 2007

30   Disc-mouthed flagon (ba 240). Fabric VERWH. Ctx 2001

31   Plain-rimmed dish (jb110). Fabric VERWS. Ctx 2041

32   Spindlewhorl. Fabric GROG. Ctx 2113

33   Butt-beaker (ea 210). Fabric GROG. Ctx 2139

34   High-shouldered jar (ce 730). Fabric GROG. Ctx 2139

35   High-shoulderd jar (ce 740). Fabric GROG. Ctx 2139

36   Lid-seated jar (cj 810). Fabric GROG. Ctx 2139

37   Carinated bowl (ha 730). Fabric GROG. Ctx 2139

0                    250 mm

1:4

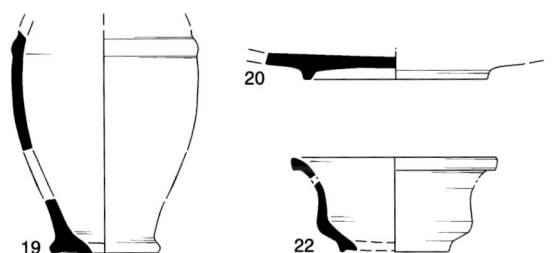

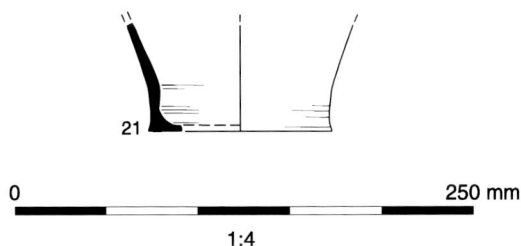

*Fig. 7.9   Late Iron Age and Roman pottery from cremations 6289 and 6293*

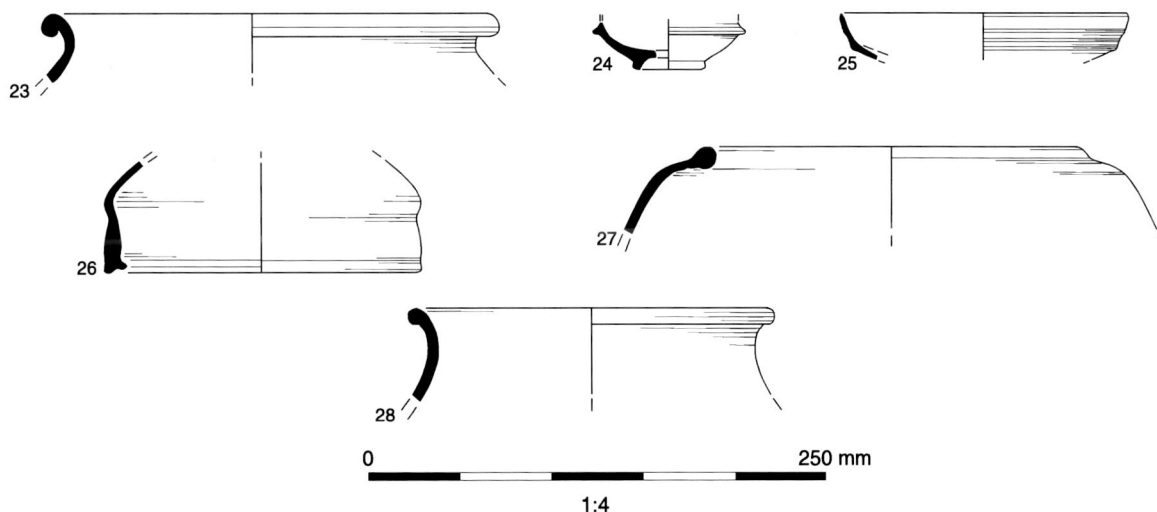

0                    250 mm

1:4

*Fig. 7.10   Late Iron Age and Roman pottery from Site M*

117

*Fig. 7.11   Late Iron Age and Roman pottery from Junction 9*

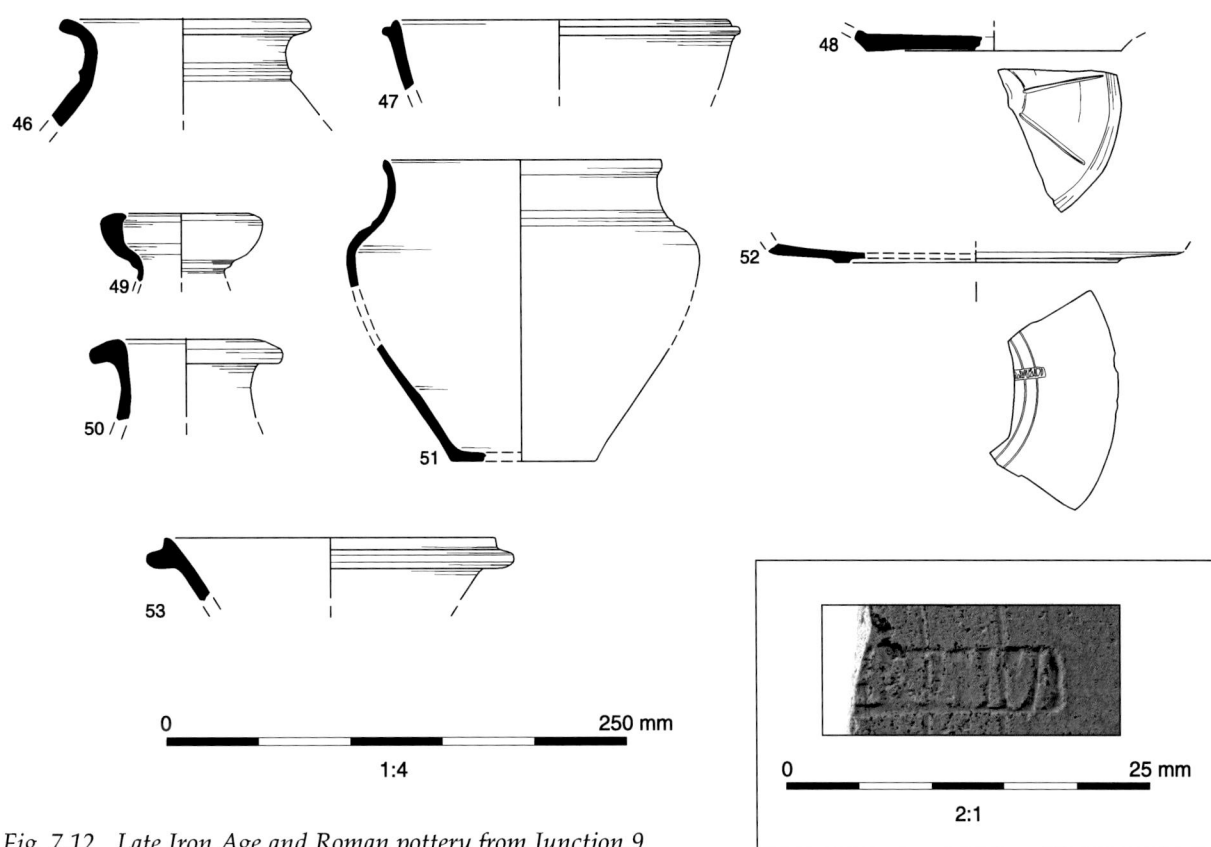

*Fig. 7.12   Late Iron Age and Roman pottery from Junction 9*

38    Thompson-type b2-4 jar. Fabric GROG. Ctx 2139
39    Lid-seated jar (cj 820). Fabric UNSREC. Ctx 2139
40    Carinated cup (fd 210). Fabric UNSREC. Ctx 2139
41    Lid-seated jar (cj 820). Fabric E40. Ctx 2139
42    Medium-mouthed jar (cd 740). Fabric E40. Ctx 2139
43    Bead-rimmed jar (ch 210). Fabric GROG. Ctx 2139
44    High-shouldered/necked jar (ce 730). Fabric GROG. Ctx 2139
45    High-shouldered/necked jar (ce 740). Fabric GROG. Ctx 2139
46    Medium-mouthed jar (cd 730). Fabric UNSREC. Ctx 2139
47    Flanged dish (jb 440). Fabric UNSREC. Ctx 2139
48    Base sherd with incised radial decoration. Fabric GROG. Ctx 2392
49    Cup-mouthed flagon (bb 242). Fabric VERWH. Ctx 2617
50    Bead-rimmed flagon (bb 242). Fabric VERWH. Ctx 2617
51    High-shouldered/necked jar (ce 730). Fabric GROG. Ctx 2036
52    Platter base with stamp (inita fe). Fabric GABTN. Ctx 2114
53    Flanged dish (ja 440). Fabric UNSREC. Ctx 2041

**Analysis of charred residue from pot 2041 by gas chromatography-mass spectrometry (GC-MS)** *by Ben Stern*

### Sample preparation

The charred residue was present within a pot recovered from context 2041. A sub-sample of 1g was solvent extracted with three aliquots of ~3ml DCM:MeOH (dichloromethane:methanol 2:1, v/v). The sample was partially soluble and the solvent became a pale orange/brown colour. The solvent extract was transferred to another vial and removed under a stream of nitrogen to leave the lipid extract. Excess BSTFA ($N,O$-bis(tri-methylsilyl)trifluoroacetamide) with 1% TMCS (trimethylchlorosilane) was added to derivatise the sample. Excess derivatising agent was removed under a stream of nitrogen. The samples were diluted in approximately 1ml of DCM for analysis by GC-MS. A method blank sample was prepared and analysed alongside the samples.

### Instrumental (GC-MS)

Analysis was carried out by GC-MS using an Agilent 7890A Series GC connected to an 5975C Inert XL mass selective detector. The splitless injector and interface were maintained at 300°C and 340°C respectively. Helium was the carrier gas at constant inlet pressure. The temperature of the oven was programmed from 50°C (2 min) to 350°C (10 min) at 10°C/min. The GC was fitted with a 15m x 0.25mm, 0.25m HP-5MS 5% Phenyl Methyl Siloxane phase fused silica column. The column was directly inserted into the ion source where electron impact (EI) spectra were obtained at 70eV with full scan from m/z 50 to 800.

## Results (GC-MS)

The results are presented as total ion chromatograms of the BSTFA derivatized solvent extract ($-Si(CH_3)_3$ derivatives). These show each separated component of the solvent extract as discrete peaks, the area under each peak being representative of the abundance (Fig. 7.13). Where identified, components have been labelled.

C = fatty acid, with carbon number and degree of unsaturation (as TMS derivatives),
* = branched isomer
MAG = monoacylglycerol, with carbon number of the fatty acid
DAG = diacylglycerol, with carbon number of the two fatty acids. Two isomers of each component.
TAG = triacylglycerol, with total carbon number of the fatty acids

The bulk of the residue was insoluble in the solvents used. However, the solvent extract of the charred residue from pot 2041 was a pale orange/brown colour. Although lipids are generally colourless the colour was a good general indication that the solvent extraction was successful in isolating solvent soluble components from the residue. The method blank contained no lipids confirming the absence of contamination during the sample preparation and analysis.

A range of triacylglycerols (labelled TAG) and their degradation products diacylglycerols (DAG), monoacylglycerols (MAG), fatty acids and glycerol were extracted from this sample. The triacylglycerols imply the presence of an animal fat or vegetable oil. Unfortunately, degradation causes the loss of the characteristic triacylglycerol distri-

bution of materials such as milk and adipose fats.

A wide range of saturated fatty acids ($C_8$ to $C_{27}$) were extracted from the sample. These are dominated by the $C_{16:0}$ and $C_{18:0}$ saturated fatty acids. Fatty acids are biologically synthesised in even carbon numbers and this indicates they come from a biological source. As fatty acids are ubiquitous at low levels in most environments, the high abundances found confirms that they originate from the sample and not from contamination. Supporting this is the absence of squalene, which is present in human fingerprints and often indicates contamination originating from recent handling. The presence of short-chain fatty acids (usually $C_4$ to $C_{14}$) may be indicative of a milk fat. Although the longer-chain fatty acids ($>C_{20}$) could also originate from a plant source.

A number of odd carbon-numbered fatty acids ($C_{15}$ and $C_{17}$) and their branched chain isomers (labelled as $C_{15*}$ $C_{17*}$, two isomers of each) were also extracted. These fatty acids are produced by bacteria which could be due to the bacterial degradation of the original oil/fat or possibly from a ruminant animal source.

Low abundances of the unsaturated fatty acid $C_{18:1}$ were extracted. The unsaturated fatty acids are preferentially degraded (over the saturated fatty acids) and this confirms that this is a degraded oil/fat. Although the ratios of abundances of the fatty acids can be used to determine the origin of the sample, this sample is degraded and, as little is known of the specific degradation pathways or their preferential degradation of one component over another (eg shorter-chain fatty acids are preferentially soluble in water than longer-chain fatty acids), this approach is not valid in this instance.

Cholesterol was also extracted from this sample. This indicated that the origin of the lipids is an

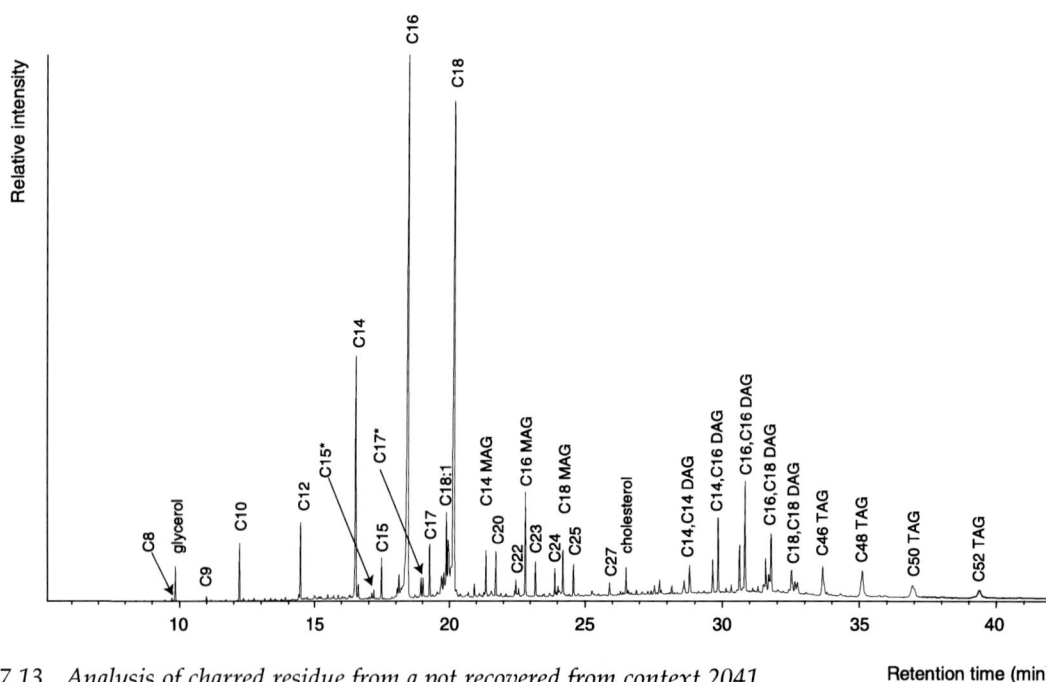

Fig. 7.13 *Analysis of charred residue from a pot recovered from context 2041*

animal source. This sample therefore contains a degraded animal fat and further analysis, such as compound-specific isotope ratio mass spectrometry of the $C_{16}$ and $C_{18}$ fatty acids, could be used to confirm the origin of the sample.

## MEDIEVAL POTTERY *by John Cotter*

### Junction 8N

#### Introduction and methodology

A total of 2152 sherds of pottery weighing 12.94kg was recovered from nearly 100 contexts on the Junction 8N site. The total rim estimated vessel equivalents (EVEs), or summation of rim circumference, was 6.06. Excluding earlier pottery, the assemblage from this particular site is entirely medieval and there is no Anglo-Saxon or post-medieval material. All the pottery was examined, spot-dated and fully catalogued (in MS Excel). For each context and fabric the total pottery sherd count and weight were recorded. Vessel form, if identifiable, was also recorded together with rim EVEs (circumference length) if present. Positive form identification was usually limited to rim sherds. As no universally accepted classification system exists for medieval pottery forms and fabrics in this area, a relatively simple site-specific system of classification was devised. The simple numeric and alphanumeric fabric codes used in the catalogue have been retained in this report but, wherever possible, cross-referenced to Museum of London (MoLAS) fabric codes, which are widely used in the London area and include several common Hertfordshire pottery fabrics (LAARC 2007). Form typology was limited to a few basic definitions (eg jar, bowl etc). More detailed codified definitions for vessel sub-parts (types of rim, base, handle etc) were also avoided as these rarely prove very useful on relatively small medieval assemblages such as that from Junction 8N. Simple descriptions of vessel sub-parts and any other attributes worthy of note (eg decoration, traces of use etc.) were, however, usually recorded in a comments field. The full pottery catalogue together with notes and sketches has been deposited in the site archive.

#### Date and nature of the assemblage

Overall the pottery assemblage is in a very fragmentary condition. The average sherd weight is only 6g, but this figure is slightly exaggerated by two contexts (6451 and 6305) containing only two or three very crushed vessels which have been counted as individual sherds (457 in total). If these are excluded the average sherd weight for the site is 7g. Many smaller sherds from the site are clearly abraded. Within the broader range, however, some larger fresher pieces have survived. These include at least two complete (reconstructable) jar/cooking pot profiles and several half profiles or significant portions of vessels. This is consistent with an assemblage largely derived from ditches, scattered pits and postholes, which appears to represent casual domestic rubbish disposal from a rural settlement context. This disposal probably took place over a century or two. The character of the pottery suggests occupation, or human activity, perhaps from as early as the later 11th century, although the main period of activity appears to have been from the late 12th-13th century. There may have been some activity into the 14th century, although the evidence for this is a little ambiguous.

#### Pottery fabrics

A relatively small number of pottery fabrics was identified. These are all local, or fairly local, apart from a Developed Stamford-ware jug and a possible exotic import. These are described and quantified in Table 7.23.

*Table 7.23: Quantification of medieval pottery fabrics from Junction 8N*

| Fabric | Name | Date | Sherds | Weight | EVEs |
|---|---|---|---|---|---|
| 1A | South Herts Greyware | *c* 1170-1350 | 1974 | 11531 | 5.07 |
| 1B | South Herts Greyware: fine | *c* 1170-1350 | 31 | 239 | 0.08 |
| 1G | Glazed greyware | *c* 1170-1350 | 9 | 85 | 0.42 |
| 2 | Chalk-tempered ware | *c* 1050-1150 | 61 | 404 | 0.21 |
| 3 | Flint-tempered ware | *c* 1050-1250? | 26 | 168 | 0.21 |
| 4 | Early med shelly ware | *c* 1075-1350 | 6 | 22 | 0.07 |
| 5 | Fine shelly-sandy ware | *c* 1050-1150? | 1 | 3 | 0 |
| 6 | Developed Stamford ware | *c* 1150-1250 | 14 | 270 | 0 |
| 7A | Oxidised sandy slipware | *c* 1200-1400? | 12 | 44 | 0 |
| 7B | Oxidised sandy ware | *c* 1200-1400? | 4 | 16 | 0 |
| 8 | Possible Islamic import | *c* 1200-1450? | 4 | 126 | 0 |
| UNID | Unidentified wares | *c* 1000-1500? | 10 | 32 | 0 |
| TOTAL | | | 2152 | 12940 | 6.06 |

*Fabric 1A. South Hertfordshire Greyware, c 1170-1350*

A medium-coarse sandy fabric. Equivalent to London fabric code SHER and SHER COAR (Vince 1985, 44). This grey reduced sandy coarse ware is easily the commonest pottery fabric from the site, as it is from most medieval sites in Hertfordshire. By sherd count it comprises 91.7% of the assemblage (or 83.7% by EVEs). The fabric and typology of this ware, or tradition, have been discussed in some detail for nearby St Albans (Havercroft et al. 1987) and a broader survey of the tradition is about to be published (Pearce and Blackmore forthcoming). A brief summary of the type and its main production sites has been published (McCarthy and Brooks 1988, 296-7), as has a detailed gazetteer of its known production sites in Hertfordshire (Turner-Rugg 1993). For the most part, the ware seen from the M1 excavations has a dense, grey to dark grey fabric with abundant, well-sorted, medium-coarse quartz sand and rare-sparse coarser quartz and flint grits. In terms of petrology, it is not a particularly distinctive fabric and given the similarity of South Hertfordshire Greywares in general it may not be possible to assign it to one or other of the several known production centres in the county on the basis of fabric characteristics alone.

In reality there is a fair bit of variation in texture, hardness and colour tone within this range, but no more than would be expected from a single production centre utilising slightly different local clay beds and sand pits over a century or more. These mostly fairly minor variations can usually be attributed to variations in the frequency and coarseness of the tempering agents (quartz mostly) and in the firing conditions in the kiln. For the purposes of this report, it has not been considered practical or necessary to divide the greyware assemblage into more than two categories: the medium-coarse Fabric 1A; and the rarer fine-medium Fabric 1B (see below). It is likely, however, that flint-tempered Fabric 3 (see below) may include sherds from the coarser end of this fabric range.

The fabric is mainly hard to very hard, but soft underfired examples also occur. Firing colour is mostly a uniform grey to dark grey but brownish-greys are also common. A few weakly oxidised, reddish-brown or orange-brown sherds also occur. Slight tonal variation is also evident on some of the most complete vessels. The internal and external surfaces often have a slightly different tone too; when this occurs the external surface is generally slightly browner than the internal surface. The core is generally slightly redder or browner than the surface colour, but sometimes just lighter or darker. A sandwich-effect firing is seen on some sherds but is not often very marked. At one end of the range, the texture of Fabric 1A can be fairly even, densely packed with abundant and well-sorted quartz grains mainly in the 0.25-1mm range, and with a slightly rough or rough feel. Most examples, however, have a fine or silty matrix with moderate to abundant coarse quartz inclusions up to 1mm, with occasional coarser quartz and flint inclusions up to 4mm across giving the fabric an abrasive feel and fairly gritty or pimply texture. At the other end of the range there is a gradual increase in very coarse inclusions including both quartz and flint grits, but such examples are fairly rare. Quartz inclusions are generally rounded to sub-rounded, occasionally sub-angular with a few worn crystals also noted. Quartz is predominantly clear and milky with lesser amounts of iron-tinted orange, brown, reddish and grey grains and occasionally red-brown iron-coated grains. Flint is generally sparse to moderate, mostly rounded, but also occurring as sparse sub-angular grits. Sparse to moderate red iron oxide or iron-rich clay pellets of varying size also occur, and occasional grey-clay pellets. Rare coarse inclusions of iron-cemented quartz grains or ironstone have also been noted, as have sparse organic inclusions. The matrix contains abundant fine mica. Despite these variations, however, the basic fabric and technology appear fairly uniform. Most vessels are clearly wheel-thrown but a few clearly have handmade bodies and wheel-finished rims.

*Sources of South Hertfordshire Greywares*

Around a dozen greyware production sites are known across Hertfordshire, most of them identified by pottery wasters and kiln furniture rather than actual kiln structures (see Turner-Rugg 1993, for most up-to-date gazetteer). Some of these have been listed in earlier summaries but sometimes, confusingly, by parish name or nearest town rather than find-spot (McCarthy and Brooks 1988, 296-7; Sheppard 1977). Production sites have also been found just outside the county. A kiln producing pottery in this tradition was excavated further south at Pinner in Middlesex (Sheppard 1977), and evidence for pottery production in this tradition has also been excavated at Uxbridge, Middlesex (Knight and Jeffries 2004). Similar grey sandy wares were also produced in neighbouring counties most notably at Limpsfield in Surrey, Denham in Buckinghamshire, and various locations in Bedfordshire and Essex.

The M1 Junction 8N site is located in the middle of west Hertfordshire. As it is more than likely that the occupants of that site obtained their greyware pottery from fairly local production sites (perhaps via local markets or itinerant traders) only those in the western part of the county will be considered as the most likely candidates. One cannot, of course, rule out the possibility of an occasional vessel or two arriving from more far-flung sources. Unfortunately, the rather uniform fabric of South Hertfordshire Greywares and their rather undiagnostic sedimentary petrology do not lend themselves to close provenancing. Minor visual and textural differences have been detected in the greyware fabrics from nearby St Albans and these, in combination with chemical analysis, may one day prove significant in identifying kiln sources (Havercroft *et al.* 1987, 32) but, to date, attempts to source greyware fabrics by simple visual comparison alone do not seem to have met with much success (A Turner-Rugg pers. comm.). Comparison of vessel typology, particularly of decorated jug handles, has some potential for sourcing (ibid.), but not all kiln-site assemblages have been adequately illustrated and published, and as the M1 assemblage has remarkably few surviving jug handles this technique is of no use in this case. Physical comparison of the M1 greywares with those of every production site known in the county is not currently a feasible option and might, in any case, be of questionable value. For the present, therefore, the most likely sources to have supplied the site are judged to have been the closest, and there were enough of these in west Hertfordshire to limit the search to this area.

The city of St Albans, only 5km east of the Junction 8N site, is easily the largest nearby consumer site of medieval pottery. Hertfordshire Greyware is by far the commonest type of pottery there on sites dated from the 12th-14th centuries and has been studied and published in some detail (Havercroft *et al.*1987). Being so close it seems logical that the sources supplying St Albans might also be those that supplied the Junction 8N site. These might, therefore, have included the kiln site at Wildhill, near Hatfield, *c* 13 km further east (Turner-Rugg 1993, 33), but to date none of the greywares from St Albans have been ascribed to a particular source. Indeed, it is possible that there was a more local kiln site supplying the city but which remains undiscovered (A Turner-Rugg pers. comm.). The closest possible production site which might have supplied the Junction 8N site is the small hamlet of Potters Crouch which lies only *c* 3.7km south-east of the site and immediately west of the village of Chiswell Green. The identification of this as a pottery production site, however, is only tentative and seems to be largely based on place-name evidence. Turner-Rugg (1993) does not mention it in her gazetteer and knows of no definite evidence for this suggestion (A Turner-Rugg pers. comm.). Although the place-name makes it an obvious candidate for a pottery-production site (as does its proximity to large modern sand/gravel quarries) the earliest reference found to this suggestion seems to be in Sheppard's (1977) article concerning the Pinner kiln in which he suggests, 'The other possible sites at Arkley, Elstree, Enfield, Potters Crouch and Wild Hill have produced kiln furniture or wasters but no actual kiln structures' (ibid., 35). He also clearly marks it as a kiln in his location map (ibid., fig. 4). McCarthy and Brooks (1988, fig. 165, no.19) also show Potters Crouch (Hertfordshire) as a production site on a location map of the south Midlands, but otherwise do not discuss it. If there were evidence in the form of kiln wasters and furniture from Potters Crouch it is unlikely that Turner-Rugg would have overlooked

it in her comprehensive 1993 gazetteer, unless the material is lost or remains in private ownership. Enquiries are currently in progress to determine the basis for these suggestions but, for the moment at least, Potters Crouch remains a possible candidate for the supply of pottery to the Junction 8N site, even if this rests solely on place-name evidence.

Two definite greyware production sites lie in different directions both only *c* 9.5km from Junction 8N. These are Nettleden, near Hemel Hempstead, to the north-west, and Chandlers Cross, near Rickmansworth, to the SSW. At Nettleden, a double-flue kiln was discovered and Greyware pottery from this site includes jugs, jars, a large storage jar and some bowls (Turner-Rugg 1993, 33, fig. 2-3). The jars/cooking pots from this kiln are mostly short necked with stubby sub-squared rims or with simpler beaded rims. Some very small jars were also produced (ibid., fig. 3.27-8). Some jars (and bowls) have applied thumbed strips. The jugs include examples with handles decorated with slashing or thumbed edges. A few body sherds with bands of combed wavy decoration are also present (ibid., fig. 3.26, 29-31). Although Turner-Rugg (ibid.) offers no specific dating for the Nettleden kiln the relatively simple rim forms and the presence of combed decoration may suggest that it dates to the first half of the 13th century rather than later. These simpler jar/cooking pot rim forms find plenty of general and even exact parallels amongst the Junction 8N assemblage and the presence of a few comb-decorated sherds in both assemblages makes Nettleden a strong candidate for the supply of at least some greywares to the Junction 8N site for at least part of the settlement's existence.

Chandlers Cross, to the south, has also produced a definite pottery kiln of the horizontal-draught type. Details of this site and its products are briefly summarised elsewhere (Havercroft *et al.* 1987, 45, fig. 3.52-63, jugs; Turner-Rugg 1993, 32, not illus.). The kiln produced South Hertfordshire Greyware including jugs, jars, bowls and curfews. Some of this greyware has linear decoration in white slip and extensive areas of dark green glaze. Potentially this source is just as likely to have supplied the Junction 8N site as Nettleden. A few sherds of glazed greyware, including a jug rim, were found at the Junction 8N site (see Fabric 1G below) and Chandlers Cross is more likely to be the source of these than any other production site in the county. A single greyware storage jar from Berkhamsted Castle, 10km north-west of our site, is possibly an underfired waster but there are no other details of its provenance (Turner-Rugg 1993, 32). It may, in any case, have come from the nearby Nettleden kiln. As one moves outside west Hertfordshire the likelihood of more distant greyware production centres supplying the Junction 8N site becomes more remote. These could, however, have included the known production centre at Gustard Wood, near Wheathampstead, *c* 14km north-east in central north Hertfordshire. This site produced greywares, some, apparently with freckles of green glaze; a massive and heavily decorated storage jar rim and a spouted vessel are also known from this site (ibid., 32). Down on the south-western border of the county, *c* 15km south-east of Junction 8 and less than 2km apart, lie the production sites of Barnet Lane, Elstree, and Elstree Hill South. Finds from the probable kiln site at Barnet Lane are in a homogenous greyware and comprise jugs with thumbed handles, jars, storage jars and socketed bowls (ibid., 31-2).

The probable kiln site at Elstree Hill South produced greyware wasters in three fabric types including a sand and flint-tempered fabric. Forms included jugs with thumbed handles, jars and bowls. Some vessels had applied band decoration and stabbed rims (ibid., 32; Salveson and Blackmore 1985). Both these sites were potential suppliers of greywares to the Junction 8N site and the presence of flint-tempered fabrics at Elstree Hill South is of particular interest given the presence of at least some flint-tempered (Fabric 3) vessels from the Junction 8N site. Other greyware production sites in central and eastern Hertfordshire are also documented (Turner-Rugg 1993), but these are much less likely to have supplied settlements in the west of the county than the more accessible production sites listed above. It is of course very likely that there were other production sites in west Hertfordshire and elsewhere in the county that remain to be discovered. In time it may be possible to identify Hertfordshire Greyware products more accurately via chemical or textural analyses as well as traditional visual and typological comparison, but most of this lies beyond the scope of the present report.

*South Hertfordshire Greyware vessel forms*

Only 270 sherds of South Hertfordshire Greyware have been assigned to a definite vessel form. These are all featured sherds, mostly rims plus a few handles or large base/body sherds. Such sherds comprise only 13.7% of the 1974 sherds in this fabric. The remainder mostly comprise body sherds and undiagnostic base sherds. Quantification by EVEs (surviving rim percent) is a more reliable approach to vessel composition, although this has the disadvantage of excluding very minor forms that might not have surviving rims. Jars/cooking pots, as expected, are easily the commonest form represented in this fabric, comprising 95.3% of the fabric EVEs total. Jugs comprise only 4.1% and bowls only 0.6%.

Jars: complete profiles are limited to only two or three examples but jars seem to have a typical medieval rounded or globular profile, sometimes slightly shouldered, with a variety of fairly simple rim types (see below) and always with a plain sagging base. The majority of jar sherds, particularly the base and lower walls, show evidence of sooting from their use as cooking vessels and a few examples show internal 'limescale' deposits. Other jars, apparently unsooted, may have been used for storage. Jars/cooking pots appear to be predominantly wheel-thrown but a few, perhaps earlier examples, clearly have handmade bodies and wheel-finished rims. The inside of one large sooted cooking pot (Fig. 7.14.1), though quite fragmentary, clearly shows two roughly horizontal rows of pinching or squeezing to build-up the lower half of the vessel, which was probably coil built; the rim, however, was finished on a turntable or wheel. Sherds from a few other jars also show this technique. One of the smallest jars in the assemblage also exhibits internal irregularities suggesting handmade manufacture (Fig. 7.14.2). Handmade but wheel-finished greyware jars of early appearance have been noted at Whormeley Wood near Stevenage in north Hertfordshire (Turner-Rugg 1993, fig. 8-11). Composite manufacture, with handmade bodies and wheel-finished rims, is also a feature of very similar coarse greywares in north Essex and is considered to be an early mode of production which disappeared soon after *c* 1250 when fully wheel-thrown vessels became the norm (Cotter 2000, 91-107). Rim diameters cover a wide size range from 110-350mm. Based on EVEs and approximate vessel counts it is clear, however, that the size range 180-280mm is common, with each 10mm subdivision represented by at least two vessels. Within this range there are two peak sizes; one at 260mm (0.61 EVEs, *c* 7 vessels) and a joint peak at *c* 210-220mm (0.56 EVEs each, *c* 7-8 vessels each). Although the highest single EVEs count is at *c* 145mm (0.75 EVEs) this is for a single small jar profile and is therefore unrepresentative of the main size trends. Jar diameters outside the 180-280mm range are fairly rare with vessels above 280mm represented by single examples only.

Rim types were not individually coded or quantified in detail (but the basic shape was described in the catalogue comments field). Most rims fell into two broad and overlapping types: thickened flat-topped rims; and sub-squared rims. Both types account individually for roughly a third each of all rim types found on jars, with the thickened flat-topped rims being perhaps slightly commoner. The remaining third comprises a variety of other less common rim types including plain everted or thickened everted types, also externally beaded rims, rare clubbed rims (probably dating to *c* 1150-1225) and more developed squared or flanged rims (Figs 7.14.1-13 and 7.16.34-51). Within the two main types of rim there are innumerable minor variations caused by the addition of internal or external bevelling, or other minor modifications caused by varying pressure from the potter's fingers as the vessel turned on the wheel. Such variation is a common feature of South Hertfordshire Greywares and many other medieval coarse ware industries.

Decoration of any sort is quite rare and not easily quantifiable as most of this occurs on body sherds, which might include sherds from rarer non-jar forms. Definite decoration, such as incised or combed decoration, is very rare but more ambiguous types of 'decoration' such as external rilling or girth grooves, and thumbed strips, are slightly more common. The rims of at least ten jars/cooking pots (0.42 EVEs) bear some sort of decoration (see also bowls below). Two jar rims appear to have light external thumbed decoration on the rim itself. One of these also has traces of incised wavy-line decoration on the neck externally (Figs 7.14.5 and 7.16.47). Another unusual jar rim has an incised wavy line on the top of the rim (Fig. 7.14.6). Two separate jar rims from the same context are decorated with a combed wavy band on the inside of the neck and incised-line or comb decoration on top of the rim (Fig. 7.16.34-5). A possible bowl also has similar internal combed decoration (see below). One other jar rim has traces of horizontal combed or finely rilled decoration on the shoulder (Fig. 7.14.4). This sort of decoration has also been noted on body sherds from at least two other vessels, probably jars, including one with bold horizontal rilling or external grooving. Marked shoulder rilling, as opposed to grooving or combing, occurs on several other jars (Fig. 7.4.7) and although this could be a by-product of wheel throwing it may also have been used to decorative effect. Rilling or 'corrugation' has been noted on greyware jars from St Albans (Havercroft *et al.* 1987, fig. 4.65-6, 68). A jar with an angle or carination on the shoulder and a plain everted neckless rim (Fig. 7.14.9) also has close parallels at St Albans (ibid., fig. 4.64) and from the Pinner kiln (Sheppard 1977, fig. 3.14-15, 17). Ten body sherds from the neck/shoulder area of perhaps half a dozen jars have applied horizontal or vertical thumbed strips. These are probably functional (to strengthen the vessels' walls) rather than decorative. A bowl or unusually large jar rim with shoulder strips is the only example of this type illustrated (Fig. 7.15.16).

Within the overall jar category are one or two other possible examples of specialised jar forms but represented by base sherds only. These include six joining sherds from the base of a small tripod-footed vessel; probably a tripod pipkin or small cauldron. The sherds include parts of two tripod feet attached to a sagging base which is heat scorched or sooted in places. The feet were formed as solid rods of clay and inserted through the vessel wall (Fig. 7.15.14). Pipkins were smallish jars with a rod-like side handle. They were probably used to prepare smaller portions of food or sauces. Although pipkins are known from St Albans, these all have plain sagging bases and so far none has been found with feet as with the example recovered from Junction 8N (Havercroft *et al.* 1997, 37). One unique sherd has been tentatively interpreted as coming from the sagging base of a large decorated storage jar (Fig. 7.15.15). This has a diameter of *c* 380-400mm with a thumbed strip applied around the basal angle and with traces of vertical combed wavy bands. Alternatively, this could be from the dome of a curfew (firecover), although it shows no traces of sooting.

Bowls: these are very rare and may not be bowls in the usual sense (shallow open forms), but possibly exceptionally large jars or storage jars since the rim forms are very similar. Only two examples were identified from rim sherds (2 sherds, 0.03 EVEs, or 0.6% of the fabric assemblage). One of these is identified from an everted jar-like rim (Fig. 7.15.16) of very large diameter (*c* 480mm). This has traces of a horizontal-applied strip on the neck and probably a vertical strip too. The other example is represented by a small sherd from a thick-walled vessel with a damaged rim and traces of combed horizontal decoration internally (Fig. 7.15.17). Typical wide greyware bowl forms, which occur at St Albans and elsewhere, were not identified.

Jugs: these are rare and only eight sherds (0.21 EVEs, or 4.1% of the fabric assemblage) have been identified with any certainty. These comprise rim sherds from five individual jugs and one detached jug handle. Because of the very small number of jugs recovered, and their fragmentary condition, none of these has the pronounced thumbed and stabbed-decorated handles that are so characteristic of South Hertfordshire Greyware jugs and which offer the best possibility of linking greyware jug assemblages to known production sites (Havercroft *et al.* 1987, 45, fig. 1-3). At the Nettleden kiln, jugs with decorated strap handles predominate, whereas at the Chandlers Cross kiln jugs with rod-section handles predominate. The single handle from the Junction 8N site (Fig. 7.15.18) and another from the nearby targeted watching brief site (see below; Fig. 7.15.19) are both of rod section and could conceivably be from Chandlers Cross, although the sample is admittedly very small and perhaps unreliable. Most of the jug rims are of simple collared form (Fig. 7.16.33) as is a glazed greyware (Fabric 1G) jug rim (Fig. 7.15.21). One rim is of simple thickened flat-topped form as is the more complete example from the targeted watching brief site at Junction 8 (see below; Fig. 7.15.19). This also has the stub of a rod-section handle with faint traces of stabbing on top. These simpler rims might be of fairly early date (perhaps *c* 1170-1225). The other handled sherd is from the lower end of a handle with a pair of thumbed impressions to secure it to the vessel wall (Fig. 7.15.18). Apart from the stabbed handle stub, none of the jugs show decoration, although some body sherds with horizontal rilling or fine grooving might have come from this form. Including the glazed jug and the watching brief example, rim diameters are in the 110-160mm range. Jugs would most commonly have been used for fetching and serving liquids. The scarcity of jugs (table wares) from this site suggests that dining and entertaining were not high priorities and that the site was probably of low status.

Miscellaneous: an odd ?basal sherd with a diameter of *c* 250mm (Fig. 7.15.20), and from the same context as the tripod pipkin (see above), appears to have been decorated on its underside with something like an unusual incised lattice design made before the vessel was fired. This was scored to a depth of 2mm with a blade. There is no external evidence of sooting, but the interior shows possible traces of sooting or boiling. It is possible that this sherd is from a lid or a curfew.

*Fabric 1B. South Hertfordshire Greyware (fine-medium fabric), c 1170-1350*

Possibly equivalent to London fabric code SHER FINE. Probably a much finer (and rarer) variant of Fabric 1A (see above), although other sources cannot be ruled out. Fine grey sandy fabric with abundant quartz mostly under 0.3mm, with rare grains up to 2mm. Other inclusions as in Fabric 1A. Sherds from perhaps seven-eight vessels represented. The only substantial vessel to survive is the upper part of a large wheel-thrown jar/cooking pot with a thickened flat-topped rim (Fig. 7.15.31). This vessel occurs in a particularly fine, light grey, almost Roman-looking fabric. A few other body sherds from other contexts have fine horizontal rilled or lightly combed decoration. These could be from jars or jugs.

*Fabric 1G. Glazed grey sandy coarse ware, c 1170-1350*

Probably a much rarer glazed variant of South Hertfordshire Greyware (Fabric 1A; see above) with nine sherds from a maximum of four vessels, possibly jugs, recovered from the site. These have a thin patchy clear glaze externally showing greyish-green against the reduced background. The only rim sherds are from a jug with a pouring lip (Fig. 7.15.21). This has a markedly collared rim and an unusual angled or carinated shoulder which bears fine horizontal rilling. Although this has been classed as a glazed greyware the fabric is a uniform leached pale brown with a few matt-black patches externally and only a few lead pellets embedded in the centre of these; it may, however, have been more extensively glazed lower down on the body. Small quantities of glazed greyware sherds have been identified from the kiln at Chandlers Cross (Turner-Rugg 1993, 32) and from excavations in St Albans (Havercroft *et al.* 1987, 32). See also Fabric 7A below.

*Fabric 2. Chalk-tempered ware, c 1050-1150*

Possibly equivalent to London fabric code EMCH (Vince and Jenner 1991, 70-2). Mainly with oxidised orange-brown surfaces and a grey core, although some pieces are greyish-brown or grey throughout. Quite a bit of textural variation. Abundant rounded chalk or algal-limestone inclusions showing white or grey, up to 4mm across but in some specimens consistently under 1mm across. The chalk is often dissolved leaving only pockmarks. Moderate to abundant fine-coarse quartz inclusions and sparse-moderate angular flint. Some specimens are much grittier than others. This fabric is common from late 11th- or early 12th-century deposits at St Albans and

is presumably fairly local (ibid.; see also Turner-Rugg 1995, 46, where they are grouped under 'calcareous wares'). The second commonest fabric from the site, but represented by only 61 sherds (2.8% of the site assemblage, or 3.5% by EVEs). Many of these are presumably residual in later contexts. Present as handmade jars/cooking pots probably, in some cases, with wheel-finished rims. A range of fairly simple thickened and flat-topped rims is represented, sometimes internally hollowed (Fig. 7.15.22-4), although one example has a more developed later-looking squared rim (Fig. 7.15.25) with equal proportions of chalk and sand. One small body sherd shows traces of combed decoration (not illus.; Key Group 6407). Unless the site was unoccupied for around 20 years, there must have been a point of overlap between the supposed end-date of chalk-tempered ware *c* 1150 and the introduction of South Hertfordshire Greywares *c* 1170. It could be that outside urban centres, like St Albans, chalk-tempered wares lingered on for another decade or two; just long enough to be contemporary with the first arrival of greyware. These may have included the sandier/grittier chalk-tempered vessels with more developed rims. Similar chalky gritty fabrics remained in production in the Winchester area, for example, as late as *c* 1225.

*Fabric 3. Flint-tempered ware, c 1050-1250?*

This falls within a group of 'early medieval unglazed sandy and gritty' wares found in St Albans and believed to date from the 11th and early 12th centuries (Turner-Rugg 1995, 48). These are thought to be of local manufacture, as some are very similar to the later South Hertfordshire Greywares. The samples from the M1 include both early medieval-looking handmade jars/cooking pots and sherds from wheel-thrown vessels that are possibly just coarser variants of South Hertfordshire Greywares, which can sometimes be flint tempered (ibid.). On this basis, the flint-tempered ware from the Junction 8N site is tentatively dated to *c* 1050-1250, but most examples probably belong to the later end of this range. This is probably equivalent to London Fabric code SHER FL (South Hertfordshire Flint-tempered Greyware), which is dated to *c* 1170-1350 (Pearce and Blackmore forthcoming). The fabric from the M1 includes a range of textures. The earlier-looking handmade examples have a fairly soft micaceous matrix with moderate very coarse angular to sub-rounded flint grits up to 4mm, moderate-abundant ill-sorted quartz up to 1mm and sparse chalk and iron compounds. Firing colour varies from dark grey to light brown. The later-looking wheel-thrown examples have the same better-sorted fabric as Fabric 1A above, but with the addition of moderate coarse angular flint up to 3mm. This fabric is fairly rare from the site (26 sherds) and possibly mostly residual.

Rims from four flint-tempered jars/cooking pots were recovered with diameters in the 160-250mm range. These include early-looking simple thickened flat-topped rims (Fig. 7.15.26-7) and a more developed wheel-thrown sub-squared/internally hollowed example (Fig. 7.15.32). Some sherds show external sooting and one has internal sooting. Despite the coarseness of this fabric a small body sherd from context 6631 is decorated with sunburst stamps in the Saxo-Norman tradition (Fig. 7.15.28). This is the only coarse-ware sherd from the site with stamped decoration. It is relatively thin walled (6mm thick) and in view of these features might perhaps be from a spouted pitcher rather than a plain jar.

*Fabric 4. Early medieval shelly ware, c 1075-1300*

Probably the same as the 'Medieval Shelly ware' (Fabric MC1) found at Great Linford in Buckinghamshire. The exact source is unknown but probably resides in the Ouse Valley, Buckingham-shire (Mynard 1992, 251). Similar fabrics also occur in Bedfordshire. It contains inclusions of Jurassic fossil shell identical to late Saxon St Neot's-type ware, possibly with the addition of crushed bivalve shell, but is generally coarser than the latter. It also contains fossil limestone, moderate fine-medium quartz inclusions and sparse flint. The shell is sometimes dissolved out. Firing colour is brown to dark grey. Some sherds are oxidised externally and reduced internally. Only six fairly small sherds were recovered from the site from just three vessels, probably wheel-thrown, including an everted jar/cooking pot rim probably with light thumbing on the apex (Fig. 7.15.29).

*Fabric 5. Fine grey sandy ware with shell. Possibly 11th-12th century?*

Present as a single small sherd from a jar/cooking pot with a flaring thickened everted rim with traces of thumbed decoration probably on the inside of the rim (context 6055, not illus.). Dark grey fabric with abundant fine-medium rounded quartz, very fine mica and sparse-moderate coarse inclusions of platy ?fossil shell up to 6mm long. Source unknown but similar to Early Medieval Sand and Shell-tempered ware (Fabric EMSS) from the London area, common there c 1075-1150 (Vince and Jenner 1991, 59-63). From a late 12th-13th-century context (6055) associated with Fabric 1A, but possibly residual.

*Fabric 6. Developed Stamford ware, c 1150-1250*

A high-quality wheel-thrown green-glazed white ware produced at Stamford in Lincolnshire. Normally traded in the form of jugs (Kilmurry 1980, 11, 130). London Fabric code DEVS (Vince and Jenner 1991, 96). The fabric is very fine and sandy with few inclusions visible to the naked eye except a few specks of red iron oxide. All 14 sherds are from the base and walls of a single jug in Key Group 6407 (Fig. 7.15.30). This has an off-white to very pale grey fabric with a glossy external clear glaze with abundant copper-green flecks. Stamford ware occurs sporadically on early medieval sites across

Hertfordshire (Turner-Rugg 1993, type not speci-fied) and also occurs at Great Linford in north Buckinghamshire, but is rare (Mynard 1992, 274). The latter does not apparently include any examples of Developed Stamford ware.

*Fabric 7A. Oxidised orange sandy slipware, c 1200-1400?*

Present as 12 body sherds apparently from glazed jugs with evidence of white-slip decoration. The fabric is fairly coarse and sandy. Most sherds are fairly worn but the slip decoration appears to be linear. One small sherd (context 6601) has an all-over external white slip with traces of narrow vertical strips in red clay under a green copper-flecked glaze in the 'highly decorated' or 'North French' style as found, for example, on London-type ware jugs of c 1250-1350 (Pearce et al. 1985). The fabric of these sherds, however, is too coarse for London-type ware or Mill Green ware (Essex) but not unlike some of the many medieval 'Essex redwares', such as medieval Harlow ware or Colchester-type ware (Cotter 2000, 107-80). Alternatively, and perhaps more likely, they could be examples of the less well-understood local glazed wares (oxidised or reduced) which also sometimes have white-slip decoration. These are thought to be a 'fine ware' variant of South Hertfordshire Greywares (Fabric 1A; see above) and have been found in very small quantities in earlier 13th-century contexts at St Albans and from the Chandlers Cross greyware kiln (Turner-Rugg 1993, 32; 1995, 48-52). A recently discovered greyware kiln at Bancroft, Hitchin, also produced a small collec-tion of glazed oxidised sandy ware with white-slip decoration (P Blinkhorn pers. comm.). Other sources, however, cannot be ruled out.

*Fabric 7B. Oxidised orange sandy ware (no visible slip), c 1200-1400?*

Otherwise as Fabric 7A above. Four body sherds present from a single glazed vessel, probably a jug. The context (6537) appears to be 13th century in date.

*Fabric 8. Possible Islamic import, c 1200-1450?*

Four abraded body sherds from a single vessel (not illus.) were recovered, three from key pit group context 6407 and one from pit context 6202, 15m distant. Pit group 6407 contained several fresh sherds from a Developed Stamford ware jug (Fabric 6; see above), a glazed South Hertfordshire Greyware sherd (Fabric 1G; see above) and a large assemblage of South Hertfordshire Greywares (Fabric 1A; see above), including jugs, and is there-fore dated to c 1170-1250. Although petrological analysis has proved inconclusive (see below), this fabric may be broadly equivalent with London Fabric code ALKG (Alkaline Glazed ware), an umbrella code for medieval alkaline glazed wares from the Islamic world including greenish-blue glazed Raqqa-type wares from Syria and Egypt, and

Maghrebi wares from north-west Africa (Vince 1985, 38, 54).

The M1 sherds are possibly from a fairly large jar or pitcher which, on balance, is probably wheel-thrown, although the surfaces exhibit many slight irregularities, particularly on the largest sherds. The curvature on the two largest sherds, probably from the lower wall of the vessel, suggests a diameter in excess of *c* 270mm at the maximum girth (higher up). The two smaller sherds are slightly thinner walled and probably from the shoulder area of the vessel, as these show fine horizontal grooving or throwing marks externally. The fabric is unusually hard and dense for a Near Eastern import and is probably overfired, giving it a sub-stoneware hardness. Despite a superficial resemblance to Near Eastern stonepaste ('fritware') fabrics, it does not appear to be an example of this class (see below). It is fine and sandy with a broad mid-grey core with paler-grey margins and surfaces. The original glazed surface has almost completely been worn off, but in pockmarks and slight surface irregularities there are tiny traces, or islands, of fine white sandy slip bearing even smaller traces of a thick greenish crystalline or aquamarine transparent glaze, apparently alkaline. The largest patch of glaze is just under 4mm across. Glaze patches occur on both the outside and the inside of the vessel suggesting it was originally glazed all over. Most of the broken edges show considerable abrasion and none of the sherds join, although it is obvious they all come from the same vessel. The sherds have a maximum thickness of 10mm and a minimum thickness of 7mm, but would have been slightly thicker with the glaze. Thin, but extensive patches, of a brownish-yellow, possibly cessy, post-deposition deposit occur on some of the sherds. Though much harder, the sherds are quite like a blue-green alkaline glazed bowl from St Gregory's Priory, Canterbury. The latter is probably of early 13th-century date and believed to come from Egypt (Cotter 2001, 237-8, 264, fig. 206.95). This accords well with the dating suggested for pit group 6407. The sherds were shown to the late Dr Alan Vince in 2008 who was also of the opinion that they might be of Near Eastern origin (pers. comm.). A thin-section report and commentary on the M1 vessel has been carried out by Rebecca Bridgman (see below). Unfortunately, this has not enabled the vessel to be assigned to a known source, although origin in the central Islamic lands was not entirely ruled out. It is fairly certain, however, that the vessel is a foreign import, perhaps from the Mediterranean, even if not Islamic. Future research may eventually determine its source. Quite how an exotic imported glazed vessel of fairly large size ended up in a medieval farmstead in rural Hertfordshire is unclear, but rare isolated finds of Near Eastern 'Raqqa' ware have previously been made on remote rural sites, such as in a peasant dwelling at Abdon in Shropshire (Hurst 1968, 198; see also Cotter 2001), as well as at several high-status sites in Britain. These would have been exotic and highly prized possessions in their time; some perhaps brought back by pilgrims or even crusaders visiting the Holy Land or the Near East. Whatever the route by which the vessel ended up at the Junction 8N site, it must, with its blue-green glaze, have appeared strikingly exotic next to the rather humdrum coarse local greywares with which it was eventually associated.

### Unidentified wares (UNID)

Ten sherds cannot be assigned to any of the above fabric groups. These are individually described in the comments field of the catalogue (details in site archive). In nearly every case the sherds are too small or worn to be confidently identified and may include misidentified Roman wares. One of two sherds may be unusually pale grey or off-cream variants of Fabric 1A. Two small glazed sherds (total weight 7g) deserve a comment however. The larger of these (6591) is soft and very worn with a very fine to fine creamy orange-buff fabric and with a small speck of clear glaze. The smaller sherd (7083) weighs less than 1g and has the same fabric as the latter but with a worn copper-green flecked glaze externally. These can probably be identified as jug sherds in either Brill/Boarstall ware from Buckingamshire (*c* 1200-1600), or as Late Medieval Hertfordshire Glazed ware (*c* 1350-1450). Unfortunately, the fabric of these two industries is too similar to distinguish in sherds as small as this (Turner-Rugg 1995, 52). Associated greywares in these contexts, however, suggest a 13th-century dating and therefore probably a Brill/Boarstall identification, although they seem slightly finer than most examples seen by the author.

### Post-medieval wares, c 1550-1900

These are absent from the Junction 8N site but a small number of these occur on other M1 sites. These comprise a few sherds of 17th/18th-century glazed red earthenwares, but mostly consist of mass-produced Victorian white earthenwares and stoneware bottles. Full details of these can be found in the project archive or are mentioned briefly in the other site reports.

### Pottery and dating in relation to the site

Pottery from contexts associated with building 6961 was examined to see if its chronology could be refined in any way and to see if there were any chronological or functional differences between pottery from the main building and its eastern 'annexe'. These contexts included three large rubbish pits (6406, 6188 and 6054) parallel to the northern wall of the building, but just outside it. The majority of the pottery recovered from the site came from these pits and from one or two others much further south of the building. The main building itself produced only small groups of pottery and the annexe just a few smallish sherds from a handful of contexts. No chronological or functional differences could be determined between the main building and annexe, or between the building and the greater majority of medieval contexts across the site. The conservative nature of South Hertfordshire Greywares makes it difficult to refine the dating within its estimated currency of *c* 1170-1350, particularly as virtually the only vessel form present is the ubiquitous jar/cooking pot. However, there is little from the site to suggest definite occupation into the 14th century and most contexts have been dated to the period *c* 1170-1300, which marks the peak of occupation on this site. In some cases, the presence of a few more developed greyware rim forms or the presence of rare glazed sherds has resulted in some contexts being dated to the 13th century. The latter include a few contexts associated with the main building. Some contexts associated with the building include definite examples of handmade greyware jars with wheel-finished rims which represent an early mode of greyware production that can probably be dated to *c* 1170-1250, and this dating fits well with the single Developed Stamford ware jug (*c* 1150-1250) from pit 6406 (context 6407). It is probably safe to conclude that the main building was occupied by *c* 1200-50 and possibly for a decade or two after this when completely wheel-thrown greyware jars became the norm.

The three large rubbish pits (6406, 6188 and 6054) parallel to the building deserve more detailed consideration, as these produced the majority of the pottery recovered from the site and include some of the largest and freshest sherds (see above). The largest of these is pit 6406, the upper fill of which (6407) is treated here as a key group with most of its pottery illustrated. This produced three of the four sherds from the possible Islamic vessel (ALKG). The fourth sherd came from a context (6202) in pit 6188 about 15m to the north-east. This is the most noteworthy cross-join recorded from the site; an observation helped by the distinctiveness of the fabric. Pit 6406 is the most westerly of the three main pits. It is of unusually oval plan, measuring 8.20 x 3 x 0.68m, with its long axis aligned with the other two pits and roughly with that of the building. Its three fills include much charcoal and rubbish so it may well be a rubbish pit, though in view of its size and unusual shape it might also originally have been a latrine pit. The quantities of pottery from each fill are given in Table 7.24.

*Table 7.24: Breakdown of medieval pottery quantities in pit 6406*

| Context | Sherds | Weight | EVEs |
|---------|--------|--------|------|
| 6407 | 299 | 2709 | 1.06 |
| 6698 | 54 | 321 | 0.56 |
| 6699 | 102 | 846 | 0.85 |
| TOTAL | 455 | 3876 | 2.47 |

The 455 sherds from pit 6406 comprise 21% of the site total. The figure for weight and EVEs is even higher (30% and 41% respectively). The average sherd weight for the whole pit is 8.5g, which is higher than the site average, with that of context 6407, at 9g, being the highest of all for a large group. The main fabrics in each of the three fills are roughly in the same proportions as those present in the overall site assemblage and so will not be considered in too much detail. The main fabric is South Hertfordshire Greyware (Fabric 1A), together with some of the finer greyware (Fabric 1B), and in each context a few sherds of chalk-tempered ware (Fabric 2) and flint-tempered ware (Fabric 3). The additional fabrics in 6407 are considered below. Context 6699, the lowest fill, mainly comprises sherds from just three greyware vessels including a complete small handmade jar/cooking pot profile (Fig. 7.14.2). It also includes the rim from a very large jar or possibly a bowl (diameter 350mm; not illus.) and another smaller jar rim. Sherds from the small jar profile in 6699 also occur in the middle fill 6698 which also produced a glazed greyware jug rim (Fig. 7.15.21).

The uppermost and main fill, context 6407, is treated here as a key group in that most of the rim sherds have been illustrated. This is the only context from the site to have produced Developed Stamford ware; a single green-glazed jug base and body sherds (Fig. 7.15.30). It also produced sherds from the only possible Islamic vessel (ALKG; not illus.). These two vessels, both probably table wares, must have been strikingly different from the mass of local greywares. Other minority wares illustrated from this group include the only substantial example of a fine South Hertfordshire Greyware jar (Fabric 1B; Fig. 7.15.31), and a developed jar rim in flint-tempered ware (Fabric 3; Fig. 7.15.32). The large South Hertfordshire Greyware element in this assemblage comprises a single jug rim (Fig. 7.16.33) and rims from at least 18 jars/cooking pots (Fig. 7.16.34-51; see Fabric 1A description above for reference to some of these).

Pits 6188 and 6095, within the same axis, will be considered more briefly. Pit 6188 is a large sub-circular rubbish pit. A sherd cross-join (ALKG) between this and Key Group 6407 was present (see above). The fills of this pit (6202, 6206 and 6207) produced 134 sherds of pottery (1095g) including three sherds of glazed greyware (Fabric 1G). Two chalk-tempered jar rims (Fig. 7.15.22-3) and two flint-tempered rims (Fig. 7.15.26-7) are illustrated, as well as several of the many greyware jar rims (Fig. 7.14.5 and Fig. 7.14.12). The only early medieval shelly ware jar rim from the site is also from this pit (Fabric 4; Fig.7.15.29). Pit 6054 lies *c* 4.5m. north-east of pit 6188 at the end of the pit axis. The fills of this pit (6055 and 6067) produced 48 sherds of pottery (413g). The only illustrated piece is a possible greyware bowl rim with internal combed decoration (Fig. 7.15.17). The only fine shelly-sandy ware jar rim also came from here (Fabric 5; not illus.).

East and south of building 6961 lay four gullies (7006, 6402, 6403 and 7704). These produced varying quantities of pottery which are indistinguishable in character from contexts associated with the building and which have therefore been similarly dated to *c* 1170-1300.

To the north of building 6961, in the angle of the enclosure, stood kiln/oven 6585. This contained a fairly small quantity of pottery, all domestic rubbish. As well as South Hertfordshire Greywares, one context (6591) also produced a small glazed sherd which may be Brill/Boarstall ware (see UNID) and if so must date after *c* 1200. Two greyware vessels from this context also have a developed, fully wheel-thrown, appearance and may date to the mid-late 13th century. In the south-eastern corner of the medieval settlement, a limekiln (6577) produced a small fresh assemblage of handmade jars in South Hertfordshire Greyware. including a profile. These probably date to *c* 1170-1250.

## Conclusions

While not the best preserved of assemblages, the medieval pottery from Junction 8N provides an essential dating framework for the site and sheds a degree of light on the economy and status of the site as well as the needs and daily concerns of its inhabitants. In medieval rural Hertfordshire, pottery, as in many other small rural settlements, was primarily functional and utilitarian and not usually the primary medium through which status and higher aspirations were expressed. The site seems to have had no early Anglo-Saxon activity. The character of the pottery suggests occupation or human activity perhaps from as early as the later 11th century. The small quantity of chalk-tempered and flint-tempered wares (both from *c* 1050, but possibly slightly earlier) do not rule out the possibility of some pre-Conquest activity. The main period of activity, however, appears to have been from the late 12th-13th century coinciding with the predominance of South Hertfordshire Greywares. There may have been some activity into the 14th century, although the evidence for this is a little ambiguous. The site is fortunate in that no later occupation or reoccupation occurred, which might have disturbed this otherwise quite narrow timeframe of medieval occupation.

There is very little diversity in the range of pottery fabrics and vessel forms available. Local coarse wares (South Hertfordshire Greywares) overwhelmingly predominate and nearly all of these are cooking pots or storage jars. The remainder comprises a small number of glazed and unglazed jugs, in some cases from slightly more distant sources, including a single green-glazed jug from Stamford in Lincolnshire and a single exotic imported vessel, which may have been a treasured personal possession. Apart from the latter there are no foreign imports. Over 90% of pottery supplied to the site came from sources probably within a *c* 4.5-9.5km radius. These very probably included greyware products from the probable nearby kiln site at Potters Crouch and from the known kilns at Nettleden, near Hemel Hempstead, and Chandlers Cross, near Rickmansworth. Only a sprinkle of more attractive glazed table wares would have come from sources beyond this (although some probably came from Chandlers Cross). These probably included other Hertfordshire kiln sites and possibly one or two sources in neighbouring counties perhaps including Essex, Buckinghamshire, and of course the one recognisable import from Lincolnshire. No London products were recognised even though glazed London-type jugs and other forms are widely distributed across south-east England. This lack of diversity, even monotony, is consistent with a fairly isolated and low-status rural settlement with little evidence for social dining and entertainment, or the fancy table wares and ceramic fripperies associated with this.

Evidence for the economy of the site is difficult to deduce from the pottery alone. Most vessels here were greyware jars and the abundant evidence for sooting on these indicates that most of these were cooking pots. Other unsooted jars may have been used for storage. A single tripod cooking vessel, a pipkin or cauldron, may have been used for making sauces. The few jugs identified would have been used for fetching and serving liquids including ale and wine. The almost complete absence of wide bowls, or indeed bowls of any sort (only two possible examples identified), is striking and puzzling and may reflect the economy of the site. On some other low-status medieval rural sites in England the presence of wide bowls in quantity has been linked to dairying practices (butter, cheese production etc; Brown 1997, 92-3), so their absence from this site requires some explanation. It has also been suggested, however, that ceramic bowls may occasionally have been used as grain measures, or 'cantels', and this was argued in the case of the rural settlement at West Cotton, Northamptonshire, where there was a high correlation between shallow ceramic bowls and bakehouses (Blinkhorn 1998-9, 44-5). In the case of our site, however, the dairying connection seems like the more plausible explanation. It could be that dairying practices, or the rearing of cattle and sheep for their milk products, were of low priority to the economy of this settlement, which may perhaps have been grain, wool or meat based. The lack of bowls might therefore be explained by the lack of concern for dairying. Wide pottery bowls were certainly available at the time and they occur in local kiln assemblages and in nearby St Albans. The low priority of dairying practices at the Junction 8N site is a possible and attractive explanation for the absence of bowls, but certainly not the only one. Pottery only ever provides a partial answer, but it generally survives much better than vessels in other materials such as wood, leather and metal. It could be that in this particular place and time wooden bowls were preferred for dairying purposes, and for eating off, but evidence for these has simply not survived. On its own the pottery evidence is inconclusive on this point, but at least provides one possible explanation. Evidence to support these suggestions might be better sought in the animal bone or other non-ceramic assemblages from the site. The fairly small assemblage of medieval animal bone includes a few horses, cattle, sheep and quite a few pigs; this evidence neither supports nor refutes the possible explanation offered here (see Chapter 8). The relatively high number of pig bones however adds some weight to the suggestion of a meat-based site economy. The lack of medieval small finds, however, is unlikely to help on this point, but does at least support the general impression of material poverty.

## Junction 8 targeted watching brief

This site produced a small assemblage of medieval pottery comprising 67 sherds weighing 296g and with a total of 0.16 EVEs. The fabrics and quantities are shown in Table 7.25.

The pottery came from a series of rubbish pits and appears to represent ordinary domestic rubbish. No medieval pottery came from the hollow-way. The condition is generally poor, with an average sherd weight of only 4.4g. Fabrics present, and the relative frequency with which they occur, mirror those on the main Junction 8N site but are restricted to the main local fabrics. The unidentified fabric is a thin-walled body sherd from a ?jar with marked external rilling. This is possibly a very pale-grey variant of South Hertfordshire Greyware and two sherds of this also occurred on the main site. South Hertfordshire Greyware vessel forms present (as rims) comprise a jar/cooking pot and a fairly simple jug rim with the stub of a rod handle (Fig. 7.15.19). A jar/cooking pot rim in flint-tempered ware is also present plus sagging base sherds, probably from jars, in chalk-tempered ware. The date range represented by the assemblage is similar to that of the main site, falling between the later 11th and 13th centuries, with the period *c* 1170-1300 best represented.

## Junction 8 Compound

This site produced only two sherds of medieval pottery weighing 24g and with a total of 0.07 EVEs.

These came from two contexts (5515 and 5521). Both sherds, which are worn, are in chalk-tempered ware (Fabric 2) and date to *c* 1050-1150 or possibly slightly later. The sherd in context 5515 is from the rim of a large jar/cooking pot with a thickened flat-topped rim with internal bevel (diameter 300mm., not illus.). The other sherd is a body sherd.

## Catalogue of Illustrated vessels (Figs 7.14-16)

1    Jar profile showing handmade body and wheel-turned rim. Fabric 1A. Dia: 340mm, Ctx 6823
2    Small jar profile showing handmade body and wheel-turned rim. Fabric 1A. Dia: 140-150mm. Ctx 6699
3    Jar, half profile. Thickened flat-topped rim. Fabric 1A. Dia: 220mm. Ctx 6823
4    Jar with sub-squared rim and horizontal combed decoration on shoulder. Fabric 1A. Dia: 230mm. Ctx 6537
5    Jar rim with traces lightly thumbed decoration on external rim and incised wavy line on neck externally. Fabric 1A. Ctx 6202
6    Jar rim with ridge on interior and incised wavy line on top of rim. Fabric 1A. Dia: 220mm. Ctx 6581
7    Jar with plain everted rim and bold external rilling. Fabric 1A. Dia: 210mm. Ctx 6503
8    Jar with plain everted rim. Fabric 1A. Dia: 180mm. Ctx 6951
9    Jar with plain everted rim and angle on shoulder. Fabric 1A. Dia: 210mm. Ctx 6591
10   Jar with squared rim. Fabric 1A. Dia: 240mm. Ctx 6111
11   Jar with early-style clubbed rim. Fabric 1A. Dia: 220mm. Ctx 7174
12   Jar with heavy-clubbed rim. Fabric 1A. Ctx 6207
13   Jar with thickened upright internal bevelled rim. Fabric 1A. Ctx 6111
14   Tripod ?pipkin or cauldron base with evidence of two inserted rod-like feet. Sooted in places. Fabric 1A. Dia: *c* 150mm. Ctx 6451
15   ?Storage jar base with applied angle strip and combed dec. Fabric 1A. Dia: *c* 380-400mm. Ctx 6947
16   Bowl/jar rim with horizontal- and vertical-applied thumbed strip decoration on neck. Fabric 1A. Dia: 480mm. Ctx 6432
17   Bowl/jar rim (damaged) with horizontal combed decoration on neck int. Fabric 1A. Ctx 6055
18   Jug handle. Lower junction with thumbed impressions. Fabric 1A. Ctx 6631
19   Jug with simple rim. Stub of rod handle with traces of stabbing on top. Fabric 1A. Dia: 160mm. Ctx 5630
20   Odd basal sherd with incised decoration under-

*Table 7.25: Medieval pottery totals from the Junction 8 targeted watching brief site*

| Fabric | Name | Date | Sherds | Weight | EVEs |
|---|---|---|---|---|---|
| 1A | South Herts Greyware | *c* 1170-1350 | 59 | 220 | 0.12 |
| 2 | Chalk-tempered ware | *c* 1050-1150 | 4 | 54 | 0 |
| 3 | Flint-tempered ware | *c* 1050-1250? | 3 | 18 | 0.04 |
| UNID | Unidentified wares | *c* 1000-1500? | 1 | 4 | 0 |
| TOTAL | | | 67 | 296 | 0.16 |

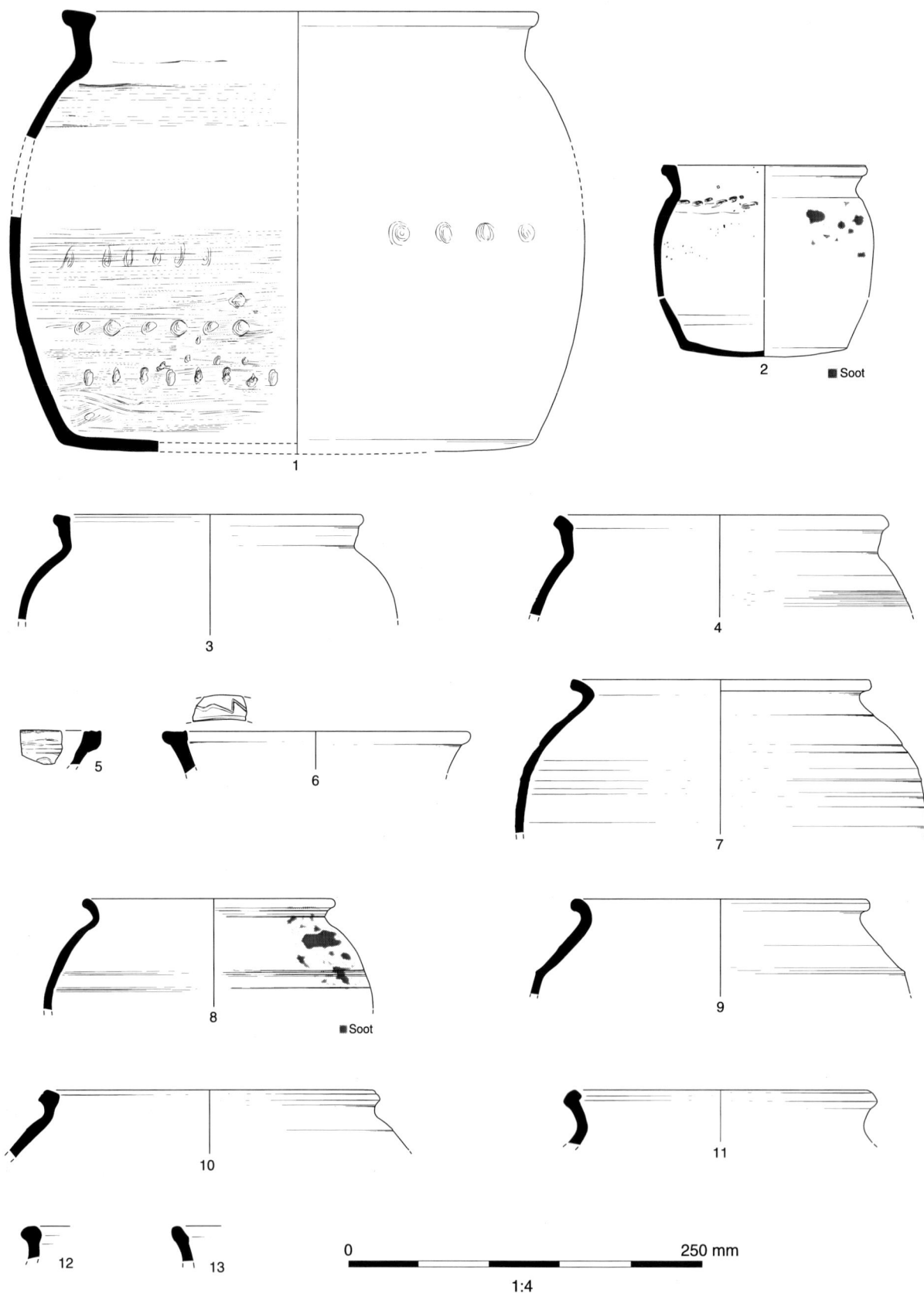

*Fig. 7.14   Medieval pottery*

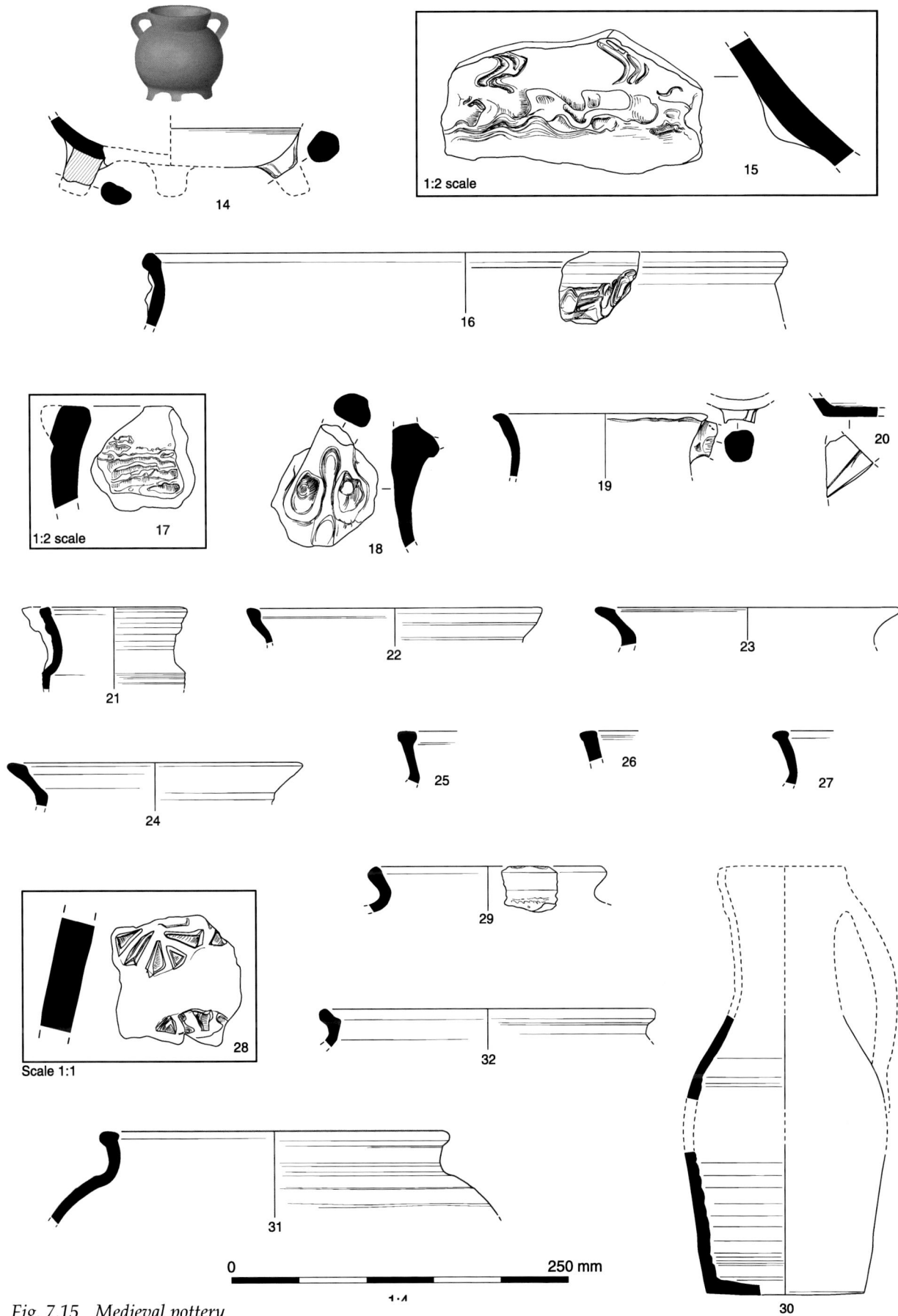

*Fig. 7.15  Medieval pottery*

side. ?Jar or curfew? Fabric 1A. Dia: c 250mm. Ctx 6451

21 Jug with collared rim, pouring lip and specks of glaze. Fabric 1G. Dia: 110mm. Ctx 6698

22 Jar with internal cupped rim. Fabric 2. Dia: 220mm. Ctx 6202

23 Jar with internal everted flat-topped rim. Fabric 2. Dia: 230mm. Ctx 6202

24 Jar with flat-topped lid-seated rim. Fabric 2. Dia: 220mm. Ctx 6662

25 Jar with squared rim. Fabric 2.Dia: 240mm. Ctx 6497

26 Jar with plain flat-topped rim. Fabric 3. Ctx 6202

27 Jar with thickened flat-topped rim. Fabric 3. Dia: 160mm. Ctx 6207

28 Body sherd with sunburst stamps. Fabric 3. Ctx 6631

29 Everted jar rim with light thumbing on apex. Fabric 4. Dia: 180mm. Ctx 6206

30 Jug. Base and shoulders. Mottled green glaze. Fabric 6. Base dia: 120mm. Ctx 6407 (Key Group)

31 Jar rim. Fabric 1B. Dia: 260mm. Ctx 6407 (Key Group)

32 Jar rim. Fabric 3. Dia: 250mm. Ctx 6407 (Key Group)

33 Jug rim. Fabric 1A. Dia: 120mm. Ctx 6407 (Key Group)

34 Jar rim with combed wavy-band decoration on internal neck and incised wavy-line decoration on top of rim. Fabric 1A. Ctx 6407 (Key Group)

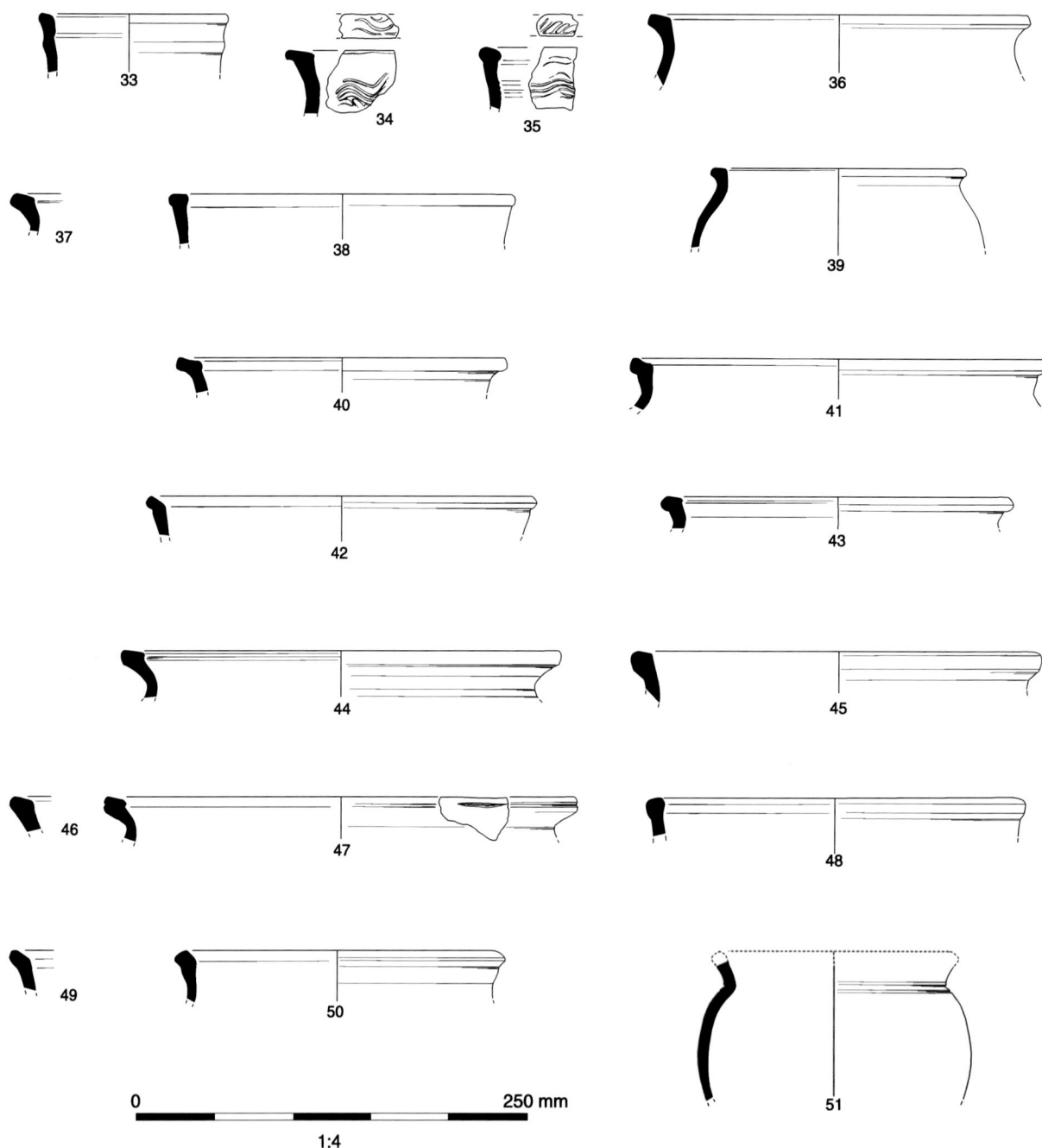

0 ──────── 250 mm
1:4

*Fig. 7.16 Medieval pottery*

35 Jar rim with combed wavy-band decoration on internal neck and possible combed decoration on top of rim. Fabric 1A. Ctx 6407 (Key Group)

36 Jar rim. Squared. Fabric 1A. Dia: 230mm. Ctx 6407 (Key Group)

37 Jar rim. Squared. Fabric 1A. Dia: 240mm. Ctx 6407 (Key Group)

38 Jar with thickened flat-topped rim. Fabric 1A. Dia: 220mm. Ctx 6407 (Key Group)

39 Jar rim. Sub-squared. Fabric 1A. Dia: 160mm. Ctx 6407 (Key Group)

40 Jar rim. Squared. Fabric 1A. Dia: 210mm. Ctx 6407 (Key Group)

41 Jar rim. Sub-squared. Fabric 1A. Dia: 260mm. Ctx 6407 (Key Group)

42 Jar with thickened flat-topped rim. Fabric 1A. Dia: 250mm. Ctx 6407 (Key Group)

43 Jar rim. Squared. Fabric 1A. Dia: 230mm. Ctx 6407 (Key Group)

44 Jar rim. Sub-squared with internal groove. Fabric 1A. Dia: 280mm. Ctx 6407 (Key Group)

45 Jar rim. Sub-squared. Fabric 1A. Dia: 260mm. Ctx 6407 (Key Group)

46 Jar with thickened flat-topped/internal-bevelled rim. Fabric 1A. Ctx 6407 (Key Group)

47 Jar rim with traces of lightly thumbed or grooved decoration on external rim. Fabric 1A. Dia: 300mm. Ctx 6407 (Key Group)

48 Jar rim with thickened clubbed form. Fabric 1A. Dia: 240mm. Ctx 6407 (Key Group)

49 Jar with squared, steeply angled rim. Fabric 1A. Ctx 6407 (Key Group)

50 Jar rim. Sub-squared with bulge below. Fabric 1A. Dia: 210mm. Ctx 6407 (Key Group)

51 Jar body. Small, c 170mm maximum girth. Groove at neck/shoulder junction. Fabric 1A. Ctx 6407 (Key Group)

**Analysis of a glazed ceramic sherd** *by Rebecca Bridgman*

*Introduction*

A ceramic sherd, with a hard grey fabric whose surface incorporated remnants of green glaze on a fine white slip, was subject to petrological analysis in order to establish production source (Fig. 7.17). A possible source in the central-Islamic lands was hypothesised and it was suggested that this sherd may be categorised as a stonepaste fabric. The aim of petrological analysis was to test this hypothesis.

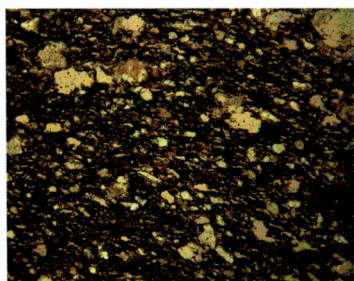

*Fig. 7.17 Photomicrograph taken in plane polarised light, area 1023x768μm*

The sherd is from a pit context (6407) associated with local wares dated *c* 1170-1250.

*Methodology*

Standard procedures were used to prepare a sample *c* 0.03mm thick, suitable for analysis using a petrological microscope (Peacock 1970, 379), based on the identification, arrangement, frequency, size, shape and composition of component inclusions (Whitbread 1995, 368). For the analysis of this sample, reference was made to the largest-scale testing of Islamic pottery carried out by Mason (2004).

*Results*

The sample tested is characterised by common quantities (20%) of poorly sorted, sub-angular quartz inclusions measuring no greater than 0.5mm in size, most frequently cracked but clear in appearance. Very few other inclusions, with a particular absence of diagnostic rock or mineral fragments, were observed making the source of production difficult to identify. As the sample contains only common quantities of quartz, it does not fall into the category of stonepaste or even proto-stonepaste fabrics that were commonly produced in central-Islamic lands from the early 11th century (ibid., 170-1). Stonepaste and proto-stonepaste fabrics are characterised by abundant (50-60%) inclusions of quartz, in some cases combined with glass fragments (ibid.). Furthermore, the inclusions observed here are not similar to those identified by Mason (ibid.) in his analyses of other fabric types from Iraq, Syria, or Iran. The closest fabric that could be compared to those tested is Mason's 'Ca-Nile 1' from Fustat, which lacks the carbonate inclusions associated with other Nile fabrics, but which does contain plagioclase feldspar (ibid., 77). Given the lack of plagioclase feldspar in the Hertfordshire sample, it seems unlikely that this could be a possible origin of this sherd. Based on current analysis, therefore, it is difficult to suggest an origin within the area defined as the central-Islamic lands as the sample tested does not match previous analysis of material from this area. Nevertheless, as the geographical area of the central-Islamic lands is very large and our understanding of ceramic production relatively poor, the possibility that the Hertfordshire sample was made in this region cannot be totally discounted.

*Observed Inclusions*

**Quartz:** present in common quantities (20%) with predominantly sub-angular grains which are poorly sorted (measuring up to 0.5mm). Includes rare (1%) polycrystalline grains and examples with significant cracking.

**Orthoclase feldspar:** present in rare quantities (1-2%) sub-rounded inclusions.

**Limestone:** present in rare quantities (1%) with sub-rounded inclusions.

**Iron-rich pellets:** sparse (3-5%) sub-rounded.

## THE CERAMIC BUILDING MATERIAL AND FIRED CLAY *by Cynthia Poole*

### Introduction and methodology

Ceramic building material (CBM) and fired clay, predominantly of late Iron Age and Roman date were recovered from the mitigation phase of excavations, at Junction 8, Junction 9, Area M and Area P. A smaller quantity of medieval/post-medieval tile was also found, mainly from the Junction 9 area. The material from the evaluation phase of the project has been incorporated with the data from the mitigation assemblage and included in the current report.

The assemblages from the mitigation excavations amounted to a total of 2886 fragments, weighing nearly 212kg, of CBM and 2543 fragments of fired clay, weighing 6783g. The material from the evaluations adds about a further 200 fragments of tile weighing *c* 13kg, but less than fifty fragments of fired clay weighing under a kilogramme. No complete tiles were recovered and thickness was the only complete dimension for the majority of pieces, though in a small number of cases length or breadth dimensions also survived. The overall mean fragment weight (MFW) of 74g for the tile reflects the relatively small size of individual pieces, though a single fragment could range from 1g to over 2kg. Nearly half the assemblage was moderately or heavily abraded. No discard policy was implemented during recording, though small shattered fragments of tile were discarded, unless they were the only pieces from an individual context.

The fired clay was extremely poorly preserved, with a very low MFW of 3g, which reflects the fact that most was recovered from sieving (sieved material had a MFW of 1.5g). However, even the material recovered by hand only had an MFW of 12g, a mean size which produces few recognisable or diagnostic fragments. Individual fragments ranged from 1g up to 140g. It was also frequently difficult to distinguish the fired clay from ceramic building material. The sieved samples were rapidly scanned and only fragments greater than 5g recorded in any detail. Much of the sieved material was discarded, retaining only shaped fragments or up to six representative fragments, where no shaped pieces survived. The tile and fired clay assemblages have been fully recorded and the data entered on an MS Excel spreadsheet.

### The fabrics

Fabrics were defined on macroscopic characteristics as well as with the aid of a x10 hand lens and additionally with a binocular microscope at x25 magnification. Eight Roman and five medieval/post-medieval tile fabrics were identified. Nearly all the Roman tile was orange or orange-red in colour and a number of fragments were classified as intermediate types between fabrics.

### *The Roman fabrics*

Fabric A: pale pink, orange pink or salmon pink clay matrix with cream-buff surface containing a moderate density of medium-coarse rose, white- or clear-quartz sand and sometimes a scatter of angular and rounded coarse stone sand and grit 0.5-3mm, plus rare scattered large grits up to 10mm of quartzite and burnt flint. The coarse sand and grit content may have derived from similar moulding sand frequently associated. This was very similar in character to Eccles ware, though whether this was indeed being brought from the Eccles kilns or was produced more locally from a similar geological clay source has not been established.

Fabric B: red-orange or maroon-red fine sandy-clay matrix containing a high density of medium quartz sand and rounded maroon iron-oxide grits or iron-rich silty clay pellets 1-8mm.

Fabric C: orange or brown-orange; fine silty-clay matrix containing a low-moderate density of medium-coarse quartz sand; occasional large clay pellets 1-10mm and rare organic impressions sometimes present.

Fabric D: light orange-brown surface; orange core; very fine sandy-silty clay fabric containing no or few inclusions apart from fine sand and very occasional coarse quartz sand (derived from moulding sand) and occasional diffuse buff clay pellets.

Fabric E: orange, red or brown in colour. The clay matrix usually contained moderate-frequent quantities of fine-medium quartz sand, and was laminated with pale orange or cream streaks enlarging into rounded globules of cream clay. Laminations varied from prominent to more diffuse and some pieces contained detached cream or ferruginous maroon-red rounded silty-clay pellets 1-7mm. The cream pellets were occasionally up to 20mm in size.

Fabric F: light brown, buff, pink and cream fine smooth clay, occasionally laminated, with few visible inclusions, but highly porous, which appeared to result from shell inclusions having been leached out in most examples. In a few some evidence of shell grit survived.

Fabric G: orange or reddish brown with cream streaks laminated clay contained a high density of white, usually coarse, quartz and other rock sand and common coarse angular flint grit up to 20mm and occasionally chalk of the same size.

Fabric H: orange-brown, diffusely laminated hard and dense sandy-clay matrix containing a high density of fine-coarse quartz sand, the coarse quartz mostly white and rose, plus rounded red-maroon iron-oxide grits up to 3mm size and rounded grits of chalk or crypto-crystalline limestone 1-8mm.

## The fired-clay fabrics

The same or very similar fabrics to the finer sandy tile group were used for much of the fired clay, which has resulted in difficulty in separating less diagnostic fragments of fired clay or tile. Fired clay normally derives from local clay sources and this similarity supports the hypothesis of a fairly local source for the tile. Some of the fired clay was assigned to fabrics distinct from the tile. These included FC:A, which consisted of a clay mixed with poorly sorted sand and small grit and on occasions containing additional organic temper (FC:A2). Another variety was FC:A3, a fine sandy-silty micaceous-clay matrix containing a low density of scattered angular flint grit 1-8mm. Occasionally chalk grit was present (FC:C).

## The medieval/post-medieval fabrics

Five exclusively post-Roman fabrics were identified, as well as a brick fabric very close in character to Fabric E, recorded as MedE in the data record.

Med1: orange-red clay matrix, which contained a high density of well-sorted coarse white-/clear-quartz sand (sub-angular-sub-rounded) 0.5-1mm, rare rounded haematite 0.5-1mm and scattered angular grits of quartz or quartzite up to 4mm.

Med2: an orange or reddish orange sandy laminated clay sometimes with cream streaks containing fine quartz sand and sub-angular-sub-rounded cream and red-clay pellets 1-5mm. This is similar to Roman fabric E, but somewhat finer.

Med3: red, brownish red very uniform fine sandy clay containing frequent fine quartz sand <1mm and rare grains of quartz and haematite 1-2mm.

Med4: red to reddish brown fine sandy clay containing poorly sorted sand comprising frequent fine-medium sand, mostly quartz but occasional dark grains, coarse angular flint grits 1-2mm and dark rounded overfired grog or slaggy inclusions *c* 2mm.

Med5: Red to brownish red, fine sandy clay containing common coarse sand grits of quartz and flint 1-2mm.

## Moulding sand

A range of the more distinctive moulding sands were noted on 186 records. The fairly standard clear/rose medium quartz sand was not normally recorded. Seven broad groups were established from the recording notes and were distinguished by the sand grade, type and the dominant colour. White-quartz sand was the most common, sometimes combined with clear or rose quartz, or a black rock sand and creating a speckled appearance in the finer varieties (MS2). The most common varieties were coarse white-quartz sand (MS5.1) or this combined with angular white-/grey-flint grits up to *c* 6mm (MS6). These were used predominantly in the Roman period, whilst in medieval/post-medieval periods only MS6 and to a lesser extent MS5.1 were at all common. None were exclusive to a particular fabric category, though some showed some slight correlation, for example MS1 and MS2 was more common on fabric D. More noticeable is the absence of these moulding sands on Fabric A.

## Discussion of the fabrics

The Roman fabrics can be allocated to three broad fabric groups. The smallest is a shelly group containing only fabric F. This was used for a few fragments found only on sites Junction 9 and Junction 8N, and may represent a minor input from production sites on the Oxford Clay to the north-west in Bedfordshire or Northamptonshire.

A second small, but significant group, is a coarse sandy group containing flint or chalk grit. This comprises fabrics A, G and H. Fabric A is distinctive with a strong similarity to Eccles ware; it is likely to derive from a single production site though it has not been confirmed that this derives from the Eccles (Kent) kilns. It was found almost exclusively at Junction 9, apart from a single fragment each at Junction 8N and Area M. Nearly three-quarters was found in early Roman phase deposits, which would be compatible with the known period of production of Eccles fabric. The absence of the white-quartz moulding sands on Fabric A also suggests a quite separate source to the other fabrics. Fabrics G and H were similar and may represent closely related clay sources. Fabric G was most common, whilst only a few pieces of H were identified. These were found at Junction 8N with lesser quantities at Junction 9 and a few fragments recovered during the evaluation. They were present throughout the Roman period, but occurred most frequently during the middle Roman phase.

The largest group, which formed over three-quarters of the assemblage, comprising Fabrics B, C, D and E, was characterised by a finer sandy fabric, often laminated with ferruginous and silty-clay pellets. These fabrics form a continuum with overlapping characteristics and are likely to represent a single geological clay source, the variations resulting from spatial differences in the clay exploited or variables in the preparation of the clay.

All occurred in moderate quantities in the early Roman phase, but are most frequent during the middle Roman phase, decreasing considerably in the late Roman phase. These fabrics formed the dominant group on all the main sites occurring in similar proportions except at Junction 8S where fabrics D and E dominated the assemblage. The white-quartz and gritty moulding sands were found on all the fabrics of this group suggesting a further connection between these fabrics.

The similarity of the main fabric group to the fired-clay fabrics suggests that the majority of the clay fabrics represent relatively local or regional production. Kilns are known at Verulamium and the surrounding area (Swan 1984, 97-8). The most likely source is the Radlett-Brockley Hill pottery and tile industry (Castle 1976) which exploited the Tertiary clays to the south of St Albans and was situated close to Watling Street.

The post-Roman fabrics are broadly similar in character to the earlier fabrics suggesting they too were manufactured in the region around St Albans. The fabrics used for roof tile were sufficiently different to have their own designations. Fabric Med1 was predominantly used for medieval roof tile, whilst fabrics Med2 and Med3 were mainly used for post-medieval tile, apparently replacing Med1. The few fragments of Med4 all appear to be medieval in character, whilst Med5 had the appearance of post-medieval tile.

## Forms and function

### The Roman tile

Examples of all major Roman tile types were found, including *tegula*, *imbrex*, flue tile, brick, *tesserae* and more unusually some examples of segmental brick, *tegula mammata* and half box-flue tile. Only the larger sites, described in more detail below, produced a wide range of forms, whilst the smaller excavations and watching briefs produced almost exclusively brick and plain flat tile, with only a few occurrences of flue tile and *tegulae*. Quantification of all the major brick and tile types from the main sites is given in Table 7.26.

### Brick and flat tile

Brick formed over two-thirds of the Roman tile assemblage, amounting to over 1200 fragments weighing nearly 150kg. It was made in all fabrics except Fabric F. No complete dimensions survived except thickness which ranged from 25mm to over 70mm (Table 7.27), with the majority measuring 35-45mm in thickness. Most pieces had a smooth flat upper surface and a more irregular rough lower

*Table 7.26: Quantification by count/weight (g) of CBM forms by site*

| Class | Site Junction 8S | Junction 8N | The Aubreys | Area M | Area P | Junction 9 | Junction 10 | Other | Total |
|---|---|---|---|---|---|---|---|---|---|
| *Roman* | | | | | | | | | |
| Brick | 18/2185 | 1062/125385 | | | 2/227 | 117/20555 | 2/129 | 4/87 | 1205/148568 |
| Brick: segmental | | 2/2935 | | | | 78/1396 | | | 80/4331 |
| Tegula mammata | 5/4130 | 14/5535 | | | | 1/49 | | | 20/9714 |
| Flat tile | 36/1074 | 347/14294 | 7/259 | 6/491 | 20/1044 | 290/9324 | | 9/684 | 715/27170 |
| Flue | 2/217 | 21/826 | | 1/120 | | 12/1342 | | 1/62 | 37/2567 |
| Tegula | 2/92 | 92/11758 | | 2/453 | | 62/7313 | | | 158/19616 |
| Imbrex | | 31/2223 | | 1/15 | | 31/2111 | | | 63/4349 |
| Tessera | | 3/60 | | | | 12/252 | | | 15/312 |
| Indeterminate | 90/328 | 422/2524 | 11/51 | 4/20 | 8/35 | 114/801 | | 8/38 | 657/3797 |
| *Total Roman* | *153/8026* | *1994/165540* | *18/310* | *14/1099* | *307/1306* | *717/43143* | *2/129* | *22/871* | *2950/220424* |
| *Post-Roman* | | | | | | | | | |
| Brick: Medieval / post-medieval | 2/1571 | 1/30 | 1/28 | | | | | 3/226 | 7/1855 |
| Brick: perforated | | | | | | | | 1/54 | 1/54 |
| Floor | | | | | | 1/87 | | | 1/87 |
| Roof: flat | 14/684 | 11/399 | 1/12 | | | 36/673 | 9/479 | 18/338 | 89/2585 |
| Roof: peg | 2/208 | | | 2/17 | | 6/105 | 4/55 | 4/192 | 18/577 |
| Roof: ridge/pantile | | 1/26 | | | | | | | 1/26 |
| Wall tile | | 1/51 | | | | | | | 1/51 |
| *Total post-Roman* | *18/2463* | *14/506* | *2/40* | *2/17* | | *43/865* | *13/534* | *26/810* | *118/5235* |
| Total | 171/10489 | 2008/166046 | 20/350 | 16/1116 | 30//1306 | 760/44008 | 15/663 | 48/1681 | 3068/225659 |

*Table 7.27: Comparison of imbrex, tegula, brick and flat-tile thickness showing the numbers of tiles within each size grade*

| Thickness | Imbrex | Tegula | Flat | Brick |
|---|---|---|---|---|
| 11-15 mm | 14 | 4 | 10 | 0 |
| 16-20 mm | 11 | 28 | 38 | 0 |
| 21-25 mm | 5 | 29 | 36 | 4 |
| 26-30 mm | 0 | 11 | 36 | 14 |
| 31-35 mm | 0 | 1 | 31 | 84 |
| 36-40 mm | 0 | 0 | 7 | 144 |
| 40-45 mm | 0 | 0 | 0 | 220 |
| 46-50 mm | 0 | 0 | 0 | 29 |
| 51-60 mm | 0 | 0 | 0 | 2 |
| 61- >70 mm | 0 | 0 | 0 | 2 |

surface; knife trimming of edges or arrises was rare. One brick, which thinned to the edges, may have been a 'Belgic brick' though it was too fragmented to be certain of this. Much of the brick had been burnt on one or more surfaces, suggesting that its prime function was for use in hearths, ovens, corn dryers or kilns. It was found mainly at Junction 8N, Junction 8S and Junction 9, with a few fragments at Junction 10, Area P and V and the Junction 8 Compound. Brick was common through all Roman phases, but was equally plentiful in medieval deposits at Junction 8N.

The flat tile fragments were without diagnostic characteristic and could derive from a variety of tile types. A comparison of the range of thickness (Table 7.27) with brick, *imbrex* and *tegula* suggests that the flat tile includes both *imbrex* and *tegula*, but the large number of tiles over 25mm in thickness suggest that a high proportion represents thin bricks.

## Segmental brick

Five examples of segmental brick amounting to 80 fragments, weighing 4331g, were found on sites Junction 8N and Junction 9. None were complete, but all appeared to be parts of semi-circular bricks. About a third survived of the most complete which had an estimated diameter of 500mm and measured 50-6mm thick. Others measured between 43mm and 45mm, or more thick, by 260-300mm in diameter. These fall within the range of sizes recorded by Brodribb (1987, 55). Surfaces were smooth, apart from the bases which tended to be rougher, but knife trimmed. They were made in fabrics C, D, E and G. Two occurred in early and middle Roman contexts, but the remainder were found residually in post-Roman contexts.

Circular and semi-circular bricks may be used as pillars or pilasters with a plaster cover, though Brodribb (ibid.) notes this does not appear to be the case in Roman Britain, where a more prosaic function as hypocaust *pilae* was the norm. Examples of *pilae* were found at Gadebridge villa in Room 9 (Neal, 1974, 15), but at Fishbourne (Cunliffe 1971,

44) it is postulated that the semicircular bricks were used as columns or pilasters in the early phase palace, though they were only found *in situ* where used for seating in the 'Third-Period' plunge bath in the East Wing. Circular bricks have been found used as paving for the threshold of a door in Room 1 of the villa at Northchurch (Neal 1976, pl. 3)

## Tegula mammata

Five examples of *tegula mammata* were found amounting to 20 fragments weighing 9714g. They were made in fabrics B, E and G. Two sizes were perhaps represented; three measuring 36-42mm were possibly a smaller variety, whilst two measuring 40-50mm thick, 266mm wide and over 258mm long may represent a larger type. All are similar in form and accord with type A as defined by Brodribb (1987, 60-2) and have evidence of only a single *mamma* towards one corner suggesting that they fall into Brodribb's (ibid.) sub-type b or possibly sub-type c. Two examples have only the oval scar of the *mamma* surviving, whilst on two others the *mamma* was sub-circular, hemispherical and roughly moulded, measuring 40-5mm wide by *c* 50mm long, and 10-18mm high. They were centred *c* 40-50mm from one edge and 75-80mm from the other. A detached *mamma* was also identified.

Brodribb (ibid.) suggests that this type of *tegula mammata* was used for flooring, though in other areas of the Roman empire such as South Gaul a similar type was used in walling as insulation, but not for heating (Bouet 1999). Most were found on site Junction 8N and one on Junction 8S. Two were in middle Roman contexts and the remainder unphased. *Tegulae mammatae* were found at Gorhambury villa in Flavian and late 1st-century contexts (Neal *et al.* 1990, 169, fig. 147.1068)

## Tegula

*Tegulae* accounted for the largest group (5%; 9% by weight) of diagnostic Roman tile forms (158 fragments, 19.6kg) and were found in greatest quantity on sites Junction 8N and Junction 9, together with a few examples from Areas G and M. No complete *tegulae* survived, the largest piece measuring no more than 195mm long by 140mm wide. The only complete dimension was thickness (Table 7.27) which was predominantly 20-25mm. Minimum numbers (MNI) based on numbers of corners by position (upper or lower L/R) and fabric indicates the following breakdown by site: Junction 9, MNI four tiles; Area M, MNI two tiles; and Junction 8N, MNI eight tiles.

A total of 51 tiles retained the flange and a further 13 had broken flanges or had been deflanged. The flange morphology (Fig. 7.18.1-9) comprised a standard range including rectangular profiles (types A and B), rounded (types D, D2, E, F) and a triangular form (type C). The sizes are summarised in Table 7.28. The type D and D2 flanges were frequently tapered and a small number of type E and F were also noted as tapered. Three unusually

*Table 7.28: Tegula flange sizes by type*

| Flange type | Flange profile | Nos | Width | Height |
|---|---|---|---|---|
| A | | 11 | 18-34mm | 40-56mm |
| A3 | | 3 | 25-8mm and 36mm | 45-58mm |
| C | | 1 | 26mm | 48mm |
| D | | 8 | 15-35mm | 30-57mm |
| D2 | | 5 | 20-30mm | 45-50mm |
| E | | 17 | 20-33mm and 40-2mm | 40-56mm and 50-2mm |
| F | | 5 | 20-7mm | 45-57mm |
| U | | 13 | 18-30mm plus one 50mm | ~ |

*Table 7.29: Summary of tegulae cutaway types and sizes (the C1 and A3 cutaways were all recorded on incomplete flanges and may be parts of composite A3/C1 type)*

| Cutaway type | Cutaway profile | Nos | Length | Width | Height/depth |
|---|---|---|---|---|---|
| A2 (Upper) | | 2<br>4<br>2<br>2<br>1<br>1 | 25-34<br>35-45<br>50-55<br>60<br>~<br>~ | 15-22<br>18-25<br>20-30<br>18-24<br>27<br>20 | 20-33<br>~<br>23<br>~<br>25<br>12-20 |
| B2 (Upper) | | 2 | >46<br>70 | 20<br>35 | ~<br>c.30 |
| C1 (Lower) | | 3* | 46 | 35 | 22 |
| A3 (Lower) | | 1* | >40 | ~ | ~ |
| A3 / C1 (Lower) | | 10 | 42<br>45<br>48<br>53<br>55*<br>60<br>~<br>~<br>~<br>~ | ~/20<br>8/30<br>2-5 / 25-40<br>~/15<br>8/16<br>~/15<br>25<br>8/30<br>8/25<br>12/30 | full/13<br>~<br>full/11-12<br>full/25<br>full/26-30<br>full/30<br>25<br>~<br>full/25<br>full/30 |
| | *plus end of flange cut to chamfer | | | | |

thick flanges, 40-50mm wide, were identified and it is possible that some damaged fragments of this type may have been mistaken for the edges of bricks, as these were not recognised until part way through the recording. Flange types do not appear to related to any phase, most occurring in the early and middle Roman phases as well as residually in post-Roman phases. The sparse occurrence in the late Roman phase merely reflects the small quantity of *tegulae* generally present in this phase.

Both upper and lower cutaways were present. Sizes of both are summarised in Table 7.29. Thirteen upper cutaways were identified, all of the conventional rectangular form (type A2) (Fig. 7.18.6 and 7.18.9) except two which were angled (type B2) (Fig. 7.18.8). One of the latter was possibly made by the tile mould, rather than being cut. Four of the type A2 cutaways were cut to shape, but five appear to have been created by the tile mould (as indicated by remnants of sanding on their surface) and subsequently knife trimmed.

The lower cutaways were all of type A3/C1 (Fig. 7.18.2-3), where completely preserved. The examples with only a C1 or A3 cutaway recorded were incomplete and may have been part of the composite type. This consists of a rectangular recess (A3) formed by the mould in the outer side of the flange, combined with an additional knife-cut wedge (C1) removed from the base angle. This equates to the group C cutaways of Warry (2006), which he suggests is one of the later types dating to AD 160-260. This is consistent with phasing for the examples from the M1 sites which have been found mainly in middle and late Roman deposits except for one in an early Roman ditch (2047), though this example may indicate later silting in the top of the ditch.

The presence of sanding on some upper cutaways and the triangular flange form may indicate that some of the tiles were made in an inverted mould such as the type F, as described by Warry (ibid., 8-34), whilst others with knife trimming along the lower edges would have been manufactured in the type D mould. Warry (ibid.) indicates that these inverted moulds were in use during the late 3rd and 4th centuries and are normally associated with his group D cutaways, none of which were present on the M1 sites.

*Imbrex*

This occurred in relatively small quantities, amounting to 63 fragments (4349g) and accounting for only 2% of the Roman tile. The tiles ranged from 8-23mm thick and in three instances the full height survived, measuring 70mm, 88mm and 110mm. All examples had a smooth outer surface, occasionally with fine longitudinal striations and one with longitudinal ribbing. Both curved and angular profiles were present. They were made in fabrics A, B, C, D and G. *Imbrices* were equally divided between sites Junction 8N and Junction 9, together with a single small fragment from Area M. They were present

through all phases of Roman occupation and occurred only rarely in post-Roman deposits.

*Flue and wall tile*

A variety of types associated with walling or cavity walling were identified, totalling 37 fragments (2567g). Box-flue tiles (*tubuli*) dominated the assemblage, but a half box or *tegula hamata* and two wall tiles were also identified.

The two small fragments of wall tile, 28mm and 45mm thick, were identified from the presence of lattice-scored keying on their back. One (2153) had a single cut line surviving (Fig.7.18.17) and the other (6816) two thick scored lines converging (Fig.7.18.18). Tiles with scored keying have been found at Gorhambury (Neal *et al.* 1990, 169) and reused in a drain at Boxmoor (Neal 1976, 85-6, 91, fig. LIII). This type of keyed brick was often used as wall jacketing in association with spacers to create cavity walling.

The single half box-flue tile or *tegula hamata* (Fig.7.18.23) was found at Junction 9. It had been deflanged in antiquity (presumably to enable reuse in general building) leaving a flange scar 180mm long and 36mm wide from the corner. The central-vent area where the flange had been cut away during manufacture survived as a slightly raised lip at the edge of the tile. A finger groove ran along the edge of the flange in the same manner as found on roofing *tegulae*. The surviving tile fragment was 28-35mm thick, >140mm wide and >235mm long. No keying was visible on the back of the tile. This type of tile was manufactured during the 1st century AD (Black 1996) and has been found at Colchester (Black 1992) and Canterbury (Black 1995), where they were found in association with distinctive thin-walled box tiles. The latter type of tile was found in the baths in Insula XIX at Verulamium (Niblett and Thompson 2005, 85), but none have been found on the M1 sites, perhaps because they may have been more prone to breakage and not so easily reused.

*Tubulus* or box-flue tile was the most common variety. All pieces were very fragmentary and ranged in thickness from 11-25mm, no other dimensions surviving. All were identified by the presence of combed keying. The keying was all of standard common combing patterns, generally of straight vertical or diagonal bands (Fig.7.18.19-22). Four examples of a straight vertical band parallel to the tile angle (type 1; Fig.7.18.22) were identified, all from Junction 8N. Five examples of two diagonal bands forming a cross (type 4; Fig.7.18.19-20) were found at Junction 8N, Junction 9, Area M and theJunction 8 Compound. One example of a less common pattern of curving bands possibly forming crossing semicircles (type 11) was found in evaluation trench 1126 (Junction 8N). A single example of a diamond with a vertical band forming a margin at each side (type 12a; Fig.7.18.21) was also found at Junction 8N, though the proposed diamond pattern could in fact be more akin to the series of crosses found on a flue tile at Gadebridge Park (Neal 1974, fig. 87.718). In most cases, the full width of the combed band did not survive, though the ratio of teeth to width indicates that most were of medium coarseness. Only three were complete; one measured 50mm wide and had 12 teeth, producing a fine combing pattern, whilst the other two were 52mm and 55mm wide both with six teeth. These both produced a very coarse combing emphasised by the wide teeth of 4-9mm spaced at 5-8mm, as compared to a more normal tooth size and spacing of 2-3mm.

Flue tiles with similar patterns of vertical bands of combing, crosses and curved or crossing semi-circles have been found at Northchurch and Boxmoor (Neal 1976, fig. XV, 73-82, fig. L, 112, 117-8) and at Gadebridge Park, (Neal 1974, 195-7, fig. 86, 715, 717, fig. 87, 718).

*Markings*

Keying has been described in relation to the flue tiles and other markings were sparse, consisting almost entirely of signature marks plus some possible tally marks and a single paw print of a dog or cat (Fig.7.18.24). A total of 23 signature marks were identified, all on tile from Junction 8N and Junction 9. The majority of signatures took the most common form of a simple semi-circle made with one or more fingers. The most common was a single groove (type 1.1), two of which were quite shallow examples with a height of 40-45mm and 55mm from the tile edge. Others were too fragmentary to gauge size. Five examples with two finger grooves (type 1.2; Fig.7.18.12) and two with three (type 1.3; Fig.7.18.13) were generally larger, measuring 90-120mm high and one was *c* 210mm wide. More unusual varieties of signature mark were each represented by a single example. These include possible examples of a looped circle (type 4), a loop (type 5), two examples of straight grooves running diagonally from the tile corner (type 12), one with two (type 12.2) and one with three finger marks (type 12.3; Fig.7.18.15) and curving zigzag (type 8; or possibly a double loop; Fig.7.18.14).

Eight examples were found on *tegulae* including types 1.1, 1.3 and 4, a single example of a type 1.3 on a *tegula mammata*, and the remaining 13 all on bricks (types 1.1, 1.2, 1.3, 5, 8 and 12). The semi-circular signatures are common on all Roman tile and appear to have been commonly used at all production sites. Types 4 and 5 are less common, though still frequently found. The other varieties of marks are much rarer. The type 12 has been found in Winchester whilst zigzags or S-shaped marks have been found in Winchester at the Cultural Centre (Poole and Shaffrey 2011) and Lankhills cemetery (Poole 2010a), and on the Isle of Wight at Combley and Newport villas (Tomlin 1987), but these have wider arcs than the example from Junction 9, which may in fact be two closely spaced tight loops. Only one tally mark was observed on a brick from Junction 8N. This was in the form of an impressed

5mm groove sloping diagonally from right to left. (Fig. 7.18.16)

### The medieval and post-medieval tile

Small quantities of medieval or post-medieval tile were recovered, mainly roof tile together with a floor tile and a few brick fragments. Seven fragments of medieval and post-medieval brick were made in fabrics Med1, Med3 and MedE. One measured 50-55mm by 110mm wide and two other pieces were 54mm and 63mm thick. The two thinner bricks may have been late medieval or Tudor, but the remainder were post-medieval in date. A modern perforated brick measuring over 65mm thick was made in a cream sandy fabric (Mod10). These were found on Areas E and F, Junction 8N and 8S, and at The Aubreys.

The roof tile was almost all in flat fragments of which a small quantity could be positively identified as peg tile. They were made in five sandy fabrics in use during the medieval and post-medieval periods. Fabrics Med1, Med2 and Med3 were found in roughly equal quantities, though the coarser sandy fabrics Med1 and Med 4 were used for medieval tile and were replaced by the finer fabrics Med 2 and Med3, which dominated the post-medieval tile. No complete tiles survived and the only measurable dimension was thickness, which ranged from 9-16mm, with a single unusually thick fragment of 19mm. Only three pieces occurred in deposits of medieval phase, though the cruder or rougher examples in later deposits are identified as medieval in date. A total of 18 fragments had evidence of pegholes, all circular, ranging from 9-15mm diameter and centred from 18-43mm from the edges. A single fragment of curved tile was probably a pantile.

### The fired clay

The poor preservation and very fragmentary character of the fired clay is reflected in the limited range of characteristics preserved. The majority of fragments (90%) retained only a single surface or were amorphous. A small number had two or three surfaces, and several were identified as oven plate and triangular oven brick. A single fragment with a wattle impression may be a part of an oven wall. Three small groups from Area Q, Junction 9 and Junction 8N, containing pieces with a flat or curving surface with finger marks, have been identified as oven lining. A number of pieces from Junction 9 and Junction 8N which have two surfaces, 30-40mm apart, joined by flat straight or curving rounded edges may be pieces of rectangular or circular oven plate. The most common diagnostic form was the triangular brick with perforations across the corners. The better preserved had a thickness of *c* 80-85mm and the perforations measured 12-16mm in diameter. Most were found at Junction 8N and one in Area Q. A few small fragments of briquetage vessel in chaff- (one fragment) and shell-tempered (four fragments) fabrics measured between 5mm and 9mm thick. These have not been traced to a salt production area though the east coast is logically the most likely source.

**The sites**

*Junction 8N*

This site produced the largest individual assemblage of both tile and fired clay, with the greatest variety of forms, compared to the other sites on the scheme. There was a total of 2059 fragments of tile weighing 173.3kg (including material from the evaluation trenches), almost entirely Roman in character. The assemblage was dominated by brick which formed 77% by weight of the tile and it is likely that much of the plain flat tile category was also thin brick. Other identifiable forms, of which *tegula* was most common (7%) included *imbrex*, flue tile, *tesserae* and more unusually a few examples of *tegula mammata*, wall tile and curved segmental bricks.

Unsurprisingly, only a few fragments of brick and *imbrex* were found in early Roman contexts. At this time it is unlikely that a site such as this would have had the resources to obtain new tile and material for reuse would not be readily available. The majority of the material was found in the middle Roman phase distributed through ditch, pit, posthole and quarry fills. It is clear that by this phase brick and tile was more readily available, as early Roman masonry buildings were refurbished, as is evidenced by the presence of early forms such as *tegula mammata* and wall tiles. Brick and tile would have been most useful in the construction of small burnt structures such as hearths, ovens and kilns. A number of such features provided evidence of this incorporating brick or tile in their construction. These included ovens 7259 and 7335 and corn dryer 6514. The corn dryer of early-mid Roman construction contained several fragments of brick, which had probably been used in the construction of an arch over the main flue or as lining for the flue.

Small amounts of brick and tile were found in late Roman contexts, reflecting the general decrease in activity on the site during this period. Nearly all was brick, including a segmental brick, together with a single example of *tegula*. Most was found in pit 6874.

Post-Roman material included 11 small fragments (332g) of medieval roof tile and a single small fragment (30g) of brick. Fabrics Med1, Med2 and Med3 were used. The roof tile was 11-14mm thick, but no evidence of pegholes survived. The small quantity of tile is perhaps surprising as this was the only site to produce evidence of medieval occupation, but the absence of CBM at this period is not unusual for the type of settlement and indicates that the buildings were constructed of other materials,

probably timber and thatch. However, the large quantity of Roman material found in medieval contexts (562 fragments; 61.5kg), representing roughly a third of the whole assemblage, points to possible reuse at this period, particularly that associated with the oven and limekiln. The oven (6585) assigned to the earlier phase of medieval activity contained 59 fragments (9.5kg) of Roman brick and tile. The limekiln (6577) belonging to phase 2 of the medieval occupation contained a smaller quantity (62 fragments; *c* 6.4kg) of brick, *tegula* and flat tile. In both structures some fragments had evidence of burning or refiring.

The fired clay (2383 fragments; 5.1kg) was mostly undiagnostic consisting of amorphous fragments or pieces with a single surface. Some pieces of possible oven plate or 'Belgic brick', possible hearth floor, triangular oven brick and briquetage were identified. The triangular brick was very badly fragmented, but two perforations measuring 14-15mm diameter were identifiable and thickness was *c* 85mm suggesting that it lay at the larger end of the size scale for this type of object. Three small flat sherds of briquetage, 9mm thick and made in a shell-tempered fabric, were recovered from pit 6817, which is dated to the late Roman phase. It is likely that the briquetage itself dates from earlier in the Roman period.

*Junction 8S*

This site produced a considerably smaller quantity of tile, amounting to 114 fragments weighing 3.1kg, whilst fired clay was negligible (84 fragments; 85g). The majority of the tile was found in quarry pits, 5025 fragments of early-middle Roman date and 5057 fragments of medieval or later date based on the tile assemblage. The remaining Roman tile formed a scatter in ditches of late Roman and post-medieval date and a tree-throw hole. The only identifiable Roman tiles were a single fragment of combed flue tile and brick, which were found in the quarry pit. There are no buildings or structures within the excavated area from which the brick and tile could derive and it seems likely that the quarry pits provided a suitable dumping ground for disposing of waste material, probably from the adjacent site at Junction 8N.

The remainder, accounting for just over three-quarters of this small assemblage, was post-Roman material comprising flat roof tile, brick and small shattered indeterminate fragments. The roof tile included two fragments with pegholes, measured 12-14mm thick and was made in a variety of fabrics. Two brick fragments measured 50-55mm thick by *c* 105mm wide and 63mm thick. The thicker brick was probably of 19th-20th-century date, though the other brick and all the roof tile could be of late medieval or early post-medieval date. The older brick had mortar on the surface. However, all the later tile was found in unphased contexts and it appears to represent material brought in as a result of agricultural activity, perhaps being used in early field drainage schemes.

### Junction 9

This site produced a substantial assemblage of tile of Roman and medieval date consisting of 760 fragments weighing 44kg, whilst fired clay amounted to 85 fragments weighing 2kg. Roman tile dominated the assemblage (almost 98% by weight) and consisted of all the most common forms including *tegula*, *imbrex*, flue tile, *tesserae* and brick. More unusually this site also produced examples of segmental brick; although one was extremely shattered, all were probably of semi-circular form. Brick and flat tile dominated the assemblage forming over 50% (68% by weight). A small fragment of *tegula mammata* and a more substantial piece of *tegula hamata* (half-box flue) were also found and suggest that the tile was being obtained from buildings originally constructed in the 1st or early 2nd centuries. Roughly half the phased Roman tile was found in early Roman contexts with a quarter each in middle and late Roman contexts.

There were two foci of tile distribution, one in the northern area of the Roman enclosures and the second in the southern area, though scattered fragments of tile occurred in the intervening areas. The greatest quantity (56% by weight) was found in ditch fills and the remainder was scattered through a range of features including pits, postholes, layers and topsoil. The largest single deposit (85 fragments; 5.35kg; 11% by weight) occurred in the waterhole 2004, but in general the tile formed a light scatter of a few fragments in each feature. A rather greater than average quantity of tile (42 fragments; 2.8kg) occurred in the curvilinear ditches (2555, 2246 and 2204) at the southernmost end of the site, perhaps indicating more intensive activity in association with this enclosure.

The material represents a general use of brick and flat tile within the occupation areas of the enclosures, that came to be discarded in the boundary ditches and other features. It is perhaps surprising that no tile had been used in the structure of the kiln 2638/2644, as it is most likely that brick and tile was reused in the construction of hearths, ovens or kilns on this type of rural site rather than in other building work. Approximately 18% (by weight) of tile was burnt reflecting the use of tile in such structures. Only the tile in direct contact with the heat source (floors and flue lining) is likely to show evidence of burning. Tile from context 2474 was the only material found in direct association with such a structure. The tile from this furnace had all been burnt, suggesting that it formed part of the structure, either as wall lining or floor, or had been used as oven furniture, possibly as covers for flue or vent holes.

Fired clay included oven plate or possibly 'Belgic brick' fragments, oven wall structure and lining, hearth floor and three sherds of briquetage. The briquetage is from a thin-walled vessel (5-7mm) in a shelly fabric. The fired clay appears to be concentrated more towards the northern area of enclosures and most was found in ditch fills with only small amounts in waterholes, postholes, pits and other deposits. The majority of the fired clay was found in early Roman contexts, decreasing significantly in quantity thereafter. It was associated with Roman tile, suggesting that it is of Roman date rather than originating from the preceding prehistoric phases.

A moderate quantity of medieval or early post-medieval roof tile amounting to 42 fragments (778g) and a single floor-tile fragment (87g) were also recovered, the majority from topsoil or subsoil deposits (particularly layer 600), though a few were found in ditches and a pit of Roman date, possibly from the final silting of these features. No significant medieval or later occupation, or structural remains, were encountered in the excavations and it is likely the spread of tile relates to agricultural practice, possibly early field drains, which frequently utilised roof tile in their bases.

### The Aubreys

Only a small quantity of tile (20 fragments; 350g) was found in this area consisting predominantly of non-diagnostic Roman flat tile, nearly all found in ditch fills and much of it in the terminus of an early Roman ditch (42). However, the tile is moderately or heavily abraded and it is unlikely that it was incorporated in the fill at that date; rather it may have been deposited during a later period of soil accumulation in the silted ditch.

### Areas B and T

Two small fragments (88g) of medieval/post-medieval roof tile were found, both made in fabric Med2, moderately to heavily abraded, and including a peg tile with a circular perforation 15mm diameter.

### Areas E and F

Apart from a fragment (130g) of non-diagnostic Roman flat tile, all the material (15 fragments; 533g) from this area was of medieval/post-medieval date. It was found in ditches, pits and a quarry pit, which were dated solely on the CBM. The material consisted of fragments of post-medieval brick, possible floor tile, flat roof tile, including peg tile with circular pegholes, with 10-14mm diameters and a modern thick perforated brick with circular perforations, measuring 20mm and 26mm in diameter, possibly a ventilation brick or for a malting kiln floor. Abrasion was generally moderate. It is unlikely that the group represents anything more than post-medieval agricultural practices such as manuring, field drainage, or maintenance of farm tracks.

## Area M

CBM and fired clay were recovered from enclosure and trackway ditches, concentrated mainly in the ditches defining an enclosure extending to the east outside the excavated area. The CBM totalled 16 fragments, weighing 1116g, and the fired clay nine fragments, weighing 68g.

The fired clay was non-diagnostic; one fragment had a single surface surviving and another two surfaces at right-angles. All the fragments are probably derived from oven or hearth type structures. The CBM all comprised Roman tile, except for two small fragments of peg tile. The group comprise a mixture of brick/flat tile, *tegula*, box flue and *imbrex*. The pieces have suffered only low or moderate abrasion, suggesting that they derived from a settlement situated within the enclosure. Though the dated ditches are assigned to the early Roman period, the single fragment of box-flue tile is of a type that did not become commonplace until the 2nd century. This suggests that the enclosure ditches continued to silt up beyond the 1st century, a process possibly not completed until the medieval period, if the fragments of peg tile are not intrusive.

## Area P

A small quantity of Roman tile (30 fragments; 1306g) comprising brick and flat tile was found mainly in the ditches defining the trackway and the pit between them. Abrasion was variable. No indication of occupation was found in the area, though significant amounts of pottery were found in the ditches suggesting that a settlement may have be situated nearby. The amount of tile, although not great, reinforces this and may represent the remnants of metalling on the track or material used to infill potholes.

## Area S (Junction 10)

No tile was found during the mitigation excavation, but a scatter was found in the evaluation trenches. Most of this was post-medieval flat roof tile (13 fragments; 534g), measuring 12-15mm thick and including a peg tile with circular peghole with a 22mm diameter. Two fragments of Roman brick were found towards the south of the area. One was possibly shaped to form a coarse *tessera* measuring 35 x 35mm.

## Area V

This area produced two fragments of post-medieval roof tile and two fragments of Roman brick and tile.

## Area W (Buncefield Depot)

A fragment of a Roman brick was found in hollow-way 124204, a piece of post-medieval flat roof tile was found in the fill of feature 126406 and a few scraps of indeterminate CBM were found in ditch 126404.

## Discussion

The Roman assemblage has a certain homogeneity in that it is dominated by brick and flat forms that could be used in a similar manner, and suggests deliberate selection of these forms for reuse. However, there is an element of heterogeneity in respect of occasional oddities such as the segmental bricks, the *tegulae mammatae*, the half-box flue and wall-tile fragments. The proportion of *tegula* to *imbrex* is not consistent with the ratios normally required for a roof. All in all this suggests the opportunistic selection or acquisition of any suitable tile that could be reused on the respective sites. It is probable that such material was reused in the construction of small structures such as ovens, hearths, corn dryers or kilns, which is the common pattern on minor rural agricultural settlements. Such use is attested by the extensive evidence of burning and refiring on the material from all excavation areas. It would seem that some had possibly been reused in a medieval oven/kiln at Junction 8N.

The presence of a range of unusual or less common forms suggests that the tile was obtained from a variety of sources, which could have included any of the villas in the region, either during their refurbishment or rebuilding, or possibly from redevelopment in Verulamium itself. The relationship of the settlements to a higher-status site or sites, or the mechanism whereby the low-status sites obtained such material is unclear. At Cotswold Community (Poole 2010b) outside Cirencester it has been suggested that there may have been an element of waste disposal from the urban centre and there is a slight hint of similar oddities in the M1 assemblage. However, these oddities may represent nothing more than opportunistic salvaging of waste building material and the greater variety of forms in use in the earlier phase of the Roman occupation in this part of the country, rather than any formal waste disposal arrangements for Verulamium. There is clearly deliberate selection for brick and flat tile that could most easily be used as general building material.

Unsurprisingly, there was a scatter of medieval/post-medieval tile and (less commonly) brick along the length of scheme, with occasional pieces in the evaluation trenches. These are likely to represent nothing more than material inadvertently incorporated in the ploughsoil as a result of manuring or more deliberately as part of field drainage. However, greater concentrations of medieval roof tile at Junction 9 suggest that it was used for roofing to a limited extent. It is unclear whether the slightly raised quantities at Junction 8N, Junction 8S, Junction 10 and Area E merely

Fig. 7.18   Ceramic building material and fired clay

reflect the more extensive areas excavated compared to the evaluation, or whether they indicate more intensive use. Where tile was used for roofing it is likely that the majority of it was very thoroughly removed for reuse elsewhere, when a building went out of use.

It is worth noting that a number of large groups of Roman tile were found in medieval features, in particular in the kiln (6591) at Junction 8N, as well as occurring more generally in ditch and features fills in the later medieval phase at this site. This may indicate the reuse of Roman brick in the medieval phase.

**Catalogue of illustrations** (Fig. 7.18)

1  *Tegula*. Flange A1. Ctx 2130
2  *Tegula*. Flange A3, cutaway A3/C1. Ctx 7784
3  *Tegula*. Flange B/E, cutaway A3/C1. Ctx 2474
4  *Tegula*. Flange C. Ctx 7316
5  *Tegula*. Flange D. Ctx 2038
6  *Tegula*. Flange D2, cutaway A2. Ctx 2247
7  *Tegula*. Flange E. Ctx 6606
8  *Tegula*. Flange F, cutaway B2. Ctx 2112
9  *Tegula*. Flange D/E, cutaway A2. Profile through flange indicating area of cutaway and position of knife trimming. Ctx 6168
10  Segmental brick. Semi-circular brick. Ctx 6499. SF 6105.
11  *Tegula mammata*. Showing *mamma* in corner quadrant. Ctx 7781
12  Signature mark. Type 1.2 on brick. Ctx 6607
13  Signature mark. Type 1.3 on *Tegula mammata*. Ctx 6607
14  Signature mark. Type 8 brick. Ctx 2048
15  Signature mark. Type 12a on brick. Ctx 6173
16  Tally mark. Diagonal impressed line on tile edge. Ctx 7084
17  Keyed surface. Knife-scored line on subsequently burnt surface. Ctx 2153
18  Keyed surface. Two knife-scored incised lines forming X. Ctx 6816
19  Keyed surface. Type 4? Two bands of coarse combing crossing. Ctx 2139
20  Keyed surface. Type 4 or 5. Two bands of medium combing crossing. Ctx 5506
21  Keyed surface. Type 12a? Two bands of coarse combing, one vertical and one diagonal. Ctx 6173
22  Keyed surface. Type 1. Corner of flue tile with combing on one face. Ctx 7472
23  *Tegula hamata*. Half-box flue with scar from de-flanging. Ctx 2451
24  Imprint. Animal paw print, probably cat paw print. Ctx 2112

**WORKED STONE** *by Ruth Shaffrey*

**Summary**

Amongst this assemblage are a minimum of 30 rotary querns and a number of flakes indicating quern manufacture. There are also whetstones and general processors including one saddle quern. All stone was fully recorded and details entered into a MS Access database

*Table 7.30: Total fragment count and numbers of contexts producing worked stone*

| Type | Mid Roman | Late Roman | Medieval 2 | Unphased | Total |
|---|---|---|---|---|---|
| Rotary quern | 10 (6) | 1 | 17 (9) | 29 (6) | 57 (22) |
| Saddle quern | | | 1 | 1 | |
| Whetstone | 1 | | 1 | | 2 |
| Other | 2 | | | | 2 |
| Processor | 1 | | | | 1 |
| Unworked | | | | 1 | 1 |
| Grand Total | 14 | 1 | 18 | 31 | 64 (29) |

**Junction 8N**

Junction 8N produced the largest quantity of worked stone including 57 quern fragments from a total of 22 contexts and a small number of other items (Table 7.30).

*Roman*

The site at Junction 8N produced the largest number and most substantial examples of rotary querns. Of the 22 records, eight are groups of very small weathered lava fragments and one group comprises three small fragments of Old Red Sandstone; none of these are specifically identifiable as rotary-quern fragments, although they are made of stone known only to have been used in this way. Each group from a single context has been treated as a single record for the purposes of analysis. The remaining 13 rotary-quern fragments are larger and more clearly identifiable. Of these, six are Millstone Grit, four are Lava and three are Old Red Sandstone.

Rotary-quern fragments were recovered most commonly from medieval contexts (nine contexts) with a significant number from both mid-Roman (six contexts) and unphased contexts (six contexts). Only one fragment was recovered from a late Roman context, which reflects the general lack of activity on the site at that time. Although rotary querns are indicative of simple domestic activity, the examples found at Junction 8N are almost all small worn fragments, many heavily so, suggesting secondary deposition. Two fragments survived sufficiently for something of their style to be determined; one is a projecting hopper-style lava quern (6823) and the other is of Millstone Grit with pronounced concentric grooving (SF 6114). An almost complete Old Red Sandstone lower quern of lozenge shape was found during the evaluation (SF 101); these are almost always of 1st- or 2nd-century date (Shaffrey 200 * ADD PAGE NUMBER). A neatly broken half saddle quern is made of quartzite, almost certainly gathered from the glacial gravels. It was found in the fill of unphased pit 6632 (6631), but seems most likely to have been associated with Roman or earlier activity.

## Medieval

Of the nine medieval contexts producing rotary-quern fragments, seven are groups of small weathered lava fragments recovered from foundation and ditch fills. It seems most likely that these represent residual evidence of earlier (presumably Roman) activity, rather than being directly related to activity associated with the medieval building. Two fragments of Millstone Grit comprise a more substantial fragment of an upper stone, which demonstrates wear associated with use, with a smaller lower stone (6382). These may be connected to medieval activity.

Other domestic activity is demonstrated by a single Norwegian Rag whetstone (SF 6082; Fig. 7.19.1). This has a partial perforation and is notched at the upper end. There is evidence for wear across the top, suggesting use for sharpening fine implements, as well as wear across the main body of the whetstone. It would not have been appropriate for sharpening agricultural tools and is more likely to be associated with the settlement.

## Discussion

Although there is a larger than average assemblage of rotary querns from Junction 8N, they are all heavily worn. They are examples of stone types commonly found in the general area and, although largely residual, they suggest a domestic element to the Junction 8N site during the Roman period. The remainder of the worked stone assemblage at this site, including whetstones and other processors, is also typical of domestic sites. None of these finds is unusual and the majority of utilised stones would have been either locally available or are imported items commonly used in the region at the time.

## Junction 9

The worked stone assemblage from Junction 9 is strikingly different to that from Junction 8N and represents a few rotary querns and processors along with unusual struck Hertfordshire Puddingstone. Only five contexts produced fragments of rotary querns, three contexts containing lava, one containing puddingstone and one containing sandstone; only the lava-quern fragments can be absolutely identified as rotary querns because they were imported specifically for this purpose. However, all the quern fragments are tiny and very highly weathered suggesting that they are residual and possibly not associated with grinding at this particular site. Other worked stone includes one pecked item of indeterminate function and two hammerstones/processors from unphased contexts, which may have been associated with the puddingstone working (see below).

The most significant component of the worked-stone assemblage from Junction 9 is a group of Hertfordshire Puddingstone fragments recovered from a total of five contexts. Thirteen flakes of Hertfordshire Puddingstone, plus a number of chips, were recovered from ditches 2006 and 2114 (contexts 2007, 2113 and 2114) all late Iron and early Roman in date. Because the matrix of puddingstone is chemically similar to that of the flint pebbles it contains, it tends to fracture equally well across the matrix and the flints. This means that a strike to the rock can result in flaking such as that seen here. The flakes also show evidence of deliberate removal including bulbs of percussion and removal scars. None of the struck material can be refitted. In addition to the flakes, a number of small fragments of puddingstone were recovered from a further two contexts on this site (2557 and 2911); these could be fragments of broken up rotary quern, but it is not possible to be sure.

The two types of debris recovered, especially the flakes, are evidence that the stone was being worked on site. More than one petrological type of puddingstone is represented amongst the flakes and they are not from immediately adjacent contexts, suggesting that the working was more than a single isolated event. The recovery of struck flakes of puddingstone is hitherto unknown in an archaeological context and, although the flakes do not appear to have been worked into tools, some have damage to the edges, which may result from use. The most likely interpretation, especially given that the date of use fits well with the known use of puddingstone for rotary querns (Major 2004), is that querns were being manufactured at this site. Although not a single definite puddingstone rotary quern was recovered from Junction 9 (or from other M1 sites), no substantial rotary querns of any lithology were found, suggesting that the domestic emphasis of the Junction 9 site was elsewhere. A study of the distribution of puddingstone querns does not reveal a particular concentration in this area, as might be expected around a manufacture site, but the Junction 9 site is conveniently located close to Watling Street for ease of distribution. Puddingstone querns do occur on nearby sites, particularly at Verulamium (eg Frere 1972; Adamson 1999, 214), and at Gadebridge Park (Neal 1974, 193) and Gorhambury (Neal *et al.* 1990, 166).

The source of the Hertfordshire Puddingstone is hard to identify because it is a difficult material to find geologically *in situ* (Robinson 1994, 77) and there are no known substantial exposures near the site. However, small outliers of Reading Beds are located within 4km of the Junction 9 site with a possible capping of Reading Beds some 3km to the south-west at Gaddesden Row, where fragments of Hertfordshire Puddingstone were observed in an exposure (Sherlock 1922, 34). In addition, a seam of large puddingstone boulders was exposed approximately 1.5m below the surface at Folly Lane (Niblett pers comm), approximately 10km to the south-west. Fragments of puddingstone can also occur in the Quaternary clay-with-flints deposits which overlie the Reading Beds (Hopson *et al.* 1996, 72-4) and boulders of it have been moved around by glacial action, so that they now occur in the glacial gravels, stratigraphically above the clay-with-flints (Sherlock and Pocock 1924, 33). These are seen on the surface of fields in the area, however they are not geologically in situ and thus impossible to provenance. Thus, the question of the source of the worked puddingstone found at Junction 9 is a complex one.

No large pieces of puddingstone were recovered from Junction 9 and it is possible that all the worked fragments exploited easily obtainable and relatively small fragments. However, the most likely reason for the working of puddingstone during the Roman period is that rotary querns were being manufactured. In this case, the stone may have been brought in from some distance, depending on availability of suitably sized pieces. In addition to the multiple sources for the puddingstone described above, the rock itself is also extremely variable. Recent work along the construction of the A10, about 30km to the east of M1 Junction 9, exposed a dozen large boulders of puddingstone interpreted as being geologically *in situ* (Lovell and Tubb 2006, 185).

They have not been studied in detail but a visual inspection confirms that they vary enormously, and it is this variability that makes a provenance difficult to establish. A possible extraction location has been exposed near Puckeridge where a group of depressions appeared to be targeting the deposits containing puddingstone (Cushion 2008, 3) and there was evidence suggesting a routeway for the extracted material to Ermine Street (Lovell and Tubb 2006, 186). However, none of the puddingstone from the Puckeridge source is sufficiently similar to that at Junction 9 to establish a link. The most that can be said at present, is that the puddingstone presumably had a relatively local source within either the Reading Beds outliers or a stratigraphically later deposit.

## Catalogue of illustrated items (Fig. 7.19)

*Junction 8N*

1    **Primary whetstone.** Schist, probably Norwegian Rag. Elongate tapered whetstone, very thin at one end with a sub-square cross-section. The other end is notched and although it maybe a spokeshave

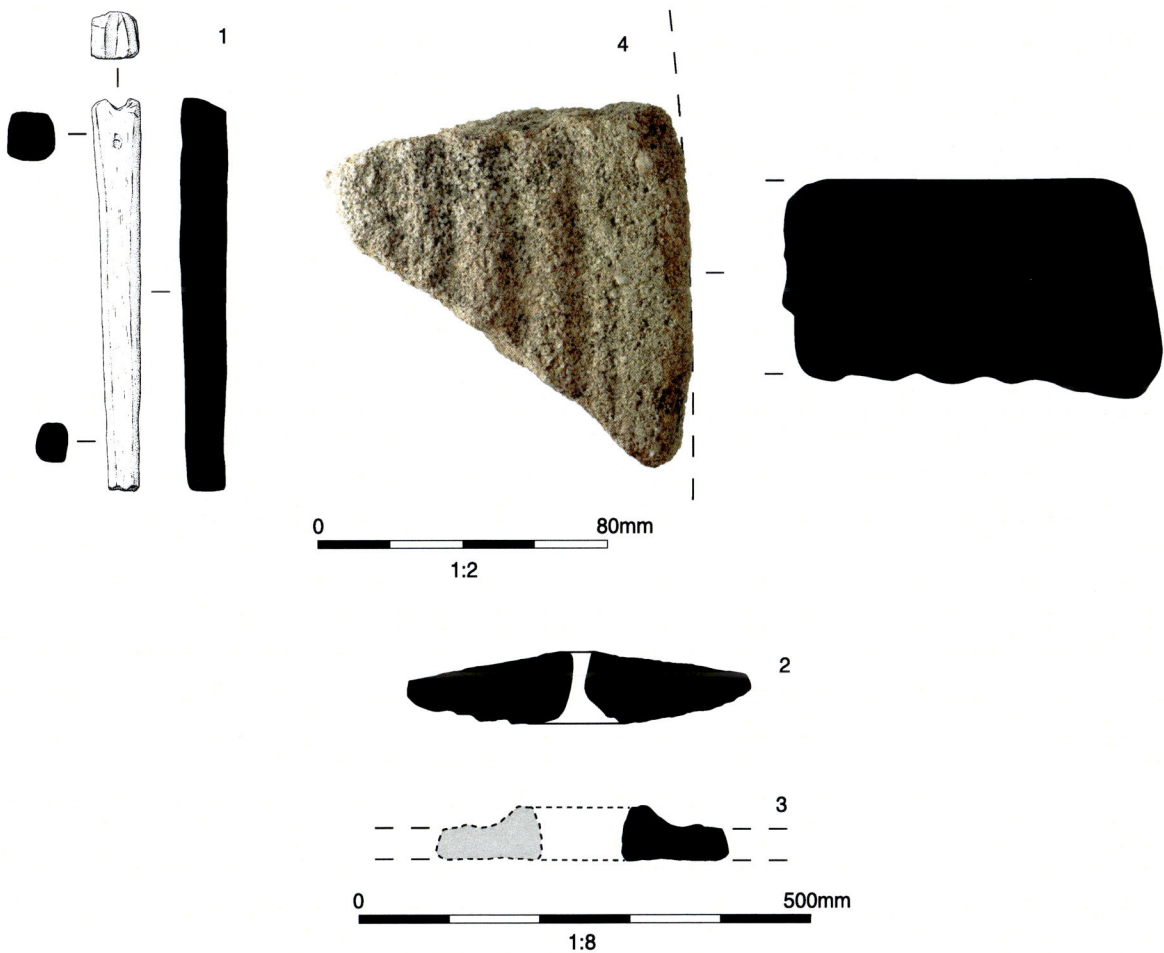

Fig. 7.19  Worked Stone

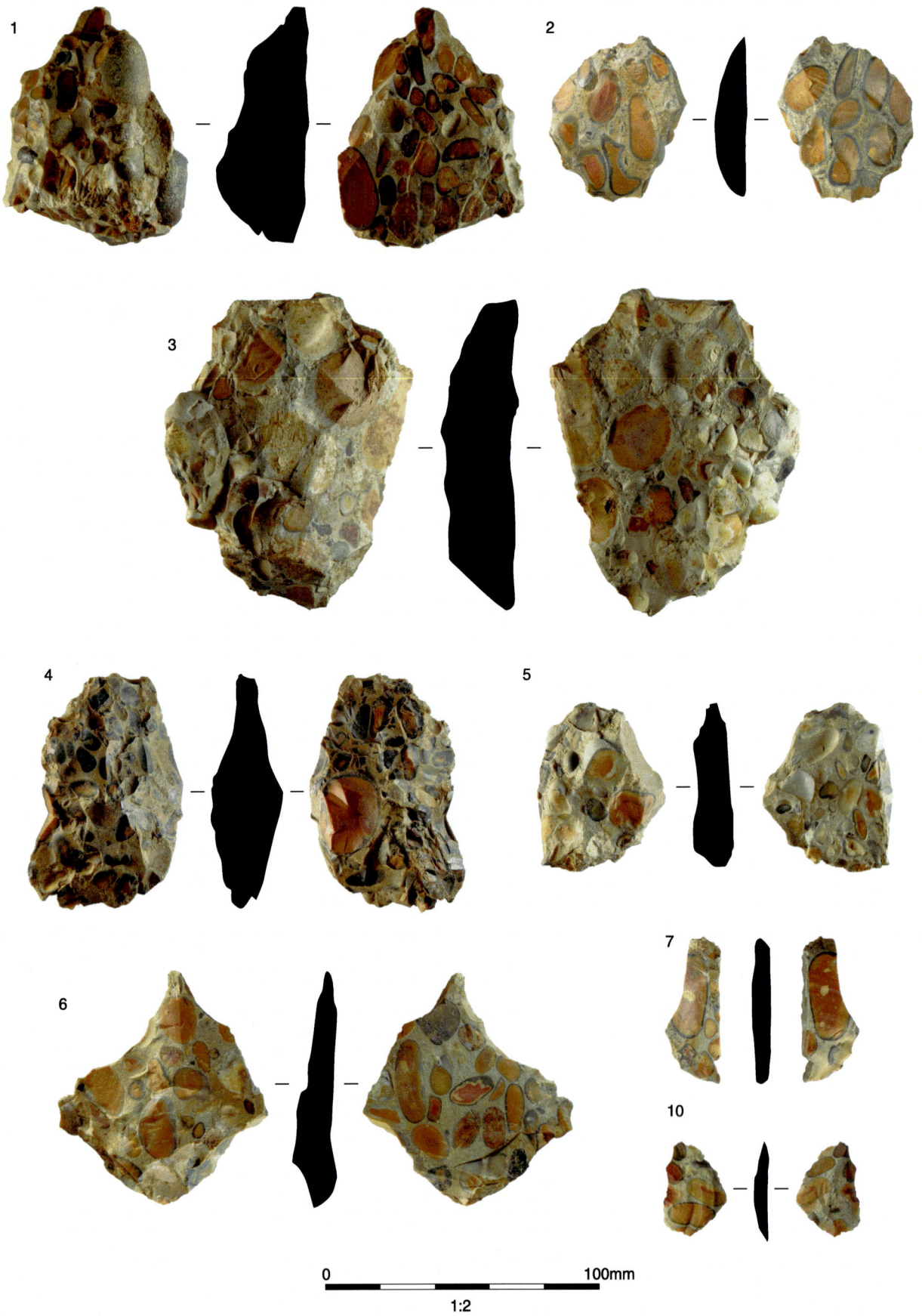

*Fig. 7.20   Puddingstone Flakes*

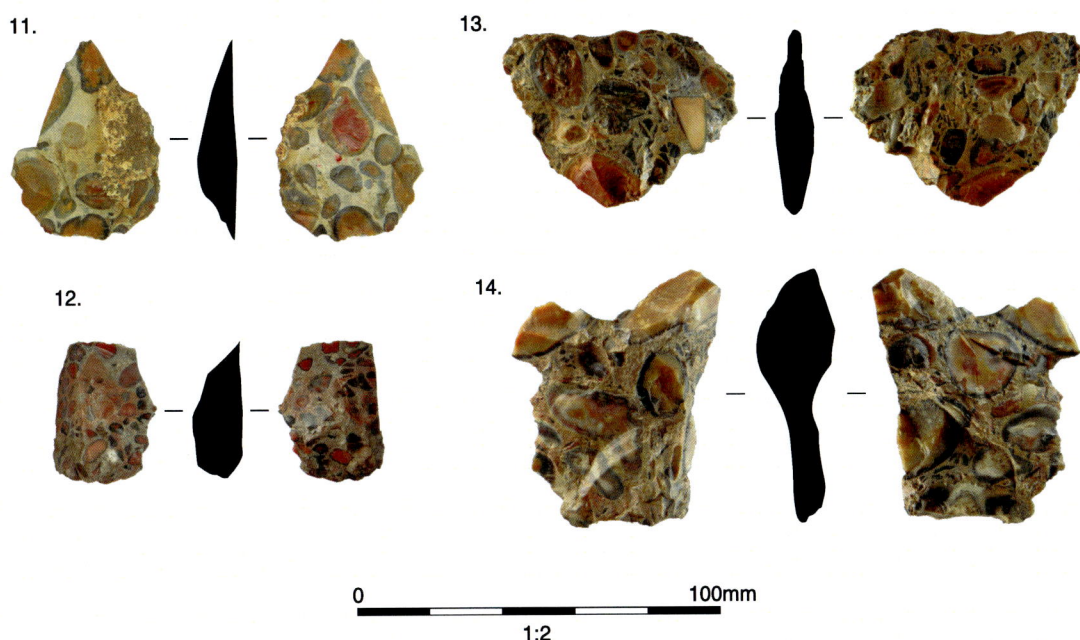

*Fig. 7.21 Puddingstone Flakes*

(used to work arrows etc) the main areas of use are on the long surfaces. There is some evidence that blades were drawn through the notch as well. There is also evidence for a partial perforation just below the notched end. Ctx 6649. SF 6082

2 **Upper rotary quern fragment.** Lava. Pronounced projecting hopper. Rim 20mm high. Edge too damaged to determine diameter, but looks crudely worked. Measures 57mm maximum thickness on hopper. Ctx 6823

3 **Incomplete lower rotary quern.** ORS QC. 80% survives. Of lozenge (type 2b) style. Almost always of 1st-2nd-century date. Rough convex base, pecked convex grinding surface with slight lip around cylindrical perforation turning into conical shape at the base. Edges are straight and quite thin (20mm). Pecked edges. Eye has a 24mm diameter (35mm on base). Th: 70mm max. Dia: 380mm. Ctx 112202. SF 101

4 **Upper rotary quern fragment.** Millstone Grit. Fragment of disc-style quern with straight edges leaning in slightly and with very smooth flat top suggesting reuse as a whetstone or similar. The grinding surface has the remains of at least four rounded channels each about 10mm wide and 1mm (max) deep. These are deliberate and not a result of wear. Concentric grooves. Th: 58mm max. Dia: indeterminate. US. SF 6114

*Junction 9*

1. **Flake / possible crude tool.** Hertfordshire Puddingstone. Striking platform at one end with some ripples and partial bulbal scar. Damaged along one edge. Ctx 2114.ER
2. **Flake / possible crude tool.** Hertfordshire Puddingstone. Curved profile with slight bulb of percussion. One edge is damaged with possible use wear. Ctx 2114. ER
4. **Flake.** Hertfordshire Puddingstone. Possible scarring where smaller flakes have been removed. Ctx 2114. ER
5. **Flake.** Hertfordshire Puddingstone. Slightly curved but with little other evidence of use or working. Ctx 2114. ER
3. **Flake / tool.** Hertfordshire Puddingstone. Large flake, thickening towards larger end and with one sharp edge. Ctx 2114. ER
6. **Flake.** Hertfordshire Puddingstone. Large flake. One face is concave, the other slightly convex. No bulb of percussion or radial scarring and no retouch. Ctx 2114. ER
7. **Flake.** Hertfordshire Puddingstone. Small narrow flake with radial scarring on one face. Ctx 2007.ER
10. **Flake.** Hertfordshire Puddingstone. Very small flake with radial scarring on one face. Ctx 2007. ER
11. **Flake.** Hertfordshire Puddingstone. Small flake with radial scars across the length of one surface and whole flake is curved. Some damage to edges but no retouch. Ctx 2007. ER
12. **Flake.** Hertfordshire Puddingstone. This is a thick concave chunk with some radial scarring. Ctx 2007. ER
14. **Flake.** Hertfordshire Puddingstone. Larger flake with prominent radial scarring and damage to some edges. Ctx 2113. LIA/ER
13. **Flake.** Hertfordshire Puddingstone. Slim flake with radial scarring. Damaged along one sharp edge. Ctx 2113. LIA/ER

## ROMAN COINS *by Paul Booth*

Only 12 Roman coins were recovered during the excavation phase of the project, supplementary to two coins found in the evaluation phase (one of Domitian, from Trench 1130, subsequently within the area of Junction 8N excavation and an undated, but probably 4th-century piece from Trench 1363, subsequently within the Junction 9 excavation area). In addition, a ?19th-century penny, worn totally flat, was found. The coins were in very variable condition, some relatively well preserved and others completely eroded. Where possible, complete identifications were made. Three coins were too eroded for any meaningful identification beyond broad period. The Roman coins are listed in site and context order in Table 7.31.

None of the sites produced a meaningful assemblage, the largest group being of nine coins from Junction 9. Single early Roman coins included a copy of a Claudian *as* from Junction 9. This was a Grade II copy in Sutherland's scheme (cf Boon 1974, 103) and although at least moderately worn had a weight of 7g. Another *as*, probably dated AD 84-5, came from an evaluation context at Junction 8N. Much less certainly of 1st-2nd-century date is an extremely eroded piece from Area P, the only coin from this site. The only certain 3rd-century coin was a regular antoninianus of Probus. Two very eroded coins, one each from Junction 8N and Area M, could have been of later 3rd- or 4th-century date, although the latter is perhaps more likely in both cases.

Eight coins were certainly of 4th century date, all but one from Junction 9. They ranged in date from the early 4th century up to the end of the Constantinian period, with probable and possible irregular issues of the mid 4th century. There were no coins of the houses of Valentinian and Theodosius. Coins of 4th-century date that could be assigned to a mint were from Trier (3) and Lyons (2).

The relative absence of early Roman coinage, despite the fact that this is the period of most intensive activity at all of the main sites, is characteristic of assemblages from lower-status rural settlements. The breakdown of the Junction 9 group, with the single Claudian copy, the single coin of Probus and seven certain or probable 4th-century pieces, is quite typical of rural coin-loss profiles, even though the extent of 4th-century activity at this site was relatively limited. The overall numbers are too small, however, to allow meaningful comparison with other assemblages from the region. Nevertheless, it may be significant that the scarcity of later 4th-century coinage at Junction 9 is reflected in the much larger assemblage from nearby Gorhambury, where coins of the house of Valentinian were scarce and those of the house of Theodosius completely absent (Curnow 1990, 112). This is a pattern also seen at Dicket Mead, but not to the same extent in the other sites discussed by Curnow (ibid., 109-10) as comparanda for Gorhambury.

## METALWORK *by Ian Scott*

### Junction 9

The metal finds number 238, and included 12 copper-alloy pieces (Table 7.32). All but 16 of the items are from late Iron Age or Roman contexts. The majority are from contexts assigned to middle Roman or late

*Table 7.31: Roman coins*

| Context | Site | SF no | Denomination |
|---|---|---|---|
| Evaluation 113010 | Junction8N | 103 | 24mm as |
| 7082 | Junction8N | 6108 | 17-19mm AE3 |
| 7234 | Junction 8N | 6113 | 12mm+ |
| Evaluation 136311 | Junction9 | 105 | 9mm+ |
| 2005 | Junction 9 | 2001 | 13mm+ |
| 2005 | Junction9 | 2004 | 16mm AE3 |
| 2005 | Junction9 | 2042 | 18mm AE3 |
| 2005 | Junction9 | 2005 | 15mm AE3 |
| 2007 | Junction9 | 2002 | 26mm as |
| 2107 | Junction9 | 2010 | 23-25mm antoninianus |
| 2107 | Junction9 | 2021 | 20mm+ AE2 |
| 2545 | Junction9 | 2048 | 10mm |
| 3044 | Area M | 3001 | 14mm+ |
| 4002 | Area P | 4001 | 22mm+ |

Roman phases. The assemblage is dominated by nails or nail fragments of which there are 201.

There are a few tools, including a probable carpenter's gouge (Fig. 7.22.1; context 2048), a small hammer (Fig. 7.22.2; context 2038) and an ox-goad (context 2007) from contexts of Roman date. There is also part of a pair of scissors (SF 2041; context 2447), the latter fragment is medieval or later in date and from an unphased context. The only item relating to transport is a possible wing from a hipposandal (Fig. 7.22.4).

Personal items number ten and include five hobnails (Table 7.33). The remaining personal items comprise a tiny fragment of copper-alloy buckle bow (SF 2011), identified by its distinctive cross-section, fragments of two broad bangles or armlets (Fig. 7.23.5-6) of Roman date, a very well-preserved Roman bow brooch of unusual form (Fig. 7.23.7) and a probable finger ring (Fig. 7.23.8; context 2557). One of the bangle fragments (Fig. 7.23.6) is from an unphased context, but it is identification and dating are certain. The single household item is the tine from a table fork of post-medieval date (SF 2003; context 2007), although from a context assigned a late Roman date. It is probably intrusive.

There are some structural items (clamps, holdfasts, looped pin and a washer) and miscellaneous fragments. The nails are overwhelmingly from contexts of Roman date (Table 7.34). Finally amongst the objects of uncertain identification is an unusual flat circular object with decorative cutouts and a lined central hole (Fig. 7.23.9). Its purpose is far from clear, but merits further discussion. The object was found in the fill of a late Roman ditch. A number of similar objects are known, but all the published examples are from late Iron Age contexts. Most have been found in late Iron Age cremation burials; examples from Biddenham Loop, Beds (Luke 2008, 222-3, fig. 9.13, RA 118) and Monkston Park, Milton Keynes (Wardle in Bull and Davis

| ?Date | Obverse | Reverse | Mint | Comment |
|---|---|---|---|---|
| ?84-85 | ..DOMITI]ANAUGGE[R.... | ?Moneta l, with cornucopia in l hand, r hand extended holding ?scales, SC | Rome | ?RIC II, 242A, 248, 270 |
| 324-330 | head l | PROVIDENTIAE AUGG | ? | |
| l 3-4C | | | | eroded |
| ?330+ | ? | figure(s), cf Gloria Exercitus | | eroded |
| 350-364 | eroded | Victoriae DD NN Aug et Cae | irregular | |
| 330-335 | FLIULCONSTA]NTIUSNOBC | GLORIA EXERCITUS 2 standards | Lyons | LRBCI, 189 |
| 330-335 | CONSTANTINUSIUNNOBC | GLORIA EXERCITUS 2 standards | Trier | as LRBCI, 68 |
| 341-348 | CONSTAN] SPFAUG | VICTORIAE DD NN AUGG Q NN | ?Trier | LRBCI, 149 |
| c 43-64 | TICLAUDIUS]CAESARAUGPM[TRPIMP | Minerva r, S C | irregular | as RIC I (2nd ed.), 100 |
| 276-282 | IMPCPROBUSPFAUG | MARS VICTOR Mars r | Lyons | RIC Vii, 38 |
| 313-315 | ?IMPCONSTANTINUSAUG | SOLI INV[ICTO CO]MITI | Trier | RIC VII Trier, 39 or 40 |
| ?330-364 | CON[ head l | eroded | irregular | size suggests FTR copy of c 350-364 |
| l 3-4C | ? | ? | | eroded |
| ??1-2C | ?head r | ? | | eroded |

*Table 7.32: Junction 9. Metalwork assemblage by function and phase*

| Phase | Tool | Transport | Personal | Household | Function Structural | Nails | Misc | Query | Total |
|---|---|---|---|---|---|---|---|---|---|
| LIA/ER | | | 2 | | 1 | 8 | 1 | | 12 |
| LIA/ER? | | | | | | 1 | | | 1 |
| MR/LR | 1 | | 2 | | 1 | 64 | 1 | 1 | 70 |
| LR | 2 | 1 | 5 | 1 | 2 | 118 | 6 | 4 | 139 |
| UN | 1 | | 1 | | | 9 | 1 | 3 | 15 |
| Topsoil | | | | | | 1 | | | 1 |
| Total | 4 | 1 | 10 | 1 | 4 | 201 | 9 | 8 | 238 |

*Table 7.33: Junction 9. Personal finds by type, phase and context*

| Phase | Context | Context type | bow brooch | armlets | Identification buckle | finger ring | hobnails | Total |
|---|---|---|---|---|---|---|---|---|
| LIA/ER | 2721 | kiln | | | | | 1 | 1 |
| | 2907 | pit | 1 | | | | | 1 |
| *LIA/ER* | *Total* | | *1* | | | | *1* | *2* |
| MR/LR | 2528 | ditch | | | | | 1 | 1 |
| | 2557 | ditch | | | | 1 | | 1 |
| *MR/LR* | *Total* | | | | | *1* | *1* | *2* |
| LR | 2041 | waterhole | | | | | 2 | 2 |
| | 2048 | ditch | 1 | | | | | 1 |
| | 2112 | ditch | | | 1 | | | 1 |
| | 2130 | ditch | | | | | 1 | 1 |
| *LR* | *Total* | | *1* | | *1* | | *3* | *5* |
| UN | 2488 | layer | | 1 | | | | 1 |
| *UN* | *Total* | | | *1* | | | | *1* |
| Total | | | 1 | 2 | 1 | 1 | 5 | 10 |

153

2006) have been published recently. There are other examples from the cemeteries at King Harry Lane (cremation 325; Stead and Rigby 1989, 358, fig. 157, no. 10) and Verulam Fields, Verulamium (burial iv; Anthony 1968, 14), at Dellfield, Berkhamsted, (burial group I; Thompson and Holland, 1976, 142-3, fig. viii, no. 1), Maldon Hall Farm, Essex (burial 3; Lavender 1991, 205-6, fig. 4, no. 2), Hinxton Rings, Cambs, (cremation 2; Hill *et al.* 1999, 253-6, fig. 10) and a burial at St Lawrence, Isle of Wight (Jones and Stead 1969, 354, fig. 2, no. 5). Discs have also been found at the Iron Age settlement at Puddlehill, Bedfordshire (Matthews 1976, 117-8, fig. 73, no. 11), in the hillfort at Spettisbury Rings, Dorset (Gresham 1939, 113, pl. vi, no. 5) and at Danebury (Cunliffe 1984, 370, fig. 7.23, no. 2.174).

It has been suggested that these objects could be knives or circular cutters similar to a modern pizza cutter (eg Luke 2008, 222) and the objects do appear to have a cutting edge around their circumference. In some cases the central hole has an inserted collar, which suggests that the disc was intended to be mounted on a rod or axle and were probably intended to revolve. In the case of the examples from Biddenham (ibid.) and from St Lawrence on the Isle of Wight (Jones and Stead 1969, 354, fig. 2, no. 5) this collar is made of iron, while in the case of the M1 example the collar is non-ferrous. The disc from King Harry Lane has no notch or cut-out in its circumference, which supports the idea that it could have been a circular knife.

More relevant, perhaps, are the examples of discs with notches on the circumference. Examples from Biddenham (Luke 2008, 222) and from burial 3 in the Iron Age cemetery at Alkham, Kent (Philp 1991; Ian Stead *in litt.*; James and Rigby 1997, fig. 42) both have distinctive notches. The discs from Puddlehill (Matthews 1976, 117-8) and Spettisbury (Gresham 1939, 113) are also notched. Unpublished examples from Beckford, Worcestershire, and Norton Road, Stotfold, Bedfordshire, noted by Luke (2008, 222) also apparently have notches.

The notches appear to have been carefully made. The example from Biddenham has two circular cut-outs joined together to form a large cut-out with a raised point in the centre. The Alkham example has a wide cut-out with a small V notch in the middle, forming an ogee shape. The M1 example has two adjacent circular cut-outs with a notch between.

If the discs are circular knives, the notches would seem to serve no purpose beyond the decorative. In cremation 2 at Hinxton Rings, the perforated circular disc was associated with a small oval disc with a central perforation, as well as four iron brooches, a pair of copper-alloy tweezers and a nail cleaner (Hill *et al.* 1999, 253-6, fig. 10). The oval disc might be symbolic rather than practical. Possibly the discs are circular knives but have some additional symbolic significance. A late Iron Age cremation burial from the excavations on the line of the A2 in Kent (Allen *et al.* forthcoming, grave 4298) was found with four copper-alloy brooches, the

poorly preserved fragments of an iron brooch, small cooper-alloy clamps or staples and a small notched and perforated copper-alloy disc (diameter 28mm). The latter was not a circular knife. The metal is thin, of uniform thickness and has no sharpened edge, the perforation is lightly off-centre, and there are

*Table 7.34: Junction 9. Nails by phase and context*

| Phase | Context | Context type | Nails |
|---|---|---|---|
| LIA/ER | 2017 | ditch | 1 |
| | 2114 | ditch | 2 |
| | 2511 | layer | 2 |
| | 2616 | layer | 1 |
| | 2664 | layer | 1 |
| | 2905 | pit | 1 |
| *LIA/ER* | *Total* | | *8* |
| LIA/ER? | 2585 | layer | 1 |
| *LIA/ER?* | *Total* | | *1* |
| MR/LR | 2038 | ditch | 21 |
| | 2118 | ditch | 1 |
| | 2170 | ditch | 2 |
| | 2173 | ditch | 1 |
| | 2205 | ditch | 1 |
| | 2352 | ditch | 5 |
| | 2353 | ditch | 3 |
| | 2354 | ditch | 3 |
| | 2364 | pit | 1 |
| | 2406 | ditch | 4 |
| | 2513 | ditch | 1 |
| | 2557 | ditch | 20 |
| | 2591 | ditch | 1 |
| *MR/LR* | *Total* | | *64* |
| LR | 2005 | pit | 10 |
| | 2007 | pit | 59 |
| | 2033 | ditch | 1 |
| | 2036 | ditch | 2 |
| | 2041 | waterhole | 9 |
| | 2048 | ditch | 27 |
| | 2129 | ditch | 2 |
| | 2130 | ditch | 2 |
| | 2139 | ditch | 1 |
| | 2152 | ditch | 1 |
| | 2153 | ditch | 1 |
| | 2168 | pit | 3 |
| *LR* | *Total* | | *118* |
| UN | 2043 | pit | 1 |
| | 2447 | pit | 2 |
| | 2448 | layer | 2 |
| | 2488 | layer | 4 |
| *UN* | *Total* | | *9* |
| US | 2001 | topsoil | 1 |
| *US* | *Total* | | *1* |
| Total | | | 201 |

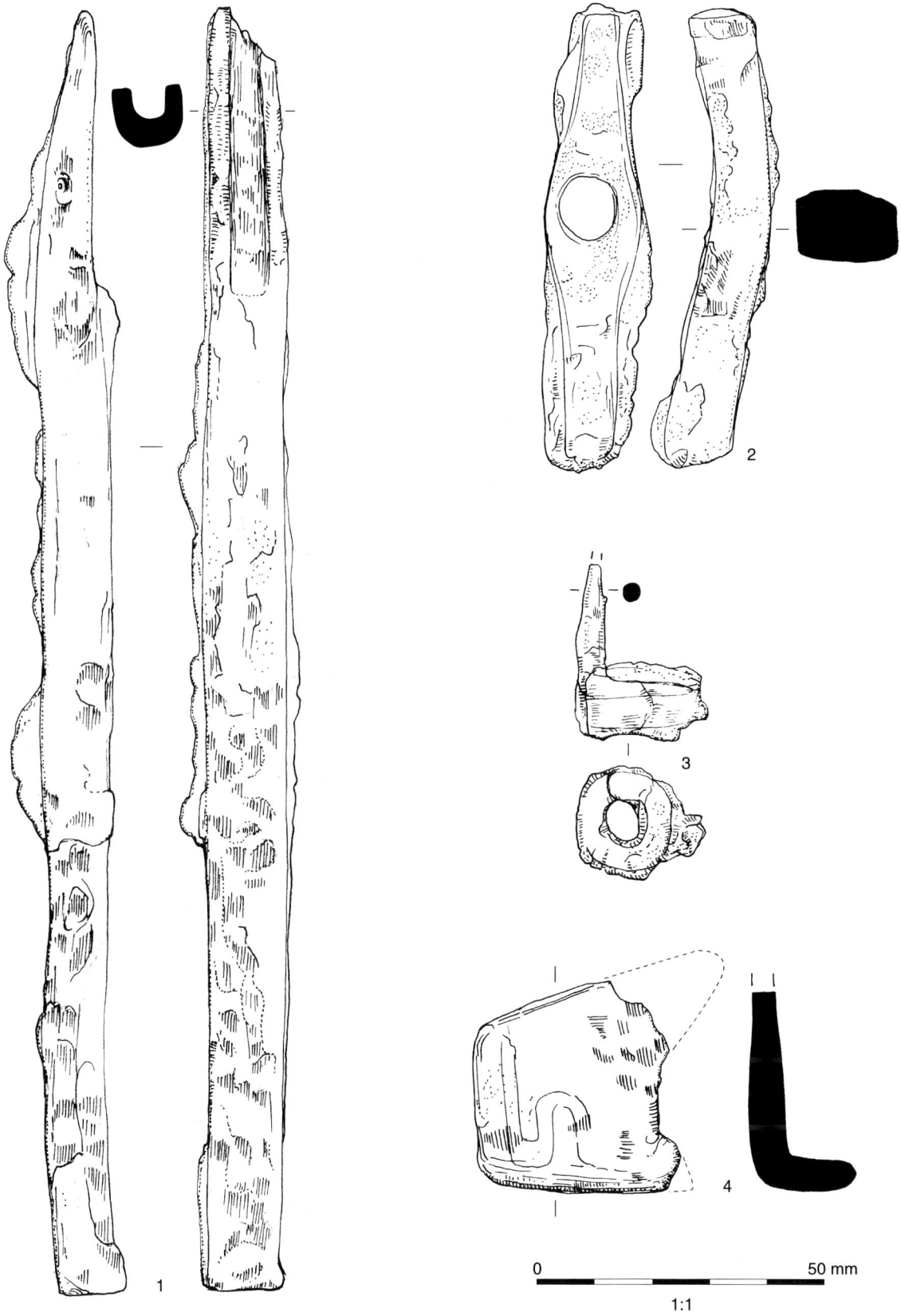

*Fig. 7.22   Metalwork from Junction 9*

three V-shaped notches spaced around the circumference. The purpose of this object is unclear but it could be seen as an echo of the circular iron ones found elsewhere, and as such might hint at some further symbolic significance to the circular iron knives or discs.

The metalwork assemblage is comparatively small, especially if the nails are excluded, and has a limited range of object types. This makes it difficult to characterise the assemblage with any degree of confidence. The material hints at domestic occupation, but given the comparatively small number of the objects, this can only be a suggestion.

## Catalogue of illustrated finds (Figs 7.22-3)

1   **Gouge.** [ID 102]. Rectangular section at top, grooved for much of length, changing to hollow half round section towards edge. Carpenter's tool? Fe. L: 214mm. Ctx 2048. Phase: late Roman. SF 2047

2   **Small hammerhead with circular eye.** [ID 81]. Jeweller's hammer? Fe. L: 75mm. Ctx 2038. Phase: middle-late Roman

3   **Ox-goad with simple collar.** [ID 69]. Fe. L: 29mm; Dia: 19mm. Ctx 2007. Phase late Roman

4   **Hipposandal wing.** [ID 98]. Curved and shaped plate. Fe. L extant: 38mm. Ctx 2048. Phase: late Roman

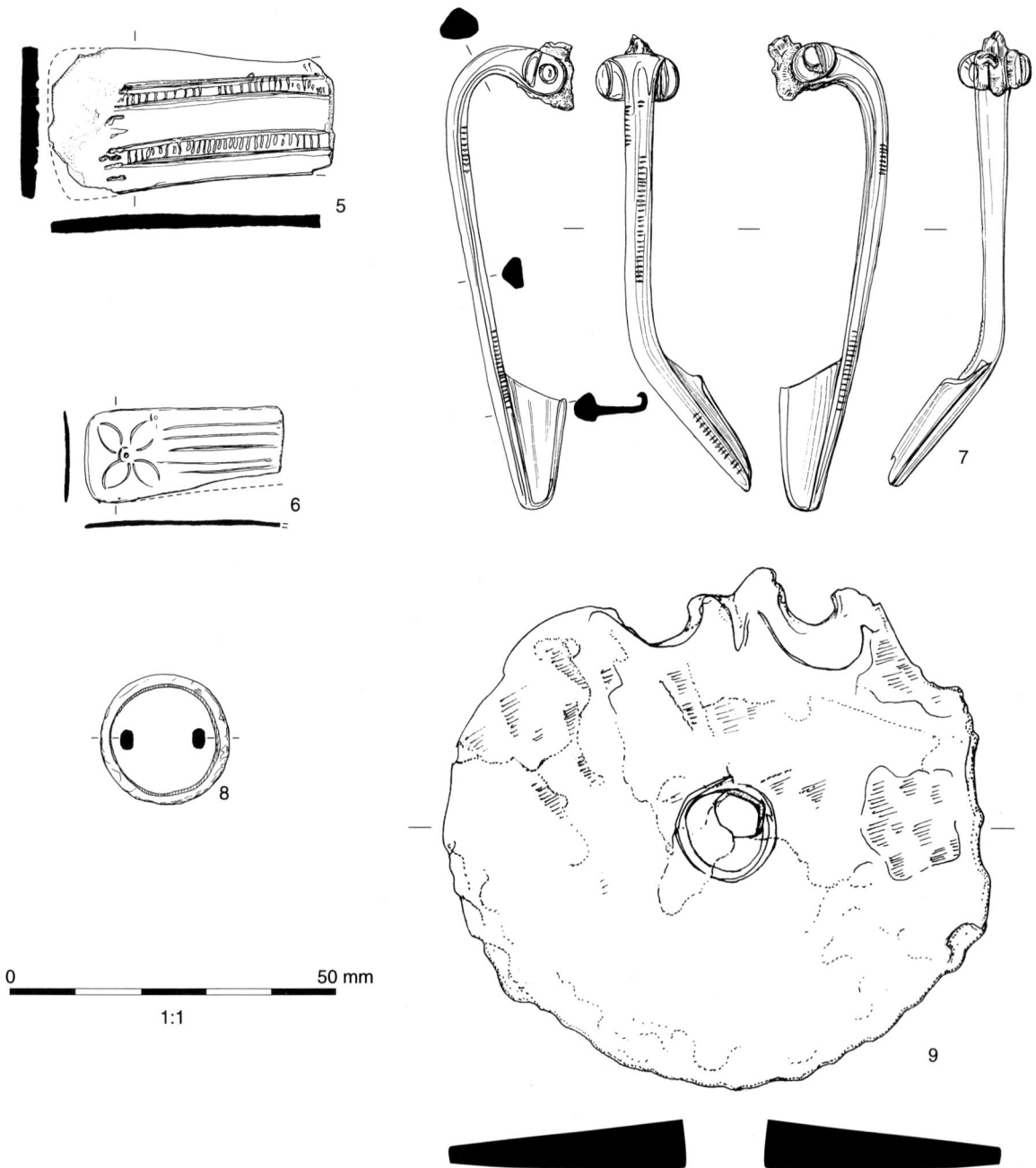

Fig. 7.23   *Metalwork from Junction 9*

156

*Table 7.35: Junction 8N. Metalwork assemblage by function and phase*

| | | | | Function | | | | |
|---|---|---|---|---|---|---|---|---|
| Phase | Transport | Personal | Household | Structural | Bindings | Nails | Misc | Total |
| LIA/ER | | | | 1 | | | 1 | 2 |
| ER/MR | | 118 | 1 | 1 | 1 | 19 | 2 | 142 |
| MED | 6 | 1 | | 3 | | 31 | 5 | 46 |
| MED* | | 1 | | | | 4 | | 5 |
| UN | 2 | 1 | | | 1 | 16 | 2 | 22 |
| Total | 8 | 121 | 1 | 5 | 2 | 70 | 10 | 217 |

5 **Terminal of broad armlet.** [ID 339]. Rounded square-end decorated with four-petal flower with central dot. Parallel lines along band aiming for centre of flower. The broad flat band decorated with parallel lines and slightly expanded at the terminal is typical of Romano-British armlets of early date. Early bracelets or armlets have been discussed recently by Crummy (2005, 98-101), who has argued that they are military armillae. This particular example falls into Crummy's Group B, with a single central band (ibid.). It has the terminal decorated with a four-petal floret. This is a 1st-century type and its presence in a late Roman context suggests that it was either residual or a long retained heirloom. Cu alloy. L: 30mm; B: 14mm. Ctx 2048. Phase: late Roman. SF 2008

6 **Terminal of broad armlet with two parallel engraved bands.** [ID 344]. A broad flat armlet or armilla similar to No. 5 above. Its terminal is incomplete but does not show any signs of decoration. The armlet is decorated with two parallel engaved bands and falls into Crummy's group A (ibid., 96). Cu alloy. L: 43mm; B: 22mm. Ctx 2488. Unphased. SF 2050

7 **Bow brooch with hinged iron pin.** [ID 346]. The bow is straight, tapers and has a triangular section. The bow has been bent laterally. The catchplate is solid and has a plain undecorated terminal. There are very small wings flanking the head of the brooch. The brooch is extremely well preserved and has small panels of rocker decoration at points on the bow. The brooch is unusual and does not fit into any of the well-defined groups of Romano-British bow brooches. The vestigial wings suggest that the brooch should have had a sprung pin, which it clearly does not, and there is no other evidence for a sprung pin. It was clearly made with a hinged pin, but with the wings associated with a sprung pin. The straight bow and the plain catchplate are all distinct features, which together make an unusual piece. Cu alloy. L: 68mm. Ctx 2907. Phase: late Iron Age-early Roman. SF 2072

8 **Finger ring.** [ID 345]. Simple band, possibly with pattern of radial lines or cable pattern decoration. The possible cable pattern suggests that this a small finger ring, comparable to rings from Higham Ferrers (Scott 2009, 209, 235, fig. 5.38: 268-9) and Colchester (Crummy 1983, 49, fig. 50: 1770). Encrusted Cu alloy. Dia: 20mm. Ctx 2557. Phase: middle-late Roman. SF 2045

9 **Almost circular plate with central round perforation.** [ID 114]. The plate is thicker in the middle and thins to the edges. The perforation is lined with a small rolled and overlapped (non-ferrous?) collar, which is clearly visible on the X-ray plate. On the edge are two almost circular cut-outs with a notch between them. Function unclear. Fe. Dia: 76-80mm. Ctx 2139. Phase: late Roman

## Junction 8N

There are three copper-alloy finds and 213 iron finds from this excavation. Although the largest part of the assemblage is from late Iron Age or Roman contexts, there is a sizeable component from medieval contexts (Table 7.35).

The largest single functional category is personal (n = 121), almost exclusively from early/middle Roman contexts. Three of these items are of copper alloy; a pin or needle stem (SF 6101) from an early or mid-Roman context (6816), and a hollow decorative stud (Fig. 7.24.1) and pair of tweezers (Fig. 7.24.2) from medieval contexts. Both of these latter items are of medieval date. The remaining personal items are hobnails, which number a minimum of 118; there are at least 152 fragments of hobnail. Most of the hobnails are from three locations in ditches: context 6020 (min. n = 43; max. n = 44); context 6316 (min. n = 49; max. n = 82); and context 6420 (min. n = 25; max. n = 27) (Table 7.36). There is a single hobnail from context 6697.

Items relating to transport (n = 8) comprise horse-shoe nails, almost certainly all late medieval or post-medieval in date. A single household object, an incomplete small knife blade (Fig. 7.24.3), came from an early Roman context (7305).

*Table 7.36: Junction 8N. Hobnails by phase and context*

| Phase | Context | Context type | Hobnails (min) | Hobnails (max) |
|---|---|---|---|---|
| | 6020 | Ditch | 43 | 44 |
| ER/MR | 6316 | Ditch | 49 | 82 |
| | 6420 | Ditch | 25 | 27 |
| *Total* | | | *117* | *151* |
| UN | 6697 | Tree-throw hole | 1 | 1 |
| *Total* | | | *1* | *1* |
| Total | | | 118 | 152 |

Structural items (n = 5) include a modern wall hook, as well as clamps and a possible hinge fragment. There are two fragments of bindings comprising strips with nail holes. Nails number a relatively modest 70 pieces, some from Roman contexts, but more from medieval or later contexts. Otherwise the assemblage includes nine miscellaneous iron items (strip, sheet, rod, etc) and a single length of lead wire.

The assemblage, excluding the hobnails, is too small to characterise. The groups of hobnails, although not intrinsically the most interesting objects, are the most interesting feature of the assemblage. The groups are from early or mid-Roman contexts 6020, 6316 and 6420. The circumstance under which the hobnails were deposited is unknown, though it is possible that they discarded as loose items or as parts of nailed shoes.

### Catalogue of illustrated finds (Fig. 7.24)

1   **Hollow domed decorative stud probably from a belt.** [ID 333]. Medieval or late medieval date.

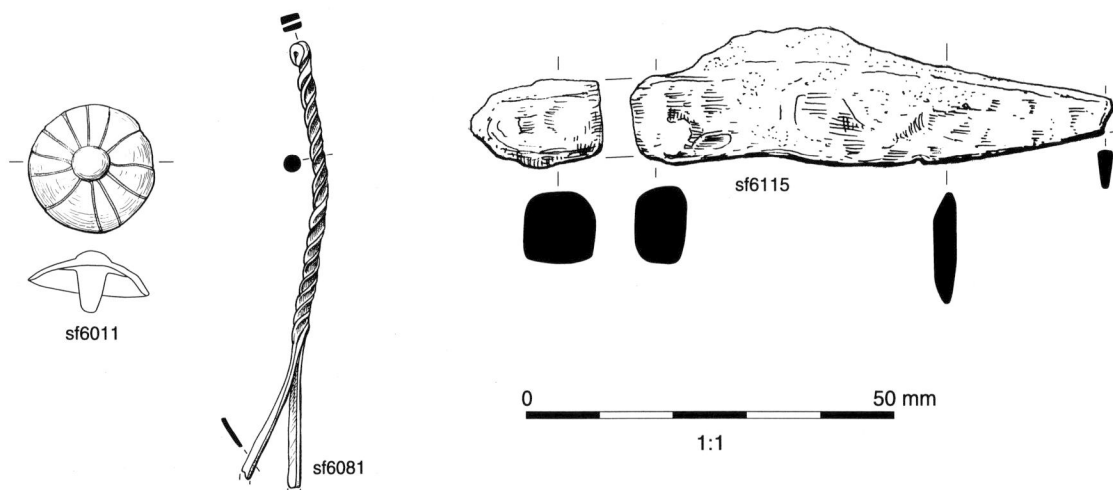

*Fig. 7.24   Metalwork from Junction 8N*

*Table 7.37: Evaluation. Metalwork assemblage by function and context*

| Total | Context | Tool | Transport | Personal | Function Binding | Nails | Misc | Query |
|---|---|---|---|---|---|---|---|---|
| 112202 | | | | | 1 | 4 | | 5 |
| 113012 | | | | | 1 | | | 1 |
| 118105 | | | | | | 1 | | 1 |
| 118106 | | | | | 1 | | | 1 |
| 118607 | | | | | 1 | | | 1 |
| 118705 | | | | | | | 2 | 2 |
| 118706 | | | | | 1 | | | 1 |
| 126403 | | | | | | 1 | | 1 |
| 127008 | | 3* | | | | | | 3 |
| 133205 | | | 1 | | | | | 1 |
| 135607 | | | | | 5 | 4 | 1 | 10 |
| 135611 | | | | | 2 | | | 2 |
| 135612 | | | | | 1 | | | 1 |
| 136214 | | | | | 1 | | | 1 |
| 136305 | | | | | 3 | | | 3 |
| 136311 | | | | 1 | 8 | 1 | 1 | 11 |
| 136315 | | | | | 2 | | | 2 |
| 151005 | 1* | | | | | | | 1 |
| US | | | 4 | | | | | 4 |
| Total | 1 | 3 | 5 | 1 | 27 | 11 | 4 | 52 |

Divided into irregular segments by fine lines. Cu alloy. Dia: 17mm. Ctx 6055. Phase: medieval. SF 6011

2   **Tweezers/earscoops.** [ID 331]. Has twisted stem and short splayed jaws, and is made from a single thin strip of metal. Compares with the implement from Swan Lane, Upper Thames Street, London (Egan and Pritchard 1991, 381, fig. 252: 1774). Cu alloy. L: 59mm; B: 4mm. Ctx 6490. Phase: medieval. SF 6081

3   **Small whittle tang knife.** [ID 306]. Tapering blade of triangular section with angled straight back and curved edge. Although heavily encrusted, the form of the blade is quite clear. Fe. L: 64mm. Ctx 7305. Phase: early-middle Roman. SF 6115

## Evaluation

The evaluation trenches produced 48 objects (Table 7.37). These include part of a cast 19th- or 20th-century ploughshare (context 151005) and three post-medieval horseshoes (context 127008). Personal items comprise a much eroded Romano-British bow brooch (Cat. No. 1; context 133205) and 4 hobnails (SF 6014, unstratified). Amongst the objects of uncertain identification is a fragmentary circular copper-alloy mount with raised beaded border (Cat No. 2; context 136311). The other two unidentified objects are extremely poorly preserved. The remaining finds comprise a small oval iron collar or binding, 27 nails and 11 miscellaneous fragments.

### Catalogue of selected finds

1   **Bow brooch.** [ID 39]. Eroded. Probably two-piece sprung, with eroded remains of hook at head. Eroded wings. Bow of oval section. Catchplate missing. Possibly part of a two-piece Colchester brooch, but too poorly preserved for certainty. Cu alloy. L: 31mm; B: 8mm. Ctx 133205. Phase: late Roman. SF 109

2   **Circular mount.** [ID 40]. Formed from thin sheet, with punched pellet border around circumference. Larger fragment comprises almost half the object. The second fragment is smaller with no original edge. There are two round raised spots or pellets within the otherwise flat field, one on each fragment. No other evidence for decoration. Two small pinholes in the larger fragment; spacing suggests originally four pinholes just inside the pellet border equally spaced around the mount. Cu alloy. Dia: 34mm. Ctx 136311. Phase: late Roman. SF 106

## GLASS *by Ian Scott*

### Introduction

There are 42 sherds of glass from the various archaeological interventions (Table 7.38). There are six sherds from the evaluation trenches, two sherds from Junction 8N and one from the watching brief on Junction 8. The remaining 33 pieces are from the excavations at Junction 9.

*Table 7.38: Glass type by site, phase and context*

| Site | Phase | Vessel | Window | Total |
|---|---|---|---|---|
| Junction 9 (Exc) 18 | LR | 18 | | |
| | MR/LR | 13 | 1 | |
| 14 | US | | 1 | 1 |
| Junction 9 (Exc) Total | | 31 | 2 | 33 |
| Evaluation trenches | ER | 1 | | 1 |
| | LR | 1 | | 1 |
| | PMED | 3 | 1 | 4 |
| Evaluation Trenches Total | | 5 | 1 | 6 |
| Junction 8N (Exc) | ER/MR | 1 | 1 | 2 |
| Junction 8N (Exc) Total | | 1 | 1 | 2 |
| Junction 8 watching brief | RO/MED | | 1 | 1 |
| Junction 8 watching brief Total | | | 1 | 1 |
| Total | | 37 | 5 | 42 |

### Evaluation trenches

The glass from the evaluation trenches includes four modern pieces from post-medieval contexts. The remaining two sherds include a small indented base sherd from a beaker or jug in pale-blue-green glass, almost colourless, with small bubbles in the metal, which might suggest a late Roman date. However, the sherd is from an early Roman context (136305) and may therefore be earlier in date or intrusive. The second sherd is an undiagnostic body sherd in blue-green glass from a late Roman context (136311). The sherd appears to have been heated causing partial blurring of the sharp edges.

### Junction 8N and Junction 8 watching brief

The sherds from Junction 8 are all very small and comprise two pieces of modern window glass and

*Table 7.39: Junction 9. Glass type by phase and context*

| Phase | Context | Context type | Vessel | Window | Total |
|---|---|---|---|---|---|
| MR/LR | 2038 | ditch | 10 | 1 | 11 |
| | 2353 | ditch | 1 | | 1 |
| | 2354 | ditch | 1 | | 1 |
| | 2406 | ditch | 1 | | 1 |
| *MR/LR Total* | | | *13* | *1* | *14* |
| LR | 2007 | pit | 14 | | 14 |
| | 2048 | ditch | 3 | | 3 |
| | 2129 | ditch | 1 | | 1 |
| *LR Total* | | | *18* | | *18* |
| US | 2001 | topsoil | | 1 | 1 |
| *US Total* | | | | *1* | *1* |
| Total | | | 31 | 2 | 33 |

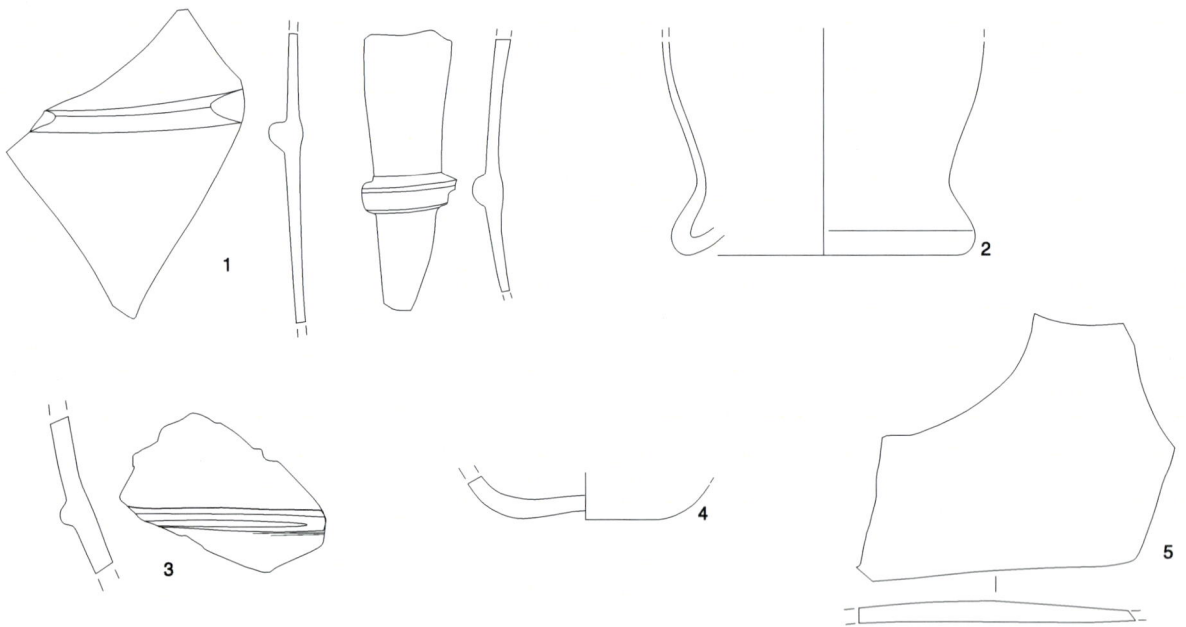

*Fig. 7.25   Glass*

small undiagnostic sherd of brown glass from a vessel. All three sherds could be intrusive.

## Junction 9 excavations

The glass from Junction 9 comprises 31 sherds of vessel glass and two sherds of window glass or possible window glass (Table 7.39). All but one sherd are from contexts dated to the Roman period.

### *Middle-late Roman contexts*

The middle to late Roman phase produced 14 sherds including 11 sherds from one context (2038). Six of these appear to be from a single vessel in yellow-brown glass with self-coloured trails (Fig. 7.25.1). The vessel form is uncertain and it is not possible to closely date the glass within the Roman period. The remaining glass from the context includes a piece of possible blue-green cast window glass (Fig. 7.25.5) and small undiagnostic vessel body sherds, one in deep-blue glass, the others in blue-green glass.

There is a tiny colourless undiagnostic body sherd from context 2406, a small vessel body sherd in yellow-green glass from context 2353, and larger body in deep-blue glass from context 2354. The latter sherd is undiagnostic to vessel form.

### *Late Roman contexts*

There is a total of 18 sherds of vessel glass from late Roman contexts. There is no identifiable window glass. Fourteen sherds come from context 2007. These include two sherds from the base of a small beaker or jug in blue-green glass (Fig. 7.25.2) and 12 small undiagnostic body sherds in blue-green glass. The variation in wall thickness between these sherds suggest that they derive from more than one vessel.

Three body sherds from context 2048 comprise one of yellow-green glass with a self-coloured trail (Fig. 7.25.3), and two body sherds of pale-blue-green glass. The latter have possible traces of wheel cutting or grinding, which are late Roman features. Finally, there is a sherd from the base of a possible unguent bottle in pale-green glass with tiny bubbles in the metal (Fig. 7.25.4).

### *Unstratified glass*

There is a single unstratified sherd of blue-green matt glossy window glass of Roman type.

## Conclusions

The glass assemblage is not large and contains only two possible pieces of window glass. Most of the vessel sherds are small, and there is little that can be firmly identified to vessel form. As with the metalwork from this site the glass hints at domestic occupation, and its presence suggests at least some pretensions to status. Beyond this its significance is uncertain.

## Catalogue of illustrated sherds (Fig. 7.25)

1   Body sherds (n = 6) slightly curved. They comprise four sherds with applied self-coloured trails and two very small sherds. There are no obvious joins, and therefore the form of the vessel is not certain. Yellow-brown glass. Largest sherd: L: 30mm; B: 28mm; Th: 1-1.5mm. Junction 9; Ctx 2038. Phase: middle-late Roman

2   Body/base sherds from a small vessel with an open base ring. Probably from a beaker/jug. Blue-green glass. Two joining sherds. Ht: 28mm; B: 35mm; Th: 1mm. Junction 9; Ctx 2007. Phase: late Roman

3   Small curved body sherd with single self-coloured trail. Undiagnostic to form. Yellow-green glass. One sherd. L: 28mm; B: 24mm. Junction 9; Ctx 2048. Phase: late Roman

4   Small indented base, possibly from an unguent bottle, small flask or beaker. Bubbles in metal. One sherd. Pale-green glass. L: 30mm; B: 27mm. Junction 9; Ctx 2129. Phase: late Roman

5   Possible window glass, though perhaps rather thin. Flat on one face, slightly curved on the opposite face. Bubbles in the metal. One sherd. Blue-green glass. L: 44mm; B: 33mm; Th: 2mm. Junction 9; Ctx 2038. Phase: middle-late Roman

## SLAG *by Luke Howarth*

Some 7.4kg of slag were recovered during the excavation phase of the project, with a smaller quantity (just over 1kg) from the evaluation. Over 90% of the material (by weight) came from Junction 9, with most of the rest from Junction 8N. The great majority of the material from the evaluation also came from the Junction 9 area (in Trenches 1356, 1357 and 1363). The material was recorded by number of fragments per context in terms of functional categories, where these could be determined. This information is summarised in Table 7.40.

The material was mostly recovered by hand excavation, but slag fragments were also recovered from environmental samples. The larger fragments are described in Table 7.40, but in some cases small fragments of metalworking debris were also found in the finest fraction (2-0.5mm) of the environmental samples and these residues have been retained. The residues were weighed and then 10% by weight of the residues was examined using a magnet and a x10 hand lens to pick out any metalworking debris.

All of the residues retained specifically for such further examination contained some evidence of metalworking, four samples in particular contained large concentrations of hammerscale, and these are listed in Table 7.41.

### Summary of the material

The morphology of the slags from this site indicates

*Table 7.40: Summary description of slag*

| Context | Sample No | .No. of fragments | Comments |
|---|---|---|---|
| 600 | | 1 | Possible fragment of hearth bottom |
| 1362 | 112 | 5 | No diagnostic form |
| 1362 | 112 | 5 | No diagnostic form |
| 2038 | | 6 | No diagnostic form |
| 2038 | | 10 | Small hearth bottom |
| 2044 | | 4 | Possible fragment of hearth bottom |
| 2048 | | 4 | Undiagnostic |
| 2048 | | 1 | Abraded fragment of Fe slag? |
| 2138 | | 2 | Undiagnostic form; some pale-green oxide (copper?) |
| 2139 | 2002 | 4 | No diagnostic form |
| 2139 | | 1 | Tabular fragment of slag with CBM annealed to one surface – fabric of structure |
| 2156 | | 10 | Vitrified CBM and fuel-ash slag (FAS) |
| 2279 | | 1 | Bun-shaped smithing hearth bottom |
| 2332 | 2024 | 1 | No diagnostic form |
| 2437 | | 3 | No diagnostic form |
| 2437 | | 1 | No diagnostic form |
| 2448 | 2036 | 2 | Fragment of hearth bottom |
| 2448 | 2036 | 11 | No diagnostic form |
| 2474 | | 7 | Vitrified CBM |
| 2488 | | 23 | Smithing-hearth bottom |
| 2488 | | 1 | FAS |
| 2488 | | 2 | Lump of iron surrounded with Fe oxide and CBM |
| 2511 | | 14 | No diagnostic form |
| 2511 | | 2 | No diagnostic form |
| 2513 | | 3 | No diagnostic form; iron-rich slag |
| 2513 | | 25 | Mixture of vitrified CBM; some fragments of nail and undiagnostic fragments of Fe-rich slag |
| 2579 | | 35 | Small hearth bottom |
| 2583 | 2039 | 1 | No diagnostic form |

iron working on small hearths. Some slags clearly represent smithing, but others are more ambiguous in character. The residues retained for metal-working debris all contained hammerscale and four samples contained relatively high concentrations of this material (Table 7.41). Hammerscale is significant as it is associated with refining of slags. The slag is predominantly indicative of iron working, though there is some evidence for the presence of copper in some of the slags. This may indicate that different ores were being worked at times, though copper and iron do occur together in some ores. The great majority of material comes from Roman deposits, the largest groups coming from features of 2nd-century date at Junction 9. A very small proportion of the slag from Junction 8N was from medieval deposits, but it is possible that this material was residual. The assemblage as a whole is relatively homogenous and is consistent with smithing of iron in small hearths rather than large-scale primary smelting.

*Table 7.40: Summary description of slag – continued*

| Context | Sample No | .No. of fragments | Comments |
|---|---|---|---|
| 2587 | | 12 | Fe slag with CBM annealed to one edge |
| 2587 | | 1 | Vitrified CBM |
| 2605 | | 5 | FAS |
| 2616 | | 6 | Iron fragments and partially vitrified CBM |
| 2616 | | 13 | No diagnostic form; Fe-rich slag and FAS |
| 2616 | | 1 | Partially vitrified |
| 2619 | | 1 | No diagnostic form |
| 2664 | | 1 | No diagnostic form |
| 2705 | | 11 | Small hearth bottoms |
| 3051 | | 1 | No diagnostic form |
| 3064 | | 1 | No diagnostic form |
| 5026 | | 15 | Fe fragments |
| 5235 | 2069 | 1 | No diagnostic form |
| 6055 | 6027 | 2 | No diagnostic form |
| 6061 | 6039 | 1 | No diagnostic form |
| 6067 | | 1 | Partly vitrified CBM |
| 6154 | | 1 | Vitrified CBM; furnace fabric. |
| 6169 | | 1 | Bun-shaped hearth bottom; cooling joints perpendicular to surface |
| 6189 | | 1 | No diagnostic form |
| 6215 | | 1 | Abraded fragment of Fe slag? |
| 6219 | | 2 | No diagnostic form |
| 6295 | 6007 | 1 | No diagnostic form |
| 6347 | | 2 | Abraded fragment of Fe slag? |
| 6356 | 6037 | 1 | No diagnostic form; Fe-rich slag |
| 6475 | | 1 | No diagnostic form; Fe-rich slag |
| 13615 | | 2 | No diagnostic form; Fe-rich slag |
| 126304 | | 1 | No diagnostic form |
| 135605 | 111 | 25 | No diagnostic form; Fe-rich slag |
| 135605 | 111 | 19 | Fragment of smithing-hearth bottom? |
| 135605 | 111 | 45 | No diagnostic form; Fe-rich slag |
| 135607 | 111 | 19 | Mostly undiagnostic fragments, ;some possible fragments of smithing-hearth bottom |
| 135607 | | 3 | No diagnostic form |
| 135607 | | 5 | No diagnostic form |
| 135612 | | 1 | No diagnostic form |
| 135705 | | 1 | Possible fragment of smithing-hearth bottom |
| 136313 | | 16 | No diagnostic form |

*Table 7.41: Residues retained for metalworking debris*

| Context | Sample No. | Wt of 10% metalworking debris picked out | Wt of hammerscale present in the sorted metal-working debris | % of |
|---|---|---|---|---|
| 2139 | 2002 | 38 g | 2 g | ~75% |
| 1362 | 112 | 33 g | 2 g | ~80% |
| 2375 | 2033 | 60 g | 1 g | ~25% |
| 7336 | 6081 | 56 g | 3 g | ~30% |

# Chapter 8: Environmental Evidence

## MAMMAL AND BIRD BONES *by Lena Strid*

### Introduction

The animal bone assemblage largely derives from Junction 8N and Junction 9, and the majority of the material comes from Roman and medieval contexts (Table 8.1). A full record of the assemblage, documented in a MS Access database, can be found within the site archive.

### Methodology

The majority of bones were recovered by hand during the excavation. A number of soil samples were taken and sieved through a 0.5mm mesh, but these samples produced little identifiable bone. Identification of the mammal and bird bone was undertaken at OA with access to the reference collection and published guides. All the animal remains were counted and weighed, and where possible identified to species, element, side and zone (Serjeantson 1996). Ribs and vertebrae were only recorded to species when they were substantially complete and could accurately be identified, or were from an identifiable articulated skeleton in which there could be no doubt as to their species. Undiagnostic bones were recorded as small (small

*Table 8.1: Number of identified bones/taxa in the M1 assemblages*

| Species | Junction 9 Roman | Junction 8N Roman | Junction 8N Medieval | Total |
|---|---|---|---|---|
| Cattle | 95 | 27 | 5 | 127 |
| Sheep/goat | 56 | 2 | 5 | 63 |
| Sheep | 1 | | | 1 |
| Goat | 4 | | | 4 |
| Pig | 19 | 3 | 12 | 34 |
| Horse | 18 | 49 | 3 | 70 |
| Cat | | | 1 | 1 |
| Domestic fowl | 1 | | 1 | 2 |
| Indeterminate bird | 3 | 2 | 6 | 11 |
| Small mammal | | | 1 | 1 |
| Medium mammal | 52 | 3 | 36 | 91 |
| Large mammal | 150 | 45 | 21 | 216 |
| Indeterminate | 569 | 159 | 163 | 890 |
| Total fragment count | 968 | 290 | 254 | 1512 |
| Total weight (g) | 7296 | 1379 | 1634 | 10309 |

mammal size), medium (sheep size) or large (cattle size). The separation of sheep and goat bones was undertaken using the criteria of Boessneck (1969) and Prummel and Frisch (1986), in addition to the use of the reference material housed at OA. Where distinctions could not be made, the bone was recorded as sheep/goat.

The condition of the bone was graded on a six-point system (0-5). Grade 0 equating to very well-preserved bone, and grade 5 indicating that the bone had suffered such structural and attritional damage as to make it unrecognisable. The minimum number of individuals (MNI) was calculated on the most frequently occurring bone for each species, using Serjeantson's (1996) zoning guide, and taking into account left and right sides. For the calculation of the number of identified fragments per species (NISP) all identifiable fragments were counted, although bones with modern breaks were refitted.

For ageing, Habermehl's (1975) data on epiphyseal fusion were used. Three fusion stages were recorded: unfused; in fusion; and fused. In fusion indicates that the epiphyseal line is still visible. Tooth wear was recorded using Grant's (1982) tooth-wear stages and correlated with tooth eruption (Habermehl 1975). Age was estimated using the methods of Halstead (1985), Payne (1973) and O'Connor (1988) for cattle, sheep/goat and pig respectively.

Measurements were taken according to von den Driesch (1976), using digital callipers with an accuracy of 0.01mm. Large bones were measured using an osteometric board, with an accuracy of 1mm.

### Preservation

The Roman assemblages showed a great range of bone condition (Table 8.2). Most bones were fairly to poorly preserved. The Junction 8N assemblage had a larger ratio of poorly preserved bones than Junction 9. There was little difference in the ratio of gnawed bones between these two sites, suggesting that the difference in bone condition is related to natural taphonomic factors. In all three assemblages, there were very few bones with gnaw marks from carnivores, probably dogs, suggesting that waste was disposed of securely soon after discard. There were no gnawed bones in the Roman Junction 8N assemblage, although the poor preservation may have obscured any traces of gnawing that were

*Table 8.2: Preservation level for bones from the M1 assemblage*

| Site | Date | N | 0 | 1 | 2 | 3 | 4 | 5 |
|------|------|---|---|---|---|---|---|---|
| Junction 9 | Roman | 968 | 1.2% | 18.3% | 45.2% | 22.4% | 11.9% | 0.9% |
| Junction 8N | Roman | 290 | 0.7% | 15.5% | 14.1% | 34.8% | 26.2% | 8.6% |
| Junction 8N | Medieval | 254 | 0.8% | 30.7% | 52.0% | 3.5% | 13.0% | |

originally present. A total of 23 bones had been burnt. Most of these occurred in the Junction 9 assemblage, although they only comprised 2.2% of the total number of fragments. The low number of burnt bones suggests that common cooking methods included boiling of meat or deboning before cooking.

## Junction 8N: Roman assemblage

The Junction 8N Roman assemblage comprises 290 fragments (Table 8.3). All but four fragments derive from the early-mid-Roman phase. The majority of the identified bone consists of teeth. This may be connected to the overall poor bone preservation of the assemblage (see above), since enamel is more resistant to taphonomic destruction than bone. The cattle teeth in particular were very fragmented.

The Roman assemblage is dominated by cattle and horse, although due to the biased element preservation the intra-site species ratio cannot be discussed further. The lack of wild mammals is not unusual for Roman rural sites, excluding villas (King 1991, 16-18), indicating that game provided at most a very minor contribution to the diet, if any.

Two first phalanges, one of cattle and one of horse, were fused, and thus belonged to animals older than 20-24 months and 12-15 months of age respectively. Dental age estimation was possible for three cattle mandibles, showing a range of slaughter ages from young adult to old adult.

## Junction 8N: medieval assemblage

The medieval assemblage from Junction 8N comprises 254 fragments (Table 8.4). A small number of bones from most of the common domestic species were present at the site, although dog was only indirectly represented in the form of gnaw marks on four bones. While not all body parts are present for the six taxa, there is no over-representation of skeletal elements that would suggest bias in the assemblage. The few ageable bones consist of a fused cattle first phalanx (>20-24 months at death), an unfused sheep/goat metapodial (<20-24 months at death) and a juvenile pig metacarpal. Sex estimation could be carried out on two pig teeth; one mandibular canine from a sow and one maxillary canine from a boar. A vertical cut mark below the P4 on the cat mandible indicates that the cat was skinned. Cat skins were common in the medieval period, albeit not associated with a high-social status (Luff and Moreno 1995; Hatting 1990; Magnell 2006).

*Table 8 3: Junction 8N, Roman assemblage. Anatomical distribution of all species, including NISP, MNI and weight. Skeletal element used for MNI is marked with an asterisk*

| | Cattle (*Bos taurus*) | Sheep/goat (*Ovis aries/ Capra hircus*) | Pig (*Sus domesticus*) | Horse (*Equus caballus*) | HBird | Medium mammal | Large mammal | Indeterminate |
|------|------|------|------|------|------|------|------|------|
| Mandible | 3* | | | | | | | |
| Loose teeth | 23 | 2 | 3 | 47 | | | 1 | |
| Rib | | | | | | 2 | | |
| Astragalus | | | | 1 | | | | |
| Phalanx 1 | 1 | | | 1 | | | | |
| Long bone | | | | | 2 | 1 | 44 | |
| Indeterminate | | | | | | | | 159 |
| | | | | | | | | |
| Total (NISP) | 27 | 2 | 3 | 49 | 2 | 3 | 45 | 159 |
| MNI | 2 | 1 | 1 | 1 | | | | |
| Weight (g) | 564 | 5 | 3 | 479 | 0 | 1 | 134 | 193 |

*Table 8.4: Junction 8N, medieval assemblage. Anatomical distribution of all species, including NISP, MNI and weight. Skeletal element used for MNI is marked with an asterisk*

| | Cattle (Bos taurus) | Sheep/goat (Ovis aries/Capra hircus) | Pig (Sus domesticus) | Horse (Equus caballus) | Cat (Felis catus) | Domestic fowl (Gallus gallus) | Bird | Small mammal | Medium mammal | Large mammal | Indeterminate |
|---|---|---|---|---|---|---|---|---|---|---|---|
| Skull fragments | | | | 1 | | | | | | | |
| Mandible | 1 | | | 1 | 1 | | | | | 1 | |
| Loose teeth | 1 | 2 | 5 | | | | | | | | |
| Vertebra | | | | | | | | 1 | | 2 | |
| Rib | | | | | | | | | 2 | 3 | |
| Scapula | | | | | | | | | 1 | | |
| Humerus | | | 3* | | | | 1 | | 1 | | |
| Radius | | 2 | 1 | | | | | | | | |
| Ulna | | | 1 | | | | | | | 2 | |
| Metacarpal | 1 | | 1 | | | | | | | | |
| Pelvis | | | | | | | | | | 1 | |
| Femur | 1 | | 1 | | | | | | | | |
| Tibia | | | | | | | | | 1 | | |
| Tarsometatarsus | | | | | | 1 | | | | | |
| Phalanx 2 | 1 | | | | | | | | | | |
| Indeterminate metapodial | | 1 | | 1 | | | | | | | |
| Long bone | | | | | | | 5 | | 31 | 11 | |
| Indeterminate | | | | | | | | | | 1 | 163 |
| Total (NISP) | 5 | 5 | 12 | 3 | 1 | 1 | 6 | 1 | 36 | 21 | 163 |
| MNI | 1 | 1 | 3 | 1 | 1 | 1 | | | | | |
| Weight (g) | 90 | 20 | 88 | 1009 | 2 | 0 | 0 | 0 | 95 | 217 | 113 |

## Junction 9: Roman assemblage

In contrast to the Junction 8N assemblage, no specific phase group dominates the Junction 9 material, which ranges from late Iron Age-late Roman in date (Table 8.5). As the individual phase groups are rather small the assemblage was analysed as a single unit.

As expected, domestic mammals dominate the assemblage (King 1991, 16-18) (Table 8.6). The paucity of wild taxa is consistent with Junction 8N, although considering the relatively small number of identified fragments, the perceived lack of evidence for hunting at these sites should be regarded with caution. Cattle is the most numerous taxon regardless of quantification method, followed by sheep/goat. The change in ratio between cattle and sheep/goat from two earlier phases to the late Roman phase is consistent with King's (1991) established theory of Romanisation in Britain leading to a reduction in the importance of sheep/goat and an increase in cattle and pig.

Both sheep and goat are present at the site. The four goat bones were recovered from the same late Iron Age/early Roman pit (2004; fill 2168), suggesting that they might derive from a single individual. Goats were rare in Iron Age and

*Table 8.5: Number of identified bones/taxa in the Junction 9, Roman assemblages*

| Species | LIA/ER | ER | MR | LR | RO |
|---|---|---|---|---|---|
| Cattle | 23 | 28 | 7 | 36 | 1 |
| Sheep/goat | 14 | 34 | 4 | 3 | 1 |
| Sheep | 1 | | | | |
| Goat | 4 | | | | |
| Pig | 4 | 8 | | 7 | |
| Horse | 3 | 4 | 3 | 8 | |
| Domestic fowl | | | | 1 | |
| Indeterminate bird | | 1 | | 2 | |
| Medium mammal | 8 | 33 | 7 | 4 | |
| Large mammal | 23 | 81 | 15 | 31 | |
| Indeterminate | 130 | 124 | 81 | 232 | 2 |
| Total fragment count | 210 | 313 | 117 | 324 | 4 |
| Total weight (g) | 2159 | 2499 | 750 | 1868 | 20 |

Roman Britain (King 1991, 16) and, as they have a higher milk yield than sheep (White 1970, 313), they may have been utilised mainly for dairy products.

Most body parts of cattle, sheep/goat and horse were present in the assemblage, indicating that

*Table 8.6: Junction 9, Roman assemblage. Anatomical distribution of all species, including NISP, MNI and weight. Skeletal element used for MNI is marked with an asterisk.*

| | Cattle (Bos taurus) | Sheep/goat (Ovis aries/ Capra hircus) | Pig (Sus domesticus) | Horse (Equus caballus) | Cat (Felis catus) | Domestic fowl (Gallus gallus) | Bird | Small mammal | Medium mammal | Large mammal | Indeterminate |
|---|---|---|---|---|---|---|---|---|---|---|---|
| Horn core | 1 | | | | | | | | | | |
| Skull fragments | 3 | 2 | | | 3 | 1 | | | | 53 | |
| Mandible | 8* | 8* | | | | | | | | 1 | |
| Loose teeth | 45 | 20 | | | 12 | 6 | | | | | |
| Axis | 1 | | | | | 1 | | | | | |
| Vertebra | | | | | | | | | 3 | 12 | |
| Rib | | | | | | | | 1 | 14 | 20 | |
| Sterum | | | | | | | | | 1 | | |
| Scapula | 3 | 3 | | | 1 | | | | | | |
| Humerus | 6 | 2 | | 1 | 2 | 3* | | | | | |
| Radius | 4 | 7 | | 1 | | 1 | | | | 1 | |
| Ulna | | 2 | | | | | | 1 | | | |
| Carpal | | | | 1 | | | | | | | |
| Metacarpal | 5 | | | 1 | | 2 | | | | | |
| Pelvis | 6 | 1 | | | | | | | | | |
| Femur | | | | | 1 | | 1 | | | | |
| Tibia | 4 | 4 | | | | 1 | | | | | |
| Calcaneus | 1 | 1 | | | | | | | 1 | | |
| Astragalus | | 1 | | | | | | | | | |
| Metatarsal | 5 | 3 | 1 | | | 3 | | | | | |
| Phalanx 1 | 3 | | | | | | | | | | |
| Phalanx 2 | | 2 | | | | | | | | | |
| Long bone | | | | | | | | 1 | 33 | 63 | |
| Indeterminate | | | | | | | | | | | 569 |
| Total (NISP) | 95 | 56 | 1 | 4 | 19 | 18 | 1 | 3 | 52 | 150 | 569 |
| MNI | 5 | 3 | | | 1 | 2 | 1 | | | | |
| Weight (g) | 3075 | 301 | 3 | 59 | 205 | 1548 | 2 | 1 | 94 | 1022 | 986 |

*Table 8.7: Junction 9, Roman assemblage. Cattle epiphyseal fusion*

| | Unfused | Fusing | Fused | % unfused |
|---|---|---|---|---|
| Early fusion (<1.5 years) | | | 5 | 0% |
| Mid fusion (2-2.5 years) | | | 6 | 0% |
| Late fusion (>3 years) | 1 | | | 100% |

*Table 8.8: Junction 9, Roman assemblage. Sheep/goat epiphyseal fusion*

| | Unfused | Fusing | Fused | % unfused |
|---|---|---|---|---|
| Early fusion (<1 year) | | | 4 | 100% |
| Mid fusion (1-2 years) | | 1 | 3 | 0% |
| Late fusion (>3 years) | 2 | | 2 | 50% |

*Table 8.9: Junction 9, Roman assemblage. Pig epiphyseal fusion*

| | Unfused | Fusing | Fused | % unfused |
|---|---|---|---|---|
| Early fusion (<1 year) | | | 3 | 0% |
| Mid fusion (1-2.5 years) | | | | |
| Late fusion (>3 years) | 1 | | | 100% |

these animals were slaughtered and butchered at the site. The pig bones derive from the skull and from meat-rich limb bones. The presence of skull elements suggests that despite the lack of foot bones, pigs were slaughtered on site, rather than brought in as meat.

Epiphyseal fusion data suggest that cattle and sheep/goat were mostly slaughtered as sub-adults and/or adults, whereas pigs were mostly slaughtered as sub-adults (Tables 8.7-9). The sheep/goat dental data show a wide age distribu-

*Table 8.10: Junction 9, Roman assemblage. Dental analysis of cattle, using Halstead (1985)*

| N | 0-1 months | 1-8 months | 8-18 months | 18-30 months | 30-36 months | Young adult | Adult | Old adult | Senile |
|---|---|---|---|---|---|---|---|---|---|
| 5 | | | | 3 | | 1 | | | 1 |

*Table 8.11: Junction 9, Roman assemblage. Dental analysis of sheep/goat, using Payne (1973)*

| N | 0-2 months | 2-6 months | 6-12 months | 1-2 years | 2-3 years | 3-4 years | 4-6 years | 6-10 years |
|---|---|---|---|---|---|---|---|---|
| 4 | | 1 | | 1 | 1 | | 1 | |

*Table 8.12: Measurements of sheep/goat bones from Junction 9 and from late Iron Age-early Roman sites in the ABMAP database*

| | Species | Element | Measurement | N | Mean | Min | Max |
|---|---|---|---|---|---|---|---|
| Junction 9 | Goat | Metacarpal | Greatest length (GL) | 1 | 105.5 | | |
| ABMAP | Sheep/goat | | | 15 | 115.8 | 104.9 | 126.1 |
| Junction 9 | Goat | Metacarpal | Greatest breadth of the distal end (Bd) | 1 | 25.2 | | |
| ABMAP | Sheep/goat | | | 20 | 22.2 | 20.6 | 24.9 |
| Junction 9 | Sheep/goat | Tibia | Greatest breadth of the distal end (Bd) | 1 | 22.4 | | |
| ABMAP | | | | 100 | 23.0 | 19.9 | 29.8 |

tion, whereas the cattle are dominated by 18-30 month old animals (Table 8.10-11). Juvenile remains were recovered from the early Roman phase, comprising one calf metacarpal, one sheep/goat scapula and one pig skull fragment. Two mandibular pig canines from the late Iron Age/early Roman phase belonged to boars, whereas one mandibular canine from the late Roman phase derived from a sow.

The measurable bones from Junction 9 are similar in size to contemporary bones from Romano-British sites in the Animal Bone Metrical Archive Project (ABMAP) database (Tables 8.12-13) (ABMAP 2009). The short length and large distal breadth of the goat metacarpal in comparison to contemporary measurements suggests that the measurements from the ABMAP database mainly derive from sheep, as they are more slender than goats. During the Roman period there is some evidence for increases in animal size, believed to be a result of focussed animal breeding, including the import of breeding animals (Maltby 1981, 185-92). As a result of the small sample size this trend is not visible in the M1 assemblages, and in any case the pattern is far from universal.

Butchering marks were recorded on eight bones. An early Roman cattle first phalanx had transverse cut marks mid bone on the lateral side. These probably derived from skinning. Cut marks on the proximal end of a late Roman horse metatarsal could derive from skinning or from disarticulation. The same context group (2040) also contained two other horse metapodials and a skull fragment, but no horse bones from meat-rich parts of the body.

*Table 8.13: Greatest length of horse metacarpal at Junction 9 and from late Iron Age-early Roman sites in the ABMAP database*

| | N | Mean | Min | Max |
|---|---|---|---|---|
| Junction 9 | 1 | 213.5 | | |
| ABMAP | 12 | 200.2 | 181.0 | 211.0 |

Cut marks at the glenoid on an early Roman pig scapula and distally on the medial side of a late Iron Age/early Roman goat humerus suggest disarticulation of these joints. One late Iron Age/early Roman sheep/goat tibia had cut marks on the distal part of the bone, which may have occurred during filleting or disarticulation. Filleting was otherwise recorded on one rib from a large mammal, which displayed transverse cut marks mid rib. Four parallel transverse heavy-cut/chop marks on the medial side of the ilium on a late Roman cattle pelvis would most likely derive from portioning of the carcass.

Small exostoses, possibly related to infection and/or muscle trauma, were found on the upper third half of the shaft on a late Roman horse metatarsal. Non-metric congenital traits were recorded on two early Roman sheep/goat mandibles, that had a foramen on the buccal side of the ramus below the premolars. Halstead and Collins (2002, 549) have suggested that this placement of an extra foramen is a characteristic indicator for sheep rather than goat.

## Discussion

The two Roman settlements, Junction 8N and Junction 9, are difficult to compare. Although the main domestic taxa are present at both sites, the composition of the assemblages varies greatly, probably mostly due to preservation differences. Large assemblages in the area include those from Gorhambury villa, just north-west of Verul-amium (Locker 1990) and from the Folly Lane shrine within Verulamium (Locker 1999). There are also minor reports on bones from secular deposits in Verulamium (Locker 1999; Wilson 1984).

With the exception of the shrine deposits, cattle is the dominant taxon in the Gorhambury and Verulamium assemblages. A predominance of sheep/goat is normally associated with a native economy, which continues in the Roman period on the rural non-Romanised sites (King 1991). However, the Iron Age phase at Gorhambury shows a predominance of cattle, and Locker (1990, 210) suggests that the environment in the area is particularly suitable for cattle compared to sheep. The predominance of cattle at Junction 8N and Junction 9 does not therefore necessarily indicate a high level of Romanisation at these settlements.

The high representation of pigs at Gorhambury suggests that the villa inhabitants were utilising nearby woods for pannage, while the low numbers of pigs at Junction 9, might indicate that the local landscape was less suitable for intensive pig farming. Another possibility is that the Junction 9 inhabitants were not able to use the existing landscape optimally for their own purposes, if the local resources were to an extent controlled by the occupants of villas, such as that at nearby Redbourn. Pigs are generally more frequent on villa sites than on other rural settlements (Cool 2006, 82-4). This might be connected to the fact that villa estates controlled more land than smaller settlements, which would enable them to keep larger number of animals. Alternatively, villas may have focussed on different agricultural products, and bought pigs for slaughter from surrounding settlements.

Medieval animal bone assemblages from Hertfordshire are rare. The few that have been published mostly derive from ecclesiastical or high-status sites (English Heritage 2008), and are thus not directly comparable to those from rural settlements. There is a small assemblage of 333 speciable bones from a croft at Gorhambury (Locker 1990), but there are not enough bones to allow an inter-site comparison of numbers of cattle, sheep/goat and pig. The NISP data suggest that sheep/goat were the most common taxa and that pigs were almost as common as cattle (ibid., 210). A large ratio of pig bones could indicate that there were forests suitable for pannage in the region.

## CHARRED PLANT REMAINS *by Wendy Smith*

### Introduction

In total 176 samples were collected during excavations and 116 of these were assessed (Smith 2008) for charred plant remains (CPR), the majority of which are of Roman date. Twenty-one of the samples assessed produced moderate to abundant CPR (excluding charcoal). Although several different areas of the M1 sites were sampled, these remains are only from two areas; Junction 8N and Junction 9. Several samples of 'moderate' quality (eg producing *c* 50-100 identifications in total) were excluded from the analysis, either because: the contexts remained unphased (evaluation sample 100); only relatively small quantities of CPR (sometimes poorly preserved) were available (in five medieval samples); or plant remains of this phase were already well represented (Roman samples). As a result, this report will only consider the 14 richer archaeobotanical assemblages recovered.

The results from 12 samples dating from the late Iron Age-early Roman/late Roman and two medieval samples (of 12th-13th-century date) are presented. Sample volumes range from 10-40l, but typically are 30-40l in volume. Samples are from a variety of features including a middle Roman corn dryer (corn dryer 7782 – samples 6088 and 6089), ditches (late Iron Age-early Roman/late Roman samples 2002, 2037, 2038 and 6024), a medieval kiln (sample 6017), a middle Roman organic layer (sample 102036), pits (late Iron Age-early Roman/late Roman pits samples 2001, 2033, 6018 and 6052, and medieval pit sample 6020) and a waterhole (late Iron Age-early Roman sample 2024). The analysis of archaeobotanical data from lesser rural Roman sites is considered to be limited in England (van der Veen *et al*. 2007, 207, fig. 2); therefore, the data presented are of regional and national importance.

### Method

Samples were processed at OA using a modified Siraf-style flotation machine. The flot (the material which floats) was washed over a 0.25mm mesh sieve and the heavy residue (the material which does not float) was retained in a 0.5mm flexible nylon mesh. The heavy-residue fraction was then subsequently wet-sieved over a series of graduated rigid sieves at >10mm, 10-4mm, 4-2mm and >0.5mm. Both flots and heavy-residue fractions were dried at 30°C. Heavy residues were sorted by eye by staff at OA; where abundant CPR were noted, the relevant heavy-residue fraction was retained.

Samples were sorted under a low-power binocular microscope at magnifications between x10 and x20. All sorted samples were then rechecked by the author to ensure that all identifiable plant remains had been extracted. Checking sorted flots and identification of sorted CPR was made using a low-power Leica EZ4D microscope at magnifications between x12.5 and x35. In addition, the author sorted the 4-2mm heavy-residue fraction for sample 6052 under a low-power binocular microscope at x12.5 magnification.

Several of the flots clearly were very rich and/or contained highly fragmented plant remains that were exceedingly time-consuming to sort. As a result, the riffling method (eg van der Veen 1984; van der Veen and Fieller 1982) was adopted, with a notional target of at least 250-300 quantifiable items, ideally 500, extracted. In all cases of sub-samples, the scores recorded in the tables are only for that portion of the flot sorted and are not factored back up to 100% of the flot/heavy residue. In two cases (samples 2001 and samples 6018) <200 quantifiable plant macrofossils were sorted from the sub-sample selected; however, both samples were extremely difficult to sort because of the highly fragmentary nature of CPR (including minute charcoal fragments) present. In addition, the initial estimate counts from primary sorting for both samples were artificially inflated by the inclusion of clearly modern seeds with black seed coats (eg *Chenopodium* spp./*Atriplex* spp.), which were subsequently disregarded for the analysis. Although it would have been satisfactory to return and sort a further sub-sample from each of these samples, it was considered that this would be unlikely to generate data that would greatly change the results already produced.

All CPR samples were fully quantified (with the proviso that highly fragmentary remains such as

awns, glumes and minute fragments of indeterminate cereal/large grass caryopses were semi-quantified) and scores were based on whole seeds or plant parts. Quantification of cereal grain and grass caryopses was based on the apical end, primarily because the majority of cereal grain was missing the embryo end. Estimate counts (where fragmentary material was quantified in terms of whole seeds or plant parts) are indicated in the tables by an 'E' after the score. In a few cases, especially where modern seeds are black, the antiquity of the CPR is in question and this has been indicated by a '?' after the score in the tables.

Quantification of cereal grain sprouts (coleoptiles) was made on those coleoptiles which have the trefoil-shaped base (two rootlet bases and the base of the acrospire) fully preserved. This most likely under represents the quantity of coleoptiles present, but avoids quantification of highly fragmentary sprouts as if they were the same as the largely intact sprouts. The length of the coleoptiles has not been measured. In all cases the tip of the coleoptile was absent.

Identifications were made in comparison with the OA reference collection and illustrations or photographs in Floras and standard keys (eg Cappers *et al.* 2006; Stace 1997). Nomenclature for the plant remains follows Stace (1997) for indigenous species and Zohary and Hopf (2000) for cultivated species. The traditional binomial system for the cereals is maintained, following Zohary and Hopf (2000, 28, table 3; 65, table 5).

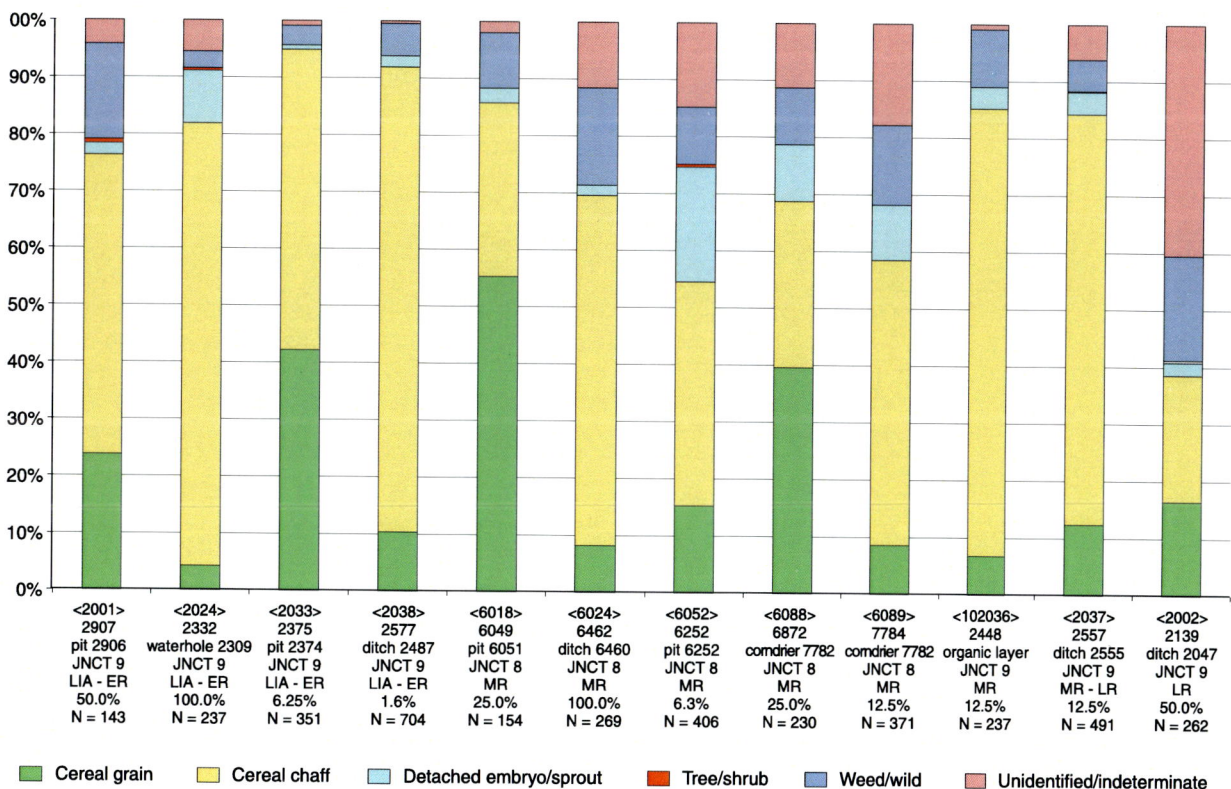

*Fig. 8.1  Relative proportions of plant remain categories in late Iron Age/early Roman-late Roman samples from all sites*

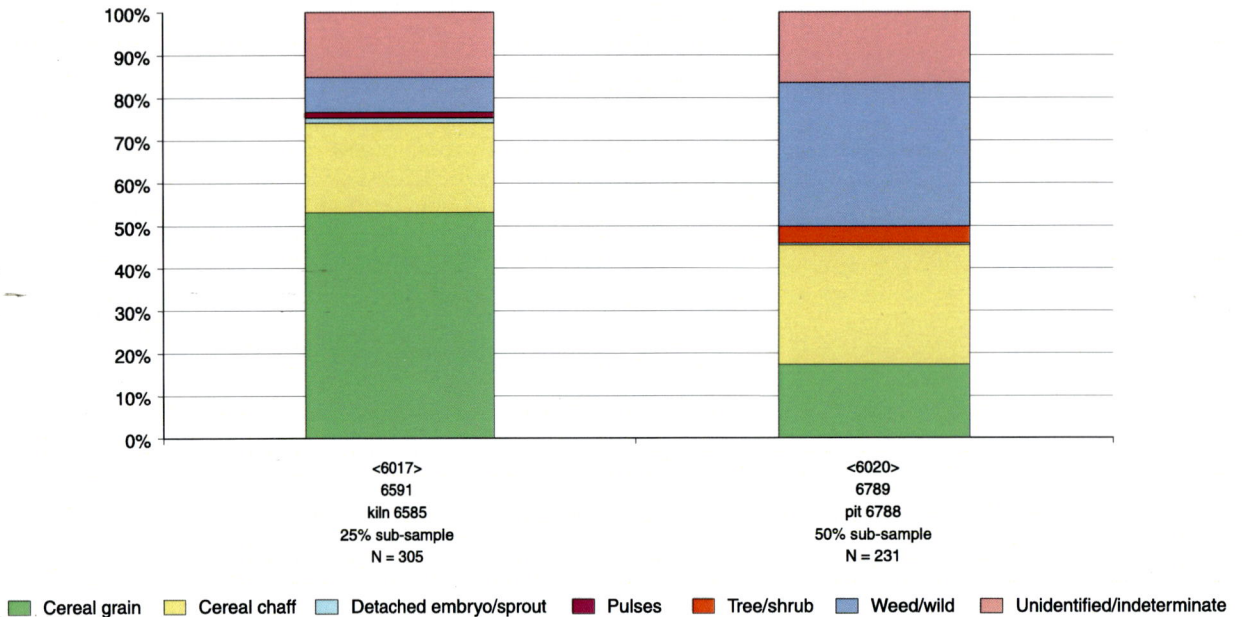

*Fig. 8.2 Relative proportions of plant remain categories from medieval samples from Junction 8N*

## Results

The CPR recovered clearly separate out into Roman and medieval periods on the basis of the wheat (*Triticum* spp.) cultivated. Table 8.14 presents the quantified taxa list for all 12 late Iron Age-early Roman/late Roman samples analysed from the scheme. Table 8.15 and Fig. 8.1 present the relative proportion of various categories of plant remains (eg cereal grain, cereal chaff, weed/wild plants, etc) recovered. Table 8.16 presents the quantified taxa list for the two medieval (12th-13th-century) samples fully analysed. Table 8.17 and Fig. 8.2 present the relative proportion of various categories of plant remains recovered from the medieval CPR assemblage.

The late Iron Age-early Roman/late Roman CPR assemblage includes several samples (n = 8) dominated by cereal chaff remains, primarily of spelt wheat (*Triticum spelta* L.). One sample was clearly dominated by cereal grain (sample 6018 from pit 6051, context 6049) and the four remaining samples were fairly mixed assemblages of cereal grain (including detached embryos/sprouts), cereal chaff and accompanying weed seeds. The weed/wild component was often relatively small (Table 8.15 and Fig. 8.1) and may be inflated by the inclusion of indeterminate cultivated/wild oat (*Avena* spp.) and/or brome grass (*Bromus* spp.), both of which can be cultivated or considered a tolerated impurity of the main crop.

The two medieval assemblages are most likely not a reliable reflection of the full range of plant-related activities carried out in the medieval settlement centred on Junction 8N. Nevertheless, both samples are clearly dominated by remains of free-threshing-type wheat (*Triticum* spp. grain and

rachis nodes), and smaller quantities of rye (*Secale cereale* L.). One possible barley (cf *Hordeum* sp.) grain was noted, but barley chaff was not observed in these samples. Sample 6017, from kiln 6585, was primarily comprised of cereal grain and chaff, with only a small weed/wild component (n = 25 or 8.2% of all identifications). Sample 6020, from pit 6788, was a fairly even mixture of cereal chaff (n = 65 or 28.1%) and weed/wild plant seeds (n = 78 or 33.8%), with a good deal of cereal grain (n = 40 or 17.3%) also present.

## Discussion

The Roman assemblages appear to primarily comprise charred crop-processing by-products, with only one sample (pit sample 6018) strongly dominated by a single product, in this case primarily poorly preserved cereal and/or cereal/large grass caryopses. Consideration of the context and distribution of these remains may be informative. The weed/wild component from these Roman assemblages is limited, but is consistent with other results from Hertfordshire. The consistent presence of indeterminate cultivated or wild oat (*Avena* spp.) and/or brome grass (*Bromus* spp.) in the weed flora may suggest a tolerated impurity, if not a cultivated crop in their own right.

### Crop-processing by-products vs. products in Roman samples

Cultivation of cereal crops for grain generates abundant waste or by-product material. In the case of the Roman samples, spelt (*Triticum spelta* L.) is the main cereal identified. Spelt is a hulled wheat which generally has two grains in each spikelet (segment)

*Table 8.14: Late Iron Age-early Roman/late Roman CPR*

| Sample | 2001 | 2024 | 2033 | 2038 | 6018 | 6024 | |
|---|---|---|---|---|---|---|---|
| Context | 2907 | 2332 | 2375 | 2577 | 6049 | 6462 | |
| Context description | Pit 2906 | Waterhole 2309 | Pit 2374 | Ditch 2487 | Pit 6051 | Ditch 6460 | |
| Site | Jnct 9 | Jnct 9 | Jnct 9 | Jnct 9 | Jnct 8N | Jnct 8N | |
| Phase | LIA-ER | LIA-ER | LIA-ER | LIA-ER | MR | MR | |
| Sample vol. (l) | 40 | 40 | 40 | 15 | 30 | 40 | |
| Flot vol. (ml) | 40 | 8 | 300 | 325 | 100 | 55 | |
| Proportion of sample sorted | 50% | 100% | 1/16th | 1/64th | 25% | 100% | |
| Seeds per litre of sediment | 71.5 | 237.0 | 21.9 | 11.0 | 38.5 | 269.0 | |
| **LATIN BINOMIAL** | | | | | | | **ENGLISH COMMON NAME** |
| **FLOT** | | | | | | | |
| **Cereal grain** | | | | | | | |
| cf *Hordeum* sp. | - | - | 3 | - | - | - | possible barley |
| *Triticum* cf *dicoccum* Schübl | - | - | - | - | - | 1 | possible emmer |
| *Triticum dicoccum* Schübl./*spelta* L. | - | - | 1 | - | - | - | indeterminate emmer/spelt |
| *Triticum dicoccum* Schübl./*spelta* L. - tail grain | - | - | - | - | - | 4 | indeterminate emmer/spelt |
| *Triticum spelta* L. | - | - | - | - | - | - | spelt |
| *Triticum* spp. - indeterminate grain fragments (est. whole grain) | 2 | - | 8 | 9 | 16 E | - | indeterminate wheat |
| *Triticum* spp. - indeterminate, germinated grain (est. whole grain) | - | - | 2 | 1 | 1 | - | indeterminate wheat |
| *Triticum* spp. - indeterminate tail grain | - | - | - | 1 | - | - | indeterminate wheat |
| Cereal - indeterminate | 12E | - | 59 E | 32 E | 43 E | 7 | cereal |
| Cereal/ POACEAE - indeterminate fragments (est. whole grain / caryopsis) | 20 E | 10 E | 75 E | 30 E | 25 E | 10 E | cereal/large grass |
| Cereal/ POACEAE - indeterminate (semi-quantified minute fragments) | +++ | - | ++++ | +++ | +++ | ++ | cereal/large grass |
| **Cereal chaff** | | | | | | | |
| *Triticum* cf *dicoccum* Schübl. - glume base | 1 | - | - | - | - | - | possible emmer |
| *Triticum dicoccum* Schübl./*spelta* L. - glume fragments (unquantified) | - | - | - | ++++ | - | - | indeterminate emmer/spelt |
| *Triticum dicoccum* Schübl./*spelta* L. - glume base | 36 E | 78 E | 71 E | 270 | 20 E | 91 E | indeterminate emmer/ spelt |
| *Triticum dicoccum* Schübl./*spelta* L. - spikelet fork (=2gb)** | 1 | - | 3 | 1 | - | 1 | indeterminate emmer/ spelt |
| *Triticum dicoccum* Schübl./*spelta* L. - terminal spikelet fork (=2gb)** | - | - | 2 | - | - | - | indeterminate emmer/ spelt |
| *Triticum spelta* L. - glume base | 2 | 6 | 20 | 102 | 5 | 15 | spelt |
| *Triticum spelta* L. - spikelet fork (= 2 gb)** | - | 0 | - | - | - | 1 | spelt |
| *Triticum* cf *spelta* L. - glume fragments | - | - | - | - | - | ++ | possible spelt |
| *Triticum* cf *spelta* L. - spikelet fork (=2 gb)** | - | - | - | - | - | 1 | possible spelt |
| *Triticum* spp. - rachis nodes (often highly fragmented, estimate whole node) | 25 E | 100 E | 84 E | 150 E | 21 E | 30 E | indeterminate wheat |
| *Triticum* spp. - awn (unquantified) | - | - | 5 E | ++ | - | + | indeterminate wheat |
| Cereal - unidentified rachis internode fragment | 9 E | - | - | 50 E | - | 25 | cereal |
| Cereal - unidentified basal rachis node | - | - | - | - | - | - | cereal |
| Cereal/ POACEAE - indeterminate, culm node | 1 | - | - | - | - | - | cereal/large grass |

| Sample<br>Context | 2001<br>2907 | 2024<br>2332 | 2033<br>2375 | 2038<br>2577 | 6018<br>6049 | 6024<br>6462 | |
|---|---|---|---|---|---|---|---|
| Cereal / POACEAE - indeterminate, culm base | - | - | - | - | 1 | - | cereal/large grass |
| Cereal / POACEAE - indeterminate, rachilla | - | - | - | 1 | - | 1 | cereal/large grass |
| **Deatched embryo/sprout** | | | | | | | |
| Cereal / POACEAE - indeterminate detached embryo | 2 | 7 | 2 | 10 | 4 | 4 | cereal/large grass |
| Cereal / POACEAE - indeterminate detached coleoptile | 1 | 8 | 1 | 1 | - | 1 | cereal/large grass |
| cf Cereal / POACEAE - indeterminate, detached sprout | - | - | - | 1 | - | - | possible cereal/large grass |
| cf Cereal / POACEAE - indeterminate, small detached embryo/sprout | - | 7 | - | 2 | - | - | possible cereal/large grass |
| **Pulses** | | | | | | | |
| Pisum sativum L. | - | - | - | - | - | - | garden pea |
| Vicia spp. / Pisum sativum L. | - | - | - | - | - | - | vetch/garden pea |
| **Tree/shrub** | | | | | | | |
| Corylus avellana L. - nutshell fragments (est. whole nut) | 1 | - | - | - | - | - | hazel |
| cf Corylus avellana L. - nutshell fragments (est. whole nut) | - | 1 | - | - | - | - | possible hazel |
| Sambucus nigra L. | - | - | - | - | - | - | elder |
| **Weed/wild plants** | | | | | | | |
| Ranunculus subgenus RANUNCULUS | - | - | - | - | - | 1 | buttercup |
| cf Urtica dioica L. - internal structure | - | - | - | - | - | - | possible common nettle |
| Chenopodium spp. / Atriplex spp. - internal structure | - | - | - | - | - | - | indeterminate goosefoot/orache |
| Atriplex spp. | - | - | 3 E | 1 | 1 | - | orache |
| Stellaria media L. | 1 | - | - | - | - | - | common chickweed |
| CARYOPHYLLACEAE - unidentified, small-seeded | - | - | - | - | - | - | pink family |
| cf Fallopia convolvulus (L.) Á. Löve - highly fragmented, est. whole seed | - | - | - | - | - | - | possible black-bindweed |
| Polygonum spp. | - | - | - | - | - | - | knotgrass |
| cf Polygonum sp. | - | - | 1 | - | - | - | possible knotgrass |
| Polygonum spp. / Rumex spp. / Carex spp. - internal structure | - | - | - | - | - | - | knotgrass/dock/sedge |
| Rumex cf. acetosella L. | 1 | - | - | - | - | - | possible sheep's sorrel |
| Rumex spp. | - | - | - | 1 | 2 | - | dock |
| cf Rumex spp. - small-seeded/immature | - | - | - | - | - | - | possible dock |
| Vicia cf hirsuta (L.) Gray | - | - | - | - | - | - | possible hairy tare |
| Vicia spp. / Lathyrus spp. | 2 | - | 5 E | - | - | - | vetch/vetchling |
| Melilotus spp. / Medicago spp. / Trifolium spp. | - | - | - | - | - | 3 | melilot/medick/clover |
| Lotus spp. / Melilotus spp. / Medicago spp. / Trifolium spp. | - | - | - | - | - | - | bird's-foot-trefoil/ melilot/medick/clover |
| FABACEAE - detached hilum (?ancient) | - | - | - | - | - | 4? | pea family |
| cf FABACEAE - immature | 1 | - | - | - | - | - | possible pea family |

| Taxon | | | | | | Common name |
|---|---|---|---|---|---|---|
| APIACEAE - unidentified, small-sized | 1 | - | - | - | - | carrot family |
| *Prunella vulgaris* L. | - | - | - | - | 1 | selfheal |
| LAMIACEAE - small sized | - | - | - | - | - | mint family |
| *Plantago major* L. | - | - | - | 1 | - | greater plantain |
| *Plantago media* L./*lanceolata* L. | - | - | - | - | - | hoary/ribwort plantain |
| *Euphrasia* spp./*Odontites* spp. | - | - | - | - | - | eyebright/bartsia |
| *Galium* spp. | 1 | - | - | - | - | bedstraw |
| cf *Arctium lappa* L. | 1 | - | - | - | 1 | possible greater burdock |
| *Carduus* sp./*Cirsium* sp. | - | - | 1 | - | - | thistle |
| *Tripleurospermum inodorum* L. | 1 | 1 | - | - | - | scentless mayweed |
| ASTERACEAE - internal structure, small-sized achene | 1 | - | - | - | - | daisy family |
| ASTERACEAE - internal structure, medium-sized achene | - | - | - | - | - | daisy family |
| cf *Lolium* sp. - rachis node | 1 | - | - | - | - | possible rye-grass |
| cf *Poa annua* L. | 1 | - | - | - | 10 | possible annual meadow-grass |
| *Avena* cf *fatua* L. - pedicel fragment | - | - | - | - | 1 | possible wild oat |
| *Avena* spp. - awn (semi-quantied fragments) | ++ | + | + | + | ++ | indeterminate wild/cultivated oat |
| *Avena* spp. - floret base | - | - | 1 | - | - | indeterminate wild/cultivated oat |
| cf *Avena* spp. - floret-base fragment | - | - | - | - | - | possible indeterminate wild/cultivated oat |
| *Avena* spp./*Bromus* spp. | 2 | - | 27 | 5 E | 4 E | indeterminate wild/cultivated oat/brome grass |
| *Bromus* spp. | 1 | 2 E | 9 | - | - | brome grass |
| cf *Bromus* spp. | 10 | 3 | - | - | - | possible brome grass |
| POACEAE - small-sized caryopsis | - | 1 | - | 6 | 21 | grass family |
| POACEAE - medium-sized caryopsis | - | 1 | - | - | 1 | grass family |
| POACEAE - large-sized caryopsis | 1 | 1 | - | - | - | grass family |
| POACEAE - basal rachis node | 1 | - | - | - | - | grass family |
| *Carex* spp. - three sided | 1 | - | - | - | - | sedge |
| Unidentified | 1 | 2 | 2 | 3 | 11 | - |
| Unidentified - seed coat fragment | 1 | - | 2 | - | - | - |
| Unidentified - ?bark/?leaf, curled fragment | - | - | - | - | - | - |
| Unidentified - bud | 1 | - | - | - | - | - |
| Unidentified - bud fragments | - | - | - | - | - | - |
| Unidentified - bud scale | 1 | - | - | - | - | - |
| Unidentified - capsule fragment or pod | - | 1 | - | - | - | - |
| Unidentified - possible thorn | - | - | - | - | - | - |
| Indeterminate | - | 10 E | 1 | - | 20 | - |
| Indeterminate - highly vitreous, amorphous | 2 | - | - | - | - | - |

**Other charred remains**

| Taxon | | | | | | |
|---|---|---|---|---|---|---|
| Fungal body (unquantified) | +++ | - | - | - | + | |
| Unidentified - insect larva | - | 1 | - | - | - | |

173

**HEAVY RESIDUE**

| Sample | 2001 | 2024 | 2033 | 2038 | 6018 | 6024 | ENGLISH COMMON NAME |
|---|---|---|---|---|---|---|---|
| Context | 2907 | 2332 | 2375 | 2577 | 6049 | 6462 | |
| **Cereal grain** | | | | | | | |
| Triticum cf dicoccum Schübl. - germinated grain | - | - | - | - | - | - | possible emmer |
| Triticum spelta L. | - | - | - | - | - | - | spelt |
| Triticum sp. - indeterminate | - | - | - | - | - | - | indeterminate wheat |
| Cereal - indeterminate | - | - | - | - | - | - | cereal |
| Cereal / POACEAE - indeterminate | - | - | - | - | - | - | cereal/large grass |
| **Cereal chaff** | | | | | | | |
| Triticum cf. spelta L. - glume base | - | - | - | - | - | - | possible spelt |
| **Tree/shrub** | | | | | | | |
| cf Corylus avellana L. - nutshell fragments (est. whole nut) | - | - | - | - | - | - | possible hazel |
| **Weed/wild** | | | | | | | |
| Avena spp./Bromus spp. | - | - | - | - | - | - | indeterminate cultivated/wild oat/brome grass |
| Bromus sp. | - | - | - | - | - | - | brome grass |

| Sample | 6052 | 6088 | 6089 | 102036 | 2037 | 2002 |
|---|---|---|---|---|---|---|
| Context | 6252 | 6872 | 7784 | 2448 | 2557 | 2139 |
| Context description | Pit 6252 | Corn dryer 7782 | Corn dryer 7782 | Organic layer | Ditch 2555 | Ditch 2047 |
| Site | Jnct 8N | Jnct 8N | Jnct 8N | Jnct 9 | Jnct 9 | Jnct 9 |
| Phase | MR | MR | MR | MR | MR-LR | LR |
| Sample vol. (l) | 40 | 10 | 10 | 40 | 40 | 30 |
| Flot vol. (ml) | 60 | 65 | 70 | 150 | 85 | 100 |
| Proportion of sample sorted | 1/16th | 25% | 1/8th | 1/8th | 1/8th | 50% |
| Seeds per litre of sediment | 25.4 | 57.5 | 46.4 | 29.6 | 61.4 | 131.0 |

| LATIN BINOMIAL | 2001 | 2024 | 2033 | 2038 | 6018 | 6024 | ENGLISH COMMON NAME |
|---|---|---|---|---|---|---|---|
| **FLOT** | | | | | | | |
| **Cereal grain** | | | | | | | |
| cf Hordeum sp. | - | - | - | - | 1 | - | possible barley |
| Triticum cf dicoccum Schübl | - | - | - | - | - | - | possible emmer |
| Triticum dicoccum Schübl./spelta L. | 1 | 25 | - | - | - | - | indeterminate emmer/spelt |
| Triticum dicoccum Schübl./spelta L. - tail grain | - | 1 | 3 | - | - | - | indeterminate emmer/spelt |

| Taxon | 1 | 2 | 3 | 4 | 5 | 6 | |
|---|---|---|---|---|---|---|---|
| *Triticum spelta* L. | 1 | 3 | 4 | - | - | - | spelt |
| *Triticum* spp. - indeterminate grain fragments (est. whole grain) | - | - | 3 | 3 | 5 | 7 | indeterminate wheat |
| *Triticum* spp. - indeterminate, germinated grain (est. whole grain) | 5 | - | 1 | - | - | - | indeterminate wheat |
| *Triticum* spp. - indeterminate tail grain | - | - | - | - | - | - | indeterminate wheat |
| Cereal - indeterminate | - | 37 E | 5 E | 3 E | 40 E | 21 E | Cereal |
| Cereal/POACEAE - indeterminate fragments (est. whole grain/ caryopsis) | 15 E | 25 E | 14 E | 10 E | 15 E | 15 E | cereal/large grass |
| Cereal/POACEAE - indeterminate (semi-quantified minute fragments) | +++ | ++++ | +++ | ++ | +++ | +++ | cereal/large grass |
| **Cereal chaff** | | | | | | | |
| *Triticum* cf *dicoccum* Schübl. - glume base | - | - | - | - | - | - | Possible emmer |
| *Triticum dicoccum* Schübl./*spelta* L. - glume fragments (unquantified) | - | - | - | - | - | - | indeterminate emmer/spelt |
| *Triticum dicoccum* Schübl./*spelta* L. - glume base | 69 E | 14 E | 108 E | 85 | 200 | 26 | indeterminate emmer/spelt |
| *Triticum dicoccum* Schübl./*spelta* L. - spikelet fork (=2gb) ** | - | 1 | - | 2 | - | 3 | indeterminate emmer/spelt |
| *Triticum dicoccum* Schübl./*spelta* L. - terminal spikelet fork (=2gb) ** | - | - | - | - | - | - | indeterminate emmer/spelt |
| *Triticum spelta* L. - glume base | 13 | 23 | 46 | 14 | 27 | 5 | spelt |
| *Triticum spelta* L. - spikelet fork (= 2 gb)** | - | 1 | - | - | 1 | - | spelt |
| *Triticum* cf *spelta* L. - glume fragments | ++++ | - | ++ | - | +++ | - | possible spelt |
| *Triticum* cf *spelta* L. - spikelet fork (=2 gb)** | - | - | - | - | - | - | possible spelt |
| *Triticum* spp. - rachis nodes (often highly fragmented, estimate whole node) | 75 E | 27 E | 30 E | 75 E | 100 E | 15 E | indeterminate wheat |
| *Triticum* spp. - awn (unquantified) | ++++ | + | ++ | - | - | + | indeterminate wheat |
| Cereal - unidentified rachis internode fragment | - | - | - | - | 10 E | 9 | cereal |
| Cereal - unidentified basal rachis node | - | 1 | 1 | - | - | - | cereal |
| Cereal/POACEAE - indeterminate, culm node | 1 | 1 | - | - | - | - | cereal/large grass |
| Cereal/POACEAE - indeterminate, culm base | - | - | - | - | - | - | cereal/large grass |
| Cereal/POACEAE - indeterminate, rachilla | 1 | 1 | - | - | - | - | cereal/large grass |
| **Deatched embryo/sprout** | | | | | | | |
| Cereal/POACEAE - indeterminate detached embryo | - | 9 | 18 | 2 | 1 | 3 | cereal/large grass |
| Cereal/POACEAE - indeterminate detached coleoptile | 10 | 13 | 1 | - | 13 | 3 | cereal/large grass |
| cf Cereal/POACEAE - indeterminate, detached sprout | - | - | - | 1 | - | - | possible cereal/large grass |
| cf Cereal/POACEAE - indeterminate, small detached embryo/ sprout | 72 | 1 | 17 | 6 | 5 | - | possible cereal/large grass |
| **Pulses** | | | | | | | |
| *Pisum sativum* L. | - | - | - | - | - | - | garden pea |
| *Vicia* spp./ *Pisum sativum* L. | - | - | - | - | - | - | vetch/garden pea |
| **Tree/shrub** | | | | | | | |
| *Corylus avellana* L. - nutshell fragments (est. whole nut) | - | - | - | - | - | - | hazel |
| cf *Corylus avellana* L. - nutshell fragments (est. whole nut) | 1 | - | - | - | 1 | - | possible hazel |
| *Sambucus nigra* L. | - | - | - | - | - | 1 | elder |
| **Weed/wild plants** | | | | | | | |
| *Ranunculus* subgenus RANUNCULUS | - | - | - | - | - | - | buttercup |

175

| Sample | 6052 | 6088 | 6089 | 102036 | 2037 | 2002 | |
|---|---|---|---|---|---|---|---|
| Context | 6252 | 6872 | 7784 | 2448 | 2557 | 2139 | |
| cf *Urtica dioica* L. - internal structure | - | - | - | - | - | 1 | possible common nettle |
| *Chenopodium* spp./*Atriplex* spp. - internal structure | - | - | - | - | - | 2 | indeterminate goosefoot/orache |
| *Atriplex* spp. | - | 1 | - | - | - | 2 | orache |
| *Stellaria media* L. | - | - | - | - | - | 1 | common chickweed |
| CARYOPHYLLACEAE - unidentified, small-seeded | - | - | - | - | - | 1 | pink family |
| cf *Fallopia convolvulus* (L.) Á. Löve - highly fragmented, est. whole seed | - | - | - | - | - | 1 | possible black-bindweed |
| *Polygonum* spp. | - | - | - | - | - | 1 | knotgrass |
| cf *Polygonum* sp. | - | - | - | - | - | - | possible knotgrass |
| *Polygonum* spp./*Rumex* spp./*Carex* spp. - internal structure | - | - | 1 | - | - | 1 | knotgrass/dock/sedge |
| *Rumex* cf *acetosella* L. | - | - | - | - | - | - | possible sheep's sorrel |
| *Rumex* spp. | 2 | - | 1 | 7 E | 3 E | - | dock |
| cf *Rumex* spp. - small seeded / immature | - | - | - | - | - | 1 | possible dock |
| *Vicia* cf *hirsuta* (L.) Gray | - | - | - | - | - | 1 | possible hairy tare |
| *Vicia* spp./*Lathyrus* spp. | - | 3 | - | - | - | 2 | vetch/vetchling |
| *Melilotus* spp./*Medicago* spp./*Trifolium* spp. | - | - | - | 1 | - | - | melilot/medick/clover |
| *Lotus* spp./*Melilotus* spp./*Medicago* spp./*Trifolium* spp. | - | - | - | - | 1 | - | bird's-foot-trefoil/melilot/medick/clover |
| FABACEAE - detached hilum (?ancient) | - | - | - | - | - | - | pea family |
| cf FABACEAE - immature | - | - | - | - | - | - | possible pea family |
| APIACEAE - unidentified, small sized | - | - | 1 | - | - | - | carrot family |
| *Prunella vulgaris* L. | - | - | - | - | - | - | selfheal |
| LAMIACEAE - small sized | - | 1 | - | - | - | - | mint family |
| *Plantago major* L. | - | - | - | - | - | - | greater plantain |
| *Plantago media* L./*lanceolata* L. | - | - | 2 | - | - | - | hoary/ribwort plantain |
| *Euphrasia* spp./*Odontites* spp. | - | - | - | - | - | 1 | eyebright/bartsia |
| *Galium* spp. | - | - | - | - | - | 2 | bedstraw |
| cf *Arctium lappa* L. | - | - | - | - | - | - | possible greater burdock |
| *Carduus* sp./*Cirsium* sp. | - | - | - | - | - | - | thistle |
| *Tripleurospermum inodorum* L. | - | - | - | - | 2 | 1 | scentless mayweed |
| ASTERACEAE - internal structure, small-sized achene | 1 | 1 | - | - | 1 | - | daisy family |
| ASTERACEAE - internal structure, medium-sized achene | - | - | - | - | - | - | daisy family |
| cf *Lolium* sp. - rachis node | - | - | - | - | - | 1 | possible rye-grass |
| cf *Poa annua* L. | 5 | - | - | 2 | 2 | - | possible annual meadow-grass |
| *Avena* cf. *fatua* L. - pedicel fragment | - | - | - | - | - | - | possible wild oat |
| *Avena* spp. - awn (semi-quantied fragments) | ++ | ++ | ++ | + | ++ | ++ | indeterminate wild/cultivated oat |
| *Avena* spp. - floret base | 2 | - | 1 | - | 1 | - | indeterminate wild/cultivated oat |
| cf *Avena* spp. - floret-base fragment | - | - | - | - | - | 1 | possible indeterminate wild/cultivated oat |
| *Avena* spp./*Bromus* spp. | 5 E | 3 | 5 E | 1 | 9 | 1 | indeterminate wild/cultivated oat/brome grass |

| Taxon | | | | | | Description |
|---|---|---|---|---|---|---|
| *Bromus* spp. | 4 | - | - | 3 | 2 | brome grass |
| cf *Bromus* spp. | - | 1 | - | - | 4 | possible brome grass |
| POACEAE - small-sized caryopsis | 16 | 40 | 10 | 3 E | 14 | grass family |
| POACEAE - medium-sized caryopsis | 3 E | - | 2 | 2 | 5 | grass family |
| POACEAE - large-sized caryopsis | - | - | - | - | 2 | grass family |
| POACEAE - basal rachis node | - | - | - | - | - | grass family |
| *Carex* spp. - three sided | 1 | 1 | 1 | - | - | sedge |
| Unidentified | 30 E | 25 | 1 | 15 E | 90 E | - |
| Unidentified - seed coat fragment | - | - | - | - | - | - |
| Unidentified - ?bark / ?leaf, curled fragment | - | 1 | - | - | 1 | - |
| Unidentified - bud | - | - | - | - | 4 | - |
| Unidentified - bud fragments | - | - | - | - | + | - |
| Unidentified - bud scale | - | - | - | - | 1 | - |
| Unidentified - capsule fragment or pod | - | - | - | - | 1 | - |
| Unidentified - possible thorn | - | - | 1 | - | - | - |
| Indeterminate | 30 E | 40 E | - | 15 E | 5 E | - |
| Indeterminate - highly vitreous, amorphous | - | - | - | - | 4 | - |
| **Other charred remains** | | | | | | |
| Fungal body (unquantified) | - | - | +++ | - | - | - |
| Unidentified - insect larva | - | - | - | - | 1 | - |
| **HEAVY RESIDUE** | | | | | | |
| **Cereal grain** | | | | | | |
| *Triticum* cf *dicoccum* Schübl. - germinated grain | 1 | - | - | - | - | possible emmer |
| *Triticum spelta* L. | - | 1 | - | - | - | spelt |
| *Triticum* sp. - indeterminate | 5 | - | - | - | - | indeterminate wheat |
| Cereal - indeterminate | 27 E | - | - | - | - | cereal |
| Cereal/POACEAE - indeterminate | 8 E | - | - | - | - | cereal/ large grass |
| **Cereal Chaff** | | | | | | |
| *Triticum* cf. *spelta* L. - glume base | 1 | - | - | - | - | possible spelt |
| **Tree/ Shrub** | | | | | | |
| cf *Corylus avellana* L. - nutshell fragments (est. whole nut) | 1 | - | - | - | - | possible hazel |
| **Weed/ Wild** | | | | | | |
| *Avena* spp./ *Bromus* spp. | 2 | - | - | - | - | indeterminate cultivated/ wild |
| | | | | | | oat/brome grass |
| *Bromus* sp. | 1 | - | - | - | - | brome grass |

*Table 8.15: Summary statistics for late Iron Age-early Roman/late Roman CPR*

| Sample | 2001 | 2024 | 2033 | 2038 | 6018 | 6024 | 6052 | 6088 | 6089 | 102036 | 2037 | 2002 |
|---|---|---|---|---|---|---|---|---|---|---|---|---|
| Context | 2907 | 2332 | 2375 | 2577 | 6049 | 6462 | 6252 | 6872 | 7784 | 2448 | 2557 | 2139 |
| Context description | Pit | Waterhole | Pit | Ditch | Pit | Ditch | Pit | Corn dryer | Corn dryer | Organic layer | Ditch | Ditch |
| | 2906 | 2309 | 2374 | 2487 | 6051 | 6460 | 6252 | 7782 | 7782 | | 2555 | 2047 |
| Site | Jnct 9 | Jnct 9 | Jnct 9 | Jnct 9 | Jnct 8N | Jnct 8N | Jnct 8N | Jnct 8N | Jnct 8N | Jnct 9 | Jnct 9 | Jnct 9 |
| Phase | LIA-ER | LIA-ER | LIA-ER | LIA-ER | MR | MR | MR | MR | MR | MR | MR-LR | LR |
| Sample vol. (l) | 40 | 40 | 40 | 15 | 30 | 40 | 40 | 10 | 10 | 40 | 40 | 30 |
| Flot vol. (ml) | 40 | 8 | 300 | 325 | 100 | 55 | 60 | 65 | 70 | 150 | 85 | 100 |
| Proportion of sample sorted | 50.0% | 100.0% | 6.25% | 1.6% | 25.0% | 100.0% | 6.3% | 25.0% | 12.5% | 12.5% | 12.5% | 50.0% |
| Seeds per litre of sediment | 71.5 | 237.0 | 21.9 | 11.0 | 38.5 | 269.0 | 25.4 | 57.5 | 46.4 | 29.6 | 61.4 | 131.0 |
| | | | | | | | | | | | | |
| TOTAL COUNT (FLOT) | 143 | 237 | 351 | 704 | 154 | 269 | 360 | 230 | 370 | 237 | 491 | 262 |
| TOTAL COUNT (HR) | 0 | 0 | 0 | 0 | 0 | 0 | 46 | 0 | 1 | 0 | 0 | 0 |
| TOTAL COUNT BOTH FLOT & HR | 143 | 237 | 351 | 704 | 154 | 269 | 406 | 230 | 371 | 237 | 491 | 262 |
| | | | | | | | | | | | | |
| **Summary by plant category (for both Flot + HR)** | | | | | | | | | | | | |
| Cereal grain | 34 | 10 | 148 | 73 | 85 | 22 | 62 | 91 | 32 | 16 | 61 | 43 |
| Cereal chaff | 75 | 184 | 185 | 574 | 47 | 165 | 159 | 67 | 185 | 186 | 353 | 58 |
| Detached embryo/sprout | 3 | 22 | 3 | 14 | 4 | 5 | 82 | 23 | 36 | 9 | 19 | 6 |
| Pulses | 0 | 0 | 0 | 0 | 0 | 0 | 0 | 0 | 0 | 0 | 0 | 0 |
| Tree/shrub | 1 | 1 | 0 | 0 | 0 | 0 | 2 | 0 | 0 | 0 | 1 | 1 |
| Weed/wild | 24 | 7 | 12 | 40 | 15 | 46 | 41 | 23 | 52 | 24 | 27 | 48 |
| Unidentified/indeterminate | 6 | 13 | 3 | 3 | 3 | 31 | 60 | 26 | 66 | 2 | 30 | 106 |
| | | | | | | | | | | | | |
| **RELATIVE PROPORTION (for both Flot + HR)** | | | | | | | | | | | | |
| Cereal grain | 23.8% | 4.2% | 42.2% | 10.4% | *55.2%* | 8.2% | 15.3% | 39.6% | 8.6% | 6.8% | 12.4% | 16.4% |
| Cereal chaff | *52.4%* | *77.6%* | *52.7%* | *81.5%* | 30.5% | *61.3%* | 39.2% | 29.1% | *49.9%* | *78.5%* | *71.9%* | 22.1% |
| Detached embryo/sprout | 2.1% | 9.3% | 0.9% | 2.0% | 2.6% | 1.9% | 20.2% | 10.0% | 9.7% | 3.8% | 3.9% | 2.3% |
| Pulses | 0.0% | 0.0% | 0.0% | 0.0% | 0.0% | 0.0% | 0.0% | 0.0% | 0.0% | 0.0% | 0.0% | 0.0% |
| Tree/shrub | 0.7% | 0.4% | 0.0% | 0.0% | 0.0% | 0.0% | 0.5% | 0.0% | 0.0% | 0.0% | 0.2% | 0.4% |
| Weed/wild | 16.8% | 3.0% | 3.4% | 5.7% | 9.7% | 17.1% | 10.1% | 10.0% | 14.0% | 10.1% | 5.5% | 18.3% |
| Unidentified/indeterminate | 4.2% | 5.5% | 0.9% | 0.4% | 1.9% | 11.5% | 14.8% | 11.3% | 17.8% | 0.8% | 6.1% | 40.5%† |

†The unidentified component of this flot was biased toward the recovery of 90 unidentified fragments of seed coat/internal structure of seed, which possibly are better considered as weed/wild. With this revision, approximately 52% of the plant remains recovered would be weed/wild. However, because there is no certainty what this seed coat may be, it has been scored here as unidentified/indeterminate. Bold italic indicates the dominant plant category (>50% of all identifications) for a sample

*Table 8.16: CPR from medieval deposits*

| Sample | 6017 | 6020 |
|---|---|---|
| Context | 6591 | 6789 |
| Context description | kiln 6585 | pit 6788 |
| Site | J8N | J8N |
| Phase | MED phase 1 | MED phase 1 |
| | L12-13C | L12 - 13C |
| Sample vol. (l) | 40 | 30 |
| Flot vol, (ml) | 75 | 200 |
| Proportion of sample sorted | 25% | 50% |
| *Seeds per litre of sediment* | *40.7* | *15.4* |

| LATIN BINOMIAL | | | ENGLISH COMMON NAME |
|---|---|---|---|
| **FLOT** | | | |
| **Cereal grain** | | | |
| cf *Hordeum* sp. | 1 | - | possible barley |
| *Secale cereale* L./*Triticum* spp. | 1 | - | indeterminate rye/wheat |
| *Triticum* sp. - free-threshing type | 79 | 23 | free-threshing-type wheat |
| *Triticum* sp. - free-threshing type, tail grain | 1 | 1 | free-threshing-type wheat |
| Cereal - indeterminate | 55 | 8 | cereal |
| Cereal/POACEAE - indeterminate | 25 E | 8 E | cereal/large grass |
| Cereal/POACEAE - indeterminate, minute fragments | ++++ | - | cereal/large grass |
| Cereal/POACEAE/?FABACEAE - indeterminate, minute fragments | - | ++ | cereal/large grass |
| | | | |
| **Cereal chaff** | | | |
| *Secale cereale* L. - rachis node | 3 | 7 | rye |
| cf *Secale cereale* L. - rachis node | 2 | 8 | possible rye |
| *Triticum* sp. - indeterminate, free-threshing-type rachis node | 37 E | 6 E | free-threshing-type wheat |
| *Triticum* sp. - indeterminate, rachis node fragments (est. whole rachis node) | 12 | - | free-threshing-type wheat |
| Cereal - indeterminate, basal rachis node | 5 | - | cereal |
| Cereal - indeterminate rachis internode | 5 | 13 | cereal |
| Cereal/POACEAE - culm node | - | 26 | cereal/large grass |
| Cereal/POACEAE - culm base | - | 5 | cereal/large grass |
| | | | |
| **Detached embryo/sprout** | | | |
| Cereal/POACEAE - detached embryo | 4 | 1 | cereal/large grass |
| | | | |
| **Pulses** | | | |
| *Vicia* spp./*Pisum sativum* L. | 4 E | - | vetch/garden pea |
| | | | |
| **Tree/shrub** | | | |
| *Crataegus monogyna* Jacq. | - | 9 | hawthorn |
| | | | |
| **Weed/wild Plants** | | | |
| *Chenopodium* spp. | 1 | - | goosefoot |
| CHENOPODIACEAE/CARYOPHYLLACEAE - internal structure family | 1 | - | indet. goosefoot family/pink |
| *Montia fontana* L. | - | 1 | blink |
| CARYOPHYLLACEAE - unidentified, small-sized | - | 1 | pink family |
| *Polygonum* spp./*Rumex* spp./*Carex* spp. - indeterminate, internal structure | 1 | 1 | knograss/dock/sedge |
| *Rumex* spp. | 1 | 2 | dock |
| cf *Rumex* spp. | - | 1 | possible dock |
| *Vicia* spp./*Lathyrus* spp. | 2 | 1 | vetch/vetchling |
| *Lotus* spp./*Medicago* spp./*Melilotus* spp./*Trifolium* spp. medick/melilot/clover | 1 | - | bird's-foot-trefoil/ |
| *Euphrasia* spp./*Odontites* spp. | - | 2 | eyebright/bartsia |
| *Galium* spp. | 1 | - | bedstraw |

*Table 8.16: CPR from medieval deposits – continued*

| Sample<br>Context | 6017<br>6591 | 6020<br>6789 | |
|---|---|---|---|
| *Lapsana communis* L. | - | 1 | nipplewort |
| *Anthemis cotula* L. | 8 E | - | stinking chamomile |
| *Tripleurospermum inodorum* (L.) Sch. Bip. | - | 28 | scentless mayweed |
| ASTERACEAE - unidentified, small flower calyx (ribbed) | - | 1 | daisy family |
| *Avena* spp./*Bromus* spp.<br>oat/brome grass | 7 | - | indet. cultivated/wild |
| POACEAE - unidentified, small-sized caryopsis | 2 | 39 | grass family |
| Unidentified | 30 E | 11 | - |
| Unidentified - capsules/seed pod - fragments | 4 | 1 | - |
| Unidentified - four-chambered capsule fragment (? *Ilex aquifolium* capsule top) | 1 | - | - |
| Indeterminate | 10 E | 25 E | - |
| Indeterminate - congealed, highly fragmented/clinkered (?pulse & cereal frags) | 1 | - | - |
| Indeterminate - congealed, high vitreous amorphous object | - | 1 | - |
| **OTHER REMAINS** | | | |
| Fungal bodies (unquantified) | - | +++ | - |

of the cereal ear. Although rarely grown today, hulled wheats do have a number of properties which would have been advantageous to past farmers. In particular they can tolerate poor soil conditions and can resist a range of fungal diseases (Nesbitt and Samuel 1996, 42). During threshing, cereal ears of spelt will break up into individual segments known as spikelets, which contain grains surrounded by tough chaff. At this point the farmer could either store or further process the spikelets of hulled wheat. Storage of hulled wheat in spikelet form is well known archaeobotanically and may serve to protect the grain from insect predation (Nesbitt and Samuel 1996, 52).

The Roman plant remains are primarily dominated by crop-processing by-products (cereal chaff and weed seeds), even when the samples were taken from deposits directly associated with corn dryer 7782. The generally poor preservation and highly fragmented nature of these remains (not just cereal grain, but including chaff and weed/wild seeds) makes speculation on which particular stage in the crop-processing sequence (*sensu stricto* Hillman 1981; 1984; 1991; Jones 1984; 1987; 1996) problematic. Regardless, a pattern of recovering charred cereal by-products is apparent from both the Junction 8N and Junction 9 samples from all Roman phases (Table 8.15 and Fig. 8.1).

One exception to this pattern is middle Roman pit sample 6018 (from pit 6051) where cereal grain dominates (n = 85 or 55.2%). It is notable that the cereal grain group from this sample consists almost entirely of fragmented indeterminate cereal and/or cereal/large-grass caryopses. Indeed, in the case of the latter grouping, minute fragments of indeterminate cereal/large-grass caryopses were particularly

*Table 8.17: Summary statistics for medieval samples*

| Sample | 6017 | 6020 |
|---|---|---|
| Context | 6591 | 6789 |
| Context description | kiln 6585 | pit 6788 |
| Site | JNCT 8 | JNCT 8 |
| Phase | MED phase 1<br>L12 - 13C | MED phase 1<br>L12 - 13C |
| Sample vol. (l) | 40 | 30 |
| Flot vol. (ml) | 75 | 200 |
| Proportion of sample sorted | 25.0% | 50.0% |
| Seeds per litre of sediment | 40.7 | 15.4 |
| **TOTAL COUNT** | **305** | **231** |
| **Summary by plant category** | | |
| Cereal grain | 162 | 40 |
| Cereal chaff | 64 | 65 |
| Detached embryo/sprout | 4 | 1 |
| Pulses | 4 | 0 |
| Tree/shrub | 0 | 9 |
| Weed/wild | 25 | 78 |
| Unidentified/indeterminate | 46 | 38 |
| **RELATIVE PROPORTION** | | |
| Cereal grain | *53.1%* | 17.3% |
| Cereal chaff | 21.0% | 28.1% |
| Detached embryo/sprout | 1.3% | 0.4% |
| Pulses | 1.3% | 0.0% |
| Tree/shrub | 0.0% | 3.9% |
| Weed/wild | 8.2% | 33.8% |
| Unidentified/indeterminate | 15.1% | 16.5% |

Bold italic indicates the dominant plant category (>50% of all identifications) for a sample

abundant, and they are frequently observed in nearly all of the Roman-period samples. Whether the fragmented grain and/or cereal/large-grass caryopes reflect poor preservation or mechanical damage during excavation and/or processing, or are representative of the conditions of deposition, is not clear.

It is likely that at these M1 sites spelt was stored in a partially threshed state, with the spelt grain still encased within its spikelet (individual segments of the cereal ear, with two grains contained within their surrounding chaff). Spelt stored in this way would then need to be processed (most likely by pounding the spikelets) producing spelt grain (the product) and a by-product of spelt glume bases, intact spikelets and any accompanying weeds of crop (eg Nesbitt and Samuel 1996). There are a number of uses for such by-products (eg Hillman 1984), many of which would not include charring and therefore are unlikely to be detected archaeobotanically. However, it is also possible to use such material as fuel and this would be one of the easiest means of disposing of unwanted cereal crop-processing by-products and may also have advantages for cereal parching/malting, since cereal chaff fuels would have a taste-neutral impact on parched or malted grain (eg Hillman 1982, 138). Subsequently, when the firing chambers of kilns/ovens were raked out, the spent fuel could be disposed of, if the ash was not of use. In this case, disposal appears to have taken the form of dumping into features such as pits and ditches.

In general, there appears to be a pattern where CPR recovered from what are deemed secondary contexts (eg ditches and pits; n = 8 samples), but possibly also the waterhole and 'organic layer' samples (Table 8.15 and Fig. 8.1), produce samples that are either dominated by cereal chaff remains (primarily of spelt *Triticum spelta* L. and/or indeterminate wheat (*Triticum* spp.) rachis node fragments) or are composed of fairly even mixtures of cereal grain, cereal chaff and any accompanying weed seeds. In addition, the samples from the corn dryer (most likely a primary context) have a substantial cereal chaff component (n = 185 or 49.9% for sample 6089 and n = 67 or 39.2% for sample 6088), although clearly occurring in mixtures with cereal grain and weed seeds. This pattern suggests that the late Iron Age-early Roman/late Roman inhabitants of settlements centred on Junction 8N and Junction 9 were using crop-processing by-products as fuel. Given the recovery of similar remains from both corn dryer samples (samples 6088 and 6089), it seems likely that the cereal crop-processing by-products were regularly used as fuel, most likely in the corn dryer(s) on site.

### Weed/wild plants in the Roman samples

The weed/wild flora is generally fairly limited, in all cases <20% of an assemblage was categorised as weed/wild plants and in many cases this compo-

nent was 10% or less of the assemblage. With the exception of brome grasses (*Bromus* spp.) and indeterminate cultivated/wild oat (*Avena* spp.) which is discussed separately below, most of the weed/wild plant remains are consistently dominated by limited number of taxa. The samples frequently include goosefoot and/or orache (*Chenopodium* spp./*Atriplex* spp.; n = 5 samples) and dock (*Rumex* cf. *acetosella* L./*Rumex* spp.; n = 7 samples), but almost always include small-sized grass caryopes (n = 13 samples). Where preservation is good to excellent, several of these small-sized caryopes have been securely identified as annual meadow-grass (*Poa annua* L.) type on the basis of the cell pattern, size and shape of the caryopsis and in comparison with modern comparative specimens. The inclusion of such small-sized weed seeds (c 1.6 x 0.6mm; information from Cappers *et al.* 2006) suggests that these may have arrived with the spelt still within the seed head (technically a panicle).

### Oat and brome: a tolerated impurity or a crop in its own right?

Indeterminate cultivated/wild oat (*Avena* spp.) and brome grass (*Bromus* spp. – also known as 'chess' or 'rye brome', although specifically this refers to *Bromus secalinus* L.) and variously indistinguishable oat/brome (*Avena* spp./*Bromus* spp.) caryopes were recovered from all 14 Roman-period M1 samples. Both oat and brome grass can in fact be crops in their own right or, at the very least, a tolerated impurity which is of similar size to cereal grain, does not adversely affect the taste of the cereal-based product and, possibly more relevantly, is difficult to fully remove from cereal grain (eg Campbell 2000, 48; de Moulins 2006, 69-71). At present both brome and the indeterminate wild/cultivated oat are classified as a weed/wild plants primarily because it cannot be assumed that they were actually cultivated intentionally; however, given their relative abundance in some samples (eg n = 36 out of 40 weed/wild identifications in sample 2038) perhaps they should be considered as a crop in their own right, even if not necessarily for human consumption. Certainly, Campbell (2000, 50) has speculated that brome was cultivated for fodder at early Iron Age Danebury (and environs) and was then replaced by oat in the late Iron Age. At the M1 sites, when identifications could be made to species level, oat (*Avena* spp.) was more frequently identified. Whether the generally low level of oat/brome in these samples indicates a tolerated contaminant, a relict from a previous crop or separate crops inadvertently mixed in storage, remains unclear.

### Comparison of Roman M1 assemblages with other Hertfordshire Roman assemblages

Charred assemblages of Roman date are relatively scarce in Hertfordshire (English Heritage 2004).

Two sites have produced results that are not directly comparable. At St Albans, a report by Lambert and Godwin (nd) on plant macrofossils from a high-status 1st-century AD cremation burial remains unpublished and a small assemblage of mineralised plant remains (believed to be from cess) has been reported from Folly Lane (Murphy and Fryer 1999).

Two other sites in Hertfordshire, however, have assemblages which are more directly comparable to the M1 Roman CPR assemblage. An assemblage of charred cereal grain, with no chaff and very few contaminants was studied from a 3rd-4th century AD (dating based on van der Veen 1989) corn dryer stokehole at Foxholes Farm by Monk (1989). The assemblages were relatively small with both emmer (*Triticum dicoccum* Schübl.) and spelt (*Triticum spelta* L.) grain identified. Analysis of samples from a corn dryer and a well from Boxfield Farm, Chells, Stevenage (Murphy 1999), has produced results remarkably consistent with those generated from the M1 samples. Most notably, the Boxfield Farm assemblages are strongly dominated by spelt (*Triticum spelta* L.) and Murphy (ibid., 137, 142) interprets the abundant remains of spelt glume bases/spikelet forks recovered from the corn dryer as evidence for the use of cereal-processing waste mixed with wood fuel for grain parching/malting. As in the M1 Roman CPR assemblages, emmer wheat was not identified in the Boxfield Farm assemblages. A charred assemblage associated with a well (Well CAB) was also recovered at Boxfield Farm, and included spelt chaff, as well as culm fragments of grasses and/or cereals, which Murphy (ibid., 142) interpreted as 'cereal processing and spoilt hay, burnt as refuse' subsequently redeposited into the well, possibly after it fell out of use. Although it would be tempting to view the charred spelt remains from Well CAB as spent fuel, other possibilities are plausible as Murphy (ibid.) rightly points out.

### Medieval CPR

Medieval assemblages from Hertfordshire are limited (eg English Heritage 2004[1]) and are primarily from waterlogged deposits from major towns (eg Hertford; Robinson 1977) or villages (eg King's Langley; Paradine 1977). CPR from 2l samples from an oven, believed to be of similar date to the Junction 8N samples (12th-13th century), were analysed from Abbey Mill, St Albans (Murphy 1993). Unfortunately, most of the cereal grain recovered could not be securely identified to species and the weed/wild plants were much more diverse. The M1 samples only produced small quantities of vetch/vetchling (*Vicia* spp./*Lathyrus* spp.), whereas the Abbey Mill medieval oven produced a wider range of taxa, with stinking chamomile (= stinking mayweed; *Anthemis cotula* L.) and goosefoot/fat hen (*Chenopodium* spp.) frequently observed.

### Conclusions

Late Iron Age-early Roman/late Roman CPR assemblages from Junction 8N and Junction 9 have produced assemblages dominated by spelt (*Triticum spelta* L.), suggesting that at least in this area of Hertfordshire spelt was cultivated throughout the entirety of the Roman period. Only one assemblage was dominated by cereal grain, eight were clearly dominated by cereal chaff remains and the remainder contained mixtures of varying proportions of cereal grain, cereal chaff and accompanying weeds of crop. It is notable that two corn dryer deposits had different compositions with one sample dominated by cereal chaff (sample 6089; n = 185 or 49.9%), whilst the other comprised a mixture of cereal grain (sample 6088; n = 91 or 39.6%), cereal chaff (n = 67 or 29.1%) and weed/wild plants (n = 23 or 10.1%). It is proposed that these remains indicate the regular use of spelt crop-processing by-products as fuel (possibly with the inclusion of accidentally charred grain) and, indeed, this also appears to be the case for a series of samples studied from a corn dryer at Boxfield Farm, Chells (Murphy 1999).

The two 12th-13th-century samples are dominated by remains of free-threshing-type wheat (*Triticum* spp.), but some evidence for rye (*Secale cereale* L.) is also present. Like the Roman samples, these assemblages are mixtures of cereal grain, cereal chaff and weed/wild plants. The only other published medieval assemblage of this date is from a kiln at Abbey Mill, St Albans (Murphy 1993).

### THE WOOD CHARCOAL *by Denise Druce*

#### Introduction

Following the assessment of over 100 samples by Challinor (2008), 15 samples were selected for further charcoal analysis. The selected samples came from a number of different feature types, including pits, ditches, a hearth and a kiln, plus four from cremation burials. The material ranged in date from the Neolithic to the medieval period. The samples were selected for full analysis to determine the taxonomic composition of the material in order to provide information about the selection of wood fuels, and to see if there were possible changes in wood taxa available or selected over time.

#### Methodology

The samples were processed using a modified Siraf flotation machine, the flots being collected onto a 250μm mesh, air-dried, and sub-sampled where necessary. Analysis of the samples followed standard procedure where *c* 100 fragments >2mm in size were extracted and identified. The charcoal was initially sorted into groups based on the features visible in transverse section using a Leica MZ6 binocular microscope at up to x40 magnification. Representative fragments of each group were then fractured to reveal both radial and tangential sections, which were examined under a Meiji incident-light microscope at up to x400 magnification. Identifications were made with reference to Schweingruber (1990), Hather (2000), and modern reference material.

## Results

The results of the analysis by fragment count are shown in Tables 8.18-20. Eleven taxa were positively identified, including six to species level. The results are discussed chronologically. The taxonomic level of identification varied according to the observed genera/family and/or the state of preservation. In many cases the fragments could only be taken to an approximate level of identification (ie to family level) as some of the key diagnostic features that are needed to distinguish the species were not observed. In other cases, the level of identifications was limited due to the similarities of species within a family or subgroup, such as Maloideae (referred to as hawthorn-type in the text), which could be hawthorn, apple, pear or one of the whitebeams, as charcoal from these cannot be separated anatomically. In general, the

*Table 8.18: Charcoal analyses. Neolithic, Bronze Age and late Bronze Age-early Iron Age samples. Numbers given are actual counts. h = heartwood present, s = sapwood present, r = roundwood present*

| Date | | Neolithic | MBA | LBA-EIA | LBA-EIA | LBA-EIA |
|---|---|---|---|---|---|---|
| Feature type | | Cremation | Cremation (unurned) | Cremation Pit | Pit | Pit |
| Sample number | | 2053 | 2052 | 117 | 2080 | 119 |
| Context number | | 5082 | 5067 | 117909 | 5423 | 119711 |
| Cut/feature number | 5081 | 5066 | 117908 | 5422 | 119712 | |
| Location | | Jnct 8S | Jnct 8S | Jnct 8S | Jnct 8S | Jnct 8S |
| % >2mm flot identified | | 100% | 50% | 6.25% | 25% | 12.5% |
| *Corylus avellana* | hazel | 1 | 1 | 11 | | |
| *Fagus sylvatica* | beech | 1 | | | 179 | |
| Maloideae | hawthorn, apple, pear etc | 3 | | 35r | | |
| cf *Prunus avium* | wild cherry | | | 2 | | |
| *Prunus spinosa* | blackthorn | 1 | | | | |
| *Quercus* sp. | oak | 31h | 207h | 64h | 1 | 137h |
| Indeterminate | | 3 | 3 | 9 | 7 | 1 |
| **Total** | | **40** | **211** | **121** | **187** | **138** |

*Table 8.19: Charcoal analyses. Late Iron Age-early Roman and mid-Roman samples. Numbers given are actual counts. h = heartwood present, s = sapwood present, r = roundwood present*

| Date | | LIA/ER | LIA-ER | LIA-ER | MR | MR | MR |
|---|---|---|---|---|---|---|---|
| Feature type | | Beam-slot | Ditch | Kiln | Cremation (urned) | Hearth | Hearth |
| Sample number | | 103 | 102037 | 2042 | 6008 | 6021 | 6084 |
| Context number | | 112217 | 2725 | 2721 | 6292 | 6753 | 7366 |
| Cut/feature number | | 112215/7229 | 2644 | 2638 | 6289 | 6752 | 7365 |
| Location | | Jnct 8N | Jnct 9 | Jnct 9 | Jnct 8N | Jnct 8N | Jnct 8N |
| % >2mm flot identified | | 6.25% | 25% | 0.4% | 100% | 3.125% | 1.562% |
| *Corylus avellana* | hazel | | | | 12 | | |
| *Alnus/Corylus* | alder/hazel | 1 | | | 1 | | |
| *Fagus sylvatica* | beech | | | | | 1 | |
| *Fraxinus excelsior* | ash | 79r | | | | | |
| Maloideae | hawthorn, apple, pear etc | | 1r | 9 | 2r | | |
| *Quercus* sp. | oak | 14h/r | 267r | 121r | 63h | 193h/r | 221h |
| Salicaceae | willow/poplar | | 1 | | | | |
| cf Salicaceae | | | 2 | | | | |
| *Ulex* sp./*Cytisus scoparius* | gorse/broom | 3 | | | | | |
| Indeterminate | | 21 | 8 | 4 | 4 | 6 | 1 |
| Total | | 118 | 279 | 147 | 70 | 199 | 222 |

*Table 8.20: Charcoal analyses. Late Roman and medieval samples. Numbers given are actual counts. h = heartwood present, s = sapwood present, r = roundwood present*

| Phase | | LR | MED Phase 1 (L12-13C) | MED Phase 2 (L12-13C) |
|---|---|---|---|---|
| Feature type | | Ditch | Kiln/oven | Pit |
| Sample number | | 2002 | 6017 | 6014 |
| Context number | | 2139 | 6591 | 6408 |
| Cut/feature number | | 2047 | 6585 | 6406 |
| Location | | Jnct 9 | Jnct 8, north | Jnct 8, north |
| % >2mm flot identified | | 25% | 50% | 12.5% |
| *Acer campestre* | field maple | 2 | | |
| *Corylus avellana* | hazel | 5r | 2r | |
| *Alnus/Corylus* | alder/hazel | 18 | | |
| *Fagus sylvatica* | beech | | 83r | 169r |
| *Fraxinus excelsior* | ash | 20r | | 1 |
| Maloideae | hawthorn, apple, pear etc | 16r | 4r | |
| *Prunus avium* | wild cherry | 11 | | |
| *Prunus spinosa* | blackthorn | 3 | | |
| *Prunus* sp. | blackthorn/wild cherry | | | 2r |
| *Quercus* sp. | oak | 30r | 1 | 20h |
| Salicaceae | willow/poplar | | | 2 |
| *Ulex* sp./*Cytisus scoparius* | gorse/broom | | | 1 |
| cf *Ulex/Cytisus* | | | | 3 |
| Indeterminate | | 11 | 10 | 5 |
| Total | | 116 | 100 | 203 |

preservation was good. The fragments categorised as indeterminate came either from distorted wood, from very small roundwood, or were highly vitrified.

### Neolithic

The charcoal assemblage from the Neolithic pit (context 5082) was radiocarbon dated (NZA-32714) to 3800-3640 cal BC (95.4% confidence; or 3760-3650 cal BC, 68.2% confidence), though relatively small (only 40 fragments >2mm in size), was dominated by oak heartwood (*Quercus* sp.) with a few fragments of hawthorn-type (Maloideae) and other short-lived species such as hazel (*Corylus avellana*) and blackthorn (*Prunus spinosa*). A single fragment of beech (*Fagus sylvatica*) charcoal was also identified, which, if contemporary with the feature, is an early record for beech. Beech pollen has been recorded in the south-east of England in deposits as early as the middle Neolithic (Birks 1989; Rackham 2003), but records for it are still quite patchy. More importantly, one of the earliest identifications of beech charcoal comes from Hazelton North, Gloucestershire, which was dated to the early Neolithic. Beech charcoal has been found from later Neolithic deposits at Abingdon, Oxfordshire and Mount Pleasant in Dorset (Smith 2002).

### Bronze Age

The charcoal from the middle Bronze Age unurned cremation burial (context 5067), radiocarbon dated (NZA-32713) to 1370-1090 cal BC (95.4% confidence; or 1260-1130 cal BC, 68.2% confidence), was dominated by oak heartwood with a single fragment of hazel. The material is consistent with other evidence from Bronze Age cremation features discovered to date. Oak charcoal was the dominant wood fuel used in Bronze Age cremations at Pepperhill/Cobham (Challinor forthcoming), Dartford (Druce 2011), and at Barrow Hills and Gravelly Guy, Oxfordshire (Thompson 1999; Gale 2004). There is increasing evidence to suggest that wood was being specifically selected for pyre construction during the Bronze Age period. The existing studies suggest that the presence of a single species, such as oak, may indicate the selection of a single tree or shrub for the bulk of the pyre construction (Thompson 1999), which itself may have been related to the status, sex or age of the body (Gale 2007).

### Late Bronze Age-early Iron Age

The assemblage from the late Bronze Age-early Iron Age cremation pit 117908 (fill 117909) was quite mixed and although dominated by oak and hawthorn-type contained several fragments of hazel and wild/bird cherry (*Prunus avium/padus*). The identification of the latter is potentially significant as bird cherry tends to be restricted to northern England and Wales (Hather 2000) and until recently wild cherry was thought to be a Roman introduction; although there are now enough prehistoric finds of its wood and stones to dispel this theory (Rackham 2003).

The charcoal assemblage is clearly quite different to the middle Bronze Age cremation deposit, and may indicate less stringent species selection or a differing approach to the cremation process. Again, this could have been based on the status, sex or age of the body, or may just reflect a temporal change. It is interesting to note that the second dominant wood species in the assemblage is hawthorn-type (which includes hawthorn, apple, pear or white-beam), and although its presence is less common, it has been associated with other Bronze Age cremation deposits in southern England (Challinor forthcoming). Challinor (2007) suggests that hawthorn wood, though quite dense, would not have been the ideal choice for the pyre structure and that it was more likely to have been used for fuel; its abundance in this context would most certainly correlate with this. It has also been suggested that apple or pear wood, which is included in this type, may have been selected for its pleasant aroma when burnt (ibid.).

The late Bronze Age-early Iron Age pit 5422 (fill 5423), was overwhelmingly dominated by beech charcoal, with a single fragment of oak. The burning efficiency of seasoned beech wood has already been highlighted (see above), and although there is no direct evidence of industrial activity associated with the pit, it is possible that the material represents some sort of industrial debris.

The other late Bronze Age-early Iron Age assemblage, from pit 119712 (fill 119711), which formed part of a pit scatter, consisted exclusively of oak. The material may, again, be derived from 'industrial' or non-domestic activity, but this interpretation must remain tentative given the lack of other evidence.

### Late Iron Age-early Roman

The sample from the late Iron Age-early Roman possible beam-slot (context 112217) was the only sample dominated by ash (*Fraxinus excelsior*) charcoal, including ash roundwood. The sample also contained frequent oak charcoal fragments and one fragment of alder/hazel (*Alnus glutinosa/Corylus avellana*). It was also the only prehistoric/Roman sample to contain fragments of gorse/broom (*Ulex sp/Cytisus scoparius*). The dominance of ash from this feature is interesting, as, after oak, ash was the preferred timber tree (Rackham 2003). However, if the charcoal is the remains of burnt timber then it is hard to explain the presence of roundwood.

The other recorded fragments may represent residual material, or burnt domestic debris, fallen into the void left by the beam. This may be supported by the unique presence of gorse/broom in this context, which is commonly used as fodder or as brushwood (Edlin 1949). Its presence indicates that heathland had developed in parts of the surrounding area by the late Iron Age-early Roman period, which is broadly consistent with evidence from other sites in the south-east such as Dart-

ford (Druce 2011) and Pepperhill/Cobham, Kent (Challinor forthcoming).

The late Iron Age-early Roman ditch fill (context 2725) was overwhelmingly dominated by oak charcoal, but the observed lack of tyloses on the wood may suggest that the material came from either immature wood or branchwood. The assemblage taken from the late Iron Age-early Roman kiln (2721), which cut the ditch, contained a very similar assemblage of immature oak/oak sapwood. It is certainly possible that oak wood was specifically selected for firing the kiln. It is also possible that the ditch assemblage represents the waste material generated by the same or similar activity. The abundance of immature oak wood or oak sapwood in the samples is interesting and may reflect the use of branch wood rather than trunk wood. If this was the case, it is possible that the material represents the waste or off-cuts generated from another activity such as construction. Both samples contained some short-lived species, including willow/poplar, hawthorn-type and, in the case of the kiln, hazel. It is possible that these fragments are incidental and represent general debris or that they represent the remains of kindling.

### Middle Roman

The three mid-Roman samples from Junction 8N were all dominated by oak charcoal; the two hearth contexts (6753 and 7366) contained no other wood species, however, the urned cremation fill (6292) contained two fragments of hawthorn-type (Maloideae) roundwood and one fragment of beech. Tyloses were observed on some of the fragments in all three of the samples, which suggests that at least some of the wood came from mature trees.

There is no direct evidence of industrial activity associated with the hearths and if they served purely a domestic function the presence of mature oak wood suggests that there was very little pressure on local oak woodland resources in the area during the Roman period. A similar picture is emerging from the south-east in general, where the overall dominance of mature oak in many Roman samples, such as those from Stansted/Braintree (Challinor 2007), Pepper Hill (Challinor 2006) and Dartford (Druce 2011), may indicate a plentiful supply of mature oak woodland.

The oak-dominated cremation burial deposit is in keeping with many other Roman cremation burial assemblages from the London area (Robinson 1996; Challinor 2006; 2011), and the south-east generally (Challinor 2007), where a single species, usually oak or ash, is used for the pyre. The presence of a few fragments of short-lived wood is also common and may represent the remains of kindling or fuel wood.

### Late Roman

The assemblage from the fill (context 2139 in cut 2047) of late Roman ditch 2490 at Junction 9 was, like that from the medieval rubbish pit (see below), much more mixed than those from earlier periods. It contained a relatively diverse range of taxa including abundant oak, ash, hawthorn-type and alder/hazel (including five positively identified hazel fragments). The sample also contained a number of wild cherry fragments, a few blackthorn-type fragments and was the only sample from the site containing field maple (*Acer campestre*). This sample contained abundant CPR, which suggests that at least some of the charcoal may represent crop-processing or cooking debris (Challinor 2008).

The assemblage was notable for its abundant roundwood, and, like the assemblage from the medieval rubbish pit is likely to represent the debris generated from a number of domestic activities. The material was probably gathered from nearby, easily accessible, resources and may be representative of the surrounding landscape during this period, which appears to have supported oak, ash and hazel woodland, and hawthorn-/blackthorn-type and field maple. Ash trees often develop as secondary woodland in areas that were once cleared. Hawthorn, blackthorn and field maple are commonly found at woodland margins or form part of hedgerows. The charcoal evidence indicates a formerly cleared and, probably, well-managed landscape containing woodland and hedgerows.

### Medieval

The sample taken from the medieval kiln/oven (context 6591) contained mainly beech charcoal, a single fragment of oak, and a few fragments of hazel and hawthorn-type roundwood. The excellent burning properties of seasoned beech have already been mentioned (see above), and beech is likely to have been specifically chosen to provide the sustained heat required to fire the kiln. Although beech is recorded in earlier features (as evidenced from this and other sites), there is an increasing body of evidence to suggest that it became more commonly used during the medieval period in southern England (see summary tables in Smith 2002; Challinor forthcoming; Druce 2011). This shift may have been as a consequence of pressure on other local woodland resources such as oak (Challinor forthcoming) and/or changes in the nature of the wooded environment due to decades of woodland management.

Although the sample from the medieval pit (context 6408) was also dominated by beech, it generally contained a much more mixed assemblage (six species/types). As well as beech, it contained abundant oak, a single fragment of ash, and several fragments of gorse/broom, willow/poplar (Salicaceae) and blackthorn type (*Prunus* sp). The pit is one of several surrounding a post-built structure and has been interpreted as a rubbish pit. The charcoal evidence tends to corroborate this, the diverse assemblage being likely to have originated from a number of different activities.

### Conclusion

The charcoal assemblages from the prehistoric and mid-Roman cremation burial features were dominated by a single taxon, which is consistent with other Bronze Age and Roman cremation assemblages, and may represent the selection of a single tree, in this case oak, for pyre construction. The assemblage from the late Bronze Age-early Iron Age cremation pit was dominated by oak and hawthorn-type and may represent the remains of both pyre and fuel wood.

The charcoal assemblages from many of the other, non-cremation, features from all periods of the site were also dominated by a single taxon of either oak or beech. The material may represent the debris associated with some sort of industrial use, as is the case for the medieval kiln, as both oak and seasoned beech burn particularly well, and would have provided the sustained heat required. However, this interpretation must remain tentative given the lack of other supporting evidence.

The dominance of ash in the late Iron Age-early Roman beam-slot is potentially quite interesting in that this was the only feature in which ash formed the bulk of the assemblage, and may represent the remains of the timber. The other material from the beam-slot, however, is likely to represent the debris generated from a range of different activities associated with the structure. The presence of gorse/broom in this context is consistent with other charcoal evidence from the south-east, and indicates the development of areas of heathland by the late Iron Age-early Roman period.

Although the pollen and charcoal evidence for beech points to its presence in the south-east by the middle Neolithic, its history and spread in Britain are still relatively poorly understood. There are very few prehistoric charcoal assemblages dominated by beech, therefore the evidence significantly adds to the existing datasets and suggests that it was locally available in the area, possibly from the Neolithic period and most certainly from the Bronze Age.

### THE CREMATED HUMAN BONE *by Nicholas Márquez-Grant*

#### Introduction

Cremated remains came from two contexts of possible late Bronze Age-early Iron Age date at Junction 8S, from single late Iron Age-early Roman deposits at Junction 9 and Area M, and from two early Roman burials (represented by four contexts) at Junction 8N.

#### Methods

All the cremation burials were examined. Table 8.21 presents the contexts that were examined in this study, alongside other observations.

*Table 8.21: Summary of cremated human bone*

| Context | Site | Context type | Period | Weight of human bone (g) | Observations |
|---------|------|--------------|--------|--------------------------|--------------|
| 2013 | Junction 9 | Fill of 2012 | LIA-ERB | 7.5 | - |
| 3040 | Area M | Ditch 3036 | MIA-LIA | 1 | - |
| 5067 | Junction 8S | Fill of 5066 | LBA | 56 | - |
| 5243 | Junction 8S | ?stakehole | Unphased | 15 | - |
| 6291 | Junction 8N | Fill of 6289 | ERB-MRB | 223 | contents of cremation urn SF 6051 |
| 6292 | Junction 8N | Fill of 6289 | ERB-MRB | 17 | ?part of above |
| 6295 | Junction 8N | Fill of 6293 | ERB-MRB | 233 | associated with cremation urn SF 6054 |
| 6298 | Junction 8N | Fill of 6289 | ERB-MRB | 10 | ?associated with ancillary vessel SF 6052 |

The aim was to ascertain the minimum number of individuals (MNI) represented by the cremated bone sample, the demographic profile of those individuals and any information regarding lifestyle as suggested by pathological lesions, and other osteological indicators, as well as to identify evidence relation to the cremation process.

In accordance with recommended practice (McKinley and Roberts 1993), samples were wet sieved and sorted into >10mm, >4mm and >2mm size categories. The sorted bone and the residues were then examined. Osteological analysis was undertaken by following the recommendations set out by McKinley (2004) and using standard methodologies for ageing and sexing etc. Detailed records for each deposit are contained in the project archive.

Material smaller than 4mm was not sorted and analysis at this level only focused on the general colour and bone elements represented. Any identifiable fragments such as dental crowns, hand and foot bones and other fragments that may provide additional useful data such as the MNI count and age determination were also noted. All data were recorded on OA laboratory recording sheets for cremation deposits.

## Results

### Weight and skeletal part representation

The deposits ranged in weight from 1-233g (Table 8.22). The most-represented bone fragment on the basis of weight (obviously there is more bone in a femur than in a radius) is the lower limb, followed by skull fragments and upper-limb bones. The axial skeleton is also represented.

The fragments from the skull were mainly from the frontal, parietal and occipital bones. No temporal bones were identified. Some skull fragments revealed the coronal, sagittal ad lambdoid sutures. Very few skeletal landmarks were identified in the bones, with only the surpraorbital margins present in some deposits (contexts 6291 and 6295). Facial bones, such as the maxilla were rarely present (only in context 6295). A right zygomatic (context 6295) was recovered. The mandible was also poorly represented. Few parts were present and these were mainly parts of the body with alveoli (again from context 6295). Some dental roots were recovered and did provide some data on the age of the individual. In addition, contexts 6291 and 6295 included some dental fragments representing at least one tooth in each context.

Vertebrae and ribs were incomplete, very fragmented and also poorly represented. Most remains belonged to pedicles and bodies of vertebrae and shafts of ribs. No atlas or axis vertebrae were identified.

Shoulder as well as the pelvic girdle was poorly represented. Some body portions of the scapula and some clavicle shaft fragments (in context 6291) represented the shoulder girdle. With regard to the pelvis, no sciatic notch, no acetabulum and no pubis were identified, and neither was the sacrum, there-

*Table 8.22: Summary of weights for each of the human cremated bone deposits*

| | Context number | | | | | | | | Total |
|---|------|------|------|------|------|------|------|------|-------|
| | 2013 | 3040 | 5067 | 5243 | 6291 | 6292 | 6295 | 6298 | |
| Skull | 0 | 0 | 7 | 0.5 | 53 | 2 | 19 | 0 | 81.5 |
| Axial | 0 | 0 | 2 | 0 | 7 | 0.5 | 13 | 0 | 22.5 |
| Upper limbs | 3 | 1 | 5 | 0.5 | 28 | 0 | 39 | 3 | 79.5 |
| Lower limbs | 4 | 0 | 10 | 7 | 24 | 10 | 75 | 5 | 135 |
| Long bone (unidentified) | 0 | 0 | 9 | 6 | 5 | 2 | 14 | 2 | 38 |
| Unidentified | 0.5 | 0 | 23 | 1 | 25 | 3 | 73 | 0 | 125.5 |
| TOTAL (g) | 7.5 | 1 | 56 | 15 | 223 | 17 | 233 | 10 | 562.5 |

fore most of these fragments were from the body of the ilium.

All the major long bones in the skeleton, including the humerus, radius, ulna, femur, tibia and fibula, were clearly identified. Many of the epiphyses were missing post-mortem, but there were two portions of the distal epiphysis of a humerus (context 5067) and a portion of articular surface probably belonging to a proximal radius (context 6295).

Hand bones were identified in a number of deposits. A possible carpal bone (lunate?) was found in context 6295. Metacarpal shafts were identified in contexts 6291 and 6295, while a portion of a metacarpal head was identified in context 5067. Portions of proximal hand phalanges (shaft and head portions) were also found in these three latter contexts. Amongst the foot bones, only metatarsal shafts were represented, these coming from contexts 6291 and 6295.

Many fragments (22.3%) could not be identified. These came largely from the sorted 4-2mm-sieve size, and were largely long-bone fragments. Other common unidentified fragments were portions of trabecular bone.

The largest fragment measured 29.5mm (a humerus shaft from context 3040), followed by a tibia shaft from context 6291, measuring 28.4mm.

### MNI, sex and age determination

None of the deposits included the remains of more than one individual. The material from 6291, 6292 and 6298 is consistent with derivation from a single (adult) individual. On this basis, the remains derive from a minimum of six individuals, four of whom are likely to be adults (>18 years of age) on the basis of bone dimensions and the texture of the skull and long-bone fragments. Unfortunately, no epiphyses were preserved to appreciate fusion of the epiphyses with the shaft and also no third molars were available to confirm the adult age (>18 years) of the individuals. With regard to cranial suture closure, although in context 6291 enough fragments with sagittal and lambdoid sutures appeared to be open, this is insufficient to indicate this was a young adult. Two individuals (3040, and 5243) could not be aged, although the dimensions of the bones suggest that they are older than a child.

Although maxillary and mandibular fragments from context (6295) preserved a total of five alveoli, indicating that the teeth were lost post-mortem, tentatively this may indicate that the individual was probably not a person of old age (>46 years) when he or she died, since considerable tooth loss may be regarded as an indicator of old age. No sex could be attributed to the adult skeletons as diagnostic bones were absent.

### Non-metric traits

Only one non-metric trait, the supraorbital foramen, could be scored for presence or absence. The left supraorbital margin found in deposit 6291 presented a supraorbital foramen.

### Palaeopathology

Most of the recovered fragments could not be observed for pathological changes. There was no evidence for ante mortem tooth loss (in five dental sockets from 6295).

### Fragmentation

Fragments between 4mm and 10mm in length were the most frequent, with the exception of context 3040 where only one fragment was recovered (Table 8.23). This was in fact the longest shaft fragment, measuring 29.5mm, and was probably part of a humerus. This was followed by fragments from contexts 6291 and 6295 with maximum fragments measuring 28.4mm (humerus) and 23.1mm (tibia) respectively.

[Table 8.23]

### Colour

Most of the cremated bone was white in all contexts, or predominantly white, with hues of blue/grey in contexts 3040, 5243 and 6295. There were no fragments in darker colours such as deep blue, brown or black. Thus, for the assemblage complete or intense combustion of all the organic component of the bone had taken place. This generally occurs at temperatures above 700°C (Holden *et al.* 1995).

*Table 8.23: Percentage of human bone fragments larger than 10mm, between 10mm and 4mm, and smaller than 4mm*

| | Context number | | | | | | | |
| | 2013 | 3040 | 5243 | 5067 | 6291 | 6292 | 6295 | 6298 |
|---|---|---|---|---|---|---|---|---|
| >10mm | 0g (0) | 1g (100) | 0g (0) | 0g (0) | 29g (13.0) | 0g (0) | 8g (3.4) | 0g (0) |
| 10-4mm | 7.5g (100) | 0g (0) | 15g (100) | 56g (100) | 113g (50.6) | 17g (100) | 184g (78.9) | 10g (100) |
| <4mm | 0g (0) | 0g (0) | 0g (0) | 0g (0) | 81g (36.3) | 0g (0) | 41g (17.5) | 0g (0) |
| TOTAL (g) | 7.5 | 1 | 15 | 56 | 223 | 17 | 233 | 10 |

## Discussion

Overall, there was no clear pattern of under representation of skeletal elements, although truncation was a factor affecting most if not all of the deposits examined. Unsurprisingly, therefore, bone weights were low, the largest individual deposit (6295) weighing 233g and the three contexts from burial 6289 producing a combined total of 250g of cremated bone. The weight of bone of an adult cremation from modern crematoria ranges from about 1000 to 3600g (McKinley 2000, 404), therefore none of these contexts can be considered as fully recovered or presenting most of the individual. In some cases, it is possible that only 'token' deposits had been buried, but generally the effects of truncation make it impossible to judge the extent to which this practice may have been observed. It is very doubtful that the tiny amount of material from Area M indicates the original presence of a burial in this context.

Bone fragments were usually not large, with only a few deposits having fragments larger than 10mm. Amongst the factors that affect fragmentation are the cremation itself, collection and burial of the human remains, deliberate fragmentation by the mourners or grave diggers, taphonomic factors (for example, soil characteristics and ploughing) and the much later process of archaeological excavation, and post-excavation processing (McKinley 1994). It is possible that cremated bone was fragmented deliberately in order to fit it into its urn. This may have been the case for some of the recovered cremations.

Further information on the funerary rite is limited, due to the truncation affecting the material and the limited sample size. However, the clear fissuring of some of the larger bone fragments suggests that the bodies were cremated while fleshed. Little warping, which is also a typical pattern observed in cremated bone that was fleshed when burning (Reverte 1986; Ubelaker 1989), was observed, but this may be due to the high fragmentation and lack of >10mm fragments to allow more accurate observation of this effect.

---

[1] The record for post-medieval Hemel Hempstead reported by Scaife (2003) is incorrect as only a late Bronze Age/early Iron Age sample is reported.

# Chapter 9: Radiocarbon dating

*by Seren Griffiths, Dan Stansbie and Rebecca Nicholson*

## INTRODUCTION

OA commissioned 11 accelerator mass spectrometry (AMS) radiocarbon dates on material derived from contexts examined in the mitigation phase of the M1 widening project. Ten results were produced initially, with an 11th to examine the stratigraphic integrity of one result. The radiocarbon results were produced on charred plant macrofossils from pits containing Mesolithic lithic assemblages (at Junction 9) and on cremated human skeletal remains, and a charred cereal grain of intrinsic archaeobotanical interest. These dates and the sample details are listed in Table 9.1 and the results summarised in Fig. 9.1. The objectives of the dating programme were:

- to establish the period of activity associated with the Mesolithic lithic assemblages/pit use;

- to establish the period of the cremation burial traditions at Junction 8S;

- to estimate the age of the spelt wheat <2017> in pit 2064 at Junction 9.

## SAMPLING

Material from the pits excavated during the project was selected for dating by OA, to investigate the chronology of the features and microlith technology. Mesolithic-period negative features are rare (Allen and Gardiner 2002), particularly those with demonstrable Mesolithic material culture (eg Allen and Green 1998), and traditions of Neolithic pit digging and infilling have been suggested to have had their origins in Mesolithic deposition in tree-throw holes (Lamdin-Whymark 2008). Furthermore, material from Neolithic features has been suggested to indicate storage in 'pre-pit' deposits (cf Garrow 2006), such as middens (eg Allen *et al.* 2004). While no examples of Mesolithic pre-pit contexts have been mooted for the M1, the material from the pits could be older than the archaeological phase of pit digging; there is no functional relationship between the dated material and the features from which they were recovered (cf Waterbolk 1971). Strictly speaking the results from these features form *termini post quos* for the infilling of the pits and deposition of the material.

After the production of the initial ten radiocarbon results, a series of simulated radiocarbon results (using the R_Simulate parameter in OxCal v4.1) was produced for the Mesolithic-period activity. These models (e.g. Fig. 9.2) employed errors based on the materials analysed and measurement technique (eg single/multiple run AMS). The modelling illustrated the location of the existing and simulated radiocarbon assemblage on a plateau in the 52nd century cal BC. Given the available informative archaeological model, further

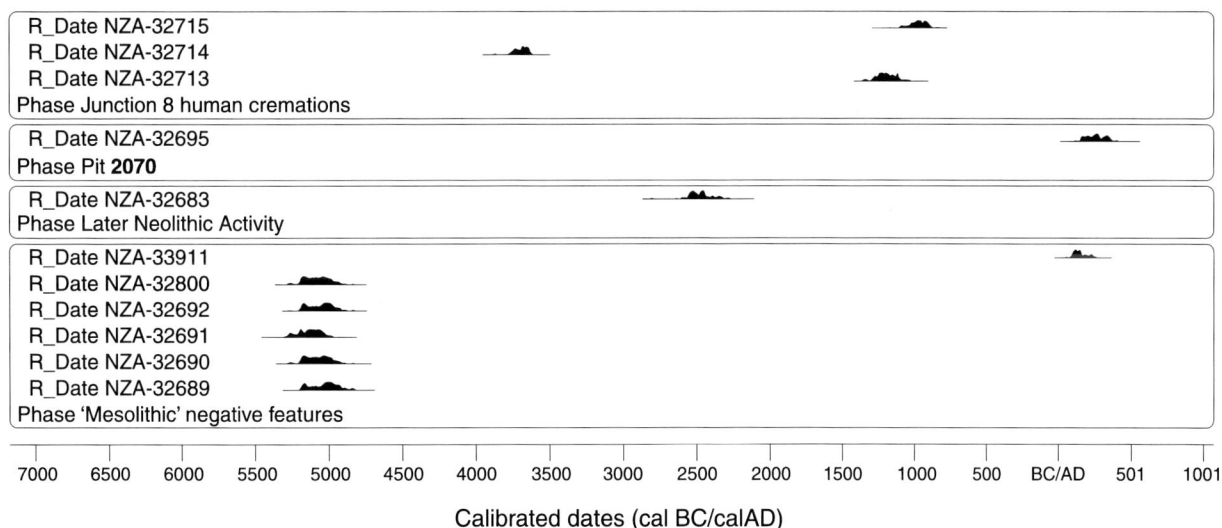

*Fig. 9.1 Probability distributions from the M1*

191

*Table 9.1: Radiocarbon data*

| Laboratory code | Context and sample | Material | Description | δ13C | Radiocarbon age BP | Calibrated date range | Preferred posterior density estimate (cal BC; 95.4% probable). |
|---|---|---|---|---|---|---|---|
| NZA-32683 | MOW05 <2004> (2051) | Charred *Corylus avellana* nutshell | Fill of pit 2052. No functional association with deposit – *terminus post quem* for infilling of pit, and deposition of broad flint flakes, and burnt flint | -22.1 ‰ | 3976 ± 50 | 2620-2340 cal BC (95.4% confidence; 2570-2460 cal BC, 68.2% confidence) | |
| NZA-32689 | MOW05 <2008> (2195) | Charred *Corylus avellana* nutshell | Fill of gully 2196. No functional association with deposit – *terminus post quem* for infilling of pit, and deposition of small charcoal and small scalene triangle assemblage | -27 ‰ | 6108 ± 55 | 5220-4850 cal BC (95.4% confidence; 5210-4940 cal BC, 68.2% confidence) | 5220-4960 cal BC |
| NZA-32690 | MOW05 <2011> (2093) | Charred *Corylus avellana* nutshell | Fill of pit 2094. No functional association with deposit – *terminus post quem* for infilling of pit, deposition of a scalene microlith, hazel nutshell and indeterminate cereal grains | -26.7 ‰ | 6142 ± 55 | 5230-4980 cal BC (95.4% confidence; 5210-4990 cal BC, 68.2% confidence) | 5220-4990 cal BC |
| NZA-32691 | MOW05 <2012> (2095) | Charred *Corylus avellana* nutshell | Fill of pit 2096. No functional association with deposit – *terminus post quem* for infilling of pit, deposition of hazel nutshell, indeterminate cereal grains and 56 worked flints | -26.4 ‰ | 6201 ± 50 | 5310-5000 cal BC (95.4% confidence; 5230-5060 cal BC, 68.2% confidence) | 5230-5000 cal BC |
| NZA-32800 | MOW05 <2017> (2063) | Charred *Triticum spelta* grain | Fill of pit 2064. No functional association with deposit – *terminus post quem* for infilling of pit. This measurement was supposedly produced on a charred cereal grain. It is probable that material for NZA-32800 was mixed up with charred hazel nutshell at some point in the sample selection (see NZA-33911). 6th millennium BC spelt is not proved at the site | -18.6 ‰ | 6147 ± 55 | 5290-4940 cal BC (95.4% confidence; 5220-5000 cal BC, 68.2% confidence) | 5230-4930 cal BC (94.5% probable; 5290-5270 cal BC, 0.9% probable) |
| NZA-33911 | MOW 05 <2017> (2063) | Charred *Triticum* sp. glume base | Fill of pit 2064. No functional association with deposit – *terminus post quem* for infilling of pit. To investigate NZA-32800, NZA-33911 was commissioned. On the basis of NZA-33911 it is suggested charred hazel nutshell associated with Mesolithic activity was accidentally dated, rather than the cereal grain recorded on the sample submission form | -24.2 ‰ | 1883 ± 30 | Cal AD 50-230 (95.4% confidence; cal AD 70-140 68.2% confidence) | |
| NZA-32695 | MOW05 <2014> (2069) | Charred seeds | Fill of pit 2070. No functional association with deposit – *terminus post quem* for infilling of pit | -22.5 ‰ | 1789 ± 45 | Cal AD 120-380 (95.4% confidence; cal AD 130-330, 68.2% confidence) | |
| NZA-32692 | MOW05 <2041> (2317) | Charred *Corylus avellana* nutshell | Fill of pit 2316. No functional association with deposit – *terminus post quem* for infilling of pit, deposition of charred hazel nutshell, possible | -25.1 ‰ | 6125 ± 50 | 5210-4930 cal BC (95.4% confidence; 5200-4990 cal BC, 68.2% confidence) | 5220-4980 cal BC |

*Table 9.1: Radiocarbon data – continued*

| Laboratory code | Context and sample | Material | Description | δ13C | Radiocarbon age BP | Calibrated date range | Preferred posterior density estimate (cal BC; 95.4% probable). |
|---|---|---|---|---|---|---|---|
| | | | grains of spelt wheat, indeterminate wheat seeds, and a scalene microtriangle | | | | |
| NZA-32713 | MOW05 <2052> (5067) | Cremated human bone | Dates death of individual | -22.1 ‰ | 2979 ± 35 | 1370-1090 cal BC (95.4% confidence; 1260-1130 cal BC, 68.2% confidence) | |
| NZA-32714 | MOW05 <2053> (5082) | Cremated animal bone | Dates death of individual | -27.6 ‰ | 4931 ± 40 | 3800-3640 cal BC (95.4% confidence; 3760-3650 cal BC, 68.2% confidence) | |
| NZA-32715 | MOW05 <2073> (5245) | Cremated human bone | Dates death of individual | -21.1 ‰ | 2836 ± 40 | 1130-900 cal BC (95.4% confidence; 1050-920 cal BC, 68.2% confidence) | |

results would provide no significant improvement in precision.

## RESULTS

The samples were pre-treated with acid-base-acid (cf http://www.rafterradiocarbon.co.nz/samprep.htm.). The calibrated ranges are shown in Fig. 9.1 and are cited in accordance with the international standard known as the Trondheim convention (Stuiver and Kra 1986). They are conventional radiocarbon ages (Stuiver and Polach 1977).

### Calibrations

The calibrated results were produced using the Reimer *et al.* (2004) curve and the computer program OxCal (v4.1 build 44; Bronk Ramsey 1995; 1998; 2001). Ranges are quoted in accordance with the Mook (1986) protocol, with end points rounded out to ten years if the error term is greater than or equal to 25 radiocarbon years, or to five years if the error term is less than 25 years. Ranges in italics are *posterior density estimates* produced from the Bayesian statistical model (see below). Ranges in plain text are maximum intercepts (cf Stuiver and Reimer 1986).

The calibrated probabilities are presented graphically. The graphs have been generated using the error terms estimated by the laboratory for the uncertainty associated with all aspects of age calculation, and the shape of the calibration curve. In themselves, these probability estimates are the radiocarbon results; there is no a priori reason why any part of the date ranges of these graphs should be more or less probable. It is possible to refine the data with reference to explicit archaeological prior beliefs, as part of a Bayesian statistical model. The resultant posterior density estimates are refinements of the probability distributions expressing archaeological interpretation and not absolute dates.

### Bayesian modelling

Chronometric data are not absolute, not least because all results are accompanied by an error term derived from the uncertainties in measurement. Within the result range, there is a point in time when the event, which is measured chronometrically, occurred. For example, all other things being equal, the result measured on a bone is the date when the animal died. The date measured on a cereal grain is the point in time the grain was removed from the plant. There can be a time lag between the measurement and the archaeological event in question; therefore a result produced on residual material within a context, will not date the context. Bayesian modelling of chronometric data relies on the archaeological interpretation of the association between dated event and archaeological event. This interpretation derives from the

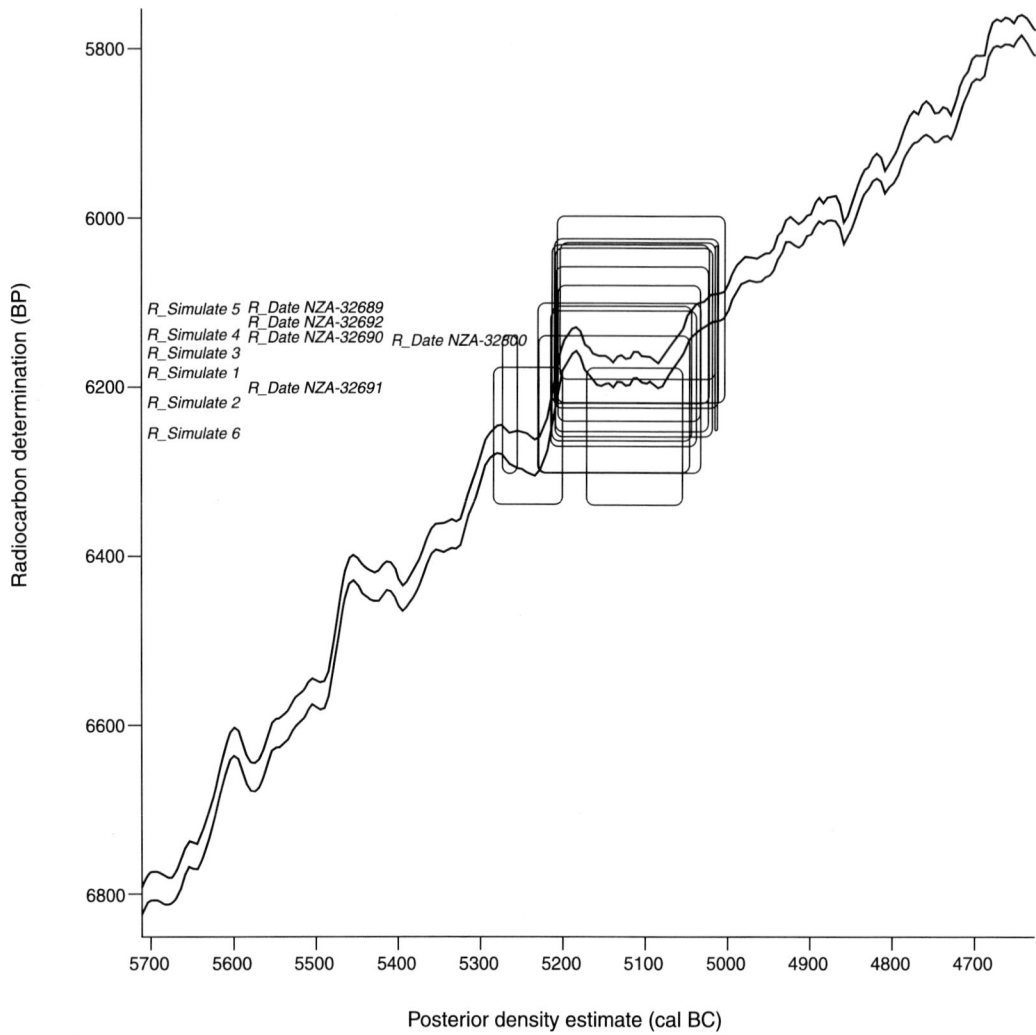

Fig. 9.2 *Probability distributions from the M1 and predictive modelling of six simulated 'Mesolithic' radiocarbon results*

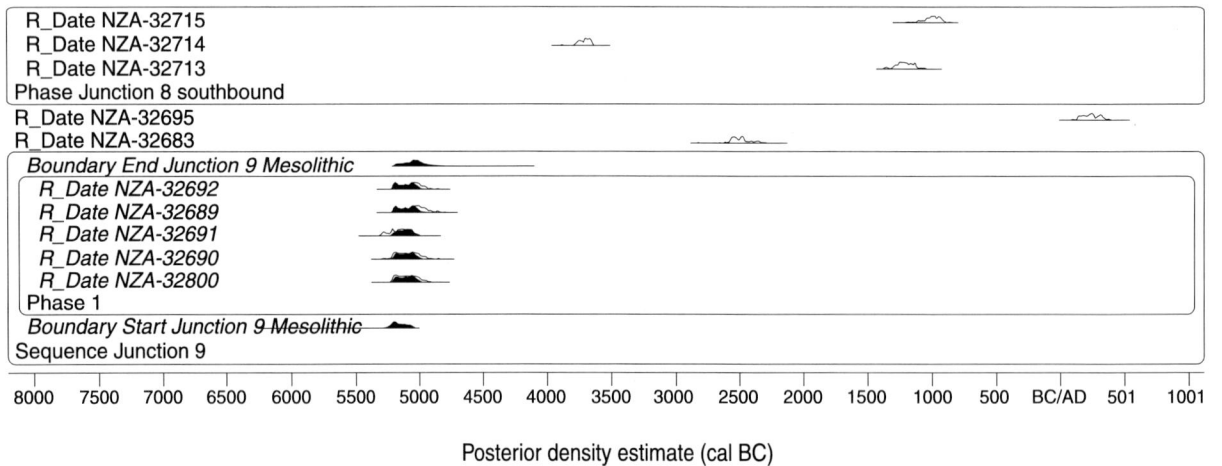

Fig. 9.3 *Probability distributions of dates from the site model A*

nature of dated material, taphonomy and deposit formation, and stratigraphic relationships, including the inferred relationships which constitute an archaeological phase. The seemingly neutral assumption of an archaeological phase can have important implications for the precision of chronometric data (if data are related as part of an archaeological event or phase, they are not independent estimates of this phase or event) and their probability estimates are related. Importantly, the statistical scatter generated from an assemblage of chronometric data (all the independent error term data) will be an artefact of the radiocarbon measurement process rather than the archaeological activity. Without accounting for statistical scatter, false imprecision will make archaeological events appear to start earlier, end later, and go on for longer than was really the case (Bayliss *et al.* 2007). OxCal v4.1, and other Bayesian programs, provide explicit, quantifiable, probabilistic methods of relating data, refining precision and estimating other chronometric aspects of archaeological interest.

The Bayesian modelling presented uses Markov Chain Monte Carlo sampling, applied in OxCal v4.1, details of which can be found on the online manual (http://c14.arch.ox.ac.uk/; Bronk Ramsey 1995; 1998; 2001). The consistency of the results has been tested, as outlined by Ward and Wilson (1978). The structure of the model described below is shown in Fig. 9.3.

**The samples and their stratigraphic relationships**

*Mesolithic negative features*

Six radiocarbon results were produced on material recovered from pits excavated at Junction 9. At this site were a cluster of pits, and four gullies. From many of the pits were recovered lithics and limited amounts of pottery and charred plant remains. Only 13 of the features contained diagnostic lithics; ten pits contained Mesolithic assemblages and three contained Neolithic assemblages.

A few of these features were interpreted as post-pits, because of the recognition of post-pipes (in features 2070, 2080 and 2182 and possibly in 2078, 2337, 2110 and 2148). Most of the pits were interpreted as deliberately backfilled in a single event. Despite the evidence for some post-pipes, no coherent structures were identified, though the activity at the site was considered as relating to occupation in the loosest sense.

The seven pits (2064, 2090, 2094, 2096, 2100, 2110 and 2316) from which Mesolithic material culture was recovered were located within the main concentration of pits (see Fig. 5.4). Some of the features contained fragmentary pottery and cereal grains. It is thought that these are intrusive, rather than that all the material had been redeposited. Possible mechanisms for this intrusion could include root action (see below).

*Pit 2094*

A single result (NZA-32690; 5230-4930 cal BC, 95.4% confidence; or 5210-4990 cal BC, 68.2% confidence) was produced on charred hazel nutshell from 2094. The feature contained hazel nutshell, modern root fragments, and a few indeterminate cereal grains. A scalene microlith, of Jacobi's (1978) type 7a2, was recovered from context 2093.

*Pit 2316*

A single result (NZA-32692; 5220-4930 cal BC, 95.4% confidence; or 5210-4990 cal BC, 68.2% confidence) was produced on charred hazel nutshell from pit 2316. The pit contained a few possible grains of spelt wheat, and indeterminate wheat seeds, as well as a type 7a2 (ibid.) scalene microtriangle.

*Pit 2096*

A single result (NZA-32691; 5310-5000 cal BC, 95.4% confidence; or 5230-5060 cal BC, 68.2% confidence) was generated on charred hazel nutshell from pit 2096. The feature contained hazel nutshell and indeterminate cereal grains. Worked flints (56 in total) including blades and narrow flakes were recovered from the feature.

*Gully 2196*

From gully 2196 a single result (NZA-32689; 5220-4850 cal BC, 95.4% confidence; or 5210-4940 cal BC, 68.2% confidence) was produced on hazel nutshell. The gully contained a small charcoal assemblage and a small type 7a2 (ibid.) scalene triangle.

*Pit 2064*

Two results were produced from pit 2064 (NZA-32800 and NZA-33911). These results are both recorded to have been produced on spelt wheat macrofossil fragments. The first result (NZA-32800), supposedly produced on a charred wheat seed, dated to 5290-4940 cal BC (95.4% confidence; or 5220-5000 cal BC, 68.2% confidence). A 6th millennium BC radiocarbon result on domesticated cereals would be nationally important, broadly contemporaneous with *Linearbandkeramik* activity on the Continent. Further, this feature contained a lightly burnt type 5c (ibid.) scalene triangle. Other charred plant remains included indeterminate wheat glume bases, and hazel nutshells. To investigate this, another result was commissioned on an indeterminate wheat glume base from the same sample as the original spelt grain (NZA-33911). This produced the range cal AD 50-230 (95.4% confidence; or cal AD 70-140, 68.2% confidence).

On this basis it is suggested that a charred hazel nutshell associated with Mesolithic activity on the site was accidentally dated, rather than the cereal grain recorded on the sample submission form. The presence of 6th millennium spelt on the site is discounted. Result NZA-32800 is poorly understood.

### Later Neolithic and later activity

Within the main concentration of pits, pit 2052 contained broad flint flakes and burnt flint. It was assessed as late Neolithic on the basis of this material, and a radiocarbon result (NZA-32683) produced on hazel nutshell provides a *terminus post quem* for its infilling of 2630-2320 cal BC (95.4% confidence; or 2560-2410 cal BC, 68.2% confidence).

### Pit 2070

A single result (NZA-32695) on charred seeds produced a *terminus post quem* for the infilling of pit 2070 of cal AD 110-370 (95.4% confidence; or cal AD 160-310, 68.2% confidence). This result indicates later activity in the vicinity of the Mesolithic-period pits. NZA-32695 and NZA-33911 are statistically consistent (T'=3.0; T'5%=3.8; n=1; Ward and Wilson 1978), and could measure material derived from the same archaeological event. If this were so, it would be more appropriate to take a weighted mean prior to calibration. An estimate for such an event would be cal AD 80-240 (95.4% confidence; or cal AD 120-220, 68.2% confidence). The consistency of these Roman-period data suggests a background scatter of later activity in the area that was earlier a focus for Mesolithic people (rather than errors in measurement, or contamination resulting in NZA-32695 and NZA-33911).

### Deposit formation and interpretation

It is assumed, as with the dated cereal example from pit 2064, that all other cereal grains from the Mesolithic pits are intrusive. Models resulting in the presence of intrusive material could include on-site sampling contamination, or unconsolidated matrixes (into which material from overlying activity might move). Mixing could have been augmented by disturbance from overlying occupation, as evidenced by activity in the vicinity and the dated material from posthole 2070.

## Junction 8S

### Human and animal cremations

Dates were obtained on three deposits of cremated bone; one of animal bone and two of human bone.

Cremated animal bone <2053> (5082) was dated to 3780-3640 cal BC (95.4% confidence; or 3760-3650 cal BC, 68.2% confidence; NZA-32714).

Cremated human bone <2052> (5067) was dated to 1380-1090 cal BC (95.4% confidence; or 1270-1130 cal BC, 68.2% confidence; NZA-32713).

Cremated human bone <2073> (5245) was dated to 1130-900 cal BC (95.4% confidence; or 1050-920 cal BC, 68.2% confidence; NZA-32715).

All the radiocarbon results on the cremated skeletal material from Junction 8S are statistically significantly different (T'=1913.7%; T'5%=6.0; n=2; NZA-32713, -NZA32714 and NZA-32715; Ward and

Wilson 1978). Even the two later results (NZA-32713 and NZA-32715) are statistically significantly different (T'=7.2; T'5%=3.8; n=1; ibid.). The results indicate that cremation burials were deposited at Junction 8S over a very considerable period of time from the earlier Neolithic until the Bronze Age. It seems most probable that these data represent highly episodic, unrelated practices, which are structured within a landscape, at a location that was perhaps physically marked, maybe preserved in some form of memory work over many generations (cf Pollard 2008). It is possible that the two later results present a single phase of activity – a tradition of burial practice – with principles structuring post-mortem rites more closely related, but the density of radiocarbon dates is not sufficient to support such an interpretation.

## DISCUSSION AND INTERPRETATION

### Mesolithic activity

The five radiocarbon results associated with Mesolithic activity at Junction 9 (including NZA-32800, produced on uncertain material) are statistically consistent (T'=1,9; T'5%=9.5; n=4; Ward and Wilson 1978). Because the results were all on short-lived material they might measure the same point in time – that is to say, it is possible that they represent a very short-lived archaeological event of a duration less than the ten-year optimum precision of this part of the calibration curve. There is, however, limited archaeological evidence for such a single episode of activity and there is no evidence to relate activity associated with these features other than as a spatially defined broad archaeological phase.

The archaeological interpretation is further complicated by the presence of later Neolithic activity, and indeed much later Roman activity in the vicinity. It seems that some of the Romano-British material, including domesticated cereal grains, was later incorporated into earlier features. The presence of significant Mesolithic lithic assemblages, in numerous features, including cores, and waste material (see Chapter 7) suggests *in situ* Mesolithic activity including flint working. The similar, homogeneous pit fills provide further evidence of Mesolithic tools, hazel nutshells and fills generically *in situ*.

The material sampled by NZA-32800 is uncertain, though it is suggested to be hazel nutshell. If all the material thought to represent *in situ* Mesolithic activity (ie all the results thought to have been produced on hazel) represented the same archaeological event, it would be more appropriate to take a weighted mean prior to calibration. An estimate for this event would be *5210-5010 cal BC* (95.4% probable; or *5210-5100 cal BC*, 39.8% probable; or *5080-5030 cal BC*, 28.3% probable; T'=1.9; T'5%=9.5; n=4).

Another interpretation is that these data represent *in situ* Mesolithic activity of a longer, unknown, duration. An estimate for the start of this activity is

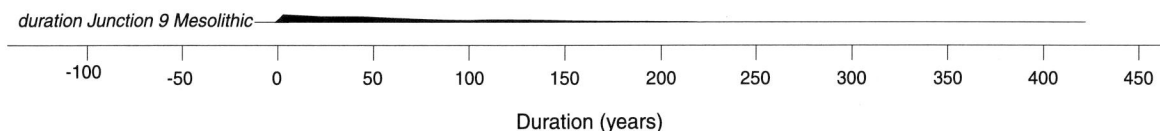

*Fig. 9.4   Probability distribution for the duration of Mesolithic activity at the site*

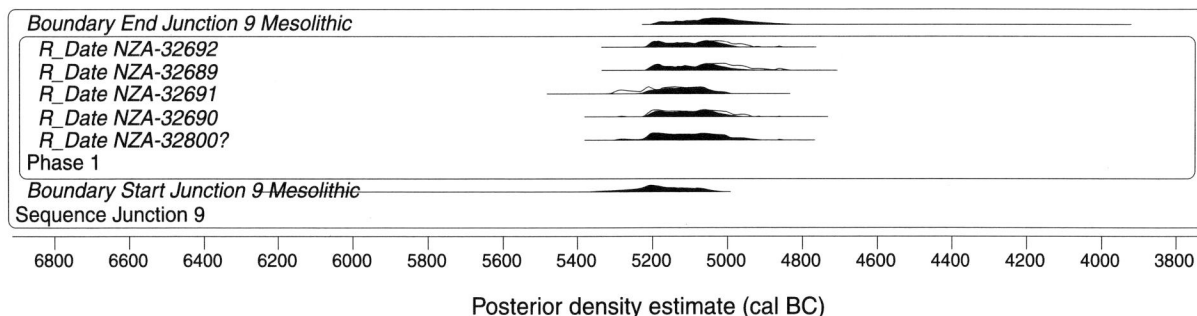

*Fig. 9.5   The site model B, excluding NZA-32800*

*5330-5020 cal BC* (95.4% probable; or *5230-5070 cal BC*, 68.2% probable; Start Junction 9 Mesolithic A; Fig. 9.3). An estimate for the end of this activity is *5210-4870 cal BC* (95.4% probable; or *5170-5160 cal BC*, 1.4% probable; or *5130-4960 cal BC*, 66.8% probable; End Junction 9 Mesolithic A; Fig. 9.3). The activity sampled went on for under 210 years (95.4% probable) or most probably under 100 years (68.2% probable; duration Junction 9 Mesolithic A; Fig. 9.4). If datum NZA-32800 is removed from the model, slightly different posteriors are produced, as activity begins *5410-5010 cal BC* (95.4% probable; or *5240-5070 cal BC*, 68.2% probable; Start Junction 9 Mesolithic B; Fig. 9.5). The end of this phase is estimated as *5210-4790 cal BC* (95.4% probable; or *5140-4950 cal BC*, 68.2% probable; End Junction 9 Mesolithic B; Fig. 9.5). The duration of this activity was under 220 years (95.4% probable), most probably under 110 years (68.2% probable; duration Junction 9 Mesolithic B; Fig. 9.6). NZA-32800 is not significant in model A's function; the parameters from model B are less precise because the model contains fewer likelihoods.

The earlier prehistoric activity indicated by the dated charred plant remains was of a relatively short duration. It could be truly contemporaneous (ie the material was harvested on the same day). It is possible that the activity took place at the optimal precision of this part of the calibration curve (ie over a period of under 10 years). Certainly this phase occurred over a period of less than 200 years (Figs 9.4 and 9.6). It is most probable that this activity occurred over a period of some 100 years (Figs 9.4 and 9.6).

The significance of the association of the radio-carbon results with the diagnostic Mesolithic

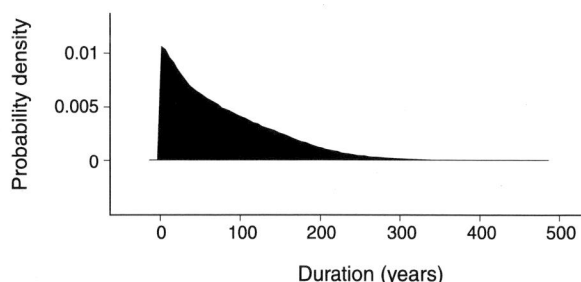

*Fig. 9.6   Probability distribution for the duration of Mesolithic activity at the site*

material culture recovered from these pits is more difficult to ascertain. The burnt hazel nutshells and wood demonstrate that people were active in the area (excluding the possibility of lightning strikes) but how this activity relates to the lithic industries is unknown. The presence of later charred plant remains from at least one of these features is demonstrated by NZA-33911, from pit 2064, from which were also recovered small sherds of intrusive pottery. It is therefore difficult to argue that these features represent sealed contexts, with excellent association between the lithic material and the radiocarbon results. These results are *termini post quos* for the infilling of the features and the deposition of associated lithic assemblages.

NZA-32690, NZA-32689 and NZA-32682 are *termini post quos* for the deposition of assemblages that include Jacobi's type 7a2 (1978) scalene triangle microliths. The infilling of these features and deposition of scalene microtriangles most probably occurred after the 52nd-51st centuries cal BC.

# Chapter 10: Overview

*by Dan Stansbie, Paul Booth and Seren Griffiths*

## LATE MESOLITHIC ACTIVITY *by Seren Griffiths and Dan Stansbie*

### The landscape context

Late Mesolithic activity defined by the presence of diagnostic flint was relatively widespread within the M1 widening corridor. Late Mesolithic/early Neolithic flint was found at Junction 8N, Junction 8S and Area P, but this material was all residual within later features, or distributed within the topsoil. The only evidence for *in situ* late Mesolithic activity came from Junction 9. Despite the lack of evidence for definite late Mesolithic settlement (except at Junction 9) from the M1 widening sites, which represent a relatively large excavated area, there is good and widespread evidence for similar settlement within the wider locality (Holgate 1995b, 8). Late Mesolithic sites in the region are located in the principal river valleys which cut the Chiltern dip slope from north to south, including the Ver valley (ibid.). Five sites (Stratford's Yard, Chesham; Redbourn; Low Farm, Fulmer; Gerrard's Cross; and Tolpit's Lane Site B, Moor Park) have produced substantial *in situ* assemblages of flint (ibid.). The site at Tolpit's Lane produced over 2000 flints, along with wild cattle and deer remains and carbonised hazelnut shells. Charcoal from the site was radiocarbon dated to 4380 ± 80 BC. At Stratford's Yard in the Chess valley a land surface buried by colluvium had a concentration of flint-working debris lying on it and a pit, possibly with a post-pipe, was cut into the same surface (Stainton 1989, 50). Artefacts from this site included an assemblage of 4000 flint tools, including narrow blades, and bones of wild cattle (one of which produced a radiocarbon date of 3940 ± 100 BC), red deer, pigs and charred hazelnut shells. Other late Mesolithic sites in the Ver valley include settlement at Redbourn and Friar's Wash (Holgate 1995b, 9).

It is therefore clear that late Mesolithic settlement was extensive in the region and that the people visiting the sites along the M1 widening corridor may have existed in what was, for the late Mesolithic period, a relatively densely utilised landscape. However, given the relatively poor chronological resolution of these sites in comparison to that from Junction 9, it is impossible to say whether or not they were in fact directly contemporaneous.

### 6th- and 5th-millennium pit sites in England and Wales

Allen and Gardiner (2002) have reviewed the evidence for Mesolithic pits in the south of England and to these features can be added recently excavated sites in the south, and several northern sites. Allen and Gardiner (ibid.) suggested that features, such as the pits located within the Stonehenge car park and those from the Dorset cursus area, could be evidence of early monumentalisation of landscape prior to the construction of 'Neolithic' megalithic and non-megalithic structures. Less certain examples of 'pits' have been recorded at Hambledon Hill (cf Mercer and Healy 2008). Monumentalisation of aspects of the 'natural' world is concurrent with Bradley's (2000) thesis of a changing conceptualisation of landscape. Evidence for posts, rather than pits, is not always present, and many examples of cut features might be better understood as fire pits or hearths. Several smaller Mesolithic pits, such as at March Hill Carr (Griffiths in prep.), Kingsdale (Howard 2007) and on the A30 in Cornwall (Griffiths 2006) contain significant quantities of burnt flint, and it may be that processing flint was part of these features' purposes.

### Site layout and organisation

Site layout and organisation cannot be considered at sites other than Junction 9, as activity at the other sites was represented by flint scatters which were residual in later features. However, low-level late Mesolithic/early Neolithic activity was fairly widespread across the landscape examined during the M1 widening.

The late Mesolithic activity at Junction 9 consisted of the excavation of at least seven pits and three gullies and their subsequent backfilling with cultural material comprising flint-working debris, diagnostic flint tools and charred hazelnut shells. However, these features were part of a much larger pit group, comprising 69 pits and two gullies, some of which produced undiagnostic flint-working debris. The late Mesolithic activity could therefore have been much more extensive than the minimum number of ten features would suggest. The dating of these features has been established by a series of radiocarbon dates (see Chapter 9) and by the presence of diagnostic artefacts. Contemporary chronometric data have been produced from several pits recently excavated at Gobowen, Shropshire (L Hayes pers. comm.).

Bayesian modelling of the radiocarbon dates from these features suggests that late Mesolithic activity probably took place over a period of 100 years, but could have taken place over a period of less than ten years during the 52nd century cal BC (see Chapter 9). Given this dating evidence and the fact that the dated features were relatively dispersed throughout the larger pit scatter, it seems likely that they represent several discrete episodes of activity. Their proportions, proximity and number might suggest repeated occupation, with groups of people moving into the area and stopping to create and repair tools and consume wild resources, and then moving on. Alternatively, there is the possibility that all of this activity represents a single archaeological phase, perhaps with spatially zoned tasks, or areas of activity. The presence of a possible post-pipe in one of the pits (2110) would seem to argue for a greater degree of permanence, but this possible posthole does not appear to be part of any coherent pattern of pits or postholes, whether dated to the late Mesolithic or not, that might form a structure. Furthermore, the dimensions of the M1 widening pits make it unlikely that these features are 'monumental' in the sense implied by Allen and Gardiner (2002).

The majority of the late Mesolithic pits had a single fill, although pits 2094 and 2064 each had two fills. Flint-working debris, flint tools and hazelnut shells were distributed evenly throughout the fills of all the features and there was no evidence for any of the artefacts or ecofacts having been deliberately placed. This suggests that the material was incorporated into the fills as part of a soil matrix and, given its state of preservation, it seems likely that this was secondary deposition, after initial discard on the ground surface. A similar process is argued to have occurred at the early Neolithic site of Kilverstone, Norfolk (Garrow *et al.* 2005). At this site, the material which formed the basis for the pit fills is characterised as 'mess' rather than midden material, although it is acknowledged that the concept of a midden may be appropriate (ibid., 150) in some ways. The hazelnuts at Kilverstone were also sometimes found within charcoal-rich lenses (ibid., 144), a characteristic that is used to argue for the backfilling of the pits with dumps of cultural material, which is missing from the Junction 9 pits. However, differences in soil conditions, or taphonomic factors, could account for this absence. The evidence from Kilverstone suggests repeated visits to the site by a mobile group or groups of people (ibid., 155) and a similar scenario can perhaps be envisaged at Junction 9 (see above), with the difference between a Mesolithic and a Neolithic way of life (ie lack of pottery at Junction 9), the presence of domesticated animals/crops at Kilverstone, and possibly greater numbers of people, accounting for the differences in density of material culture accumulated.

## Subsistence and economy

Unfortunately, evidence for subsistence and economy is limited to flint tools and flint-working debris and hazelnut shells, with no faunal remains or other environmental indicators available. The presence of scalene triangles, amongst the flint assemblage, indicates the repair and/or the manufacture of hunting tools and the hazelnut shells demonstrate the gathering and use of wild resources. The quantities of flint recovered (see Chapter 7) perhaps indicate a relatively long-term occupation for purposes of rest and retooling, rather than a short-term 'hunting camp'. The kinds of tools manufactured at Junction 9, however, (ie blades, scalene triangles and an obliquely blunted point) might be argued to represent evidence for a 'hunting camp'. Given this, perhaps, it would be better to see the evidence as representing a variety of different activities, which could occur in particular parts of the landscape, but could equally occur within the same locale, as proposed for early Mesolithic activity in the Vale of Pickering (Conneller and Schadla-Hall 2003).

## Scalene microlith chronology

In 1979, Switsur and Jacobi wrote their seminal analysis of microlith typologies, in which they defined a number of spatially and temporally transgressive microlith clusters. The M1 microlith assemblage is dominated by scalenes, with a few probable rods. We may, in this sense, define it as one of Switsur and Jacobi's (1979, 47) cluster B sites which were '...distributed over southern England' and which chronologically 'cover the time period 6500 B.C. (Broomhill, Hampshire) to the end of the Mesolithic'. Switsur and Jacobi's (ibid.) also suggest that, 'in addition to possessing numerous later microlith shapes (classes 5-8, occasionally 9), the sites retain a noticeable, often high, proportion of early microlith shapes...'. As a later cluster B site, the M1 could also overlap temporally with the Pennines scalene dominated sites such as March Hill Carr, Pule Bents and other Pennines sites (Griffiths in prep.).

The only other English sites which have robustly dated later microlith assemblages, are rod-dominated March Hill Top (ibid..), and the scalene assemblage from March Hill Carr (ibid.). The temporal difference between these results could be evidence of changes in regional styles of lithic technology, or represent chronological development. Switsur and Jacobi (1979, 45) classified their scalene-dominated March Hill II and Lominot sites as cluster D because of the Pennines and Clevelands typology, raw material and relative absence of rods. Clearly two well-dated sites do not provide an adequate or robust sample for these cluster types or scalene typology.

Other sites with radiocarbon dates (Table 10.1), stratigraphically associated with apparently later scalene dominated assemblages are Windmill Farm (cf Smith 1984, 179), Dean and Dan Cloughs (Griffiths in prep.), Lominot IV (Switsur and Jacobi

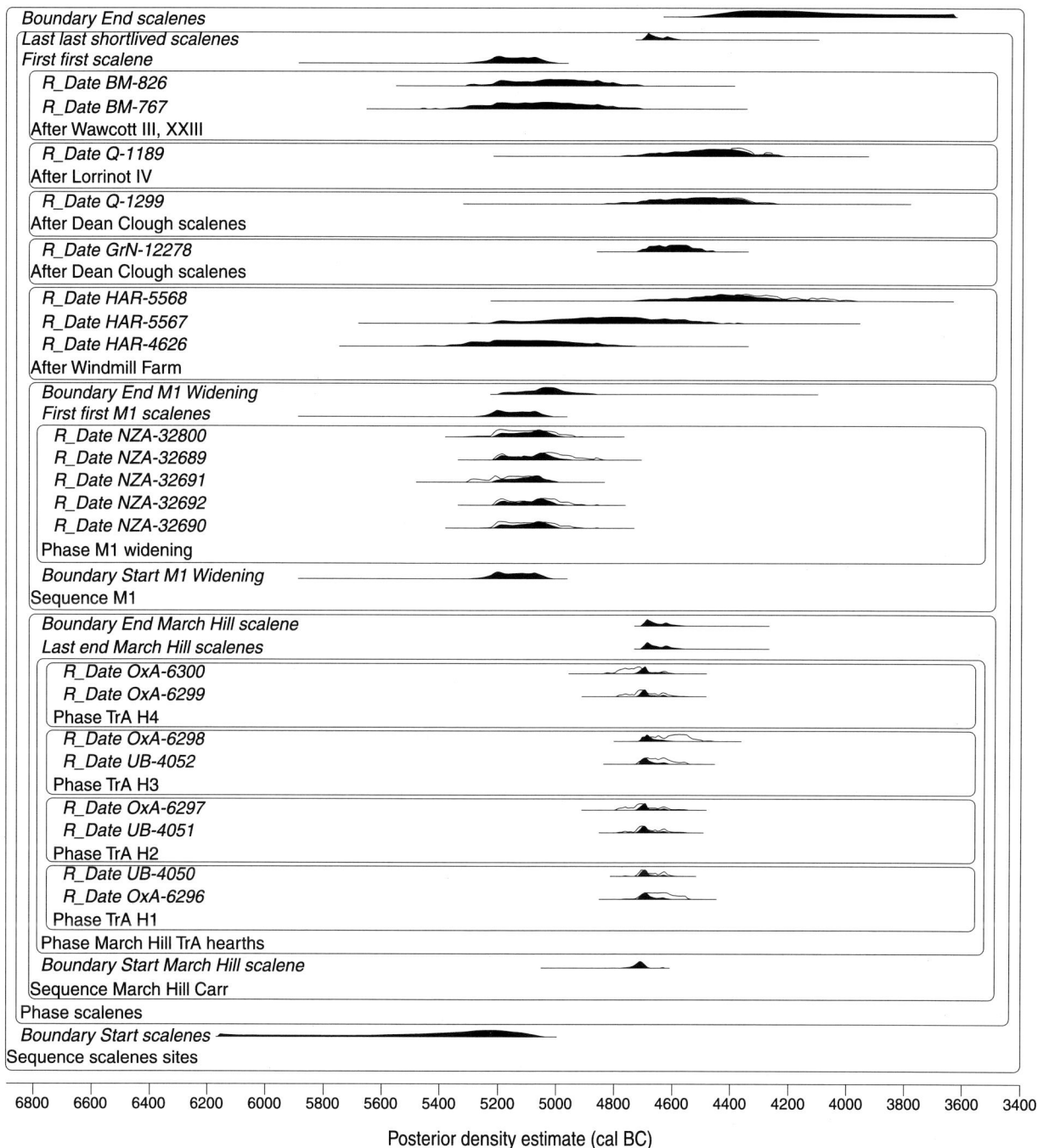

*Fig. 10.1 Probability distributions associated with scalene triangle assemblages*

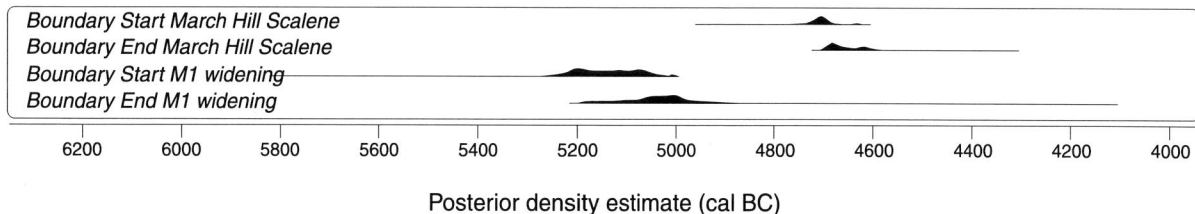

*Fig. 10.2 Probability distributions for estimated first and last use of scalene microliths*

1975; Griffiths in prep.) and Wawcott III and XXIV (Froom 1976, 164). Unfortunately, the radiocarbon results from these sites have poor association with any archaeological event in the published sources. Furthermore, the radiocarbon dates from these sites were produced on unspeciated charcoal of uncertain maturity or on oak charcoal. These results could all have inbuilt age offsets (ie have been derived from old wood), between the archaeological event (ie the gathering of the wood for fuel) and the radiocarbon age of the material. In the model comparing the scalene chronologies, these results are used as *termini post quos*; effective likelihoods on the last dated event associated with scalene use, but not effective on the earliest dated event associated with scalene use. The data from Broom Hill (O'Malley and Jacobi 1978) are not discussed, because it is not possible, from the published report, to associate radiocarbon results with microliths. Other sites exist with poorly understood associations between radiocarbon samples and later Mesolithic material culture (cf Gardiner nd). Together with the data from the March Hill Carr hearths, the Junction 9 pits are arguably one of only two well-understood, chronometric assemblages associated with scalene triangle use in England. These two sites currently provide the chronometric end points for scalene use. Junction 9 provides the earliest accurate estimation for scalene triangle use in England of *5220-5060 cal BC* (68.2% probable; first scalene; Figs 10.1-2). The last accurate dated event associated with scalene triangle use is provided by the March Hill Carr estimate of *4710-4610 cal BC* (68.2% probable; end March Hill scales; Figs 10.1-2). Together these sites demonstrate that scalene triangle dominated assemblages were in use at least for some *390-570 years* (68.2% probable; duration scalenes; Fig. 10.3).

### Wider social networks

The majority of evidence for Mesolithic occupation in England derives from surface collected lithic scatters and stratified deposits or material from features is significantly rarer. The proximity of the features at Junction 9 might suggest an area favoured either by a group of people or repeatedly visited over a period of time, perhaps seasonally. Interpretation of Mesolithic settlement evidence has predominantly followed the thesis of Clark (eg 1954), who suggested a transhumance model, intimately linked with resource scheduling. Recent

critiques have attempted to deconstruct this model, emphasising the complexity of an 'economic' model (eg Joachim 1976), variability in ancient animal and plant populations (Carter 2001), and the limitations of seeing Mesolithic populations as predominantly semi-nomadic microlith-wielding hunters (Clarke 1976; Finley 2006; Conneller 2005). Evidence for repeated occupation at sizeable early Mesolithic structures in favoured locations, such as Howick (Waddington *et al.* 2003) and East Barns (Gooder 2007), also forces us to problematise the nature of occupation and the structures which are envisaged (cf Taylor and Gray Jones 2009). It is notable that most Mesolithic structural evidence from England seems to be associated with much earlier Mesolithic activity. It is from pit or posthole sites, such as those discovered at Junction 9, that the evidence for later Mesolithic occupation is derived.

The absence of structural settlement evidence in England is especially pertinent when the range of later Mesolithic Continental examples is compared. These include stone-built hut-rings, and stake-built structures presumably associated with organic covers. Grøn (2003, 688) has also emphasised that even considerable wooden structures may leave very limited earth-fast features.

The Junction 9 features are nationally important because of their contribution to the chronology of later Mesolithic tool typologies and the probable demonstration of repeated occupation of favoured locales (cf Wickham-Jones 2005). The location of the Junction 9 pits, at the head of a now dry valley, might provide some indication of natural features that drew people repeatedly to this place. Barton *et al.* (1997) have emphasised that as well as more utilitarian resources, Mesolithic people created 'persistent places' because of socialised interactions with their landscape (cf Pollard 2000). Whether this site represents the deposition of material in pits by a large group of people occupied in retooling, or the repeated revisiting of the location over several generations, the Junction 9 Mesolithic pits are rare indications of the complex relationships that Mesolithic people engaged with over the course of their lifetimes.

### EARLY NEOLITHIC ACTIVITY *by Dan Stansbie*

Stratified evidence for early Neolithic activity was restricted to a single pit (5081) from Junction 8S. The pit lay in the southern central part of the site, and

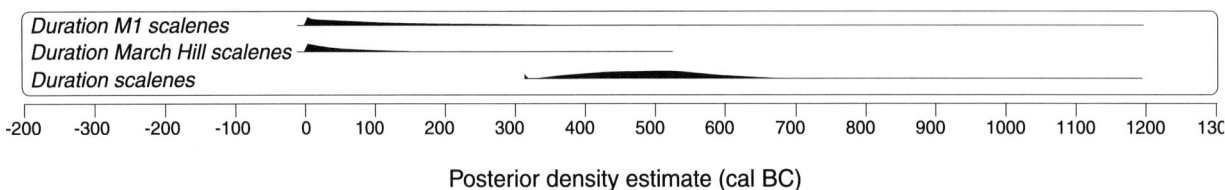

*Fig. 10.3 The duration of use of scalene triangles as calculated from the parameters shown in figure 10.1*

*Table 10.1: Comparative radiocarbon data*

| Site | Lab code | Context and sample | Material | Description | δ13C | 14C age BP | Calibrated date range |
|---|---|---|---|---|---|---|---|
| March Hill Carr | OxA-6296 | Fill of hearth 1, trench A, defined by a circle of stones, overlain by peat | *Corylus avellana* charcoal | The hearth contained flakes consistent with the refitted assemblage. Dates firing of hearth and ?production of lithic assemblage (English Heritage unpublished data; Griffiths in prep.). | -24.4 | 5790±35 | |
| March Hill Carr | UB-4050 | Fill of hearth 1, trench A, defined by a circle of stones, overlain by peat | Hazel/ *Prunus* sp. charcoal | The hearth contained flakes consistent with the refitted assemblage. Dates firing of hearth, and ?refitting flints (English Heritage unpublished data; Griffiths in prep.). | | 5813±22 | |
| March Hill Carr | UB-4051 | Hazel charcoal sample taken from the fill of hearth, Tr. A H2, composed of a circle of built-up stones, sealed under 40-50cm peat | *Corylus avellana* charcoal | The hearth is of a similar style to those previously dated by Switsur (Q-788), which was probably adjacent to this area. Dates firing of hearth (English Heritage unpublished data; Griffiths in prep.). | | 5824±28 | |
| March Hill Carr | OxA-6297 | Hazel charcoal sample taken from the fill of hearth Tr. A H2 composed of a circle of built-up stones. Sealed by 40-50cm peat | *Corylus avellana* charcoal | The hearth is of a similar style to those previously dated by Switsur, which was probably adjacent to this area. Dates firing of hearth (English Heritage unpublished data; Griffiths in prep.). | -24.4 | 5835±35 | |
| March Hill Carr | UB-4052 | Hazel charcoal sample located within hearth Tr. A H3; an oval pit. Contained a scalene triangle, and was surrounded by a scalene triangle assemblage | *Corylus avellana* charcoal | The association suggests hearth date contemporary with scalene production. Dates firing of hearth; ?date of scalene manufacture (English Heritage unpublished data; Griffiths in prep.). | -26.8±0.2 | 5796±29 | |
| March Hill Carr | OxA-6298 | Hazel charcoal sample located within hearth Tr. A H3; an oval pit. Contained a scalene triangle, and was surrounded by a scalene triangle assemblage | *Corylus avellana* charcoal | The association suggests hearth date contemporary with scalene production. Dates firing of hearth; ?date of scalene manufacture (English Heritage unpublished data; Griffiths in prep.). | -24.6 | 5745±35 | |
| March Hill Carr | OxA-6299 | Hazel charcoal sample from Tr. A H4; a very small pit, filled with charcoal. Burnt flints were collected from the hearth fill. The burning of the flint might be part of a deliberate pretreatment process | *Corylus avellana* charcoal | Dates firing of the hearth and burning of flints (English Heritage unpublished data; Griffiths in prep.). | -25.3 | 5830±35 | |
| March Hill Carr | OxA-6300 | Hazel charcoal sample from Tr. A H4; a very small pit, filled with charcoal. Burnt flints were collected from the hearth fill. The burning of the flint might be part of a deliberate pretreatment process | *Corylus avellana* charcoal | Dates firing of hearth and burning of flint (English Heritage unpublished data; Griffiths in prep.). | -26.0 | 5855±40 | |
| Dean Clough SE 0065 812715 | GrN-12278 | The date material came from the floor of a definite hearth with a flagged floor; scalene triangles were recovered from the site | *Quercus* sp. charcoal | TPQ firing of hearth, and ?use of scalenes (Smith–Deenen pers. comm. 2009 Unpublished data; Griffiths in prep.). | | 5750±50 | 4720–4460 cal BC |
| Dean Clough SD 9949 1289 | Q-1299 | Charcoal from a hearth, collected from three squares of the excavation area (Stonehouse 1986, 8) | Bulk charcoal | The site produced 932 flints; 13 were identified as scalene triangles. Micro burins and cores were also recovered. Conjoining pieces (109 in total) were identified, and knapping debris suggests *in situ* working (Griffiths in prep.). ?TPQ firing of hearth, and flint working | | 5645±140 | |

*Table 10.1: Comparative radiocarbon data – continued*

| Site | Lab code | Context and sample | Material | Description | δ13C | 14C age BP | Calibrated date range |
|------|----------|--------------------|----------|-------------|------|-----------|-----------------------|
| Wind-mill Farm | HAR-4626 | A number of features produced a lithic assemblage including scalene triangles, lancolate, straight-backed and obliquely backed pieces. | Charcoal | Date is ?TPQ for burning and lithic assemblage (Smith 1984, 179). | | 6160±150 | |
| Wind-mill Farm | HAR-5567 | A number of features produced a lithic assemblage including scalene triangles, lancolate, straight-backed and obliquely backed pieces | Charcoal | Date is ?TPQ for burning, and lithic assemblage (Smith 1984, 179). | | 5920±180 | |
| Wind-mill Farm | HAR-5568 | A number of features produced a lithic assemblage including scalene triangles, lancolate, straight-backed and obliquely backed pieces | Charcoal | Date is ?TPQ for burning and lithic assemblage (Smith 1984, 179). | | 5510±150 | |
| Lomi-not IV | Q-1189 | ? A scalene-dominated assemblage not fully reported by Switsur and Jacobi (1975) | ? | TPQ uncertain activity (Switsur and Jacobi 1975; Griffiths in prep.). | | 5610±120 | |
| Waw-cott III | BM-767 | Base of pit 2; associated with a dominance of scalenes over isosceles forms | Charcoal-carbonaceous material, including hazel nutshells | TPQ infilling pit, and deposition numerous Mesolithic flints including microlith points, triangles, crescents and rectangles, distinct from Thatcham industries (Froom 1976, 160) | | 6120±134 | |
| Waw-cott XXIII | BM-826 | Hearth associated with Mesolithic flint industry including scalene triangles similar to that of Wawcott III | Charcoal | ?TPQ infilling pit, deposition scalenes? (Froom 1976, 164) | | 6079±113 | |

was shallow, with a flat base. The pit fill produced a radiocarbon date (NZA-32714) of 3780-3640 cal BC (95.4% confidence; or 3760-3650 cal BC, 68.2% confidence) on burnt animal bone and also produced worked flint. A single pit cannot be taken as evidence of settlement, but it does show a human presence in the area in the early Neolithic, and the presence of burnt animal bone suggests that people were in the area long enough to accumulate and burn occupation debris. The fragmented nature of the animal bone suggests that it was not a placed deposit. In addition, unstratified worked flint from Junction 8S, Junction 8N and Area P indicates possible early Neolithic activity (see Chapter 7), but this material is all residual in later features or stratified in the topsoil (see late Mesolithic activity above) so its significance is uncertain.

## LATER NEOLITHIC AND EARLY BRONZE AGE ACTIVITY *by Dan Stansbie*

### The landscape

Definitive evidence of late Neolithic-early Bronze Age activity within the M1 widening corridor was scarce, but four pits from the excavations at Junction 9 are dated to the late Neolithic period. Three of these are dated on the basis of late Neolithic worked flint from their fills and one (pit 2052) was dated on the basis of a fragment of hazelnut shell from its secondary fill, which produced a radiocarbon determination (NZA-32683) of 2620-2340 cal BC (95.4% confidence; or 2570-2460 cal BC, 68.2% confidence). In addition, five pits (5064, 5088, 5096, 5172 and 5226 ) from Junction 8S were possibly of Neolithic to early Bronze Age date on the basis of worked flint from their fills or, in the case of pit 5226, burnt unworked flint. Finally, undated pits from the Aubreys produced worked flint of late Neolithic-early Bronze Age date, raising the possibility that they may date to this period, a suggestion supported by the occurrence of eight small sherds of pottery from one of these pits. These were not closely dated, but a late Neolithic-Bronze Age date is suggested by Webley and Brown (see Chapter 7). The occurrence of the flint, in particular, recalls the evidence for Neolithic flintwork recorded in earlier work at this site (see Chapter 1).

### Site organisation

Like the scatter of late Mesolithic pits described above the late Neolithic pits from Junction 9 were part of a scatter of 69 pits and two gullies, many of which could have dated either to the late Mesolithic or the late Neolithic periods. However, on their own the late Neolithic pits represent evidence for limited late Neolithic settlement activity, relating to a small group, or groups of people moving through the landscape. These pits may have related to very similar activity to that described for the late Mesolithic (see above). The presence of flint-working debris, along with tools, burnt flint and hazelnuts from throughout the pit fills, indicates, as with the Mesolithic pits, that the material had been introduced into the pits as part of a soil matrix and probably therefore represents secondary deposition of material originally deposited on the ground surface. Similarly, possible late Neolithic-early Bronze Age pits from Junction 8S and The Aubreys may relate to relatively short-lived occupation by mobile groups, with the dispersed nature of these pits indicating more than one occupation event.

## Subsistence and economy

As with the late Mesolithic evidence, the lack of faunal remains and environmental indicators (apart from hazelnuts) makes the drawing of inferences about subsistence and economy problematic. However, the presence of flint tools and hazelnut shells at Junction 9 indicates repair and/or manufacture of tools and the consumption of wild resources. The presence of burnt flint also suggests that any occupation lasted long enough for the accumulation and burning of debris. Similar activities can be imagined taking place at Junction 8S and The Aubreys, although at these sites the hazelnut shells are absent.

## LATER PREHISTORIC ACTIVITY *by Dan Stansbie*

### Distribution of evidence

Evidence for later prehistoric activity along the route of the M1 widening corridor was limited. Much of it came from the vicinity of Junction 8, with the great majority from Junction 8S, where scattered isolated pits, along with two more substantial groups of pits, two four-post structures and two unurned cremation burials, provided evidence of fairly dispersed settlement over a wide area dating to the late Bronze Age-early Iron Age. This is very much in keeping with evidence from elsewhere in the area (R Niblett pers. comm.). A scatter of late Bronze Age-early Iron Age pottery, intrusive in the upper fills of Mesolithic and Neolithic pits at Junction 9, attests to limited activity of that date in this area and four pits, and a short stretch of ditch, also dating to the late Bronze Age-early Iron Age were excavated during a watching brief at the Buncefield Depot, to the north of Junction 8. Some residual late Bronze Age-early Iron Age and middle Iron Age pottery was also found in the late Iron Age-early Roman features at Junction 8N (see Chapter 3). Excavation of the outer ditch of the

hillfort at The Aubreys provided no dating evidence, but the ditch is assumed to be of Iron Age date by association with the hillfort.

## Site organisation

The evidence from Junction 8S suggests that late Bronze Age-early Iron Age activity was distributed across the excavated area fairly widely, but also fairly thinly. The main concentrations of activity comprised two groups of pits, located in the north-western corner (7785) and in the north-eastern part (7786) of the site. Both pit groups produced moderate amounts of late Bronze Age-early Iron Age pottery and also worked flint, and to judge from their profiles represent shallow scoops dug for the deposition of rubbish, or possibly midden material (see Chapter 7). Other isolated pits, a gully and a tree-throw hole were scattered across the area, representing similar activity. Two post-built structures, presumably for crop storage, were found in the south-eastern corner of the excavation area and two cremation burials, probably relating to the same settlement, were placed in the south-western and north-central parts of the site respectively. The lack of evidence for structures, apart from the four- and five-post storage structures (see above), requires some explanation and is perhaps best accounted for by truncation from medieval and later ploughing which, judging from the shallowness of many of the features, was severe enough to entirely remove shallow postholes and other features. Overall the evidence suggests that a small-scale late Bronze Age-early Iron Age farmstead was present at Junction 8S. The small scatter of pits and single ditch from the Buncefield Depot watching brief may perhaps have been part of the same dispersed settlement, but the character of the feature assemblages there suggest a different type of activity from that indicated at Junction 8S.

Late Bronze Age-early Iron Age settlement is reasonably well known in the Chilterns and such settlements have been excavated at Puddle Hill, Foxholes Farm, Cole Green, Pea Lane and Bottom House Lane (Bryant 1995, 19), and also include the hillfort at Ivinghoe Beacon (Cotton and Frere 1968). Much closer, at Buncefield Lane, Hemel Hempstead, pits, postholes, a ditch and a buried soil horizon were dated to the late Bronze Age/early Iron Age (McDonald 2003, 51). Similar sites have also been excavated along the route of the Berkhamsted to Kings Langley bypass. These include ditches, pits and three possible rectangular post-built structures at Rucklers Lane, late Bronze Age-early Iron Age pits, postholes and ditches near Wood Lane End and two late Bronze Age round-houses and eight four-post structures at Oakwood, Berkhamsted (McDonald 1996). In addition, a late Bronze Age roundhouse was excavated in West-wood Quarry, about 500m west of The Grove site near Watford. Environmental evidence from this site suggests arable farming, with finds of emmer

emmer and barley, but no field systems were identified (R Niblett pers. comm.). These settlements (with the exceptions of Buncefield Lane, Rucklers Lane and Wood Lane End) all produced evidence of circular post-built structures, which were absent from the Junction 8S site. However, all the extensively excavated sites of the period also produced four- and six-post granaries, which can be paralleled at Junction 8, although only one site (Totternhoe) had any form of enclosure (Bryant 1995, 19). This evidence suggests a fairly extensive population at least on the valley slopes and plateau edges, but not occupation of such density or character that regular definition of sites with enclosures was required.

The small amount of late Bronze Age-early Iron Age pottery from Junction 9, mostly intrusive in the tops of the fills of earlier prehistoric features, suggests the possibility of similar settlement activity at this site, but in this case the extensive Roman activity in the area may have obliterated all trace of features related to such settlement. Activity at The Aubreys, possibly but not demonstrably of this date, was also restricted to pits and postholes, but with an absence of any coherent structures. Although the presence of a hearth among the northernmost group of pits suggests that this activity was related to settlement, the quantity of material culture recovered was exceedingly small and the date of the hearth is very uncertain.

### Site economies and diet

There was no direct evidence for late Bronze Age-early Iron Age economy or diet, as no faunal remains or other environmental remains were recovered.

### Ritual and burial practices

There is no evidence for later prehistoric structured deposits from either Junction 8S or The Aubreys. Two pits from Junction 8S (5023 and 5106) produced sherd groups representing fragments of single vessels, but their degree of fragmentation suggests that they were deposited as part of a backfill of midden, or occupation soil (see Chapter 7), and the lack of large volumes of animal bone, human bone and small finds from any of the deposits would seem to support this argument (although the general scarcity of bone is also in part a consequence of poor-preservation conditions). At Buncefield Depot two further pit groups contained notable concentrations of sherds, including a large part of a single early Iron Age vessel in pit 532. It is possible that the latter represents some kind of structured deposit, but there was no other associated material that might have shed further light on this possibility.

The evidence for burial practices is limited to the two late Bronze Age cremation burials (5066 and 5244) also from Junction 8S. A single unurned cremation burial (5066) occurred in the south-western corner of the site and produced a radiocarbon date (NZA-32713) of 1380-1090 cal BC (95.4% confidence; or 1270-1130 cal BC, 68.2% confidence) and a second unurned cremation burial (5244) was found in the northern central part of the site, producing a radiocarbon date (NZA-32715) of 1130-900 cal BC (95.4% confidence; or 1050-920 cal BC, 68.2% confidence). It is now widely acknowledged that there was a tradition of cremation burial without grave goods in late Bronze Age southern England and that these are typically found singly or in small groups (Webley *et al.* 2007, 139). The examples from Junction 8S are paralleled in Hertfordshire at Gadebridge (Bryant 1997) and more widely in southern England (Webley *et al.* 2007, 139). Of the two radiocarbon dates from Junction 8S only the second, from cremation 5244, falls within the 11th-9th-century cal BC date range expected for such burials (ibid.), with the first example falling somewhat earlier, within the 13th-12th centuries cal BC. However, both seem to fit within the tradition of late Bronze Age cremation burials in all other respects, although the dates of their deposition were probably significantly different.

### Wider social networks

In view of the lack of evidence for substantial late Bronze Age-early Iron Age activity within the M1 widening corridor from anywhere other than Junction 8S, assessing the place of the settlement within the wider contemporary community is problematic. It is possible that the earliest occupation of The Aubreys overlapped chronologically with early Iron Age occupation at Junction 8S, but given the lack of dating evidence from the excavation at The Aubreys, and the late Bronze Age radiocarbon dates from Junction 8S, this must remain speculative. If the two sites were contemporary at any point then it might be argued that The Aubreys served as a centre for ritual and communal activities, which may have involved people from the Junction 8S site, only *c* 3.5km distant. Although perhaps in large part a consequence of the paucity of excavation, the absence of evidence for sustained settlement within The Aubreys may suggest only sporadic occupation. Its siting between two dry valleys, which may have had at least seasonal streams in the past, may have lent significance to its location. Evidence for status, or hierarchy, at Junction 8S is lacking, with the material culture assemblages not showing any particular characteristics that can be readily interpreted in these terms, nor any differentiation between different parts of the site. Lack of evidence for buildings also makes status differences difficult to address, but the absence of enclosure ditches may suggest a lack of differentiation. The evidence for possible later prehistoric settlement at The Aubreys is even more problematic, with the extreme paucity of the material culture assemblage making inferences about status and hierarchy, or exchange, impossible to sustain, and even its chronology quite uncertain.

## LATE IRON AGE AND ROMAN ACTIVITY
*by Dan Stansbie and Paul Booth*

### Settlement pattern

The majority of evidence for Roman activity along the route of the M1 widening corridor came from Junction 8N and Junction 9, where enclosures, boundary ditches and corn drying ovens indicated relatively intensive agriculturally related activity, with pits and smaller ovens within enclosure 7700 at Junction 8N possibly indicating domestic occupation. Evidence for Roman activity was also uncovered at Areas M and P, Junction 10 and Junction 8S. Ditches at Area M represented agricultural activity dating to the early Roman period, while similar activity from Area P dated to the middle Roman period. At Junction 10, a fenceline was tentatively assigned to the late Iron Age-early Roman period and at Junction 8S a sub-rectangular enclosure and a ditch produced early-middle Roman pottery. At The Aubreys, ditches of a possible field system respecting the position of the earthworks may also have been of Roman date.

Evidence for the intensity of occupation in this period in the wider landscape beyond the M1 corridor is variable. There is little evidence for the immediate impact of the Roman conquest in the Verulamium hinterland, with the majority of settlements continuing from the late Iron Age until the early 2nd century, when settlement shift occurred (eg Niblett 2005a, 156). Pollen evidence from the Ver floodplain and from the fill of the mid-1st-century funerary shaft at Folly Lane indicates a largely agricultural landscape with only remnant woodland, and animal dung and trampled soil from the same feature suggest the presence of stockyards (Niblett 1999, 62). At a slightly later date evidence from villas in the area supports the view that the rural economy was dominated by mixed farming. There is some evidence for agricultural exploitation in the form of rectangular fields and trackways to the south of Verulamium, known from aerial photographs and from archaeological evaluations, at Smallford Farm, Jersey Farm, Turners Farm and Fairfolds Farm, Sandridge, although at the first two sites the evidence is undated and at all four it is fragmentary. Field boundaries to the north of Verulamium, which run at right-angles to the line of Watling Street, may also be Roman in date (R Niblett pers. comm.). Williamson (2000, 146, fig. 24) has suggested that field layouts on the line of the watershed between the Ver and the Gade predate the Norman conquest, although there is no firm evidence of a Roman date for these features. Williamson's (2010, 185) recent expansion of his earlier work gives a more nuanced approach to the chronology of 'relict field systems', suggesting that

these '...probably have complex origins. Rather than dating from a single "period", they are the result of many centuries of development, and their distinctive form is largely a consequence of the natural topography'. Such evidence does not permit the reconstruction of wide-ranging field systems of Roman date, although the existence of such systems is very probable.

Excavated lower-status rural sites and farmsteads belonging to the Roman period are rare in the vicinity of the M1 corridor, although such sites have been more extensively investigated in the immediate vicinity of St Albans. This pattern may be attributable to a long-standing tradition of archaeological research with both methods and priorities which, until relatively recently, have favoured work on villas at the expense of other settlement types, although extensive truncation due to medieval and post-medieval ploughing in the Verulamium hinterland may also have contributed to the pattern of data in this area. Rural settlement is, however, known from Harpenden, Redbourn, Kettlewells and Bladder Wood (Hunn 1995a, 84). Sites with evidence for masonry buildings include Old Jeromes West, 0.5km north of Gorhambury, and a rectangular enclosure at Prae Wood (ibid., 83), as well as the possible structure in the vicinity of Junction 8 (see above). The character of this last group of sites is uncertain, however, and evidence to confirm or contradict their definition as distinct from villas is lacking. The wider landscape of the Chiltern dip slope was fairly densely settled. A survey of north-west Essex estimated 1.3 Roman settlements per square km (Williamson 1984, 228) and Hunn (1996, 52) recorded 43 settlements, over 40 square miles, near Stevenage. However, Roman sites recorded along pipeline easements in the St Albans area and along the Kings Langley to Berkhamsted bypass are comparatively scarce and this may suggest that the boulder clay areas of north-east Hertfordshire were more agriculturally attractive than the clay-with-flints areas, which cover much of the dip slope further to the south (eg Williamson 2010, 64-6). In several areas, for example Ashridge and Berkhamsted golf course and Marshalls Heath Wood, Wheathampstead, which have been woodland since the medieval period and therefore not ploughed, Roman, or at least pre-medieval, enclosure banks survive. Earthworks also survive at Piggott's Hill Wood, Harpenden, and excavations at Aldwickbury golf course nearby heave revealed a trackway, an enclosure and three ovens dating to the Roman period (West 2008, 15), suggesting a low-status settlement at this site as well.

Evidence for religious sites in the landscape includes the temple complex at Annables Cottages, near Friars Wash approximately 1km to the southeast of the Junction 9 site, the faunal assemblage from which was dominated by pig bones (Wessex Archaeology 2009, 13), as well as the temple at Wood Lane End, to the west of Junction 8 (Neal

1983; 1984). A temple/mausoleum complex also existed at Rothamstead, Harpenden (Lowther 1937).

By the late 3rd century rural settlement in the region shows evidence of variable fortunes, with a number of the villas in the Verulamium hinterland showing decline in this period, followed by a possible revival in the early 4th century and decay from the mid 4th century (Williamson 2010, 68). Nevertheless, there are suggestions of late 4th- or early 5th-century activity (though not necessarily of typical 'villa' character) at some of these sites, including Gadebridge (Neal 1974, 76-83), Park Street (O'Neil 1947, 29-30) and Mackerye End (R Niblett pers. comm.). Change was also extensive in the lower-status rural settlements from the late 3rd century, as shown by evidence from Fairfolds Farm, Sandford, which went into decline around this time, and sites at Crawley Lane, Wiggington and Stoney Lane, Bourne End, which declined in the early 4th century. Local industries were also in decline by this period with, for example, the iron deposits in the Bulbourne Valley perhaps having been exhausted by, or at least not exploited beyond, the later 3rd century (Branigan 1985, 161). The Verulamium region pottery industry may have ceased production a little later, in the first half of the 4th century (Lyne 2006, 123).

## Site layout, function and organisation

The six sites with Roman occupation encountered along the M1 widening corridor were spatially discrete and will therefore be discussed separately in geographical order from south to north.

Late Iron Age-early Roman activity at Junction 8N consisted of a substantial SW-NE-orientated linear ditch (7676) fronting a row of evenly spaced square postholes indicating a fenceline or possible bank revetment, with vestigial possible structural features just to the south. To the north-west of this was an irregular north-south-aligned boundary (7187), defined by a segmented ditch. The relationship of these features is unclear. In fact the spatial logic of the plan strongly suggests that the segmented boundary should be assigned to the succeeding early Roman phase and formed part of a series of irregular enclosures. Even if this was not the case, the fact that the fence/palisade associated with ditch 7676 lay on its south side suggests that other associated activity also lay in this direction. The absence of any other contemporary elements that might have formed related parts of enclosure boundaries appears problematic, but the problem may be misconceived; instead 7676 was perhaps part of a system of linear boundaries dividing the landscape, rather than enclosing individual settlement units within it. Such boundaries, as is clearly the case at Junction 8N, could have been substantial, but need not have been continuous over substantial distances. The scale, however, is more modest than that of the linear earthworks associated with some of the late Iron Age 'site clusters' discussed by Bryant (2007).

A single beam-slot and a few associated postholes lying just south of ditch 7676 may have represented part of an associated building, but are otherwise difficult to interpret. The function of a large sub-rectangular pit lying north of ditch 7676 is also uncertain. within the putative enclosure was ambiguous. Unfortunately, the finds assemblages are also unhelpful in addressing the nature of the late Iron Age activity as they are sparse. Pottery from this phase consists entirely of grog-tempered ware and where rim sherds are present they come from multi-functional medium-mouthed jars, suggesting that any settlement was not of particularly high status. No animal bone, charred plant remains or charcoal were recovered from any of the contexts associated with this activity.

Activity of early-middle Roman date at Junction 8N comprised a series of sub-rectangular enclosures (7700, 7277, 66624, 6622, 6150 and 6104), field boundaries (6768 and 6713) probably utilising elements of late Iron Age boundary 7187 (if indeed that boundary was not entirely of this phase), a trackway (6364 and 6365) and a corn dryer (6514). It appears that some elements of this enclosure system were laid out earlier than others, although overall it was early-middle Roman in date. The earliest element was probably enclosure 7700, which was possibly contemporary with corn dryer 6514, lying outside it to the south. Enclosures 7277, 6624 and 6622 were probably next in the sequence, with enclosures 6150 and 6104 laid out last. The field boundaries and trackway ditches have no stratigraphic relationship with the enclosures, but their spatial relationship with enclosure 7700 is fairly clear. The lack of evidence for structures within the enclosures makes it tempting to interpret them as part of a field system, but as with the late Iron Age-early Roman period, described above, shallow postholes could have been truncated by later ploughing. The form of the smaller enclosures, in particular, may suggest that they functioned as paddocks. The gaps between the segments of ditch 7187 on the north-western boundary raise questions about control of movement through this boundary, but may suggest a relatively complex system of stock control in this part of the site, the gaps, mostly relatively small, being closed with hurdles or similar structures as required. Either way, these ditches probably formed an outer ring of enclosures at the periphery of a larger settlement with its nucleus to the east of the excavated area, beneath the original line of the M1. The quantity and state of preservation of pottery from the fills of enclosure ditch 7700 and the presence of rubbish pits within the enclosure, however, suggest that it at least was the focus of some kind of settlement, although this could have been subsidiary to a main focus located close by. Although the constrained area of excavation does not allow certainty on this point, the apparent absence of further boundaries extending away westwards, from the ring of possible paddocks, suggests that there was no particular need for a well-defined network of fields immediately adjacent to the settlement/paddock complex. This presumably reflected characteristics of the agricultural regime practised. Combined with the evidence of the character of ditch 7187 this suggests a concern with pastoralism, notwithstanding the presence of the corn dryer to the south.

Junction 8S also produced evidence of probable agricultural activity, very likely relating to the same nucleus of settlement located beneath the M1 between the Junction 8N and Junction 8S sites. The latter contained part of a sub-rectangular enclosure (5500) and a linear ditch (5501) producing small and abraded assemblages of early-middle Roman pottery and small amounts of animal bone. This material could have been incorporated into the fills of the field boundary through the spreading of midden material.

Enclosure and trackway ditches from Area M probably represented part of an agricultural landscape. In the first phase of activity, dating to the middle-late Iron Age, two slender ditches, 3022 aligned NNE-SSW and 3008 orientated east-west, before returning to the SSW, probably demarcated an enclosure. A gap between the two ditches, later blocked by a short east-west-orientated linear feature (3024), may have contained a stock-handling gate. The second phase of activity, dating to the early Roman period, may have represented either two trackways and a sub-rectangular enclosure or, more likely, successive phases of enclosure boundary with an adjacent trackway to the west, contiguous with the north-western corner of the principal enclosure. Activity in this phase is also likely to have been related to agriculture, with the small amount of Roman pottery from the ditch fills suggesting that any settlement focus must have been some distance away.

Roman features at Area P consisted merely of four ditches, all aligned roughly NE-SW, and a scatter of pits. The nature of the activity is therefore difficult to ascertain, but was again presumably agricultural in character. Two of the ditches may have bounded a NE-SW-aligned trackway. It is probable that all of the features were of early-middle Roman date.

The excavation at Junction 9 revealed evidence for a more-intensively utilised agricultural landscape, although the very narrow excavation transect made meaningful interpretation difficult. The principal features were a series of long-lived field boundaries initially set out in the late Iron Age and maintained and developed into the later 3rd century. Late Iron Age-early Roman activity was concentrated at the north-western and south-eastern ends of the excavation and comprised a series of probable field boundary and trackway ditches. At the north-western end of the excavation, ditches 2008 and 2188 probably formed a NE-SW-orientated trackway, south-east of which lay an isolated cremation burial (2012) in a grog-tempered pedestal urn. Immediately to the south-east of these

features, ditches 2757, 2739 and 2114 probably defined a series of paddocks or enclosures and at the south-eastern end of the site ditches 2745 and 2747 may have defined the north-western boundary of an enclosure lying to their south-east, with ditch 2749 forming an internal division of the putative enclosure.

In the early Roman period the field systems at the north-western end of the site were augmented with a series of linear and L-shaped ditches. Ditch 2738 probably formed part of a sub-rectangular enclosure lying largely beyond the limit of excavation to the east, while ditches 2490, 2740, 2126 and 2594 supplemented, or reinforced, the late Iron Age-early Roman enclosure system to the south-east of ditch 2738. In the central part of the excavation, L-shaped ditch 2741 may have defined part of a sub-rectangular enclosure similar to that enclosed by ditch 2738. At the south-eastern end of the site, late Iron Age-early Roman ditches 2745, 2746 and 2749 were replaced by ditches 2748, 2750 and 2751, defining parts of two sub-rectangular enclosures. To the north of ditch 2748 was a large kiln/oven, which possibly functioned as a limekiln or corn dryer, while south of the ditch was a large waterhole, indicating that the enclosures may have functioned in part as paddocks for stock. There is no evidence for further modification of the enclosures at the northern end of the site during the mid-Roman period, but these enclosures probably remained in use, as they were subsequently modified in the late Roman period. In the central part of the excavation, the probable enclosure represented by ditch 2741 was remodelled by ditch 2742. However, the most extensive middle Roman reorganisation took place at the south-eastern end of the excavation, where early Roman ditches 2750 and 2751 were cut by curvilinear ditch 2752, which may have formed a sub-circular enclosure with ditches 2753 and 2754 extending beyond the limit of the excavation to the south-west. To the north of these ditches curvilinear ditch 2650 cut early Roman ditch 2748. Nearby hollows (2706, 2608 and 2657) were also of this date. Immediately to the north-west of these features, linear ditches 2755 and 2278 may have defined a NE-SW-orientated trackway running beyond the limits of excavation to the north-east.

Late Roman activity at Junction 9 was confined to the northern end of the site where L-shaped ditch 2737 may have defined two sides of a sub-rectangular enclosure. Lying immediately to the south of this enclosure was a well (2004), adjacent to an earlier ditch (2490), which continued to fill in this period. The character of the late Iron Age and Roman activity at Junction 9, particularly the putative trackways, the well and the waterhole suggests that the landscape was being used for the keeping of stock, while the kiln/oven indicates complementary activities probably associated with arable production. That the agricultural regime was mixed is indicated by the evidence of both animal bones and the presence of charred plant remains found in association with the possible corn dryer, and also elsewhere. The lack of evidence for buildings and the small quantities of material culture also point towards an agricultural as opposed to a settlement function for this area, although the frequency and variety of reworking of enclosures and linear boundaries suggests that a domestic focus lay close by. It should also be borne in mind that, as at Junction 8N, shallow post-holes and foundation trenches may well have been removed by later truncation.

Activity of this period at Junction 10 was confined to a fenceline comprising 13 postholes, which produced two sherds of late Iron Age-early Roman pottery. The context of this structure is most likely to have been agricultural, but the evidence for its date is extremely limited.

## Agricultural economy and diet

The evidence of Roman enclosures and field systems at Junction 8 and Junction 9 attests to fairly intensive and long-lived use of the local landscape for agriculture, including both crop growing and animal husbandry, from at least the late Iron Age until the end of the 3rd century when it is possible that there was a widespread reorganisation of the landscape, which would fit well with the evidence from some other rural sites in the Verulamium hinterland (R Niblett pers. comm.). These include indications of changes in the organisation of the villa estate at Gorhambury at this time (Neal *et al.* 1990, 77), and it is possible that such changes had implications for the use of the landscape in the M1 area in the 4th century.

Faunal assemblages were recovered from the late Iron Age, early Roman and middle Roman phases at Junction 8S, Junction 8N and Junction 9, but unfortunately not from the other Roman sites (see Chapter 8). The assemblage from Junction 8N consisted of a mere 290 fragments, largely deriving from the early-middle Roman phase and largely consisting of teeth. This assemblage is dominated by cattle and horse, indicating that cattle and horse husbandry may have been one of the activities associated with the enclosures at Junction 8N, but the poor state of preservation of the material makes it clear that much, if not all, bone from medium-sized and smaller animals (of which sheep/goat would have been the most important) is likely to have been lost to adverse soil conditions, so it is impossible to judge the relative importance of the main domestic species at this site.

The faunal assemblage from Junction 9 was in better condition. It was dominated by cattle and sheep/goat, with sheep/goat remains being more common in earlier contexts. A wider range of body parts was present in this assemblage and evidence of butchery suggests that a settlement focus must have lain very close to the site. Some pig bone was also present. Again the evidence indicates that animal husbandry was one of the activities undertaken

within the field systems. High proportions of cattle remains are often taken as a sign of high status, urban or military functions (King 1999, 180), although a general increase in the representation of cattle, as seen at Junction 9, can be characteristic of the later Roman period on sites of a variety of types in southern Britain. In the local context, this pattern may perhaps be explained in terms of some kind of connection between the Junction 9 field system and the villa at Gorhambury (Neal *et al.* 1990), where the faunal assemblage was also cattle dominated, with a further connection in terms of husbandry geared to the provision of resources for Verulamium, where cattle appear to dominate the faunal assemblages from the beginning of occupation onwards, although they are also of major importance in the late Iron Age (Niblett 2005a, 132-3). Whether the Junction 8N site formed part of a similar agricultural regime cannot be determined and evidence for the other sites is lacking altogether. Burnt residue from a Verulamium-region white ware vessel recovered from well 2004 at Junction 9 was analysed for lipids and produced evidence of degraded animal fat (see Chapter 7). Unfortunately, the specific type of fat could not be determined, but this result adds to the evidence for exploitation of animals at the site.

The charred plant assemblages from Junction 8N and Junction 9 indicate that spelt wheat was the dominant cereal product on both sites (see Chapter 8), with corn dryers from both sites demonstrating that crop-processing activities were being undertaken. The charred grain assemblages may be seen as fairly typical of the region, where other local assemblages are dominated by spelt or spelt and emmer (see Chapter 8). Taken together, the faunal and plant remains indicate a mixed-farming regime, with elements of crop processing and animal husbandry being undertaken at both Junction 8N and Junction 9. Fragments of quern stones from Junction 8 and Junction 9, with 57 fragments coming from Junction 8, supplement the evidence for crop processing on both sites. Such activity may, however, have involved little more than routine conversion of grain to flour and meal on a day-to-day basis. There is, for example, no evidence from the corn dryers for their use in the malting process.

A further aspect of the economy of these settlements is illustrated by the evidence for manufacture of querns of Hertfordshire Puddingstone at Junction 9 (see Chapter 7). The occurrence of flakes of more than one variant of this stone type, in a number of dispersed contexts, suggests at least intermittent, rather than one-off, production. The fact that fragments of the querns themselves were not found does not reveal much about the nature of this production, but the general rarity of direct evidence for quern production sites in Roman Britain, and the location of the site close to Watling Street, might suggest that quern production was at least a semi-specialised task and might have been a significant supplement to the agricultural economic base of the site.

## Ritual and burial practices

There was little evidence for ritual activity in the form of 'structured' deposits of large groups of pottery, animal bone and human bone, or small finds in the ditch fills or pits of any of the late Iron Age or Roman field systems within the M1 widening corridor. However, pit 7124, which was situated within enclosure 7700 at Junction 8N, contained materials that clearly suggested structured deposition. This material included pottery, human skull fragments and a quern stone in the pit's basal fill, along with a charcoal-rich lens incorporating a cattle mandible and humerus, and 75 fragments of unidentified animal bone. Other evidence for ritual activity came from three late Iron Age-early Roman cremation burials, two from Junction 8N (6289 and 6293) and one (2012) from Junction 9. Burials 6289 and 2012 were contained within, and 6293 was accompanied by a grog-tempered ceramic vessel dating to the late Iron Age-early Roman period. Cremation burials 6289 and 6293 were found within enclosures 7277 and 6624 respectively, but could have predated them. It is possible that these burials were placed within a functioning field system. Burial 2012, in a late Iron Age pedestal urn, was contemporary with late Iron Age enclosures at Junction 9. The iron disc from a later Roman ditch at the same site (see Chapter 7), some 60m south of burial 2012, might possibly, in view of the associations of the majority of the known objects of this type, have been derived from a further disturbed burial of late Iron Age date.

## Wider networks

The character of the narrow M1 widening scheme transect limits the extent to which the evidence contained within it can be used to support wider conclusions about the nature of exploitation of the landscape in this period. Nevertheless, the indication of increased numbers of sites of late Iron Age and Roman date, and of more intensive activity within most of them compared to the evidence from earlier periods, support, at least superficially, a more general model of intensification of landscape use at this time. A remarkable increase in the number of sites of late Iron Age date, compared to those of middle Iron Age date, has been noted in the Chilterns (cf Bryant 1995, 26). Despite the relative difficulties concerning the material culture of the earlier period (ibid.; Masefield 2008, 192) the broad validity of this pattern has been recognised more widely in south-east England by Hill (2007, 24), who sees parts of Hertfordshire as amongst those regions which 'seem to have had relatively little permanent settlement *c* 300-100 BC' and links the apparently rapid expansion of settlement patterns thereafter with large-scale social change at this time.

The M1 evidence is consistent with such a model. It also underlines the importance of what seems likely to have been a particularly significant compo-nent of the physical manifestation of intensification of landscape use, the definition of trackways with linear ditches. Such ditches are a key feature of the M1 sites at Junction 8S, Areas M and P, and Junction 9. There is no evidence from the present project for trackways defined in such a way (or indeed in any way) before this time. This is not to doubt the existence of defined routes through the middle Iron Age and earlier landscapes, but the means of such definition in a less-intensively exploited landscape (following Hill 2007) do not seem to have involved extensive provision of archaeologically detectable features. A characteristic related to the widespread introduction of ditched trackways is the use of ditched enclosures to define settlement locations. In the context of a national survey of Romano-British rural settlement enclosed sites are defined as representing 'a significant majority of the classifiable settlements' in Hertfordshire (Taylor 2007, 49). This characterisation is again of a 'broad-brush' nature, but is once more supported by the M1 evidence.

The M1 sites include no complete settlement enclosures, but suggest that these were potentially of varied form, apparently having an organic, agglomerative character at Junction 8S, while appearing more rectilinear at Area M and Junction 9, although curvilinear features did occur at the southern end of the latter site in the middle Roman period. The artefact assemblages, associated with these different sites and areas, are insufficiently large or distinctive to shed light on the possible significance of these morphological variations, whether in terms of specific functions or of social or economic status-related characteristics.

A further characteristic of the M1 sites is the evidence for field systems. In the case of Junction 8N, the small sub-rectangular enclosures are perhaps best seen as paddock-like additions to a settlement nucleus (see above), rather than forming part of a wider system of fields. The position at Areas M and P and at Junction 9 is less clear, though in all cases it is possible that some of the linear ditches at these sites formed parts of field boundaries rather than (or as well as) defining settlement enclosures and trackways. At The Aubreys, however, it seems more likely that linear ditches outside the hillfort to the east and tentatively dated to the Roman period formed part of a system of rectilinear fields, given that there was no indication of contemporary settlement related activity in the near vicinity. Again the definition of fields using ditched boundaries may be seen as more characteristic of the late Iron Age and early Roman periods than earlier, as has also been suggested as a result of survey work undertaken north of Berkhamsted (Morris and Wainwright 1995, 70-1).

In terms of general aspects of early chronology and demarcation of settlement and agricultural landscape, the M1 sites therefore supplement the information on known patterns of development, but are of value in providing this evidence in the context of broadly lower-status settlement types.

Good structural evidence remains elusive, a problem which can be characteristic of such sites but is exacerbated by the nature of the excavated sample, as structures could have been located close by rather than within the transect. Careful examination of the ceramic building material shows that much of it was brick and it is likely that all this material (concentrated at Junction 8N and Junction 9) had been recycled for use in features such as hearths and ovens. It therefore reveals little about the buildings of the Roman period on these sites, but instead raises the question of how far people were prepared to carry such material for reuse. It is possible that in the case of Junction 8 the brick and tile derived from the enigmatic building at Breakspeares (cf Hunn 1995a, 83). If this was the case, it may be appropriate to characterise this latter site as a small villa, although it remains unclear if the Roman features at Junction 8N would have formed an integral part of this site or lay adjacent to it. Potential sources of brick and tile for Junction 9 are not so easily identified, but a number of substantial buildings (including the temple at Friar's Wash less than 1km away) lay within a fairly short distance of this site, and its proximity to the line of Watling Street would have made transport of building material relatively straightforward. The question of whether any of the fragments of window and vessel glass from Junction 9 can also be explained as obtained through recycling is less certain, but may perhaps be worth consideration. The absence of indicators of moderate status amongst the metal and pottery assemblages from this, as well as the other M1 sites, suggests that the glass may be anomalous, but once again the constraints of the excavated areas mean that any such assessment can only be tentative.

## MEDIEVAL ACTIVITY *by Dan Stansbie*

### The landscape

Evidence for medieval activity discovered during the course of the project was concentrated around Junction 8, to the west of medieval St Albans and within the hinterland of the town, which lay only 5km to the east. Unfortunately, the inevitable restrictions of linear scheme excavation give tantalising glimpses of the medieval settlement pattern, rather than a broader understanding of the landscape that a larger concentrated development scheme might yield. Nevertheless, evidence from Junction 8N, the Junction 8 Compound and the Junction 8 watching brief offers some insight into the dispersed and possibly related medieval settlement pattern in this area. Junction 8N produced the most substantial evidence for settlement, including a post-built structure, pits, and enclosure and a limekiln. Immediately to the north of this settlement, at the Junction 8 Compound, was a north-south-aligned ditch and a group of pits probably also representing medieval settlement and dating to

the 11th-13th centuries. To the north of this activity the Junction 8 targeted watching brief revealed a short stretch of a NW-SE-orientated hollow-way of possible medieval date, and a group of pits, possibly representing a small building and possibly also of medieval date, just to the south. Together this evidence gives the impression of small-scale and dispersed settlement and agricultural activity, perhaps suggesting the existence of several peasant hamlets in the area.

### Junction 8N: settlement layout, function and organisation

The settlement at Junction 8N provides the most extensive evidence for medieval activity, including at least one croft, a limekiln and attendant rubbish pits and drainage ditches. The occupation was divided into two phases, the later dating to the late 12th-13th centuries and the earlier, which produced no secure dating evidence, predating this, but probably also belonging to the late 12th-13th centuries. The first phase of activity, situated towards the northern end of the Junction 8N excavation area, comprised two east-west-aligned ditches (6095 and 6449) spaced approximately 26m apart, with a small kiln/oven (6585) lying between them, close to the eastern end of ditch 6449. Both ditches ran beyond the limit of excavation to the west and east. The interpretation of these features is difficult, given their fairly ephemeral nature, but the lack of evidence for domestic occupation from this phase, including a lack of structures, rubbish pits and finds or environmental evidence, suggests activity of broadly agricultural character. The parallel alignment of the ditches and the distance between them of 26m, or approximately 28 yards, may be taken to suggest that they bounded a strip field, albeit one that had been turned over to small-scale occupation by the late 12th century. The presence of the kiln within this strip is problematic, but it is situated close to the northern boundary and may also have been associated with agricultural activity, perhaps serving as a crop drying oven, an interpretation supported by the recovery of cereal grains and chaff from the upper fill (6591) of the oven (see Chapter 8). By the late 12th century the field strip, if that is what it was, had been replaced by a small settlement, though the evidence does not allow its character, whether as individual farmstead or hamlet, to be determined. This perhaps represented a 'daughter settlement' built to accommodate a son unable to find his own holding, or parents who had given up their holding (Stamper 1999, 257).

The second phase of medieval occupation included a post-built structure (6961) orientated SW-NE, presumably representing a peasant dwelling or croft, or possibly two such structures erected end to end. The building was accompanied by two phases of drainage ditches to its south-east. An initial phase of curvilinear drainage ditches

(6300, 6403, 7006 and 7704) on a roughly SW-NE alignment, ran parallel to the structure. Having silted up or been backfilled, ditches 7006 and 6403 were replaced with a NW-SE-orientated linear ditch (6402). North-east of structure 6961 and at right-angles to it a slight linear ditch (6515) may have represented a palisade slot, while similarly ephemeral ditches 6538 and 6524 probably served a similar function. Several large pits (6030, 6054, 6188, 6497, 6451, 6276 and 6406) surrounding structure 6961 had regular profiles and may have been dug to extract building materials, but also served as rubbish pits, all of them producing assemblages of pottery and animal bone. Pit 6406, a large oval-shaped feature situated immediately to the south-west of structure 6961, contained multiple layers of deliberate backfill material which incorporated a substantial assemblage of late 12th-13th-century pottery. Given the size and shape of this feature, along with its location, it may be interpreted as a latrine pit, but there is no evidence for any structure surrounding the pit and there is no environmental evidence to support this interpretation.

The medieval occupation continued beyond the limit of excavation to the south-west, and possibly incorporated more buildings, and agricultural working areas, as shown by evaluation trench 1126, which revealed several NE-SW-aligned gullies and a layer containing 13th-century pottery. Within the excavated area the settlement was enclosed to the north-east and north-west by an L-shaped ditch (6109), presumably representing a toft boundary, and to the south-east by the presumably still visible line of Roman trackway boundary 6364. A limekiln (6825) was situated in the south-east corner of the enclosure, close to ditches 6109 and 6364. Reuse of Roman enclosure boundaries during the medieval period can be paralleled at nearby Gorhambury (Neal *et al.* 1990, 83) and it has been suggested that the extensive co-axial landscape in the area of Shenley Ridge, North Mimms and Aldenham incorporates the remains of a planned Roman system of land allotment in later fields (Williamson 2000, 146-7).

The evidence suggests that this activity represents a small peasant holding, possibly comprising a single toft/croft, of a type typical of the dispersed landscape of the Chiltern dip slope (Hunn 1995b, 50), but under represented in the archaeological record of Hertfordshire. Building 6961 almost certainly represented the dwelling place of a single peasant family and probably comprised a simple post- and clay-built structure of two bays. The surrounding drainage gullies indicate that the settlement may have had problems with surface water, possibly over an extended time period given the evidence for remodelling of the drainage system. However, such an arrangement is paralleled at Gorhambury, where large linear ditches were laid out at right-angles close to a small rectangular post-built structure of late 11th-early 14th-century date (Neal *et al.* 1990, 84) and at Caldecote

in North Hertfordshire, near Baldock, where 11th-early 12th-century post-built structures were provided with large curvilinear drainage ditches (Beresford 2009, 61). The large but relatively scarce rubbish/clay extraction pits are harder to parallel on rural settlements from Hertfordshire and their contents probably do not represent all the rubbish produced by the household, much of which must have been placed on middens and spread onto the fields. Given the late 12th-13th-century date range of the pottery from the fills of the pits they need represent little more than a single generation's occupation.

Limekilns, such as kiln 6825, are traditionally interpreted as being used for the production of lime mortar for construction, with a by-product being lime for use in the lime washing of wattle and daub buildings. However, given the lack of evidence for stone-built structures on the site, and notwithstanding the fact that such structures may have lain beyond the limit of excavation, it seems possible that lime production at the settlement was intended for agricultural use. A limekiln was also discovered at Gorhambury (Neal *et al.* 1990, 85-6) and a kiln was excavated at Caldecot (Beresford 2009, 63), although in this case it was interpreted as a corn drying or malting oven.

## Junction 8 Compound and targeted watching brief

Activity at the Junction 8 Compound comprised a single length of ditch and a scatter of pits, which produced a small amount of medieval pottery, while excavations at the targeted watching brief produced a further scatter of pits and a hollow-way/trackway of possible medieval date. The ephemeral nature of these features and the small scale of the excavations make interpretation difficult. However, the general impression gained is one of low-key settlement activity, probably also relating to a farmstead/farmsteads and confirming the picture of dispersed medieval settlement in the area.

## Structural components

As stated above structure 6961 probably represents a post-built peasant dwelling, possibly comprising two structures built end to end, but more likely a single structure of two bays, with a cross-entry approximately halfway down its length. The construction was of timber posts, probably set in clay walls, which would account for the slight irregularity of the post-lines (Beresford 2009, 64) and also for the fact that there is little evidence for any repair, or the replacement of the posts. Unfortunately, there is no evidence for how the structure from Junction 8N would have been roofed, although it might be expected to have had a thatched roof of straw or reeds (Dyer 1986, 26). The structure is paralleled at Gorhambury, where a post-built structure (Building 56), slightly smaller than the example from Junction

8N, was dated to the early 12th-14th centuries (Neal *et al.* 1990, 85). Four similar houses dating to the 11th-early 12th centuries were excavated at Caldecote (Beresford 2009, 58-63), although again the structures were all considerably smaller than the example at Junction 8N. Larger houses of similar construction dating to the 12th-mid 14th centuries were also excavated at Caldecote (ibid., 85-6).

### Agricultural economy, diet and status

Unfortunately, all the charred plant remains of medieval date from Junction 8N come from kiln 6585 and pit 6788, which was probably part of the kiln and therefore from the first phase of medieval activity, before the establishment of the settlement. They cannot therefore be compared directly with the evidence of the small animal bone assemblage, which comes entirely from contexts associated with the second phase of activity. However, the assemblage does give some insight into the agricultural use of the area before the establishment of the settlement and may be relevant to understanding of the second phase settlement if it is assumed that there was no radical difference in agricultural practice between the two phases. The cereal assemblages from oven 6585 and pit 6788 are dominated by spelt wheat, with some rye, and are a mixture of cereal grain, cereal chaff and weeds/wild plants (see Chapter 8) indicating a fairly standard medieval arable economy. Some vetch/garden pea is also present. The assemblage can be compared with cereal remains from Caldecote which are sparse, partly due to the fact that widespread sampling was not standard practice at the time of that excavation (Martin 2009). The Caldecote assemblage was also dominated by wheat, although bread/club wheat was dominant over emmer/spelt (ibid., 227) and rye, barley and oats are also present. The evidence of the charred plant remains from Junction 8N indicates that a fairly standard range of crops was cultivated and processed on the site before the second phase settlement was established. Fragments of rotary quern recovered from medieval contexts are likely to represent residual Roman material, and it is possible that crop-grinding activities took place off site, or else that evidence of medieval grinding implements did not survive. The lack of charred plant remains associated with the settlement itself is problematic, but it may be assumed that the inhabitants had access to a similar range of crops to those from Caldecote, including wheat, barley, oats, peas and beans (Beresford 2009, 231). Charcoal from oak, ash and beech, among other species (see Chapter 8), recovered from kiln/oven 6585 and pit 6406 shows that a wide range of timber was available for exploitation.

The medieval animal bone assemblage only numbers 254 fragments, suggesting that much of the material derived from secondary deposition, an interpretation backed up by the presence of dog gnawing marks on some of the bones. Cattle, pig, sheep/goat, horse and domestic fowl are all present, with pig being the most common species by NISP and sheep/goat being as common as cattle. This presents an interesting contrast to the assemblage from Gorhambury, where this pattern is reversed (see Chapter 8). The assemblage suggests a standard mixed-farming economy, with the dominance of sheep/goat and pig perhaps being attributable to the location of the settlement in the upland environment of the Chiltern dip slope, an interpretation backed up by the comparable relative lack of cattle at Gorhambury. A mandible of a cat with a cut mark, which indicates that the animal had been skinned, suggests that the inhabitants of the farmstead were exploiting animal resources for clothing as well as food products. The probable deposition of the majority of animal remains on middens may explain the relatively small size of the assemblage, although poor preservation as a consequence of adverse soil conditions, already noted in relation to assemblages of Roman date, was presumably also a significant factor.

Further light is thrown on the economy of the medieval settlement by the composition of the pottery assemblage, which largely comprises cooking pots and storage jars in South Hertford-shire greywares, but shows a notable lack of wide bowls, a form usually associated on medieval rural settlements with dairying (see Chapter 7). This lack of wide bowls tallies with the paucity of cattle bone from the animal bone assemblage to confirm the picture of a more sheep/goat- and pig-based animal economy, perhaps more suited to the upland landscape of the area. Pigs would have been particularly suited to an environment with a relatively high proportion of woodland.

As has already been suggested, the structural evidence indicates a peasant toft/croft, probably accommodating a single family operating a subsistence farming regime. The pottery evidence broadly confirms this picture, with the pottery assemblage being dominated by cooking/storage jars in South Hertfordshire grey wares, with only a few regional imports including some green-glazed jugs. Four body sherds from a probable imported vessel, perhaps of Middle Eastern origin (see Chapter 7) from the fills of pits 6406 and 6188 form an exception to this pattern, but the small amount of this material (representing a single vessel) means that its presence, despite being intrinsically interesting, does not really alter the overall picture. A single medieval whetstone from ditch 6645 and made from Norwegian rag is likely to have been used for sharpening fine implements, but is not necessarily out of place in a settlement of this type (see Chapter 7). Few metal objects were recovered from medieval contexts and those that were, including a decorative stud and a pair of tweezers, are common enough finds on comparable medieval settlements (Cool *et al.* 2009, 179-209). Overall the evidence of the finds confirms the picture of a relatively low-status peasant household suggested by the structural evidence.

**The settlement in the wider landscape**

The medieval settlement pattern on the Chiltern dip slope in the 11th century, particularly within the hinterland of St Albans, was dispersed, with relatively few settlements (Redbourn and Sandridge) acquiring village-like characteristics by the 14th century (Hunn 1995, 50). Wheathampstead, probably an early minster within a Saxon estate centre (eg Williamson 2010, 157) arguably also had such characteristics (R Niblett pers. comm.), while at Hemel Hempstead there was a market by about 1300 (Williamson 2010, 243). The remaining settlement pattern was characterised by small dispersed hamlets, in character more like the medieval settlement from Gorhambury (Neal *et. al.* 1990) and unlike the nucleated village at Caldecote, which was located on the north Hertfordshire chalk lands (Beresford 2009, 21). Indeed Lewis *et al.* (2001, 10) state that, 'the absence of large medieval villages, deserted, shrunken or inhabited in such districts as the Chilterns must mean that nucleated settlement never existed there'. This pattern is seen by Hunn (1995b, 50) as being heavily influenced by the presence of St Albans, which provided a relatively large central focus discouraging the development of larger villages. However, it may also be seen as a response to the upland landscape, which was perhaps less suitable for large-scale cultivation than other lower-lying areas of the region. The settlement at Junction 8N may therefore be seen as typical of the area.

The wider landscape of the St Albans area has been seen as exhibiting many of the characteristics of a woodland landscape (ibid., 50) and the limited charcoal evidence from the Junction 8N settlement does not contradict this pattern, with beech, oak, ash, hazel, hawthorn-type, gorse/broom, willow/poplar and blackthorn-type all being recovered. It should be remembered, however, that the bulk of this material was recovered from kiln 6585, which belonged to the initial agricultural phase of medieval activity, and from one other context, pit 6404. Field systems in the St Albans area were characterised by open common arable fields, interspersed with smaller units, sometimes enclosed with hedges (ibid,, 53). Elements of enclosure were therefore present in the landscape from an early stage. The evidence gained from the excavations at Junction 8N fits neatly into this picture, adding to our understanding of a landscape populated with small dispersed peasant hamlets. While the evidence from Caldecote (Beresford 2009) provides parallels in terms of building techniques and material culture, the settlement at Gorhambury (Neal *et al.* 1990) provides a closer overall parallel for the settlement at Junction 8N. Although the evidence gained from the M1 excavations is unsurprising and fits into already established understandings of settlement in the area, it remains important as a relatively rare example in the region.

# Bibliography

Adamson, S, 1999 The small finds from the lower slope, in Niblett 1999, 196-216

Ager, B M, 1989 The Anglo-Saxon cemetery, in Stead and Rigby 1989, 219-39

Allen, M and Gardiner, J, 2002 A sense of time - cultural markers in the mesolithic of southern England, in D Bruno and M Wilson (eds), *Inscribed landscapes: marking and making place*, University of Hawaii Press, Honolulu, 139-53

Allen, M and Green, M, 1998 The Fir Tree Farm Shaft: the date and archaeological and palaeo-environmental potential of a chalk swallowhole features, *Proc Dorset Nat Hist Archaeol Soc* **120**, 25-38

Allen, T and Welsh, K, 1998 Eton Rowing Lake, Dorney, Buckinghamshire, third interim report, *SouthMidlands Archaeol* **28**, 75-84

Allen, T, Barclay, A and Lamdin-Whymark, H, 2004 Opening the wood, making the land: the study of a Neolithic landscape in the Dorney area of the Middle Thames Valley, in J Cotton and D Field (eds), *Towards a new stone age: aspects of the Neolithic in south-east England*, CBA Res Rep **137**, York, 82-98

Allen, T, Donnelly, M, Hayden, C and Powell, K, forthcoming *A road through the past: high status late Iron Age and early Roman burials, Bronze Age enclosures, Iron Age, Roman and medieval settlements on the line of the A2 Pepperhill to Cobham Widening Scheme, Gravesend, Kent*, Oxford Archaeol Monogr, Oxford

Animal Bone Metrical Archive Project (ABMAP) http://ads.ahds.ac.uk/catalogue/specColl/abmap/index.cfm, accessed June 2009

Anthony, I E, 1960 Rural Hertfordshire in the Iron Age and Roman period, *Hertfordshire's Past* **1**, 2-9

Anthony, I, 1968 Excavations at Verulam Fields, St Albans, 1963-4, *Hertfordshire Archaeol* **1**, 9-50

AOC Archaeology Group, 2002 The Grove, [Watford], archaeological investigations 2002, http://web.archive.org/web/20040806075702/archaeologyatthegrove.com/archaeology/index.html, accessed October 2010

Atkins, 2005 M1 6a-10 Widening, Archaeological Design: Evaluation Strategy

Atkins, 2006 M1 6a-10 Widening, Archaeological Design Part 2: Mitigation Strategy,

Bagshawe, T, 1928 Early Iron Age objects from Harpenden, *Antiq J* **8**, 520-2

Baker, J T, 2006 *Cultural transition in the Chilterns and Essex region, 350 AD to 650 AD*, Univ Hertfordshire Press Stud Regional Local Hist **4**, Hatfield

Barrett, J, 1980 Pottery of the later Bronze Age in lowland England, *Proc Prehist Soc* **46**, 297-319

Barton, R N E, 1995 The long blade assemblage, in T Allen, *Lithics and landscape: archaeological discoveries on the Thames water pipeline at Gatehampton Farm, Goring, Oxfordshire 1985-92*, Oxford Archaeol Unit Thames Valley Landscapes Monogr **7**, Oxford, 54-64

Barton, R N E, Price, C and Proctor, C, 1997 Wye Valley Caves Project: investigations at King Arthur's Cave and Madawg Rock Shelter, in G S Lewis and D Maddy (eds), *The Quaternary of the South Midlands and the Welsh Marches*, Quaternary Research Association, London, 63-75

Bayliss, A, Bronk Ramsey, C, van der Plicht, J and Whittle, A, 2007 Bradshaw and Bayes: towards a timetable for the Neolithic, in Bayliss and Whittle 2007, 1-28

Bayliss, A and Whittle, A (eds), 2007 Histories of the dead: building chronologies for five southern British long barrows, *Cambridge Archaeol J* **17**(1: supplement)

Beresford, G, 2009 *Caldecote the development and desertion of a Hertfordshire village*, Soc Medieval Archaeol Monogr **28**, Leeds

Biddulph, E, 2001 Roman pottery, in Smith 2001, 34-5

Bird, D, 2005 Reflections on the choice of Brockley Hill as a pottery production site, *J Roman Pottery Stud* **12**, 22-5

Birks, H J B, 1989 Holocene isochrone maps and patterns of tree-spreading in the British Isles, *J Biogeography* **16**, 503-40

Black, E W, 1992 Keyed tile fragments, in P Crummy (ed.), *Excavations at Culver Street, The Gilberd School, and other sites in Colchester 1971-85*, Colchester Archaeol Rep 6, 261-272

Black, E W, 1995 *Cursus Publicus, the infrastructure of government in Roman Britain*, Brit Archaeol Rep (Brit Series) **241**, Oxford.

Black, E W, 1996 Box Flue-tiles in Britannia: the Spread of Roman Bathing in the First and Second Centuries, *Archaeol J* **153**, 60-78

Blinkhorn, P, 1998-9 The trials of being a utensil: pottery function at the medieval hamlet of West Cotton, Northamptonshire, *Medieval Ceram* **22-3**, 37-46

Boessneck, J, 1969 Osteological differences between sheep (*Ovis aries Linne*) and goat (*Capra hircus Linne*), in D Brothwell and E Higgs (eds), *Science in Archaeology*, Thames and Hudson, London, 331-85

Boon, G C, 1974 Counterfeit coins in Roman Britain, in J Casey and R Reece (eds), *Coins and the archaeologist*, BAR Brit Ser **4**, Oxford, 95-171

Booth, P, 2007 Oxford Archaeology Roman pottery recording system, Oxford Archaeology, unpublished document (revised)

Bouet, A, 1999 *Les matériaux de construction en terre cuite dans les thermes de la Gaule Narbonnaise*, Scripta Antiqua **1**, Ausonius–Publications, Bordeaux

Bradley, R, 2000 *An archaeology of natural places*, Routledge, London

Branigan, K, 1985 *The Catuvellauni*, Alan Sutton, Gloucester

Brodribb, G, 1987 *Roman brick and tile*, Alan Sutton, Stroud

Bronk Ramsey, C, 1995 Radiocarbon calibration and analysis of stratigraphy: the OxCal program, *Radiocarbon* **37**, 425-30

Bronk Ramsey, C, 1998 Probability and dating, *Radiocarbon* **40**, 461-74

Bronk Ramsey, C, 2001 Development of the radiocarbon calibration program OxCal, *Radiocarbon* **43**, 355-63

Brossler, A, Laws, G and Welsh, K, 2009 An Iron Age and Roman site at Leavesden Aerodrome, Abbots Langley, *Hertfordshire Archaeol Hist* **16**, 27-56

Brown, D H, 1997 Pots from houses, *Medieval Ceram* **21**, 83-94

Bryant, S, 1995 The late Bronze Age to the middle Iron Age of the north Chilterns, in Holgate 1995a, 17-27

Bryant, S, 1997 Iron Age, in J Glazebrook (ed.), *Research and archaeology: a framework for the eastern counties. 1. Resource assessment*, East Anglian Archaeol Occ Papers **3**, Scole, 23-4

Bryant, S, 2007 Central places or special places? The origins and development of 'oppida' in Hertfordshire, in C Haselgrove and T Moore (eds), *The later Iron Age in Britain and beyond*, Oxbow, Oxford, 62-80

Bryant, S and Niblett, R, 1997 The late Iron Age in Hertfordshire and the north Chilterns, in A Gwilt and C Haselgrove (eds), *Reconstructing Iron Age societies*, Oxbow Monogr **71**, Oxford, 270-81

Bull, R and Davis, S, 2006 *Becoming Roman: excavation of a Late Iron Age to Romano-British landscape at Monkston Park, Milton Keynes*, Mus London Archaeol Service Archaeol Stud Ser **16**, London

Campbell, G, 2000 Plant utilization: the evidence from charred plant remains, in B Cunliffe (ed.), *The Danebury Environs Programme: The Prehistory of a Wessex Landscape. Volume 1: Introduction*,

English Heritage and Oxford University Committee for Archaeol Monog No. **48**, 45-59

Cappers, R T J; Bekker, R M and Jans, J E A, 2006 *Digital seed atlas of the Netherlands*, Barkhuis Publishing and Groningen University Library, Groningen

Carter, R J, 2001 Human subsistence and seasonality in Mesolithic northwest Europe based on studies of mandibular bone and dentition in red deer (*Cervus elaphus*) and roe deer (*Capreolus capreolus*), Unpublished PhD thesis, University of London

Castle, S A, 1976 Roman pottery from Radlett, 1959, *Hertfordshire Archaeol* **4** (1974-6), 149-52

Challinor, D, 2006 Wood charcoal from Pepper Hill, CTRL specialist report series, in CTRL digital archive, Archaeology Data Service, http://ads.ahds.ac.uk/catalogue/projArch/ctrl

Challinor, D, 2007 Charcoal, in J Timby, R Brown, E Biddulph, A Hardy and A Powell, *A Slice of rural Essex: archaeological discoveries from the A120 between Stansted Airport and Braintree*, Oxford/Wessex Archaeology, Oxford, Chapter 7 on CD-Rom

Challinor, D, 2008 Charcoal, in OA 2008

Challinor, D, 2011 Wood charcoal, in A Simmonds, F Wenban-Smith, M Bates, K Powell, D Sykes, R Devaney, D Stansbie and D Score, *Excavations in north-west Kent 2005-2007: one hundred thousand years of human activity in and around the Darent Valley*, Oxford Archaeol Monogr **11**, Oxford, 273-4

Challinor, D, forthcoming The wood charcoal, in Allen *et al.* forthcoming

Clark, G (ed.), 1954 *Excavations at Star Carr; an early Mesolithic site at Seamer near Scarborough, Yorkshire*, Cambridge University Press, Cambridge

Clarke, D, 1976 Mesolithic Europe: the economic basis, in G de G Sieveking, I H Longworth and K E Wilson (eds), *Problems in economic and social archaeology*, Duckworth, London, 449-81

Conneller, C, 2005 Moving beyond sites: Mesolithic technology in the landscape, in N Milner and P Woodhouse (eds), *Mesolithic studies at the beginning of the twenty-first century*, Oxbow, Oxford, 42-55

Conneller, C and Schadla-Hall, T, 2003 Beyond Starr Carr: the vale of Pickering in the tenth millennium BP, *Proc Prehist Soc* **69**, 85-105

Cool, H E M, 2006 *Eating and drinking in Roman Britain*, Cambridge University Press, Cambridge

Cool, H, Blanche, E, Pearce, J and Zeepvat, R, 2009 Medieval and post-medieval artefacts, in Beresford 2009, 179-209

Coombs, D, 1979 A late Bronze Age hoard from Cassiobridge Farm, Watford, Hertfordshire, in C Burgess and D Coombs (eds), *Bronze Age hoards. Some finds old and new*, BAR Brit Ser **67**, Oxford, 197-233

Cotter, J P, 2000 *Post-Roman pottery from excavations in Colchester 1971-1985*, Colchester Archaeol Rep **7**, Colchester

Cotter, J P, 2001 The pottery, in M Hicks and A Hicks (eds), *St Gregory's Priory, Northgate, Canterbury excavations 1988-1991*, Archaeol Canterbury New Ser **II**, 231-66

Cotton, M A and Frere, S S, 1968 Ivinghoe Beacon, excavations 1963-5, *Recs Buckinghamshire* **18**, 187-260

Crummy, N, 1983 *The Roman small finds from excavations in Colchester 1971-9*, Colchester Archaeol Rep **2**, Colchester

Crummy, N, 2005 From bracelets to battle-honours: military *armillae* from the Roman conquest of Britain, in N Crummy (ed.), *Image, craft and the Classical World. Essays in honour of Donald Bailey and Catherine Johns*, Monog Instrumentum **29**, Montagnac, 93-106

Cunliffe, B, 1971 *Excavations at Fishbourne 1961-1969 Volume II: The Finds*, Rep Res Comm Soc Antiq London **27**, Leeds

Cunliffe, B, 1984 *Danebury: an Iron age hillfort in Hampshire. Volume 2. The excavations 1969-1978: the finds*, CBA Research Report **52**, London

Cunliffe, B, 2005 *Iron Age Communities in Britain* (4th ed), Routledge, London

Curnow, P E, 1990 The coins, in DS Neal, A Wardle and J Hunn, 105-12

Cushion, B, 2008 Bowl's Dell Puckeridge, Archaeological Earthwork Survey, Hertfordshire County Council Environment Department, unpublished report

Davies, B, Richardson, B and Tomber, R, 1994 *A dated corpus of early Roman pottery from the City of London*, CBA Res Rep **98**, London.

de Moulins, D, 2006 Charred plant remains, in D Hurst (ed.), *Roman Droitwich: Dodder Hill fort, Bays Meadow villa, and roadside settlement*, CBA Res Rep **146**, York, 69-75

Dimbleby, G W, 1978 A pollen analysis from Verulamium (St Michaels 1966) *Hertfordshire Archaeol* **6**, 112-5

Druce, D, 2011 Charcoal, in A Simmonds, F Wenban-Smith, M Bates, K Powell, D Sykes, R Devaney, D Stansbie and D Score, *Excavations in north-west Kent 2005-2007: one hundred thousand years of human activity in and around the Darent Valley*, Oxford Archaeol Monogr **11**, Oxford, 170-3

Dyer, C, 1986 English peasant buildings in the later middle ages (1200-1500), *Medieval Archaeol* **30**, 19-45

Edlin, H L, 1949 *Woodland crafts in Britain*, Batsford, London

Egan, G, and Pritchard, F, 1991 *Dress accessories c 1150-1450*, Medieval finds from excavations in London **3**, HMSO, London

English Heritage, 2004. *Environmental Archaeology Bibliography*, http://ads.ahds.ac.uk/catalogue/specColl/eab_eh_2004, Accessed June 2009

English Heritage, 2008 *Environmental Archaeology Bibliography*, http://ads.ahds.ac.uk/catalogue/specColl/eab_eh_2004, accessed June 2009

Evans, J, 2001 Material approaches to the identification of different Romano-British site types, in S James and M Millett (eds), *Britons and Romans: advancing an archaeological agenda*, Counc Brit Archaeol Res Rep **125**, York, 26-35

Finlay, N, 2006 Gender and personhood, in C Conneller and G Warren (eds), *Mesolithic Britain and Ireland. New approaches*, History Press, Stroud, 35-60

Freeman, C E and Watson, W, 1949 Early Iron Age objects from Harpenden: a new interpretation, *Antiq J* **29**, 196-7

Frere, S, 1972 *Verulamium Excavations Vol 1*, Rep Res Comm Soc of Antiq of London **27**, London

Froom, F R, 1976 *Wawcott III : a stratified Mesolithic succession*, BAR Brit Ser **27**, Oxford

Gale, R, 2004 Charcoal from later Neolithic/early Bronze Age, Iron Age and early Roman contexts, in G Lambrick and T Allen, *Gravelly Guy, Stanton Harcourt Oxfordshire: the development of a prehistoric and Romano-British community*, Oxford, Oxford Archaeol Thames Valley Landscapes Monogr **21**, Oxford, 445-56

Gale, R, 2007 The Charcoal, in F Brown, C Howard-Davis, M Brennand, A Boyle, T Evans, S O'Conner, A Spence, R Heawood and A Lupton, *The archaeology of the A1(M) Darrington to Dishforth DBFO Road Scheme*, Lancaster Imprints **12**, Lancaster, 354-60

Gardiner, J, undated The Mesolithic in Hampshire: resource assessment. Solent Thames Hampshire Regional Research Framework, Unpublished report

Garrow, D, Beadsmoore, E and Knight, M, 2005 Pit clusters and the temporality of occupation: an earlier Neolithic site at Kilverstone, Thetford, Norfolk, *Proc Prehist Soc* **71**, 139-57

Garrow, D, 2006 *Pits, settlement and deposition during the Neolithic and early Bronze Age in East Anglia*, BAR Brit Ser **414**, Oxford

Going, C J, 1987 *The mansio and other sites in the south-eastern sector of Caesaromagus: the Roman pottery*, CBA Res Rep **62**, London

Going, C, 2003 Roman pottery in McDonald 2003, 56

Gooder, J, 2007 Excavation of a Mesolithic house at East Barns, East Lothian, Scotland: an interim report, in K L R Pedersen and C Waddington (eds), *Mesolithic studies in the North Sea basin and beyond*, Oxbow, Oxford, 49-59

Grant, A, 1982 The use of tooth wear as a guide to the age of domestic ungulates, in B Wilson, C Grigson and S Payne (eds), *Ageing and sexing animal bones from archaeological sites*, BAR Brit Ser **109**, 91-108

Green, S H, 1984 Flint arrowheads: typology and interpretation, *Lithics* **5**, 19-39

Gresham, C A, 1939 Spettisbury Rings, Dorset, *Archaeol J* **96**, 114-31

Griffiths, S, 2006 Radiocarbon determinations A30 Bodmin to India Queens (A30 BOD 05.3), in A30 Bodmin to Indian Queens road improvement scheme, Oxford Archaeology unpublished report

Griffiths, S, in prep Chronological modelling of the Mesolithic-Neolithic transition in Britain, Cardiff University PhD thesis.

Grøn, O, 2003 Mesolithic dwelling places in south Scandinavia: their definition and social interpretation, *Antiquity* **77**, 685-708

Habermehl, K-H, 1975 *Die Altersbestimmung bei Haus- und Labortieren* (2nd ed.), Verlag Paul Parey, Berlin and Hamburg

Halstead, P, 1985 A study of mandibular teeth from Romano-British contexts at Maxey, in F Pryor, *Archaeology and environment in the Lower Welland Valley*, East Anglian Archaeol Rep **27**, 219-24

Halstead, P and Collins, P, 2002 Sorting the sheep from the goats: morphological distinctions between the mandibles and mandibular teeth of adult *Ovis* and *Capra.*, *J Archaeol Sci* **29**, 545-53

Hather, J G, 2000 *The identification of the Northern European Woods*, Archetype, London

Hatting, T, 1990 Cats from Viking Age Odense, *J Danish Archaeol* **9**, 179-93

Havercroft, A B, Turner-Rugg, A and Rugg, G, 1987 Notes on Hertfordshire Greyware vessels from recent excavations in St Albans, with particular reference to size and shape as demonstrated by two new computer programs, *Medieval Ceram* **11**, 31-67

Hawkes, C F C and Hull, M R, 1947 *Camulodunum: first report on the excavations at Colchester 1930-1939*, Rep Res Comm Soc Antiq London **14**, Oxford

Hey, G, Dennis, C and Mayes, A, 2007 Archaeological investigations on Whiteleaf Hill, Princes Risborough, Buckinghamshire, 2002-6, *Rec Buckinghamshire* **47**(2), 1-80

Highways Agency, 1994 M1 Widening Junctions 6a to 10: Environmental Statement, Volume 2 Part 5: archaeological assessment, Highway Agency, unpublished report

Hill, J D, 2007 The dynamics of social change in later Iron Age eastern and south-eastern England *c*. 300 BC-AD 43, in C Haselgrove and T Moore (eds), *The later Iron Age in Britain and beyond*, Oxbow, Oxford, 16-40

Hill, J D, Evans, C and Alexander, M, 1999 The Hinxton Rings – a late Iron Age cemetery at Hinxton, Cambridgeshire, with a reconsideration of northern Aylesford-Swarling distributions, *Proc Prehistoric Soc* **65**, 243-73

Hillman, G, 1981 Reconstructing crop husbandry practices from the charred remains of crops, in R J Mercer (ed.), *Farming practice in British prehistory*, Edinburgh University Press, Edinburgh, 123-62

Hillman, G, 1982 Evidence for spelting malt, in R Leech (ed.), *Excavations at Catsgore 1970-1973: a Romano-British village*, Western Archaeol Trust Excavation Monogr **2**, Bristol, 137-41

Hillman, G, 1984 Traditional husbandry and processing of archaic cereals in recent times: the operations, products and equipment which might feature in Sumerian texts. Part I: The glume wheats, *Bull Sumerian Agriculture* **1**, 114-52

Hillman, G, 1991 A sample of carbonised plant remains, in B Philp, K Parfitt, J Willson, M Dutto and W Williams, *The Roman Villa site at Keston, Kent: first report (excavations 1968–1978)*, Kent Archaeol Rescue Unit Kent Monogr Ser Res Rep **6**, Dover, 292

Holden, J L, Phakley, P P and Clement, J G, 1995 Scanning electron microscope observations of heat-treated human bone, *Forensic Sci Inter* **74**, 29-45

Holgate, R (ed.), 1995a *Chiltern archaeology recent work: a handbook for the next decade*, Book Castle, Dunstable

Holgate, R, 1995b Early prehistoric settlement of the Chilterns, in Holgate 1995a, 3-16

Hopson, P M, Aldiss, D T and Smith, A, 1996 *Geology of the country around Hitchin: memoir for 1:50 000 geological sheet 221 (England and Wales)*, HMSO, London

Howard, C (ed.), 2007 *Kingsdale Head project. Kingsdale in the parish of Thornton in Lonsdale, North Yorkshire: a report on the excavation of a longhouse type structure with associated features identified by geophysical surveys, and three training trenches*, Ingleborough Archaeology Group, Ingleton

Hudspith, R E T, 1995 Fieldwalking in South Bedfordshire 1988-91, in Holgate 1995a, 131-39

Hunn, J, 1995a The Romano-British landscape of the Chiltern dip slope: a study of settlement around Verulamium, in Holgate 1995a, 76-91

Hunn, J, 1995b The medieval landscape of the Chiltern dip slope: a brief outline of the administration and infrastructure of the countryside around St Albans, in Holgate 1995a, 44-55

Hunn, J R, 1996 *Settlement patterns in Hertfordshire: a review of the typology and function of enclosures in the Iron Age and Roman landscape*, BAR Brit Ser **249**, Oxford

Hurst, J G, 1968 Near Eastern and Mediterranean medieval pottery found in north-west Europe, in A Martensson (ed.), 'Res Mediaevales', *Archaeologica Lundensia* **iii**, 195-204

Jacobi, R, 1978 The Mesolithic of Sussex, in P L Drewett (ed.), *Archaeology in Sussex to AD 1500*, CBA Res Rep **29**, London, 15-22

James, S and Rigby, V, 1997 *Britain and the Celtic Iron Age*, British Museum, London

Jochim, M, 1976 *Hunter-gatherer subsistence and settlement: a predictive model*, Academic Press, New York

Jones, G, 1984 Interpretation of archaeological

Jones, G, 1984 Interpretation of archaeological plant remains: ethnographic models from Greece, in W van Zeist and W A Casparie (eds), *Plants and ancient man: studies in palaeoethnobotany*, Balkema, Rotterdam, 43-61

Jones, G, 1987 A statistical approach to the archaeological identification of crop-processing, *J Archaeol Sci* **14**, 311-23

Jones, G, 1996 An ethnoarchaeological investigation of the effects of cereal grain sieving, *Circaea* **12**(2), 177-82

Jones, J D and Stead, I M, 1969, An early Iron Age warrior-burial found at St Lawrence, Isle of Wight, *Proc Prehistoric Soc* **35**, 351-4

Kilmurry, K, 1980 *The pottery industry of Stamford, Lincs. c A.D. 850-1250*, BAR Brit Ser **84**, Oxford

King, A, 1991 Food production and consumption - meat, in R F J Jones (ed.), *Britain in the Roman period: recent trends*, J R Collis Publications, Sheffield, 15-20

King, A, 1999 Diet in the Roman world: a regional inter-site comparison of the mammal bones, *J Roman Archaeol* **12**, 168-202

Knight, H and Jeffries, N, 2004 *Medieval and later urban development at High Street, Uxbridge: excavations at the Chimes Shopping Centre, London Borough of Hillingdon*, Mus London Archaeol Service Archaeol Stud Ser **12**, London

LAARC, 2007 Post 1992 Museum of London code expansions: Post-Roman pottery, www.museum oflondon.org.uk.post_rom.pdf

Lambert, C A, and Godwin, H, Plant remains from the ditch in the Roman city of Verulamium (St Albans), unpublished manuscript cited in English Heritage 2008

Lamdin-Whymark, H, 2008 *The residue of ritual action: Neolithic deposition practices in the middle Thames valley*, BAR Brit Ser **466**, Oxford

Lavender, N J, 1991 A late Iron Age burial enclosure at Maldon Hall Farm, Essex: excavations 1989, *Proc Prehistoric Soc* **57**, 203-9

Lewis, C, Mitchell-Fox, P, and Dyer, C, 2001 *Village, hamlet and field: changing medieval settlements in central England*, Windgather, Macclesfield

Lewis, J, 2007 Excavations east of Blackmoor, Charterhouse, Mendip Hills, Somerset, *Proc University of Bristol Spelaeological Society* **24**(2), 83-96

Locker, A, 1990 The mammal, bird and fish bones, in Neal *et al.* 1990, 205-10

Locker, A, 1999 The animal bone, in Niblett 1999, 324-45

Longworth, I, 1989 Pottery from the Roman settlement, in Stead and Rigby 1989, 53-79

Lovell, B and Tubb, J, 2006 Ancient quarrying of rare in situ Paleogene Hertfordshire Puddingstone, *Mercian Geologist* **16**, 185-9

Lowther, A W G, 1937 Report on the excavation of the Roman structure at Rothamsted Experimental Station, Harpenden, *Trans St Albans Hertfordshire Archaeol Architect Soc* **5**(2),108-14

Luff, R-M and Moreno Garcia, M, 1995 Killing cats in the medieval period. An unusual episode in the history of Cambridge, England, *Archaeofauna* **4**, 93-114

Luke, M, 2008 *Life in the loop: investigation of a prehistoric and Romano-British landscape at Biddenham Loop, Bedfordshire*, East Anglian Archaeol **125**, Bedford

Lyne, M, 1999 The pottery from the Lower Slope, in Niblett 1999, 233-70

Lyne, M, 2006 The pottery, in R Niblett with W Manning and C Saunders, Verulamium: excavations within the Roman town 1986-88, *Britannia* **37**, 108-23

McCarthy, M R and Brooks, C M, 1988 *Medieval pottery in Britain AD 900-1600*, Leicester University Press, Leicester

McDonald, T, 1996 *The Archaeology of the A41 Berkhamsted and Kings Langley Bypasses, Berkhamsted*, Dacorum Heritage Trust

McDonald, T, 2003 Excavations at Buncefield Lane, Hemel Hempstead, *Hertfordshire Archaeol* **13** (for 1997-2003), 47-60

McKinley, J I, 1994 Bone fragment size in British cremation burials and its implications for pyre technology and ritual, *J Archaeol Sci* **21**, 339-42

McKinley, J, 2000 The analysis of cremated bone, in M Cox and S Mays (eds.) *Human osteology in archaeology and forensic science*, Greenwich Medical Media, London, 403-21

McKinley, J I, 2004 Compiling a skeletal inventory: cremated human bone, in M Brickley and J I McKinley (eds), *Guidelines to the standards for recording human remains*, BABAO and Inst Field Archaeol Pap **7**, Birmingham, 9-13

McKinley, J I and Roberts, C, 1993 *Excavation and post-excavation treatment of cremated and inhumed human remains*, Inst Field Archaeol Techn Pap **13**, Birmingham

Magnell, O, 2006 Att befolka en stadsdel - Pälsare i det medeltida kvarteret Blekhagen, *META medeltidsarkeologisk tidskrift* **4**, Lund

Major, H, 2004 The dating of Puddingstone querns, *Lucerna* **27**, 2-4

Maltby, M, 1981 Iron Age, Romano-British and Anglo-Saxon animal husbandry – a review of the faunal evidence, in M Jones and G Dimbleby (eds), *The environment of man: the Iron Age to the Anglo-Saxon period*, BAR Brit Ser **87**, 155-203

Margary, I D, 1973 *Roman roads in Britain* (3rd ed.), Phoenix House Ltd, London

Martin, G, 2009 Botanical remains, in Beresford 2009, 226-7

Masefield, R, 2008 *Prehistoric and later settlement and landscape from Chiltern Scarp to Aylesbury Vale. The archaeology of the Aston Clinton Bypass, Buckinghamshire*, BAR Brit Ser **473**, Oxford

Oxford Archaeology, 2006i M1 Widening Scheme Junction 8 southbound: archaeological excavation, written scheme of investigation, Oxford Archaeology, unpublished report

Oxford Archaeology, 2006j M1 Widening Scheme Junction 8 northbound: archaeological excavation, written scheme of investigation, Oxford Archaeology, unpublished report

Oxford Archaeology, 2008 M1 Widening, Junction 6a to 10, Hertfordshire: archaeological post-excavation assessment report, Oxford Archaeology, unpublished report

Oxford Archaeology, forthcoming M25 DBFO Widening Section 1, post-excavation assessment and project design

Paradine, P, 1977 Seeds from cess pit 47, in D S Neal (ed.), Excavations at the Palace of King's Langley, Hertfordshire 1974-1976, *Medieval Archaeol* **21**, 136

Parminter, Y, 1990 The coarse pottery, in Neal *et al.* 1990, 174-85

Payne, S, 1973 Kill-off patterns in sheep and goats: the mandibles from Aşwan Kale, *Anatolian Stud* **23**, 281-303

Peacock, D P S, 1970 The scientific analysis of ancient ceramics: a review, *World Archaeol* **1**, 375-89

Pearce, J E and Blackmore, L, forthcoming A dated type-series of London medieval pottery, Part 5: Shelly-sandy ware and the greyware industries, *Trans London Middlesex Archaeol Soc*

Pearce, J E, Vince, A G and Jenner, M A, 1985 *A dated type-series of London medieval pottery. Part 2: London-type Ware*, London Middlesex Archaeol Soc, Spec Pap **6**, London

Philp, B, 1991 Major Iron Age site discovered near Alkham, Kent, *Kent Archaeol Rev* **103**, 50-2

Pitts, M, 2005 Pots and pits: drinking and deposition in late Iron Age south-east Britain, *Oxford J Archaeol* **24**(2), 143-61

Pollard, J, 2000 Ancestral places in the Mesolithic landscape. *Archaeol Rev Cambridge* **17**(1), 123-38

Pollard, J, 2008 Deposition and material agency in the early Neolithic of southern Britain. I., in B J Mills and W H Walker (eds), *Memory work: archaeologies of material practices*, SAR Press, Santa Fe, 41-59

Poole, C, 2010a Ceramic and stone building material in P Booth, A Simmonds, A Boyle, S Clough, H E M Cool and D Poore, *The late Roman cemetery at Lankhills, Winchester, excavations 2000-2005*, Oxford Archaeol Monogr **10**, Oxford, 334-8

Poole, C, 2010b Ceramic building material, in A Smith, K Powell and P Booth (eds), *Evolution of a farming community in the Upper Thames Valley. Excavation of a prehistoric, Roman and post-Roman landscape at Cotswold Community, Gloucestershire and Wiltshire Volume 2: the finds and environmental reports*, Oxford Archaeol Thames Valley Landscapes Monogr **31**, Oxford, 153-65

Poole, C and Shaffrey, R, 2011 Roman ceramic building material, in B M Ford, S Teague, E Biddulph, A Hardy and L Brown, *Winchester - a city in the making. Archaeological excavations between 2002 and 2007 on the sites of Northgate House, Staple Gardens and the former Winchester Library, Jewry St*, Oxford Archaeol Monogr **12**, Oxford, 290-3 and digital Part 3.7

Prehistoric Ceramics Research Group (PCRG), 1997 *The study of later prehistoric pottery: general policies and guidelines for analysis and publication*, Prehist Ceram Res Group Occ Pap **1** and **2**, Oxford

Prummel, W and Frisch, H-J, 1986 A guide for the distinction of species, sex and body side in bones of sheep and goat, *J Archaeol Sci* **13**, 567-77

Rackham, O, 2003 *Ancient Woodland, its history, vegetation and uses in England*, Castlepoint Press, Dalbeattie

Reimer, P J, Baillie, M G, Bard, L E, Bayliss, A, Beck, J W, Bertrand, C J H, Blackwell, P G, Buck, C E, Burr, G S, Cutler, K B, Damon, P E, Edwards, R L, Fairbanks, R G, Friedrich, M, Guilderson, T P, Hogg, A G, Hughen, K A, Kromer, B, McCormac, G, Manning, S, Bronk Ramsey, C, Reimer, R W, Remmele, S, Southon, J R, Stuiver, M, Talamo, S, Taylor, F W, van der Plicht, J and Weyhenmeyer, C E, 2004 IntCal04 terrestrial radiocarbon age calibration, 0-26 cal kyr BP. *Radiocarbon* **46**, 1029-58

Reverte, J M, 1986 Cremaciones prehistóricas en España, *Anales de la Escuela de Medcina Legal* **1**, 129-51

Robinson, E, 1994 Hertfordshire Puddingstone foray, Saturday 5th June, 1993, *Proc Geologists Ass* **105**, 77-9

Robinson, M, 1977 The ecology, in M R Petchey (ed.), Excavations in Hertford 1973–4, *Hertfordshire Archaeol* **5**, 166-7, 171-4

Robinson, M, 1996 The charred remains and molluscs, in C Bell, An archaeological excavation on land adjacent to Snowy Fielder Waye, Isleworth, London Borough of Hounslow, Middlesex, *Trans London Middlesex Archaeol Soc* **46**, 52-5

Salveson, G and Blackmore, L, 1985 Excavations at Elstree Hill South, 1981-1983, *Trans London Middlesex Archaeol Soc* **36**, 81-106

Scaife, R, 2003 Charred plant remains, in McDonald 2003, 58

Schweingruber, F H, 1990 *Microscopic wood anatomy* (3rd ed.), Swiss Federal Institute for Forest, Snow and Landscape Research, Birmensdorf

Scott, I R, 2009 Small finds, in S Lawrence and A Smith, *Between villa and town. Excavations of a Roman roadside settlement and shrine at Higham Ferrers, Northamptonshire*, Oxford Archaeol Monogr **7**, Oxford 199-250

Serjeantson, D, 1996 The animal bones, in S Needham and T Spence, *Refuse and disposal at Area 16 east Runnymede. Runnymede Bridge research excavations, Volume 2*, British Museum Press, London, 194-253

Shaffrey, R, 2006 *Grinding and Milling. Romano-British Rotary Querns made from Old Red Sandston*, BAR Brit Ser **409**, Oxford

Sheppard, D, 1977 A medieval pottery kiln at Pinner, Middlesex, *London Archaeol* **3**(2), 31-5

Sherlock, R L, 1922 *The geology of the country around Aylesbury and Hemel Hempstead : explanation of sheet 238*, HMSO, London

Sherlock, R L and Pocock, R W, 1924 *The geology of the country around Hertford : explanation of sheet 239*, HMSO, London

Smith, A, 2001 Excavations at Canon's Corner, Barnet, Middlesex, *Trans London Middlesex Archaeol Soc* **52**, 27-39

Smith, A, Brown, L and Brady, K, 2008 A Romano-British landscape at Brockley Hill, Stanmore, Middlesex: excavations at Brockley Hill House and the former MoD site, *Trans London Middlesex Archaeol Soc* **59**, 81-152

Smith, G, 1984 Excavation at Windmill Farm, Predannack Moor, *Cornish Archaeol* **23**, 179

Smith, W, 2002 *A review of archaeological wood analysis in southern England*, English Heritage Centre Archaeol Rep **75/2002**, Portsmouth

Smith, W, 2008 Assessment of charred plant remains, in Oxford Archaeology 2008

Stace, C, 1997 *New Flora of the British Isles* (2nd ed.), Cambridge University Press, Cambridge

Stainton, B, 1989 Excavation of an early prehistoric site at Stratford's yard, Chesham, *Rec Buckinghamshire* **31**, 49-74

Stamper, P, 1999 Landscapes of the middle ages: rural settlement and manors, in J Hunter and I Ralston (eds), *The archaeology of Britain: an introduction from the upper Paleolithic to the industrial revolution*, Routledge, London, 247-63

Stead, I M and Rigby, V, 1989 *Verulamium: the King Harry Lane site*, English Heritage Archaeol Rep **12**, London

Stratascan, 1995 A report for St Albans Museums on a geophysical survey carried out on M1 field evaluation, April/May 1995, Stratascan, unpublished report

Stuiver, M and Kra, R S, 1986 Editorial comment, *Radiocarbon* **28**(2B), ii

Stuiver, M and Polach, H A, 1977 Discussion, reporting of $^{14}$C data, *Radiocarbon* **19**(3), 355-63

Stuiver, M and Reimer, P J, 1986 A computer program for radiocarbon age calculation, *Radiocarbon* **28**, 1022-30

Swan, V, 1984 *The pottery kilns of Roman Britain*, Roy Comm Hist Monuments Eng Supp Ser **5**, HMSO, London

Switsur, V R and Jacobi, R M 1975 Radiocarbon dates for the Pennine Mesolithic, *Nature* **256**, 32-4

Switsur, V R and Jacobi, R M, 1979 A radiocarbon chronology for the early postglacial stone industries of England and Wales, in R Berger and H E Suess (eds), *Radiocarbon dating: proceedings of the ninth international conference, Los Angeles and La Jolla, 1976*, University of California Press, Berkeley, 41-68

Taylor, B and Gray Jones, A, 2009 Definitely a pit, possibly a house? Recent excavations at Flixton School House Farm in the Vale of Pickering, *Mesolithic Misc* **20**(2), 21-6

Taylor, J, 2007 *An atlas of Roman rural settlement in England*, CBA Res Rep **151**, York

Tebbutt, C F, 1932 Early Iron Age settlement on Jack's Hill, Great Wymondley, Herts., *Proc Prehist Soc East Anglia* **6**, 371-4

Thompson, A and Holland, E, 1976 Excavation of an Iron Age site at Dellfield, Berkhamsted, *Hertfordshire Archaeol* **4** (1974-6), 137-48

Thomas, J, 1999 *Understanding the Neolithic*, Routledge, London

Thompson, G B, 1999 The analysis of wood charcoals from selected pits and funerary contexts, in A Barclay and C Halpin, *Excavations at Barrow Hills, Radley, Oxfordshire, Oxford. The Neolithic and Bronze Age Monument Complex*, Oxford Archaeol Thames Valley Landscapes Monogr **11**, Oxford, 247-53

Thompson, I M, 1979 Wheathampstead revisited, *Bull Inst Archaeol* **16**, 158-85

Thompson, I M, 1982 *Grog-tempered 'Belgic' pottery of south-eastern England*, BAR Brit Ser **108**, Oxford

Tomber, R and Dore, J, 1998 *The national Roman fabric reference collection: a handbook*, Mus London Archaeol Services Monogr **2**, London

Tomlin, D J, 1987 *Roman Wight: a guide catalogue to "The Island of Vectis, very near to Britannia"*, Isle of Wight County Council, Isle of Wight

Turner-Rugg, A, 1993 Medieval pottery in Hertfordshire. A gazetteer of the principal collections, *Hertfordshire Archaeol* **11**, 30-53

Turner-Rugg, A, 1995 Medieval pottery from St Albans, *Medieval Ceram* **19**, 45-65

Ubelaker, D H, 1989 *Human skeletal remains. Excavation, analysis, interpretation* (2nd ed.), Taraxacum, Washington

van der Veen, M, 1984 Sampling for seeds, in W van Zeist and W A Casparie (eds), *Plants and ancient man: studies in palaeoethnobotany*, Balkema, Rotterdam, 193-9

van der Veen, M, 1989 Charred grain assemblages from Roman-period corn driers in Britain, *Archaeol J* **146**, 302-19

van der Veen, M and Fieller, N, 1982 Sampling seeds, *J Archaeol Sci* **9**, 287-98

van der Veen, M, Livarda, A and Hill, A, 2007 The archaeobotany of Roman Britain: current state and identification of research priorities, *Britannia* **38**, 181-210

Viatores, The, 1964 *Roman roads in the south-east midlands*, Gollancz, London

Vince, A G, 1985 The Saxon and medieval pottery of London: a review, *Medieval Archaeol* **29**, 25-93

Vince, A G and Jenner, A, 1991 The Saxon and early medieval pottery of London, in A G Vince (ed.), *Aspects of Saxon and Norman London 2: finds and environmental evidence*, LAMAS Spec Pap **12**, 19-119

von den Driesch, A, 1976 *A guide to the measurement of animal bones from archaeological sites*, Peabody Museum of Archaeology and Ethnology, Harvard University, Havard


Waddington, C, Bailey, G, Bayliss, A, Milner, N, Pedersen, K, Shiel, R and Stevenson, T, 2003 A Mesolithic settlement at Howick, Northumberland: a preliminary report, *Archaeol Aeliana* **32**, 1-12

Ward, G K and Wilson, S R, 1978 Procedures for comparing and combining radiocarbon age determinations: a critique, *Archaeometry* **20**, 19-31

Warry, P, 2006 *Tegulae: Manufacture, typology and use in Roman Britain*, Brit Archaeol Rep Brit Ser **417**, Oxford

Waterbolk, H T, 1971 Working with radiocarbon dates, *Actes du VIII^e congrès international des sciences préhistoriques et protohistoriques* **1**, 11-25

Waugh, K, 1999 Roman coarse pottery, in C J Going and J R Hunn, *Excavations at Boxfield Farm, Chells, Stevenage, Hertfordshire*, Hertfordshire Archaeol Trust Rep **2**, Hertford, 88-135

Webley, L, Timby, J and Wilson, M, 2007 *Fairfield Park: later prehistoric settlement in the eastern Chilterns*, Bedfordshire Archaeol Monog **7**, Oxford

Wessex Archaeology, 2009 Friars Wash, Redbourn, Hertfordshire; Archaeological evaluation and assessment of results, Wessex Archaeology, unpublished report

West, S, 2008, A multiperiod landscape at Aldwickbury golf course, near Harpenden, *Hertfordshire Archaeol Hist* **15** (2006-8), 5-20

Whitbread, I K, 1995 *Greek transport amphorae: a petrological and archaeological study*, Brit Sch Athens Fitch Lab Occ Pap **4**, Athens

White, K D, 1970 *Roman farming*, Thames and Hudson, London.

Wickham-Jones, C, 2005 Summer walkers? mobility and the Mesolithic, in N Milner and P Woodman (eds), *Mesolithic studies at the beginning of the 21st century*, Oxbow, Oxford, 30-41

Wilkinson, D (ed.), 1992 *OAU Field Manual*

Williamson, T, 1984 The Roman countryside: settlement and agriculture in north-west Essex, *Britannia* **15**, 225-30

Williamson, T, 2000 *Origins of Hertfordshire*, Manchester University Press, Manchester

Williamson, T, 2010 *The origins of Hertfordshire*, Hertfordshire Publications, Hatfield

Wilson, B, 1984 Bones from Verulamium, in S Frere, *Verulamium excavations, Vol. III*, Oxford Univ Comm Archaeol Monogr **1**, 294-5

Wingfield, C, 1995 The Anglo-Saxon settlement of Bedfordshire and Hertfordshire: the archaeological view, in Holgate 1995a, 31-43.


Young, C J, 1977 *The Roman pottery industry of the Oxford region*, BAR Brit Ser **43**, Oxford


Zohary, D and Hopf, M, 2000 *Domestication of plants in the Old World: the origin and spread of cultivated plants in West Asia, Europe, and the Nile Valley* (3rd ed.), Clarendon Press, Oxford

# Index